2000

revised & expanded edition

BISEXUAL
RESOURCE
GUIDE

**3rd edition
Robyn Ochs,
editor**

Bisexual Resource Center

Bisexual Resource Center
P.O. Box 400639
Cambridge, MA 02140
United States of America

© 1999

ISBN 0-9653881-2-3

Printed in the United States of America

Contents

GLBT Library
GLBT Student Support Services
Indiana University
705 East 7th Street
Bloomington, IN 47405-3809

Contents

BI STUFF
from the
Bisexual Resource Center

Liz Nania's design of the classic pink and blue bi-angles has been modified by Jonathan Urbach to include the Bisexual/Lesbian/Gay/Transgendered Rainbow in each triangle. On black 100% cotton tees in four styles, lots of sizes, and all at ONLY $15 each.

PO Box 400639
Cambridge, MA
02140
617•424•9595

www.biresource.org/bookstore
www.biresource.org/videostore
www.biresource.org/musicstore

The Bisexual Resource Center, in conjunction with Amazon Books, is pleased to bring you the first on-line Bisexual Bookstore and Music Store. Also, with Reel.com, we offer the first on-line Bisexual Video Store. Think of the BRC Website as the one place that stocks virtually every bi book, video, and music CD available. And we have many of these products at below list price. In addition, through arrangements made with Amazon Books and Reel.com, the BRC earns a commission on every sale, which goes to support our award-winning work. As always, we urge you to support your local queer bookstore — but if you can't get to one, or you can't find what you're looking for, please consider shopping here.

bumperstickers

2 styles, with
or without text.
$1.50 ea.

For an order form, information, color images of the merchandise, and more, call us, write to us, send us email, or visit our website.
www.biresource.org
www.biresource.org/biproducts
email: brc@biresource.org

Introduction

In the mid 1980s I was at a conference on bisexuality sponsored by what is now known as the Bisexual Resource Center and someone said, "Wouldn't it be great if someone made a list of all of the bi groups out there? That way we could all keep in touch with each other." I remember thinking, "What a good idea! SOMEBODY should do that." Well, that somebody turned out to be me. I pulled together the first edition of the *International Directory of Bisexual Groups* later that year. It was six pages long and listed about 40 groups in a handful of countries.

Things change. Movements grow. Listing over 300 bi groups and 1750 bi-inclusive groups in 56 countries, as well as hundreds of electronic resources, the *Bisexual Resource Guide 2000* is evidence that the bi movement has indeed come a long way. The growth in the number of bi groups is evidence of a burgeoning movement, but perhaps even more powerful a statement is the number of groups which formerly ignored (or even denied access to) bisexual people which now include us. This expansion of "community" is an international trend, and it will help to make it easier for bisexual people to identify as such, and easier for all of us – lesbian, gay, bi-sexual, heterosexual, transgendered, queer, and questioning – to find comfort with ourselves and a sense of community with others, even if and when our identities change over our lifetimes.

An Asian woman recently wrote to me, wondering why we would be interested in including Asian resources in a Guide produced in the United States. It is my belief that we are all empowered by the knowledge that there is widespread organizing by bisexuals and other sexual minorities in so many countries throughout the world. We can gain nourishment and strength by looking across oceans, and sometimes even by looking across town in our own communities. This book is evidence that we are not alone, and we are in good company.

This guide includes several other important sections: an extensive bibliographic section, an annotated list of recommended films, advertising, information on safer sex, photos, great quotes, cartoons by Alison Bechdel and Roberta Gregory, an electronic resources section, and of course listings of 2100+ resources in 56 countries.

The *Bisexual Resource Guide 2000* is truly a community undertaking. More than 150 people contributed their time and talents to make it happen. A list of some of these people follows. This project couldn't have happened without you! And we need even more people to help with the next *Guide*. Besides giving of your money (hint, hint!), you can also help by writing to me and giving me feedback. I especially need the input of folks outside the U.S. What other information would *you* like to see in the next edition of this guide? What books and films have you read that you think should appear on the lists (but don't yet)? Are there groups that you know about that I don't? Are there listings that are incorrect? I won't know unless you tell me. You can write to me c/o BRC, or you can write to me directly at: PO Box 391611, Cambridge MA 02139 (USA) or send me e-mail at: ochs@bi.org.

Bi for now,

Robyn Ochs

Words of Thanks

The thing I most value about this project is that the production of this Guide is a community effort. More than 150 people in various parts of the world have given generously of their time and energies to make it happen. The following people particularly deserve thanks:

Top: Assistant editor Linda Dyndiuk

Middle: Wayne Bryant at 5th International Conference on Bisexuality, 1998

Right: Local volunteer Lori Ann Lima

Assistant Editor:
Linda Dyndiuk

Interior layout/design:
Kathleen Hepburn

Cover design & graphic design:
Mary-Ann Greanier; David Reiffel (uc@world.std.com)

Writers:
Film section: Wayne Bryant
Bi The Book: Robyn Ochs & Ron Fox
Safer & Sexier: Cianna Stewart
Getting Bi on the Internet: Audrey Beth Stein, Gilly Rosenthal, John Valentine & Kathryn Foote

Advertising:
Jeliza Patterson & Arthur Cohen

Promotion:
Arthur Cohen; Mary-Ann Greanier; Dorian Solot

Proofreading, research, data entry, envelope stuffing, etc.:
'Tina Blanco, Emily Cook, Sophia Cordoni, Amber Crabbe, Larry Deck, Linda Dyndiuk, Meghan Foley, Elizabeth Garcia, Mary Ann Greanier, Amatul Hannan, Amy Harris, Jennifer M. Koerber, Sheeri Kritzer, Libby Larson, Michael Leibensperger, Lori

Ann Lima, Cana McCoy, Graham McKay, Robyn Ochs, Denise Overturf, Peg Preble, Kathryn Schnaible, Carl Sciortino, Harriet Tanzman, Thea Tremain, Keja Valens, Karen Weeks, Ethan Weker, Sara Meyers Wolfson. (For the record, this list includes lesbians & straight women, as well as many bi people).

Photography:
Robyn Ochs, Hilde Vossen, Wayne Bryant, Peg Preble and others.

Regional editors:
▼ ARGENTINA: Alejandra Sarda <escrita@arnet.com.ar> ▼ AUSTRALIA: QL: Wayne Roberts; NSW/ACT: Michael Scheper [MikZ] <mikz@poboxes.com>; WA: Anna Hepworth <mouse@cygnus.uwa.edu.au>; SA: Glenn Vassallo <glenv@queer.org.au>; NT: Wayne Roberts; TAS: Teddy; VIC: Cath Lawrence ▼ BELGIUM: Maria Brattemark ▼ CANADA: QUE: Sophie Richard <4uonly@bigfoot.com>; ONT: Stephen; Eastern: Tania Trépanier <ttrepani@is2.dal.ca>; Cent/West: Carolyn Reitzel; CHINA: You Yun;

Top: Robyn Ochs with local volunteer Meghan Foley

Middle, left: Alejandra Sarda, editor for Argentina

Middle, right: Gert Danielsen, editor for Costa Rica, Guatemala, Nicaragua and Norway

Bottom: At 5th International Conference on Bisexuality, 1998: Catherine Deschamps (France), Robyn Ochs (US), Alejandra Sarda (Argentina), Angelica Ramirez Roa (Mexicao), and Ann Bensussan (France)

COLOMBIA: Diego in Medellin ▼ COSTA RICA: Gert Danielsen <gd10@st-andrews.ac.uk> ▼ FINLAND: Linda Eklöf <linda@seta.fi> ▼ FRANCE: Anne Bensoussan ▼ GERMANY: Axel Griessman <axl@axl.org> ▼ GUATEMALA: Gert Danielsen <gd10@st-andrews.ac.uk> ▼ HONG KONG: Verdy Leung ▼ ICELAND: Samtokin '89 <gayice@mmedia.is> ▼ INDIA: Sherry Joseph <sherry@vbharat.ernet.in> & Deep Purkayasta ▼ IRELAND: Brian J. Saccente ▼ ISRAEL: Jared Goldfarb <jared@pobox.com> ▼ JAPAN: Luka Koba ▼ KOREA: Christina ▼ MEXICO: Mafer Cepeda ▼ NETHERLANDS: Maurice Snellan <maurice@LNBI.demon.NL> & Hanneke Van der Sterre ▼ NEW ZEALAND: Robyn Ochs, with help ▼ NICARAGUA: Gert Danielsen <gd10@st-andrews.ac.uk> ▼ NORWAY: Gert Danielsen <gd10@st-andrews.ac.uk> ▼ PHILIPPINES: Daniel Ocampo <dannyo@surfshop.net.ph> ▼ RUSSIA & UKRAINE: Vlad Somov <v-vs@usa.net> ▼ SINGAPORE: Iris Verghese ▼ SOUTH AFRICA: Benjamin Conradie & Nigel Hertz ▼ SWITZERLAND: Sandrine Pache <vogay@worldcom.ch> ▼ ZIMBABWE: Oliver Phillips <oliverph@dircon.co.uk> ▼ UNITED KINGDOM: Kevin Lano <klano@hotmail.com>

UNITED STATES:

Danielle Bautier (CA-SF area); Shannon Bayless <garulf@prodigy.net> (OK); Melinda Brown <mel@psicorps.org> (TN); Marcella Bucknam <quest15@juno.com> (AR, NB & ND & SD); Sarah Buxbaum (OH); Arthur Cohen <arthurc@mediaone.net> (MA-east); Wendy Curry <madamec@earthlink.net> (MA); Larry Deck <mshenga@lionking.org> (NH); Lisa Diguardi <diguardi@yahoo.com> (CO); Lisa Ehren <Latarra@globaldialog.com> (WI); Holly Naneette Ferris (MI); Christine "Stine" Lea Fletcher <cfletcher@Library.MsState.Edu> (LA & MS); Heather Franek (UT); Stephanie Moore-Fuller (MI); Elizabeth Garcia (MA-east-colleges); Pete Glass <pglass@ccmail.nevada.edu> (NV); Alexei Guren

At BiNet USA meeting

Courtesy of Robyn Ochs

Right: Guide staff, L-R, front: Tom Limoncelli, Robyn Ochs (ed.); back: Maurice Snellan, Linda Eklöf, Elyn Rabinowitz, Bobbi Keppel, Brett Beemyn, Arthur Cohen, Gary North.

Peg Preble

<alexei_guren@msn.com> (WA & OR); Emily C. Hadley <sativa@rocketmail.com> (KS); Jennifer Hadlock (CT); Steve Haley (FL); Georgea Harrison (IL-Chicago); Zandra Hawkins <zanhawk@kiva.net> (IN); Linda Hower (NH); Jim Hohl <jim@bi.org> (NYC); Sandy James <sandals@dmi.net> (ID); Elaine Holliman <holliman@earthlink.net> (MN); Steve Kadar <stevekadar@geocities.com> (VA); Bobbi Keppel <71612.340@compuserve.com> (ME); Sheeri Kritzer <sheeri@brandeis.edu> (MA- Boston); Charles Anders Kupperman <ck17Wpahesz.net> (NC); Susan Lander, Esq. (DC); Michelle LeBlanc (AK); Julie Levitt <bifemme@hotmail.com> (OR); Tom Limoncelli <tal+brc@plts.org> (NJ); Diana Lomarcan (AL); Sandra M. <axal@mailexcite.com> (PR); Jess Meyer (TX); E. Grace Noonan (MA-central & western); Gary North <bisexuals@aol.com> (CA-southern); Ron Owen <rtoaz@aol.com> (AZ); Linda Powers <linda@netins.net> (IA); Ellyn Rabinowitz (NYC); S.C. Ranger (SC); Kim Regan (MO); Aimee Ricciardone <aricciar@fas.harvard.edu> (VT); Leah Robin (GA); Frank E. Ross (KY); Cassie Shadows (CA-central); E. C. Sheeley (NM); Bob Shoemaker (DE & PA-Philadelphia); Karen Snelbecker <iguana@voicenet.com> (PA-Philadelphia); Marijah Sroczynski <marijah@juno.com> (PA-other); Steve Kadar (VA); Kim Ward <biwarriors@aol.com> (VT); Julie Waters <julie@drycas.club.cc.cmu.edu> (RI); Sean Whitcomb (CO); Ariella Wurmser <ariella@multicom.org> (NY state dx NYC area); Anonymous (MD)

Thanks to the following for their various roles in helping move this project along: Brett Beemyn (for his repeated offers to help out!), Linda Blair, Wayne Bryant, 'Tina Blanco and Sabrina Santiago (BRC Treasurers), Beth Firestein (for her editorial talents), Ron Fox, Sheeri Kritzer, Graham McKay, Brigitta Meyer, Vladislav Ortanov, Terri Lyn Balash Laymen, UpperCase Production & Design, Inc., Richard Curran, Ren Yamin, and to those who wished to remain anonymous and to those whose names I simply forgot to include (sorry).

To all of the board members and volunteers of the Bisexual Resource Center.

For financial support, special thanks to Dr. Fritz Klein and the American Institute of Bisexuality.

To my domestic partners, Luca (now departed, sadly) and Emma, for serving as paperweights.

```
 ^ ^         ^ ^
=O= ____)  =O= _____}
```

SPECIAL THANKS TO THE ESPECIALLY WONDERFUL:

This project would not have been possible without the support and brilliance of Kathleen (the extremely great) Hepburn. She designed the data base in which over 2000 listings reside. She has walked me through technical questions, made me laugh when I needed to. And, of course, she made this Guide look the way it does;

Linda Dyndiuk who tirelessly and relentlessly dug up volunteers, scheduled them week after week, and chased down overdue listings and "missing" editors, and worked every single Monday evening for at least a year on this project!;

David Rothscheck and Arthur Cohen for their endless patience and boundless energy as they stepped in at the eleventh hour and helped with some of the meta-organizing, taking on everything from securing advertising, to soliciting volunteers, and keeping me calm.

And of course, I'll take a bit of credit too as the mother and editor of this book, and its previous 13 incarnations as the *The Bisexual Resource Guide* and as *The International Directory of Bisexual Groups.*

This Guide is dedicated to my mother, Sonny Ochs and to my partner in crime and life, Peg Preble, neither bisexual, and both two of my strongest supporters.

What is Bisexuality?

bi Robyn Ochs

Some people are attracted to men. Some people are attracted to women. And some people are attracted to men and to women. And some of us go through periods in our lives when we aren't particularly attracted to anyone.

Simple.

Sexologist Alfred Kinsey and his colleagues tried to chart this diversity by developing what ended up being called "The Kinsey Scale," a seven point scale in which people who were exclusively heterosexual in their attractions and behaviors were assigned a zero, people who were exclusively homosexual a six, with lots of combinations of heterosexuality and homosexuality in the one to five range. One of the most surprising findings of the *Kinsey Report* was that almost half of his male respondents, and about one-fourth of his female respondents reported adult sexual experience with both men and women. And this was in the late 1940s! Kinsey addressed the fluidity of sexuality in the following statement:

> *Males do not represent two discrete populations, heterosexual and homosexual. The world is not divided into sheep and goats. Not all things are black, nor all things white. It is a fundamental of taxonomy that nature rarely deals with discrete categories. Only the human mind invents categories and tries to force facts into separated pigeon-holes. The living world is a continuum in each and every one of its aspects. The sooner we learn this concerning human sexual behavior the sooner we shall reach a sound understanding of the realities of sex.*

Similarly, anthropologist Margaret Mead stated in a 1975 article in *Redbook*,

> *Even a superficial look at other societies and some groups in our own society should be enough to convince us that a very large number of human beings – probably a majority – are bisexual in their potential capacity for love. Whether they will become exclusively heterosexual or exclusively homosexual for all their lives and in all circumstances or whether they will be able to enter into sexual and love relationships with members of both sexes is, in fact, a consequence of the way they have been brought up, of the particular beliefs and prejudices of the society they live in and, to some extent, of their own life history.*

Given statements like this, it is surprising that Western culture has held on to its dichotomous concept of sexual orientation, which posits that everyone is *really* either gay or straight. In this mode of thinking, bisexuality exists only as an oddity, a transitional phase, a blip in the natural order of things.

But those who attempt to dichotomize sexuality are closing their eyes to the very real experiences of some very real people. Anthropologist Esther Newton wrote that "desire, we begin to think, is less like a heart, throbbing the same everywhere, and more like music, and every culture has its own—not only songs, but tonality, instruments and occasions." Not only does every culture and every subculture have its own understanding of sexuality and its meaning, but every individual is different, with our own unique sexuality. We each have the right to use the labels we choose, and to live as we choose, providing that all parties involved are fully consenting adults.

My advice to you is this:

Be good to yourself.

Be good to your loved ones.

Be honest.

Be thoughtful.

Play safe.

Communicate.

Get the support and information you need.

And celebrate the gift of your sexuality!

And that's the purpose of this book.

How to Start a Bisexual Support Group

bi Robyn Ochs

Bisexual support groups are springing up all over the world. Is there one in your town? If not, you may want to start one. Here are some pointers to help you create the safe space essential for creating a positive bisexual identity.

What is a Support Group?

It's up to you to decide what type of group you want. It can be a social group, a facilitated or unfacilitated discussion group, it can be closed or open to newcomers. Each type of group will require different skills to run.

Rule Number One: There Are No Rules.

There is no simple formula for the successful creation of a bisexual support group. Even within a given country, every community has its own character. Organizing in Minneapolis is not the same as organizing in a small town in New Hampshire. And a small town in Manitoba may be different from a small town in Quebec. Therefore, what follows are guidelines and suggestions, not hard and fast rules. You will need to adapt this information to your own community's resources and needs, and to your own personal desires.

A Group will be More Successful if its Members Feel a Sense of Ownership.

If you are beginning a group, do everything possible to make sure that the group, and not one person, shares responsibility and decision making. Therefore, while it is important to go into your first meeting with some ideas about what you would like a group to be, be open to other people's ideas. Failure to do so will result in a situation where all members will not get what they need from the group, and you will get stuck doing all of the work, because other people will not feel invested in the group. And if you burn out or lose interest, the group may cease to exist.

Logistics

The first step in forming a new group is to organize a meeting. This process of organization has several components: finding a space, letting people know that the meeting is going to happen, and deciding upon the actual agenda for the meeting.

Finding a space: In many communities it is possible to obtain meeting space at little or no charge. Public libraries, schools, city or town halls, someone's home, women's or progressive bookstores, food cooperatives, religious meeting houses (Quakers and Unitarian Universalists are usually particularly receptive) may have meeting space available. Keep in mind issues such as safety, accessibility to public transportation and wheelchair accessibility, and try to select a place which is fairly neutral, to allow closeted people, or people new to bisexual identity the maximum possible safety. When you have found a meeting space, make sure to leave time to advertise. Usually 6-8 weeks is sufficient.

Contact information. It can be very helpful to list a telephone number or post office box which people can contact for more information. Should you list your own address or phone number? Some people feel comfortable doing this, others do not. One woman lists her telephone number with a pseudonym. That way she knows immediately whether someone is calling as a result of her ads or posters, and she feels safer because she is not giving out her real name. If you list your own number and have restrictions on when you are willing to be called, state that clearly in the flier or ad, such as "for info. call Maria at 222-2222 between 6 pm and 9 pm." Another option is to rent a voice mailbox (approximately $10/month), or to ask a local (or not too far away) lesbian/gay hotline, or lesbian/gay center, or women's center to serve as your contact phone number, at least for a limited time. Whatever method you choose, be sure to return all calls promptly, and to be discreet. Remember: homophobia exists, and not everyone is out to his/her roommate, parents, spouse, etc.

Covering Expenses: Keep expenses as low as possible, then "pass the hat" at the meeting. State what your expenses were, and propose a suggested amount, asking people to pay what they can.

Getting the Word Out: Advertising

Once you have located a site for your first meeting, you must let as many people as possible know that it is happening. There are a number of ways to do this, mostly through newspapers, fliers, and word of mouth.

Newspaper calendars and classified ads. Many newspapers will list events open to the public in a "calendar" section. Check your local newspaper to see whether they do this. Calendar listings are usually free. If a calendar listing is not possible, you my want to consider placing a brief classified ad. Keep it as short and inexpensive as possible, for example:

> *BISEXUAL support/discussion group forming. First meeting November 22, 7:30 p.m. at Local High School Cafeteria. Call (789)456-1234 for info.*

Try to get this listing into as many publications as possible: the newspapers of nearby colleges, the nearest gay paper (even if it is based in another city or town), regional e-mail lists or bulletin boards, any local or regional newsletters (does a nearby Unitarian Universalist Church have a newsletter? Is there a women's center newsletter published nearby?)

Fliers. Make up a clear, concise 8 1/2 x 11 inch or other standard size poster about the meeting. State the time and place of the meeting, whether it is wheelchair accessible, what its purpose is: "to discuss the possible formation of an ongoing bisexual support group." Statements about confidentiality may be helpful, especially in a more conservative environment. Get these posters up in as many locations as possible: on bulletin boards in local progressive stores, on local campuses, in bookstores, at the nearest food coop, gay bars, etc. Use your imagination. One place you may want to consider postering is the inside of bathroom stalls. They sometimes stay up longer before getting pulled down, you will have a captive audience, and interested people can read them and copy down the information in total privacy.

Remember: when choosing where to place calendar listings and to hang posters, keep in mind that bisexual people are a very diverse group, and to reach the maximum number of people you will want to get the word out in many different locations. This means reaching people from all economic, racial, and ethnic backgrounds who are bi, gay, and straight identified.

Your First Meeting

Come to your first meeting prepared. Arrange chairs in a circle so that everyone can see each other and everyone is included. Here is one possible format for a first meeting: ▼ **Welcome everyone.** Discuss ground rules (respect for one another, confidentiality, sharing air time, no one has to speak who does not wish to.) Review the evening's agenda. Many people feel more comfortable when they know what to expect. Make sure that everyone is comfortable physically: let them know where the bathroom is, where they may and may not smoke, that they may get up and leave the room if they wish to, etc. ▼ **Do some sort of "go-around"** in which each person gets a chance to speak. Have each person say their name and answer a question or two (why they came, what they would like to get out of the meeting, an interesting fact about themselves.) One exercise which can be a good icebreaker is to have people divide into pairs. Within each pair, have each person interview the other for 3 minutes, then switch roles. When each has interviewed a partner, come back to the

main group and go around the room, having each person introduce her/his partner: "This is Teresa. She is the mother of two children. She hates lima beans and likes to play rugby and the violin." ▼ **Have a moderated discussion**. Most people in a new group have had little or no opportunity to talk about issues related to bisexuality and are starving for a chance to talk. ▼ **Set aside time to decide on the next step.** Do people want to have another meeting, to start a group, etc.? Make sure that you do not leave the meeting without scheduling your next meeting. Pass around a phone list so that you (or someone else who is designated) have a way to reach people interested in meeting again.

Make sure that this meeting does not last more than 2 hours, or people will start to drift out and will miss the planning segment of the meeting. Keep an eye on the time, and try to leave 40 minutes or so for the planning segment. You may have to cut off an interesting conversation, but explain that you are asking people to cut the current conversation short to work out a way to continue the discussion later.

Subsequent Meetings

Depending upon the needs and desires of its members, support groups usually take one of four formats: ▼ **Focus on personal support or empowerment.** A personal support group would meet regularly and might focus on "go-arounds," with each member giving an update on current issues in her or his life. Other group members would listen and, sometimes, if asked, offer comments or advice. Occasionally, issues raised in the go-arounds might lead to impassioned political discussions over sexual politics and other issues. ▼ **Focus on discussion of topics.** A discussion-focused group would pick a topic in advance of each meeting. Topics might include: a book or article that everyone agreed to read and discuss, or a subject (the politics of marriage, bisexuality and feminism, coming out to one's children, parents, friends, partners, etc., dating, gender differences in relationships, monogamy and open relationships, safer sex, being bi in the gay community, etc.) ▼ **Focus on activities.** An activity-focused group might meet regularly for social activities: going out dancing, bowling, to the movies, to the beach, or renting and watching videos. ▼ **A combination of the above.** Brief go-arounds followed by a topic discussion, or go-arounds some weeks and topic discussions on others, with periodic social activities.

The group must decide where and how often to meet, and you must decide what type of commitment is expected from members. One suggestion is to meet weekly for a fixed period of time to form a sense of community and group cohesion and then to adjust your meeting to a less-intensive schedule. Another suggestion is to begin a personal support and empowerment group with several weeks of topic discussions to allow members time to build trust. You also need to decide whether to be an open or closed group. You might begin as an open group and then decide to close the group to new members at a later date, as the group coalesces. If you decide to close your group, you may wish to set up a mechanism for helping others form their own support groups. You may choose to rotate facilitators, or to have a regular volunteer or professional facilitator.

It is important to remember that, no matter what you do, not all groups will last. The group chemistry may not be right. If this happens, you may want to try again from the beginning.

Words Of Advice

Whenever possible, **talk to other people** who have experience in what you are trying to do. Talk to people who have started bisexual support groups in areas similar to yours, or who have started other types of support groups in your own community. We can learn from others' successes and mistakes.

Embrace diversity. While it may sometimes be more comfortable to have a group filled with people who are like you in terms of class, race, politics, etc., sometimes we learn more in a group where a variety of diverse voices are present.

Try, to the greatest extent possible, to **accommodate people's needs.** Is your meeting place wheelchair accessible? Are there pets, cigarette smoke, or other environmental substances present that members may be allergic to? Is your meeting place on public transportation for members without cars?

An occasional individual may contact you or show up at your meetings whose needs cannot be met by a support group. You may wish to have the names and phone numbers of the nearest hotline and of a couple of supportive therapists so that you can provide appropriate referrals.

Be clear in your advertising, and to new members that your group is not a dating service. Some support groups have policies stating that group members should not get romantically involved with one another.

Be aware that your group will provide support for many more people than actually attend meetings. The simple knowledge that there is a bisexual group meeting out there may be affirming to more people than you will ever know. And that is another good reason to get the word out.

If your group is an open group, try to make meeting time, place and contact information consistent. Some people may be terrified at the idea of attending a bisexual support group, and it may take them months to get up the courage to come to their first meeting. Make sure these people can find you.

Once your group is established, don't forget to get listed in the *Bisexual Resource Guide.*

[Note: This information originally appeared in the form of a pamphlet published by the Bisexual Resource Center. I am aware that this information is directed primarily at readers in the United States and Canada, and that some of the information contained herein may not apply to those organizing in other countries. Readers in other countries: please take what is useful, and forgive the rest. —Robyn Ochs]

Announcements
Upcoming conferences, calls for papers, etc.

Australian Bisexual Anthology. The Australian Bisexual Network invites submissions to their project to publish an anthology of bi writing from the Australian region. Personal stories, bi theory, poetry, cartoons, photographs, etc. are welcome from bi people and their partners or family members, and from bi and bi-inclusive groups in Australia, New Zealand, Papua New Guinea, Norfolk Island and other South Pacific Islands. We hope to collect submissions from a diverse group - cultural, ethnic, (trans-)gender, age, religion, community identity, etc. Send submissions to: Jacinta Toomey, 345 Boundary Street, West End, QLD 4101, Australia. (07) 38462427.

Bi Women welcomes writings by women: poetry, short fiction (up to 3 pages), news articles, opinion pieces, book and film reviews. Send writings to BBWN, PO Box 400639, Cambridge MA 02140, USA, or you can email them to ochs@bi.org for forwarding to *Bi Women's* editor.

Bisexual Erotic Stories Wanted: Sexually explicit fiction/semi-fiction of not more than 5000 words featuring bisexual characters & a representation of bisexual desire (detailed characters & some cultural context, rather than just sex acts), aiming to present a diversity of bisexual erotic writings, and desires which have previously been hidden in other erotic anthologies. Themes could include: celibacy, monogamy, nonmonogamy, gender transgression, fluid desire, identity politics, politics of biphobia, BDSM, bisexual culture, non-Western concepts of bisexuality, etc. Any genre ok (sci-fi, cyber, crime,horror, humor, coming out stories, etc...). The editorial group is comprised of activists within the UK bi community. Please send all pieces with a SSAE to PO Box 10048, London SE15 4ZD, UK. Email: klano@hotmail.com.

Book on Black Homosexuality. Seeking contributions, min. 6000 words, including areas such as bisexuality, coming out in the Black commmunity, gay racism, etc. For further info, write to: Delroy Constantine-Simms, The University of Hertfordshire, Watford Campus, Aldenham, Aldenham Hall, Watford WD2 8AT, United Kingdom. E-mail: eduqdc1@herts.ac.uk.

Children of Stonewall. Alyson Publications, a leader in gay & lesbian publishing, seeks personal essays from lesbians, gay men, bisexuals, & transgendered people born after (or shortly before) the Stonewall Riots of 1969. Looking for varied, engaging, thoughtful, well-written, surprising, personal, funny, introspective work. Particularly interested in essays about your younger years. Let's tell the world what it's like to inherit the older generations' legacy of relative freedom & pride – and trouble. Essays should be 1-15 pages, double spaced. Write for submission guidelines to: Robin Bernstein & Seth Silberman, Eds., *Children of Stonewall*, PO Box 11172, Takoma Park MD 20913, USA.

Disabled Women's Anthology. Are you a disabled dyke, two-spirited bisexual or transgendered woman? We want your writing for an anthology!! Stories, poems, narrative, & other writing as well as visual art (in black and white). We need more submissions from disabled Asian, Latina, African Canadian, African-American and Two-Spirited women to constitute real representation. Contact: Shelly Tremain c/o Women's Press, 517 College St. Suite 233, Toronto, Ontario Canada M6G 4A2. 416-921-2425.

Life in the Closet. Carol Riels, researcher/author, is gathering research for her next book, on alternative lifestyles. If you are les/bi/gay/trans and have not always been out, but rather tried to lives as straight, or at least presented yourself to others as straight before coming out, she would like to hear your story. Areas of interest include: 1) how the deception affected you; 2) what your emotions were during this time; 3) what you had to do to keep up the facade during this time; 4) what made you finally stop denying your true identity to yourself and others; 5) how you feel now; 6) how old you were when you realized how you were feeling; 7) what you would say to others who are having difficulty being true to themselves and to others; 8) what name you would like to use; 9) where you are from. You may share all that you want. Carol will edit out what may not be relevant to the book. If your story is used in the book, you may remain anonymous, use an alias, or use all or part of your real name. If your story is used, you will be sent an autographed copy, hot off the press, provided that you send Carol your mailing address. You may e-mail your story or inquiry to manyfaces@cedar-rapids.net.

Journal of Gay, Lesbian & Bisexual Identity, Warren Blumenfeld, editor. Announcing a scholarly forum containing peer-reviewed original articles, clinical studies, & high quality research papers that address the many factors involved in the discovery & assertion of one's sexual identity. Now accepting original manuscripts. For complete submission guidelines: Warren J. Blumenfeld, Editor, *Journal of Gay, Lesbian & Bisexual Identity*, PO Box 929, Northampton MA 01061. For subscription info: Human Sciences Press, Inc., Attn, Dept. HGL94., 233 Spring St., New York, NY 10013-1578, USA.

Queer Subjects. Contributions sought for a volume of essays on the question of queer subjects (as people & "disciplines"), academic life & the job market, especially essays exploring these overlapping topics from a personal perspective while making critical analyses of the material practices of academic scholarship, professional development, & institutional change. There exists very little personal or scholarly analysis of the material & intellectual constraints that scholars doing lesbian & gay studies face in academic contexts. Because such concerns are connected to & reinforced by larger questions of homophobia, heterosexism, & the viability of any kind of "identity-politics-based" research in academic settings, we want to include a wide range of contributions & hope to hear not only from younger scholars – graduate students & recent Ph.D.'s – about how they have negotiated the current highly limited job market but also from older, more established scholars who have been pioneers in the field or have entered it only after securing tenure. Seeking essays that look at the personal experiences of practitioners in the growing & changing field of queer studies, as well as contributions that explore the personal, academic, & institutional pressures on queers who, for various reasons, are not actively pursuing queer scholarship. Manuscripts should be 15-20 pages, double-spaced. Submit 2 copies of your manuscript: 1 to Toni McNaron, Department of English, University of Minnesota, Minneapolis, MN 55401 & 1 to Scott Bravmann, 319 Church Street, San Francisco, CA 94114, USA. Email: bravmann@aol.com.

A Wideness of Spirit: Testimonies of Bisexual People of Faith is an anthology in search of writings. Those following any spiritual path, including but not limited to: Jews, Christians, Pagans, UUs, Muslims, Hindus, Buddhists, Wiccans, people in 12-step recovery, and indigenous earth based traditions are invited to send essays, poems, songs, liturgy, etc. Those most likely to be selected are those under 20 pages, double-spaced, which speak passionately and clearly about the author's understanding of the intersections between sexual orientation and spirit path. The anthology will also seek to reflect race/class/gender/age/geographic/lifestyle diversity. The deadline will be mid-1999. Contact Deb Kolodny at: 301-565-0719, DebraRuth@aol.com, or 631 Ritchie Avenue, Silver Spring, MD 20910. Completed manuscripts along with discs should be sent to that address as well.

MEETINGS & CONFERENCES

April 23-25, 1999 (& annually in April): BECAUSE (Bisexual Empowerment Conference: A Uniting, Supportive Experience) A conference for bisexual, transgender and other queer & queer-friendly people in Minneapolis/St. Paul, Minnesota and the entire Midwest! Robyn Ochs and Fritz Klein are the keynote speakers in 1999. For info. contact: BECAUSE, PO Box 23172, Richfield MN 55423, USA. (612) 813-1383. Email: Lunn-1@tc.umn.edu.

Australia Bi Conference held annually in March. Contact: Australian Bisexual Network (see listings).

1st weekend of September, annually: Northwest Bisexuals Campout. Northwest US bisexuals hold their annual gathering & campout in the Wenatchee National Forest near Mt. Ranier National Park in Washington state. Sponsored by the Bisexual Network of Oregon (BiNet), this event is held at a secluded campground between the Bumping & American rivers, 23 miles east of Chinook Pass & Mt. Ranier National Park. All bisexuals & their guests are welcome. Info: BiNet Orgeon at 503-622-5401.

November, annually: Creating Change Conference. Sponsored by the National Gay & Lesbian Task Force, this is an annual activist conference. Many wonderful workshops, speakers, and lots of how-to information for both veteran and aspiring activists from all over the United States. For more information contact: Creating Change, NGLTF, PO Box 96030, Washington DC 20090-6030, USA or NGLTF@ngltf.org.

July 16-18, 1999: **UK BiCon**. Likely to be held in Edinburgh, Scotland. For more details contact BM BiCon, London WC1N 3XX, visit their web site at http://bi.org/-bicon/ or send email to bicon2000@bi.org. Summer 2000: **BiCon 2000**, Likely to be held in September in Plymouth, United Kingdom.

Oct. 5-7, 1999, **Something Queer is Bruin': 10 Years of GLBTs in Academia** at the University of California, Los Angeles, USA. 10th anniversary conference of the University of California Lesbian, Gay, Bisexual, and Transgender Association (UCLGBTA) celebrates the first decade of LGBT academic presence on California campuses. There will be presentations in three areas of interest: (1) politics and public policy, (2) culture, arts, and media, and (3) education and student leadership, focusing on practical usefulness to educators, students, practitioners, and/or providers. Cost: TBA (No one will be turned away for lack of funds). Contact: The UCLA LGBT Campus Resource Center Homepage for Conference Links and electronic registration at <http://www.ben2.ucla.edu/~lgbt/>; or email at LGBT@UCLA.EDU; or call (310) 206-3628; or snailmail to: UCLA LGBT Campus Resource Center, 220 Kinsey Hall, Box 951579, Los Angeles, CA 90095-1579. Conference Co-Chairs: Steven Leider and Jodie Lind.

Summer 2000: **6th International Bi Conference** in Rotterdam, The Netherlands. Information on the conference will be published at http://www.lnbi.demon.nl/ibc6/. Information requests, proposals and such can be sent to ibc6@lnbi.demon.nl which will, for the moment be the central mail address. Snailmail information requests can be sent to: Dutch Bisexual Network, P.O. Box 75087, 1070AB Amsterdam, The Netherlands. Exact date to be announced.

Summer 2001: **North America Bi Conference** in Vancouver, Canada. Contact: BiNet-Vancouver at binetbc@bi.org (see listing for BiNet-Vancouver)

1999 or 2001: **South American Bi Conference** to be held in Brazil.

Robyn Ochs

Linda Blair, president of the Bisexual Resource Center, at the 5th International Conference on Bisexuality

2002: **7th International Bi Conference** to be held in Australia. Contact Wayne Roberts at ausbinet@rainbow.net.au.

February 13, 1999: **London BiFest.** For the first time ever there will be a major parade of bisexual people & their allies through the streets of the capital, not to protest, but to proudly celebrate their sexuality & increase their visibility, cumulating in the first ever London Bisexual Festival. BiFest will be held at the University of London Union and will include entertainment, music, exhibitions, performers & more. Sponsored by the London Bisexual Group, one of the oldest and longest established bisexual community groups in the UK. For more information contact Marc Turner at 0956-896-589 or email LBF@biout.demon.co.uk.

March, annually: **Children from the Shadows.** A sexual minority youth conference for youth and service providers held annually in Connecticut, USA. Lots of bi content. This nonprofit organization holds additional events during the year. Write: PO Box 1855, Manchester CT 06056-1855. 860-649-7386.

July, annually: **BiCamp.** To be held in western Massachusetts, USA. For more information call the Bisexual Resource Center at 617-424-9595.

Emergence International: Annual conferences for gay Christian Scientists. Held annually. Write: Emergence International PO Box 6061-423 Sherman Oaks, CA 91413. BILLXLS@aol.com Phone: 800-280-6653.

The Evangelican Network (T-E-N) of Biblical Churches holds two annual conferences (February in Phoenix, AZ; Autumn in Vancouver, BC). Christian Bible based organization which serves as a support network for predominantly glbt independent churches, organizations and individuals. For more information, write to: Cristo Ministries, PO Box 16104, Phoenix, AZ, 85011-6104 or phone: 602-265-2813 or 602-265-2918. On the internet: http://www.xroads.com/ten_net/cpress/htm or email ten_net@xroads.com.

In the Family: A Magazine for Lesbians, Gays, Bisexuals and their Relations, the quarterly magazine addressing lesbian, gay and bisexual families, sponsers an annual lgb family therapy conference. P.O. Box 5387, Tacoma Park, MD 20913. Phone: 301-270-4771, on the web at http://www.inthefamily.com, or e-mail Lmarkowitz@aol.com.

Pa'Fuera Pa'Lante Northeast Conference '99. Annual Regional Organizing Conference devoted to the concerns of the Latino/a Lesbian, Gay, Bisexual, & Transgender Community. For more information call: 212-614-2949 or e-mail pafuerapal@aol.com.

El Encuentro 7 International Conference: "A World Without Borders" Hosted by LLEGO. San Diego/Tijuana, October 7-11, 1999. For information contact: (202)266-8240 (Washington, DC) or (619)692-1967 (San Diego).

Creating Change. Annual Conference. The National Conference for the Gay, Lesbian, Bisexual & Transgender Movement. 1999 Conference will be held in Oakland, CA November 10-14. For more information contact NGLTF, 2320 17th Street NW, Washington DC, 20009-2702, (202)332-6483 x3329. TTY: (202)332-6219, FAX: (202)332-0207. Or visit their web site www.ngltf.org.

OTHER IMPORTANT ANNOUNCEMENTS:

$$$ Grant money available for projects related to bisexuality $$$: The American Institute of Bisexuality announces that grants (US $200-1500) are available for projects related to bisexuality, such as: publications, academic research, seed money for new bi organizations, community outreach projects, etc. Applications accepted on a continuous basis and reviewed every 4 months. Groups or individuals in all countries are welcome to apply. For application contact: AIB, 4545 Park Blvd. #207, San Diego CA 92116, USA.

Funders of Lesbian, Gay and Bisexual Programs: A Directory for Grantseekers.
Published by the Working Group on Funding Lesbian and Gay Issues. Lists over 240
foundations and corporations from across the country who have funded national,
regional or local lesbian, gay and/or bisexual programs and projects. The Directory is
available for $15.00, with discounts for orders of more than 10 copies. To order, or
for further information on the Working Group contact The Working Group on
Funding Lesbian and Gay Issues, 116 East 16th Street, 7th Floor, New York, NY
10003. Phone (212)475-2930, fax: (212)982-3321 or e-mail WGNancy@aol.com. Please
make checks payable to Astraea/Working Group.

Canadians: The Toronto Centre for Lesbian & Gay Studies announces the **Lynch
History Grant for LGBT History.** The $1000 grant is open to individuals, groups and
organizations. It is awarded every other year, and must be used for the creation for
new work which contributes to an understanding of the historical development of
lgbt sexualities, identities, politics and communities in Canada, with priority to
projects that reflect the racial, cultural, lingusitic, class or other differences which
make up queer historical experience. Projects may be: slide show, workshop,
conference, oral history project, art exhibit, popular or academic article, pamphlet,
book. For more information contact: 416-926-XTRA, ext. 2810 or email:
ejackson@inforamp.net.

African-American bisexual & lesbian women sought to volunteer for a doctoral
research project on the coming out process and implications for therapy done by
Ph.D. candidate at Spaulding University. To volunteer: email to Alison From
<alifrom@aol.com>, write her at 335 Olin Memorial Health Center, E. Lansing MI
48824, USA, or call 617-355-2310 and leave your name and address.

New Bi Book! Bisexuality in the United States: A Social Science Reader by Paula Rust
is coming out in 1999, from Columbia University Press. Highly recommended!

Call for participants. Your participation is needed! We are conducting a national
survey of the experiences of sexual minority people as clients in psychotherapy or
counseling. We want to know the quality of mental health services you have
received. This is an opportunity to let professional providers know how they're doing
in meeting your specific needs. For a short (4 page) questionnaire e-mail: Rita
Cowan, PhD or Melissa Lidderdale at GLBtherapy@aol.com or mail address to PO
Box 1211, Massillon, OH 44648. Confidentiality will be maintained. Deadline April
30, 1999.

Finding Bisexuality in Literature

bi Robyn Ochs

This section of the Bisexual Resource Guide contains an annotated bibliography (or Bi- bliography) of books with bisexual content: books about the subject of bisexuality as well as books with bi characters. Now it's very easy to tell if a non-fiction book is about bisexuality: it's usually called *Bisexual Lives*, or *Bisexual Politics*, or something like that. But it's a lot harder to tell if a work of fiction is a "bisexual book."

After all, how do you determine who is "really" bisexual? Is a female character who is heterosexual at the beginning of the book and then falls in love with another woman and at the end of the book is still deeply in love with that woman "really" a bisexual, or is she "really" a lesbian? If she never labels herself as lesbian or bi-sexual, the reader will obviously be making a subjective interpretation. It is important to keep in mind that the author's intent and the readers interpretations are not always the same.

This was demonstrated to me very clearly in the winter of 1996 as I was organizing a panel at the Out/Write conference here in Boston. I provided conference organizer Michael Bronski with a list of approximately one dozen fiction writers whom I thought would be appropriate for a panel on bi characters in fiction. Michael called those on my list whom he thought most likely to attend the conference, and he reported back to me that one woman whom he had called, *several* of whose novels appear on my list of books with bi characters, had wondered aloud to him why she was being asked to be on this particular panel. "I don't write about bisexuals," she said, "I write about straight women who become lesbians." Well, she certainly could have fooled me, and, to be quite honest, I felt a sense of personal hurt and rejection when Michael reported what the novelist had said, though of course I recognize the right of the author to understand her own creations as she chooses.

It would not be an understatement to say that we are starved for reflections of our lives, and as a result we grab at whatever scraps we can find.

So, how *can* you recognize a bisexual? There is a presumption in Western cultures that all people are heterosexual, expanded somewhat in this century to the presumption that all people are either heterosexual *or* become homosexual. Bisexuality, for the most part, remains invisible—invisible, that is, except as a point of conflict or transition. In other words, an action or event must occur in order to make bisexuality visible to the viewer. Thus, with rare exceptions, the only bisexuals who are seen as bisexual are those who are known to be in relationships with more than one partner (of more than one sex), and bisexuals who are leaving a partner of one sex for a partner of a different sex. Bisexuals whose lives are celibate, monogamous, and/ or non-conflictual are not read as bisexual by the outside viewer, but rather as either straight or gay. Hence, there is an inevitable association of bisexuality with non-monogamy, conflict and transition.

In our review of bisexuality in literature, certain general themes can be found.

One major theme is **triangulation**, usually accompanied by jealousy and the fracturing of one relationship for another. The bisexual person is usually located at the triangle's apex. Two examples of this are Anaïs Nin's *Henry and June*, which is about a triangulated relationship with between Henry, June and Anaïs, with June at the apex; and Earnest Hemmingway's *Garden of Eden*, with Catherine at the apex between Marita and David.

Then there's the "**discovery novel**," popular in lesbian literature of the 1970s, in which a previously heterosexual woman *discovers* her lesbianism by falling in love with a woman. Because at the end of the book she is happily paired with another woman, she is commonly read as a lesbian. But one might ask whether her previous relationships should be considered valid, as well as what questioning the stability of her identity over time: what this woman's future might hold, should her current relationship end. Despite statistical probability, because we live in a "happily ever after" culture, we are not supposed to ask this latter question. Another common character found in discovery novels is the woman (sometimes the (ex)partner of the woman described above) who can't handle the societal stigma attached to a same-sex relationship and "goes back" to men (is she *really* a lesbian unwilling to admit it, or is she really bi, or really straight?)

Another place we can sometimes find bisexuality is in **fantasy/science fiction/ Utopian** novels. Here, bisexuality is *normal*, a given, not stigmatized. By setting a story outside of the current reality, a great deal more leeway is allowed. A few examples are Starhawk's *The 5th Sacred Thing*, Samuel Delaney's *Dhalgren*, Marge Piercy's *Woman on the Edge of Time*, James Varley's *Titan, Wizard,* and *Demon Series*, and Melissa Scott's *Burning Bright* and *Shadow Man*.

Historical novels are another place to locate the elusive bisexual. Here, safely far away from the present time, men (and almost all of the historical bisexuals I've been able to located are male) are bisexual — no big deal — though they're not called bisexual or gay. Examples: most of the historical novels by Mary Renault (about ancient Greece), and Lucia St. Clair Robson's *Tokaido Road* (which is set in 17th century Japan).

And then there's what I call "**1970s bisexuality**" where bisexuality equals free love. These novels are usually written by men and, in contrast to historical novels, the bisexuals characters are almost always women who share their voluptuous bodies with both women and (primarily) with men. Authors Robert Heinlein, Tom Robbins, and John Irving would all be included under this heading.

Then there's **adolescent bisexuality**, sometimes written off as youthful teenage experimentation: Hanif Kureishi's, *The Buddha of Suburbia*, and Felice Picano's, *Ambidextrous*.

Finally, there's the **hedonistic bisexual** who is often self-destructive and may leave a trail of broken lives (including his or her own), for example, Leonard Cohen's *Beautiful Losers*, Rupert Everett's *Hello Darling, Are You Working?*, and Carole Maso's *The American Woman in the Chinese Hat*.

But few authors actually use the "B-word." Among the few who do are Emma Donohue, Larry Duplechan, E. Lynn Harris, Dan Kavanagh, M.E. Kerr, and poets Michael Montgomery & Michelle Clinton.

In *Vice Versa: Bisexuality and the Eroticism of Everyday Life,* author Marjorie Garber says that we write our life histories backward, from the present, eliminating facts that do not fit our current stories. Someone who currently identifies as a gay man, therefore, might discount all past heterosexual experience, even if it felt meaningful and "real" at the time. And authors may do the same for their characters. Unlike those of us in the real world, the authors, of course, have this right: they *can* see into their characters minds. The characters are, after all, their creations.

Perhaps one thing I learned from my experience of trying to organize the writers panel is that, in my hunger to find myself in fiction, perhaps I was focusing too hard. Perhaps I can find aspects of myself not only in fictional characters that self-identify as bisexual, but also in the experiences of characters of various sexual orientations.

Labels are tools, which help us to describe ourselves to ourselves as well as to others. They are not fixed and unchanging *essences*. The reality is that each of us is unique. Labels, however useful, will never be fully adequate to the task of describing real people, and should not be confused with reality. In that sense, we may be able to find our own bisexual experiences in fiction, regardless of the self-identification of the character or the intent of the author.

That said, I present you with a list of books that contain within their pages some degree of bisexual content.

Bisexual Stories

An annotated bi-bliography
bi Robyn Ochs

All of the books listed below deal in some way with bisexual identity and/or behavior, though few of the narrators or characters in the books listed below use the word "bisexual." Rather, each book has at least one character whose life history can be interpreted to be bisexual. This list is by no means exhaustive; rather it is a place to begin. Your suggestions for books to be listed in future editions of this *Guide* are welcome. All books listed below are in English, except as noted. Many of these books can be ordered through the "Bisexual Bookstore" on the World Wide Web: http://www.biresource.org/bookstore/index.html.

[codes: m: primarily about men; w: primarily about women; m,w: about both men and women]

BIOGRAPHIES/AUTOBIOGRAPHIES

James Broughton, **Coming Unbuttoned**. San Francisco: City Lights Books, 1993. Born in 1913, poet and independent filmmaker Broughton takes us through his life in the San Francisco Bay Area, London and Paris. Though he does not delve into the meaning of his bisexual identity, he (and many others in his story) clearly identifies as such and over the course of his life had a number of relationships with men and women.

John Cheever, **The Journals of John Cheever**. NY: Knopf: 1990. Includes discussion of writer's bisexuality and extramarital relationships. (In case you were wondering, none of Cheever's fictional writings discuss bisexuality.) (m)

Cyril Collard, **Savage Nights**. Woodstock, NY: The Overlook Press1993 (originally published in French as **Les Nuits Fauves**). French writer, film director and actor writes of his HIV diagnosis and subsequent relationships with a 17 year old woman and two young men. Set in present-day Paris, this disturbing and powerful story, includes discussions of unprotected sex, anonymous s/m sex, and the difference for the author between sex with male and female partners. The author self-identifies as bisexual. (m)

Samuel R. Delaney, **The Motion of Light in Water**. NY: Arbor House, 1988. Fascinating autobiography of science fiction writer's teens and twenties in New York City, 1957-1965. While Samuel Delaney currently identifies as gay, his history and his former identification are bisexual. (m)

Ruth Falk, **Women Loving: A Journey Toward Becoming an Independent Woman**. NY: Random House, 1975. An autobiographical account of the author's journey, including her bisexuality. (w)

Barbara Guest, **Herself Defined: The Poet H.D. and Her World**. NY: Doubleday, 1984. Biography of American expatriate writer H.D (1886-1961). Thorough and respectful representation of her significant romantic relationships, which included both women and men. (w,m)

Anchee Min, **Red Azalea**. NY: Berkeley Books, 1994. Fascinating autobiography of a woman growing up in Maoist China. The woman Min loves in her youth, and perhaps Min herself, are bisexual. (w)

Kate Millett, **Flying**. NY: Simon & Schuster, 1974. and **Sita**. NY: Simon & Schuster, 1976. (w) 2 autobiographical novels by a self-identified bi who has been a leader of the modern women's movement. (w)

Nigel Nicolson, **Portrait of a Marriage**. London: Weidenfeld & Nicolson, 1973. Biography of Vita Sackville-West & Harold Nicolson by their son. Born late 19th-century, Vita was a self-identified bi woman of the British upper class in love with Violet Trefusis. (w,m)

Anaïs Nin, **Henry and June**. NY: Harcourt, Brace, Jovanovich, 1986. Nin's diary from 1931-1932, in which she recounts her relationships with her husband, Hugo, and with Henry and June Miller. Beautiful writing, much discussion about her relationships and their meaning to her. (w)

Carol Queen, **Real live nude girl: Chronicles of sex-positive culture**. PA: Cleis Press, 1997. (w,m) Collection of autobiographical essays by a leading bi-identified exponent and proponent of sexual diversity and sex-positivity.

Wallace P. Rusterholtz, **My not-so-gay life**. Chicago: First Unitarian Society of Chicago, 1996. Rusterholtz, born in 1909, discusses his experiences as a bisexual man, his World War II service in Iran, memories of the Chicago Unitarian church, and opinions on current political and religious issues.

Blanche Weisen, **Eleanor Roosevelt** (2 volumes). NY: Penguin, 1992. Includes substantial discussion of her intimate relationships. (w)

In German:

Irmela v.d. Lühe, **Erika Mann: Eine Biografie** (luhe irmela von der 1947/ 1993). "Life of a woman with contradictions and ruptures in life who did not keep her same and other sex relationships secret yet when editing her father's letters she erased homoerotic hints. Reads like a novel."

POETRY

Michelle Clinton, **Good Sense & The Faithless**. Albuquerque, NM: West End Press, 1994). About life, about complexity, about racism, being bisexual, politics, and more.

M.S. Montgomery, **Telling the Beads**. An explicit and emotionally gripping book of sonnets, a journey across the life of one
bisexual man. Baltimore: Chestnut Hills Press, 1994. (available for $11.50 from New Poets Series, 541 Picadilly Rd., Balti-
more MD 21204)

FANTASY & SCIENCE FICTION

Gael Baudino, **Gossamer Axe**. NY: Penguin Books. 1990. Ancient Irish Pagan religion meets heavy metal. The story of a
harper born in the 6th century who has found her way to
present-day Denver, where she uses the forces of heavy metal
to try to rescue her true love from centuries of imprisonment.
Both Christa and Siudb, her love, are bisexual. (w). **Maze of Moonlight**. NY: Penguin
Books, 1993. Set in Europe during the time of the Crusades and the last days of the
Elves. A couple of the male characters are behaviorally bisexual.

Greg Bear, **Anvil of Stars**. NY: Warner Books, 1992. A ship of children are set on a
mission to locate and punish those who have destroyed Earth. These children are not
bound by the old rules, and neither monogamy nor heterosexuality is enforced, although both seem to be presented as somewhat more satisfying and, perhaps, signs
of a more mature, adult relationship. (m)

Samuel Delaney, **Dhalgren**. NY: Bantam Books, 1975. Disturbing story of a young
drifter who enters the remains of a destroyed city. Set on earth in the more or less
present time. The protagonist is bisexual, and a couple of the other characters have
bisexual histories or experiences. (m)

Diane Duane, **Door Into Fire**. NY: Tom Doherty Associates, Inc., 1979. **Door Into
Shadow**. NY: Tom Doherty Associates, Inc., 1984. **Door into Sunset**. NY: Tom Doherty
Associates, Inc., 1992. Well-written fantasy series in which most people are bisexual,
and homophobia is nonexistent. (m,w)

Robert A. Heinlein, **Friday**. NY: Ballantine Books, 1982. Set in a future society where
casual sex, polyamory and sex between women are all considered acceptable. Inter-
estingly (and a statement about the author and the time in which the book was written), heterosexual relationships are still privileged, and almost all of the women, but
none of the men in the book is actively bisexual. (w)

Ellen Kushner, **Swordspoint**. NY: Tor Books, 1987. In a society where conflicts are
settled by duels, a professional swordsman whose current relationship is with a man,
and whose past love was a woman, is involved in the intrigues of the nobles, one of
whom is a bisexual man. (m)

Mercedes Lackey and Ellen Guon, **Summoned to Tourney**. NY: Baen Publishing Enterprise (distributed by Simon & Schuster), 1992. Set in San Francisco and more or less in the present, a male elf is involved in a three way relationship with two humans (one male, one female). They are street musicians who ride magic steeds that look like motorcycles, and struggle to save San Francisco from destruction. (m)

Ursula LeGuin, **The Dispossessed.** NY: Granada Publishing, 1975. Set far in the future on a moon far from earth, this social utopian novel about anarchy involves a society in which there is no stigma attached to sexual orientation or sexual behavior. The protagonist, though primarily heterosexually oriented, has homosexual experiences as well. (m)

Vonda N. McIntyre, **Starfarers**. NY: Ace Books, 1989. Set on a research spaceship, a woman and two men are in a romantic partnership, and are considered by some old-fashioned because theirs is a closed relationship. (m)

R.M. Meluch, **Chicago Red**. NY: Roc (Penguin Books)1990. Set in post-democracy North America, where a king rules over impoverished peasants. Tow, the "king's assassin" and a not at all likeable man, is bisexual. (m)

Pat Murphy, **Nadya**. (NY: Tom Doherty, 1996). Set in the 1800s, a chronicle of the adventures of a young woman who becomes a wolf once a month. She travels from Missouri to the west coast, and in the course of her travels falls for a man, and then a woman, and then a different man. (w)

Marge Piercy, **Woman on the Edge of Time**. NY: Fawcett Cress, 1976. Sci-fi/fantasy novel about a Latina woman in a NYC mental hospital who time travels to a future utopian society in which bisexuality & homosexuality are completely accepted. (m,w)

J.F. Rivkin, **Silverglass**. NY: Ace Fantasy, 1986; **Web of Wind**. 1987; **Witch of Rhostshyl**. 1989. Sci-fi/fantasy trilogy about two women, a mercenary and a noblewoman, both of whom happen to be bisexual. (w)

Mary Rosenblum, **Chimera**. NY: Del Ray/Ballantine Books, 1993. It's the future, for many people life takes place as much in virtual reality as in the flesh world. At least one character in this book, David Chen, a virtual reality artist is clearly bisexual, though the "b-word" is not used. A good read.

Melissa Scott, **Burning Bright**. NY: Tor/Tom Doherty Associates, 1993. (mw?) Hi-tech sci-fi based on concept of virtual reality games. One male character and (likely) the female protagonist are bi. (m,w). **Shadow Man**. NY: Tor/Tom Doherty Associates, 1995. (mw) It's the future, and it has finally been determined that there are 5 sexes, not two. But the people on this one colony, unlike those on all of the other planets, haven't accepted that yet, with a resultant culture clash between indigenes and off-worlders. With 5 sexes, there are 9 different sexual orientations, including bi, omni, demi and hemi.

Starhawk, **The Fifth Sacred Thing**. NY: Bantam Books, 1993. Futuristic utopian novel with two competing cultures: one egalitarian in which bisexuality is taken for granted, and the other oppressive and authoritarian. (m,w)

John Varley, **Steel Beach**. NY: Putnam, 1992. After the invasion of the earth, humans have moved to the moon (and elsewhere). In this society, people, who can now live a very long time, can be hetero-, homo-, or bisexually oriented, and also can (and sometimes do) change sexes surgically. The main character is (almost entirely) heterosexual, and is attracted to women when he is a man, and to men when she is a woman. Other characters are differently oriented. (m, w)

Margaret Weis and Tracy Hickman, **Rose of the Prophet**, Volumes I (1988), II (1988) and III (1989). NY: Bantam Books. 20 Gods rule the world, each with different abilities and his or her own followers, but now they are at war. This trilogy is the story of this war and the people involved. Mathew, an androgynous man, is in love with the other two central characters, a woman and her husband, though he never has a sexual relationship with either.

Walter Jon Williams, **Aristoi**. Set in the far future, all sexual orientations are accepted. Gabriel, the protagonist, the creator and leader of a number of worlds, has a number of concurrent relationships with men and women.

SELECTED OTHER FICTION

(This list is far from exhaustive.)

Alice Adams, **Almost Perfect**. (NY: Fawcett, 1993) Lifestyles of the (almost) rich and famous. Daugher of Mexican mother and famous Anglo father meets Anglo commercial artist who is unpredictable, drinks too much and is somewhat of a misogynist. Oh, and he is bisexual too. (m)

Lisa Alther, **Five Minutes in Heaven**. (NY: Dutton, 1995). (m,w) Three of the four main characters could all be classified more or less Kinsey-5s, and the fourth is - who knows, but much as she'd like to be, she's not a Kinsey 0. **Bedrock**. NY: Ivy Books, 1990. (w) 2 married women, best friends, & their love for each other. **Other Women**. NY: Knopf (Random House), 1984. (w) A woman with a bi history comes to terms, through therapy, with herself & her love for women. **Original Sins**. NY: Signet, 1982 (m,w) Story of 5 people growing up in Tennessee, including 2 with bisexual experiences. **Kinflicks**. NY: Knopf, 1976. (w). Woman with bi history struggles to understand herself & her relationship with her mother.

Carol Anshaw, **Aquamarine**. NY: Washington Square Press, 1992. (w) Interesting and thought-provoking novel which takes the life of a competitor in the 1968 Olympics and projects 20 years into her future. Three different possible futures are presented, each based on the reverberations of choices made shortly after the Olympics. In each of her equally possible futures, she has married or remained single, loved women or men, become a parent or not, stayed in her Missouri hometown or moved to New York City. **Seven Moves**. NY: Mariner Books (Houghton Mifflin), 1996. A lesbian therapist's lover disappears. One of her best friends (a minor character) is a woman married to a man who is also seeing another woman.

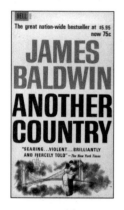

James Baldwin, **Another Country**. NY: Dell, 1985. (m) From 1960, about race, sexuality & friendship between men. **Giovanni's Room**. NY: Dell, 1988 (1956) (m). Two male expatriates in France, one from the US, one Italian, fall in love. One is engaged to be married to a woman. Beautifully written, lots of internal struggle and self-hatred. **Tell Me How Long The Train's Been Gone**. NY: Dell, 1968. (m) About an African American man who becomes an actor. Probably the most clearly bisexual of all of Baldwin's characters.

Ann Bannon, **Odd Girl Out** (Tallahassee: Naiad, 1983 — originally 1957) and **Beebo Brinker** (Tallahassee: Naiad, 1986 — originally 1962). Two in a series of 5 novels published in the late 50s and early 60s, these are fascinating representations of gay and bisexual life in that time period. **Odd Girl Out** is the story of two young college women who have a relationship until one leaves the other for a man. **Beebo Brinker** is the story of a lesbian in NY's Village scene. Several of the characters in the book could be characterized as bisexual. But beware: none of these characters are overly loveable.

Pat Barker, **The Eye in the Door**. NY: Plume/Penguin, 1993. Set in England during World War I, psychological novel about Billy Prior, an intelligence agent who is bisexual, as is one other male character. **The Ghost Road**. More about Billy Prior. Both of these books are excellent reads. (m)

Christopher Bram, **Almost History**. NY: Plume/Penguin, 1993. (m) Fascinating historical novel about a gay American diplomat who spends much of his career in the Marcos-controlled Philippines. Beginning in the 1950s and moving forward in time to just beyond the fall of the Marcos regime, many of the secondary male characters are bisexual in identity and/or behavior.

Rita Mae Brown, **Rubyfruit Jungle**. Plainfield, VT: Daughters, Inc., 1973. Most of the characters behave bisexually. About sexuality & growing up poor. **Six of One**. US & Canada: Bantam Books, 1978. (w) Set in a small southern town & spanning 1909-1980, the book has 2 bi women: the narrator and Ramelle. **Southern Discomfort**. NY: Bantam Books, 1982. (w) Set in Alabama,in the early 20th century, two secondary characters, Grace and Payson, are bisexual. **Venus Envy**. NY: Bantam Books, 1993. (w) Set in present day Virginia, about a woman's relationships with family and friends.

Jackie Calhoun, **Lifestyles**. Tallahassee, FL: The Naiad Press, 1990. Can be read as a bisexual or lesbian coming out story. A woman who has been left by her husband of many years meets and falls in love with another woman. (w)

Susan Taylor Chehak, **Dancing on Glass**. NY: Fawcett Crest, 1993. Man goes back to the town of his childhood to resurrect his family name. Falls in love with a woman whose family is historically interwoven with his, marries her, but then becomes obsessed with a teenaged boy. Kind of soap-operatic. (m)

Leonard Cohen, **Beautiful Losers**. NY: Vintage, 1966. Yes, *that* Leonard Cohen. The songwriter. Poetic, erotic and disturbing novel set in Montreal. Both of the male characters are bisexual. (m)

Nicole Conn, **Claire of the Moon**. Tallahassee: The Naiad Press, Inc., 1993. A (formerly) straight woman discovers love with a lesbian therapist (no, not hers) at a writers retreat. Just like the movie of the same name. (w)

Emma Donohue, **Stir Fry**. NY: HarperCollins, 1994. In Dublin, a 17-year-old woman begins university, discovers her 2 new women roommates are a couple. One of these self-identifies as bi. **Hood**. NY: Harper Collins, 1996. A lesbian in Ireland's life partner is a woman who has has a history with both men and women. Note: Emma Donohoe is a contributor to the **Bisexual Horizons** anthology. (w)

Larry Duplechan, **Eight Days A Week**. (Boston: Alyson, 1985). Takes place in Los Angeles, in the pre-AIDS era. Johnny Ray Rousseau, a 22 year old African-American nightclub singer by night, legal secretary by day, meets and falls for a blond bisexual banker who is portrayed as somewhat of a jerk not, however, because he is bisexual, but because he is possessive and wants Johnny Ray to give up his nightclub career to be home with him at night. Explicit sexuality and lots of musical references. (m).

Andrew Dworkin, **Mercy**. NY: Four Walls, Eight Windows, 1990. Unsettling story written in the first person of a girl who grows up and is abused by one man after another. Some of her various sexual relationships are with women. Well-written, upsetting, very graphic.

Brett Easton Ellis, **The Rules of Attraction**. NY: Penguin, 1987. Pretty depressing book about students at a private college with no direction who take lots of drugs, sleep with each other (while drunk or high), and never go to class. Most of the men sleep with lots of men and women; the women sleep with the men. (m)

Rupert Everett, **Hello Darling, Are You Working?** NY: Avon Books, 1992. The British narrator, Rhys, is a bisexual actor, drug addict, and sometimes prostitute. (m)

Harvey Fierstein, **Torch Song Trilogy**. NY: Villard Books, 1983. (A play.) The protagonist's lover/ex-lover Ed is a self-identified bisexual. He is also closeted and would prefer to be straight, but he makes makes progress through the play. Some focus on Arnold's unwillingness to accept that Ed might actually be bisexual. (m)

E.M. Forster, **Maurice**. NY: W.W. Norton & Co., 1971. About a homosexual man in love with another homosexual man who "goes straight." Is he bisexual? Historically. Is he in denial of his homosexual feelings? Probably. Are his heterosexual feelings "real"? Probably. Listed here mainly because it was written in 1913-1914, is beautifully written, and is one of the only early gay-themed novels that ends happily. (m)

Paul Goodman, **Making Do**. NY: Macmillan, 1963. Set in the very early 60s, several of the male characters are bisexual, none of the women. This book is definitely disturbing, replete with racism, misogyny, violence, though interesting as a look at a specific time and place in history. Certainly helps you to understand the subsequent rise of feminism & lesbian separatism. (m)

Stephanie Grant, **The Passion of Alice**. NY: Houghton Mifflin, 1995. Set in Massachusetts in the mid 1980s. About a hospitalized anorexic woman. Maeve, a bulimic woman on the same ward, and a major character in this book, is behaviorally bisexual, though there is no discussion of identity. (w)

Carol Guess, **Seeing Dell**. Pittsburgh: Cleis Press, 1995. Dell, a taxi driver, has died suddenly, leaving behind two lovers, one male, one female. Set in a small town in the midwestern United States, it's refreshing to see a novel about working class people. (w)

Diana Hammond, **The Impersonator**. NY: Doubleday, 1992. Story of a sexually compelling man who lacks inner direction and gets through life by dissembling and by attaching himself to various lovers, one of whom is a man. There are 2 male characters who could be called bisexual. (m)

Joseph Hansen, **Job's Year**. NY: Plume Fiction, 1983. About a primarily gay actor with other bi characters as well) (m,w); **A Smile in His Lifetime**. NY: Plume Fiction, 1981. A married man dealing with his homosexuality. (m) **Backtrack**. London: GMP, 1982 and NY: The Countryman Press, 1987. A primarily gay young man trying to find out who murdered his primarily gay father. (m) **Steps Going Down**. NY: Penguin Books, 1982. There are two bisexual men in this crime book, both utterly unlikeable - but then this book contains unlikeable characters of several sexual orientations. (m)

E. Lynn Harris, **Invisible Life**. NY: Doubleday, 1991 (m) and **Just As I Am** (NY: Doubleday, 1994) (m) A middle class African American man struggles to deal with his bisexuality and with issues of coming out. Issues such as: relationships, being in the closet, dis/honesty, HIV, etc. **And This Too Shall Pass** (NY: Doubleday, 1996). A pro football player comes to identify as gay. A few of the other male characters in the book could be identified as bisexual, especially Basil, the closeted and dishonest man who appears in Harris' earlier books.

Ernest Hemingway, **The Garden of Eden**. NY: Collier Books, 1986 (written 1961). His last work, about a male/female couple & a woman who enters their relationship. Transgender issues, jealousy, bisexuality. (w). Also, among his collections of short stories is one called "The Sea Change" in which a woman tells her male beloved that she has fallen in love with a woman.

Greg Johnson, **Pagan Babies**. NY: Plume (Penguin), 1993. Since their days together in Catholic school, Janice and Clifford's lives are intertwined. Janice is straight, and Clifford gay—well, except that he and Janice are boyfriend/girlfriend for years, with an active sexual relationship during some of that time. This novel is about growing up Catholic in the US, about AIDS, friendship, expectations and disappointments. (m)

Dick Kavanagh (pseudonym of Julian Barnes), **Duffy**. NY: Pantheon Books, 1980., **Fiddle City, Putting the Boot In** NY: Penguin, 1987, and **Going to the Dogs** (1987). Standard English detective fare, except that the protagonist, Duffy, is a bisexual ex-cop. (m)

M.E. Kerr, **Hello, I Lied**. NY: Harper Collins, 1997. A teenaged boy summering in East Hampton in a cottage on an estate where his mother is employed as cook for a retired rock star, has a boyfriend back in New York, is dealing with what it means to have a gay identity, and then falls in love with a French girl who is a guest of the rock star. Oops, is he really gay? What are his friends going to think now? (m)

James Kirkwood, **P.S. Your Cat is Dead**. NY: Warner Books, 1972. An underemployed NYC actor/writer catches the (bi) burglar who is in the process of robbing him (not for the first time), and ties him up in his kitchen. The actor's recently deceased best friend and one other character, are also bisexual. Entertaining. (m)

Edith Konecky, **A Place at the Table**. NY: Ballantine Books, 1989. Middle aged Rachel is "a perfectly ordinary woman who sometimes falls in love with other women." (w)

Hanif Kureishi, **The Buddha of Suburbia**. NY, London, etc.: Penguin Books, 1990. In suburban London, the story of the bi son of an Indian father & English mother. (m,w)

D.H. Lawrence, **The Fox**. NY: Bantam Books, 1923, 1951. In rural England, two women living together as a couple. Tensions arise with the arrival of a man who courts one of the women. No explicit bisexuality, but the two women are obviously, sexual or not, a couple. (w)

Jane Lazarre, **The Powers of Charlotte**. Freedom, CA: The Crossing Press, 1987. A psychological novel about a woman from a Jewish Communist family. Bisexuality is not a central theme, but 4 characters have varying degrees of bisexual histories. (m,w)

Rosamond Lehman, **Dusty Answer**. London/NY: Harcourt Brace Janovich, Inc., 1927. A young wealthy English woman's search for love. Both the man and the woman with whom she falls in love are, ultimately, unattainable. Quite an amazing book, considering it was published in 1927. I'm surprised it isn't better known. (w, m)

Jennifer Levin, **Water Dancer**. NY: Penguin Books, 1994. A marathon swimmer, training for a race, stays with her trainer and his wife. This book is about motivation, about relationships, about swimming, and has a bisexual character. (w)

Erika Lopez, **Flaming Iguanas: An Illustrated All Girl Road Novel Thing.** NY: Simon & Schuster, 1997. Two twenty-something Puerto Rican women from New Jersey take off across the US on newly acquired motorcycles. Tomato Rodriguez, the narrator, is trying to figure out whether she's bisexual. This book is unique and highly entertaining. (w)

Daniel Magida, **The Rules of Seduction.** Boston: Houghton Mifflin, 1992. Jack Newland is a wealthy New York socialite who has had relationships with both men and with women, as have some of his male friends. (m)

Dacia Maraini, **Women at War.** NY: Italica Press, 1988. (originally published in Italian as **Donna in guerra**). A working class schoolteacher and her mechanic husband vacation in the Bay of Naples. Previously passive and unpolitical, Vannina meets various people and begins to develop a feminist and political consciousness. This book has female and male bisexual characters. **Letters to Marina** (originally published in Italian in 1981 as **Lettere a Marina**) (Freedom, California, 1988: The Crossing Press). A feminist woman talks about her past and current experiences in the form of a series of letters to Marina, a woman who is her ex-lover. She, and some of her past and present lovers, love both men and women. This book was referred to me by the author as a book with bisexual characters, when I told her of this project.

Carole Maso, **The American Woman in the Chinese Hat.** NY: Penguin Books, 1994. Shortly after her brother's death from AIDS, a New York writer named Catherine leaves her woman lover of 12 years and comes to the French Riviera, where she comes apart, having a number of affairs, with men and women, in the process. (w)

Carole Spearin McCauley, **The Honesty Tree.** Palo Alto, CA: Frog in the Well Books, 1985. Novel about 2 women in a relationship. (w)

Valerie Miner, **Movement.** Trumansburg, NY: The Crossing Press, 1982. A decade in the life of a journalist who is married to a draft resister in the 60s & 70s. She, and one of her woman friends have bisexual experience/attractions. (w)

Elias Miguel Munoz, **Crazy Love.** Houston, TX: Arte Publico Press (Univ. of Houston, Houston TX 77004), 1988. About growing up in one Cuban American family. Focus on family dynamics and expectations, and on his sexual experiences, both consensual (with women and men) and nonconsensual (with men), while growing up and as an adult. (m)

Gloria Naylor, **Bailey's Cafe.** NY: Vintage Contemporaries (Random House), 1993. A book about suffering & survival, with a bi character, Jesse Bell. (w)

O'Brien, Edna, **The High Road.** NY: Plume, 1988. An Irish woman goes to an island in Spain to recover from a broken heart caused by a relationship with a man, becomes attracted to a Spanish woman. Also **Casualties of Peace**, 1966 in **An Edna O'Brien Reader.** NY: Warner Books, 1994. O'Brien is an Irish author whose books were banned in Ireland in the 1960s. From an Irish woman's perspective, she deals quite explicitly with life, sexuality, and emotion. (w)

Felice Picano, **Late in the Season**. NY: Gay Presses of New York, 1984. Gay-identified man in a long term relationship with a man meets and gets involved with a college aged woman. (m) **Ambidextrous**. NY: Gay Presses, 1985. A currently-gay identified man looks back on his bisexual childhood and adolescence in NYC. (m)

Marge Piercy, **Summer People**. NY: Fawcett Crest, 1989. The story of 2 women & a man in a triad relationship. (m,w)

Manuel Puig, **Kiss of the Spider Woman**. NY: Vintage Books, 1980. Story of 2 men, a homosexual window dresser & a heterosexual revolutionary who are imprisoned in the same cell in a Latin American prison. Involves situational bisexuality. (m)

Jane Ransom, **Bye Bye**. NY: New York University Press, 1997. A psychological satire of NYC and its art scene. The story of a New York woman thrown out by her "too-perfect" husband because of her nonconsensual infidelities, who decides to change her identity. She disappears, and then reappears as "Rosie" and has three lovers, two women and a man. (f)

Mary Renault, **The Persian Boy**. NY: Vintage Books, 1972. A fictionalized version of the story of the Persian king Darius and Alexander the Great, told from the eyes of the eunoch slave boy Bagoas. Darius and Alexander are both portrayed as bisexual, with Alexander way up there on the Kinsey Scale, and Darius somewhere in the middle. (m) **The Last of the Wine**. NY: Vintage Books, 1975 (first published in 1956). Set in ancient Athens, some men are heterosexual, some homosexual, and some bisexual. Lysis, the male lover of the male protagonist, is bisexual. (m)

Tom Robbins, **Even Cowgirls Get the Blues**. NY, etc.: Bantam Books, 1976. A straight man's perspective of female bisexuality. (w)

Lucia St. Clair Robson, **The Tokaido Road**. NY: Ballantine Books, 1991. Set in 17th-century Japan, many of the male characters are behaviorally bisexual. (m)

Jane Rule, **The Young in One Another's Arms**. Tallahassee: Naiad Press, 1984. About a multigenerational boarding-house-becomes-communal-group in Vancouver. There are two women who have relationships with women (each other) and with men. This book deals with triangulation, with redefinition of "family." (w). **This is Not for You.** Tallahassee: Naiad, 1982. Set in the US and London, the story of a group of friends beginning in their college years. The narrator is a lesbian?/bisexual? woman who is in love with another woman from college but refuses to allow a romantic or sexual relationship to develop, despite the reciprocity of feeling. The narrator later has a relationship with a woman married to a man. (w)

May Sarton, **Mrs. Stevens Hears the Mermaids Singing**. New York: W.W. Norton and Company, 1965. A poet looks back over her long life and recalls her past loves, male and female, trying to understand their relationship to the development of her poetry and her self. Sarton herself self-identified, at various times, as lesbian and bisexual. (w)

Cathleen Schine, **Rameau's Niece**. NY: A Plume Book (Penguin), 1994. A present day 28-year old New Yorker, who has published a bestselling book on 18th century French fiction, is married to a 39 year old English professor. Her life begins to get caught up in and confused with the story in a manuscript she is reading, and her life spins away from normalcy. Her sexual fantasies run rampant, their subjects are both male and female. (w)

Sarah Schulman, **People in Trouble**. NY: E.P. Dutton, 1990. One of the 3 main characters is Kate, an artist and married woman who loves her husband and also falls in love with a lesbian AIDS activist named Molly. As is the case with all of Schulman's books, this is a fascinating if sometimes depressing look at NYC life. (w)

Dani Shapiro, **Playing With Fire**. NY: Doubleday, 1989. Two young women meet at Smith College, one from a religious Jewish family, the other a Christian socialite. They begin to fall in love with each other, and then are pulled apart by a third party. A novel about family and boundaries, set in high society. (w)

Tom Spanbauer. **The Man Who Fell in Love With the Moon**. NY: Atlantic Monthly Press, 1991. Several bi characters in this novel set in 19th-century Idaho. (m,w)

Darcy Steinke, **Suicide Blonde**. NY: Washington Square Press, 1992. Set in San Francisco, a (possibly, kinda) bisexual woman is obsessed with her lover, a bisexual man. Full of compulsion, alcohol and drugs, and destruction. Disturbing. (m,w)

Junichiro Tanizaki, **Quicksand**. NY: Alfred A. Knopf, 1993 (originally 1947). Set in Japan in the 1920s, a female married art student falls in love with a woman. A story of obsession and betrayal. Both women are bisexual. (w)

Carla Tomaso, **Matricide**. One of the narrator's sidekicks is a woman just out of high school who self-identifies as bisexual. (w)

Alice Walker, **The Color Purple**. New York: Harcourt Brace Janovich, 1982. Shug, a major character, is bisexual. (w)

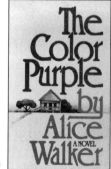

Edmund White, **The Beautiful Room.is Empty**. NY: Ballantine Books, 1988. The narrator's best female friend, Maria, self-identifies as bisexual. Also minor male bisexual character. Autobiographical novel about growing up gay in New York in the 50s and 60s. (m,w)

Stevie White, **Boy Cuddle**. London: Penguin, 1992. British novel about a bisexual boxer in love with a prostitute who has sex with men for money and an ongoing relationship with the protagonist, who also becomes seriously involved with a female prostitute. About life on the streets of South London. The front cover says "Amoral. Bisexual. In love ...?" (m)

Mary Wings, **She Came By The Book**. NY: Berkeley Prime Crime Book, 1996. Set in San Francisco's gay community, this murder mystery includes a **very, very** minor bisexual plot twist. It's interesting nonetheless, if you're interested in a story that's not too far off from real life community politics.

Jeanette Winterson, **The Passion**. NY: Vintage International (Random House), 1987. (w) Set in France and Italy during Napoleon's reign, one of the protagonists is a bisexual woman. **Written on the Body**. NY: Vintage International (Random House), 1992. Set in the present, a tale of love between the narrator and a married woman. The name and gender of the narrator (who talks of past relationships with men and with women) is never stated. Reading this book is an interesting and somewhat unsettling experience. **Gut Symmetries**. NY: Knopf, 1997. Two physicists, one male, one female, have an affair. He is married, she is single. She meets and falls in love with his wife. Beautifully written story of a romantic triangle. (w)

Shay Youngblood, **Soul Kiss**. Young African American girl is left at age 7 by her addict mother with two "aunts" (actually a couple). This book is about her growing up, her search for love, and the development of her sexuality. I'm not sure whether she would call herself bisexual, but her experience is bisexual. This book is beautifully written. (w)

Eda Zahl, **Fluffy Butch**. London: Mandarin Fiction, 1994. Quirky novel about a young woman living in Los Angeles who dates men and women. The back cover says: "How do you learn to love men? Mary learns by shaving her head, moving to Los Angeles and dating women. To her amazement bald Mary begins to view the world from a man's point of view. She even begins to sympathise with them. Worse, she starts to date them again. Mary finds herself having affairs with men and women, sometimes women and men—who knows who she'll end up with?" (w)

SHORT STORIES:

Ruthann Robson, **Eye of a Hurricane**. Ithaca, New York: Firebrand Books, 1989. Some of these short stories have bisexual characters. (w)

Jane Rule, **Inland Passage**. Tallahassee, FL: Naiad Press, 1985. "His Nor Hers," "Puzzle," and possibly also "Inland Passage" have bisexual characters.

If you have trouble finding any of the books in this section at your local bookstore, many are available through the Bisexual Resource Center's on-line Bisexual Bookstore at http://www.biresource.org/bookstore. Books purchased through the Bisexual Bookstore generate money that helps the BRC produce conferences, pamphlets, and this Bisexual Resource Guide.

A Queer World

The Center for Lesbian and Gay Studies Reader
Edited by Martin Duberman
Contributors include Jewelle Gomez, Vivien Ng, Cindy Patton, Walt Odets, Jeffrey Escoffier, Judith Roof, and Douglas Crimp.
0-8147-1875-2 / $24.95 PAPER

Queer Representations

Reading Lives, Reading Cultures
A Center for Lesbian and Gay Studies Book
Edited by Martin Duberman
Contributors include Dorothy Allison, Samuel R. Delany, Joan Nestle, David Halperin, Dale Peck, Sarah Schulman, and B. Ruby Rich.
0-8147-1883-3 / $22.95 PAPER

Carryin' On in the Lesbian and Gay South

Edited by John Howard
0-8147-3560-6 / $18.95 PAPER

Queer Theory

An Introduction
Annamarie Jagose
0-8147-4234-3 / $14.95 PAPER

Heroic Desire

Lesbian Identity and Cultural Space
Sally R. Munt
0-8147-5607-7 / $18.50 PAPER

Islamic Homosexualities

Culture, History, and Literature
Edited by Stephen O. Murray & Will Roscoe
0-8147-7468-7/ $19.95 PAPER

Freedom to Differ

The Shaping of the Gay and Lesbian Struggle for Civil Rights
Diane Helene Miller
0-8147-5596-8
$18.50 PAPER

Opposite Sex

Gay Men on Lesbians, Lesbians on Gay Men
Edited by Sara Miles and Eric Rofes
0-8147-7477-6 / $16.95 PAPER

The Queer Renaissance

Contemporary American Literature and the Reinvention of Lesbian and Gay Identities
Robert McRuer
0-8147-5555-0 / $18.95 PAPER

Virginia Woolf

Lesbian Readings
Edited by Eileen Barrett & Patricia Cramer
with an Afterword by Jane Marcus
0-8147-1264-9 / $18.95 PAPER
The Cutting Edge: Lesbian Life & Literature Series

Gay Macho

The Life and Death of the Homosexual Clone
Martin P. Levine
Edited with an Introduction by Michael S. Kimmel
0-8147-4695-0 / $17.95 PAPER

NYU Press
1-800-996-NYUP [6987]   www.nyupress.nyu.edu

A Reader's Guide to Non-Fiction Books, Chapters, and Journal Articles on Bisexuality

bi Ronald C. Fox with Robyn Ochs

Copyright ©1999 Ronald C. Fox and Robyn Ochs

The following books, book chapters, and journal articles are a diverse collection of recommended non-fiction readings that focus on bisexual identity and/or behavior and take an affirmative approach to bisexuality and bisexual issues. We have highlighted a few items in each section with a ▼ symbol that we consider good places to begin. All materials listed below are in English, except as noted. This list is by no means exhaustive; rather it is a work in progress. Your suggestions for books, chapters, and journal articles to be listed in future editions of the *Guide* are welcome, including in languages other than English. Many of the books listed can be ordered through the "Bisexual Bookstore" on the World Wide Web, located at: http://www.biresource.org/bookstore/index.html.

Codes: (w): Primarily about women; (m) Primarily about men; (w,m); About both women and men

NON-FICTION BOOKS SPECIFICALLY ON BISEXUALITY

Aggleton, Peter. (Ed.). (1996). **Bisexualities & AIDS: International perspectives**. London: Taylor & Francis. (m) Collection of essays and reviews of the research literature on bisexual behavior among men in a number of modern cultures, including Australia, Brazil, Canada, China, Costa Rica, the Dominican Republic, France, India, Mexico, Papua New Guinea, Peru, the Philippines, and the U. K.

Bi Academic Intervention (Phoebe Davidson, Jo Eadie, Clare Hemmings, Ann Kaloski, & Merle Storr). (Eds.). (1997). **The Bisexual Imaginary: Representation, identity, and desire.** London: Cassell. (w,m) Collection of essays on bisexuality in history, literature, film, and cultural studies.

▼ Bisexual Anthology Collective (Leela Acharya, Nancy Chater, Dionne Falconer, Sharon Lewis, & Leanna McLannan, Susan Nosov) (Eds.). (1995). **Plural desires: Writing bisexual women's realities.** Toronto: Sister Vision Press. (w) An anthology of writings by a diverse group of Canadian & US women.

Bode, Janet (1976). **View from another closet: Exploring bisexuality in women.** New York: Hawthorne. (w) One of the first books on bisexuality, based on the author's interviews with bisexual women.

Bryant, Wayne. (1997). **Bisexual characters in film: From Anaïs to Zee.** New York: Harrington Park Press. (w,m) What it says. More descriptive than analytical.

Cantarella, Eva. (1992). **Bisexuality in the ancient world.** New Haven, CT: Yale University Press. (w,m) Translated from the Italian. A scholarly examination of bisexuality in ancient classical Greece & Rome.

▼ Firestein, Beth A. (Ed.). (1996). **Bisexuality: The psychology and politics of an invisible minority.** Thousand Oaks, CA: Sage. (w,m) A collection of essays that provides the most comprehensive overview and review of bisexuality and psychology to date, with chapters by Ron Fox, Loraine Hutchins, Carol Queen, Maggie Rubenstein, Paula Rust, Robyn Ochs, and others.

Garber, Marjorie. (1995). **Vice versa: Bisexuality & the eroticism of everyday life.** New York: Simon & Schuster. (w,m) If you are interested in an in-depth look at bisexuality in literature, popular culture, or psychoanalysis, this book is for you.

Geller, Thomas. (Ed.). (1990). **Bisexuality: A reader & sourcebook.** Ojai, CA: Times Change Press. (w,m) Collection of interviews & articles.

George, Sue. (1993). **Women & bisexuality.** London: Scarlet Press. (w) An examination of bisexual identity and relationships, based on the author's survey study of 150 self-identified bisexual women in the United Kingdom.

Haeberle, Edwin J., & Rudolph Gindorf. (1998). **Bisexualities: The ideology and practice of sexual contact with both men and women.** New York: Continuum. (w,m) Translated from the German. Collection of essays by participants in the 1990 International Berlin Conference for Sexology. Most chapters reflect the beginnings of the shift in scholarly thinking about bisexuality that has come about as a result of subsequent and more current research on bisexuality and bisexual identity.

Hall, Donald. E., & Maria Pramaggiore. (Eds.). (1996). **RePresenting bisexualities: Subjects & cultures of fluid desire.** New York: NYU Press. (w,m) Collection of essays on bisexuality in queer theory, literature, film, and cultural studies.

▼ Hutchins, Lorraine, & Lani Ka'ahumanu. (Eds.). (1991). **Bi any other name: Bisexual people speak out.** (w,m) Boston: Alyson. Diverse collection of 75 essays and autobiographical narratives by bi-identified people from the United States.

Klein, Fritz. (1993). **The bisexual option (2nd ed.).** New York: Harrington Park Press. (see display ad elsewhere in this *Guide*.) (w,m) Second edition of the one of the first published books on bisexuality (1978) written from an affirmative perspective (Charlotte Wolff's 1979 book, **Bisexuality: A Study,** listed below, is the other). The author is also the creator of the well-known Klein Sexual Orientation Grid (KSOG), a multi-dimensional scale of sexual orientation & sexual identity (see Klein, Sepekoff, & Wolf, 1986 below under "Sexual orientation: Non-dichotomous approaches" for their original article).

Klein, Fritz, & Timothy J. Wolf. (Eds.). (1985). **Two lives to lead: Bisexuality in men and women.** New York: Harrington Park Press. (w,m) The first published scholarly collection of reports on 1980s research on bisexuality. Originally a special issue of the prestigious *Journal of Homosexuality* (1985, Vol. 11, Issue 1/2).

▼ Kohn, Barry, & Alice Matusow. (1980). **Barry & Alice: Portrait of a bisexual marriage.** Englewood Cliffs, N.J.: Prentice-Hall. (w,m) An autobiographical account of the authors' marriage and the impact on their relationship of their coming to terms with their bisexuality.

▼ Ochs, Robyn. (1999). **Bisexual Resource Guide (3rd ed.).** Cambridge, MA: Bisexual Resource Center ($12.95, BRC, POB 400639, Cambridge, MA 02140). (w,m) Contains an extensive bibliography of books, chapters, and journal articles with bi content, list of recommended films, announcements, and relevant notices, and listings of more than 2000 bisexual & bi-inclusive groups & electronic mail lists. (Yes, we *know* that's what you're reading right now, but we listed it just in case this bi-bliography gets reproduced and distributed somewhere else).

Off Pink Collective. (1988). **Bisexual lives.** London: Off Pink Publishing. (w,m) Collection of personal narratives by bisexual women and bisexual men in the U. K.

▼ Rose, Sharon, Cris Stevens. & The Off-Pink Collective. (Eds.). (1996). **Bisexual horizons: Politics, histories, lives.** London: Lawrence & Wishart. (w,m) Diverse collection of 54 essays and autobiographical narratives by bi-identified people, mostly from the U. K.

Rust, Paula C. (1995). **Bisexuality & the challenge to lesbian politics: Sex, loyalty & revolution** . New York: NYU Press. (w) The author traces the origins of the controversy about bisexuality among lesbians to the 1970s lesbian feminist debates, out of which, she argues, developed an environment in which bisexuality inevitably became a challenge to lesbian politics. She also discusses likely for the sexual politics of the future.

▼ Rust, Paula C. (Ed.). (1999). **Bisexuality in the United States: A Social Science Reader**. New York: Columbia University Press. (w,m) Comprehensive collection of classic journal articles and book chapters on bisexuality, including many for which the original references are included in this reading list. Highly recommended.

Sigma Research. (1993). **Behaviourally bisexual men in the UK: Identifying need for HIV prevention**. London: UK Health Education Authority. (m) Results of a government sponsored survey study of sexual behavior and HIV/AIDS awareness.

Tielman, Rob A. P., Manuel Carballo. & Aart C. Hendriks. (Eds.). (1991). **Bisexuality & HIV/AIDS: A global perspective**. (m) Buffalo, NY: Prometheus. Collection of essays and reviews of research on bisexual identity and behavior among men in a number of modern cultures, including Australia, India, Indonesia, Latin America, Mexico, the Netherlands, New Zealand, Sub-Saharan Africa, Thailand, the United Kingdom, and the United States.

▼ Tucker, Naomi, with Liz Highleyman & Rebecca Kaplan. (Eds.). (1995). **Bisexual politics: Theories, queeries, & visions**. New York: Harrington Park Press. (w,m) (Order info: 1-800-342-9678). Diverse collection of essays exploring the history, philosophies, visioning, and strategies of bisexual politics in the United States.

Weinberg, Martin S., Colin J. Williams, & Douglas W. Pryor. (1994). **Dual attraction: Understanding bisexuality**. New York: Oxford University Press. (w,m) Results of the authors' interview and survey research on bisexual identity and relationships in 1980s San Francisco. Includes personal narratives, the authors' views on how bisexual identity develops, comparison of bisexual, heterosexual, and lesbian/gay patterns of sexual attractions and relationships, and a portrait of the impact of HIV/AIDS on the lives of individuals from their original interviews.

Weise, Elizabeth R. (Ed.). (1992). **Closer to home: Bisexuality & feminism**. Seattle: Seal Press. (w) Collection of 23 essays by bisexual feminist women on bisexuality, feminism, & their intersection.

▼ Wolff, Charlotte. (1979). **Bisexuality: A study**. London: Quarter Books. (w,m) One of the first books on bisexuality written from an affirmative perspective (Fritz Klein's **Bisexual Option**, listed above, is the other), based on the author's survey research on bisexual women and bisexual men in the U. K.

In Dutch:

▼ Hanson, Hannie (Ed.). (1990). **Bisexuele levens in Nederland**. [Bisexual lives in the Netherlands]. Amsterdam: Orlando. (w,m) Portrait of bisexual identity and relationships, based on the author's interviews with bisexual women and men.

Kuppens, A. (1995). **Biseksuele identiteiten: Tussen verlangen en praktijk**. [Bisexual identities: Between desire and behavior]. Nijmegen: Wetenschapswinkel. (w,m) Theoretical overview and discussion of bisexual identities, based on interviews with bisexual women and bisexual men.

van Kerkhof, Marty P. N. (1997). **Beter Biseks. Mythen over biseksualiteit ontrafeld.** [Better bisexuality: Myths about bisexuality revealed]. Amsterdam: Schorer Boeken. (w,m) Examination of bisexual identity and relationships, based on interviews with bisexual women and bisexual men.

In French:

▼ Mendès-Leité, Rommel, Catherine Deschamps, & Bruno-Marcel Proth. (1996). **Bisexualité: Le dernièr tabou.** [Bisexuality: The last taboo]. Paris: Calmann Levy. (w,m) Portrait of bisexual identity and behavior among bisexual men in France today, based on the authors' interviews.

In German:

▼ Feldhorst, Anja. (1996). (Ed.). **Bisexualitäten.** [Bisexualities]. Berlin: Deutsche AIDS-Hilfe. (w,m) Collection of essays on bisexual identity, relationships, and communities in Germany.

Geissler, Sina-Aline. (1993). **Doppelte Lust: Bisexualität heute— Erfahrungen und Bekenntnisse.** [Dual desire: Bisexuality today: Experiences and confessions]. Munich: Wilhelm Heyne. (w,m) An exploration of bisexuality in Germany today, based on author's interviews with bisexual women and bisexual men.

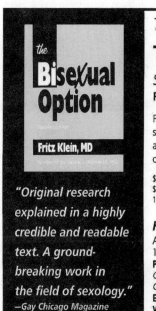

▼ Gooß, Ulrich. (1995). **Sexualwissenschaftliche Konzepte der Bisexualität von Männern.** [The concept of bisexuality in scientific discourse about human sexuality]. Stuttgart: Ferdinand Enke. (w,m) Scholarly examination by a German psychiatrist of the origins and development of the concept of bisexuality in the fields of psychology and sexology, including an overview of current theory and research.

Haeberle, Erwin J., & Rolf Gindorf. (Eds.). (1994). **Bisexualitäten: Ideologie und Praxis des Sexualkontes mit beiden Geschlectern.** [Bisexualities: Theory and practice of sexual relations with both sexes]. Stuttgart: Gustav Fischer Verlag. (w,m) A collection of scholarly essays on bisexuality by participants in the 1990 International Berlin Conference for Sexology. English translation is listed above.

Honnens, Brigette. (1996). **Wenn die andere ein Mann ist: Frauen als Partnerinnen bisexueller Männer.** [When the other person is a man: Women partners of bisexual men]. Frankfurt: Campus. (w,m) Explores the experiences of women in marriages with bisexual men in Germany, based on the author's interviews.

▼ Hüsers, Francis & Almut König. (1995). **Bisexualität.** [Bisexuality]. Stuttgart: Georg Thieme. (w,m) A sociologist and a psychiatrist provide a comprehensive and affirmative picture of and guide to bisexuality in Germany today.

In Spanish:

Archivo Lesbico y de Mujeres Diferentes. (1998). **Escrita en el cuerpo.** [**Written in the body**]. Retrieved from the World-Wide Web: http://www.bi.org/~ba.biwomen/ (w) Collection of original and translated articles, in Spanish, on bisexuality and bisexual issues.

BI-INCLUSIVE NON-FICTION BOOKS

Psychology, Sociology, and Sexual Orientation

▼ Bohan, Janet S. (1996). **Psychology & sexual orientation: Coming to terms.** New York: Routledge. (w,m) Excellent bi-inclusive historical and contemporary overview of the field of sexual orientation and sexual identity.

Cabaj, Robert P., & Terry S. Stein (Eds.). (1996). **Textbook of homosexuality and mental health.** Washington, DC: American Psychiatric Press. (w,m) A ground-breaking LGB-affirmative book, with chapters by Ron Fox (on bisexual identity) and Dave Matteson (on bisexual counseling issues) and other bi-inclusive chapters on a diverse range of LGB psychiatry and psychology issues.

Eliason, Michele J. (1996). **Who cares?: Institutional barriers to health care for lesbian, gay, and bisexual persons.** New York: NLN Press. (w,m) A bi-inclusive thorough examination of obstacles to quality health care for lesbians, gay men, bisexual women, and bisexual men.

Kominars, Sheppard B., & Kathryn D. Kominars. (1996). **Accepting ourselves and others: A journey into recovery from addictive and compulsive behaviors for gays, lesbians and bisexuals.** Center City, MN: Hazelden. (w,m) A bi-inclusive LGB-centered guide to the process of recovery.

Rust, Paula C. (Ed.). (1997). **Sociology of sexuality & sexual orientation: Syllabi & teaching materials.** Washington, DC: American Sociological Association. (w,m) Collection of college course syllabi, including the syllabus for Robin Ochs' course "Contexts and constructs of identity: Bisexuality."

Savin-Williams, Ritch C., & Kenneth M. Cohen. (Eds.). (1996). **The lives of lesbians, gays, and bisexuals: Children to adults.** Fort Worth, TX: Harcourt Brace. (w,m) A bi-inclusive collection addressing developmental issues of lesbians, gay men, bisexual women, and bisexual men over the lifespan.

Identity

Atkins, Dawn. (1996). (Ed.). **Looking Queer: Body Image and Identity in Lesbian, Bisexual, Gay and Transgender Communities.** New York: NYU Press. (w,m) An excellent collection that includes a number of bi voices (including the editor's): Greta Christina, Kate Woolfe, Catherine Lundoff, Nina Silver, Susanna Trnka, Julie Waters, Morgan Holmes, Raven Kaldera, Laura Cole, Layli Phillips, Ganapati Durgadas and Jill Nagle (those are just the ones we know about, or whose essays deal directly with bisexuality). Over 400 pages of excellent reading.

Burch, Beverly. (1994). **On Intimate Terms: The Psychology of Difference in Lesbian Relationships.** (Urbana & Chicago: University of Illinois Press. (w) Burch, a psychotherapist, draws a distinction between "primary" and "bisexual" lesbians, and posits that there may be a complementarity, or attraction, between the two. She sees "bisexual lesbians" as women who identify as lesbian later than "primary lesbians" and may have had significant heterosexual relationships and/or continue to recognize heterosexual relationships as a possibility. Primarily about women who identify as lesbian rather than bisexual, but extensive discussion of bisexuality.

D'Augelli, Anthony R., & Charlotte J. Patterson. (Eds.). (1995). **Lesbian, gay, and bisexual identities over the lifespan: Psychological approaches** New York: Oxford University Press. (w,m) Groundbreaking LGB psychology book that includes a chapter by Ron Fox on bisexual identities.

▼ Esterberg, Kristin G. (1997). **Lesbian & bisexual identities: Constructing communities, constructing selves.** Philadelphia: Temple University Press. (w) An in-depth study of lesbian and bisexual identity development, based on the author's interviews with a diverse group of women in a Northeastern community in the U.S.

▼ Johnson, Brett K. (1997). **Coming out every day: A gay, bisexual, or questioning man's guide.** Oakland, CA: New Harbinger. (m) The queer man's comprehensive & bi-inclusive guide to coming out and maintaining a positive self-accepting identity.

Norris, Stephanie, & Emma Read. (1985). **Out in the open: People talking about being gay or bisexual.** London: Pan. (w,m) A diverse collection of profiles of gay men, lesbians, bisexual men and bisexual women in the United Kingdom.

Van Gelder, Lindsay & Pamela Robin Brandt. (1996). **The Girls Next Door: Into the Heart of Lesbian America.** New York: Simon & Schuster. (w) This entertaining book about lesbians in America includes substantial discussions about lesbians who sleep with men but self-identify as lesbians, attitudes of lesbians about bisexuals, and, in general, the fluidity, for many of us, of our sexual desire. It's a fun read, with discussions of the Michigan Womyn's Music Festival, the Dinah Shore Party Circuit and the Lesbian Avengers, among other things.

Wishik, Heather & Carol Pierce. (1991). **Sexual orientation & identity: Heterosexual, lesbian, gay, & bisexual journeys.** Laconia, NH: New Dynamics. (w,m) An in-depth and affirmative exploration of sexual orientation and the development of sexual identity with interwoven theory and personal narratives.

Sexuality

Bright, Susie. (1992). **Susie Bright's sexual reality: A virtual sex world reader.** Pittsburgh, PA: Cleis Press. (w) Collection of bi-affirmative autobiographical essays on sexuality and sexual diversity.

Laumann, Edward O., John H. Gagnon, Robert T. Michael, & Stuart Michaels. (Eds.). (1994). **The social organization of sexuality: Sexual practices in the United States.** Chicago: University of Chicago Press. (w,m) This interesting and controversial book contains results of the most recent large-scale study of sexuality in the U. S. The study was carried out, with private funding, after United States Congress refused to provide public funding. Chapter 9 titled "Homosexuality" includes the most recent statistics from research of this type on same-sex behavior and relationships, bisexual attractions and behavior, and LGB self-identification.

▼ Marrow, Joanne. (1997). **Changing positions: Women speak out on sex & desire.** Holbrook, MA: Adams Media. (w) Comprehensive and enlightening contemporary portrait of women's sexuality, based on the author's interviews with bisexual, lesbian, and heterosexual women.

Pasle-Green, Jeanne, & Jim Haynes. (1977). **Hello, I love you: Voices from within the sexual revolution.** New York: Times Change Press. (w,m) Diverse collection of 1970s personal narratives on sexual behavior, relationships, and bisexuality.

▼ Queen, Carol., & Lawrence Schimel. (Eds.). (1997). **Pomosexuals: Challenging assumptions about gender and sexuality.** San Francisco: Cleis Press. (w,m) A bi-affirmative, bi-inclusive collection of essays celebrating gender and sexual diversity.

Relationships and Families

Abbott, Deborah, & Ellen Farmer. (Eds.). (1995). **From wedded wife to lesbian life: Stories of transformation.** Freedom, CA: Crossing Press. (w) Collection of personal narratives of 43 women about their coming out experiences.

Buxton, Amity P. (1994). **The other side of the closet: The coming out crisis for straight spouses & families.** New York: John Wiley & Sons. (w,m) An exploration of the issues involved in heterosexual marriages in which of one of the partners comes out as gay or bisexual, with a focus on the experiences of the female spouses of gay & bisexual men.

Cassingham, Barbee J. & Sally M. O'Neil. (Eds.). (1993). **And Then I Met This Woman.** Racine, WI: Mother Courage Press. (w) About previously married women's journeys into same-sex relationships. Most of the women in the book identify as lesbian, a few identify also as bisexual. First person accounts, may be helpful for women coming out from heterosexual identities.

Faderman, Lillian. (1991). **Odd girls & twilight lovers.** New York: Penguin. (w) Fascinating history of lesbian life in 20th-century U. S. Includes numerous references to bisexuality, especially in the 1920s and 1980s.

Gochros, Jean Schaar. (1989). **When husbands come out of the closet.** New York: Harrington Park Press. (w,m) Study of the impact of the coming out process on the spouses of gay and bisexual men and their marital relationship.

Scott, Jane. (1978). **Wives who love women.** New York: Walker. (w) Based on the author's interviews with married lesbian and bisexual women.

Strock, Carrie. (1998). **Married women who love women.** New York: Doubleday. (w) Portrait of currently lesbian-identified married women, their attractions and relationships with other women, and the impact of these experiences on their heterosexual marriages. Based on interviews and the author's personal experiences. May be helpful for women with current or past similar experiences.

Polyamory

Anapol, D. M. (1997). **The new love without limits: Secrets of sustainable intimate relationships.** San Rafael, CA: IntiNet Resource Center. (w,m) A bi-inclusive classic on polyamory.

▼ Easton, Dossie & Catherine A. Liszt. (1997). **The ethical slut: A guide to infinite possibilities.** San Francisco: Greenery Press. (w,m) An comprehensive bi-inclusive guide to polyamorous relationships.

Foster, Barbara M., Michael Foster, & Letha Hadady. (1997). **Three in love: Menages à trois from ancient to modern times.** (w,m) New York: Harper Collins. Overview of threesomes throughout history.

▼ Lano, Kevin, & Claire Parry. (Eds.). (1995). **Breaking the barriers to desire: Polyamory, polyfidelity & non-monogamy— New approaches to multiple relationships.** Nottingham, England, UK: Five Leaves Publications. (w,m) Collection of the essays on diverse forms of multiple relationships.

Nearing, Ryam. (1992). **Loving more: The polyfidelity primer.** Boulder, CO: Loving More. (w,m) Another classic guide to committed polyamorous relationships.

West, Celeste. (1995). **Lesbian polyfidelity.** San Francisco: Booklegger Press. (w) Comprehensive guide to committed polyamorous relationships among women.

Youth

▼ Bass, Ellen & Kate Kaufman. (1996). **Free your mind: The book for gay, lesbian, and bisexual youth—and their allies.** (w,m) New York: Harper Perennial. A broad-ranging bi-inclusive contemporary guide for LGB youth, allies, and families.

Bernstein, Robin, & Silberman, Seth Clark. (Eds.). (1996). **Generation Q: Gays, lesbians, and bisexuals born around 1969's Stonewall riots tell their stories of growing up in the age of information.** Boston: Alyson. (w,m) Diverse collection of personal narratives by gay, lesbian, and bisexual youth.

Findlen, Barbara. (Ed.). (1995). **Listen Up: Voices From the Next Feminist Generation.** Seattle: Seal Press. (w) An anthology of autobiographical writings by feminists in their 20s. Several contributors self-identify as bisexual, including Anastassia Higgenbotham, Laurel Gilbert, Jee Yeun Lee, and Christine Doza.

Pollack, Rachel, & Cheryl Schwartz. (1995). **The journey out: A guide for and about lesbian, gay and bisexual teens.** New York, N.Y: Viking. (w,m) A bi-inclusive guide to coming out and LGB identity for teenagers, their families, and their friends.

Sherrill, Jan-Mitchell, & Craig A. Hardesty. (1994). **The gay, lesbian & bisexual students' guide to colleges, universities, & graduate schools.** New York: NYU Press. (w,m) Comprehensive guide to LGB affirmative institutions of higher learning.

Transgender Persons and Identities

Denny, Dallas. (Ed.). (1998). **Current concepts in transgender identity.** New York: Garland. (w,m) An up-to-date collection of essays representing emerging affirmative approaches to transgender identities and issues, including chapters on gender identity and sexual orientation by Ira Pauly and Jamison Green.

Wilchins, Riki Ann. (1997). **Read my lips: Sexual subversion and the end of gender.** Ithica, NY: Freehand Books. (w,m) Collection of autobiographical essays by a bi-identified transgender activist celebrating sexual and gender diversity.

Ethnic, Racial, & Cultural Diversity

▼ Asian & Pacific Islander Wellness Center. (1997). **Understanding Asian & Pacific Islander sexual diversity: A handbook for individuals.** San Francisco: Asian & Pacific Islander Wellness Center. (w,m) An excellent overview of historical and contemporary sexual diversity in the Asian and Pacific Islander communities, including a list of community organizations and a reading list.

Lim-Hing, Sharon. (Ed.). (1994). **The very inside: An anthology of writing by Asian & Pacific Islander lesbian & bisexual women.** Toronto: Sister Vision Press. (w) A collection of essays and poetry that includes several pieces by bi-identified women.

Ratti, Rakesh (Ed.). (1993). **Lotus of another color: An unfolding of the South Asian Lesbian & Gay Experience.** Boston: Alyson. (w,m) An anthology that includes three essays by bi-identified people.

Attitudes toward Homosexuality and Bisexuality

Colker, Ruth. (1996). **Hybrid: Bisexuals, multiracials, & other misfits under American law.** New York: NYU Press. (w,m) An examination of how the legal system treats and mistreats those who don't fit standard categories, including bisexual and multiracial people.

Gamson, Joshua. (1998). **Freaks Talk Back: Tabloid Talk Shows and Sexual Nonconformity.** Chicago: University of Chicago Press. (w,m) Well-written and chock full of stories about US talk shows and their treatment of lesbian, gay, bi and transgendered people. Explores the issues from many angles, including how, while being used by talk shows, LGBT activists in return use talk shows to educate the public about LGBT issues. Includes substantial discussion of how bi's in particular are treated, including a number of entertaining behind the scenes stories.

Queer Theory/Cultural Studies/Literary Criticism

▼ Beemyn, Brett, & Mickey Eliason. (Eds.). (1996). **Queer studies: A lesbian, gay, bisexual, & transgender anthology.** NY: NYU Press. (w,m) Includes essays by Paula Rust, Amanda Udis-Kessler, Ruth Goldman, Amber Ault, Christopher James, Warren J. Blumenfeld and others. An impressive bi-inclusive mixed orientation collection, with several chapters on bisexuality in the context of queer studies.

Lesbian, Gay, and Bisexual Communities

Working Group on Funding Lesbian & Gay Issues. (1997). **Funders of lesbian, gay & bisexual programs: A directory for grantseekers (3rd ed.).** New York: Working Group on Funding Lesbian & Gay Issues. (w,m) Available for $10 from the Working Group on Funding Lesbian & Gay Issues, 666 Broadway, Suite 520, New York, NY 10012. Phone: 212-475-2930.

BOOK CHAPTERS AND JOURNAL ARTICLES ON BISEXUALITY

Complete information is provided for all listed chapters and articles, with the exception of chapters from the following anthologies:

Hutchins & Ka'ahumanu, **Bi any other name**; Rose, Stephens, & the Offpink Collective, **Bisexual horizons**; Tucker, **Bisexual politics**; Weise, **Closer to home**; The Bisexual Anthology Collective, **Plural desires**; Bernstein & Silberman, **Generation Q**; Findlen, **Listen up**; Beemyn & Eliason, **Queer studies**; and Hall & Pramaggiore, **RePresenting bisexualities.**

For chapters from these anthologies, the authors' names, chapter titles, book titles, and page numbers are given, and the reader is referred to the relevant book sections above for complete references. For books that were already described above in the book sections, a list of authors and titles are given at the beginning of each section, and the reader is referred to the book sections for complete references.

Special Issues of Journals and Magazines

Asian Pacific Journal. (1993, Spring/Summer, Vol. 2, No. 1). Special issue titled **"Witness aloud: Lesbian, gay & bisexual Asian/Pacific American writing."** A collection primarily by lesbian and gay identified authors. Includes writing by bi authors Indigo Chih-Lien Som and Jee Yeun Lee.

Journal of Gay, Lesbian, and Bisexual Identity. (1997, Vol. 2, Issue 1). **Special issue on bisexual theory**: Collection of essays, articles, poetry, and book reviews on bisexuality in literature, film, autobiography, community, and cultural studies.

Journal of Homosexuality (1985, Vol. 11, Issue 1/2). **Special issue on bisexuality**: Collection of scholarly reports on 1980s research on bisexuality.

Lavender Network: Oregon's Lesbian and Gay Newsmagazine. (1993, January) **Special issue on bisexuality**. Includes articles by Sharon Sumpter, Elias Farajajé-Jones, and others.

Loving More: New Models for Relationships. (1997, Fall). Special issue, titled **"Bi love."** Includes articles by Loraine Hutchins, Mark Silver and others.

Open Hands: Reconciling Ministries with Lesbians and Gay Men. (1991, Fall). **Special issue on bisexuality**. Includes articles by Beth Weise and others.

Open Hands: Reconciling Ministries with Lesbians and Gay Men. (1998, Summer). Special issue titled **"Bisexuality: Both/and rather than either/or."** Includes articles by Amanda Udis-Kessler, Ben Roe, and others.

Sexual Orientation: Multidimensional Approaches

For Books on sexual orientation, see the Bi-Inclusive Books section above: Under *Psychology, Sociology, & Sexual Orientation*: Bohan, 1996; Rust, 1997.

Psychological and Sociological Perspectives

Berkey, Braden R., Perelman-Hall, Terri, & Kurdek, Lawrence A. (1990). **The multidimensional scale of sexuality.** *Journal of Homosexuality, 19*(4), 67-87.

Coleman, Eli. (1987). **Assessment of sexual orientation.** *Journal of Homosexuality, 14*(1/2), 9-24.

▼ Klein, Fritz, Sepekoff, Barry, & Wolf, Timothy J. (1985). **Sexual orientation: A multi-variable dynamic process.** *Journal of Homosexuality, 11*(1/2), 35-50.

Rust, Paula C. (1996). **Finding a sexual identity & community: Therapeutic implications & cultural assumptions in scientific models of coming out.** In E. D. Rothblum, & L. A. Bond (Eds.), *Preventing heterosexism & homophobia* (pp. 87-123). Thousand Oaks, CA: Sage.

Sell, Randall L. (1996). **The Sell Assessment of Sexual Orientation: Background and scoring.** *Journal of Gay, Lesbian, & Bisexual Identity, 1*(4), 295-310.

Shively, Michael, & DeCecco, John. (1977). **Components of sexual identity.** *Journal of Homosexuality, 3*(1), 41-48.

Personal and Political Perspectives

▼ Gibian, Ruth. (1992). **Refusing certainty: Toward a bisexuality of wholeness.** In *Closer to home* (pp. 3-16).

Kaplan, Rebecca. (1995). **Your fence is sitting on me: The hazards of binary thinking.** In *Bisexual politics* (pp. 267-280).

Bisexual Identity

Psychological and Sociological Perspectives

For Books on bisexual identity, see also the following sections above: Books Specifically on Bisexuality: Bode, 1976; George, 1993; Klein, 1993; Klein & Wolf, 1985; Rust, 1995, 1999; Weinberg, Williams & Pryor, 1994. In *Dutch*: Hanson, 1990; Kuppens, 1995; van Kerkhof, 1997; Wolff, 1979. In *French*: Mendès-Leité, Deschamps, & Proth, 1996. In *German*: Feldhorst, 1996; Geissler, 1993; Gooß, 1995; Hüsers & König, 1995. Bi-Inclusive Books: Under *Identity*: Atkins, 1996; Burch, 1994; Esterberg, 1997; Johnson, 1997; Wishik & Pierce, 1991. Under *Ethnic, Racial, & Cultural Diversity*: Asian & Pacific Islander Wellness Center, 1997.

Blumstein, Philip W., & Pepper Schwartz. (1977). **Bisexuality: Some social psychological issues.** *Journal of Social Issues, 33*(2), 30-45.

Schwartz, Pepper, & Philip Blumstein. (1998). **The acquisition of sexual identity: Bisexuality.** In E. J. Haeberle, & R. Gindorf (Eds.), *Bisexualities: The ideology and practice of sexual contact with both men and women* (pp. 182-212). New York: Continuum.

Coleman, Eli. (1998). **Paradigmatic changes in the understanding of bisexuality.** In E. J. Haeberle, & R. Gindorf (Eds.), *Bisexualities: The ideology and practice of sexual contact with both men and women* (pp. 107-112). New York: Continuum.

▼ Firestein, Beth A. (1996). **Bisexuality as paradigm shift: Transforming our disciplines.** In B. A. Firestein (Ed.), *Bisexuality: The psychology & politics of an invisible minority* (pp. 261-291). Thousand Oaks, CA: Sage.

▼ Fox, Ronald C. (1995). **Bisexual identities.** In A. R. D'Augelli, & C. J. Patterson (Eds.), *Lesbian, gay, and bisexual identities over the lifespan: Psychological perspectives* (pp. 48-86). New York: Oxford University Press.

▼ Golden, Carla. (1996). **What's in a name? Sexual self-identification among women.** In R. C. Savin-Williams, & K. M. Cohen (Eds.), *The lives of lesbians, gays, & bisexuals: Children to adults* (pp. 229-249). Ft. Worth, TX: Harcourt Brace.

Ochs, Robyn. (1997). **Contexts & constructs of identity: Bisexuality.** In P. Rust (Ed.), *Sociology of sexuality & sexual orientation: Syllabi & teaching materials* (pp. 100-107). Washington, DC: American Sociological Association.

▼ Paul, Jay P. (1996). **Bisexuality: Exploring/exploding the boundaries.** In R. C. Savin-Williams, & K. M. Cohen (Eds.), *The lives of lesbians, gays, & bisexuals: Children to adults* (pp. 436-461). Ft. Worth, TX: Harcourt Brace.

Queen, Carol. (1995). **Sexual diversity and bisexual identity.** In *Bisexual politics* (pp. 151-160).

Rust, Paula C. (1992). **Who are we & where do we go from here? Conceptualizing bisexuality.** In *Closer to home* (pp. 281-310).

▼ Rust, Paula C. (1996). **Sexual identity & bisexual identities: The struggle for self-description in a changing sexual landscape.** In B. Beemyn, & M. Eliason (Eds.), *Queer studies: A lesbian, gay, bisexual, & transgender anthology* (pp. 64-86). New York: NYU Press.

Shuster, Rebecca. (1987). **Sexuality as a continuum: The bisexual identity**. In The Boston Lesbian Psychologies Collective (Eds.), *Lesbian psychologies: Explorations & challenges* (pp. 56-71). Urbana & Chicago, IL: University of Illinois Press.

Wishik, Heather R. (1996). **Life maps: Tracking individual gender and sexual identity construction in the contexts of cultures, relationships, and desires**. *Journal of Gay, Lesbian, & Bisexual Identity, 1*(2), 129-152.

Personal and Political Perspectives

For Books with personal and political perspectives on bisexual identity, see also the following sections above:
Books Specifically on Bisexuality: Bisexual Anthology Collective, 1995; Hutchins & Ka'ahumanu, 1991; Off Pink Collective, 1988; Rose, Stevens & the Off-Pink Collective, 1996; Tucker, 1995; Weise, 1992. In *Spanish*: Archivo Lesbico y de Mujeres Diferentes, 1998.
Bi-Inclusive Books: Under *Identity*: Norris & Read, 1985; Van Gelder & Brandt, 1996. Under *Youth*: Findlen, 1995. Under *Ethnic, Racial & Cultural Diversity*: Lim-Hing, 1994; Ratti, 1993.

Chater, Nancy, & Lilith Finkler. (1995). **"Traversing wide territories": A journey from lesbianism to bisexuality**. In *Plural desires* (pp. 14-36).

Cooper, Laurie A., Michelle E. Hynes, & Edith R. Westfall. (1995). **The Kinsey three**. In *Plural desires* (pp. 261-275).

▼ Eadie, Jo. (1996). **Being who we are (and anyone else we want to be)**. In *Bisexual horizons* (pp. 16-20).

▼ Fox, Ann. (1991). **Development of a bisexual identity**. In *Bi any other name* (pp. 29-36).

Hamilton, Louis. (1996). **Deaf bisexuality**. In *Bisexual horizons* (pp. 144-148).

McKeon, Elizabeth. (1992). **To be bisexual and underclass**. In *Closer to home* (pp. 27-34).

Montgomery, Michael S. (1996). **An old bottle for old wine: Selecting the right label**. In *Bisexual horizons* (pp. 21-24).

Queen, Carol A. (1991). **The queer in me**. In *Bi any other name* (pp. 17-21).

▼ Shuster, Rebecca. (1992). **Bisexuality and the quest for principled loving**. In *Closer to home* (pp. 147-154).

Starr, Christina. (1995). **Making a sexual choice**. In *Plural desires* (pp. 185-190).

▼ Sumpter, Sharon F. (1991). **Myths/realities of bisexuality**. In *Bi any other name* (pp. 12-13).

▼ Udis-Kessler, Amanda. (1996). **Challenging the stereotypes**. In *Bisexual horizons* (pp. 45-57).

Zipkin, Dvora. (1992). **Why bi?** In *Closer to home* (pp. 55-73).

Bisexual Attractions and Behavior

Psychological and Sociological Perspectives

Findings of research on bisexual attractions & behavior. For a review of the social science literature on bisexual identity, see Fox, "Bisexuality in perspective" (cited in this section).

For <u>Books</u> on bisexual attractions and behavior, see also the following sections above:
<u>Books Specifically on Bisexuality</u>: Aggleton, 1996; Bode, 1976; George, 1993; Haeberle & Gindorf, 1998; Klein, 1993; Klein & Wolf, 1985; Rust, 1995; Sigma Research, 1993; Tielman, Carballo & Hendriks, 1991; Weinberg, Williams & Pryor, 1994; Wolff, 1979. In *French*: Mendès-Leité, Deschamps, & Proth, 1996.
<u>Bi-Inclusive Books</u>: Under *Sexuality*: Laumann, Gagnon, Michael & Michaels, 1994; Marrow, 1997.

Binson, Diane, Stuart Michaels, Ron Stall, Thomas J. Coates, John H. Gagnon, & Joseph A. Catania. (1995). **Prevalence & social distribution of men who have sex with men: United States & its urban centers**. *Journal of Sex Research, 32*(3), 245-254.

Blumstein, Philip & Pepper Schwartz. (1976). **Bisexuality in women**. *Archives of Sexual Behavior, 5*(2), 171-181.

Blumstein, Philip & Pepper Schwartz. (1976). **Bisexuality in men**. *Urban Life, 5*(3), 339-358.

▼ Doll, Lynda S., Lyle R. Petersen, Carol R. White, Eric S. Johnson, John W. Ward, & The Blood Donor Study Group. (1992). **Homosexually & nonhomosexually identified men who have sex with men: A behavioral comparison**. *Journal of Sex Research, 29*(1), 1-14.

▼ Fox, Ronald C. (1996). **Bisexuality in perspective: A review of theory & research**. In B. A. Firestein (Ed.), *Bisexuality: The psychology & politics of an invisible minority* (pp. 3-50). Thousand Oaks, CA: Sage.

Gagnon, John H., Cathy S. Greenblat, & Michael Kimmel. (1998). **Bisexuality: A sociological perspective**. In E. J. Haeberle, & R. Gindorf (Eds.), *Bisexualities: The ideology and practice of sexual contact with both men and women* (pp. 81-106). New York: Continuum.

Gindorf, Rolf. & Alan Warran/ (1998). **Bisexualities: Heterosexual contacts of "gay" men, homosexual contacts of "heterosexual" men**. In E. J. Haeberle, & R. Gindorf (Eds.), *Bisexualities: The ideology and practice of sexual contact with both men and women* (pp. 213-220). New York: Continuum.

McKirnan, David J., Joseph P. Stokes, Lynda Doll, & Rebecca G. Burzette. (1995). **Bisexually active men: Social characteristics & sexual behavior**. *Journal of Sex Research, 32*(1), 65-76.

Messiah, Antoine, & Emmanuelle Mouret-Fourme. (1993). **Homosexualité, bisexualité: Éléments de socio-biographie sexuelle [Homosexuality, bisexuality: Elements of a sexual social biography].** Population, 48(5), 1353-1380.

▼ Queen, Carol. (1996). **Bisexuality, sexual diversity, & the sex-positive perspective.** In B. A. Firestein (Ed.), *Bisexuality: The psychology & politics of an invisible minority* (pp. 103-124). Thousand Oaks, CA: Sage.

Rogers, Susan M., & Charles F. Turner. (1991). **Male-male sexual contact in the U.S.A.: Findings from five sample surveys, 1970-1990.** *Journal of Sex Research, 28*(4), 491-519.

Ross, Michael W., & Paul, Jay P. (1992). **Beyond gender: The basis of sexual attraction in bisexual men & women.** *Psychological Reports, 71,* 1283-1290.

▼ Rust, Paula C. (1992). **The politics of sexual identity: Sexual attraction & behavior among lesbian & bisexual women.** *Social Problems, 39*(4), 366-386.

Sell, Randall L., Wells, James A., & David Wypij. (1995). **The prevalence of homosexual behavior & attraction in the United States, the United Kingdom & France: Results of national population-based samples.** *Archives of Sexual Behavior, 24*(3), 235-248.

Wellings, Kaye, Julia Wadsworth, & Anne M. Johnson. (1994). **Sexual diversity & homosexual behaviour.** In A. M. Johnson, J. Wadsworth, K. Wellings, & J. Field, *Sexual attitudes & lifestyles* (pp. 183-224). Oxford: Blackwell Scientific Publications.

Personal and Political Perspectives

For <u>Books</u> with personal and political perspectives on bisexual attractions and behavior, see also the following sections above:
<u>Books Specifically on Bisexuality</u>: Bisexual Anthology Collective, 1995; Hutchins & Ka'ahumanu, 1991; Off Pink Collective, 1988; Rose, Stevens & the Off-Pink Collective, 1996; Tucker, 1995; Weise, 1992.
<u>Bi-Inclusive Books</u>: Under *Sexuality*: Bright, 1992; Marrow, 1997; Pasle-Green & Haynes, 1977; Queen & Schimel, 1997.

Barragan III, C. J. (1991). **More than a footnote.** In *Bi any other name* (pp. 17-21).

▼ Christina, Greta. (1995). **Bi sexuality.** In *Bisexual politics* (pp. 161-166).

Field, Nicola. (1996). **Trade secrets.** In *Bisexual horizons* (pp. 133-141).

▼ Goswami, Changini. (1991). **My underself.** In *Bi any other name* (pp. 60-63).

Hutchins, Loraine. (1991). **Love that kink.** In *Bi any other name* (pp. 335-343).

Johnson, Laura. (1991). **Making my own way.** In *Bi any other name* (pp. 40-42).

▼ Klassen, Karen. (1991). **Talking about sex, gender, and desire.** In *Bi any other name* (pp. 329-334).

▼ Ripley, Rebecca. (1992). **The language of desire: Sexuality, identity and language.** In *Closer to home* (pp. 91-102).

Stone, Dave. (1996). **Living with the Janus people.** In *Bisexual horizons* (pp. 127-132).

Tan, Cecilia. (1995). **Bisexuality and S/M: The bi switch revolution.** In *Bisexual politics* (pp. 167-170).

Yost, Lisa. (1991). **Bisexual tendencies.** In *Bi any other name* (pp. 74-76).

Bisexual Relationships and Families

Psychological and Sociological Perspectives

For <u>Books</u> on bisexual relationships and families, see also the following sections above:
<u>Books Specifically on Bisexuality</u>: Bode, 1976; George, 1993; Klein, 1993; Klein & Wolf, 1985; Rust, 1995; Weinberg, Williams & Pryor, 1994. In *Dutch*: Hanson, 1990; Kuppens, 1995; van Kerkhof, 1997; Wolff, 1979. In *French*: Mendès-Leité, Deschamps, & Proth, 1996. In *German*: Feldhorst, 1996; Geissler, 1993; Honnens, 1996.
<u>Bi-Inclusive Books</u>: Under *Relationships & Families*: Burch, 1994; Buxton, 1994; Faderman, 1991; Gochros, 1989.

Coleman, Eli. (1985). **Bisexual women in marriages.** *Journal of Homosexuality, 11*(1/2), 87-99.

Coleman, Eli. (1985). **Integration of male bisexuality & marriage.** *Journal of Homosexuality, 11*(1/2), 189-208.

▼ Rust, Paula C. (1996). **Monogamy & polyamory: Relationship issues for bisexuals.** In B. A. Firestein (Ed.), *Bisexuality: The psychology & politics of an invisible minority* (pp. 127-148). Thousand Oaks, CA: Sage.

▼ Wolf, Timothy J. (1985). **Marriages of bisexual men.** *Journal of Homosexuality, 11*(1/2), 135-148.

Personal and Political Perspectives

For <u>Books</u> on bisexual relationships and families, see also the following sections above:
<u>Books Specifically on Bisexuality</u>: Bisexual Anthology Collective, 1995; Bode, 1976; Hutchins & Ka'ahumanu, 1991; Kohn & Matusow, 1980; Off Pink Collective, 1988; Rose, Stevens & the Off-Pink Collective, 1996; Tucker, 1995; Weise, 1992.
<u>Bi-Inclusive Books</u>: Under *Relationships & Families*: Abbott & Farmer, 1995; Cassingham & O'Neil, 1993; Scott, 1978; Strock, 1998. Under *Sexuality*: Pásle-Green & Haynes, 1977; Under *Polyamory*: Anapol, 1997; Easton & Liszt, 1997; Foster, Foster & Hadady, 1997; Lano & Parry, 1995; Nearing, 1992; West, 1995.

▼ Arden, Karen. (1996). **Dwelling in the house of tomorrow:** Children, young people and their bisexual parents. In *Bisexual horizons* (pp. 247-257).

Bassein, Richard S. (1991). **A day in the life.** In *Bi any other name* (pp. 171-173).

Brewer, Michael. (1991). **Two-way closet.** In *Bi any other name* (pp. 140-143).

▼ Bryant, Wayne. (1991). **Love, friendship, and sex.** In *Bi any other name* (pp. 69-73).

Cade, Felicity. (1996). **Marriage and bisexuality.** In *Bisexual horizons* (pp. 114-118).

Girard, Chris. (1991). **A few brave and gifted people.** In *Bi any other name* (pp. 167-170).

Glenn, Roland. (1991). **Proud father of a bisexual son.** In *Bi any other name* (pp. 254-257).

▼ Gonsalves, Sharon. (1992). **Where healing becomes possible.** In *Closer to home* (pp. 115-125).

▼ Jones, Billy, & Peaches Jones. (1991). **Growing up with a bisexual dad.** In *Bi any other name* (pp. 159-166).

Key, Mattie. (1991). **Never, never boring.** In *Bi any other name* (pp. 174-176).

Montgomery, Michael S. (1997). **The marrying kind: Bisexual life, partnered identity.** *Journal of Gay, Lesbian, & Bisexual Identity, 2*(1), 77-82.

▼ Nachama. (1991). **Double quest.** In *Bi any other name* (pp. 79-82).

Norrgard, Lenore. (1991). **Can bisexuals be monogamous?** In *Bi any other name* (pp. 281-284).

Rose, Sharon. (1996). **Against marriage.** In *Bisexual horizons* (pp. 119-121).

▼ Silver, Nina. (1992). **Coming out as a heterosexual.** In *Closer to home* (pp. 35-46).

Trnka, Susanna. (1992). **"A pretty good bisexual kiss there...".** In *Closer to home* (pp. 103-113).

▼ Weise, Elizabeth R. (1991). **Bisexuality, *The Rocky Horror Picture Show*, and me.** In *Bi any other name* (pp. 134-139).

Yoshizaki, Amanda. (1991). **I am who I am— A married bisexual teacher.** In *Bi any other name* (pp. 25-26).

Bisexual Youth

Bi-inclusive resources on and for bisexual youth. For Books on bisexual youth, see also the following book section above:
Bi-Inclusive Books: Under *Identity*: Johnson, 1997. Under *Youth*: Bass & Kaufman, 1996; Pollack & Schwartz, 1995; Sherril & Hardesty, 1994.

Psychological and Sociological Perspectives

▼ D'Augelli, Anthony R. (1996). **Enhancing the development of lesbian, gay, & bisexual youths.** In E. D. Rothblum, & L. A. Bond (Eds.), *Preventing heterosexism & homophobia* (pp. 124-150). Thousand Oaks, CA: Sage.

Evans, Nancy J., & Anthony R. D'Augelli. (1996). **Lesbians, gay men, & bisexual people in college.** In R. C. Savin-Williams, & K. M. Cohen (Eds.), *The lives of lesbians, gays, & bisexuals: Children to adults* (pp. 201-226). Fort Worth, TX: Harcourt Brace.

Harbeck, Karen M. (1993). **Invisible no more: Addressing needs of gay, lesbian & bisexual youth & their advocates.** *High School Journal, 77*(1-2), 169-176.

Pope, Raechele L., & Amy L. Reynolds. (1991). **Including bisexuality: It's more than just a label.** In N. J. Evans, & V. A. Wall (Eds.), *Beyond tolerance: Gays, lesbians, and bisexuals on campus* (pp. pp. 205-212). Alexandria, VA: American College Personnel Association.

Savin-Williams, Ritch C. (1995). **Lesbian, gay male, & bisexual adolescents.** In A. R. D'Augelli, & C. J. Patterson (Eds.), *Lesbian, gay, & bisexual identities over the lifespan: Psychological perspectives* (pp. 165-189). New York: Oxford University Press.

▼ Savin-Williams, Ritch C. (1996). **Self-labeling & disclosure among gay, lesbian, & bisexual youths.** In Laird, J. & R-J. Green (Eds.) *Lesbians & gays in couples & families: A handbook for therapists* (pp. 153-182). San Francisco: Jossey-Bass.

Personal and Political Perspectives

For Books with personal and political perspectives on bisexual youth, see also the following sections above:
Books Specifically on Bisexuality: Bisexual Anthology Collective, 1995; Hutchins & Ka'ahumanu, 1991; Rose, Stevens & the Off-Pink Collective, 1996; Tucker, 1995; Weise, 1992.
Bi-Inclusive Books: Under *Youth*: Findlen, 1995; Bernstein & Silberman, 1996.

▼ Arnaoot, Nadya. (1996). **Me and my gender(s).** In *Generation Q* (pp. 221-223).

Arnaoot, Nadya. (1996). **Stone.** In *Generation Q* (pp. 146-148).

▼ Cooper, Charlotte. (1996). **Fitting.** In *Generation Q* (p. 59-64).

Doza, Christine. (1995). **Bloodlove.** In *Listen up* (pp. 249-257).

▼ Gilbert, Laurel. (1995). **You're not the type.** In *Listen up* (pp. 102-112).

▼ McDade, Pete. (1996). **A difficult floating garden.** In *Generation Q* (pp. 102-105).

▼ Medina, Dalissa. (1996). **Tune in, get off, come out: California dreamin' and my age of Aqueerius.** In *Generation Q* (pp. 59-64).

Pemberton, Sarah. (1996). ***Rocky Horror* schoolgirl.** In *Generation Q* (pp. 69-72).

Older Bisexual Women and Bisexual Men

Psychological and Sociological Perspectives

For Books on older bisexual women and bisexual men, see also the following section above:
Bi-Inclusive Books: Under *Relationships & Families*: Buxton, 1994; Gochros, 1989; Marrow, 1997.

Boxer, Andrew M. (1997). **Gay, lesbian, and bisexual aging into the twenty-first century: An overview and introduction.** *Journal of Gay, Lesbian, & Bisexual Identity, 3* (3/4), 187-197.

Linsk, Nathan L. (1997). **Experience of older gay and bisexual men living with HIV/AIDS.** *Journal of Gay, Lesbian, & Bisexual Identity, 3* (3/4), 265-285.

Personal and Political Perspectives

For Books with personal and political perspectives on older bisexual women and bisexual men, see also the following sections above:
Books Specifically on Bisexuality: Bisexual Anthology Collective, 1995; Hutchins & Ka'ahumanu, 1991; Kohn & Matusow, 1980; Off Pink Collective, 1988; Rose, Stevens & the Off-Pink Collective, 1996; Tucker, 1995; Weise, 1992.
Bi-Inclusive Books: Under *Relationships & Families*: Abbott & Farmer, 1995; Cassingham & O'Neil, 1993; Faderman, 1991; Scott, 1978; Strock, 1998.

▼ Keppel, Bobbi. (1991). **Gray-haired and above suspicion.** In L. Hutchins & L. Ka'ahumanu. (Eds.), *Bi any other name* (pp. 154-158).

▼ Utz, Cornelius. (1991). **Ninety-three people = 110% acceptance.** In *Bi any other name* (pp. 22-24).

Bisexuality & Transgender Persons and Identities

Psychological Perspectives

For Books addressing transgender persons and identities, see also the following section above:
Bi-Inclusive Books: Under *Transgender Persons & Identities*: Denny, 1998.

Bentler, Peter M. (1976). **A typology of transsexualism: Gender identity theory and data.** *Archives of Sexual Behavior, 5,* 567-584.

Coleman, Eli, Walter O. Bockting, & Louis Gooren. (1993). **Homosexual & bisexual identity in sex-reassigned female-to-male transsexuals.** *Archives of Sexual Behavior, 22*(1), 37-50.

▼ Denny, Dallas, & James Green. (1996). **Gender identity & bisexuality.** In B. A. Firestein (Ed.), *Bisexuality: The psychology & politics of an invisible minority* (pp. 84-102). Thousand Oaks, CA: Sage.

▼ Devor, Holly. (1993). **Sexual orientation identities, attractions, & practices of female-to-male transsexuals.** *Journal of Sex Research, 30*(4), 303-315.

Green, Jamison. (1998). **FTM: An emerging voice.** In D. Denny (Ed.), *Current concepts in transgender identity* (pp. 145-162). New York: Garland.

Pauly, Ira B. (1990). **Gender identity and sexual preference.** In D. Denny (Ed.), *Current concepts in transgender identity* (pp. 237-248). New York: Garland.

Personal and Political Perspectives

For <u>Books</u> with personal and political perspectives on transgender persons and identities, see also the following section above:
Bi-Inclusive Books: Under *Transgender Persons & Identities*: Wilchins, 1997.
See also Patricia Kevena Fili's column *TransBiLine* in the bi magazine *Anything That Moves*.

▼ Antoniou, Laura. (1997). **Antivenom for the soul.** In C. Queen, & L. Schimel (Eds.), *Pomosexuals: Challenging assumptions about gender and sexuality* (pp. 114-121). San Francisco: Cleis Press.

Franek, Heather. (1998, Summer). **Talking about the issues no one's expressing: Telling it like it is in the world of bi-trans romance.** *Anything That Moves,* 28-31.

Harrison, David. (1997). **The personals.** In C. Queen, & L. Schimel (Eds.), *Pomosexuals: Challenging assumptions about gender and sexuality* (pp. 129-137). San Francisco: Cleis Press.

▼ Hemmings, Clare. (1996). **From lesbian nation to transgender liberation: A bisexual feminist perspective.** *Journal of Gay, Lesbian, & Bisexual Identity, 1*(1), 37-60.

Martin-Damon, Kory. (1995). **Essay for the inclusion of transsexuals.** In *Bisexual politics* (pp. 241-250).

Michaela-Gonzalez, Andrea. (1998, Summer). **It's what you think you see that counts: True tales from the edges of the bi-trans continuum.** *Anything That Moves,* 22-25.

▼ O'Connor, Rachel. (1996). **The transgender identity as a political challenge.** In *Bisexual horizons* (pp. 243-246).

Valerio, Max Wolf. (1998, Summer). **The joker is wild: Changing sex and other crimes of passion.** *Anything That Moves,* 32-36.

▼ Wilchins, Riki Anne. (1997). **Lines in the sand, cries of desire.** In C. Queen, & L. Schimel (Eds.), *Pomosexuals: Challenging assumptions about gender and sexuality* (pp. 138-149). San Francisco: Cleis Press.

Bisexuality and Ethnic, Racial, & Cultural Diversity

For <u>Books</u> on bisexuality and ethnic, racial, & cultural diversity, see also the following sections above:
<u>Books Specifically on Bisexuality</u>: Aggleton, 1996; Cantarella, 1992; Tielman, Carballo & Hendriks, 1991.
<u>Bi-Inclusive Books</u>: Under *Ethnic, Racial, & Cultural Diversity*: Asian & Pacific Islander Wellness Center, 1997.

Overview

▼ Rust, Paula C. (1996). **Managing multiple identities: Diversity among bisexual women & men.** In B. A. Firestein (Ed.), *Bisexuality: The psychology & politics of an invisible minority* (pp. 53-83). Thousand Oaks, CA: Sage.

Psychological and Sociological Perspectives

▼ Carballo-Diéguez, Alex. (1995). **The sexual identity & behavior of Puerto Rican men who have sex with men.** In G. M. Herek, & B. Greene (Eds.), *AIDS, identity, & community: The HIV epidemic & lesbians & gay men* (pp. 105-114). Thousand Oaks, CA: Sage.

▼ Kochems, Lee M., & Jacobs, Sue-Ellen. (1997). **Gender statuses, gender features, & gender/sex categories: New perspectives on an old paradigm.** In S. E. Jacobs, W. Thomas, & S. Lang (Eds.), *Two-spirit people: Native American gender identity, sexuality, & spirituality* (pp. 255-264). Urbana, IL: University of Illinois Press.

▼ Lang, Sabine. (1997). **Various kinds of Two-spirit people: Gender variance & homosexuality in Native American Communities.** In S. E. Jacobs, W. Thomas, & S. Lang (Eds.), *Two-spirit people: Native American gender identity, sexuality, & spirituality* (pp. 100-118). Urbana, IL: University of Illinois Press.

Liu, Peter. & Connie S. Chan. (1996). **Lesbian, gay, & bisexual Asian Americans & their families.** In Laird, J. & R-J. Green (Eds.) Lesbians & gays in couples & families: A handbook for therapists (pp. 137-152). San Francisco: Jossey-Bass.

Manalansan IV, Martin F. (1996). **Double minorities: Latino, Black, & Asian who have sex with men.** R. C. Savin-Williams, & K. M. Cohen (Eds.), *The lives of lesbians, gays, & bisexuals: Children to adults* (pp. 393-415). Fort Worth, TX: Harcourt Brace.

▼ Morales, Eduardo S. (1996). **Gender roles among Latino gay & bisexual men: Implications for family & couple relationships.** In Laird, J. & R-J. Green (Eds.) *Lesbians & gays in couples & families: A handbook for therapists* (pp. 272-297). San Francisco: Jossey-Bass.

Williams, Walter L. (1996). **Two-spirit persons: Gender nonconformity among Native American & Native Hawaiian youths.** In R. C. Savin-Williams, & K. M. Cohen (Eds.), *The lives of lesbians, gays, & bisexuals: Children to adults* (pp. 416-435). Ft. Worth, TX: Harcourt Brace.

Zamora-Hernandez, Carlos E., & Davis G. Patterson. (1996). **Homosexually active Latino men: Issues for social work practice.** In John F. Longres (Ed.), *Men of color: A context for service to homosexually active men* (pp. 69-91). New York: Harrington Park Press.

Anthropological and Cross-Cultural Perspectives

Aggleton (1996) contains chapters on bisexuality in Australia, Brazil, Canada, China, Costa Rica, the Dominican Republic, France, India, Mexico, Papua New Guinea, Peru, the Philippines, and the U. K. Tielman (1991) contains chapters on bisexuality in Australia, India, Indonesia, Latin America, Mexico, the Netherlands, New Zealand, Sub-Saharan Africa, Thailand, the U. K., and the United States.

Adam, Barry D. (1985). **Age, structure, & sexuality: Reflections of the anthropological evidence on homosexual relations.** *Journal of Homosexuality, 11*(3/4), 19-34.

Blackwood, Evelyn. (1985). **Breaking the mirror: The construction of lesbianism & the anthropological discourse on homosexuality.** *Journal of Homosexuality, 11*(3/4), 1-18.

▼ Callender, Charles, & Lee M. Kochems. (1985). **Men & not-men: Male gender-mixing statuses & homosexuality.** *Journal of Homosexuality, 11*(3-4), 165-178.

▼ Carrier, Joseph M. (1985). **Mexican male bisexuality.** *Journal of Homosexuality, 11*(1/2), 75-86.

De Cecco, John P. (1998). **Bisexuality and discretion: The case of Pakistan.** In E. J. Haeberle, & R. Gindorf (Eds.), *Bisexualities: The ideology and practice of sexual contact with both men and women* (pp. 152-156). New York: Continuum.

Herdt, Gilbert H. (1984). **A comment on cultural attributes & fluidity of bisexuality.** *Journal of Homosexuality, 10*(3/4), 53-62.

Wong, Joseph. (1998). **Bisexuality in early Imperial China: An introductory overview.** In E. J. Haeberle, & R. Gindorf (Eds.), *Bisexualities: The ideology and practice of sexual contact with both men and women* (pp. 140-151). New York: Continuum.

Personal and Political Perspectives

For <u>Books</u> with personal and political perspectives on bisexuality and ethnic, racial, & cultural diversity, see also the following sections above:
<u>Books Specifically on Bisexuality</u>: Bisexual Anthology Collective, 1995; Hutchins & Ka'ahumanu, 1991; Rose, Stevens & the Off-Pink Collective, 1996; Tucker, 1995; Weise, 1992.
<u>Bi-Inclusive Books</u>: Under *Ethnic, Racial, & Cultural Diversity*: Lim-Hing, 1994; Ratti, 1993.

▼ Acharya, Leela, Amina, Amita, Farzana Doctor, & Gogia. (1995). **"Purifying" the (identi)ghee: South Asian feminists** *Gup-shup*. In *Plural desires* (pp. 101-118).

Alexander, Christopher. (1991). **Affirmation: Bisexual Mormon.** In *Bi any other name* (pp. 193-197).

Barlow, Valerie. (1996). **Bisexuality and feminism: One Black women's perspective**. In *Bisexual horizons* (pp. 38-40).

Blasingame, Brenda. (1991). **The palmist knew**. In *Bi any other name* (pp. 144-146).

Chaudhary, Kamini. (1993). **The scent of roses**. In R. Ratti (Ed.), *A lotus of another color: An unfolding of the South Asian gay and lesbian experience* (pp. 145-150).

Chaudhary, Kamini. (1993). **Some thoughts on bisexuality**. In R. Ratti (Ed.), *A lotus of another color: An unfolding of the South Asian gay and lesbian experience* (pp. 54-58).

Chen, Shu Wei— Andy. (1991). **A man, a woman, attention**. In *Bi any other name* (pp. 179-180).

▼ Choe, Margaret Mihee. (1992). **Our selves, growing whole**. In *Closer to home* (pp. 17-26).

▼ Dajenya. (1991). **Sisterhood crosses gender preference lines**. In *Bi any other name* (pp. 247-251).

Fehr, Tracy Charette. (1995). **Accepting my inherent duality**. In *Plural desires* (pp. 128-129).

▼ Gollain, Françoise. (1996). **Bisexuality in the Arab world: An interview with Muhammed** . In *Bisexual horizons* (pp. 58-61).

Gorlin, Rebecca. (1991). **The voice of a wandering Jewish bisexual**. In *Bi any other name* (pp. 252-253).

▼ Jadallah, Huda, & Pearl Saad. (1995). **A conversation about the Arab Lesbian and Bisexual Women's Network**. In *Plural desires* (pp. 252-259).

▼ Ka'ahumanu, Lani. (1991). **Hapa haole wahine**. In *Bi any other name* (pp. 306-325).

▼ Lakshmi & Arka. (1993). **Extended family**. In R. Ratti (Ed.), *A lotus of another color: An unfolding of the South Asian gay and lesbian experience* (pp. 265-278).

Lee, Jee Yeun. (1995). **Beyond bean counting**. In B. Findlen (Ed.), *Listen up: Voices from the next feminist generation* (pp. 205-211). Seattle: Seal Press.

▼ Leyva, Obie. (1991). **¿Que es un bisexual?** In *Bi any other name* (pp. 201-202).

Paul. (1996). **On being bisexual and black in Britain**. In *Bisexual horizons* (pp. 95-99).

▼ Pollon, Zélie. (1995). **Naming her destiny: June Jordan speaks on bisexuality**. In *Plural desires* (pp. 77-82).

▼ Prabhudas, Yasmin. (1996). **Bisexuals and people of mixed-race: Arbiters of change**. In *Bisexual horizons* (pp. 30-31).

Reichler, Rifka. (1991). **A question of invisibility**. In *Bi any other name* (pp. 77-78).

▼ Rios, Joe. (1991). **What do Indians think about?** In *Bi any other name* (pp. 37-39).

▼ Silver, Alan. (1991). **Worth the balancing.** In *Bi any other name* (pp. 27-28).

Som, Indigo Chih-Lien. (1995). **The queer kitchen.** Bisexual Anthology Collective (Eds.), *Plural desires* (pp. 84-88).

▼ Tucker, Naomi. (1996). **Passing: Pain or privilege? What the bisexual community can learn from the Jewish experience.** In *Bisexual horizons* (pp. 32-37).

Uwano, Kei. (1991). **Bi-loveable Japanese feminist.** In *Bi any other name* (pp. 185-187).

▼ Whang, Selena J. (1991). **[untitled].** In *Bi any other name* (pp. 177-178).

Bisexuality & HIV/AIDS

For Books on bisexuality & HIV/AIDS, see also the following sections above: Books Specifically on Bisexuality: Aggleton, 1996; Sigma Research (1996); Tielman, Carballo & Hendriks, 1991.

Overview

Bajos, N., J. Wadsworth, B. Ducot, A. Johnson, F. Le Pont, K. Wellings, A. Spira, & J. Field. (1995). **Sexual behaviour & HIV epidemiology: Comparative analysis in France & Britain.** The ACSF Group. *AIDS, 9*(7), 735-43.

▼ Doll, Lynda S., Ted Myers, Meaghan Kennedy, & Dan Allman. (1997). **Bisexuality & HIV risk: Experiences in Canada & the United States.** *Annual Review of Sex Research, VIII*, 102-147.

Bisexuality, Women, & HIV/AIDS

▼ Gómez, Cynthia A., Delia Garcia, Valerie J. Kegebein, Starley B. Shade, & Sandra R. Hernandez. (1996). **Sexual identity versus sexual behavior: Implications for HIV prevention strategies for women who have sex with women.** *Women's Health: Research on Gender, Behavior, & Policy, 2*(1/2), 91-110.

Moore, Jan, Dora Warren, Sally Zierler, Paula Schuman, Liza Solomon, Ellie E. Schoenbaum, & Meaghan Kennedy. (1996). **Characteristics of HIV-infected lesbians & bisexual women in four urban centers.** *Women's Health: Research on Gender, Behavior, & Policy, 2*(1/2), 49-60.

Rila, Margo. (1996). **Bisexual women & the AIDS crisis.** In B. A. Firestein (Ed.), *Bisexuality: The psychology & politics of an invisible minority* (pp. 169-184). Thousand Oaks, CA: Sage.

Ziemba-Davis, Mary, Stephanie A. Sanders, & June Machover Reinisch. (1996). **Lesbians' sexual interactions with men: Behavioral bisexuality & risk for sexually transmitted disease (STD) & Human Immunodeficiency Virus (HIV).** *Women's Health: Research on Gender, Behavior, & Policy, 2*(1/2), 61-74.

Bisexuality, Men, & HIV/AIDS

▼ Aoki, Bart, Chiang Peng Ngin, Bertha Mo, & Davis Y. Ja. (1989). **AIDS prevention models in Asian-American communities.** In V. M. Mays, G. W. Albee, & S. F. Schneider (Eds.), Primary Prevention of AIDS: Psychological Approaches (pp. 290-308). Newbury Park, CA: Sage.

▼ Boulton, Mary, Graham Hart, & Ray Fitzpatrick. (1992). **The sexual behaviour of bisexual men in relation to HIV transmission.** *AIDS Care, 4*(2), 165-175.

Chu, Susan Y., Thomas A. Peterman, Lynda S. Doll, James W. Buehler, & James W. Curran. (1992). **AIDS in bisexual men in the United States: Epidemiology & transmission to women.** *American Journal of Public Health, 82*(2), 220-224.

Davis, Mark, Gary Dowsett, & Ullo Klemmer. (1996). **On the beat: A report on the Bisexually Active Men's Outreach project.** In *Bisexual horizons* (pp. 188-199).

▼ Diaz, Theresa, Susan Y. Chu, Margaret Frederick, Pat Hermann, Anna Levy, Eve Mokotoff, Bruce Whyte, Lisa Conti, Mary Herr, Patricia J., Cornelis A. Rietmeijer, Frank Sorvillo, & Quaiser Mukhtar. (1993). **Sociodemographics & HIV risk behaviors of bisexual men with AIDS: Results from a multistate interview project.** *AIDS, 7*(9), 1227-1232.

Kegeles, Susan M., & Catania, Joseph A. (1991). **Understanding bisexual men's AIDS risk behavior: The risk-reduction model.** In R. A. P. Tielman, M. Carballo, & A. C. Hendriks (Eds.), *Bisexuality & HIV/AIDS: A global perspective* (pp. 139-147). Buffalo, NY: Prometheus.

▼ Magaña, J. Raul, & Joseph M. Carrier. (1991). **Mexican & Mexican American male sexual behavior & spread of AIDS in California.** *Journal of Sex Research, 28*(3), 425-441.

Matteson, David R. (1997). **Bisexual and homosexual behavior and HIV risk among Chinese-, Filipino- and Korean-American men.** *Journal of Sex Research, 34*(1), 93-104.

Morales, Eduardo S. (1990). **HIV infection & Hispanic gay & bisexual men.** *Hispanic Journal of Behavioral Sciences, 12*(2), 212-222.

Peterson, John L. (1995). **AIDS-related risks & same-sex behaviors among African American men.** In G. M. Herek, & B. Greene (Eds.), *AIDS, identity, & community: The HIV epidemic & lesbians & gay men* (pp. 85-104). Thousand Oaks, CA: Sage.

Stokes, Joseph P., Kittiwut Taywaditep, Peter Vanable, & David J. McKirnan. (1996). **Bisexual men, sexual behavior, & HIV/AIDS.** In B. A. Firestein (Ed.), *Bisexuality: The psychology & politics of an invisible minority* (pp. 149-168). Thousand Oaks, CA: Sage.

Tafoya, Terry. (1989). **Pulling coyote's tale: Native American sexuality & AIDS.** In V. M. Mays, G. W. Albee, & S. F. E. Schneider (Eds.), *Primary prevention of AIDS: Psychological approaches* (pp. 280-28). Newbury Park, CA: Sage.

▼ Wood, Robert W., Leigh E. Krueger, Tsilke C. Pearlman, & Gary Goldbaum. (1993). **HIV transmission: Women's risk from bisexual men.** *American Journal of Public Health, 83*(12), 1757-9.

▼ Wright, Jerome W. (1993). **African-American male sexual behavior & the risk for HIV infection.** *Human Organization, 52*(4), 431-431.

Bisexual Youth & HIV/AIDS

▼ Cochran, Susan D., & Vicki M. Mays. (1996). **Prevalence of HIV-related sexual risk behaviors among young 18 to 24year-old lesbian & bisexual women.** *Women's Health: Research on Gender, Behavior, & Policy, 2*(1/2), 75-90.

Cranston, Kevin. (1991). **HIV education for gay, lesbian, & bisexual youth: Personal risk, personal power, & the community of conscience.** *Journal of Homosexuality, 22*(3/4), 247-259.

▼ Hayes, Robert B., & Susan M. Kegeles. (1991). **HIV/AIDS risks for bisexual adolescents.** In R. A. P. Tielman, M. Carballo, & A. C. Hendriks (Eds.), *Bisexuality & HIV/AIDS: A global perspective* (pp. 165-174). Buffalo, NY: Prometheus.

▼ Rotheram-Borus, Mary Jane, & Cheryl Koopman. (1991). **Sexual risk behavior, AIDS knowledge, & beliefs about AIDS among predominantly minority gay & bisexual male adolescents.** *AIDS Education & Prevention, 3*(4), 305-312.

Personal and Political Perspectives

Bishop, Dolores. (1991). **Another senseless loss.** In *Bi any other name* (pp. 258-260).

Danzig, Alexis. (1990). **Bisexual women & AIDS.** In *The ACT UP/New York Women and AIDS Book Group* (pp. 193-198). Boston: South End Press.

Dutton, Jackie. (1996). **It's about numbers.** In *Bisexual horizons* (pp. 169-175).

George, Sue. (1996). **HIV, AIDS and safer sex: Introduction.** In *Bisexual horizons* (pp. 159-165).

Highleyman, Liz. (1996). **Bisexuals and AIDS.** In *Bisexual horizons* (pp. 166-168).

Lourea, David. (1991). **Just another lingering flu.** In *Bi any other name* (pp. 99-102).

Sands, David. (1996). **Tony.** In *Bisexual horizons* (pp. 211-213).

Stewart, Hap. (1991). **A healing journey.** In *Bi any other name* (pp. 147-150).

Bisexuality and Psychology

For Books on bisexuality and psychology, and on affirmative approaches to counseling and psychotherapy with bisexual women and bisexual men, see also the following sections above:
Books Specifically on Bisexuality: Firestein, 1996; Klein, 1993; Wolff, 1979. In German: Gooß, 1995; Hüsers & König, 1995.
Bi-Inclusive Books: Under *Psychology, Sociology, and Bisexuality:* D'Augelli & Patterson (1995), Cabaj & Stein (1996), Eliason (1996); Kominars & Kominars (1996); Savin-Williams & Cohen, 1996.

Falco, Kristine L. (1996). **Psychotherapy with women who love women.** In R. P. Cabaj & T. S. Stein, *Textbook of homosexuality & mental health* (pp. 397-412). Washington, DC: American Psychiatric Press.

▼ Lourea, David. (1985). **Psycho-social issues related to counseling bisexuals.** *Journal of Homosexuality, 11*(1/2), 51-62.

▼ Markowitz, Laura M. (1995). **Bisexuality: Challenging our either/or thinking.** *In the Family: A Magazine for Lesbians, Gays, Bisexuals & their Relations,* 1(1), 6-11, 23.

▼ Matteson, David R. (1996). **Counseling & psychotherapy with bisexual & exploring clients.** In B. A. Firestein (Ed.), *Bisexuality: The psychology & politics of an invisible minority* (pp. 185-213). Thousand Oaks, CA: Sage.

Nichols, Margaret. (1989). **Sex therapy with lesbians, gay men, & bisexuals.** In S. R. Leiblum, & R. C. Rosen (Eds.), *Principles & practice of sex therapy: Update for the 1990s (2nd ed.).* (pp. 269-297). New York: Guilford.

Weasel, Lisa H. (1996). **Seeing between the lines: Bisexual women & therapy.** *Women & Therapy, 19*(2), 5-16.

Wolf, T. J. (1987). **Group counseling for bisexual men.** *Journal of Homosexuality, 14*(1/2), 162-165.

Wolf, T. J. (1987). **Group psychotherapy for bisexual men & their wives.** *Journal of Homosexuality, 14*(1/2), 191-199.

Attitudes toward Bisexuality: Biphobia, Heterosexism, Discrimination

For <u>Books</u> on attitudes toward bisexuality, see also the following sections above:
<u>Books Specifically on Bisexuality</u>: For psychological and sociological perspectives: Colker (1996), Eliason (1996), and Rust (1995).Firestein, 1996; Klein, 1993; Wolff, 1979. In German: Gooß, 1995; Hüsers & König, 1995. For personal and political perspectives: Archivo Lesbico y de Mujeres Diferentes, 1998; Bisexual Anthology Collective, 1995; Hutchins & Ka'ahumanu, 1991; Off-Pink Collective, 1988; Rose, Stevens & the Off-Pink Collective, 1996; Tucker, 1995; and Weise, 1992.
<u>Bi-Inclusive Books</u>: Under *Psychology, Sociology, and Bisexuality*: Bohan, 1996; D'Augelli & Patterson (1995), Cabaj & Stein (1996), Eliason (1996); Savin-Williams & Cohen, 1996.

Blasingame, Brenda M. (1992). **The roots of biphobia: Racism & internalized heterosexism.** In *Closer to home* (pp. 47-54).

Eliason, Michele J. (1996). **A survey of the campus climate for lesbian, gay, & bisexual university members.** *Journal of Psychology & Human Sexuality, 8*, 39-58.

▼ Eliason, Michele J. (1997). **The prevalence & nature of biphobia in heterosexual undergraduate students.** *Archives of Sexual Behavior, 26*(3), 317-325.

▼ Kaplan, Rebecca (1992). **Compulsory heterosexuality & the bisexual existence: Toward a bisexual feminist understanding of heterosexism.** In *Closer to home* (pp. 269-280).

▼ Ochs, Robyn. (1996). **Biphobia: It goes more than two ways.** In B. A. Firestein (Ed.), *Bisexuality: The psychology & politics of an invisible minority* (pp. 217-239). Thousand Oaks, CA: Sage.

Ochs, Robyn, & Deihl, Marcia. (1992). **Moving beyond binary thinking.** In W. Blumenfeld (Ed.), *Homophobia: How we all pay the price* (pp. 67-75). Boston: Beacon.

▼ Spalding, Leah R., & Peplau, Letitia Anne. (1997). **The unfaithful lover: Heterosexuals' perceptions of bisexuals & their relationships.** *Psychology of Women Quarterly, 21*(4), 611-625.

Udis-Kessler, Amanda. (1991). **Present tense: Biphobia as a crisis of meaning.** In *Bi any other name* .

Bisexuality and Feminism

For books on bisexuality & feminism, see also the following sections above: Books Specifically on Bisexuality: Bisexual Anthology Collective, 1995; George, 1993; Hutchins & Ka'ahumanu, 1991; Rose, Stevens & the Off-Pink Collective, 1996; Tucker, 1995; and Weise, 1992. In *Spanish*: Archivo Lesbico y de Mujeres Diferentes, 1998. Bi-Inclusive Books: Under *Identity*: Atkins, 1996; Burch, 1994; Esterberg, 1997. Under *Youth*: Findlen, 1995. Under *Ethnic, Racial, & Cultural Diversity*: Lim-Hing, 1994; Ratti, 1993.

Armstrong, E. (1995). **Traitors to the cause? Understanding the lesbian/gay "bisexuality" debates.** In *Bisexual politics* (pp. 199-218).

Ault, Amber. (1996). **Ambiguous identity in an unambiguous sex/gender structure: The case of bisexual women.** *Sociological Quarterly, 37*(3), 449-463.

Ault, Amber. (1996). **Hegemonic discourse in an oppositional community: Lesbian feminist stigmatization of bisexual women.** In B. Beemyn, & M. Eliason. (Eds.), *Queer studies: A lesbian, gay, bisexual, and transgender anthology* ((pp. 204-216). New York: NYU Press.

Baker, Karin. (1992). **Bisexual feminist politics: Because bisexuality is not enough.** In *Closer to home* (pp. 255-268).

Bisexual Anthology Collective. (1995). **Toward a feminist bisexual politic: A discussion.** In *Plural desires* (pp. 210-225).

Bower, Tamara. (1995). **Bisexual women, feminist politics.** In *Bisexual politics* (pp. 99-108).

Came, Heather. (1996). **Towards a free and loose future.** In *Bisexual horizons* (pp. 25-29).

Choe, Margaret Mihee. (1992). **Our selves, growing whole.** In *Closer to home* (pp. 17-26).

Elliott, Beth. (1991). **Bisexuality: The best thing that ever happened to lesbian-feminism?** In Hutchins & Ka'ahumanu (Eds.), *Bi any other name* (pp. 324-328). Boston: Alyson.

Elliott, Beth. (1992). **Holly near and yet so far.** In *Closer to home* (pp. 233-254).

Friedland, Lucy, & Liz A. Highleyman. (1991). **The fine art of labeling: The convergence of anarchism, feminism, and bisexuality.** In *Bi any other name* (pp. 285-298).

▼ Golden, Carla. (1994). **Our politics and choices: The feminist movement and sexual orientation.** In B. Greene G. M. Herek (Eds.), *Lesbian and gay psychology: Theory, research, and clinical applications* (pp. 54-70). Thousand Oaks, CA: Sage.

Gregory, Deborah. (1983). **From where I stand: A case for feminist bisexuality.** In S. Cartledge, & J. Ryan (Eds.), *Sex and love: New thoughts on old contradictions* (pp. 141-156). London: The Women's Press.

Hemmings, Clare. (1995). **Locating bisexual identities: Discourses of bisexuality and contemporary feminist theory.** In D. Bell, & G. Valentine (Eds.), *Mapping desire: Geographies of sexualities* (pp. 41-54). London: Routledge.

Higgenbotham, Anastassia. (1995). **Chicks goin' at it.** In B. Findlen (Ed.), *Listen up: Voices from the next feminist generation* (pp. 3-11). Seattle: Seal Press.

▼ Kaplan, Rebecca. (1992). **Compulsory heterosexuality and the bisexual existence: Toward a bisexual feminist understanding of heterosexism.** In *Closer to home* (pp. 269-280).

Matteson, Dave. (1991). **Bisexual feminist man.** In Hutchins & Ka'ahumanu (Eds.), *Bi any other name* (pp. 43-50). Boston: Alyson.

Murray, Annie S. (1995). **Forsaking all others: A bifeminist discussion of compulsory monogamy.** In *Bisexual politics* (pp. 293-304).

Ochs, Robyn. (1992). **Bisexuality, feminism, men and me.** In *Closer to home* (pp. 127-132).

Parr, Zaidie. (1996). **Feminist bisexuals in the U.K.— Caught between a rock and a hard place?** In *Bisexual horizons* (pp. 274-280).

Schneider, Anne. (1991). **Guilt politics.** In *Bi any other name* (pp. 275-278). Boston: Alyson.

▼ Sturgis, Susan. M. (1996). **Bisexual feminism: Challenging the splits.** In *Bisexual horizons* (pp. 41-44).

Terris, Ellen. (1991). **My life as a lesbian-identified bisexual fag hag.** In *Bi any other name* (pp. 56-59). Boston: Alyson.

▼ Udis-Kessler, Amanda. (1992). **Closer to home: Bisexual feminism and the transformation of hetero/sexism.** In *Closer to home* (pp. 205-232).

Uwano, Kei. (1991). **Bi-lovable Japanese feminist.** In *Bi any other name* (pp. 185-187). Boston: Alyson.

▼ Weise, Elizabeth R., & Bennett, Kathleen. (1992). **Feminist bisexuality: A both/and option for an either/or world.** In *Closer to home* (pp. 205-231).

Yoshizaki, Amanda. (1992). **Breaking the rules: Constructing a bisexual feminist marriage.** In *Closer to home* (pp. 155-162).

▼ Young, Stacey. (1992). **Breaking silence about the "B-word": Bisexual identity and lesbian-feminist discourse.** In *Closer to home* (75-87).

Woodard, Victoria. (1991). **Insights at 3:30 a.m.** In *Bi any other name* (pp. 83-86). Boston: Alyson.

Zabatinsky, Vashti. (1992). **Some thoughts on power, gender, body image and sex in the life of one bisexual lesbian feminist.** In *Closer to home* (pp. 133-146).

Bisexuality and Spirituality

Chapman, Guy. (1996). **Roots of a male bisexual nature.** In *Bisexual horizons* (pp. 62-69).

de Sousa, Elehna. (1995). **In the spirit of Aloha: to love is to share the happiness of life here & now.** In *Plural desires* (pp. 145-149).

Drake, Kelly. (1996). **Bisexuality and spirituality.** In *Bisexual horizons* (pp. 111-113).

Fehr, Tracy Charette. (1995). **Accepting my inherent duality.** Bisexual Anthology Collective (Eds.), *Plural desires* (pp. 128-129).

Hurley, Karen. (1991). **Coming out in spirit and in flesh.** In *Bi any other name* (pp. 94-102). Boston: Alyson.

Hutchins, Loraine. (1991). **Letting go: An interview with John Horne.** In *Bi any other name* (pp. 112-116). Boston: Alyson.

Perlstein, Marcia. (1996). **Integrating a gay, lesbian, or bisexual person's religious and spiritual needs and choices into psychotherapy.** In C. J. Alexander (Ed.), *Gay and lesbian mental health: A sourcebook for practitioners* (pp. 173-188). New York: Harrington Park Press.

Rose, Sharon. (1996). **Against marriage.** In *Bisexual horizons* (pp. 119-121).

Starhawk. (1995). **The sacredness of pleasure.** In *Bisexual politics* (pp. 325-329).

Tirado, Leonard. (1991). **Reclaiming heart and mind.** In *Bi any other name* (pp. 117-123). Boston: Alyson.

Wheaton United Methodist Church Reconciling Congregation Task Force. (1991, Fall). **One church's journey toward including bisexuals.** *Open Hands: Reconciling Ministries with Lesbians and Gay Men, 16.*

Queer Theory/Cultural Studies/Literary Criticism

For Books on queer theory, cultural studies, and literary criticism, see also the following sections above:
Books Specifically on Bisexuality: Bi Academic Intervention, 1997; Bryant, 1997; Garber, 1995; Hall & Pramaggiore, 1996. See also the special issue of the *Journal of Gay, Lesbian, and Bisexual Identity* (1997).
Bi-Inclusive Books: Under *Queer theory*: Beemyn & Eliason, 1996.

▼ Ault, Amber. (1996). **Hegemonic discourse in an oppositional community: Lesbian feminist stigmatization of bisexual women.** In *Queer studies* (pp. 204-216).

Carroll, Traci. (1996). **Invisible sissy: The politics of masculinity in African American bisexual narrative.** In *RePresenting bisexualities* (pp. 180-204).

▼ Connerly, Gregory. (1996). **The politics of Black lesbian, gay, and bisexual identity.** In *Queer studies* (pp. 133-145).

▼ du Plessis, Michael. (1996). **Blatantly bisexual; or, Unthinking queer theory.** In *RePresenting bisexualities* (pp. 19-54).

Eadie, Jo. (1997). **Living in the past: Savage nights, bisexual times.** *Journal of Gay, Lesbian, and Bisexual Identity, 2*(1), 7-26.

Fraser, Miriam (1996). **Framing contention: Bisexuality displaced.** In *RePresenting bisexualities* (pp. 253-271).

▼ Hall, Donald E. (1996). **Graphic sexuality and the erasure of a polymorphous perversity.** In *RePresenting bisexualities* (pp. 99-123).

▼ Hemmings, Clare. (1993). **Resituating the bisexual body: From identity to difference.** In J. Bristow, & A. R. Wilson (Eds.), *Activating theory: Lesbian, gay, bisexual politics* (pp. 119-138).

Hemmings, Clare. (1997). **Bisexual theoretical perspectives: Emergent and contingent relationships.** In Bi Academic Intervention (Ed.), *Bisexual imaginary: Representation, identity and desire* (pp. 14-31). London: Cassell.

▼ James, Christopher. (1996). **Denying complexity: The dismissal and appropriation of bisexuality in queer, lesbian, and gay theory.** In *Queer studies* (pp. 217-240).

Kaloski, Ann. (1997). **Bisexuals making out with cyborgs: Politics, pleasure, con/fusion.** *Journal of Gay, Lesbian, and Bisexual Identity, 2*(1), 47-64.

▼ Loftus, Brian. (1996). **Biopia: Bisexuality and the crisis of visibility in a queer symbolic.** In *RePresenting bisexualities* (pp. 207-233).

Morris, Sharon, & Merl Storr. (1997). **Bisexual theory: A bi academic intervention.** *Journal of Gay, Lesbian, & Bisexual Identity, 2*(1), 1-6.

Pramaggiore, Maria. (1996). **Straddling the screen: Bisexual spectatorship and contemporary narrative film.** In *RePresenting bisexualities* (pp. 272-297).

Bisexual Community & Bisexual Politics

For <u>Books</u> on bisexual community & politics, see also the following sections above:
<u>Books Specifically on Bisexuality</u>: For psychological and sociological perspectives: Rust, 1995. In German: Feldhorst, 1996; Hüsers & König, 1995. For personal and political perspectives: Bisexual Anthology Collective, 1995; Hutchins & Ka'ahumanu, 1991; Ochs, 1999; Rose, Stevens, & Off Pink Collective, 1996; Tucker, 1995; Weise, 1992. In *Spanish*: Archivo Lesbico y de Mujeres Diferentes, 1998.
<u>Bi-Inclusive Books</u>: Under *Identity*: Esterberg (1997). Under *LGB Communities*: Working Group on Funding Lesbian & Gay Issues, 1997.

Geographic Bisexual Communities

Barr, George. (1985). **Chicago Bi-ways: An informal history.** *Journal of Homosexuality, 11*(1/2), 231-234.

Berry, Dave. (1996). **A history of the Edinburgh Bisexual Group.** In *Bisexual horizons* (pp. 281-286).

Esterberg, Kristin G. (1996). **Gay cultures, gay communities: The social organization of lesbians, gay men, & bisexuals.** In R. C. Savin-Williams, & K. M. Cohen (Eds.), *The lives of lesbians, gays, & bisexuals: Children to adults* (pp. 337-392). Fort Worth, TX: Harcourt Brace.

Euroqueer, A. (1996). **Bisexuality in Brussels.** In *Bisexual horizons* (pp. 287-288).

Hüsers, Francis. (1996). **Bisexual associations in Germany.** In *Bisexual horizons* (pp. 293-297).

Kaal, Wouter. (1996). **A history of the bi movement in the Netherlands.** In *Bisexual horizons* (pp. 289-292).

Roberts, Beth C. (1997). **"The many faces of bisexuality": The 4th International Bisexual Symposium.** *Journal of Gay, Lesbian, and Bisexual Identity, 2*(1), 65-76.

Roberts, Wayne. (1996). **The making of an Australian bisexual activist.** In *Bisexual horizons* (pp. 149-153).

Rubenstein, Maggi, & Cynthia A. Slater. (1985). **A profile of the San Francisco Bisexual Center.** *Journal of Homosexuality, 11*(1/2), 227-230.

Tucker, Naomi. (1995). **Bay Area bisexual history: An interview with David Lourea.** In *Bisexual politics* (pp. 47-62).

Weise, Beth R. (1996). **The bisexual community: Viable reality or revolutionary pipe dream?** In *Bisexual horizons* (pp. 303-313).

The Broader Bisexual Community and Bisexual Politics

Arnesen, Cliff. (1991). **Coming out to Congress.** In *Bi any other name* (pp. 233-239). Boston: Alyson.

Chandler, Paul. (1996). **Coming in from the cold: Bisexuality and the politics of diversity.** In *Bisexual horizons* (pp. 277-235).

▼ Donaldson, Stephen. (1995). **The bisexual movement's beginnings in the 70s: A personal retrospective.** In *Bisexual politics* (pp. 31-46)

Eadie, Jo. (1993). **Activating bisexuality: Towards a bi/sexual politics.** In J. Bristow, & A. R. Wilson (Eds.), *Activating theory: Lesbian, gay bisexual politics* (pp. 139-170).

▼ Farajajé-Jones, Elias. (1995). **Fluid desire: Race, HIV/AIDS, and bisexual politics.** In *Bisexual politics* (pp. 119-130).

Hemmings, Clare, & Warren J. Blumenfeld. (1996). **Reading "monosexual".** *Journal of Gay, Lesbian, & Bisexual Identity, 1*(4), 311-321.

Highleyman, Liz A. (1995). **Identity and ideas: Strategies for bisexuals.** In *Bisexual politics* (pp. 73-92).

▼ Highleyman, Liz, Robert Bray, David Chapman, Adrienne Davis, Lani Ka'ahumanu, & Elliot Ramos. (1996). **Identity and ideas: A roundtable on identity politics.** *Journal of Gay, Lesbian, & Bisexual Identity, 1*(3), 235-253.

Hutchins, Loraine. (1995). **Our leaders, our selves.** In *Bisexual politics* (pp. 131-142).

▼ Hutchins, Loraine. (1996). **Bisexuality: Politics & community.** In B. A. Firestein (Ed.), *Bisexuality: The psychology & politics of an invisible minority* (pp. 240-259). Thousand Oaks, CA: Sage.

Ka'ahumanu, Lani. (1995). **It ain't over 'til the bisexual speaks.** In *Bisexual politics* (pp. 63-68).

Lano, Kevin. (1996). **Bisexual history: Fighting invisibility.** In *Bisexual horizons* (pp. 219-226).

Ochs, Robyn, & Highleyman, Liz. (1999). **Bisexual Movement.** In B. Zimmerman (Ed.), *The encyclopedia of lesbianism.* New York: Garland.

Orlando, Lisa. (1991). **Loving whom we choose.** In *Bi any other name* (pp. 223-232). Boston: Alyson

Shuster, Rebecca. (1991). **Considering next steps for bisexual liberation.** In *Bi any other name* (pp. 266-274). Boston: Alyson.

▼ Udis-Kessler, Amanda. (1996). **Identity/politics: Historical sources of the bisexual movement.** In *Queer studies* (pp. 52-63).

If you have trouble finding any of the books in this section at your local bookstore, many are available through the Bisexual Resource Center's on-line Bisexual Bookstore at http://www.biresource.org/bookstore. Books purchased through the Bisexual Bookstore generate money that helps the BRC produce conferences, pamphlets, and this Bisexual Resource Guide.

Notable Films with Bisexual Characters

compiled bi Wayne Bryant

The following is a list of notable films containing one or more bisexual characters. Most of these films are available on video and described in further detail in the author's book, **Bisexual Characters in Film: from Anaïs to Zee**. Not all of the bi characters in these films portray positive images of bisexuality. Some of these have been included because of their historical or social significance. Those which are particularly negative are noted. For each film listed, the format is as follows:

Name of film (alternate name, if any) • *Country* • Director • Year of release

If you have trouble finding bi films at your nearby lackluster video store, nearly all of the movies listed here are available for rent or purchase at the Bisexual Videostore on the web. The URL is:

http://www.biresource.org/videostore

Videos rented or purchased through this site help to finance projects of the Bisexual Resource Center, such as this Bisexual Resource Guide.

Comedy

Beyond Therapy • *USA* • Robert Altman • 1986
Offbeat comedy starring Jeff Goldblum as the bisexual and Glenda Jackson as his therapist.

California Suite • *USA* • Herbert Ross • 1978
A star-studded cast including Michael Caine, Bill Cosby, Jane Fonda, Walter Matthau, Richard Pryor, and Alan Alda. Based on a Neil Simon play.

© New World Pictures
Beyond Therapy

Chasing Amy • *USA* • Kevin Smith • 1997
Ostensibly the story of a straight male cartoonist who falls in love with a lesbian female cartoonist. Beneath the surface it's really about the two guys, their complex relationship, and the difficulty of defining one's sexuality. Highly recommended.

Dallas Doll • *Australia* • Ann Turner • 1994
Bisexual actress Sandra Bernhard stars as an American golf pro who moves in with an Australian family and ends up sleeping with all the ones who are of legal age.

Entertaining Mr. Sloane • *USA* • Douglas Hickox • 1970

An adaptation of Joe Orton's play about a handsome bisexual killer who is in relationships with a brother and sister.

Even Cowgirls Get the Blues • *USA* • Gus van Sant • 1993

Uma Thurman plays Sissy Hankshaw, a bisexual woman who was born to travel. Based on the Tom Robbins novel. Uneven acting throughout, but excellent music by kd lang.

Even Cowgirls Get the Blues

French Twist (Gazon Maudit) • *France* • ÊJosiane Balasko • 1995

A French farce in which a housewife falls in love with a lesbian whose van broke down at her doorstep. Stars Victoria Abril. A fun film despite some heavy-handed stereotypes.

Go Fish • *USA* • Rose Troche • 1993

A humorous look at lesbian relationships in the 90s. Lesbian attitudes toward bisexual women are examined through a character who also sleeps with men.

Grief • *USA* • Richard Glatzer • 1993

Alexis Arquette plays the bi character in this comedy about the soap opera going on behind the production of a TV soap opera. Paul Bartel, who has directed other films with bisexual characters, plays the judge.

The Hotel New Hampshire • *USA* • Tony Richardson • 1984

Includes a love scene between Jodie Foster and Nastassja Kinski. Also starring Rob Lowe and Wallace Shawn.

The Incredibly True Story of Two Girls in Love • *USA* • Maria Maggenti • 1995

Same-sex love crosses race and class boundaries. Bisexual characters. The director identifies as "omni-sexual."

Late Bloomers • *USA* • Julia Dyer • 1997

Two married women discover the unexpected pleasures of a same-sex relationship.

Love and Human Remains • *Canada* • Denys Arcand • 1993

Combination comedy and thriller. A serial killer is stalking the streets of Toronto. Ruth Marshall plays the main character's bisexual roommate.

May Fools (Milou en Mai) • *France* • Louis Malle • 1990

"Mommy, why does Auntie Claire tie up her friend at night?" With Miou-Miou as the arch-conservative sister.

My Father is Coming • *Germany/USA* • ÊMonika Treut • 1990

A German woman's father is coming to visit her in New York and doesn't know that she is single and unemployed. Co-stars Annie Sprinkle as herself.

New Year's Day • *USA* • Henry Jaglom • 1990

A Californian (Jaglom) rents an apartment in Manhattan, only to discover that the previous tenants have not yet moved out. "Everybody out there [Los Angeles] is bisexual."

The Opposite of Sex • *USA* • Don Roos • 1998

Christina Ricci stars as a bad-assed teen who seduces her brother's boyfriend.

Relax, It's Just Sex • *USA* • P.J. Castellaneta • 1998

Sex and relationships in the '90s. Serena Scott Thomas plays the bi character.

A Rose By Any Other Name • *USA* • Kyle Schickner • 1997

A straight man and a "lesbian" fall in love. Their friends don't get it. Written and directed by a bisexual who definitely does (get it).

Scenes from the Class Struggle in Beverly Hills • *USA* • Paul Bartel • 1989

It's the servants vs. the elite in this sex farce starring Jacqueline Bisset, Mary Woronov, Wallace Shawn, and Ed Begley Jr.

Their First Mistake • *USA* • George Marshall • 1932

Laurel and Hardy perform simply the finest gender-bending roles of their era.

Biographical:

Becoming Colette • *Germany/France/USA* • Danny Huston • 1991

The story of a young bisexual woman who became one of France's greatest writers.

Carrington • *UK* • Christopher Hampton • 1995

This historical drama ignores its Bloomsbury Group setting and curiously neglects Carrington's bisexuality, while highlighting her husband's. Starring Emma Thompson.

Chanel Solitaire • *France/UK* • George Kaczender • 1981

The story of a young bisexual woman who became one of France's greatest designers.

Henry and June • *USA* • Philip Kaufman • 1990

The story of a young bisexual woman who kept one of France's greatest diaries. Stars Uma Thurman as June.

Henry and June

Total Eclipse • *UK* • Agnieszka Holland • 1995

A film about the stormy relationship between poets Paul Verlaine and Arthur Rimbaud. Not the most positive portrayal of bisexuals.

Wilde • *UK* • Brian Gilbert • 1998

The best of several films about the tribulations and trials of Oscar Wilde.

Musical:

The Adventures of Priscilla, Queen of the Desert • *Australia* • 1994

Three drag queens (a gay man, a bisexual, and a transsexual) lip sync their way across the Australian outback. Great music and fabulous costumes, but gratuitous sexism.

Cabaret • *USA* • Bob Fosse • 1972

Based on stories by gay author Christopher Isherwood. Stars Joel Grey, Liza Minelli, and Michael York.

Zachariah • *USA* • George Englund • 1970

Billed as "the first electric western." Stars drummer Elvin Jones. Great music by the New York Rock Ensemble, Country Joe and the Fish, The James Gang, and Doug Kershaw.

Historical:

The Bostonians • *UK* • James Ivory • 1984

Written by gay author Henry James, the main character is based on his bisexual sister. Like most Ivory films, it is a period piece with beautiful costumes and scenery.

Queen Christina • *USA* • Rouben Mamoulian • 1933

Greta Garbo stars as the bisexual queen of Sweden. She kisses the countess and dresses in male drag.

Spartacus • *USA* • Stanley Kubrick • 1960 (restored 1991)

The restored version depicts Crassus (Laurence Olivier) as bisexual, attempting to seduce his slave. This scene was cut from the original release. Also stars Peter Ustinov, Laurence Olivier, Tony Curtis, Woody Strode, Charles Laughton and Kirk Douglas.

A Special Day (Una Giornata Particolare) • *Italy* • Ettore Scola • 1977

Marcello Mastroianni plays a gay man who falls for the charms of Sophia Loren. Set in Mussolini's Italy.

Drama:

Advise and Consent • *USA* • Otto Preminger • 1962

A political struggle in the U.S. Senate causes the revelation of many secrets. Stars Henry Fonda, John Granger, and Charles Laughton (as the Jesse Helms character).

All Over Me • *USA* • Alex Sichel • 1997

Major teen angst about sexuality, drugs, home life and more.

Bar Girls • *USA* • Marita Giovanni • 1994

A lesbian film with lots of bi women and "sudden conversions." Most of the action takes place in an upscale L.A. lesbian bar. Look for a cameo by Chastity Bono.

Basic Instinct • *USA* • Paul Verhoeven • 1992

Every bisexual or lesbian woman in the film is a killer. Stars Sharon Stone and Michael Douglas.

Bound • *USA* • Andy & Larry Wachowski • 1996

A gangster moll conspires with a female ex-convict to steal a fortune from the mob. In the process they fall in hot, passionate lust.

Chantilly Lace • *USA* • Linda Yellen • 1993

Made for TV movie about women and friendship in the 90s. Lots of improvised dialogue. The b-word is actually used.

Claire of the Moon • *USA* • Nicole Conn • 1992 • 102m

An anal-retentive lesbian and a sloppy bisexual woman share a cabin at a writers retreat. They are at each other's throats until they finally fall in lust. The ending, though highly predictable, is worth the wait.

Crash • *Canada/UK/France* • David Cronenberg • 1996

The story of group of people (some of whom are bisexual) who with a fetish for bodies which have been deformed by car crashes. Decidedly not for the weak of stomach.

The Crying Game • *UK* • Neil Jordan • 1992

A bisexual British soldier is taken hostage by the Irish Republican Army. His captor's life is changed forever.

Dakan • *Guinea* • Mohamed Camara • 1997

A rare African film with bi male characters. Sori and Manga are schoolmates who are attracted to women, but ultimately come to understand that their first love is each other.

Desert Hearts

Desert Hearts • *USA* • Donna Deitch • 1985

Breakthrough film about a conservative woman going through a divorce who falls in love with a wild, young lesbian (Patricia Charbonneau) in the desert.

El Diputado (The Deputy or **Confessions of a Congressman)** • *Spain* • Eloy de la Iglesia • 1978

A married Spanish congressman with a particular interest in young men is framed by the fascists.

Dog Day Afternoon • *USA* • Sidney Lumet • 1975

Al Pacino plays a bisexual who robs a bank to get money for his lover's sex-change operation. Based on a true story.

The Doom Generation • *USA* • Gregg Araki • 1995

It isn't easy to shock movie-viewers these days, but Araki gives it his best shot. This road movie features foul-mouthed teens, psycho killers, and sweaty bi sex.

Erotique • *USA/Germany/Hong Kong* • Lizzie Borden, Monika Treut & Clara Law • 1993

Three short films by women directors. Two have bisexual characters. The first of these, "Let's Talk About Sex" was co-written by bisexuals, Lizzie Borden and Susie Bright.

Exotica • *Canada* • Atom Egoyan • 1995 • 103m

An excellent film about some very disturbed people who work at, or frequent a strip club. This movie is a study in eroticism, secrecy, and despair.

Flirting with Disaster • *USA* • David O. Russell • 1996

The character called Tony actually calls himself bisexual. Not the world's most likable guy, but no worse than the other characters.

The Fourth Man (De Verde Man) • *Netherlands* • Paul Verhoeven • 1983

A man falls in love with another man whom he passes on a train, only to find that they are both in love with the same dangerous woman.

High Art • *USA* • Brandon Williams • 1998

A young and aspiring magazine writer learns that her drugged-out upstairs neighbor was once a well-known photographer. The two women mix work with play.

Higher Learning • *USA* • John Singleton • 1995

A film about racism and the struggle for identity. Loaded with cardboard characters, including a student who is "confused" about her sexuality.

I've Heard the Mermaids Singing • *Canada* • Patricia Rozema • 1982

Polly, an inept temp worker, falls in love with her new boss. She later discovers the woman's darkest secrets.

Law of Desire (La ley del deseo) • *Spain* • Pedro Almodóvar • 1987

Almodóvar's semi-autobiographical film about the loves and losses of a gay film director. A wide range of sexualities are represented.

Lost Language of Cranes • *UK* • Nigel Finch • 1991

Based on David Leavitt's novel about a gay man and his father who come out to each other.

Mass Appeal • *USA* • Glenn Jordan • 1984

Jack Lemon as a parish priest who hates confrontation, but finds himself defending a bisexual divinity student.

Nea • *France* • Nelly Kaplan • 1976

Comic drama about a teenage girl who writes a best-selling erotic novel. She encourages her mother's love for another woman.

Nowhere • *USA* • Gregg Araki • 1997

The third film in Araki's generation X trilogy. Bisexual characters abound (along with sex, drugs, music, and a space alien). Shortly after the film was released, the director, known as a gay icon, revealed that he has a girlfriend.

Paris France • *Canada* • Gerard Ciccoritti • 1993

Lucy decides that her writer's block can be broken if she can just recreate the wild sexuality of her Paris years. Her husband and lover are both bi.

Peter's Friends • *UK* • Kenneth Branagh • 1992

Peter invites his old school friends for a New Year's reunion and the sharing of revelations. An appalling bit of overacting by the director.

Pigalle • *France/Switzerland* • Karim Dridi • 1994

Fifi, the bisexual hustler, Vera, the private dancer, and Divine, the transvestite hooker are among the denizens of this seedy Paris neighborhood.

The Pillow Book • *France/UK/Netherlands* • Peter Greenaway • 1997

A sumptuous visual treat, this is the story of a Japanese woman obsessed with the human body as calligraphy canvas. Her father and lover are both bisexual.

The Rainbow • *UK* • Ken Russell • 1989

Amanda Donohoe and Sammi Davis play teacher and student who fall in love. Glenda Jackson as the mother.

Savage Nights (Les Nuits Fauves or **Wilde Maechte)** • *France* • Cyril Collard • 1993

Writer/director/star Collard's story of a self-absorbed bisexual man who is HIV positive and makes no attempt to protect his lovers. Won four Cæsar awards just days after Collard's death.

Steam • *Italy/Turkey/Spain* • Ferzan Ozpetek • 1997

Francesco inherits a Turkish bath from his aunt. He leaves his wife in Rome and heads for Istanbul to dispose of his property. When he sees the bathhouse, he falls in love with it, and the caretaker's son.

Street Kid (Gossenkind) • *Germany* • Peter Kern • 1991

A young bi hustler with fabulous hair earns his living in the streets of Dusseldorf, Germany.

Sunday Bloody Sunday • *UK* • John Schlesinger • 1971

The trials of triads. Murray Head appears in the role of a young artist whose older lovers are played by Peter Finch and Glenda Jackson.

Three of Hearts •. *USA* • Yurek Bogayevicz • 1993

A lesbian hires a male "escort" to seduce and then dump her bisexual ex-lover in hopes that she can win her back.

Threesome • *USA* • Andrew Fleming • 1994

A woman is mistakenly assigned to the dorm room of two men. Each becomes attracted to the roommate who is not attracted to them. The bisexual character is treated as "confused."

La Truite (The Trout) • *France* • Joseph Losey • 1982

Frederique is so attractive that her gay husband falls in love her. So do lots of other people, of various sexualities.

Victim • *UK* • Basil Dearden • 1961

Dirk Bogarde plays a bisexual lawyer whose marriage and career are threatened by a blackmail scheme.

A Village Affair • *UK* • Moira Armstrong • 1997

Martin and Alice move to the country, where his roving eye comes to rest on Clodagh, the daughter of wealthy neighbors. But Clodagh only has eyes for Alice.

The Watermelon Woman • *USA* • Cheryl Dunye • 1997

A young African-American woman searches for the identity of an actress identified in old film credits only as The Watermelon Woman. In the process she finds a lot more, including (briefly) a bisexual lover.

When Night is Falling • *Canada* • Patricia Rozema • 1995

Love story between a previously-straight woman who teaches at a religious school and a lesbian who is a performance artist in a circus. Unjustly rated NC-17. Highly recommended.

Wild Things • *USA* • John McNaughton • 1998

Neve Campbell, Kevin Bacon, and Matt Dillon star in this less-than-thrilling thriller. The bisexuality is treated matter-of-factly, but the sex is mostly gratuitous.

Women in Love • *UK* • Ken Russell • 1970

Based on the D.H. Lawrence novel. Features an extended nude male wrestling scene. Stars Alan Bates and Glenda Jackson.

X, Y & Zee (Zee and Company) • *USA* • Brian Hutton • 1971

Elizabeth Taylor seduces Susannah York in order to get her away from Michael Caine. A decidedly bad and dated film that must be seen.

Your Friends and Neighbors • *USA* • Neil LaBute • 1998

If you have friends and neighbors like this, run far away, change your name, and start a new life. Definitely *not* a date movie. Excellent acting by Amy Brenneman and the ensemble.

X, Y and Zee

Cult:

Black Lizard • *Japan* • Kinji Fukasaku • 1968

An actor in drag plays a bisexual female master thief. One of the campiest films of all time. Screenplay by bisexual author, Yukio Mishima, who also appears in the film.

Cult of the Damned (Angel, Angel, Down We Go) • *USA* • Robert Thom • 1969

Holly Near plays the spoiled daughter of a wealthy couple. Her boyfriend and father are bi. Embarrassingly bad movie.

The East Is Red • *Hong Kong* • Ching Siu-Tung & Raymond Lee • 1993

A classic Hong Kong martial arts film in which the hero is a transgendered bisexual. Lots of blood.

Faster Pussycat! Kill! Kill! (Leather Girls, Mankillers) • *USA* • Russ Meyer • 1965

The classic 60s sexploitation film. Three go-go dancers (one lesbian, one bi, and one straight) drive their sports cars into the desert and terrorize everyone they meet.

Flesh • *USA* • Paul Morrissey • 1968

A young and beautiful Joe Dallesandro plays a bisexual hustler who is trying to raise money for an abortion for his wife's girlfriend. One of the best of the Warhol films.

Liquid Sky • *USA* • Slava Tsukerman • 1983

Alien beings in search of opiates discovers that orgasms produce the very best. They lands atop the apartment building of the bisexual Margaret and change her life.

The Rocky Horror Picture Show • *UK* • Jim Sharman • 1976

This science fiction parody is the queen of camp cult films, starring Tim Curry and Meatloaf as two of many bisexual characters. Great music by Richard O'Brien, who plays Riff Raff.

The Sticky Fingers of Time • *USA* • Hilary Brougher • 1997

This low-budget, campy sci-fi flick features several bisexual characters. A writer goes out for a cup of coffee in 1953 and ends up in the East Village in 1997, unaware that a nuclear explosion has mutated her soul.

Mysteries:

The Color of Night • *USA* • Richard Rush • 1994 • 136m

Bruce Willis as a psychologist who takes over his murdered friend's therapy group to discover who killed him. Jane March is excellent as the bisexual character, Rose.

Deathtrap • *USA* • Sidney Lumet • 1982

Michael Caine is a writer who plans a murder in order to overcome a bad case of writer's block. But who is the intended victim? His wife? His lover? Lots of great plot twists.

Deathtrap

The Last Of Sheila • *USA* • Herbert Ross • 1973

James Cockburn sets an elaborate trap to discover the hit-and-run driver who killed his wife. Many more discoveries are made along the way. Star-studded cast.

Horror:

Blood and Roses (Et Mourir de Plaisir) • *France/Italy* • Roger Vadim • 1960

Carmilla is obsessed with her vampire ancestor of two hundred years earlier. She is taken over by the vampire's spirit.

Dracula's Daughter • *USA* • Lambert Hillyer • 1936

The first in a long tradition of female bisexual vampires on film. She falls in love with her (male) doctor and seduces a (female) prostitute.

The Hunger • *USA* • Tony Scott • 1983

Beautifully filmed story about a bisexual vampire in search of a new lover. Hot love scene between Catherine Deneuve and Susan Sarandon. Also starring David Bowie.

Interview With the Vampire • *USA* • Neil Jordan Scott • 1994

Starring Tom Cruise, Brad Pitt, and Antonio Banderas. Not as explicitly bisexual as the book, but the erotic tension can be cut with a knife.

Lair of the White Worm • *UK* • Ken Russell • 1988

Amanda Donohoe is a vampirish snake-woman who seduces her prey, both male and female before feeding them to the snake god.

Lust for a Vampire (To Love a Vampire) • *UK* • Jimmy Sangster • 1970

A student seduces and kills classmates and teachers at a boarding school.

The Vampire Lovers • *UK* • Roy Ward Baker • 1970

A young woman is left at houses of the wealthy by her mother. She seduces their daughters and drains their blood.

Vampyres, Daughters of Dracula • *UK* • Joseph Larraz • 1975

A pair of female vampires live in a castle together in England. They are lovers, but also enjoy the men they seduce before killing them.

Most of the films mentioned in this section are available for purchase or rental through the Bisexual Resource Center's on-line Bisexual Video Store at http://www.biresource.org/videostore. Videos purchased or rented through the Bisexual Video Store earn money that helps the BRC produce conferences, pamphlets, and this Bisexual Resource Guide.

Wayne M. Bryant
c/o Bisexual Resource Center
P.O. Box 400639
Cambridge, MA 02140
bryant@tdint.com

SAFER & SEXIER

bi Cianna Stewart

Get nude.

Ask yourself a few questions:

Do you like having sex?

Do you feel like you deserve to have a good time during sex?

What kind of sex do you like?

Do you know what you like during sex?

Do you like your body?

Do you know what will make you feel good during sex?

Do you feel like you should be able to get what you want during sex?

Do you know how to ask for what you want?

Do you know how to say that something does not feel good?

Do you know how to say something would feel better if...

Do you like to talk during sex?

Do you like to talk before having sex?

Do you hate to talk about sex?

What words to you use for your body?

What words to you use for someone else's body?

What words to you use to for different sexual/sensual acts?

What kind of sex makes you feel unsafe?

What are your boundaries?

What are your partner's boundaries?

Are you more willing to stop doing something altogether, or to try doing it with latex?

You know, it's OK to have a hard time with safer sex. In fact, you would be unusual if you never had any difficulty either introducing the topic or in being 100% consistently safe.

What is most important is to recognize that getting to be safe is a series of steps. Even those of us who have been doing it for a while started somewhere, and even we have to negotiate with every new partner. Many of us still have some things that are hard for us, and most of us have gone through some kind of grieving over that "other" kind of sex.

So there's this thing out there called HIV, and while it seems like it's everywhere, you can actually track its path, and stop it before it gets to you. Really.

Who me?

HIV has no biases for or against a group of people. It does, however, have a particular fondness for bodily fluids which have a high level of white blood cells, and for activities which transmit those fluids from one person to another. It therefore affects all people doing certain "unsafe" activities, regardless of sexual identity, gender, age, race, ability, class or regional location.

Yes, you.

"Bodily Fluids"?

HIV lives in white blood cells. Fluids with a high concentration of white blood cells are blood, semen, vaginal fluids (i.e. cum, discharge, ejaculate, etc.). HIV may be transmitted through breast milk. Menstrual blood contains regular blood, and could easily transmit HIV. Saliva, tears, and sweat have such low traces of white blood cells that you'd have to drink gallons to put yourself seriously at risk. Urine is sterile and does not transmit HIV. Feces, however, often have blood in them and are therefore unsafe.

"Unsafe Activities"?

A short (and incomplete) list of activities which are potentially unsafe when engaged in without the use of a barrier:

- Intercourse between a man and a woman or between two men
- Anal finger play or fisting
- Vaginal finger play or fisting
- Oral sex on a man or woman
- Sharing any part of a rig used for injection drugs
- Cuttings, piercings, or whipping until blood is drawn
- kissing while there are open sores on the mouth.

Safer Injecting

Injection drug use is responsible for a higher percentage of new HIV infections than any other activity. This is especially true in urban areas, and for women. While many people think of addicts when hearing about needle use, the number of people who use drugs recreationally at dance clubs and parties is growing, and many of them are sharing their works.

Bleach will kill HIV, but only if it stays in the rig for at least 30 seconds. Drawing up alternatively water and bleach at least 5 times will usually fill the time minimum.

The most effective way to stay safe if you inject drugs either recreationally or regularly is to own your own rig, and not to share needles, syringes, cottons, cookers, or water with anyone else. Having works doesn't mean you're addicted, just that you care about staying alive.

Safer Sex: What it means and doesn't mean

"Safer sex" means using barriers during sex to keep yourself and your partner(s) from exchanging bodily fluids which carry HIV. Using safer sex also protects you from many other sexually transmitted diseases.

Safer sex does not mean asking your partners about who they've slept with and then deciding, based on that information alone, that it's okay to have unsafe sex. This ignores the fact that there are a number of ways to contract HIV, including sharing rigs while using injection drugs. This also does not ask what kinds of sex they had, whether safe or not, and does not at all address what partners their partners have had. This is also not a safe method for many bis, since both homophobia and biphobia on the part of our partners can affect how we answer and/or how they answer us. Beyond that, people have been known to change answers based on whether they think you'll still sleep with them if they answer honestly.

Safer sex does not mean simply being in a monogamous relationship. You may have been monogamous for all of two weeks. Or perhaps either you or your partner is a serial monogamist, who still has been known to have many partners in one year.

Safer sex means educating yourself, planning enough to get the supplies, and keeping them close at hand. If you have to get out of bed, go into another room, or if you simply left the stuff at home, you're giving yourself one more excuse to not play safely. Keep some next to your bed, in the kitchen, out by the pool, on your person, in your car, at the office, wherever you have sex. (Lucky you — at the office?)

Safer sex means being okay with talking about what you want. That can include "let's use this" and "I don't want to do that" and "a little more to the left..."

Safer Sex

Condoms

So available, so colorful, so user friendly. Condoms have gotten a bad rap in some circles about their tendency to break. But most of the times that a condom breaks, it's because it was used incorrectly. Always be sure to use a lubricated condom, or some lube with unlubed condoms. Be sure you NEVER use a petroleum-based lube with latex (like Vaseline, baby oil, Pennzoil, whatever your fetish) — it breaks down the latex and will cause it to tear.

Gloves

For all "digital play" (i.e. using your fingers in someone's vagina or anus) wear a latex glove, and use lots of lube. Gloves can be cut open by removing the fingers and thumb and cutting open one side to give you a nice, large, stretchy piece of latex for oral sex on women or for rimming. I love gloves because they make everything smoother, silkier. They are a fashion statement, especially when you coordinate the colored ones with your outfit. Tips/ideas: You can get boxes of gloves at beauty supply houses. If you're sensitive to the powder on gloves (or on latex), pre-rinse them in water, then let them dry. They'll be all ready to use when the occasion arises. If you'll be changing orifices mid-play (e.g. anus to vagina, one butt to another, etc.), put on two gloves at the beginning. Then, when you want to switch, just take one off, and you're ready. Try lube on the inside of the glove. You'll feel more, and the **glove seems thinner.**

Lubricant

For a lot of sex play, especially with latex, using a lubricant of some kind is highly recommended. Use a water-based one, because petroleum products break down latex.

Tips and ideas:

▼ Many lubes contain Nonoxynol-9, which does help fight HIV, but may also cause an allergic reaction. Women are especially sensitive to it. Check the ingredient list.

▼ Keep some water near wherever you have sex in a spray bottle or a squirt gun. If your lube begins to dry out, add water.

▼ For your travel pack, pick up lube samples from anywhere you buy lube. You can also often get some for free from health offices, AIDS outreach services, and from HIV testing sites.

▼ Lube makes everything wet and slippery. I can feel more. So can my partner(s). I can play longer. A lot longer. I have become a major lube fetishist. So can you.

Going Down on a Woman (a.k.a. oral sex/eating out/muff diving)

What's the big deal with this? Is it really not safe? I haven't heard anything that proves it.

OF COURSE NOT, because there have been almost no official (read: government) studies. But women who are HIV+ have a high rate of vaginal infections, and so there's a high rate of white blood cells and HIV just waiting for your mouth to suck them in.

You can use dental dams, if you like sex to taste like bubble gum. Or you can use the new dams made especially for oral sex. Or you can use plastic wrap (name brand, not generic, please, Mary). It's cool stuff because it doesn't taste like anything, you can see through it, and it comes in big long strips and neat colors. You can cut the tip off a condom and then cut it up the side to get a stretchier, thinner dam. Tip: Put some lube on her vagina or butt before covering it up, and everything will feel fabulous.

Dams

For years dental dams have been the standard barrier for oral sex on women or oral/anal play with women or men (rimming). Originally developed for use in dentistry, they are square sheets of latex which make an effective, if unappealing barrier. The main complaints about dental dams is that they are too thick and taste bad.

More recently, dams have come available which are made especially for oral sex. Two thin, plastic dams available on the market are Eros Veils and Rim Me. Recently a new latex product called Sheer Glyde Dams (known as Lollyes in Australia) has been approved by the FDA. These are larger than dental dams (6 x 10 inches), much thinner, and virtually taste-free.

As with any latex products, a little water-based lubricant between the skin and the latex will improve sensitivity and make the barrier feel even thinner. But be sure to avoid oil-based lubricants, which dissolve latex.

Plastic Wrap

Already around many households, plastic wrap can be used for oral sex on women or for oral/anal play with men or women (rimming). On the microwavable/non debate: you only have to worry about microwavable wrap becoming porous if your body heats up over 165 degrees Fahrenheit.

Tips/ideas:

▼ Take it out of the box to unroll and cut it by tearing it, so you don't get cut by the little razor edge on the box.

▼ Put some lube on his/her skin before wrapping. It'll feel better.

▼ Don't stretch the wrap tight, just lay it against the skin, sticking it on with the lube. This will help keep it from tearing, and you'll also be licking all those nooks and crannies, not a flat sheet of plastic.

▼ Plastic wrap is clear, thin, strong, and doesn't taste like latex. You can see through it. You can smell through it. It also comes in rolls so you aren't restricted on size. Plastic wrap is also useful as a restraint...

There's so much more I could tell you, but that's all I have room for now. Play a lot. Play safe. Have a good time. Wake up. Take some responsibility. Stay healthy. Learn to talk about sex and to ask for what you want. Sex gets better if you do. Now isn't that an excellent side effect from having safer sex?

Cianna Stewart has worked as a Peer Safer Sex Slut with Lyon-Martin Women's Health Services and the Gay Asian Pacific Alliance Community HIV Project in San Francisco. She is currently doing HIV prevention work in the Philippines. She swears that she's never enjoyed sex as much as she does now. Parts of this article previously appeared in Anything that Moves magazine. Reprinted by permission.

[Editor's note: In the US, the phone number of the National AIDS Hotline is (800) 342-AIDS (in Spanish: 800-344-SIDA; for Native Americans: 800-354-7889; for hearing impaired: 800-AIDS-TTY).]

Roberta Gregory

Getting Bi
on the Internet

What's out there in cyberspace for bisexuals, and how to get to it

The Internet has become a wonderful and popular place to share ideas, discussion and resources. But although it is a great place to find bi and bi-related information it can also be quite overwhelming to the newcomer. Without a good working knowledge of how to use search engines and navigate the Internet, it is very easy to just become lost and not find anything useful at all!

The resources here are listed by type: web pages, e-mail lists, IRC (chat), and newsgroups. Each section has a description of what that type of resources are listed and how to use them, with a list of some of the most popular and useful bisexual-related items.

Since there's way too much on the Internet to cover here, and because it's always changing, we've attempted to compile only what we think are some of the most general and helpful resources to someone new to the Internet (or to bisexuality!). By no means is this an attempt to include ALL bisexual or bi-inclusive Internet resources, but just to provide some good jumping-off points to get you started.

Web

bi Audrey Beth Stein

URLs for all sites mentioned in boldface are included at the end of this section.

The web has become a great resource for bisexuals in recent years. **The Bisexual Resource Center (BRC)**, which publishes the Bisexual Resource Guide, also publishes a number of pamphlets on the web and in print. Titles include "Bisexuality: Some Questions Answered," "10 Things Your Congregation Can Do To Become More Welcoming," and "How to Start a Bisexual Support Group." The BRC also hosts an online bisexual bookstore in conjunction with amazon.com and the Bisexual Resource List which is part of the Queer Resource Directory.

PlanetOut is self-described as "the largest worldwide online community of gay, lesbian, bisexual, and transgendered people." Sections of PlanetOut include travel, movies, finance, news, radio, chat, and links to other bi and queer sites.

GLAAD, the Gay & Lesbian Alliance Against Defamation, advertises itself as a "national organization that promotes fair, accurate and inclusive representation as a means of challenging discrimination based on sexual orientation or identity." Their web site "invite[s] you to utilize these pages to access information about how the media portrays the gay, lesbian, bisexual and transgender community or how you can respond to media defamation and affirmation."

The **Queer Resources Directory** "is an electronic library with news clippings, political contact information, newsletters, essays, images, hyperlinks, and every other kind of information resource of interest to the GLBT community. Information is stored for the use of casual network users and serious researchers alike." Among other things, it includes a list of LGBT+ mailing lists.

The **BiNet USA** site includes a brief history of the bisexual movement and activist central with "instant email" to make it easier to be informed and speak out on various bi issues. "The Mission of BiNet USA is to collect and distribute information regarding Bisexuality; to facilitate the development of Bisexual community and visibility; to work for the equal rights and liberation of Bisexuals and all oppressed peoples; and to eradicate all forms of oppression inside and outside the Bisexual community. We are committed to being affirmatively inclusive of a multicultural constituency and political agenda."

Digital Queers promotes equal rights for queers and the queer community through strategic and effective use of digital technology and communications.

There are a number of collections of links and resources available on the web; more substantial ones include **bi.org**, **Bisexual Options**, **Bisexual Hell**, **Bi All Means**, and **Rainbow Query**.

The goal of the **bi.org** is "to serve the worldwide bisexual community by providing a free Internet presence for bisexual individuals, groups and non-profit organisations. As well as providing free WWW space, there is a large set of pages detailing resources (groups, organisations, magazines, Internet newsgroups), and @**bi.org** email addresses and majordomo mailing lists are also available." **Bi.org** is centered in Europe while **Bisexual Options**, "your internet guide for everything bisexual," hosts web sites for nonprofit bi organizations in North America. **Bisexual Options** also includes links to resources and dates and contact information for upcoming conferences. Together the two sites provide a "City Bi City" guide, personal ads, and international news. **Bi.org**'s collection of links (organized by topic) includes a list of webrings, which are a good way to find personal sites of random bi folk.

Bisexual Hell is purely a link-list, while **Bi All Means** is a good collection of resources by category, including bi-specific, health, polyamory, and youth. **Rainbow Query** is a search engine which searches by category (including "bisexual") or by keyword.

While there are more and more bi-related sites cropping up on the web, and there is even an e-directory of lesbigay scholars, finding sites with unique or intellectual content is still a challenge. The October 1994 issue of **Bad Subjects** includes an article entitled "Bisexuality and How To Use It: Toward a Coalitional Identity Politics" by Annalee Newitz and Jillian Sandell. The **National Journal of Sexual Orientation Law** is one place to find new content on a regular, if infrequent basis. **ELIGHT** plugs itself as "an e-zine for the web created by and for gay youth and young adults in cyberspace." While bisexuals aren't mentioned in the title we are pretty well represented in the 'zine itself, which includes coming out stories, writings (both fiction and non-fiction), poetry, and personals. The **Rainbow Icon Archive** chronicles the history of many queer symbols, and **!OUTPROUD! The National Coalition for Gay, Lesbian, Bisexual, and Transgender Youth** includes book recommendations, a community role models archive, message boards, and a school resource library.

The **Fine Art of Being Come Out To: A Straight Person's Guide To Gay Etiquette** by Susan Harris includes an entire chapter on the bisexual coming out. There's a tremendous irony to the existence of this guide; if you pick it up on your own you probably don't need to read it, and if you should be reading it someone is probably trying to figure out the safest way to get it into your hands. That said, **The Fine Art Of Being Come Out To** is both hilarious and quite useful, and if more people read it, this world might be a better place.

The URL list

Bisexual Resource Center **http://www.biresource.org/**

Bisexual Bookstore **http://www.biresource.org/bookstore/**

Bisexual Resource List **http://www.qrd.org/qrd/www/orgs/brc/brl-toc.html**

Planet Out **http://www.planetout.com/**

GLAAD **http://www.glaad.org/**

Queer Resources Directory **http://www.qrd.org/qrd/**

Queer Resources Directory -- list of electronic mailing lists **http://www.qrd.org/qrd/electronic/mail/**

BiNet USA **http://www.binetusa.org/**

Digital Queers **http://www.dq.org/**

Bi.org **http://bi.org/**

Bisexual Options **http://www.bisexual.org/**

Bisexual Hell **http://www.tiac.net/users/danam/bisexual.HTML**

Bi All Means **http://www.biallmeans.org/**

Rainbow Query **http://www.glweb.com/rainbowquery/index.html**

Bisexuality and How To Use It: Toward a Coalitional Identity Politics **http://eserver.org/bs/16/Sandell.html**

Rainbow Icon Archive **http://www.enqueue.com/ria/**

National Journal of Sexual Orientation Law **http://sunsite.unc.edu/gaylaw/**

E-Directory of Lesbigay Scholars **http://newark.rutgers.edu/~lcrew/lbg_edir.html**

ELIGHT **http://www.elight.org/**

!OUTPROUD! **http://www.outproud.org/**

Khushnet - Extensive listings for South Asian GLBs. Includes Nepal, Australia, India, Malaysia, Pakistan, Singapore, Sri Lanka and more. **http://www.khushnet.com/**

The Fine Art of Being Come Out To: A Straight Person's Guide To Gay Etiquette **http://www.io.com/~wwwomen/queer/etiquette/intro.html**

Bi Mailing Lists

bi Gilly Rosenthol

Imagine being able to have a conversation with other people just like you all over the world - observant Jewish bisexuals, bi librarians, bi women with male partners. Or people who just share a similar interest - other people who want to chat about bi theory, activism, or local events. How can you do that without running up a phone bill to challenge the national debt? Join some email lists!

An email list is way of talking via email with not just one person at a time, but a whole group. You can sit back and just read the messages that come by, or be an active participant in the conversation. You send messages to a central address that sends them out to everyone who's subscribed to the list. Some lists are closed - only women, or bisexuals, or bisexual women with purple hair, are allowed to join, and subscriptions requests are filtered through a human being. Others are open, and anyone who's interested can join. Some have an option for digest format - you get one email with a bunch of messages, rather than thirty email messages throughout the day.

In addition to the address used to send messages to the list, there is usually a separate address for administrative tasks such as joining and leaving the list. This address usually goes to one of two common programs used to maintain mailing lists, Majordomo and Listserv. If the subscription address is in the form of listserv@anywhere.com, you can send an email with the body "info listname" for more information, or "sub listname your name" to subscribe. It the address is majordomo@anywhere.com, the format for information is the same, and to subscribe simply write "subscribe listname your-email-address" in the body of your message. Try not to include your .signature file, if you use one; it will only confuse the computer. Very quickly, you should get back information about where to send messages that you want to go to the list, and how to unsubscribe. Save this message - it makes it much easier once you're getting three hundred messages a day and need to cut down on your mailing lists!

The Mailing List list

Regional mailing lists are included in the Directory section with their respective regions; general and topic-specific mailing lists are listed below.

biachad Biachad ▼ which means "together" in Hebrew, is an international discussion list for religious Jews that are bisexual or bi-curious. Regular topics of discussion are religion, sexuality, culture, and politics. In the future, we are hoping that the list will also grow to include regional, national, and possibly international gatherings. majordomo@byz.org subscribe biachad your-email-address http://www.nwlink.com/~apwills/biachadindex.html

BIACT-L ▼ Bisexual Activists Discussion List listserv@brownvm.brown.edu info biact-l

BIFEM-L ▼ A discussion list for issues of interest to bisexual women. listserv@brownvm.brown.edu info bifem-l

BISEXU-L ▼ A general discussion list on issues of interest to bisexuals. listserv@brownvm.brown.edu info bisexu-l http://drycas.club.cc.cmu.edu/~julie/bisexu-l.html

BITHRY-L ▼ Bisexual Theory Discussion List listserv@brownvm.brown.edu info bithry-l

disabled-bi ▼ The Disabled Bisexual list is open to anyone who defines themselves as disabled. Disabled is defined as anything that impairs your standard of living majordomo@queernet.org subscribe disabled-bi

pagan-bi ▼ The Pagan Bisexual list is for any Bisexual, male or female, who defines themself as Pagan. Open to any path. majordomo@queernet.org subscribe pagan-bi

bi-pagan ▼ For pagan bisexuals. Based in the UK. listserv@ogham.org subscibe bi-pagan {your name}. http://www.maghmell.demon.co.uk/bi-pagan/

RuBlfruit ▼ Moderated mailing list for bi women only. majordomo@queernet.org info rubifruit

sotts mailing list ▼ The SOTTS Mailing List is an Internet mailing list for bisexual, gay, or lesbian partners in mixed orientation relationships who are trying to keep their marriages intact and for keeping the relationship positive for those couples who are separating or divorcing. The SOTTS List is not moderated; it is a closed list so that only lesbigay spouses will be members. The subscription list is private. majordomo@mailinglist.net subscribe sotts E-Mail questions concerning SOTTS to MGRSOTTS@MailingList.net http://www.glpci.org/~ssn/

ssml mailing list ▼ The Spouse Support Mailing List (SSML) is an Internet mailing list for straight spouses and their bisexual, gay, or lesbian partners who are trying to keep their marriages intact and for keeping the relationship positive for those couples who are separating and divorcing. The List also includes couples where one is bisexual and the other gay or lesbian and where both are bisexual and working through issues in their relationship. Membership is confidential. Majordomo@mailinglist.net subscribe ssml Email questions concerning SSML to MGRSSML@MailingList.net. http://www.mailinglist.net/ssml

STR8S ▼ The STR8S Mailing List is an Internet mailing list for straight spouses of bisexual, gay, or lesbian partners who are trying to keep their marriages intact and for keeping the relationship positive for those couples who are separating and divorcing. The Str8s List is not moderated; it is a closed list so that only straight spouses will be members. The subscription list is private. majordomo@mailinglist.net subscibe str8s http://www.mailinglist.net/str8s Email questions concerning STR8S to MGRSTR8S@MailingList.net.

BiW-MP ▼ This is a list for bi women in relationships with men to discuss any particular issues which relate to these relationships, covering general issues like relationships with the lesbian community, contradictions in being a feminist dyke in love with a man, and handling one's desires for women whilst maintaining a relationship with the male partner. majordomo@bi.org http://bi.org/biw-mp/

Bisexuelle ▼ French-language list for bisexuals, bi-curious and their supporters. listserv@anargo.qc.ca subscribe bisexuelle yourname http://www.bisexuelle.qc.ca/melo/maillist.html

WOMBAT ▼ "Women of Beauty And Temptation" Wombat is a women-only list for discussion of bisexuality. While only women are allowed, it's not required that you be bisexual to join. Info: WomBAT-request@listserv.aol.com Subscribe: listserv@listserv.aol.com SUBSCRIBE WomBAT your name http://drycas.club.cc.cmu.edu/~julie/wombat.html

Gay, Lesbian, Bisexual People of Color ▼ Subscribe: majordomo@abacus.oxy.edu with the text "subscribe glbpoc" or for information on the list, with the text "info glbpoc".

Nice Jewish Girls ▼ Discussion list for lesbian & bi Jewish women. Members only. For more information, send e-mail to majordomo@zoom.com with "info nicejg" in the body of the message.

APLBN: Asian Pacific-Islander Lesbian & Bisexual Women's Network ▼ Messages include various discussion topics, announcements of community events, and networking. Requests for subscription or info: APLB-REQUEST@kwaj.engr.sgi.com. APLBN is human run; please send a human-readable message. Web page: expage.com/page/aplbn.

Vidaguei List ▼ Spanish-language discussion group. VIADGUEI@listbot.com.

Activistaguie List ▼ Spanish-Language e-mail list intended for the sharing of political and activist information. ACTIVISTAGUE@listbot.com.

IRC

bi John Valentine

Interrelay chat, or IRC, is very much in flux. Anyone at anytime can create a channel (chat room)...and the channels are constantly changing. There are some "reliable" bi channels under the names **#bi**, **#bisexual**, and **#bisexuals_anonymous**. To complicate matters, there are hundreds of IRC servers around the world. There seem to be three main networks of IRC servers: DALnet, Undernet, and EFnet. Each of these three networks seem to have the three above mentioned channels on a regular basis as well as dozens of other bisexual related channels that come and go.

The character of the channels varies. Some are for non-sexual discussion only, while others are purely sexual. The channels listed above seem to be the most tame and friendly to people new to IRC.

Web sites where one can learn about IRC, download IRC software, and search for currently available channels include

http://www.liszt.com/chat/

http://www.irchelp.org

http://www.funet.fi/~irc

http://light.lightlink.com/irc/

Newsgroups

bi Kathryn Foote

Newsgroups, like e-mail lists (listservs), are electronic forums through which people all over the world can connect on the basis of common interests and characteristics. Newsgroups, however, are easier to use than e-mail lists in some ways. As long as a particular newsgroup exists on the server to which your computer is networked (for example, on the aol.com server if your internet access is through America Online) all it takes to get started is to locate it on the list of groups available and then click to subscribe. That group you selected is then instantly accessible for you to participate in at your convenience (although "netiquette" generally dictates that you "lurk"--that is, just read--a given group for a month or so before posting yourself). So, with a newsgroup, there is no waiting for a listowner or listserv program to process your subscription request--and no danger of hundreds of messages suddenly appearing in your personal mailbox, as with a high-volume mailing list.

Despite these advantages, or in some measure because of them, the trend for sexuality-related discussion is currently toward listservs and away from newsgroups. Ease of access makes newsgroups (especially unmoderated ones) obvious targets for "spam" (irrelevent, irritating, and often commercial messsages sent to many newsgroups at once, much like traditional direct mail), "hate-mail" posts by bi/homophobic bigots, and sometimes a combination of the two. Relatedly, e-mail lists afford their subscribers greater privacy than do newsgroups. They also offer a better opportunity to discuss narrowly-focused topics (such as bis/LGBTs in a certain profession or religion) without being interrupted by someone relatively clueless who is "just passing by" in cyberspace.

Nevertheless, there are still several internationally oriented bisexual and related newsgroups on the internet that are usually filled with more posts than you could read in one sitting. Some regional/national newsgroups (described in the regional sections of this guide) still get a fair number of legitimate posts as well. You will also be able to find out about new/other groups through your newsreader's search program or through search engines like Yahoo! on the worldwide web.

The primary bisexually focused newsgroup on the internet is **soc.bi**. (There is also **alt.personals.bi**, but even many of the non-spam posts there are of the "bi-curious" and/or "seeking hot bi babe" variety and so may not be of interest to many.) The discussion is wide-ranging (from bi self-definition, to politics, to gossip) and often quite interesting and informative. The group can seem, however, to have wild mood swings--from threads (groups of related posts) composed of little more than allusions to newsgroup in-jokes, to protracted and vicious "flamewars" (exchanges of nasty, often ad-hominem attacks), sometimes over seemingly minor differences. It is an especially good idea, therefore, to read the FAQ (Frequently Asked Questions) document that is posted periodically to the newsgroup itself and is permanently on the web at http://bi.org/~jon/soc.bi (the soc.bi homepage). Doing so will allow you to familiarize yourself with some of the pet peeves and the folklore that have developed among longtime posters. (Reading a newsgroup's FAQ, when one exists, is always advisable.)

There are two other newsgroups that are not just about bisexuality but are explicitly inclusive of bis. These are **soc.women.lesbian-and-bi** (swlab) and **soc.support.youth.gay-lesbian-bi** (ssyglb). Unlike soc.bi, these forums are moderated. That is, posts to the group get forwarded to a moderator who filters out the spam, hate mail, and anything else that is deemed inappropriate or irrelevant. Please note, however, that these groups are not exclusive in terms of who can post. Swlab will post messages from men or heterosexual women as long as they are civil and concern the group's topic: the lives of lesbians and bi women. Ssyglb, as the title suggests, focuses on support, discussion, news and networking for LGB youth but does not prohibit appropriate messages from older people (like those who are thirty or even more ancient). The FAQs for swlab and ssyglb are on the web at http://www.mtholyoke.edu/~wjfraser/swlab and http://www.youth.org/ssyglb/ssyglb-faq.html, respectively. These FAQs are quite comprehensive, chock full of links and other resources, and are great resources in and of themselves.

Finally, there are two other well-populated groups that may be of interest to bisexuals and that already have many bi posters: **soc.motss** and **alt.polyamory**. The "motss" in soc.motss stands for "members of the same sex," and is an acronym generally understood on the net to pertain at least to lesbians and gay men and often extended (as in the case of this newsgroup) to include bisexual, transgender, and other. Soc.motss is for social discussion among LGBTO people.

Alt.polyamory is a group for discussions of interest to polyamorous people. The FAQ provides the basics on polyamory (and beyond), so that those new to the concept can be prepared to engage in meaningful discussion.

If you do not have newsgroup access or your system does not carry one of the newsgroups described here, you can still read and post through a web site called dejanews (http://www.dejanews.com) as long as you can provide them with an e- mail address. If you do not have an e-mail address, or if that server is busy, you can still read some groups through search engines on the web.

However you get there, here's hoping you have a happy experience in bi newsgroup land.

Directory of Bisexual and Bi-Inclusive Groups

About the listings: what's here, what's not, and how they were chosen.

An enormous number of individuals from all over the world volunteered to work as regional editors. What follows is the result of their work combined with some work done on this end. Editors were asked to verify and add listings of bi and bi-inclusive groups in their geographic region. You may notice that regions differ in terms of what is and what is not included—that is because we tried to respect the editor's judgement. In general, we were much more restrictive in scope in areas that have many resources. For example, in Boston, an organization that calls itself "lesbian and gay" rather than "lesbian, gay, bisexual & transgender" was unlikely to be included. However, in India we were so happy to find any resources at all that we included groups regardless of their name.

Organizations are arranged as follows: International groups are listed first. Countries follow alphabetically, with national groups listed first, then local groups. In some instances organizations that we feel should be given priority have been moved to the front of their section. With this exception, groups are then alphabetized by the city in which they are located, then further alphabetized by group name. You should be creative in searching: for example, many groups located within New York City may be listed under city neighborhoods such as Flushing, or Brooklyn, rather than under New York City, and other listings may not have a city name listed at all and would thus be listed at the beginning of their region.

If your group is not listed and should have been please do not take offense. Rather, just send us information so that we can include it in our next edition! Likewise, if there are errors in the listings, please let us know. Groups come and go and change their names, addresses, email and phone numbers daily - you can help us keep our information current.

Boston Pride, 1997

INTERNATIONAL

Bisexual Resource Center   EA💻▼
PO Box 400639
Cambridge MA 02140
tel: 617-424-9595
e-mail: brc@biresource.org
URL: www.biresource.org
BRC educates general public & interested organizations about bisexuality through providing resources & creating public forums for discussion. Produces pamphlets, organizes conferences, publishes the Bisexual Resource Guide, facilitates Boston area support groups for people who are or think they might be bi, houses the bisexual archives. Website has resources & links to "The Bisexual Bookstore" with 700+ titles. **Publication(s):** *The Bisexual Resource Guide*

BiNL-L   ▼💻
e-mail: listserv@bi-link.tdcnet.nl
Bisexuality Discussion in Dutch. For more information, send to above e-mail address with only "info binl-l" in the body of the message. To subscribe send message with only "subscribe binl-l" to above e-mail.

bisexual@onelist.com   ▼💻
ON
tel: 519-743-4967 (via Bell relay); fax: 519-743-6506
e-mail: aladrisa@home.com
URL: www.onelist.com
"Another worldwide discussion list for the bisexual community."

Bisexual Pen-Pals   ▼
Pen-Pal Scheme/ EBG
58a Broughton Street
Edinburgh Scotland EH1 3SA
Send SASE for more info.

euro-bi   💻
England
e-mail: majordomo@bi.org
URL: bi.org/euro-bi
For discussions about bisexuality, or of interest to bisexuals, specifically related to the UK & europe. Aims to be a bi-positive, sex-positive safe space. To subscribe, send a message to majordomo@bi.org.

Affirmation: Gay & Lesbian   🌐💻
Mormons
P.O. Box 526175
Salt Lake City UT 84152
tel: 213-255-7251
URL: members.aol.com/wasatchweb
International social & support organization for GLBT people with a Mormon/LDS background, whether they currently identify themselves as Mormon or not. Frequent meetings throughout Utah & chapters throughout the US. The SLC group also sponsors a Gay Mormon Father's Group that meets separately.

Association of College Unions: 🎓
International Gay, Lesbian &
Bisexual Concerns Committee
send mail to: ACU: IGLBCC
c/o Jane Stachowiak
Berklee College of Music, Student Activities
1140 Boylston Street, Box 360
Boston MA 02215
tel: 617-747-2096; fax: 617-262-3083

Campaign to End Homophobia   EY🔵💻
P.O. Box 53170
Washington DC 20009-3170
e-mail: rlking@aol.com
URL: www.endhomophobia.org
Works to end homophobia through education. Develops & distributes educational materials affirming lesbian & gay youth, information for teachers, & curriculum for anti-homophobia workshops.

Emergence International   🌐💻
(Gay Christian Scientists)
PO Box 6061-423
Sherman Oaks CA 91413
tel: 800-280-6653
e-mail: BILLXLS@ix.netcom.com
URL: www.geocities.com/WestHollywood/1892/emerge.html
Annual conferences. Publishes bi-monthly journal "Emerge" & monthly newsletter "The In Between Times".

Key to symbols: ▼ = bi   ♀ = women   ♂ = men   🌐 = religious/spiritual
💧 = for allies   **M** = for married bis   ♥ = for partners of bis   **Y** = youth   **C** = people of color
✎ = school   🎓 = college/university   **P** = professional   **E** = educational
A = activist/political   **H** = health (incl. HIV)   📰 = media/press   💻 = internet resource

Robyn Ochs

Poet Sheila Mabry at 5th International Conference on
Bisexuality 1998.

EQUAL! at Lucent Technologies   P 🖳
tel: 500-346-5232
e-mail: equal@ equal.lucent.com
URL: www.equal.org
*Educational / support group that addresses
workplace environment affecting GLBT
employees or their family, friends or colleagues .
Local chapters all over the globe & an international structure.*

Family Pride Coalition (formerly Gay &   Y 🖳
Lesbian Parents Coalition International)
PO Box 34337
San Diego CA 92163
tel: 619-296-0199; fax: 619-296-0699
e-mail: pride@familypride.org
URL: www.familypride.org/
*Supporting & protecting glbt people & their
families. Advocacy & support groups. Pagina en
español, informazzione in italiano. Over 85
chapters. International info & referrals on
custody, adoption, surrogacy, AI, rights of co-
parents. Mailing list is completely confidential.*
Publication(s): *Quarterly newsletter.*

Gender, Sexuality & Identity: 👓 E 🖳
Study Abroad Program in the Netherlands
School for International Training, Kipling Road
PO Box 676
Brattleboro VT 05302-0676
tel: 800-336-1616
e-mail: csa@sit.edu
URL: www.sit.edu
*16 credit undergraduate program held in
Amsterdam. Focus on integrating strong cultural
immersion with strong academics. Includes
seminar on sexuality, gender & identity.*

Intel Gay, Lesbian or Bisexual   PE 🖳
Employees (IGLOBE)
c/o L. Parrish
Intel Corporation, M/S RN5-08
2200 Mission College Blvd.
Santa Clara CA 95052
tel: 408-765-4199 (Liz Parrish, President)
e-mail: iglobe-request@intel.com or
liz.parrish@intel.com
URL: www.glyphic.com/iglobe
*"An Intel-sanctioned employee diversity group
for networking of Intel employees. A forum for
Intel employees in affirmation of Intel's
commitment to equality, diversity & making
Intel a great place to work."* **Publication(s)**:
*The Rainbow Connection A benefit for members
published monthly, lists activities at Intel sites
worldwide.*

International Gay Attorneys Network   P
tel: Helmut Graupner: ++43/676/309 4737; fax:
+43 1 876 3061
e-mail: a8301536@unet.univie.ac.at
*In formation: A worldwide network of gay & bi
attorneys which will enable each participating
attorney to serve clients not only locally but
worldwide. Colleagues already participating
from Berlin, Geneva, Munich, Prague, San
Francisco & Vienna.*

International Gay & Lesbian   A 🖳
Human Rights Commission
1360 Mission St.
Suite 200
San Francisco CA 94103
tel: 415-255-8680; fax: 415-255-8662
e-mail: ilglhrc.@iglhrc.org
URL: www.iglhrc.org
*NGO whose mission is to protect & advance the
human rights of all people & communities
subject to discrimination or abuse on the basis of
sexual orientation, gender identity, or HIV
status.* **Publication(s)**: *Unspoken Rules, Action
Alert various*

Key to symbols: ▼ = bi   ♀ = women   ♂ = men   ☯ = religious/spiritual
◊ = for allies   **M** = for married bis   ♥ = for partners of bis   **Y** = youth   **C** = people of color
110   **The Bisexual Resource Guide 2000**

International Lesbian & Gay Association   AE
81, rue Marche-au-Charbon
B-1000Brussels
tel: +32-2-502-2471; fax: same
e-mail: ilga@ilga.org
Umbrella organization. "A federation of over 300 glbt groups from 75 countries fighting for the rights of lgbt people. We also have over 100 supportive associate & individual members. Will you join us?" World/regional conferences, information clearing house, lobbying of international orgs/institutions to fight descrimination based on sexual orientation. Bisexual Information Pool of ILGA c/o ABN, PO Box 490, Lutwyche, Queensland Australia 4030. Email: ausbinet@rainbow.net.au.
Publication(s): *ILGA Bulletin*

International Sexual Minorities   ⌨
Information Resource (ISMIR)
PO Box 81869
Pittsburgh PA 15217-0869
tel: 412-422-3060; fax: 412-359-3878
e-mail: info@ismir.aol.com
URL: www.ismir.org
Information resource for glbt individuals. Maintains interactive website database of over 7,000 addresses. **Publication(s):** *ISMIR Events Calendar; ISMIR Chronicle*

Interweave   ☻
c/o Unitarian Universalist Association
164 Milk St, #406
Boston MA 02109
Membership organization affiliated with the UUA, dedicated to the spiritual, political, & social well-being of UU's who are confronting oppression as lgbt persons, & their heterosexual allies. Celebrates the culture & the lives of its members. **Publication(s):** *Interweave World*

Journal of Gay, Lesbian &   ↵YCPE✑
Bisexual Identity
Warren J. Blumenfeld, Editor
PO Box 929
Northampton MA 01061
tel: 413-585-9121; fax: 413-584-1332
e-mail: blumenfeld@educ.umass.edu
Interdisciplinary journal. Peer-reviewed original articles, personal essays, clinical studies, research papers, etc. For submission guidelines write to editor, above. For subscription information, write: Human Sciences Press, Inc., Attn. Dept. HGL94, 233 Spring St., New York, NY, 10013-1578.

Lickity Spit: the lean clean bi zine   ▼
& other comix
c/o Alleged Literature attn: Damian Cugley
255B Banbury Rd
OxfordOX2 7HN England
e-mail: damian.cugley@oxfordcc.co.uk
Send SAE or 2 international reply coupons for catalogue. Or $5 US for samples, stating preference "m/f/bi. " Variety of comics w/strong sexual/humorous content. Please include over 18 statement with orders. Also produces QZ, a regularly updated list of queer zines in the UK.
Publication(s): *Zinabed, Hey Luv!, "Lickity Spit", Giant Sized Man Thing #1, etc. Publications contain comic strips, cartoons, collage & some articles. May contain scenes of graphic sex.*

Otras Ovejas   ☻E⌨
Lavalle 376 2do. E
Buenos Aires
tel: 54 1 314 59 89; fax: 54 1 314 59 89
e-mail: thanks@wamani.apc.org
URL: swiftsite.com.otrasovejas
Documentation Centers (40 in L.A.). Study groups on the Bible & other religious texts from a pro-LGB view. **Publication(s):** *Lesbigay Spirituality & The Bible Booklet. Freely distributed. Spanish translation from the original in English.*

PFLAG-USA (Parents, Families &   AE◊⌨
Friends of Lesbians & Gays)
1101 14th St NW, Suite 1030
Washington DC 20005
tel: 202-638-4200; fax: 202-638-0243
e-mail: info@pflag.org
URL: www.pflag.org
Local groups in many cities around the US & in Canada, Australia, UK, France, Argentina, Italy, Israel & South Africa. Contact the national office for locations. To subscribe to mailing list send message "subscribe pflag-announce" to majordomo@pflag.casti.com.
Publication(s): *var. publications including newsletter: Flagpole (quarterly) call, fax, or email to request catalog.*

Prime Timers Worldwide   ♂
PO Box 436
Manchaca TX 78652
tel: 512-282-2861, 8am-10pm Central time
Social organization for older gay & bi men, with chapters in major cities in Australia, Canada, Ireland, Sweden & the US. Monthly meetings on subject of interest; several other monthly special-interest events.

✎ = school   ↵ = college/university   **P** = professional   **E** = educational
A = activist/political   **H** = health (incl. HIV)   ✑ = media/press   ⌨ = Internet resource

QUEERLAW-CAN-L   **AEP** 🖳
(Queerlaw Canada mailing list)
e-mail: egale@egale.ca
URL: www.egale.ca/feedback/
mailist.htm#queerlaw-can
*Legal issues from a Canadian perspective (but
not limited to Canada) for legal academics/
professionals & anyone else interested in the
topic. E-mail or visit web page for more info.*

RFSL The Swedish Federation for   🖳
Gay & Lesbian Rights website
N-0212
URL: www.rfsl.se/defaulteng.nclk
*Extensive Swedish LGB website featuring
Webchat "Chat with other Homo & Bisexuals 10
channels - girls & boys backroms, Bisex & more"
Library w over 5,000 titles, searchable online, &
Homoguide "A searchable gay guide over
Sweden, also in English."*

Straight Spouse Network of Parents   ♥ **M** 🖳
& Friends of Lesbians & Gays
c/o Amity Pierce Buxton
8215 Terrace Drive
El Cerrito CA 94530-3058
tel: 510-525-0200
e-mail: info@ssnetwk.org
URL: www.ssnetwk.org
*International organization of heterosexual
spouses & partners whose current or former
mates are b,g,l or t. Support groups, state &
country contacts, & individual spouses provide
confidential help & resource information to
spouses & partners worldwide.* **Publication(s):**
News & Notes Published 2x/year

Unitarian Universalist Association   ☪**EA** 🖳
**Office of Bisexual, Gay, Lesbian &
Transgender Concerns**
25 Beacon Street
Boston MA 02108-2800
tel: 617-742-2100 x470 or x465; fax: 617-742-0321
e-mail: obgltc@uua.org
URL: www.uua.org/obgltc
*Provides resources for UU congregations
working toward being more affirming &
welcoming to BLGT folks.*

World Congress of GLB Jewish   ☪
Organizations
102 Buckingham Avenue
Trenton NJ 08418-3314
tel: 609-396-1972
e-mail: rjh@maxmaxpartners.com
*Aims to end homophobia with in the Jewish
community & antisemitism in the GLBT
community, worldwide.*

ARGENTINA

Amenaza Lésbica   ♀
Casilla de Correo 12
Sucursal 27 B (1427)
Buenos Aires Bueno Aires
e-mail: amenaza@artemis.wamani.apc.org
*Grupo de lesbianas que publica una revista
abierta a contribuciones por parte de mujeres
bisexuales. [Lesbian group that publishes a
magazine open to contributions from bi women.]*

Biblioteca GLTB
Paraná 157 "F"
Buenos Aires
tel: (54 1) 373 89 55; fax: same
e-mail: cha@nat.com.ar
*Library, has written material & films on bi
people (mostly men).*

Comunidad Homosexual Argentina   **A** 🖳
Parana 157 "F"
(1017) Buenos Aires
tel: 054/1-373-8955
e-mail: cha@nar.com.ar
URL: www.sensualbaires.com
*Legal defense organization for LGBT. LBGT
library/archives*

Escrita en el Cuerpo: Archivo y   **EA** ♀
**Biblioteca de Lesbianas, Mujeres Bisexuales
y Diferentes [Written on the Body: Lesbian,
Bisexual & Different Women's Archives &
Library]**
Perú 1330, 4to.
Buenos Aires
tel: (54 1) 361 36 43 or 863 91 90; fax: (54 1) 382
90 95
e-mail: ales@wamani.apc.org
*Grupos de apoyo para mujeres bisexuales,
producción y distribución de material escrito
sobre bisexualidad. [Support groups for bi
women, produces & distributes written material
on bisexuality.] Coordinates the Working Group
on Bisexuality for ILGA Latin America.*

Local

Grupo Bi   ▼ ♀
c/Escrita en el Cuerpo
Guardia Vieja 4329, 7mo H
Buenos Aires
tel: (54 1) 361 36 43; fax: (54 1) 382 90 95
e-mail: ales@wamani.apc.org
*Support group for bisexual & questioning
women. Meets every 2nd Saturday at 5 p.m. at
Peru 1330, 4to.*

Key to symbols: ▼ = bi   ♀ = women   ♂ = men   ☪ = religious/spiritual
🌢 = for allies   **M** = for married bis   ♥ = for partners of bis   **Y** = youth   **C** = people of color

Asociación Travestis Argentinas
c/o Escrita en el Cuerpo
Peru 1330 4 to.
Buenos Aires
tel: (54)1-361-36-49; fax: (54)1-382-90-95
*Grupo de personas transgenero que incluye
algunas abiertamente identificadas como
bisexuales. [Transgendered group, includes some
bi-identified people.]*

Centro Cristiano de la Comunidad LGTTB 🌀
Bernardo de Irigoyen 118, 1ero. 3
Buenos Aires
tel: (54 1) 585 6772
*Religious group, includes bi people in all its
activities & literature.*

Centro Cristiano Ecumenico de la 🌀
**Comunidad Lésbica, Gay, Bisexual y
Transgénero**
Maipu 484,
2do. (galeria)
Buenos Aires
tel: 54-1-585-67-72
*Grupo de apoyo con orientación religiosa, en la
linea de la Iglesia de la Comunidad
Metropolitana. [Support group with religious
orientation, like the Metropolitan Community
Church.]*

Gay, Lesbian, Bisexual, Transvestite & E🖼
Transexual Library
Parana 157, F (1070)
Buenos Aires
tel: 54 1 373 89 55; fax: 54 1 373 89 55
e-mail: cha@nat.com.ar
Specializes in gay/bi men materials.

Grupo Nexo E
Callao 339 4to.
Buenos Aires
tel: (54 1) 375 0366; fax: same
e-mail: nx@netline.com.ar
*Gay & lesbian group, very bi-friendly. Several bi
people are working in different cultural activities
inside this group. The newly founded Network of
GLB Psychologists can be cocntacted through
this group.* **Publication(s)***: NX The only
mainstream GLTB magazine in Argentina.
Covers bi issues in a very positive way.*

Lesbian & Bisexual Mothers Support Group ♀
Peru 1330, 4to
Buenos Aires
tel: (54 1) 361 36 43
*Support group for lesbian, bisexual & question-
ing mothers meeting every Saturday from 6-8
p.m. in Lesbianas & Escrita en el Cuerpo's
premises.*

Como las Iguanas ♀
Bolivar 553, 4to. B (5000)
Córdoba
tel: (54 51) 56 43 10
e-mail: sga@net.com.ar
*Grupo para lesbianas, mujeres bisexuales &
transgénero. LBTgroup, the 1st of its kind in
their city (& in the whole country). Includes bi
women & bi FTMs. Offers support groups, street
theater & educational activities (lectures at the
university).*

Colectivo Arco Iris HA
Pasco 994
Rosario, Santa Fe
tel: 54-41-814977; fax: 54/41-841977
e-mail: colectivoarcoiris@arnet.com.ar
*Three main areas of focus: sexuality, AIDS, &
Human Rights. Within these areas, provides
medical & legal assistance, health education/
consulting, psychological help, sex education,
hotline, social/support groups (including AA,
allies, LBGT groups, HIV, Christian), political
action groups. Also runs radio station,
publication, & Queer Studies Institute.*
Publication(s)*: INFOCAI bulletin*

"Desire...is less like a heart,
throbbing the same everywhere, and
more like music, and every culture
has its own—not only songs, but
tonality, instruments, and occasions."

—*Esther Newton (in "Yams, Grinders & Gays,"*
Out/Look, *Spring 1988)*

🌀 = school   ᗌ = college/university   **P** = professional   **E** = educational
A = activist/political   **H** = health (incl. HIV)   🖼 = media/press   ⌨ = Internet resource
The Bisexual Resource Guide 2000   **113**

AUSTRALIA

Australian Bisexual Network ▼A🖳
PO Box 490
Lutwyche, Brisbane QLD 4030
tel: +61-7-38572500; tollfree: 800-653223
e-mail: ausbinet@rainbow.net.au
URL: www.rainbow.net.au/~ausbinet/
*National network of bi men, women,
transgenders, partners, regional bi & bi-friendly
organisations & services, based in Brisbane,
providing information, some support, sexual
health education, policy, advocacy, political
action, meetings, social events, Bi Camp,
national conferences & outreach to bi & bi-
curious people/groups in the Asia-Pacific &
Indian Ocean Regions. ICQ: 16442611. IRC:
#BiNET on the Australian IRC servers-
mpx.sydney.oz.org; aussie.sydney.oz.org.*
Publication(s): *National Biways Magazine Bi-
monthly, news, events, personals. Membership/
subscription: individual/couple: $20/pa;
concessional: $15, under 21: $10; groups/svcs:
$25; overseas: $30.*

Australian Bisexual Network - ▼Y
Australian Bisexual Youth Forum
PO Box 490
Lutwyche, Brisbane QLD 4030
tel: (07) 3857 2500 or toll-free from anywhere in
Australia: 1800-653223
e-mail: ausbinet@rainbow.net.au
*The youth arm of ABN for young people under
27. Provides link-up & network for young
bisexual guys & girls, a forum for discussion of
issues, support & social activities.*

Australian Bisexual Women's ♀🖳▼
Homepage
URL: bi.org/~ozbiwomen/
Resources for Australian bi women.

#BifemPerth ▼♀🖳
*Found on IRC in some of these servers:
mpx.sydney.oz.org,
aussie.sydney.oz.org, ussr.perth.oz.org.*

#bisexual ▼🖳
*Found on the Australian IRC servers:
mpx.sydney.oz.au; aussie.sydney.oz.org.*

OZBI ▼🖳
e-mail: ozbi-owner@queer.org.au
*E-mailing list for Australian bisexuals &
friends. To subscribe, send a message to
<majordomo@queer.org.au> with the following
command in the body of the message: "Subscribe
ozbi".*

AusGBLF 🖳
e-mail: ausgblf-owner@queer.org.au
*Australian glb people & friends. While the list
has an Australian focus, overseas visitors are
welcome here. For more information about the
list, send e-mail to majordomo@queer.org.au
with only "info ausgblf" in the body of the
message*

Australian Lesbian & Gay Archives
PO Box 124
Parkville VIC 3052
Preserving the LGB history of Australia.

Australian Queer Resources Directory 🖳
queer.org.au Inc.
P.O. Box 815
Broadway NSW 2008
e-mail: ausqrd@queer.org.au
URL: ausqrd.queer.org.au/qrd
*An online library of resources for the Australian
GLBT & otherwise queer communities. It
contains news clippings, papers, articles, books/
films/plays/etc. reviews, event announcements,
resource lists, & more.*

Digital Queers Australia 🖳A
P.O. Box 1106
Darlinghurst NSW 2010
tel: 04 1117 0363
e-mail: digiqueers@queer.org.au
URL: dqa.queer.org.au
*DQA is the Digital Queers Australia announce-
ments list - Regular meetings, special events,
fundraisers, & worker bees. You will also receive
progress reports on projects & news of decisions
made at regular meetings. For more information
about the list, send e-mail to
majordomo@queer.org.au with only "info dqa" in
the body of the message.*

First Step Y♂E
GPO Box 229
Canberra ACT 2601
*6 week development course for gay/bi men under
26.*

Kinship (Australia) ☻
P.O. Box 364
Parramatta NSW 2124
tel: 800-4GAY SDA
For practicing & ex-Seventh Day Adventists.

Maybe Baby 🖳
P.O. Box 9
Darlinghurst NSW 2010
tel: 018 652 951; fax: (02) 9380 5848
e-mail: maybebaby@pinkboard.com.edu
URL: www.pinkboard.com.au/~maybebaby
*For GLBT contemplating parenthood - organizes
workshops.*

Key to symbols: ▼ = bi ♀ = women ♂ = men ☻ = religious/spiritual
🖳 = for allies M = for married bis ♥ = for partners of bis Y = youth C = people of color

Oz-Spouse Support Mailing List ♥▼▯

e-mail: oz-spouse-owner@queer.net.au
An E-mail list offering for Australian straight spouses of LBGT people. For info only, send email to <majordomo@queer.org.au> with message in the body: "info ozspouse-support". To subscribe, send a message to <majordomo@queer.org.au> with the following command in the body of the message: "Subscribe oz-spouse"

OZChat ▯

e-mail: ozchat-owner@queer.org.au
OzChat is a response to the growing need to move the lighter & more social traffic from the AusGBLF mailing list, which was intended to cater to more for information & resource sharing & serious discussion. For info, send e-mail to majordomo@queer.org.au with only "info ozchat" in the body of the message.

Pen Search ▯

P.O. Box 1103
Eastwood NSW 2122
e-mail: stevensp@tpgi.com.au
URL: www.geocities.com/WestHollywood/Heights/8149
Australian branch of international queer pen pal organization.

Queer.org.au Monthly Mailing List ▯

URL: www.queer.org.au/info/listinfo.html
Monthly mailing list information, also includes various subscription information & other news & info in DigiQueerland, Australia. To establish a mailing list contact the lists administrator at: listdude@queer.org.au.

University of Sydney: &⁄EA▯
Queer Collaborations

c/o Gay & Lesbian Officers
Sydney University SRC
Level 1, Wentworth Building
Sydney NSW 2006
tel: 02-9660-5222
02-9330-1155; fax: 02-9330-1157
URL: www.queer.org.au/qc/
Organizes annual national queer student conferences.

Women Partners of Bisexual Men ♥ ♀
Support Project

send mail to: WPBMSP
PO Box 350
Darlinghurst 2010
tel: Sara: (02) 9206 2026
(07) 3857 2500

Australian Capital Territory

Stepping Out Y ♀ E

GPO Box 229
Canberra ACT 2601
tel: 02/6257-2855; fax: 02/6257-4838
e-mail: aidsact@tpgi.com.au
6 week development course for lesbian & bi women aged 26 & under.

Local

Australian National University: &⁄
Sexuality Department

c/o Sexuality Officers, Students' Association
GPO Box 229
Canberra ACT 2601
tel: 02/6257-2855; fax: 02/6257-4838
e-mail: aidsact@tpgi.com.au
LGB group set up & funded by Student Union on campus.

MAGNet ♂

GPO Box 229
Canberra ACT 2601
tel: 02-6257 2855; fax: 02-6257 4838
e-mail: aidsact@tpgi.com.au
Mature-aged gay & bi men's group, mtgs in Acton.

The Australian National University: &⁄▯
Jellybabies

c/Clubs & Societies, Students' Association
The Australian National University
Canberra ACT 0200
tel: 02/6279-9277
e-mail: jellybabies@student.anu.edu.au
URL: student.anu.edu.au/Clubs/Jellybabies
Campus LGB group.

New South Wales

Cross-Campus Sexuality Network &⁄A

CI- Students' Union
PO Box 10
Kingswood NSW 2747
tel: 04/1463-1030; fax: 02/4736-0676
e-mail: ccsn98@hotmail.com
Umbrella group for university/college queer groups in NSW & ACT.

New England G & L Services, Inc.

PO Box W103
West Armidale NSW 2350
tel: 02/6771-1032 or
800/066-615; fax: 02/6771-1032
e-mail: negals@mpx.com.au
For GLBT in country NSW.

✎ = school &⁄ = college/university P = professional E = educational
A = activist/political H = health (incl. HIV) ✍ = media/press ▯ = Internet resource
The Bisexual Resource Guide 2000 **115**

PRIDE   **EA**⬛
P.O. Box 7
Darlinghurst NSW 2007
tel: (02) 9331 1333; fax: (02) 9331 1333
e-mail: pride@rainbow.net.au
URL: cybersyd.rainbow.net.au/pride
*Provides venue, support & other services for
groups, individuals in Sydney's GLBT
community.*

Local

Sydney Bisexual Network   ▼⬛
PO Box 281
Broadway NSW 2007
tel: 02-9565-4281 (Message w/info about current
activities)
e-mail: sbn@bi.org (Human, general info);
sbn-owner@queer.org.au (Human, newsgroup
info)
URL: bi.org/~sbn

Bi & Partners Social Club   ▼
P.O.Box 2030
Gosford NSW 2250
tel: 02-4323 9064
e-mail: statboa@exarch.com.au

Sydney Bisexual Youth   **Y▼E**⬛
PO Box 7
Darlinghurst
Sydney NSW 2010
tel: 015 677 016 (Sam [men]);
04 1466 4888 (Glenn [women])
e-mail: sby@queer.org.au
URL: www.queer.org.au/~sby
*Part of Australian Bisexual Youth Alliance
(ABYA), a network linking young bisexual people
throughout Australia.*

Guys Like Us   ♂⬛
NSW
tel: 02/6645-3863
e-mail: glu@hotmail.com
URL: www.bri.net.au/~sean/glu/
*Social group for gay, bi, & curious guys under
30, meets monthly at both MacLean & Grafton
on north coast of NSW.*

Young Guys Together   **Y**♂⬛
NSW
tel: 02/9515-3236
e-mail: bigayguy@rainbow.net.au
URL: bigayguy.rainbow.net.au/
Bi/gay/curious males aged 18-25.

Hume Phoenix Inc.   **A**
The Secretary
P.O. Box 1155
Albury NSW 2640

Asians & Friends Sydney   **C**♂
PO Box 238
Darlinghurst NSW 2010
tel: 02-9543-7980
Gay & bi Asian men & friends. Meets Fridays.

Silk Road   ♂**C**
P.O. Box 350
Darlinghurst NSW 2010
tel: (02) 9206 2000
Gay & bisexual Asian men.

Newcastle Gay Friendship Network
P.O. Box 1081
Newcastle NSW 2300
tel: (02) 4929 3464; fax: (02) 4929 4469

Macquarie University: Queer Bits
Macquarie Univ. Student's Council
PO Box 96
North Ryde NSW 2113
tel: Tim Davis: 02-9805-7629

Fun & Esteem West   **Y**♂⬛
c/o ACON Western Sydney
P.O. Box 45
Parramatta NSW 2145
tel: (02) 9204 2405 (Antony - Wed. or Thurs.)
e-mail: aconwest@acon.org.au
URL: www.rainbow.net.au/~aconwest/
For GBQ males under the age of 26.

Wayward
PO Box 4092
Parramatta NSW 2124
tel: Roger Levi: 0417-03-493 (mobile)
e-mail: rlevi@mail.usyd.edu.au
*Social support society of Western Sydney for lgbt
community in Western Suburbs of Sydney.*

West Guys Youth   ♂**HY**
Parramatta NSW
tel: Michael 02-9832-7717
Anthony 04-1241-4414
e-mail: westguys@one.net.au
*Community based support group for gay,
bisexual & questioning guys 26 & younger. Meets
2nd & 4th Tuesdays 7:30-9:30pm in the Old
Council Building, 2 Civic Place, room #3. Also
hosts a variety of workshops.*

> "The limitations of language,
> the existing terms, do not
> encompass the enormity and
> explosiveness of my sexuality....
> My sexuality is
> bigger than words."
>
> —*Sunfrog, in* Bisexual Politics

Key to symbols: ▼ = bi   ♀ = women   ♂ = men   ☽ = religious/spiritual
☙ = for allies   **M** = for married bis   ♥ = for partners of bis   **Y** = youth   **C** = people of color

GAMMA NSW ♂ M 💻
197 Albion St.
Surrey Hills NSW 2010
tel: toll-free in NSW: 1800-804617 6pm - 10pm
weeknights or
02/9207-2800
e-mail: gamma@queer.org.au
URL: gamma.queer.org.au/
*Information & support for gay or bi men who are
or have been married. Weeting on 1st & 3rd
Wednesdays at Gay&Lesbian Counselling
Service, address above.*

Gay & Bisexual Peer Support ♂
Sydney NSW
tel: (049) 29 3464

Sydney University: GLOSS/FLOSS 🎓 ♂ ♀ 💻
Lower Ground Floor
Holme Building
Sydney NSW 2006
tel: 02-9660-5222
e-mail: gloss@queer.org.au; floss@queer.org.au
URL: gloss.queer.org.au/; floss.queer.org.au/
*GLOSS is Sydney University's social & support
group for non-heterosexually identified guys.
FLOSS is Sydney Uni's social/support group for
non-hetero women.*

The BiFem Social Group ▼ ♀ 💻
Sydney NSW
e-mail: peace@one.net.au
URL: web.one.net.au/~peace/
*For bisexual women. Some social event welcome
partners &/or their children*

University of Technology: 🎓 **EA**
Bisexuals/Gays/Lesbians (BIGLUTS)
c/o Sexuality Officers, Student Assoc.
PO Box 123, Broadway
Sydney NSW 2007
tel: 9514-1155;
Nicole: 02-9330-1155
*Group for lgb & other queer students. Meets
Fridays 6pm, Common Area, Level 2, Bon
March Bldg.*

University of Wollongong: Alliance of 🎓
Lesbian/Bisexual/Gay Students
c/o Henry W. Collier , Sr. Lecturer
Department of Account & Finance
Box 1144
Wollongong NSW 2500
tel: 042-214-012
e-mail: collier@uow.edu.au
For students & staff at the University.

Queensland

QLDQueer Mailing List 💻
QLD
e-mail: qldqueer-owner@queer.org.au
*Email list for Queensland LBGT & friends. To
subscribe, send email to
<majordomo@queer.org.au> with following
command in the body of the message: subscribe
qldqueer
To unsubscribe, send email to same with
message:
unsubscribe qldqueer. Questions, email list
owner at address above.*

Queensland Association for Gay & **A** 💻
Lesbian Rights
QLD
e-mail: QAGLR@queer.org.au
URL: www.queer.org.au/~dazee/QAGLR/
Lobbying, activism, meetings, internet.

Local

Townsville Bisexual Network ▼
PO Box 1169
Townsville QL
tel: Julie: 014-971 582; Bruce 0417-748 658
*Social group for bi people & partners. Restau-
rants, drinks, movies, parties, friends, bbqs &
other events. Mts. 1st Wednesdays at Sovereign
Hotel Beer Garden, Flinders Street West,
Townsville.*

Bar Bi ▼
Fortitude Valley, Brisbane QLD
*Bar nights for bisexuals & friends held at The
Rat & Parrot Hotel, corner Constance & Ann
Streets on 2nd Sat. & 4th Wed. each month from
8-12 pm. Check with ABN for latest details at
07/3857-2550 or ausbinet@rainbow.net.au.*

Metropolitan Community Church 🕯
Rainbow Community Center
719A Stanley Street
Wooloongabba
Brisbane QLD
tel: 07/3891-2164; fax: 07/3891-2134
e-mail: mccbris@pronet.net.au
*A Christian Church with special outreach to
LGBT community. Service at 10am & 7pm Sun.
at above address.*

Queensland Institute of Technology: 🎓
Freedom Avengers
Brisbane QLD
tel: Student Guild Help Desk (07) 3684 1666
*Social group for glbt students & supporters at
the Uni.*

🔖 = school 🎓 = college/university   **P** = professional   **E** = educational
A = activist/political   **H** = health (incl. HIV)   📰 = media/press   💻 = Internet resource
The Bisexual Resource Guide 2000   *117*

Wayne Bryant

University of Queensland: ✍
Queer Sexuality Collective
Student Union
c/o Queer Tribes, Clubs & Societies
St. Lucia, Brisbane QLD 4072
tel: +61-7365-2200 x308
07-3365-2220; fax: +61-7365-2220
e-mail: yal@lingua.cltr.uq.oz.au
*Social support group for glbt HIV+ & queer
friendly students. All welcome at the Rona
Room, Student Union Building, St. Lucia
Campus. Meets Tues. & Thurs. 1pm in the Rona
Room, in the Union Complex.*

South Australia

St. Albans Anglican Church ☯
Auchenflower, Brisbane QLD
tel: 07/3870-2566
*All members of the LGBT communities welcome.
Holy Communion Sun. at 9:30am followed by
fellowship & snacks. St. Albans, corner of Milton
Road & Winholt Street.*

Stonewall Riders
Brisbane QLD
tel: Matthew 07/3847-4246
*LBGT cycling group organizing bicycle rides of
various levels as well as providing social
activities. The group is inclusive & anyone
wanting to organize & lead a ride is most
welcome. Rides start/finish at a convenient
location, include a stop for coffee. A helmet is
compulsory for all rides, a medical kit is always
on hand. Bring water & sunscreen.*

Rainbow Community Centre 🖳
Association, Inc.
PO Box 1078
Fortitude Valley Queensland 4006
e-mail: Rainbow.Centre@queer.org.au
URL: Rainbow.queer.org.au/
*LBGT Community Centre offering offices,
meeting rooms, resources, drop-in & forums for
community groups, services, & individuals.
Individual & organisation memberships
available. Open for general use: 3-6pm W, Th,
Fr, 7:30-10pm first Fridays. Street address:
Upstairs, 719A Stanley Street, Woolloongabba
(next to SE Freeway, look for Rainbow flag).*

**INQBLOT (Ipswich Network of Queers, Bi-
sexuals, Lesbians or Transgenderists)**
PO Box 817
Ipswich QL 4305
Monthly social support group for Ipswich area.

Bi The Way E-Mail List ▼🖳
Adelaide SA
e-mail: btw-owner@queer.org.au
*For Adelaide & other South Australian bisexuals
& friends. To subscribe, send email to
<majordomo@queer.org.au> with message in
body: subscribe btw. To unsubscribe, send email
to same with message: unsubscribe btw. For info,
contact list owner at above email address.*

Local

Adelaide Bisexual Support Group ▼
Adelaide SA
tel: Gillian: 08-8395-0318
e-mail: Gillian - gevans@dove.net.au or Jason -
merlin@box.net.au
*Social events & meetings for bisexual & bi-
friendly people.*

Bi The Way: Adelaide's Bi Community ▼🖳
Adelaide SA
e-mail: merlin@box.net.au
URL: www.box.net.au/~merlin/newsletter.html
*Home page of Adelaide's bi community, includes
exhaustive list of Adelaide's LBGT resources.*

Adelaide Spokes 🖳
Adelaide SA
tel: Llew: (08) 83620594 or Sue or Jo: (08)
82612268
e-mail: llew@merlin.net.au
URL: arthur.merlin.net.au/~llew/spoker
*For LGBs - regular weekend & midweek bike
rides around Adelaide & longer rides in the
country & interstate.*

Key to symbols: ▼ = bi   ♀ = women   ♂ = men   ☯ = religious/spiritual
☙ = for allies   **M** = for married bis   ♥ = for partners of bis   **Y** = youth   **C** = people of color
118   **The Bisexual Resource Guide 2000**

Adelaide University Pride   Ⓑ
c/o The Clubs Association
University of Adelaide
North Terrace
Adelaide SA 5005
tel: (08) 8303 3410
Group for non-heterosexual University students, staff & friends.

Flinders University: OUT   Ⓑ
Adelaide SA
tel: via Clubs & Societies: (08) 82012276
LGB group for students. Meets fortnightly at noon Fridays during semester.

Second Story Youth Health Centre   **YH**
PO Box 3232 Rundel Mall
Adelaide SA 5000
tel: City office: 08-8232-0233 or Elizabeth office: 08- 8255-3477 M-F 9-5.
LGB Youth Center located at 57 Hyde Street. Health & esteem education programs & support groups for people under 26.

Shangri La   ♂**C**
Adelaide SA
tel: For info or a chat: Phillip, David or Dean at 2nd Story: (08) 82320233
Social support group for young Asians who are gay or bisexual or just attracted to guys. Asian guys meet on last Saturdays 2-4:30pm & Asians & friends afterwards.

Gay & Lesbian Counselling Service of SA Library
PO Box 2011
Kenttown SA 5071
tel: (08) 8362 3223 or 1800 182 233; fax: (08) 83631046
Information for LGBT people.

BAMH (Bisexual & Married Homosexual   ♂
Men's Support Group)
c/ AIDS Council of SA
Kent Town SA 5071
Norwood SA 5067
tel: AIDS Council of SA: (08) 83621611
Meets Wednesday afternoons monthly & Thursday nights weekly.

Tasmania

Tasmanian Bisexual Support Network   ▼🖥
Tasmania
e-mail: teddles@access.net.au
URL: www.powerup.com.au/~daltoff/bi

Victoria

Australian Bisexual Men's   ▼♂**HM**♥**E**🖥
Association - GAMMA Project
The Franklin Centre
402 Elgar Rd
Box Hill VIC 3128
tel: 039-8901068; GAMMA-line: 03-98990509 or 1800-807-660 (free call w/in VIC only)
e-mail: gpnews@vicnet.net.au
URL: www.vicnet.net.au
Resource, education & counselling service for bisexual & married gay men & their partners & health care professionals working with bi men. ABMA operates the GAMMA Project & GAMMA-line info & safe sex counselling line for bi & married gay men in Victoria.

JOY-FM   📻🖥
PO Box 907
South Melbourne VIC 3206
tel: +61 3 969 00 907; fax: +61 3 9699 2646
e-mail: admin@joy.org.au
URL: joy.org.au
Melbourne G&L/Queer Radio Station. Studio & office location: 268A Coventry St.

VicQueer Mailing List   🖥
VIC
e-mail: vicqueer-owner@queer.org.au
*To subscribe, send email to <majordomo@queer.org.au> with message in body: subscribe vicqueer. To unsubscribe, send email to same with message: unsubscribe vicqueer
For info, contact list owner at above email address.*

Local

Bi & Partners Social Club Geelong   ▼♥🖥
P.O.Box 338
Drysdale VIC 3222
tel: 03/52533103
URL: www.geocities.com/WestHollywood/Village/5188/
Meeting Info: every 3rd Tues 7-9 pm at Bethany Family Services Building, Gibb Street, North Geelong

Melbourne Bisexual Network
PO Box 38 Clifton Hill
Melbourne VIC 3068
tel: Catherine (03) 95214128
e-mail: miheyla@hotmail.com
For bisexual people & their friends in Melbourne. Includes bi women's discussion group.

🐌 = school   Ⓑ = college/university   **P** = professional   **E** = educational
A = activist/political   **H** = health (incl. HIV)   📻 = media/press   🖥 = Internet resource
The Bisexual Resource Guide 2000   **119**

Melbourne Bisexual Youth (MBY) Y▼
c/o 3/13 Arkle St
Prahran VIC 3181
tel: contact: Catherine (03)9521-4128 or Hana
(03)95721352
e-mail: catherinel@union.unimelb.edu.au or
m.venn@pgrad.unimelb.edu.au
URL: www.geocities.com/WestHollywood/Village/
9202/
*Social, support group for bi & curious youth in
Melbourne. To subscribe to the MBY list, send e-
mail to majordomo@queer.org.au with
"subscribe mby" in the body of the mail.*

Frankline Centre: ▼M♥HE♂⬛
GAMMA Project
(Australian Bisexual Men's Association)
PO Box 223
Monte Albert
Victoria 3127
tel: 03/9890-1068
GAMMA: 03/9899-0509
e-mail: gpnews@vicnet.net.au
URL: www.vicnet.net.au
*Provides information, counselling & support for
bisexual & married gay & bisexual men & their
partners. Training workshops for health &
community professionals, volunteer.s*

Latrobe University: Bi-Friendly Group, ⚭
& Gay, Lesbian & Bisexual Society
c/o SRC
Bundoora VIC 3083
tel: Queer Officers: 03-94792976
e-mail: woodhouse@LATCS2.LAT.oz.au
*Safe & comfy space to discuss bi & related
issues. Non-bi members welcome.*

Hamilton District Alternative Connections ♂
PO Box 366
Hamilton VIC 3300
tel: (03) 55712349
Discreet social/ support club for gay & bi men.

Partners & Families of Gay, Lesbian & ♥♠
Bisexual People
c/o 831 High St. Road, Glen Waverly or
PO Box 571 Endeavor Hills
Kew VIC 3150
tel: Linda: (03) 9700-7190 or A/H - Nan- (03) 9802-
8523, nancy (03) 9867 7828
*Offers information & support to partners &
families of LGB people.*

GAMMA-Line M♂H
Melbourne VIC
tel: (03) 9899-0509 or 1800-807-660 (free call w/in
VIC only)
*Confidential counseling & AIDS information
service for married G/B men.*

Melbourne University: Pride Collective ⚭
Melbourne VIC
tel: Queer Officers: (03)993448159

Gippsland Gay People's Support Group
PO Box 848
Morwell VIC 3840
*GLB support & social group. Meets 1st
Tuesdays.*

Swinburne University of Technology: Gay, ⚭
Lesbian & Bisexual Support Network
c/o Student Union
Swinburne VIC
tel: Student Union: 03-9214-4440
Student group.

Warrnambool Gay Group
PO Box 1059
Warrnambool VIC 3280
Social group for LGBs. Meets 3rd Tuesdays 8pm.

Western Australia

West Australian Bisexual Network ▼
PO Box 1167
Canning Vale WA 6155
tel: Graham or Ian: 08-9354 2737
*Counselling & referrals for people coming to
terms with their sexuality. Social role passed to
Australian Bisexual Network.*

Gay & Lesbian Counselling Service (GLCS) EH
79 Stirling Street
Perth W.A. 6000
tel: (08) 9328 9044; fax: (08) 9328 1345
*Provides support services to LBGT people, rural
people, isolated people, youth, married people.
Telephones staffed Mon. - Fri. 7:30 - 10:30 pm.
Contact point for Breakaway (men under 26),
26up (men over 26), Groovy girls (women under
30). Holds courses & has shared accomodation
register.*

Western Australian AIDS Council EH♂
PO Box 1510
West Perth WA 6872
tel: (08) 9429 9900
e-mail: waac@highway1.com.au
*WAAC runs a number of services for gay & bi
identifying men to do with the issues of male to
male sex. They also run a phone line for nongay
identified men who have sex with men.*

Key to symbols: ▼ = bi   ♀ = women   ♂ = men   ☯ = religious/spiritual
♠ = for allies   **M** = for married bis   ♥ = for partners of bis   **Y** = youth   **C** = people of color
120   **The Bisexual Resource Guide 2000**

Local

BiWim ♀▼
PO Box 8369
Perth Business Centre
WA 6849
fax: (08) 9227 1835
e-mail: photogal@highway1.com.au
Social support group for bi women, women who might be bi, or women who want to know more about bisexuality. Regular meetings.

Bisexual Meeting House ♂▼
Perth W.A.
tel: Sundays only, Keith 08/9368-2575
Drop-in centre for bi men providing sexual & social contact, info. & group support.

Curtin University of Technology: Curtin ⬤⌒
Gay Lesbian & Alternative Sexuality Society
c/ Student Guild
Kent Street
Bentley WA 6102
tel: 08-9266-3385
Meets Fri. 12-2pm during termtime.

Southwest Friends ♂
PO Box 235
Bunbury WA 6231
tel: Laurie: (08) 9791 1734 after 6pm.
Social support group for gay, bi & unsure guys.

Gay/Bisexual Fathers' Support Group ♂
PO Box 1564
Canningvale WA 6155
tel: 0416-041-759
Meets fortnightly Mondays at the Carlisle Hotel.

University of Western Australia: ⬤⌒E
Wilde Alliance & Sexuality Information Department
Box 85, Guild of Undergraduates
Stirling Highway
Crawley WA 6009
tel: termtime: (08) 9380 3902; fax: (08) 9380 1041
e-mail: sid@gu.uwa.edu.au
Wilde Alliance is a student/staff LGB group. SID is a UWA Student Guild department dealing w/all issues of sexuality. Includes education, referrals, social networking, awareness & visibility campaigns, publications, community events. **Publication(s)**: *Little Boxes Monthly newsletter, typically one A4 sheet, including events & general department/club info.*

Edith Cowan University: ⬤⌒H
Amendment 23
c/o ECU Student Guild
2 Bradford Street
Mt. Lawley WA
tel: (08) 9370 6821; fax: (08) 9370 6823
e-mail: a23@amendment23.ml.org
Campus LGBT group. Has meeting room & runs social functions & awareness campaigns.

Murdoch University: Y⬤⌒
Gay & Lesbian Society (MUGLes)
Box 406
Student Guild, South Street
Murdoch WA 6150
tel: (08) 9360 6592 during term time
A safe place on campus that is open to all. Open lunch times M-Th.

Perth Outdoors Group
PO Box 47
Northbridge WA 6865
tel: (08) 9354 2737
Organizes both indoor & outdoor activities including car rallies, weekends away, walks, cable skiing, etc.

Enigma ♥
Perth WA
tel: (08) 9446 5092
Support for the spouses of bi people.

Freedom Centre Y
PO Box 1510
West Perth WA 6872
tel: (08) 9228 0354
A space for young glbt & questioning people to meet, chat, hang out & access information in a friendly environment. Contact point for Club 1526, a group of young glbt people raising awareness in the community. Open Wednesday, Friday & Saturday 3-10 pm. Street address: 134 Prisbane Street, Northbridge, Perth.

BELARUS

Belarus League for Freedom of Gays, A
Lesbians & Bisexuals — Belarus Lambda League
send mail to: BLL
PO Box 23
BY-220006
Minsk
Activist group seeking contact with foreign activists.

✎ = school   ⬤⌒ = college/university   P = professional   E = educational
A = activist/political   H = health (incl. HIV)   ✍ = media/press   🖳 = Internet resource
The Bisexual Resource Guide 2000   121

BELGIUM

Belgian Gay Motorcycle Club 'De Knalpijp'
Vlaanderenstraat 22
9000 Gent
tel: +32-(0)9-2216056
+32-(0)95-185124; fax: +32-(0)9-2226252
e-mail: d.factory@innet.be

Federatie Werkgroepen   **PEA**🖳
Homoseksualiteit
Vlaanderenstraat 22
9000 Gent
tel: +32-(0)9-2236929; fax: +32-(0)9-2235821
e-mail: fwh@innet.be
URL: www.club.innet.be/fwh/
*An umbrella-organization for Flemish societies
for glbs. that operates in the areas of emancipation & interest on three levels: 1) trying to get
their demands realized through political &
social actions; 2) supporting regional centers &
thematical groups with various information
packets; 3) personal information & service
through the publication of ZiZo, the telephone-
service & text-service on TV, also available on
the internet via http://www.vrt.be/tt2/
tt.asp?page=527 & http://www.vrt.be/tt2/
tt.asp?page=528. **Publication(s)**: ZiZo The
bimonthly magazine for lgbs in Flanders.
Informs about the movement, politics, culture &
society, the pink lifestyle & it is not without
humour & erotics. Independant editorial team. A
year's subscription costs Bfr 550. Sent under
plain cover, to receive it in a closed envelope, the
dues are Bfr 950. To subscribe, deposit the
correct amount into bank account 068-2159688-
10 of ZiZo & note the address where you want to
receive it.*

HoLeBifoon
tel: +32-(0)9-2382626
*Informational phone line for LesBiGays. They
listen to your story & redirect to other organizations if necessary.*

"Temporality becomes an
important issue in reading
bisexuality, especially since most
readers distinguish the sexual
orientation of characters in
novels based upon the desires or
relationships at the end of a
text—rather than looking at the
fluctuations and variations of
desire throughout the novel."

—*Marcy Jane Knopf, in "Bi-nary Bi-sexuality in*
Re-presenting Bi-Sexualities, *p. 157.*

Local

De Roze Drempel   🖳
P.O. Box 113
3000 Leuven 3
tel: +32-(0)16-200606
e-mail: drempel@ping.be
URL: www.ping.be/drempel/
*De Roze Drempel started as the 'Leuvense
Studenten Werkgroep Homofilie' in 1969. They
celebrated their 5th lustrum in 1994 & are thus
one of the longest existing organizations in the
lesbigay world. Having started as a small group
for university students, the group has grown into
a society for students, non-students, youth,
adults from Leuven & sometimes wide
surroundings. Meets every Thurs. from 21.00h to
01.00h in Masereelclub, Ierse Predikherenstraat
25 in Leuven.* **Publication(s)**: *De Roze Drempel
NieuwsBrief Monthly newsletter that keeps you
posted about what the group does, their activities
& gives you insight in things happening in
Flanders & the rest of the world.
For Bft 250 or Bfr 150 if you're under 26yo, you
can become a member of 'De Roze Drempel' &
receive the newsletter. Membership also entitles
you to discounts on activities. To join, deposit the
right amount to bank account 001-1697483-59 &
mention 'membership' & 'open' or 'closed'
(according to the kind of envelope they need to
send the newsletter in).*

Holebi Diest   **Y**🖳
Begijnenstraat 1a
3290 Diest
tel: +32-(0)13-313505
e-mail: holebi.diest@skynet.be
URL: surf.to/holebi/
*GLB workgroup of 'Jeugdhuis Tijl'. If you're lg
or b in the Diest area, this is the place to meet
others like you. Meets every Tues. from 20.00h to
0.00h.* **Publication(s)**: *Nieuwsbrief Subscription to the Holebi Diest newsletter is free. To
subscribe, send an e-mail with your mailing
address. Electronic subscriptions in plain text or
Word-file are available.*

Dubbeldekker   ▼ ♥ 🖳
Lombaardstraat 20
3500 Hasselt
tel: +32-(0)11-212020; fax: +32-(0)11-210054
e-mail: lach@tornado.be
URL: www.tornado.be/~lach/
*Mixed bi-group, mainly men. Meets every 1st
Thurs. of the month at 20.00h in a room over
Café Hemelrijk, Hemelrijk 11 in Hasselt.*

Key to symbols: ▼ = bi   ♀ = women   ♂ = men   ☯ = religious/spiritual
🖐 = for allies   **M** = for married bis   ♥ = for partners of bis   **Y** = youth   **C** = people of color
122   **The Bisexual Resource Guide 2000**

Nota Bene Y
P.O. Box 137
3500 Hasselt
e-mail: nota.bene@freemail.nl
*Meetings every 1st & 3rd Fri. at
'Ontmoetingscentrum Katarina', N.
Cleynaertslaan z/n in Hasselt. The meetings
start at 20.00h.*

Universitaire Campus, Diepenbeek:
We Are Gay
Gebouw D
3590 Diepenbeek
tel: +32-(0)11-268109; fax: +32-(0)11-268199
e-mail: wag@luc.ac.be
URL: www.luc.ac.be/~wag/
*LGB student organization . WAG wants to make
clear to students that being gay or bisexual is not
a problem. Focus on supporting students who are
still fighting with their being gay or bi. Call for
meeting info.*

Verkeerd Geparkeerd YE🖳
P.O. Box 535
9000 Gent
e-mail: VeGe@student.rug.ac.be
URL: student.rug.ac.be/VeGe/
*Verkeerd Geparkeerd organizes various activities
in Gent, participates in national meetings &
sometimes has weekend trips or camps. Meets
about 3 times a month during university year,
less often during vacations & exam-periods.
Some meetings are thematic (coming out, safer
sex), others are social. Under the name
'Scholenwerking' they do education on schools
about homosexuality & bisexuality.*
Publication(s): *VG-Verslag VG-Verslag is
published 8 times a year & informs members of
when & where activities take place.*

Bi Werking
Wel Jong Niet Hetero
("Young: yes, Straight: no way")
PB 323
9000 Gent 1
e-mail: wjnh@ping.be
URL: www.ping.be/wjnh
*Bi group of Wel Jong, Niet Hetero (WJNH),
which is an umbrella-organization for lesbigay
youthgroups in Flanders. They define youth as
people under 26. Groups belonging to WJNH
offer a meeting place for youngsters to meet
people their own age who understand them
because they share similar experiences. You get
to meet other lesbigay youngsters & it doesn't
matter if you are having a hard time being
lesbigay or would like to make a billboard telling
everyone. To find out about the various groups &
activities, please call, write or e-mail.*

BRAZIL

Atoba
Rua Prof. Carvalho de Melo 471
Magalhaes Bastos Rio de Janeiro CEp 21735-11
RJ
tel: (55)21-322-0787; fax: (55)21-331-15-27
e-mail: atobamehomos@ax.ibase.org.br
atoba@ax.apc.org
*Grupo gay/lésbico, abierto a personas
bisexuales. [GL group open to bis.] Hosts of the
2nd International Lesbian Bisexual & Gay
Cultural Conference June 22-28th 1998.*

Grupo Gay da Bahia
Caixa Postal 2552
40.020
Salvador Bahia
tel: 071-243-4902; fax: 071-322-3782
e-mail: iuizmott@ufba.br

Quimbanda-DuDu: Grupo Gay C
Negro da Bahia
Rua do Sodré, 45
Salvador Bahia
tel: 071-243-4902; fax: 072-433-4782
e-mail: iuizmott@ufba.br

GLB: Grupo de Lesbianas de la Bahia ♀HEA
Caixa Postal 6430 - 40.000-000
Rua Frei Vicente 24
Pelourinho
Salvador Bahia
tel: 55/071-322.2552; 321.1848; 384.6080
e-mail: janepantel@e-net.com.br
*Work in HIV/AIDS prevention, women's rights,
lesbian visibility. Publishes bimonthly newsletter
for the Brazilian lesbian community.*

BULGARIA

Local

Orchidea 2000
PO Box N 3
Panagiurishte 4500
tel: 00359/3573289; fax: 00359/3573289
e-mail: glav@pan.trakianet.bg

Flamingo Agency
Angel Bliznatchki
POB 63
Sofia 1680
tel: +359 799 74647; fax: +359 799 74647
e-mail: flamingo@mobikom.com
Organization for LGBT people.

✎ = school   🎓 = college/university   P = professional   E = educational
A = activist/political   H = health (incl. HIV)   📰 = media/press   🖳 = Internet resource
The Bisexual Resource Guide 2000   **123**

Roberta Gregory

CANADA

EGALE-L 🖥A
e-mail: egale@egale.ca
URL: www.egale.ca/feedback/mailist.htm#egale-l
*Announcements & news from the EGALE
organization & discussions about issues of
interest to LGB Canadians. E-mail or visit web
site for more info. Bilingual (French/English)
site includes membership form, archives
including back issues of their newsletter, a
breakdown of Canadian queer rights progress by
province & a list of employers providing benefits
for same-sex partners.*

Equality for Gays & Lesbians Everywhere A🖥
Suite 306, 177 Nepean Street
Ottawa ON K1N 6E2
tel: 613-230-1043; fax: 613-237-6651
URL: www.egale.ca
*National organization committed to advance-
ment of equality & justice for LGBs in Canada.
Info available in English & French. EGALE
library, text library, newsletters, related web
links & membership info are on-line.*

"Never be bullied into silence.
Never allow yourself to be made
a victim. Accept no one's
definition of your life, but define
yourself."

—*Harvey Fierstein*

LAMBDA Organization E🖥
P,O. Box 52068
Garneau Postal Outlet
Edmonton AB T6G 2T5
tel: 403-439-2616; fax: 403-434-1069
e-mail: lambda@compusmart.ab.ca
URL: gpu.srv.ualberta.ca/~cbidwell/cmb/
lambda.htm
*Encompasses LAMBDA Institute of Gay &
Lesbian Studies, which is funded by the
LAMBDA Educational Research Foundation.*

National Union of Jewish Lesbian, Gay, 🕭
Bisexual & Transgender Students
e-mail: bcherkasov@hillewl.org
See listing under USA, national.

The Canadian Gay, Lesbian & Bisexual 🖥
Resource Directory
Winnipeg MB N8C 1C7
tel: 204-488-1805 or 1-800-CGLBRD-4U (245-
2734)
URL: www.cglbrd.com
Listings of LGB groups throughout Canada.

WAYVES: The Atlantic Canadian Lesbian, 🖾
Gay, Bisexual, & Transgendered Newspaper
P.O. Box 34090
Scotia Square
Halifax NS B3J 3S1
tel: 902-827-1680, advertising;
902-826-7356, circulation
e-mail: wayves@fox.nstn.ca
*Wayves exists to inform Atlantic Canadian
LGBT people of activities in their communities,
to promote those activities & to support their
aims & objectives. An independent publication
by a non-profit collective.* **Publication(s):**
*Wayves Published 10 times per year/monthly.
Free of charge at various locations throughout
Nova Scotia.*

Lesbian, Gay, Bisexual, Transsexual & 🖥
Transgender Pride of Toronto
50 Charles Street East
P.O. Box 371, Station F
Toronto M4Y 2l8
tel: 416-92-PRIDE; fax: 416-927-7886
e-mail: pride97@gaypride.org
URL: www.torontopride.com

Alberta

Times 10 🖾EA🖥
1021-124 Street
Edmonton AB T5N 1P5
tel: 403-425-5407; fax: 403-488-6927
URL: www.times10.org
Edmonton's LGB magazine. **Publication(s):**
Times 10

Key to symbols: ▼ = bi ♀ = women ♂ = men 🕭 = religious/spiritual
♦ = for allies **M** = for married bis ♥ = for partners of bis **Y** = youth **C** = people of color
124 **The Bisexual Resource Guide 2000**

Local

Biversity ▼♀M♥
c/o Calgary Birth Control (CBC)
Suite 304, 301-14 St NW
Calgary AB T2N 2A1
tel: 403-203-5580
Monthly support group, some social activities.
Only for city of Calgary. Open to all sexual
orientations.

Gay Lines Calgary E
201-223 12th Ave SW
Calgary AB T2R OG3
tel: 403-234-8973
Info line, drop in, rap sessions.

Prime Timers ♂
1093-11444 119th St.
Edmonton AB T5G 2X6
tel: 403-426-7019 (Peter)
e-mail: mercury@planet.eon.net
Monthly meetings for G/B men over 40, meets
2nd Sundays at 3pm.

University of Alberta: Outreach ᴧE
Box 75
Student Union Bldg
University of Alberta
Edmonton AB T6G 2J7
tel: 403-988-4166
Meetings Mondays 7pm. For students & staff of
the University.

Queer North Gay & Lesbian Community
Association
Box 1492
Grand Prairie AB T8V 4Z3
tel: 403-539-3325
e-mail: spake@telusplanet.net
NW Alberta & NE British Columbia. Open
Closet Drop In.

Gay & Lesbian Alliance of Lethbridge
Lethbridge AB
tel: 403-329-4666
Peer support line, M, W 7-10pm. Open meetings
every 6 weeks. Coffee nights Thursdays 8-10 at
Carole's Bistro.

University of Lethbridge: Queers & Allies ᴧE
Club
Student Clubs
Lethbridge AB T1K 3M4

Gay & Lesbian Assoc. of Central Alberta
(GALACA)
Bx 1078
Red Deer AB T4N 6S5
tel: 403-340-2198

British Columbia

BiNetBC ▼EA🖳
(Bisexual Network of British Columbia)
P.O. Box 53515
984 West Broadway
Vancouver BC V5Z 1K0
tel: 604-875-6336
e-mail: binetbc@hotmail.com
URL: bi.org/~binetbc
The umbrella group for BiFace Support Group
(1st & 3rd Tues 7:30-9:30pm); Options
Friendship Group (meets at a local cafe 2nd &
4th Fri after 9pm); BiCycle (activity group meets
last Sun every month); & the BiLine (#above, an
info & counseling line). **Publication(s)**: *The*
Fence Post Newsletter Newsletter is also online
at website.

Victoria Pride Society A
BC
tel: PrideLine: 250-360-2393
e-mail: pride@avi.org
For Victoria's GLBT communities. Organizers of
Pride Day.

Local

Simon Fraser University: ᴧA🖳
Out On Campus
c/o SFSS
Burnaby BC V5A 1S6
tel: 604-291-5933; info line: 604-688-WEST, ext.
2064; fax: 604-291-5843 (c/o SFSS)
e-mail: out-on-campus@sfu.ca (local
announcements); out-on-campus-info@sfu.ca
(coordinators)
URL: www.sfu.ca/out-on-campus
LGBT collective of Simon Fraser University.

Douglas College: ᴧ
Lesbian, Gay & Bisexual Collective
c/o Student Society
PO Box 2503
New Westminster BC V3L 532
tel: 604-527-5111 or 604-327-5335 x4550
To support people, do community outreach,
provide a safe area.

Lesbian Gay Bi Youth Y
Vancouver BC
tel: 604-688-9378 x2102

Queer FM ◤EAᴧ🖳
CITR Radio 101.9 FM
University of British Columbia
Vancouver BC
tel: Request line: 604-822-2487
e-mail: queerfm@portal.ca
URL: www.lesbigay.com/queerfm
Variety show for glbt people. Sundays 6-8pm.

✎ = school	ᴧ = college/university	P = professional	E = educational
A = activist/political	H = health (incl. HIV)	◤ = media/press	🖳 = Internet resource

University of British Columbia: ⚲↗
Gays, Lesbians & Bisexuals of UBC
c/o Student Union Building
2075 Wesbrook Mall
Vancouver BC V6T 1Z1
tel: 604-290-9778

Vancouver Community College: ⚲↗
Lesbian, Gay & Bisexual Student Association
Student Union Building
1155 East Broadwy
Vancouver BC V5N 5V1
tel: 604-871-7171

University of Victoria: ⚲↗
Lesbian, Gay, Bisexual Alliance Centre
P.O. Box 3035
Victoria BC V8W 3P3
tel: 250-472-4393

Victoria Youth Pride Society Y🖳
c/o UVic LGBA Centre
SUB B118
Victoria BC V8W 3P3
tel: 250-472-4393
e-mail: lgba@finearts.uvic.ca
URL: kafka.uvic.ca/~lgba/
Social & support group for people 14-22 who are or think they might be glbt, 2 spirited, or questioning, & their supporters. Meets Wednesdays 7:30pm at Fairfield Community Place (just east of Moss).

Manitoba

Swerve ✍🏻
200-63 Albert Street
Winnipeg MB R3B 1G4
tel: 204-942-4599; fax: 204-947-0554
Winnipeg's LBG paper.

Local

University of Manitoba: GLASS (Gay & ⚲↗
Lesbian Associate of Students & Staff)
312 University Centre
Winnipeg MB R3T 2N2
tel: 204-474-7439
204-474-6516 (student center)
GLASS is the U of M campus connection to the LGB community of Manitoba. Provides referral services, social organization, speakers & films. Involved in community activities, peer support & small resource library.

University of Winnipeg: LGB Collective ⚲↗
UWSA General Office
RM 2624 Lockhart Hall
513 Portage Ave
Winnipeg MB R3B 2E9
tel: 204-786-9025
Sponsors several visibility events including: The HOmo Hop, Day Without Hate, & Pink Triangle Week. Info & educational opportunities about issues relating to homo/bisexuality & homophobia. There is a LGB Resource Center, which is a safe space /lounge/drop in centre.

Winnipeg Gay/Les/Bi Youth Group Y🖳
c/o Winnipeg Gay/Lesbian Resource Center
PO Box 1661
Winnipeg MB R3C 2Z6
tel: Rex: 244-4526
e-mail: wlgbyouthgroup@geocities.com
URL: www.geocities.com/capitolhill/4174
Social & support group for those under 25. Meets Thurs 7:30pm.

Winnipeg Gay/Lesbian Resource Center E🖳
#I-222 Osborne St. South
Box 1661
Winnipeg MB R3L 1Z3
tel: 204-284-5208
URL: www.uwinnipeg.ca/campus/uwsa/
lesgaybi.htm
Info line, library, legal clinic, fracophone group.

New Brunswick

Local

Northern Lambda Nord
NB
Serving people in northern Maine & northern & western New Brunswick. See complete listings, including mailing address, under "USA: Maine."

Gais.es Nor Gays Inc. (GNG)
PO Box 983
Bathurst NB E2A 4H8
tel: 506-783-7440 (Fri. 8-10pm)
Bilingual LGBT group. Holds dances, suppers & other events in northeast NB. Phone for upcoming events. Holds annual camping/ dancing/fun Labour Day weekend. Runs the only LGBT centre in Atlantic area, at the Complexe Madisco, 702 Main St, office 30, Petit-Rocher. Drop by Fri. 8-10pm. Bilingual newsletter.

FLAG (Fredericton Lesbians & Gays)
Station A
Fredericton NB E3B 5G2
tel: 506-457-2156
Socials/meetings 2nd Wed of each month, 7pm.

Key to symbols: ▼ = bi ♀ = women ♂ = men ☙ = religious/spiritual
◊ = for allies **M** = for married bis ♥ = for partners of bis **Y** = youth **C** = people of color
126 **The Bisexual Resource Guide 2000**

Fruit Cocktail: CHSR 97.9 FM   🖳
Fredericton NB
tel: 506-453-4985 off air
506-453-4979 on air; fax: 506-453-4958
e-mail: u5mc@unb.ca
URL: www.unb.ca/web/gala
*Mon 7-8PM radio show syndicated worldwide,
lesbigay news & issues, lesbigay & gay-positive
music artists.*

New Hope Metropolitan Community Church ☙
c/o Unitarian Fellowship Hall
749 Charlotte Street
Fredericton NB E3B 1M6
tel: 506-455-4622 or 465-4MCC or leave message
at FLAG LINE 506-457-2156
*Services Sun. 7pm. All welcome, regardless of
sexual orientation. Pastor is Rev. J.J. Lyons,
B.I.D.M.Div.*

PFLAG - Fredericton   ☙🖳
PO Box 1556
Station A
Fredericton NB E3B 5G2
tel: Francis 506-454-8349
e-mail: b84q@jupiter.csd.unb.ca
URL: www.unb.ca/web/P-FLAG/
*Meets 3rd Sun. 2pm in room 19E1 or Alumni
Memorial Building on UNB campus. Not related
to FLAG or FFLAG.*

University of New Brunswick: Ꮗᐤ🖳
GALA (UNB/STU Gay & Lesbian Alliance)
UNB Student Help Center
PO Box 4400
Fredericton NB E3B 5A3
tel: 506-453-4955; fax: 506-453-4958
e-mail: v0c5@unb.ca
URL: www.unb.ca/web/gala/katie/gala.html
*LGBT group providing healthy, supportive
atmosphere to come out & to meet others.
Promotes gay positive attitudes on campus.
Meets Fri. 7pm room 19E1 of the Alumni
Memorial Bldg. for speakers, videos, desserts,
discussions, etc. Last Fri., coming out group
meets for support in Room 19E1. Wheelchair
accessible except washrooms.*

Mount Allison University: Catalyst   ᏇᐤE
c/o Kris Trotter
Sackville NB E0A 3CO
tel: 506-364-2357; fax: 506-364-2216
*Provides support for LGBT students &
information about LGBT issues for members &
the university community. Organizes a yearly
public forum on LGBT issues & occasional
social activities. Meets weekly. Every second
meeting open to the public; the remainder are
closed support meetings for LGBT students.
Contact Kris Trotter for meeting info. School
term only.*

PFLAG - Moncton   ☙
Box 249
Sackville NB E0A 3C0
tel: Eldon Hay 506-536-0599; fax: 506-364-2617
e-mail: ERHay@MTA.ca (Eldon Hay)
*Meets 3rd Mon. 7:30-9:30, Room 339, Taillon
Bldg, Universite de Moncton.*

Reach Out
PO Box 6861
Saint John NB E2L 4S3
tel: 506-642-6969 (Reach Out phone line) or 506-642-1957
e-mail: z1fe@unbsj.ca (number 1, not the letter L)
*Social group for Saint John area LGB & their
families. Video nights, family-oriented activities
& other events, some of which are non-smoking
or non-alcoholic. Phone line provides info. on
upcoming AIDS Saint John & LGBT events.*

Newfoundland

Newfoundland Gays & Lesbians   AE🖳
for Equality (NGALE)
P.O. Box 6221
St. John's NF A1C 6J9
tel: 709-753-4297 (753-GAYS); fax: 709-579-0559
e-mail: ngale@geocities.com
URL: www.geocities.com/WestHollywood/4291
*Community-based, non-profit volunteer
organization dedicated to providing support,
education & advocacy to & for gays, lesbians,
bisexuals & other sexual minorities in NF. Meets
in boardrom at AIDS Committee (above
address).*

Local

**Lesbian/Gay/Bisexual/Questioning
Support & Information Line**
NF
tel: 709-753-4297 (753-GAYS)
*Live consultation from trained volunteers 7-
10pm Tues. & Thurs. Message system & pre-
recorded info. available at other times. We do not
subscribe to Call Display or Caller ID.*

**BGLAS : Bisexual, Gay &
Lesbian Association for Support**
Box 20002
Corner Brook NF A2H 6J5
tel: 709-634-1066

Memorial University: Ꮗᐤ🖳
**LGBT-MUN (Lesbians, Bisexuals, Gays &
Transgenders at Memorial University**
St. John's NF A1C 5S7
tel: 709-754-5896
e-mail: lbgtmun@plato.ucs.mun.ca
URL: www.ucs.mun.ca/~lbgtmun

🌢 = school   Ꮗᐤ = college/university   **P** = professional   **E** = educational
A = activist/political   **H** = health (incl. HIV)   ⧳ = media/press   🖳 = Internet resource
The Bisexual Resource Guide 2000   **127**

Robyn Ochs

PFLAG - St. John's &
PO Box 6221
St. John's NF A1C 6J9
tel: 709-753-4297
e-mail: ngale@geocities.com

Nova Scotia

Homosexualist Agenda **EA**
RR#1
Scotsburn NS B0K 1R0
tel: Joyce: 902-485-8202
e-mail: hugmor@north.nsis.com
*Goals are to promote freedom & equality for
Nova Scotia's LGBT & two-spirited population,
confront homophobia & mean-spirited attacks,
public education campaign aimed at destroying
stereotypes. Future plans include providing
support & outreach for members of local Pictou
County queer community, forming links with
other groups also fighting for civil rights &
participating in the political process to advance
the cause of queer liberation.*

JUKA; Nova Scotia Black Gay, **CHE**
Lesbian & Bisexual Association
c/o AIDS Coalition of Nova Scotia
#600-5675 Spring Garden Road
Halifax NS B3J 1H1
tel: 902-454-5882: Les Gray or 902-429-7922: Val
Jackson; fax: 902-422-6200
*Monthly social events include pool, coffee & other
events. Also provides peer counseling, community workshops, open houses, newsletter articles
& support for those infected, affected or
concerned with AIDS. "JUKA" is an African
term that means "Rise up. Stand up."*

Men's Sex Project, ♂**EH**
c/o AIDS Coalition N.S. (Nova Scotia)
Ned MacInnis
5675 Spring Garden Rd.
6th Floor
Halifax NS B3J 1H1
tel: 902-425-4882; fax: 902-422-6200
e-mail: acns@kayhay.com
*HIV/AIDS prevention, education & support
project for gay & bisexual men in Nova Scotia.*

Nova Scotia Rainbow Action Project **A**
(NSRAP)
c/o Wayves
RPO Box 34090
Scotia Square
Halifax NS B3J 3S1
tel: 902-453-3953, or 902-429-7091, or 902-351-
2714
*Meets once every 3 months. The mandate of the
group is to foster change in our communities &
society so that people of all sexual orientations
are valued & included through community
development, networking, & political action.*

OUTline **YH**
c/o Planned Parenthood, Nova Scotia
6156 Quinpool Road, Suite 100
Halifax NS B3L 1A3
tel: 1-800-566-2437;902-492-0444; fax: 902/492-
7155
e-mail: am253@ccn.cs.dal.ca
*Toll-free support line for LGBT youth in Nova
Scotia; sponsored by the Lesbian, Gay &
Bisexual Youth Project, Planned Parenthood
Nova Scotia & the AIDS Coalition of Nova
Scotia. 25 years old & under staffed by peer
volunteers 25 years old & under Saturdays 5:30-
9:30pm.*

Planned Parenthood Nova Scotia **EH**
6156 Quinpool Road, Suite 100
Halifax NS B3L 1A3
tel: 902-492-0444
e-mail: ppns@istar.ca
*Open 9am-4pm, Mon.-Fri. Sexuality informa-
tion, resource library on sexuality issues, videos,
books pamphlets, government reports, LGBT
Youth Project resources & workshops on
sexuality issues.*

Key to symbols: ▼ = bi ♀ = women ♂ = men ☯ = religious/spiritual
& = for allies **M** = for married bis ♥ = for partners of bis **Y** = youth **C** = people of color
128 **The Bisexual Resource Guide 2000**

Local

PFLAG-Amherst   ♿
183 East Victoria St.
Amherst NS B4H 1Y7
tel: Dr. Maida Follini 902-667-1608; Murial
Goodwin 902-546-2344
e-mail: ERHay@MTA.ca (Eldon Hay)
Meets monthly, 3rd Thurs., 12 LaPlance Street,
Amherst.
Also, PFLAG-Annapolis Valley (Contact Roger
Bouthillier 902-679-2292, outreach@atcon.com).

Dalhousie University: Bisexual, Gay &   🎓
Lesbian Association of Dalhousie (BGLAD)
Student Union Building, Rm. 320
6136 University Av.
Halifax NS B3H 4J2
tel: 902-494-6662 (c/o NSPIRG)
e-mail: bglad@is2.dal.ca
A social & support group for LGB university
students. Meetings held in Student Union Bldg.
on Monday evenings, room 316.

Gay, Lesbian & Bisexual Youth Group at   Y
Queen Elizabeth High School
1929 Robie Street
Halifax NS
tel: 902-421-6797
Contact J. Buffet, guidance counselor.

Human against Homophobia (HAH!)   EA🖳
c/o NSPIRG
6136 University Ave., Rm. 315
Halifax NS B3H 4J2
tel: 902-494-6662; fax: 902-494-6662
e-mail: nspirg@is2.dal.ca
URL: chebucto.ns.ca/CommunitySupport/NSPIRG
BLG & straight persons working to dispel sexual
myths & stereotypes in Halifax. HAH! functions
as a collective & focuses on education &
awareness while promoting a multiplicity of
expressions & realities.

Lesbian, Gay & Bisexual Youth Project   YAE🖳
c/o Planned Parenthood, Nova Scotia
6156 Quinpool Road
Suite 100
Halifax NS B3L 1A3
tel: 902-492-0444; fax: 902/492-7155
e-mail: ppns@istar.ca
URL: ccn.cs.dal.ca/communitySupport/LGBYP/
lgbyp.html
Offers two social, support & educational groups
for lgb youth 25 years & under; conducts
educational workshops for groups & schools;
provides support, resources, & advocacy for
individuals & youth workers. Resource library.

Lesbian Outdoor Club   ♀ 🎓
send mail to: Drawer LOC
Wayves
Box 34090
Scotia Square
Halifax NS B3J 1S1
tel: 902-466-7644: Joan
Bi-positive organization.

Lesbians & Children Together   ♀
Halifax NS
tel: 902-469-5764: Lena
e-mail: 73654.2033@CompuServe.com
Social gatherings for lesbians (& supporters)
with children; meets about once a month for
parents & children to meet other lesbian
families. Bi-positive organization.

Maritime School of Social Work: 🎓APE
Lesbian, Gay & Bisexual Caucus
c/o Rusty Neal
6414 Coburg Road
Halifax NS B3H 2A7
tel: 902-494-1193; fax: 902-494-6709
e-mail: rusty.neal@dal.ca
Acts as a social & support network for social
work students, advocates for curriculum,
practice & policy changes in social work. Some
caucus members are also available to conduct
workshops on homophobia & heterosexism for
groups & schools. Caucus meets regularly &
holds social events.

PFLAG   ♿EA
Halifax NS
tel: 902-479-1856 (Done or Sylvia) or 902-443-
3747 (Ron)
e-mail: ab247@chebucto.ns.ca
Bi-positive & inclusive.

Queer News   📰🎓
c/o CKDU
6136 University Avenue
4th Floor
Halifax NS B3H 4J2
tel: 902-494-6479; fax: 902-494-1110
e-mail: ckdufm@is2.dal.ca
Interviews & news from GLBT communities,
locally & internationally. Currently airs
Wednesdays from 12:05pm to 12:30 pm (subject
to change) on CKDU FM97.5.

♿ = school   🎓 = college/university   P = professional   E = educational
A = activist/political   H = health (incl. HIV)   📰 = media/press   🖳 = Internet resource
The Bisexual Resource Guide 2000   **129**

St. Mary's University: 🖐
St. Mary's Campus Outreach Society
Room 516 (5th Floor)
Student Union Building
St. Mary's University
Halifax NS B3H 3C3
tel: 902-496-8717
e-mail: K_melans@squid.stmarys.ca (Ken
Melanson) or outreach@bass.stmarys.ca
Provides a safe environment for GLB students to interact & discuss ideas important to them & shows them that they are not alone. Call for meeting schedule & location.

Red Door Adolescent Health Center **YEH**
28 Webster Court
Kentville NS B4N 1H7
tel: Tim: 902-679-1411
Information & resources; support on all aspects of sexuality. Youth group meets Tues. 4pm.

Cape Breton MsM Group **E♂**
AIDS Coalition of Cape Breton c/o Jean MaQueen
106 Townsend St. Suite 10
Sydney NS B1P 6H1
tel: 902/567-1766
A support, educational & social group for gay, bi & non-gay/bi identified men who have sex with men.

Acadia University: Outlet 🖐
Wolfville NS B0P 1X0
tel: 902-542-2200 ext 2142
e-mail: 012100b@axe.acadiau.ca (Steven Benedict)
Acadia University's LGBT group.

Ontario

Ontario Bisexual Network ▼
519 Church Street.
Toronto ON M4Y 2C9
tel: 416-925-XTRA x2049
e-mail: steve@bi.org
Looking to create a true sense of bisexual community within Ontario. Member groups include: BEST (Windsor), Bisexual Women of Toronto, Bisexual & Lesbian Women of York Region, Toronto Bisexual Network, BiVerse (Peterborough), Bytown Bis (Ottawa), Ottawa Bi Women's Discussion Group.

Coalition for Lesbian & Gay Rights in Ontario **A**
Box 822, Station A
Toronto ON M5W 1G3
tel: 416-533-6824 or
416-925-XTRA x2037
Works toward feminism/LGB liberation. Meets 1st/3rd Wednesday of month, 6-8pm at the 519 Church St. Community Center.

Lesbian Gay Bi Youth Line of Ontario **Y🖳**
PO Box 62, Station F
Toronto ON M4Y 2L4
tel: 800-268-YOUTH; 416-962-YOUTH; fax: 416/
962-7967. TDD on all lines
e-mail: LGBLine@icomm.ca
URL: www.icomm.ca/lgbline
Peer support/information to LGBT youth in Ontario. Sun-Fri, 4-9:30pm.

Local

Toronto Bisexual Network ▼A
519 Church Street.
Toronto ON M4Y 2C9
tel: 416-925-9872 x2015; fax:
e-mail: steve@bi.org
For bisexual women, men, their families, friends & lovers. Support, socials, activism & discussion. Meets 3rd Thurs. 8pm at 519 Church St. Community Center. Fully accessible.

London Bisexual Network ▼
London ON
tel: 519-433-3762
e-mail: LBN_halo@hotmail.com
Support, discussion & networking group, open to all bi & bi-curious men & women. Meets at HALO (649 Colborne St. 2nd flor), 3rd Thurs. 8-10pm.

Ottawa Bi Women's Discussion Group ♀▼
c/o Pink Triangle Services
71 Bank Street, 2nd Floor
Ottawa ON
tel: 613-237-9872 x 2117
e-mail: bp418@freenet.carleton.ca
Meets 3rd Fridays at above address.

Bisexual Women of Toronto ▼♀AE
c/ OBN
519 Church Street
Toronto ON M4Y 2C9
tel: 416-925-9872 x2198
e-mail: kmtaves@yorku.ca
Support & social network for all bisexual women or women who are interested in bisexuality to discuss & listen to various perspectives on current bisexual issues. We are a diverse group of women from the gay & straight communities who try to foster inclusivity by welcoming & encouraging differences. Transsexual & transgendered women welcome. Meetings 1st Thursday at 8pm at the 419 Church St. Community Center.

BiTO ▼🖳
Toronto ON
A discussion group for the Toronto-area bisexual community. For info on how to join: http://www.egroups.com/list/bito.

Key to symbols: ▼ = bi ♀ = women ♂ = men ☯ = religious/spiritual
🖐 = for allies **M** = for married bis ♥ = for partners of bis **Y** = youth **C** = people of color
130 **The Bisexual Resource Guide 2000**

Healthier Sex Network for ▼H
Bisexual Men & Women
Toronto ON
tel: 416-925-9872 x 2139
e-mail: hsn2000@hotmail.com

Ottawa Bi-Poly Group ▼
Ottawa ON
e-mail: nataliep@impertinent.com
Meets last Sun. 6pm at Maxwell's Restaurant on Elgin St.

Gay, Lesbian & Bisexual Youth of Durham Y
Durham ON
tel: 905-665-0051

Humber College LGB Club 🎓💻
c/o SAC
205 Humber College Blvd.
Etobicoke ON M9W 5L7
tel: 416-675-6622x5051
e-mail: lgbclub@hcol.humberc.on.ca
URL: hcol.humberc.on.ca/html/lgbclub
A positive club for LGB students providing support & education on LGB issues to the college community & organize social events in which LGB students at Humber College can meet & network.

McMaster University: Gay, Lesbian 🎓📰💻
& Bisexual Association of McMaster
Box 313
Hamilton ON LBS 1CO
tel: 905-525-9140x27397
URL: www-msu.mcmaster.ca/services/glbam/glbam.htm
Social, support groups, including "A Different Voice" radio show & "10% Plus" newsletter.
Publication(s): *10% Plus*

RESPECT
276 Hunter Street, West
Hamilton ON L8P 1S3
tel: 905-521-1520
Rejuvenate, Excel, Survival, Purpose, Examination, Change, Triumph (RESPECT). A structured facilitated discussion group with a series of set discussion topics aimed at GLBT people. Meeting times: alternate Wednesdays, at Melrose United Church, 80 Homewood Ave.

Kingston Lesbian, Gay &
Bisexual Association
51 Queen's Crescent
Kingston ON K7L 3N6
tel: 613-531-8981

Queen's University: 🎓
Lesbian, Gay & Bisexual Issues Committee
c/o Education Commission Office
Kingston ON K7L 3N6
tel: 613-545-4816
e-mail: lgbic@www.ams.quensu.ca
URL: www.cglbrd.com
Responsible for raising awareness & educating on LGB issues on campus (& beyond).

Sisters in Strength ♀
51 Queen's Crescent
Kingston ON K7L 3N6
A non-judgemental, all womyn's group that tries to provide a safe space for womyn at all stages of discovering their sexuality. Mostly social, but attempts to provide all information needed or requested. A good entry point into the lesbian/bisexual womyn's community. Womyn only, usually youth, but all ages are welcome.

Out & About CKWR FM 98.7 📰
Kitchener/Waterloo ON
LGB entertainment, community info & newsmagazine show.

Positivity About Youth Sexual Orientation Y
c/o ACOL, 343 Richmond St.
London ON N6A 3C2
tel: David Brownstone: 519-434-1601
Meetings 8pm Fridays, 2nd fl., 343 Richmond St.

Rainbow Radio Network 📰
Unversity of Western Ontario
Rm. 255
UCC
London ON N6A 3K7
tel: 519-661-3601 business; 661-3600 on-air
CHRW, 94.7 FM, 10-midnight, Tuesdays.

University of Western Ontario:

▼**Gay, Lesbian & Bisexual** 🎓E
Student Affairs
UWO, Room 340 UCC
London ON N6A 3K7
tel: 519-661-3574; fax: 519-661-3816
Support group for GLB students.

▼**University of Western Ontario: uwOUT!** 🎓
Room 340 UCC
London ON N6A 3K7
tel: 519-432-3078

Coalition for Gay, Lesbian Y
& Bisexual Youth in Peel
c/o Peel Health Dept.
Mississanga ON
tel: 905-791-7800x7436-2; fax: 905-848-9176
e-mail: norm.blain@peelsb.com
Meets 3rd Tues. 4-6pm.

🎓 = school   🎓 = college/university   P = professional   E = educational
A = activist/political   H = health (incl. HIV)   📰 = media/press   💻 = Internet resource
The Bisexual Resource Guide 2000   *131*

Peel Pride: Gay, Lesbian   **YEA**
& Bisexual Youth in Peel
c/o Peel Health Dept.,
3038 Hurontario St., 3rd floor
Mississauga ON L5B 3B9
A coalition of Peel youth social agencies &
interested individuals who provide support,
education & advocacy on behalf of LGB youth.
Services include a drop-in centre (call 416-925-
9872 ext 2142).

GLIS - Gays, Lesbians in Support
Oakville ON
tel: 905-815-4040x3817
e-mail: jack.hellewell@sheridanc.on.ca
Social/support groups for GLB & our positive
friends. Meetings held weekly at the Trafalgar
Road Campus of Sheridan College in Oakville.

Al-Anon - Lesbian, Gay & Bisexual
Ottawa ON
tel: Information: 613-237-XTRA 2031
Meets Tuesdays 8pm at St. Pierre Community
Center
172 Gate St. Al-Anon: 12-Step self help group for
lesbians, gays & bisexuals affected by someone
else's drinking. All welcome. FMI about these &
other neighborhood groups, call the main office
(number above).

Association of Lesbians, Gays,   **A**
Transgendered & Bisexuals
PO Box 2919 Station D
318 Lisgar, 2nd Floor
Ottawa ON KIP 5W9
Home of many LGBT artistic & cultural events.
Publication(s): *Go Info*

Carleton College: Gay, Lesbian,   ⚥🖳
Bisexual & Transgendered Centre
c/o 401 Unicentre Bldg.
Ottawa ON K1S 5B6
tel: 613-520-3723; fax: 613-520-3704
URL: www.carleton.calglb

Pink Triangle Services   **E**
71 Bank Street, 2nd Floor
Ottawa ON
tel: 613-563-4818
Social services agency w/resources including
gayline, peer counseling, discussion groups,
lending library, speakers bureau. Meeting place
for the Ottawa Bi Women's Discussion Group.

Pink Triangle Youth   **Y🖳**
c/o Pink Triangle Services
71 Bank Street
Ottawa ON ONT K1P 6H6
tel: 613-563-4818
e-mail: pty@doubt.com
URL: www.gayottawa.net/PTY

Sex Addicts Anonymous (SAA)
PO Box 20477
Ottawa ON K1N 1A3
tel: 613-786-1060
Sex Addicts 12-Step self help group for LGBs
who require support to stop compulsive sex
behavior. All welcome.

University of Ottawa: ⚥A
Pride Centre/Centre de la Fierte
Box 22, Room 07
85 University Priv.
Ottawa/Hull ON K1N 6N5
tel: 613-562-5966; fax: 613-562-5969
e-mail: pride@aix2.uottawa.ca
Coming out & discussion groups, guest speakers,
political action, social events, poster campaign.

Rainbow Service Organization   🖳
Peterborough ON
tel: Paul Cummings: 705-876-1845
e-mail: rmccaugherty@trentu.ca
URL: www.geocities.com/WestHollywood/3131
Agency catering to needs of LGBs in counties of
Peterborough, Northumberland, Victoria &
Haliburton. Counseling & social events; monthly
dances.

Trent University: Trent Queer Collective   ⚥🖳
Peterborough ON
tel: 705-743-5414
e-mail: queer@trentu.ca
URL: www.trentu.ca/queer

Community Outreach Project
of Algoma (COPA)
Sault Ste. Marie ON
tel: 705-946-7006
For the lesbigay community of Sault Ste. Marie.
Free phone line, social, recreational & gay-
positive services.

Gay, Lesbian, Bisexual Youth Group   **Y**
203-211 Elm Street
Sudbury ON P3C 1T3
tel: 800-465-2437; 705-688-0500
Meets every Monday night. For youth 14-19
years old. Sponsored by AIDS Committee of
Sudbury.

Laurentian University: Pride Association   ⚥🖳
Sudbury ON
tel: 705-673-6506
e-mail: pridelu@geocities.com
URL: www.geocities.com/WestHollywood/3859
Meets monthly for students on campus.

Key to symbols: ▼ = bi   ♀ = women   ♂ = men   ☻ = religious/spiritual
🖐 = for allies   **M** = for married bis   ♥ = for partners of bis   **Y** = youth   **C** = people of color
132   **The Bisexual Resource Guide 2000**

Lakehead University: Pride Central   * ☐*
Lesbian, Gay & Bisexual Centre
c/o LUSU, 955 Oliver Road
Thunder Bay ON P7B 5E1
tel: Jen: 807-343-8813; fax: 807-343-8598
e-mail: bgllu@gale.lakeheadu.ca
URL: www.geocities.com/WestHollywood/3859
*Promotes safety on campus & broadens
awareness of LGB issues with the help of a paid
Centre coordinator. LGB library.*

519 Church Street Community Center
519 Church Street
Toronto ON M4Y 2C9
tel: 416-392-6874
*City-funded community center. M-F 9am-
10:30pm. Sat. noon-6pm. Sun. 10am-5pm.*

Coalition of Jewish Gay,   **Y** ☺
Lesbian & Bisexual Students
Toronto ON
tel: 416-925-XTRA x2114

Gay, Lesbian, Bi-Youth   **Y**
Support Group York Region
Toronto ON
tel: 416-925-XTRA x2249

Gays, Lesbians & Bisexuals
International (GLInt)
Toronto ON
tel: 416-925-XTRA x2187
*Support group for interested students, visible
minorities & people whose first language is not
English.*

LesBi Youth Peer Support (LYPS)   **Y** ♀ ☐
519 Church Street
Toronto ON M4Y 2C9
tel: 416-925-9872
URL: www.cglbrd.com/entries/889.html
*For l/b women under 26. Women of color over 26
who are exploring coming out issues are
welcome. Dances, coming out groups, films, peer
support, weekly groups,anti-racist workshops &
more.*

Lesbian, Gay, Bisexual Youth Line   **Y** ☐
PO Box 62
Station F
Toronto ON M4Y 2L4
tel: 416-925-YOUTH or toll free 800-268-YOUTH
e-mail: lgbline@iComm.ca
URL: www.icomm.ca/lgbline

Lesbian, Gay & Bisexual Youth of Toronto   **Y**
Toronto ON
tel: 416-925-XTRA x2880

Outspoken: **A**
Lesbian, Gay & Bi Media Watch Group
Toronto ON
tel: 416-925-XTRA x2212

Parkdale Gay, Lesbian & Bisexual Group
Toronto ON
tel: 416-925-XTRA x2012

Portuguese Lesbians, Gays & Bisexuals
Toronto ON
tel: 416-925-XTRA x2236

Scarborough College: Freedom Alliance   * ☐*
Toronto ON
tel: 416-925-XTRA x2105
e-mail: fafc_lgb@fissure.scar.utoronto.ca
URL: www.scar.utoronto.ca/~fafc_lgb

Toronto Poly Discussion Group   ▼☐
Toronto ON
e-mail: siobhan@interlog.com
*New group forming for socials, support &
discussion.*

University of Toronto: *&*
Rainbow Triangle Alumni Association
Toronto ON
tel: 416-925-XTRA x2238

BGLOW: Bisexual, Gay & Lesbian   **Y**
Organization of Woodstock
send mail to: BGLOW
377 Buller Street
Woodstock ON N4S 4M9
tel: 519-539-6121; 1-800-755-0394

Quebec

Local

Montreal Bi Association   ▼☐
Montreal QC
e-mail: canalbisex@anargo.qc.ca
URL: www.bisexuelle.qc.ca

Bishop's University: *&*
The Pink Triangle Association
Box 2133
Lennoxville QC J1M 1Z7
e-mail: Heather <co941454@ubishops.ca>
*"Our organization is open to everyone regardless
of sexual orientation. We are a support network
& social club for gays, lesbians, bisexuals, trans,
straight & queer students."*

✎ = school	*&* = college/university	**P** = professional	**E** = educational
A = activist/political	**H** = health (incl. HIV)	☎ = media/press	☐ = Internet resource

The Bisexual Resource Guide 2000   **133**

Concordia College: &⏚
Concordia Queer Collective
c/o C.S.U., suite 637
1455 de Maisoneuve Blvd.
Montreal QC H3G 1M8
tel: 514-848-7414; fax: 514-848-7450
e-mail: qcoll@alcor.concordia.ca
URL: alcor.concordia.ca/~qcoll/
Office: 2020 Mackay. For the queer community
on & off campus. Open to everyone. People
invited to drop the office by for a chat, coffee & to
help out in organizing events such as dances (on
campus & at clubs), wine & cheeses, inviting
guest speakers, movie showings, an annual art
show, & helping out around the office. General
CQC Meeting - Fridays at 5:30pm, 2030 Mackay.
Every other week, we plan to screen queer-related
films.

L'Universite de Montreal, HEC et &
Polytechnique: Le Triangle
B.P. 49511 C.P. du Musee,
5122 Cote-des-Neiges
Montreal QC H3T 2A7
tel: 514-389-1964
e-mail: lefebvpa@ere.umontreal.ca
Association etudiantes pour la protection des
droits des gaies, lesbiennes et bisexuels/les. Des
activites sont regulierement organisées (films,
discussion, sorties culturelles ou sportives).
[Student associatoin for the protection of glb
rights. Regular activities (films, discussions,
events].

McGill University: Lesbians, Bisexual, &⏚
Gays & Transgendered Students of McGill
University Centre, Room 429
3480 McTavish Street
Montréal QC H3A 1X9
tel: 514-398-6822; fax: 514-398-7490
e-mail: lbgtm@vub.mcgill.ca
URL: ssmu.mcgill.ca/lbgtm
LBGTM organizes social events, discussion
groups, & political responses for Undergraduate
& Graduate students of McGill University as
well as for members of the LBGT community of
Montreal. **Publication(s)**: *Queery Newsletter*
2x/yr.

Saathi (South Asian Gays, Lesbians ⏚
& Bisexuals of Montreal/Gais, Lesbiennes
et Bisexuels Sud-Asiatiques de Montreal)
Montreal QC
URL: www.total.net/~courage/saathi.html
Provides a safe space where South Asian Queers
may get together socially.

Groupe 14-17 YE
CISC
55 che. Ste-Foy
Quebec QC G1R 1S9
tel: 641-2572
Meets Wed. 7:15-9:30. Personal development.

Key to symbols: ▼ = bi ♀ = women ♂ = men ☻ = religious/spiritual
⚐ = for allies **M** = for married bis ♥ = for partners of bis **Y** = youth **C** = people of color

Groupe d'entraide 18-25 ans   Y
Quebec QC
tel: 418-641-0784 ext. 509
Groupe de support, d,entraide et de référence pour les jeunes agés de 18-25 ans se questionnant sur leur orientation sexuelle. L'objectif est d'offrir soutien et compréhension dans un climate sérieux, agréable et réconfortant. Support group for people between 18 & 25 years of age who have questions about their sexual orientation. Gives help in an atmosphere of sharing & mutual understanding.

Parents d'Enfants Gais   ♦
55 chemin Ste-Foy #202
Quebec QC G1R 1S9
tel: 418-641-2572
Meetings once a month, themes, guest speakers, for parents of gay kids. **Publication(s)**: *Groupe de soutien pour parents d'enfants gais Gives info about the themes chosen & guest speakers*

Saskatchewan

Perceptions
PO Box 8581
3rd Floor, 241-2 Ave. S.
Saskatoon SK S7K 6K7
tel: 306-244-1930; fax: 306-665-9976
e-mail: perceptions@the.link.ca
Publication(s): *Perceptions 8x/year. Free distribution. Subscriptions Can. $22/yr.*

Local

University of Saskatchewan: Gays &   &⌢
Lesbians at the University (GLUS)
PO Box 639
RPO University
Saskatoon SK S7N 4J8
tel: 306-652-6080
Support for faculty & staff at the University.

"For now I look you in the eye
and say
I will not be the skeleton in our
family closet
I will not be your homo or
heterosexual assumption
I will not be your scapegoat
I will not be controlled
I will not be contained
I will not betray my truth"

—*Lani Ka'ahumanu, from "That Naked Place"*

CHINA

bi You Yun
Beijing Hotline: 010-64266958. It's called an "AIDS hotline", but people know that it's about sexual minorities, too. It's actually a pager number, not a phone line. I was told that the volunteers received thousands of phone calls from all over China in the months after the number was publicized in a popular magazine, so the volunteers had a hard time finding enough funding to cover their returning calls. This number was established in 1997 or 1996, but until the summer of 1998 was only publicized by word of mouth within the community.

In Mainland China, although the visible glbt community has been developing for a few years, there have not been any formally-named groups until very recently, because forming non-governmental organizations is a very sensitive matter there. The first named lesbian group is Beijing Sister, established in October 1998, after the first national lesbian conference in China held on October 2 & 3, 1998. The gay male communities are a lot larger than the lesbian ones in terms of size & number of members, but, to my knowledge, there are also no self-named gay male groups within Mainland China to this day.

Bisexual identity seems to carry somewhat different meanings in China than in the West. To a large extent, the gay or lesbian community does not exclude bisexual people. The absence of the so-called "biphobia" which exists in the West seems obvious, although such an absence is apparently not complete. Indeed, because, in China, the general public still strongly disapproves of same-sex love, some bisexual people see their

✎ = school   &⌢ = college/university   P = professional   E = educational
A = activist/political   H = health (incl. HIV)   ☎ = media/press   ⌨ = Internet resource
The Bisexual Resource Guide 2000   **135**

being able to form heterosexual marriages as real advantage. Although not every bisexual person in China may think that way, it's extremely rare for bis to be accused by gays or lesbians for being "not brave enough to admit." Practically, the prevailing heterosexism puts all people who have same-sex romantic passion in the same boat.

In addition, the Chinese lgbt people (not only in Mainland China, but also in Hong Kong, Taiwan, & some other Asian countries) conceptualize their sexual identity now by a term "Tongzhi" (meaning "comrade." "Tong" meaning "homo", & the Chinese term homosexuality, "tongxinglian," also starts with the same character "tong"), in some sense similar to the English term "queer", but not totally equivalent. In the lgbt context, Tongzhi means people who are not traditionally heterosexual, therefore including gays, lesbians, bisexuals, transgenders & transsexuals, crossdressings, even S/M, even heterosexual people who are willing to accept sexual minorities. In other words, the Tongzhi community includes bisexual people.

Since the late 1980s, gay bars have appeared in almost all major cities in China, while there has not been a single lesbian-exclusively bar. Meanwhile, other alternative community-building means like discussion groups are also developing. For example, in the summer of 1998, a group of glbt people gathered in Lemon Tree Cafe in Beijing for discussion & began a monthly discussion gathering that welcomes anybody to attend. Some activists & scholars have also brought LGBT issues into the

discussion in other public settings like the Women's Tea House.

There are regular social gatherings for lgbt people in big cities like Beijing. However, most lgbt people in smaller cities or rural areas still live in tremendous isolation, let alone possible discrimination if one's identity is exposed. So community activists are trying to develop a broader communication network for LGBT people to reduce the isolation most of them have to face in their everyday lives.

As in most other parts of the world, the Internet has also been playing a very important role in connecting LGBT people in China. Here is an incomplete list of the major lgbt websites in China:

http://bbs.gzsums.edu.cn/~bbs/. Click "Eden Garden" then click "Homosexuality". There are quite a few serious gay novels & other good articles. Please note that this website is in mainland China & any erotic materials or radical articles in it may cause its shut-down! I suggest reading the articles while remaining silent, don't cause it to be focused on by security administration. (I quote this entire paragraph from somebody else who is on a Chinese lgbt e-mail list I'm also on.)

http://aizhi.sis.com.cn This site is the online version of the AIZHI newsletter, the oldest lgbt advocate newsletter in China started in 1994. This website started in the summer of 1998.

http://www.youmail.com.cn/cafe

http://www.youmail.com.cn/friends The newsletter "Friends" by dermatologist Dr. Beichuan Zhang, a more academic-oriented newsletter that not only discusses issues related to

Key to symbols: ▼ = bi ♀ = women ♂ = men ☸ = religious/spiritual
♠ = for allies M = for married bis ♥ = for partners of bis Y = youth C = people of color
136 The Bisexual Resource Guide 2000

homosexuality but also intends to bring people in sexual minorities & the so-called "mainstream" together.

http://www.zg169.net/~les This is a lesbian & bisexual women – female Tongzhi – website, established in last August 1998. It's pretty active now.

Besides those in Mainland China, there is a US-based website mainly devoted to the Tongzhi community in Mainland China & the LGBT in the US who are from Mainland China at **http://www.csssm.org**. The organization's name is "the Chinese Society for the Study of Sexual Minorities" (CSSSM), started in September 1997. (I'm one of the founders & current members). The CSSSM publishes a bilingual (Chinese & English), bi-weekly webzine "Tao Hong Men Tian Xia" (direct translation is "pink color all over the world," meaning "we lgbt people are anywhere").

"Lavender Phoenix" is another US-based group, "a network for lesbians & bisexual women in & from Mainland China," started in May 1997 by five lesbians & bisexual women from China in the US (I was one of them). It doesn't have a webpage yet, it has a few contact e-mail addresses: **lavender_phoenix@hotmail.com** & **lavenderphoenix@juno.com**.

COLOMBIA

Proyecto Lambda - Liga Colombiana de   **HA**
Lucha contra el SIDA [Colombian League for the Fight Against AIDS]
Ave. 32, No. 14-16
Bogotá
tel: 57 1 287 05 01; fax: 57 1 338 04 32
e-mail: ligasida@latino.net.co

Local

Comunidad del Discipulo Amado   ◉
Apdo Aereo 57280
Bogota
tel: 91-768-2100
Gay/bi support group with a religious orientation. Meets at a local church.

Equilateros   **EHA**
Apdo Aereo 25770
Bogota
tel: 91-768-2100
e-mail: velandia.sexosida@urc.net.co
Gay-bi group providing support, AIDS education, & activism.

Gados   🖳
Apdo Aereo 241889
Bogota
tel: 91-505-1222 (voicemail)
URL: www.prof.uniandes.edu.co/~gados/
Internet-based group with regular meetings in Bogota.

Gaeds
Apdo Aereo 76811
Bogota
tel: 91-500-9100
Lesbigay group.

RIT   **P**
Apdo Aereo 57724
Bogota
tel: 94-500-7927 (voicemail)
Gay/bi group that publishes gay information booklet & coordinates gay conferences, groups, etc. **Publication(s)***: Info G&L*

Grupo de Apoyo Paisa
Apdo Aereo 59188
Medellin
tel: 94-241-3021 (voicemail)
LGB support group, holds monthly meetings.

COSTA RICA

Colectivo Bisexual   ▼
send mail to: CB
Apartado #1476-2050
San Pedro de Montes de Oca
San José

"This is the new bisexual movement in a nutshell: hard fought, hard thought, and distinctly individual."

—John Leland, Newsweek 7/17/95

✎ = school   ✐ = college/university   **P** = professional   **E** = educational
A = activist/political   **H** = health (incl. HIV)   ✐ = media/press   🖳 = Internet resource
The Bisexual Resource Guide 2000   **137**

Asociación de la Lucha por el Respeto a la 🖳
Diversidad Sexual (ALUDIS) [Association for
the Fight for Respect for Sexual Diversity]
Apartado 1766-2050
San José
tel: 506-223-8419
Marco Castillo; fax: 506-256-4824
e-mail: asibehu@sol.rasca.co.cr
  Publication(s): *Boletin YKE (versions in*
  English & Spanish) Print & on-line bi-monthly
  publication. (Call (xx506) 283-1471 for
  subscription). Editions for sale at 50 Colones
  each (about: 0.25 $) + postage.

Asociación Triángulo Rosa   **EAH**🖳
Apartado Postal 1619-4050
Alajuela
tel: 506-258-0214; fax: 506-258-0635
e-mail: atrirosa@sol.rasca.co.cr
URL: www.losangeles.org/triangulo-rosa/
  Para gente LesBiGay, no importa el colór,
  religión, profesión, contamos con actividades
  sociales, culturales, grupos de apoyo, educación,
  activista, salud, etc. Brindamos un espacio físico
  seguro y fuera de prejuicios, donde los y las
  asistentes pueden aprender, relacionarse y
  desarrollarse tal y como son. [For LGB people of
  any color, religion, or profession, we offer
  support groups, education, activism & health. A
  space that is safe & free from prejudice where
  poeple can learn, relate & develop as they are.] C

Asociación Triangulo Rosa - San José   **EAHY**
13 Calle, 2 Avenida
San José
e-mail: rastern@sol.rasca.co.cr
  Contact person: Carl Vincent.

Hotel Casa Blanca de Manuel Antonio, S.A. 🖳
Apdo. 194
6350 Quepos
Manuel Antonio
tel: 506-777-0253, 777-1316, or 777-1790; fax: 506-777-0253
e-mail: cblanca@sol.racsa.co.cr
URL: www.hotelcasablanca.com
  A gay owned/operated resort on the Pacific coast
  of Costa Rica for gays, lesbians, & their friends.

Instituto Lationamericano de   **EH**
Prevención y Educación en Salud (ILPES)
[Latin American Institute for Prevention &
Education in Health]
Apartado Postal 561-1002
tel: 253 86 62 or 283 53 05; fax: 253 76 25
e-mail: ilpes@sol.rasca.co.cr
  Tiene una serie de publicaciones muy
  interesantes. [Has a series of very interesting
  publications.]

CZECH REPUBLIC

Local

Promluv   ♀ **H**
c/o Jana Stepanova
Promluv
V Olsinach 50
Prague 10 100 00
  For lesbians & bisexual women. Focuses on
  physical & emotional health, contacts &
  referrals, publication of a magazine (Promluv),
  & disseminating accurate information about
  lesbians. "Our goal is to buy or lease space to
  start a center offering an information service,
  AIDS hot line, library, meeting & club rooms, a
  cafe, & possibly a fitness center, & space for
  short-term accommodation. Donations welcome."
  Publication(s): *Promluv*

ECUADOR

Fundación Ecuatoriana de Acción y   **HA**
Prevención para la Promoción de la Salud
(FEDAEPS) [Ecuadorian Action & Prevention
Foundation for the Promotion of Health]
Baquerizo 166 y Tamayo
Quito
tel: 593 2 223 298; fax: same
e-mail: admin@fedaeps.ecuanex.net.ec
  Action/prevention health group.

EL SALVADOR

Entre Amigos [Among Friends]   ♂ **H**
Urbanizacion Elisa
Pasaje 'A', casa 23
Colonia Layco
San Salvador
tel: 503-225-15-67 or
503-226-08-64
e-mail: fundasida@sal.gmb.net
  Dutch government-funded 18 page glossy
  publication, produced by the gay/bisexual
  program of El Salvador's Foundation for AiDS
  Prevention, Education & Management
  (FUNDASIDA). Covers activism, safer sex,
  community events, & social & legal matters.

Key to symbols: ▼ = bi   ♀ = women   ♂ = men   ☯ = religious/spiritual
🖑 = for allies   **M** = for married bis   ♥ = for partners of bis   **Y** = youth   **C** = people of color
138   The Bisexual Resource Guide 2000

FINLAND

Finnish Bi mailing list ▼ 💻
e-mail: bi-lista@seta.fi
URL: Under construction
*The main language of this list is Finnish.
Subscribe by sending the message "subscribe bi-
lista" to majordomo@seta.fi.*

Local

Bi Group at SETA ▼ 💻
Hietalahdenkatu 2 B 16
0053100180 Helsinki
tel: +358-9-6123233(SETA Office); fax: +358-9-
6123266
e-mail: linda@seta.fi/
URL: www.seta.fi
*Meets 2nd & 4th Thursdays (except July) at
18L99 at the above address.*

Tampere Bi Group ▼ 💻
c/o Tampereen SETA
Hämeenpuisto 41a 47
Tampere 33101
tel: 4358-3-2148-721
e-mail: llyheiko@info1.info.tampere.fi
URL: treseta.oldhouse.sgic.fi/
ryhmat.html#BIRYHMA (in Finnish)
*Meets Mondays at 7pm on even numbered weeks
at the above address.*

Women's Bi Group of Helsinki ▼ ♀
c/o Naisasialiitto Unioni
Bulevardi 11A
00120Helsinki
Meets 3rd /tyesdats at tge above address.

FRANCE

Bi'Cause ▼A💻
c/o Centre Gai et Lesbien
3 Rue Keller
Paris 75 011
tel: 01-43-57-21-47
e-mail: annebens@club-internet.fr
URL: www.pelnet.com/bicause/Index.html
*2 meetings per month—1 Mon. 8pm at the CGL
(discussion, film, introductions), 1Thurs. in a
bar. Free monthly writing workshop. Free social
support workshop every 2 months, with
psychologist. Monthly political workshops.
(Bastille/Voltaire or Ledru Rollin metro stop).*
Publication(s): *Bi'Cause Black & White: 4-8 pp
quarterly; News, association info, outline, books,
agenda: available at the CGL*

Let it Bi 💻▼
Paris
e-mail: letitbe@geocities.com
URL: www.geocities.com/WestHollywood/Heights/
3537
*French language news on web. Bibliography,
books & bisexuality in the press. Lis of bi
celebrities, bi films, bi organizations & bi web
sites.*

Au dela du personnel Y▼A
c/o Leo Vidal
11 rue de l'annonciade
Lyon 69001
tel: 04 72 008965; fax: 04 72 00 89 65
e-mail: lthiers@hol.fr
*Libertarian Movement; reflections about
feminism, bisexuality, non-monogamy,
anarchism.*
Publication(s): *Au dela du personnel Book:
Editor ACL, 1998 issue*

Groupe Action Gaie (GAG)
Initiatives Plurielles
Maison Des Associations
46 Ter Rue Ste Catherine
Orleans 45 000
tel: 02 38 53 2024
Movie club; welcome meetings.
Publication(s): *Le Petit Rose Black & White;
association's news; activities programme*

Local

Bi-France ▼
c/o M. Leo
1, Montee des Carmelites
Lyon 69001

GERMANY

BiNE - Bisexuelles Netzwerk e. V. ▼ 💻
Postfach 610214
1092310923 Berlin
tel: Bi Helpline 030-2117405 M, W 5-6:30pm, or
Jurgen, Bettina: 030-2117405; fax: 49-30-2117405
e-mail: bine@roiss.ikw.tu-freiberg.de
URL: www.bi.org/~bine/
*Media management: Patricia 06703-960721 or
Thomas 030-8592018. Foreign contacts: Peter
Bell 030-6814291.* **Publication(s):** *Bijou /
Bisexuelles Journal/Newsletter For more info
about Bijou, contact Frank Buhlrich, Gerhard-
van-der-Poll-Str. 29., 28332 Achim.*

Bisexual-Helpline ▼
*Berlin: Montag und Mittwoch 4-6pm - 030-
2117405 (Jurgen). Munchen: Dienstag &
Donnerstag 9-10am - 089-334384 (Katja)*

✎ = school   ✍ = college/university   P = professional   E = educational
A = activist/political   H = health (incl. HIV)   ☎ = media/press   💻 = Internet resource
The Bisexual Resource Guide 2000   **139**

German language Bi homepage ▼ 🖳
URL: bi.org/~bine/

Local

Bisco Berlin (Bi Disco) ▼
10115 Berlin
*3rd Sat of month, starts at 9pm
Ackerkeller, Ackerstr. 12-13,
Hinterhaus. More info through BiNe.
Im*

Bi-Frauen Gruppe Berlin ▼ ♀
Frieda Frauenzentrum e. V.
Proskauer Str. 7
10247 Berlin (Friedrichshain)
*Open discussion groups (call for
times) & bi women's dances.*

Offener Gespräechskreis ▼
Bisexualität
c/oSonntags-Club e.V.
10437 Berlin
tel: 030-4497590; fax: 030-4485457
*Meets Thurs 7pm at infoLaden Kopenhagenerstr.
14 Berlin (Prenzlauer Berg).*

Bi-Gruppe fuer Frauen und ▼
Maenner Hamburg
KISS Altona, Blauer Raum
Gausstr. 21
22765 Hamburg
tel: Andreas: 040-4221744
Meets 1st & 3rd Mondays 8-10pm.

Bi-Gruppe Oldenburg ▼
c/o Naünd e.V. /Kneipe "Hempels"
Ziegelhofstr. 83
26121 Oldenberg
tel: Thomas 0441/883368
Meets 2nd & last Tuesday 8pm

Bi-Gruppe Laatzen ▼
c/o Kontaktzentrum
Kiefernweg 2
30880 Laatzen
tel: Volker 05102-3799
Meets. 2nd Wednesdays at 7:30pm.

Bi-ings, Bi-Gruppe Hildesheim ▼
c/o Hindesheimer AIDS-Hilfe
Zingel 14
31134 Hildesheim
tel: Birgit Jost: 05121-133127

Christopher Street Day 1998 in Köln, Germany

Bi-Gruppe Göttingen ▼
Gemiendehaus der reformierten Gemeinde
Untere Karspuele 11
37073 Göttingen
tel: 0551-5311924 (Johanna)
Meets 1st Thursday of month 8:30-10:30pm.

Bi-Gruppe Braunschweig ▼
c/o Braunschweiger AIDS-Hilfe
Eschternstr. 15
38100 Braunschweig
tel: Norbert 0531-311535
Call for meeting times.

Bi-gruppe Gelsenkirchen ▼
c/o AIDS-Hilfe Gelsenkirchen
Husemann Str. 39-41
45879 Gelsenkirchen
tel: 0209/19446 (AIDS-Hilfe) or 0209/206880 Heiki
Contact: 0209/206880 Heiki
Meets 1st Sundays at 7pm.

Uferlos Party Köln ▼
Schultz Koelner Schwulen- und Lesbenzentrum
Karthaeuserwall 18
50678 Köln/Cologne (Ehrenfeld)
tel: Peter 0214-47140
*Meets 3rd Fridays 10pm at Schulz, Koelner
Schwulen- und Lesbenzentrum.*

Bi-Stammtisch Mainz-Wiesbaden ▼
c/o Krokodil
Soemmeringplatz
55118 Mainz
tel: Werner: 0611-598947
Meets 2nd Wednesdays 8pm.

Key to symbols: ▼ = bi   ♀ = women   ♂ = men   ☯ = religious/spiritual
♦ = for allies   M = for married bis   ♥ = for partners of bis   Y = youth   C = people of color
140   **The Bisexual Resource Guide 2000**

Stammtisch bisexueller ▼
Frauen und Maenner
Weinstube im Hinterhof
Egenolffstr. 17
60316 Frankfurt (Nordend)
tel: Thomas: 06192/242868; Andrea & Bini:069/
503602
Meets 1st & 3rd Mondays 8:30pm.

Bi-Gruppe Stuttgart ▼
c/o KISS, Raum 4
Marienstr. 9
70178 Stuttgart
tel: 0711-2621355 (Andreas) or 0711-560141
(Claudia)
*Meets 1st Mon. 7:30pm. Bi-Stammtisch
Stuttgart meets at Rittersteuble, Ritterstr. 7,
70199 Stuttgart-Heeslach, 3rd Mondays 7:30pm.
Contact Claudia (above) for info.*

Bi Stammtisch - München ▼
80469 München
tel: 089 651 9222 (Heiner)
*Meets 3rd Monday at 7:30pm at Cafe Glück,
Palmstr. 4.*

Bi-Gruppe München ▼
c/o SUB
Muellerstr 43
80469 München
tel: 089-2603056
Open meetings every 1st & 3rd Monday.

Bi-Gruppe Nürnberg ▼
Morrison Glockenhofstr. 39
90478 Nürnberg
tel: Christina: 0911-4180091; Edwin: 0911-
3609944; Fred: 0911-3939271
Mtgs. 1st Tuesdays 8pm.

Uferlos Stammtisch Köln ▼
Köln
tel: Peter 0214-47140
*Meets last Thursdays 8pm at Otto's, Ottostr. 72,
50823 Köln (Ehrenfeld).*

Bi-Gruppe Potsdam ▼
Potsdam
tel: 0331-2701324 (Hilke); 0331-296653 (Udo)

Potsdam Bi-Frauen-Gruppe ▼ ♀
Autonomes Frauenzentrum Potsdam
Zeppelinstr. 189
14461 Potsdam
*Meets every 2nd & 4th Thursday at above
address.*

Bisexuellen-Stammtisch Berlin ▼
im Cafe Vierlinden,
Erkelenzdamm 47
10999 Berlin
tel: 030-2117405
*Meets every 1st Friday from 8pm. Call BiNe for
more info.*

Bi-Gruppe-Bremen ▼
c/o Rat und Tat Zentrum
Theodor-Koerner-Strasse 1
28203 Bremen
tel: 0421-704170
*Meets every 2nd Thursday at 8pm. Bi Cafe meets
every 3rd Thursday at 8pm.*

Bi-Gruppe Köln ▼
c/o Bürgerzentrum Ehrenfeld
Venloer Str. 429
50823 Köln/Cologne
tel: Peter 0214 47140
Meets 8pm every 1st Monday.

Referat Für Lesben, Schwule, Bi- und 🎓
Transsexuelle der HU
Unter den Linden 6
10117 Berlin
*LGBT Support Group of the Humboldt
University.*

Selbsthilfetreffpunkt Friedrichshain, ♀ ♥
Selbsthilfegruppe für Frauen / Partnerinnen
Bisexueller Männer
send mail to: Selbsthilfetreffpunkt Friedrichshain
Boxhagener Straße 62a
10245 Berlin
tel: 030-2918348 (Ms. Luhn)
*Self help group for women & partners of bisexual
men. Meets last Fri. of month at 6pm.*

Referat Für Lesben, Schwule, Bi- und 🎓
Transsexuelle der TU
Marchstraße 6
10587 Berlin
*LGBT Support Group of the Technical
University.*

Lesbenberatung ♀
Kulmer Straße 20a
2.Hinterhof (court)
4.Stock (floor)
10783 Berlin
tel: 030-2152000; 030-4224276
*Anonymous counseling for L & B women over
the phone & by appointment. Mon, Tue & Thur
4-7pm, Fri 2-5 pm. Library, bi women's dances
& other activities, open discussion groups &
workshops.*

🖉 = school   🎓 = college/university   P = professional   E = educational
A = activist/political   H = health (incl. HIV)   📰 = media/press   💻 = Internet resource
The Bisexual Resource Guide 2000   **141**

Referat F Lesben, Schwule, Bi- und   🐌
Transsexuelle der FU
Kiebitzweg 23
14195 Berlin
LGBT Support Group of the Free University.

GUATEMALA

Asociación de Talleres Holísticos (ATH)   **YEH**
Apdo. Postal 1289
Ciudad de Guatemala
tel: 502/22-33-35; fax: 502/22-33-35
e-mail: pmpasca@guate.net
Primarily gives sessions/lecture & conductions discussions on sexuality, mostly for youth in the capital. Support & services for HIV/AIDS. Contacts: Ruben Mayorga, Fernando Arevalo, Jose Mario Maza.

Local

OASIS: (Organizacion de Apoyo   **EHYA**🖳
a una Sexualidad Integral frente al SIDA)
11 Calle 4 -51
Zona 1
Apdo Postal 1289
Ciudad de Guatemala
tel: 502/220-3263; fax: 502/232-3335
e-mail: oasis@gua.gbm.net
URL: maxpages.com/maxpage.cgi/oasis/
Works with marginalized groups including gays, lesbians, bi's, transpeople, sex workers, & ghetto youth. Various educational activities/groups: health/HIV/AIDS/sexuality education, self-esteem, codependency, alcohol/drug addiction, & human rights work. Also sponsors cultural activities: films, art shows, parties. Members of ARCEGAL (Asociacion Regional Centroamericana de Gays y Lesbianas). **Publication(s)**: *"Boletin de OASIS" bulletin*

HONDURAS

Grupo PRISMA   **E**
Apartado Postal 4590
Tegulcigalpa
tel: 504-232-8342
e-mail: prisma@sdnhon.org.hn
Social/educational group working for empowerment of the LBG community in Honduras within the greater context of human rights. Publication has articles & information about local events. **Publication(s)**: *En Ambiente Published bimonthly.*

HONG KONG

AIDS Concern   **H**♂
tel: (852) 2898 4411 or help line (852) 2898 4422
e-mail: aidscon@netvigator.com
The only NGO with outreach team for men who have sex with men.

HK-QUEER   🖳
e-mail: majordomo@sqzm14.ust.hk
For glb people in Hong Kong. To subscribe send message to majordomo@sqzm14.ust.hk. In the body of message write: "subscribe hkqueer <yourname>"

Hong Kong Blessed Minority   👁🖳
Christian Fellowship
tel: (852) 2834 6601
e-mail: minoritychurch@geocities.com
URL: www.geocities.com/WestHollywood/6262/
Christian Fellowship for GLBT.

Hong Kong Ten Percent Club
GPO Box 72207
Kowloon2314-8726
Meets Weds. from 7:30-9:30 pm. Also has a "She & Her Ladies Activities Group" organizing regular women's acitivities.

Zi Mei Tong Zhi - Queer Sisters   ♀🖳
Hong Kong Central Post Office #9313
tel: 852-23144348 (answered live Thursdays 7:30-10pm); fax: pager: 71128445 a/c1613
URL: www.qs.org.hk
Feminist organization advocateing & fighting for women's sexual rights, comprised of women who are tired of "being told to stick to one SEXual ID & one kind of feminist idea $ never can we be named or explained by one (whatever) ism. We are playful & serious, personal & political, involved in a movement fighting for a more inclusive, more open & better world with larger space for women, as sexual beings & as subjects, who have different, various & everchanging routes in the immense domain of sexuality. We believe in a never ending search for the indeterminacy, heterogeneity, multiplicity, transgressiveness & variance of sexuality & sexual choices. Projects include research, a hotline, a quarterly newsletter, workshops, fundraising parties & having fun.

> "It was a while before we came to realize that our place was the very house of difference rather than the security of any one particular difference."
>
> —*Audre Lorde, in* Zami *(Persephone Press, Watertown MA, 1982, p. 226)*

Key to symbols: ▼ = bi   ♀ = women   ♂ = men   👁 = religious/spiritual
👤 = for allies   **M** = for married bis   ♥ = for partners of bis   **Y** = youth   **C** = people of color
142   **The Bisexual Resource Guide 2000**

HUNGARY

Gay Switchboad Budapest E🖳
Postbox 752
H-1437
Budapest
tel: (36)30-32-33-34; fax: (36)1-351-20-15
e-mail: budapest@compuserve.com
URL: ourworld.compuserve.com/homepages/
budapest
*Provides hotline 4-8pm for questions ranging
from social events to HIV/AIDS education to
navigating as a tourist in Budapest (including
money, travel, weather, etc). Staff is fluent in
English, German, & Hungarian. Also responds
to email & fax, maintains a website with links.*

ICELAND

Samtokin '78: Icelandic ◍AH🖳
Organisation of Lesbians & Gay Men
Postholf 1262, 121 Reykjavik
Reykjavik 121
tel: 354-5528539; fax: 354-5527525
e-mail: gayice@mmedia.is
URL: www.mmedia.is/~gayice
*National organization w/several groups,
including a small group for bisexual people. "The
organisation of course welcomes bisexual people
in all of its activities. We have a gay center at
Lindargata 49 with a coffeeshop & a library
open M, Th 8-11pm & Saturdays 9:30pm-1am.
Also in Iceland: "semi-gay" bar at Laugavegur
22, & gay guesthouse "Room With a View" at
Laugavegur 18 (ph/; fax: +354 522 7262), gay
radio 89.3 (24 hours/day)"* **Publication(s)***:
Samtakafrettir A small newsletter of the
organisation which gives details on what's
happening each month. In Icelandic.*

INDIA

Humsafar Trust (India) ♂EH
Post Box 6913
Santa Cruz West
Mumbai Maharastra 600 056
tel: voice mail:
91-22-972-6913
e-mail: admin@humsafar.ilbom.ernet.in
*Drop-in centre for men who have sex with men
(MSM). Provides counselling, condom
distribution, telephone counselling, & outreach
work.*

Khushnet India: C🖳A
Indian South Asian Network Online
URL: www.khushnet.com/india.htm
*Extensive listings for South Asian GLB groups
in India, including Secunderabid, New Dehli,
Bombay, Lucknow, Dehli, Banglore, Calcutta,
Cochiri, etc.*

Stree Sangam ♀A
P.O. Box No 1613
Matunga
Bombay 600 019
e-mail: admin@faow.ilbom.ernet.in
A collective of lesbian & bisexual women.

Local

Counsel Club
c/o Pawan
Post Bag 10237
Calcutta 700 019
*Annual membership of Rs 200/$10 for Naya
Pravartak subscription, penpal listing, access to
archives, counseling help.*

Humrahi 🖳
Editor-Darpan
PO Box-3910,
Andrews Ganj,
New Delhi 110 049
e-mail: aka9@hotmail.com
URL: www.geocities.com/WestHollywood/Heights/
7258/
*Forum for Gays at New Delhi, India. Meets
regularly on 1st & 3rd Sat. Counseling
available. Fundraising. The group welcomes all
persons from the community.*
Publication(s): *Darpan.*

Buku Seri IPOOS Gaya Betawi ✍
send mail to: IPOOS
Kotak Pos 7631
JKBT
Jakarta Barat 11076
*Indonesian periodical put out by Indonesian gay
organization.*

"What is new
is not bisexuality but rather
the widening of our awareness
and acceptance of human
capacities for sexual love."

—*Margaret Mead (1901-1978),*
quoted 1975 in Redbook

✎ = school   ✐ = college/university   **P** = professional   **E** = educational
A = activist/political   **H** = health (incl. HIV)   ✍ = media/press   🖳 = Internet resource
The Bisexual Resource Guide 2000   **143**

IRELAND

Bi Irish   ▼ 🖳
c/o OUThouse
PO Box 4767
Dublin
tel: Darragh, (h) +353 1 670 56 80
e-mail: bi.irish.@bi.org
URL: bi.org/~bi.irish/
*"for bisexuals & others who feel not quite
straight...main focus is on the exploration &
validation of bisexual identities..." Meets first
Tuesday of the month in Outhouse (a queer
community resource centre), 6 South William
St., Dublin 2, from 8-9:30pm.*

Local

**OUThouse: LGB Community
Resource Center**
6 South William St., Dublin 2
tel: (01) 670 6377
*Organizes many support/social groups. Coffee
shop & drop-in resource center. M-F 10-6. Coffee
shop: M-Sat. 12-6, Sun. 3-6.*

Lesbian & Gay Resource Centre   ♂
8 South Main St
Cork Ireland
tel: 021-278470; fax: 021-287471
*Married Gay Men Group Wed. 7-9pm Sat 3-5
pm. Contact 021-271087.*

The Other Side Bookshop & Cafe
8 South Main St.
Cork
tel: (021) 278 470
*Open Tue-Sun 11-7:30pm. Holds a range of
community center meetings & workshops.*

**University College Cork: Orientation &   👓⁄🖳
Sexual Identity Society (OASIS)**
Box 50, Student Accomodation Office
University College
Cork
tel: +353 21 902276; +353 21 902353; fax: +353 21
274483
e-mail: oasis@www.ucc.ie
URL: www.ucc.ie/ucc/socs/oasis
*For LGB students & their friends. Informal
Tuesday lunches.*

**National University of Ireland,   👓⁄🖳
Galway: Pluto**
Galway
e-mail: plutosoc@yahoo.com
URL: www.geocities.com/WestHollywood/7116/
index.html
*LGB society of the university. Meets Tuesdays
7:30pm during termtime in Rm. 307, Tower 2.*

Les/Gay/Bi Drop-ins
c/o Galway Gay Helpline
PO Box 45, Eglington Street
Galway City
tel: (091) 564-611, Wed. 8-10pm.
*Meets Sun. 4pm for films, workshops, chats &
coffee.*

ISRAEL

**Association of Gays, Lesbians   EA 🖳
& Bisexuals in Israel ("The Agudah")**
28 Nachmani St.
PO Box 37604
Tel Aviv 61375
tel: (011) 972-36-204-327; (011)972-3-629-3681;
fax: (011) 972-3-525-2341
e-mail: sppr@netvision.net.IL
URL: www.geocities.com/WestHollywood/
Stonewall/2295
*Aims to advance legal, social & cultural rights of
GLBTs in Israel in order to become fully equal
citizens. Political action, education programs, &
collaboration with social change agents, enhance
a sense of solidarity & congregational cohesion
within the community, & to assist & support
those in need. Support groups, help lines, social
events, youth groups & pride celebrations & an
international email network. (Formerly the
Society for the Protection of Personal Rights)*

Ge'ut   A
PO Box 37413
Tel Aviv
tel: 972-3-636-0149
*Political activist lgbts within the Meretz Party,
who lobby for lgbt rights in Israel.*

HaZman HaVarod (Pink Times)   ✉◢🖳
PO Box 14595
Tel Aviv 61144
tel: 972-3-685-1807
e-mail: t_tarbut@netvision.net.il
URL: www.pinktime.co.il
Israel's national lgbt newspaper.

KLAF   🖳 ♀
PO Box 26221
Jerusalem 91062
tel: 972-2-625-1271
e-mail: klaf_israel.hotmail.com
URL: www.aquanet.co.il/vip/klaf
Israel's lesbian, feminist community.

Key to symbols: ▼ = bi   ♀ = women   ♂ = men   ☯ = religious/spiritual
☙ = for allies   **M** = for married bis   ♥ = for partners of bis   **Y** = youth   **C** = people of color
144   The Bisexual Resource Guide 2000

Local

Hebrew University: 🖉EA🖳
HaAsiron HaAcher (The Other 10 Percent)
PO Box 6916
Jerusalem 91068
tel: 972-2-653-5454
e-mail: asiron@hotmail.com
URL: www.poboxes.com/asiron
LGBT student organization.

The Jerusalem Open House   EA🖳
PO Box 33107
Jerusalem 91037
tel: 972-2-537-3906
e-mail: gayj@hotmail.com
URL: www.poboxes.com/gayj
Jerusalem's LGBT umbrella organization &
community center. Support groups, social events,
political activism, info. lines, speakers bureau,
sports clubs, art workshops, religious study,
youth groups & pride celebrations.
Publication(s): *Once Only A magazine of*
LGBT art & culture (in Hebrew). $10.

Bela Do'eget   H🖳
PO Box 37604
Tel Aviv 61375
tel: 972-3-620-4327 or 629-3681; fax: 972-3-525-2341
URL: www.geocities.com/westhollywood/
stonewall/1582
The Agudah's HIV/AIDS project, supported &
organized by the lgbt community.

Gam v'Gam   ▼E
PO Box 37604
Tel Aviv 61375
tel: 972-3-620-4327 or 629-3681; fax: 972-3-525-2341

Tel Aviv University: B.Gay   🖉EA
PO Box 37604
Tel Aviv 61375
tel: 972-3-688-8961
Student organization.

> Ultimately, the questions of
> whether someone is 'really'
> straight or 'really' gay or even
> 'really' bisexual "misrecognizes
> the nature of sexuality, which is
> fluid not fixed, a narrative that
> changes over time rather than a
> fixed identity, however complex."
>
> —*Marjorie Garber*

JAPAN

Queer Diversity
send mail to: QD
c/o #940-KSGH, 6, 615-0072
e-mail: RXT02026@nifty.ne.jp
Aims: communicating, discussing, networking,
exchanging information, organizing events &
educating people. Friendly with socially/
politically active LGBTQ&F groups &
individuals who relate to issues of sex, gender,
sexuality, sexual orientation, non-monogamy, sex
positive, etc. Communication almost all in
Japanese, but English possible.

Local

HIP's Home Page   🖳
e-mail: hibino@mbox.kyoto-inet.or.jp
URL: web.kyoto-inet.or.jp/people/hibino/
Maintained by HIBINO, Makoto. Contains 5MB
of HIBINO's literature, including essays on
sexuality & gender with LesBiGay pride march
photos. Most pages are in Japanese, some in
English.

Project P   🖳
c/o PONPOKO-House
58 Higashikubota-cho, Kita-sirakawa,
Sakyo-ku, 606-8285
Kyoto
tel: +81-75-723-4421
e-mail: hibino@mbox.kyoto-inet.or.jp
URL: web.kyoto-inet.or.jp/people/hibino/group/
Project P/
An all-welcome/active/political/friendly group
in Kyoto, Japan. We try to understand,
communicate, & enjoy our differences. Issues
with sexual orientation, gender roles, gender
identity, sex, & sexual violence are our important
interests, but not all. Events, workshops,
monthly cafes, occasional publications. (Inquiry
in English takes long time for answer.)

KOREA

*See also **South Korea** and **North Korea** listings.*

On-Line Resource List for Queer Koreans   C🖳
URL: www.hana-lei.com/qk/frame.html
Lists groups & resources for lgbt people in Korea,
& for people of Korean descent .

✎ = school	🖉 = college/university	P = professional	E = educational
A = activist/political	H = health (incl. HIV)	✍ = media/press	🖳 = Internet resource

The Bisexual Resource Guide 2000   *145*

Sappho ♀
tel: 02-574-3003 W
02-793-2836 H
e-mail: glee@gias.snu.ac.kr (until 01/99)
An organization for foreign lesbian feminists but majority are english speaking. Meets 3rd Sat. of every month & is fairly casual. Programs offered are: English / Korean exchange program & study/discussion group (feminist issues...). Alcohol is discouraged.

LITHUANIA

Lithuanian Gay League EA
P. O. Box 2862
Vilnius 2000
tel: 370/2-63-30-31; fax: 370/2-63-30-31
e-mail: eduardas@lgl.vno.osf.lt
National NGO aiming to raise awareness about LGB discrimination in Lithuanian society. Educational programming about AIDS & STDs. Activism for creating anti-discrimination legislation, project for registered partnerships.

MALAYSIA

Khushnet Malaysia: Pink Triangles 🖥A
P.O. Box 11859
Kuala Lumpur 50760
URL: www.khushnet.com/maylasia
Connections, AIDS information, counseling.

Local

Pink Triangle H
P.O. Box 11859
50760
Kuala Lumpur
Counseling, AIDS information.

MEXICO

Acion Humana Por La Comunidad H
Apartado Postal 27-131
MexicoD.F. 06761
tel: 52-5-772-0778
e-mail: amac@laneta.apc.org
Activism on HIV-AIDS, gay life, human rights.

Local

Taller Reflexivo de Mujeres Bisexuales ▼ ♀ CA
(TREMUB) de El Closet de Sor Juana
c/o El Closet de Sor Juana
Nevado 112, Depto. 8,
Col. Portales
MéxicoD.F.
tel: 525 549 11 91; fax: same
e-mail: closetsj@laneta.apc.org or
careaga@servidor.unam.mx
Cuenta con un espacio permanente sobre el ser bisexual y su inserción en otros movimentos sociales - feminista, lésbico, democrático, derechos humanos. Cuenta con un proyecto de difusión a través de una revista informativa recién iniciada. [Space for discussion about bisexual identity & involvement in other movements: feminist, lesbian, democratic, human rights. Recently produced a publication.]

Roberta Gregory

Key to symbols: ▼ = bi ♀ = women ♂ = men ☯ = religious/spiritual
🔥 = for allies **M** = for married bis ♥ = for partners of bis **Y** = youth **C** = people of color
146 The Bisexual Resource Guide 2000

NEPAL

Nepal Queer Society C☐
G.P.O. 9075
EPC 5203
Kathmandu
URL: www.khushnet.com/nepal.htm
For queer people of Nepal. Linked on Khushnet.

NETHERLANDS

Dutch Bisexuals Mailing List ☐▼
Schoonderloostraat 82
3024TX Rotterdam
e-mail: binl-l@lnbi.demon.nl
General mailing list for Dutch speaking bisexuals. To subscribe, send e-mail to majordomo@lnbi.demon.nl without subject & the text 'subscribe binl-l' in the body of the message. You will receive a confirmation message from the server.

Vereniging Landelijk Netwerk ▼A☐
Biseksualiteit
(in English: Dutch National Bi Network)
Postbus 75087
1070AB Amsterdam
tel: +31-(0)6-52766064; fax: +31-(0)10-2449059
e-mail: lnbi@lnbi.demon.nl
URL: www.lnbi.demon.nl/
*The national organization / action-group for bisexuality became a society in 1992 after having been in existence for ten years. Goals: (1) to stimulate both local & national activities for / by bisexuals & allies, to increase recognition, support & emancipation of bisexuals. (2) to change society as a whole, by breaking the hetero-norm & the gay / straight duality in order to achieve acceptance of bisexuality as an equal choice & way of life. **Publication(s)**: Bi-Nieuws Quarterly newsletter. For 35 dutch guilders you can become a member of the society & receive Bi-Nieuws by mail. Only their PO box address is mentioned on the otherwise blank envelope. By transferring the amount of 7.50 dutch guilders on giro-account 5459383 of LNBi in Amsterdam you may request a test issue of Bi-Nieuws. Exchange subscriptions are accepted, foreign memberships add 10 guilders. Bi-Nieuws is published in Dutch only.*

Local

BiGroep Amsterdam ▼
Stichting Werkgroep Biseksualiteit Amsterdam
P.O. Box 59653
1040 LD Amsterdam
tel: +31-(0)6-52766064
Organizes activities at changing times & places. Please contact them for meeting info. The meetings are very sociable & there are possibilities for talking, seriously or otherwise, & dancing.

Bi-Groep Gouda ▼♀
Gouda ZH 2806JB
tel: +31-182-527471
e-mail: novami@worldonline.nl
Women's group regularly organizes meetings during weekends with varying activities. Exchange of opinion & the chance to meet other bi-women is the main purpose. New friendships may arise.

Rotterdam Bi! ▼
P.O. Box 19068
3001 BB Rotterdam
tel: +31-(0)10-2449066; fax: +31-(0)10-2449059
e-mail: maurice@lnbi.demon.nl
Meets every 4th Sat. at the COC building during the COC-Café mixed evening. Schiedamsesingel 175, Rotterdam. Purely social meetings, for fun & meeting people. Introduction by one of the people of the organizing committee is possible.

Discussion Group ▼♀♂
'De Kringen' Amersfoort
Attn. Bi-Kringen
P.O. Box 28001
3828ZG Hoogland
tel: +31-(0)33-4805153 (until 21.00h) Theo, men
+31-(0)33-4729576 (until 21.00h) Trees, women
Discussion groups about bisexuality. Separate men's & women's groups. Please call to find out if they are taking new joiners.

GOBI Initiatiefgroep Biseksualiteit Nijmegen ▼
c/o N.V.I.H. COC
Afdeling Nijmegen
P.O. Box 552
6500AN Nijmegen
tel: +31-(0)24-3234237
"GOBI Initiatiefgroep Biseksualiteit Nijmegen" has 5 initiatives: 1) Bi-women group; 2) Bi-men group; 3) Mixed bi-group; 4) Youngsters group 'Jobi; 5) Bi-Café. Once a month, each initiative has its gathering. For information, write or call central address / number.

🖎 = school   ᔕ = college/university   P = professional   E = educational
A = activist/political   H = health (incl. HIV)   🖾 = media/press   ☐ = Internet resource
The Bisexual Resource Guide 2000   **147**

Dutch Bi Network, "Rose Zaterday," 1997

Discussion group 'De Kringen' Groningen ▼
Attn. Nico & Marja (Bi-Kring Groningen Drenthe)
P.O. Box 403
9700AK Groningen
tel: +31-(0)592-340883 (Nico)
+31-(0)50-5733012 (Marja)
Mixed discussion group about bisexuality. Please call to find out if they are taking new joiners.

Discussion Group Rotterdam ▼
Rotterdam
tel: +31-(0)187-612128 (Ali)
Independent discussion group. Meets regularly at members' home. Call to enquire if there are openings available in the group.

Bi-meeting ▼
Bi-Meeting 'De Samenkomst'
Tilburg
tel: +31-(0)13-5343405 (Ton, Jos or Judith)
Social meeting for bi's in co-operation with bar disco 'My Way'. Meets every 1st Thurs. of the month at 21.00h at Vechelstraat 1 in Tilburg.

NVSH Eindhoven
Eindhoven
tel: +31(0)2124340 (evening-hours)
Every first Sat. of the month the Eindhoven department of the NVSH (Dutch Society for Sexual Reformation) organizes an erotical sauna / nudist evening for couples & (limited) singles, especially bisexuals. Held at a farm between Weert & Roermond. Entrance fee for couples is f 25,–; men alone f 25,–; women alone f 15,–. Pushy behaviour will not be tolerated, & the possibility for sex is always there. Calling in advance is compulsory, you need to get directions or you will get lost!

Foundation Group 7152 ♀ ▯
P.O. Box 1402
3500BK Utrecht
tel: +31-(0)35-5243623 (Lon)
e-mail: tiah@cistron.nl
URL: www.geocities.com/WestHollywood/
Stonewall/2951/
To help l & b in the process of becoming aware of & accepting their feeelings for women & to offer meeting places. All women, young or old, married or single can join, with privacy respected. **Publication(s):** *Amarant Amarant is published six times per year & contains information & articles pertaining to women & lesbianism & bisexuality.*

Dutch Society Orpheus M ♥ ▯
P.O. Box 14121
3508 SE Utrecht
tel: +31-(0)20-6390765
URL: www.xs4all.nl/~orpheus/
Discussion & support group for glbs & partners. Organizes meetings for married couples in which one partner is lg or b. **Publication(s):** *Orpheus Nieuwsbrief Quarterly newsletter for their members. Membership is 45 guilders for individuals or 67,50 guilders for couples (one newsletter). Applications should be sent to: Orpheus membership administration; P.O. box 1002; 8900CA Leeuwarden, the Netherlands.*

Discussion Groups: De Kringen ▼▯
Kanaalweg 21
3526 KL Utrecht
tel: +31-(0)30-2888636 (Paul)
e-mail: kringnet@pi.net
URL: home.pi.net/~kringnet/
Meetings are held, usually monthly, at the home of one of the members. Call to enquire if there are openings available. New groups are formed regularly & usually carry on for years, but not continually with the same people.

Dutch Bi Network, "Rose Zaterday," 1997

Key to symbols: ▼ = bi ♀ = women ♂ = men ☯ = religious/spiritual
☖ = for allies **M** = for married bis ♥ = for partners of bis **Y** = youth **C** = people of color
148 **The Bisexual Resource Guide 2000**

Jongerengroep PéPé   Y
Kraneweg 56
9718JT Groningen
tel: +31-(0)50-5132620
*LGB youth group PéPé organizes a social for
youngsters every Thurs. evening from 20.00-
01.00h where you can drink, small-talk with
others, but also talk seriously with one another.
Also organize a theme-evening every 1st Sat. of
the month, same time. Activities held at the
COC-building, Kraneweg 56 in Groningen.*

Twente Technical University: HoBiHe   ⌒Y🖳
Enschede
e-mail: hobihe@student.utwente.nl
URL: www.student.utwente.nl/~srd/hobihe/
*Youth group for integration of homo- &
bisexuality. To join e-mail list to be kept
informed about their activities, send e-mail to
hobihe-lijst-request@archon.student.utwente.nl
with 'subscribe' (without quotes) in the body of
the message.*

Discussion group 'De Samenkomst'   ▼
Tilburg
tel: +31-(0)13-5343405 (Ton, Jos or Judith)
*Discussion group that organizes meetings about
once a month. Social & theme evenings are held
alternately. The group focuses on the surroundings of Tilburg.*

NETHERLANDS ANTILLES

Local

Orguyo
Montanja di Rei 447
Curaçao
tel: 599 9 67 85 43; fax: 599 9 65 05 85
e-mail: curamere@ibm.net
Gay, lesbian & bisexual organization.

NEW ZEALAND

New Zealand Bisexual Network   ▼🖳
PO Box 5426
Wellesley Street
Auckland
tel: 09-302-0590; fax: 09-302-2042
e-mail: grieve@ihug.co.nz
URL: homepages.ihug.co.nz/~grieve/
*1st & 3rd Fri 6-8pm at the Pride Centre, The
Peoples Centre Building, 33 Wyndham St,
Auckland City. Welcomes all bisexual & bi-
curious.*

AIDS Hotline   H
tel: 0800 - 802 437
*In addition to AIDS information & counselling
phone calls can be forwarded to Gayline
Auckland. This allows anyone in NZ to have toll
free access to the services of Gayline.*

New Zealand Gays, Bisexuals, Lesbians 🖳
& Friends Electronic Mail List (NZGBLF)
e-mail: To subscribe: nzgblf-sub@qrd.org.nz
For inquiries: nzgblf-info@qrd.org.nz
*E-mail list for the discussion of any issues about
the queer community in New Zealand / Aotearoa.
Overseas visitors welcome.*

New Zealand Pink Pages   🖳
URL: nz.com/NZ/Queer/PinkPages
*Web site lisitng LGBT & Queer resources in New
Zealand.*

Pride Media Team (PMT)   ✐🖳
PO Box 5426
Wellesley St.
Auckland
tel: +64-9-302-0590; fax: +64-9-303-2042
e-mail: pmt@qrd.org.nz
URL: nz.com/NZ/Queer/PMT
*Loose coalition of individuals monitoring New
Zealand's newspapers, radio & television to
ensure fair & accurate reporting on & about the
GLB communities.*

Local

Bi Group   ▼
Pride Centre
33 Wyndham Street
Auckland City
tel: Robin Hopkins 09/302-0590
*Meets twice monthly, 1st & 3rd Fri., 6-8pm at
the Pride Centre for friendly & informal get
togethers.*

Wellington Bisexual Women's Group   ▼♀
PO Box 5145
Wellington
Publication(s): *Bi-lines*

Auckland Bisexual Women's Group   ▼♀
c/o Pride Centre
P.O. Box 5426, Wellesley St.
Auckland
tel: Robyn Hopkins: 64-9-302-0590 (6-8pm)

✎ = school   ⌒ = college/university   P = professional   E = educational
A = activist/political H = health (incl. HIV)   ✐ = media/press   🖳 = Internet resource
The Bisexual Resource Guide 2000   **149**

Dunedin - Beyond the Closet ♀

Meets 1pm Mon, Cottage Lounge, Club & Socs Building. Provides safe, supportive space for women questioning or confirming their sexuality. Beyond the Closet coffee evenings begin early April at Clubs & Socs. An informal get together where topics such as law, safe sex & sexuality, women on the web, etc are discussed.

Dunedin - YES Y

tel: Kate +64-3-456-1465, or Leeann +64-3-473-0868

Social group for LGB youth. Meets fortnightly, Sun. 2pm at the Pickled Penguin on Dundas St. "We just do stuff like go to the movies or iceskating or whatever, just so people can meet other people & recognise a few faces when they get confident enough to start going to dances etc."

Gaylink Hamilton ♂ 💻

tel: (07) 8549631 or (07)8555-G4A2Y
e-mail: Colin Lowe: clowe@wave.co.nz
URL: www.geocities.com/WestHollywood/1102
Social support group for men who love men. Drop-in every Wed. 8-10pm. Support phone line open during these hours.

QRA: Guide to the GLBT 💻
communities in New Zealand
URL: nz.com/NZ/Queer

Auckland University : Uni-GoBLeT ⚥
EEO Officer
Private Bag 92019
Auckland
For staff & students.

Auckland University: ⚥ ♀
Women Loving Women
c/o Auckland University Students Association
Private Bag 92019
Auckland

Aukland Pride Centre 💻
Box 5426
Wellesley St
Auckland
tel: +64-9-302-0590
URL: nz.com/NZ/Queer/PrideCentre/
For the GLBT communities in Tamaki Makaurau/Auckland. Located at the People's Centre, 33 Wyndham Street. Social events, space for groups & projects, drop-in & phone venue, newsletter, info & referral, political lobbying.

Dinner Club for Women ♀
PO Box 68 922
Newton
Auckland
e-mail: dcw@outnet.co.nz
"A series of sensational evenings designed for women who wish to dine exclusively in the company of other women."

Express: New Zealand's Newspaper 📰
of Gay Expression
PO Box 47-514
Ponsonby
Auckland
tel: 64-9-361-0190; fax: 64-9-361-0191
e-mail: express@outnet.co.nz

Gayline Auckland
Auckland
tel: (09) 303 3584
Acts as a referral point for anyone requiring support, counselling, or information about their sexuality.

Icebreakers for Men Y♂
Auckland
tel: (09) 376-4155 (Rainbow Youth)
Social/support group for young men, 16 - 26, who think they might be gay or bisexual.

Icebreakers for Women Y♀
Auckland
tel: (09) 376 4155 (Rainbow Youth)
Social/support group for young women who think they might be lesbian or bisexual.

OUT! Magazine 📰
Private Bag 92126
Auckland
tel: +64-9-377-9031; fax: +64-9-377-7767
e-mail: out@nz.com

Rainbow Youth Auckland Y💻
Box 5426
Wellesley St.
Auckland
tel: +64-9-376-4155; infoline:+64-9-376-4156
e-mail: aniwa@outnet.co.nz
URL: nz.com/nz/queer/rainbowyouth
Publication(s): *Rainbow Youth*

B.L.G. (Bisexual, Lesbian, ⚥
& Gay Support Group)
c/o UCSA
Christchurch
tel: Nick or Rebecca: (03) 365 2620
e-mail: sbh25@student.canterbury.ac.nz
Social/support group for blgt & unlabelled students.

Key to symbols: ▼ = bi ♀ = women ♂ = men ☯ = religious/spiritual
♦ = for allies M = for married bis ♥ = for partners of bis Y = youth C = people of color
150 The Bisexual Resource Guide 2000

Christchurch BLG
Christchurch
tel: Nick or Rebecca +64-3-365-2620
e-mail: shb25@student.canterbury.ac.nz
*Meets Thurs. 6pm in International Room, 1st
floor, UCSA Building, 90 Ilam Rd.*

Icebreakers Christchurch   Y♂E🖳
c/- 198 Youth Health Centre
198 Hereford
Christchurch
tel: Gayline 379-4796 or Ettie Rout Centre 379-
1953
e-mail: icebreakers.chch@hotmail.com
URL: nz.com/NZ/Queer/ChchIcebreakers
*Support group in Christchurch, for young men
16-24 who are gay or bi, or think they may be.
The group explores issues related to sexuality &
provides a safe, secure & fun environment for
youth.*

Ice Breakers   ♂Y
PO Box 1382
Dunedin
tel: (03) 4772-077 (Gayline)
*Social/support group for young men, up to 25
yrs, who think they might be gay or bisexual.*

Otago Gaily Times
c/o The AIDS Project
154 Hanover St
Dunedin
tel: +64-3-474-7732; fax: +64-3-474-7631
Otago magazine.

University of Otago: ♂ 🎓
Gay & Bi Guys on Campus
Dunedin
tel: c/o Gayline: (03) 477-2077
Gay & bi students & staff.

Icebreakers   Y♂
New Zealand Aids Foundation
Box 41
Hamilton
tel: NZAF: +64-7-838-3557
*Social & support group for young men who think
they might be gay or bisexual.*

Waikato University: 🎓 🖳
BLG Collective/Queers on Campus
c/o Bisexual Student's Officer
Waikato Student Union, Gate 1, Knighton Road
Private Bag 3059
Hamilton East
tel: +64-7-856-9139
URL: nz.com/NZ/queer/BGL/
*Social/support group for GLBT & unlabeled
students at the Uni.* **Publication(s)**: *Q! Waikato
Students Union Queer Magazine*

Gayline Hokitika
Hokitika
tel: +64-3-755-6270
Mon, Tues, Thurs 7-10pm.

Ascent   ◕♂
Nelson
tel: Brian +64-3-548-3304
For gay/bi Catholic men.

Spectrum   ♂ 🖳
Box 4022
Nelson South
tel: Kevin:+64-3-547-2827, Nick:+64-3-545-0797
e-mail: kevin@ts.co.nz or ntilly@xtra.co.nz
URL: nz.com/NZ/Queer/Spectrum
*Social/support group for gay & bi men. Drop-in
centre Thursday 7:30-10:30pm for coffee &
conversation at 42 Franklin St. $2.00 entry.
They also put Gaytime FM on air every week.*

Rainbow Times   ✍
PO Box 6074
New Plymouth
Taranaki News Publication.

Taranaki Pride Alliance
PO Box 6074
New Plymouth
e-mail: janet.chapman@taranaki.ac.nz
Publication(s): *Rainbow Times*

Rainbow Club   ♂ 🖳
PO Box 134
Otaki Railway
tel: +64-4-293-7177 or
0800-392-333
URL: nz.com/NZ/Queer/RainbowClub/
*A social & support group for gay & bisexual men
living in the Kapiti & Horowhenua areas (north
of Wellington). Monthly newsletter to members &
other local groups. Meets mainly in members'
homes on last Sat. of each month. Welcomes
contacts especially from other groups, individuals in rural areas or prospective members.*

Manawatu Lesbian & Gay Rights Assn.   A🖳
(MALGRA)
Box 1491
Palmerston North
tel: +64-6-358-5378
URL: nz.com/NZ/queer/MALGRA/
*Umbrella organization for several groups
including a lesbian support group, a group for
gay male youth, a queer students group. A
bisexual group is in the process of being formed
(as of 1999) although at this point they are
unclear whether it will choose to be under the
umbrella of MALGRA.*

🖉 = school   🎓 = college/university   **P** = professional   **E** = educational
A = activist/political **H** = health (incl. HIV)   ✍ = media/press   🖳 = Internet resource
The Bisexual Resource Guide 2000   *151*

Tamaki Makaurau Lesbian Newsletter ♀
PO Box 44-056
Pt Chevalier, Auckland 2
e-mail: jrankine@hrc.govt.nz
Monthly newsletter, 11 issues per year,
beginning of the month.

First Out Y ♀
Wellington
tel: c/o Lesbianline: (04) 499-5567
A group for young women under 27 who think
they might be lesbian or bisexual.

Flat Out Y 🖳
PO Box 10104
Wellington
e-mail: flat-out@geocities.com
URL: www.geocities.com/WestHollywood/3384/
Group of young queer people set up by the
Wellington City Council to organise recreational
& social activities for LGBT & queer friendly
youth in the Wellington area.

Galaxies: Lesbian, Gay & Bisexual 🕭
Christian Community of Wellington
PO Box 5203
Thorndon
Wellington
tel: St. Andrews
+64-4-472-9211; fax: +64-4-472-9211
e-mail: edington@actrix.gen.nz
For GLB Christians & their families. "Non-
hierarchical, non-judgmental & open in its
theology."

Icebreakers ♂ 🖳
Icebreaker Referrals
PO Box 9247, Marion Square
Wellington
tel: Wellington Gay Switchboard: 7:30-10pm: (04)
385-0674
e-mail: ice-breakers@geocities.com
URL: www.geocities.com/WestHollywood/village/
2622/
Nationwide network of support & social groups
for young men (16-26) who are gay, bi, attracted
to other guys, or just questioning their sexuality.
Assistsin the development of a healthy self-
esteem & sexuality for young gay & bi men.
Icebreaker groups also in Hamilton, Auckland,
Dunedin & Christchurch.

Lesbian Quarterly ♀
PO Box 11-882
Wellington
Quarterly Wellington magazine & newsletter.
Formerly called the Lesbians Newsletter.

Victoria University of Wellington, UniQ 👓🖳
c/o VUWSA,
PO Box 600
Wellington
tel: Women: Suraya Singh (04) 384 4156
Men: Alastair Cameron (04) 475 2290
e-mail: uniq@sans.vuw.ac.nz
URL: www.sans.vuw.ac.nz/~uniq
A group for lgbt students as well as students
questioning their sexuality. It is run by queer
students to promote an inclusive, safe & friendly
environment for all queer people on campus.
Helps people start up more specific groups (eg. bi
men's support group, queer chocoholics, etc).

NICARAGUA

Colectivo de Mujeres Autonomas ♀
Apartado Postal Ciudad Sandino 038
Managua
Group for autonomous women; includes lesbians
& bisexual women.

Fundación Xochiquetzal HAYE
Apartado No. 112
Managua
tel: 505/2-490585; fax: 505/2-491346
e-mail: quetzal@tmx.com.ni
Non-profit NGO based in Managua w/ offices in
5 cities in northern Nicaragua. (Contact in
Matagalpa: Angela Rocha Mairena 505/61-
490585) Provides HIV testing & counselling.
Youth work, hotline, radio programs, documen-
tation of injustices. Also members of Arcegal, a
Central Amercan LGBT organization, & the
Central American Confederation of NGOs
Against AIDS. **Publication(s)**: *Fuera del Closet*
(Out of the Closet) Published 3 times/yr: March
(dedicated to women), June (to sexual prefer-
ences), Sept (to youth), Dec (to the International
Day in the Fight Against AIDS).

NORWAY

Landsforeningen for Lesbisk or EA
Homofil figjoring (LLH - Norway)
St. Olavs plass 2
Pb 6838
Oslo n-0130
tel: 47/22-36-19-47; fax: 47/22-11-47-45
National organization for liberation of LGB
people. Establishes social, political, & educa-
tional agendas. Norway's largest & most
important LBG organization. Receives state
funding, but operates independently. Coordi-
nates local adult & youth groups all over
Norway. **Publication(s)**: *BLIKK*

Key to symbols: ▼ = bi ♀ = women ♂ = men 🕭 = religious/spiritual
🝔 = for allies **M** = for married bis ♥ = for partners of bis **Y** = youth **C** = people of color
152 The Bisexual Resource Guide 2000

Local

Bikuben ▼
Postboks 296
Skoyen
N-0212Oslo

Ungdomsgruppa/LLH-Oslo YE
Postboks 0838, St. Olavs Plass
Oslo N-0130
tel: support lines:
47/90-10-02-77
47/810-00-277
*Runs a support hotline for LGB youth. Regular
meetings, social events, nights out. Part of LLH-
Norways. Membership, annual fee: NOK50.
Contact: Jan Benny Sulutvedt* **Publication(s)**:
*Medlemsposten Issued every 2-3 mo. announcing
upcoming events.*

PAKISTAN

Local

Khushnet Pakistan E🖳
Hum-Khayal Publications
Attn: Anjum
2 Jinnah Colony
Faisalabad
URL: www.khushnet.com/pakistan.htm
*Publishers of Pakistan's first book of gay poetry,
Narman, by Ifti Nasim.*

PERU

Local

Comunidad Cristiana Vida Nueva 🌐H
Casilla 2627
Correo Central
Lima 1
tel: 254.0275
e-mail: VIDANUEVA@computextos.com.pe
*Ecumenical Christian-based group providing a
supportive community for people marginalized
by sexuality issues: GLBT's & allies. Also runs
shelter for HIV-positive children.*

"Your fence is sitting on me." At US March on
Washington for Gay, Lesbian & Bi Equal Rights &
Liberation, 1993

PHILIPPINES

Bisexual Network of the Philippines ▼🖳
Manila Bi Group: Danny: sioldan@hotmail.com
Cebu Bi Group: Brian: argao@rocketmail.com
URL: www.rainbow.net.au/~ausbinet/binetph.htm
*A new network still in its formative stage but
eager to hear from bisexual & bi-curious men &
women from throughout the Republic of the
Philippines. All you have to do is register with us
to be granted membership. You are welcome to
attend any meetings & social events that may be
organised or go on our private e-mail list for
BiNet Philippines news updates. At present
BiNet Philippines is developing social groups in
the Manila Metro area & in Cebu City. It is
hoped other groups will develop as more people
contact BiNet Philippines & get involved.*

Local

**ZONE Convergence of
Gay Humanists & Friends**
42 - B Lake View Drive
Pasig City
tel: 63/2-671-73-72
e-mail: zone@misa.irf.ph.net
*To end discrimination & inequality, denounce
violence in any form be it physical, religious,
economic or sexual in origin. To move towards a
world of diversity & multiplicity in beliefs &
ideas in ethnicity, language, work, lifestyle.
Believe in freedom & the meaning of life.
Imagine a world that is flexible, changing &
responding to the dynamic needs of people. For
anyone! Including gay-friendly heteros.*

🖉 = school   = college/university   P = professional   E = educational
A = activist/political   H = health (incl. HIV)   📰 = media/press   🖳 = Internet resource

Can't Live In the Closet   E💻
P.O. Box 2356
CPO 1163
Quezon City
fax: (632) 911-6239
e-mail: CLIC@phil.gn.apc.org
Direct services for glb people through education,
information & counseling & support group
formation activities. Library & resource center,
quarterly newsletter called BreakOut. Lobbying
activities with government. Discussions,
workshops, video showings, fundraising
activities, etc.

POLAND

Local

Lambda Warsaw
24/26 Krakowskie
Przedmiescie Street
00-927 Warszawa 64

University of Warsaw: ALG Board
24/26 Krakowskie
Przedmiescie Street
00-927 Warszawa 64

Lambda Krakow
PO Box 249
30-960 Krakow 1

Lambda Wroclaw
PO Box 812
50-950 Wroclaw 2
 Ruch Lesbijek i Gejow.

Lambda Bydgoszcz
PO Box 111
85-956 Bydgoszcz 13

Lambda Torun
PO Box 115
87-116 Torun 17

Lambda Poznan
PO Box 176
Poznan 2
tel: 61/537655 (Fridays 5-8pm only)

RUSSIA

rus-bi   💻
e-mail: majordomo@bi.org
URL: bi.org/~russia/rus-bi.html
 Discussions on lesbianism & bisexuality in
 Russia
 & Russian-speaking countries.

All-Russian Amalgamation of Gays,   💻AH
Lesbians & Bisexuals
I-348
P.O. Box 17
Moscow 129348
e-mail: info@gayclub.ru
URL: www.gayclub.ru
 Provides legal assistance for GLB people.
 Participates in AIDS prevention programs.
 Spreads info. for & about GLB people. Develops
 one of the biggest Russian internet sites devoted
 to GBL issues.

Local

EGO   E
P.O. Box 264
Astrakhan 414000
e-mail: v_vk@yahoo.com
 Exchange of visits, leisure, information for &
 about GLB people. Contact person: Serguey
 Samoilenko **Publication(s)**: *Nash Mir*

Moscow Musical Festivals   💻
P.O. Box 17
Moscow 129648
tel: 7-095/188-4728; fax: 7-095/292/6511x547
e-mail: gayclub@glasnet.ru
URL: www.gayclub.ru
 Classical music promotion, support to young
 musicians, organization of musical festivals &
 other activities. GLB-friendly.

We & You   HA
Grafski per.4/9
Moscow 129626
tel: 7-095/916-4868; fax: 7-095/916-4868
e-mail: weandyou@online.ru
 Support for HIV+ GBL, spreading legal &
 medical info on AIDS & HIV in CIS countries.
 Publication(s): *Life Goes On*

"And the truth of my experience is this: my sexuality is whole. I am not
straight with men and lesbian with women; I am bisexual with both. Enjoying
sex with both women and men is no more an inherently schizophrenic form
of sexuality than enjoying both intercourse and oral sex."

—*Greta Christina* in Bisexual Politics.

Key to symbols: ▼ = bi   ♀ = women   ♂ = men   ☯ = religious/spiritual
👍 = for allies   **M** = for married bis   ♥ = for partners of bis   **Y** = youth   **C** = people of color
154   **The Bisexual Resource Guide 2000**

Megapolis agency　　　　　　　　**EA 🖳**
P.O. Box 425
Novosibirsk 630027
e-mail: orfey@online.nsk.su
URL: www.nsk.su/~orfey/
Unification & experience exchange for GBL;
information exchange with domestic &
international GLB groups; propagation for
healthy way of life, safer sex; support for non-
discrimination policy, defense of sexual
minorities' rights, change to non-homophobic
trends in the society.
Contact person: A. Grebenshikov.
Publication(s): *Sib-10 Siberian newspaper for*
gays & bisexuals, published bimonthly since
May 1996.

All Colours of Rainbow
P.O. Box 0556
Tver 170004
Computer based dating service, support for GLB
people in trouble, information & consultative
service for / on GLB groups in CIS states. Contact
persons: Alexey Vinogradov (President), Serguey
Tiotski (Vice President) **Publication(s)**: *S-*
express Monthly bulletin

Societas Thelemica Rutheniae
send mail to: S.T.R.
c/o Igor S. Anikeev
9-140 R. Luxemburg St.
Volgograd RU-40021
e-mail: Igor.Anikeev@p9.f54.n5055.z2.fidonet.org
We welcome anyone who's dedicated to the
principles of free love & is ready to accept the
Law of Thelema. We try to establish some
religious foundations for homo- / bisexuality. In
any case a person who's persecuted for his / her
sexual orientation can find a friendly community
here at the very least.

SINGAPORE

Oriental Sensation　　　　　　　　♂
134 Bukit Batok
West Avenue 6
#09-445
2365

People Like Us
PO Box 299
Raffeles City Post Office
9117

Local

Singapore: Action for AIDS　　　　**AH 🖳**
62-B Race Course Rd
Singapore S-218568
URL: www.khushnet.com/singapore.htm
AIDS action, local group. Listed in Khushnet.

SLOVAKIA

Local

Museion　　　　　　　　　　　　　♀
PO Box 410
Banska bystrica 1
Bratislava 97401
tel: (88) 43 656; 011-427-325-164; fax: 011-427-
832-175
Lesbicka organizacia.

SLOVENIA

Legebitra　　　　　　　　　　　　**Y▼**
e-mail: minus26@hotmail.com
URL: www.ljudmila.org/sigrd/legebitra.html

Local

Galfon, Gay & Lesbian Switchboard　　**E**
tel: 386/61-132-4089
Information, help, support every day 7 - 10 pm

Magnus　　　　　　　　　　　　**♂ HE**
Kersnikova 4
SI-1000
Ljubjana
tel: 386/61-132-7368; fax: 386/61-329-185
e-mail: siqrd@mila.ljudmila.org
Social organization for men only. They own a
gay club Tiffany, organize trips, work on safer-
sex education & AIDS / HIV prevention.

Roza klub　　　　　　　　　　　**A 🖳**
Kersnikova 4
SI-1000
Ljubljana
tel: 386/61-130-4740; fax: 386/61-329-185
e-mail: siqrd@mila.ljudmila.org
URL: www.ljudmila.org/sigrd/
Political & social group for women & men. Roza
klub publishes magazine Revolver, organizes gay
& lesbian film festival, works on education &
social events (clubs Roza disco & Propaganda),
co-operates at preparing law on registered
partnerships.

🖎 = school　　　⬸ = college/university　　P = professional　　　E = educational
A = activist/political　　H = health (incl. HIV)　　🖘 = media/press　　🖳 = Internet resource
The Bisexual Resource Guide 2000　　　　　　　　　　　　　　　　**155**

SKUC LL ♀ A 💻
Metelkova 6
SI-1000
Ljubljana
tel: 386/61-132-7368; fax: 386/61-329-185
e-mail: siqrd@mila.ljudmila.org
URL: www.ljudmila.org/lesbo/
Political & socal organization for women only.
They publish magazine Lesbo, work on lesbian
visibility, co-operate at preparing law on
registered partnerships. They also own lesbian
club Monokel (Eyeglass).

SOUTH AFRICA

Mazibuko Kanyiso Jara: A
Equal Rights Project National Coalition
for Gay & Lesbian Equality
P.O. Box 27811
Yeoville 2143
tel: 27/11-4873810/1/2
881/209-104 NCGLE voicemail; fax: 27/11-
4871670
Voluntary association of more than 74 LGBT
organizations in South Africa. Lobbied
successfully for the retention of sexual orienta-
tion as one of the grounds of non-discrimination
in the Constitution. Works for legal & social
equality for its members. Work includes law
reform, lobbying, litigation, advocacy,
employment equity, leadership training.

Roberta Gregory

Key to symbols: ▼ = bi ♀ = women ♂ = men ☾ = religious/spiritual
🐾 = for allies M = for married bis ♥ = for partners of bis Y = youth C = people of color

National Coalition for   **A**
Gay & Lesbian Equality
PO Box 27811
Yeoville/Bellevue 2198
tel: 27 (0) 1-4873810/1/2; vm: 0881 209 104; fax: 27 (0)11-4871670
Voluntary association of more than 74 lbgt organisations in South Africa. Successfully lobbied for the retention of sexual orientation as one of the grounds of non-discrimination in the Constitution. Mandated to work for legal & social equality for its members, including law reform, lobbying, litigation, advocacy, employment equity, leadership training & development.

Local

Assoication of Bisexuals,
Gays & Lesbians (ABIGALE)
Box 16534
Vlaeberg 8018
Cape Town
tel: Theresa or Middie on 902-241-532

Gay & Lesbian Organization
of Witwaterstrand
PO Box 23297
Joubert Park
Johannesburg 2044
tel: 011-403-4250; 011-720-6955

Lesbian, Gay & Bisexual Collective   **CA**
11 Battersea Avenue
Reservoir Hills, Durban
tel: Christopher David 31-821-309
URL: www.khushnet.com/south_africa.htm
Established to support people, do community outreach, provide a safe area.

Fata Morgana   ♂ **M**
PO Box 19003 Fisherhill
Trannsvaal/Johannesburg 1408
Support group for married gay men. Not a social club.

"When I finally began coming out to people I had the same feeling one has when, after a long hike, one takes off one's backpack. I felt light and wonderful, and surprised, because I had never realized just how much extra weight I had been carrying around."

—*Robyn Ochs*

SOUTH KOREA

See also listings under **Korea**.

ChinGu-sai   ♂ **EA**
P.O. Box # 1246
Kwanghwamun
Seoul 110-612
tel: 02/464-7916
02/462-8462; fax: 02/462-8425
e-mail: ebahn@chollian.net
Predominantly gay organization in Seoul. Various activities include: advocating gay pride, political activism, safer sex education, AIDS activism, self-esteem workshops, summer gay rights camp, phone & individual counselling **Publication(s)**: *ChinGu-sai (1994) Newsletter containing info on current events @ ChinGu-sai & other practical information for gay men.*

Kiri Kiri   ♀ **EA**
P.O. Box #1816
Kwanghwamun
Seoul 110-618
tel: 02/363-7213
02/313-3429; fax: 02/363-7213
The 1st, largest & most political lesbian org. In recognition of the exclusion of lesbian issues & agenda from gay discourse, subculture & feminism in Korea, Kiri Kiri stives for lesbian visibility & to raise lesbian rights as a social issue. Activities include: lesbophobia criticism, political activism, safer sex education, & providing a safe & supportive environment for lesbians (phone & individual counseling too). **Publication(s)**: *Alternative World 1st Lesbian publication: lesbophobia criticsm, safer sex education, practical information for lesbians, film/book/event reviews*

Queer Film Festival Organization   **EA**
Midong Building #301
195 - 1 Nakwon - Dong
Chongno - Ku
Seoul
tel: 02/766-5626; fax: 02/766-0598
e-mail: queer21@shinbiro.com
This org. planned to hold the 1st queer film festival in Seoul in 1997, but the festival was cancelled several times due to government censorship. They will continue to attempt to hold the festival. Furthmore, they wish to make the existence of queer visible in a heterosexist society such as Korea & promote a positive understanding of queer identities. **Publication(s)**: *Queer Cinenews: Irregular Magazine Official news & activities related to Queer Film Festival. Reports lates happenings in the queer cinema community.*

✎ = school   ⚲ = college/university   P = professional   E = educational
A = activist/political   H = health (incl. HIV)   ✍ = media/press   ▭ = Internet resource
The Bisexual Resource Guide 2000   **157**

Local

Yonsei University: Come Together   ⚥EA🖳
tel: 015/357-3769
URL: note.com/cometo
1st gay group in Korea, contributing greatly to raising gay rights as a social issue in Korea. Strives to provide a space where individuals can share their personal experiences & spport each other. Members also translate & read various foreign books on gay discourse. Currently trying to network with other unviersity gay/lesbian groups.

Ditto (Katten-Maum)   EAH
Pusan
tel: 051-809-2583
The meaning of ditto (katten-maum) is sameness, homogenity. All of our members are sexual minorities & we chose the name for the purpose of "becoming one". There are few local queer groups in Korea. Most of the groups exist in Seoul & Ditton (katten-maum) is a local queer group in Pusan & Kyungnam. The queer culture of this region differs from Seoul & other regions so our org. is specific to the region. Acitivites inclue: counseling, AIDS activism, aiding HIV+ people, political activism.

Dae Dong In   EA
PO Box 97
Kwanghwamun
Seoul110-600
tel: 02-923-0609; fax: 02-923-2175
Composed of members from Seoul, this organization welcomes everyone concerned about sexual minority rights. Sexual orientation or preference does not matter (transgender, queer, heterosexual...) Advocates gay/lesbian rights & strives to gain visibility. **Publication(s)***: Dyke Monthly newsletter describing various activities & news about the organization.*

Seoul National University: MaEum 006   ⚥▼
Seoul
tel: pager 015/8446-2570 or 02/965-6544
e-mail: ebahn@chollian.net
LGB student group at Seoul Nation University that welcomes all sexual minorites. The original name of this group was MaEum 001. Heterosexuals can be seen as having 100% of rights whereas homosexuals are just recently gaining rights & recognition. To symbolize this struggle, the group increases the number each time a positive social change for LGB rights happens. **Publication(s)***: MaEum 006 Newsletter for the organization: heterosexism, AIDS activism, LBG rights movement.*

SPAIN

ANAT - CP   HYE
Apdo. 126,
348805
Guardo Palencia
tel: 0034/902-11-49-49
e-mail: anat@dragonet.es
NGO whose ojectives are attention, information for people with drug dependency and/or HIV/AIDS infection. Services & activities include: information/education, rehab, youth group, social activities, self-support, education, cultural groups, sport group.

Collectiu Lambda de Gais i Lesbianes del Pais Valencia   🖳
c/ Salvador Giner, 9 b. izq.
CP 46003
Valencia, Valencia
e-mail: lambda@arrakis.es
URL: www.arrakis.es/~lambda
Various associated groups: youth, lesbian, AIDS prevention, christian gays, university groups. Telephone information, library, medical, social, & mental help services, legal assistance.

Local

HERAKLES - SAFO Assemblea per la Llibertat Sexual [Assembly for Sexual Liberty]
C/ Los Centelles 29-10
46.006 Valéncia (País Valencià)
tel: (34) 96 334 03 28; fax: same
e-mail: herasafo@arrakis.es
fils@xarxaneta.org (FILS)
Somos abiertos a todos/as los/as que estamos por la libertad sexual. Coordinados con el movimiento alternativo que denuncia le homofobia. Se ha creado el Fórum Internacional para la Libertad Sexual FILS. Nuestro grupo gestiona una base de datos con contenidos de libertad sexual y alternativos. [Open to all those who believe in sexual liberty. Works with the alternative movement that denounces homophobia. Created FILS, the International Forum for Sexual Freedom. Maintains a database of information about sexual freedom & alternatives.] Organizes concerts & a film series.

SRI LANKA

Friendship Sri Lanka   ♀
c/o Shan Gunawardane
1049 Pannipitiya Rd
Battaramulla
Colombo
For lesbians & bisexual women.

Key to symbols: ▼ = bi   ♀ = women   ♂ = men   ☯ = religious/spiritual
♦ = for allies   **M** = for married bis   ♥ = for partners of bis   **Y** = youth   **C** = people of color
158   **The Bisexual Resource Guide 2000**

Local

Companions on a Journey A💻
1003 /5 Park Lane
Welikada Rajagiriya
tel: 941-072-87675
URL: www.khushnet.com/sri_lanka.htm
Gay men & lesbians.

SWEDEN

Local

Bikupan ▼
c/o RFSL, Stockholm
Box 350, S-101 26
Stockholm
tel: Christopher Arnold: (+46) 8 628 89 08
e-mail: chris@bahnhof.se

SWITZERLAND

Bi-group-Basel ▼♂
c/o Stephan Kalt
Delsbergerallee 55
Basel Basel-Stadt 4053
tel: 061 331 66 14
e-mail: stephan@bidule.com
Weekly meetings.

BINE CH (Bisexuelles Netzwerk ▼AM♥💻
Schweiz - Antenne Bisexuel Suisse -
Bisexuel Network Switzerland)
PO 5543
Bern Bern 3001
tel: 41 31769 1033; fax: 41 31769 1037
e-mail: bine_ch@gmx.net
URL: www.bine.ch/
National organization.

Groupe Bi, vogay ▼EA💻
13 des Oiseaux
CP 894
1000 Lausanne 9
tel: 0041.21.646.25.35; fax: 0041.21646.29.29
e-mail: vogay@worldcom.ch (groupe bi)
URL: www.vogay.ch
*Meetings & information 2nd Wednesdays of the
month.*

VoGay, Jeunnes gays, bis et lesbiennes ▼♀Y
13, av des Oiseaux 13
CP 894
CH-1000 Lausanne 9
tel: 41-21/646 25 35; fax: 41-21/646 29 29
e-mail: vogay@worldcom.ch (femme bi)
URL: www.vogay.ch

Local

Bisexuelle Frauengruppe ▼♀
Postfach 2309
Luzern 6002
Monthly meetings.

Bisexualle Frauen Groupe ▼♀
Postfache 5505
3001 Berne
tel: 41-32-322-55-31

Association 360° A
CP 411
1211 Geneve 4
tel: Philippe (in France): 0033-450-38-1005
*Association open to all - promotes the idea of
acceptance of ALL sexual preferences.*

Gruppe fuer schwule Vatern, verheiratete ♂
Schwulen und bisexuelle Maenner
send mail to: HABS
P.O. Box CH-4001
Basel
tel: 061-692-6655
e-mail: steilacotschna@compuserve.com
*Heterogeneous group of men: mixed age, social
status & background. Members either switched
their lifestyle from straight to gay or define
themselves as bisexual.*

Artemesia Y♀
Sihlquai 67
Post Fach 7088
Zurich 8023
tel: 0041 (0) 1243 02 70, Tuesdays from 7pm
Phone line.

UKRAINE

Local

**The Foundation to Defend the Rights of
Sexual Minorities**
a/r 8506
Kharkov 310055
tel: 38-0572-934264; fax: 38-0572-934264
Seeking contacts & assistance from abroad.

**Kiev Regional Intellect Club for
Gays & Bisexuals**
P.O. Box #99
Kieve-80254080
e-mail: nick@nym.alias.net
*Revival of the spirituality among GLB, leisure
activities, & info. on GLB in Ukraine. Contact
person: Nickolay Yanko.*

🖉 = school   ꝏ = college/university   P = professional   E = educational
A = activist/political   H = health (incl. HIV)   ✍ = media/press   💻 = Internet resource
The Bisexual Resource Guide 2000   *159*

Lugansk Regional Club for GLB People 💻
PO Box 62
Lugansk-51348051
tel: 0642/479422; fax: 0642/479422
e-mail: editor@ourworld.lugansk.ua
URL: www.geocities.com/WestHollywood/2118/
*Lugansk regional GLB club. Contact: Andrey
Maymulakhin* **Publication(s)**: *Nash mir
monthly magazine*

UNITED KINGDOM

Bisexual Phone Lines ▼
*England: 0(1)81-569-7500 Tuesdays &
Wednesdays, 7:30-9:30pm & 10:30am-12:30 pm
Sat. Scotland: Edinburgh bi helpline 0(1)31-557-
3620, Thursdays, 7:30-9:30pm.*

Bi-Academic Intervention ▼P
send mail to: B-AI, A. Kaloski & C. Hemmings
University of York
Women's Studies Centre
5 Main St.
Heslington,York, North YorkshireYO1 5DD
England YO1 5DD
e-mail: eakn1@york.ac.uk or socs197@york.ac.uk
*Support & information network for bisexuals &
others doing research or providing resources on
bisexuality. Holds twice yearly "day schools,"
circulates bibliographies & puts like people in
touch.* **Publication(s)**: *Bi-Academic Intervention More or less monthly. Donations to cover
cost of mailing encouraged.*

Biscuits Network Y▼
PO Box 3
Herts England AL8 7DR
*Young bisexual national activities for those
under 26. Send SASE.*

UK-BI ▼💻
e-mail: listserv@ogham.org
*Mailing list for bisexuals in the UK. To
subscribe, send a message to listserv@ogham.org
with no subject, reading subscribe uk-bi
{yourname}.*

uk-smbi 💻▼
e-mail: majordomo@bi.org
URL: bi.org/uk-smbi
*Mailing list for discussions about SM-
bisexuality, or any topic of interest to SM
bisexuals, specifically related to the UK. This list
aims to be a bi-positive, SM-positive safe space.*

Bisexual Therapists Forum ▼P
England
tel: Contact through Bisexual Phoneline (London):
0(1)81 569 7500
For those involved in counseling work.

Off Pink Publishing Collective ▼
24 Shandon Rd.
Clapham Park
London England SW4 9HR
e-mail: OffPink@bi.org
*Publishers of Bisexual Lives & Bisexual
Horizons.*

South Region Bisexual Women's Network ▼♀
90 Highbury Hill
London England N5 1AT
*Network for bisexual women in UK & bi
women's groups. Organizes regular workshops &
camps.*

BASH ▼HE💻
(Bisexual's Action on Sexual Health)
PO Box 10048
London England SE15 42D
e-mail: klano@hotmail.com
URL: bi.org/~kcl/bash.html
*Promotes health of people who have sex w/both
men & women, however they identify, & of people
who are self-identified bisexuals. Safe-sex
workshops, bisexuality awareness training, HIV
prevention initiative & projects, research,
workshops, leaflets, peer education project, safer
sex workshops in Higher Education, organiza-
tional meetings monthly.*

I forgot that when we find comfort in "us" and "them,"
we are sometimes uncovering the unacknowledged chasm of differing
experience and other times we're retreating from kinship with people not so
different after all, or kin *because* of their difference, because of what they
know about how to live their different lives that might directly apply to our
lives. Sometimes what they know is the only thing that will save us or
comfort us, and we sit divided from each other by the lines in the sand,
dying of thirst next to a pitcher of water.

—Elise Matthesen

Key to symbols: ▼ = bi ♀ = women ♂ = men ☉ = religious/spiritual
👤 = for allies **M** = for married bis ♥ = for partners of bis **Y** = youth **C** = people of color

LGB National Pen Pals
PO Box 2000, Harwich
Horwich,Bolton, Greater ManchesterBL6 7PG
England BL6 7PG
tel: (01204) 667747
For all people over 18 in the UK. Members socials. Info on under 18's services. Send SAE for info.

UK-MOTSS　　　　　　　　　　　　　　　🖳
e-mail: see below
URL: uk-motss.diversity.org.uk
For more info, view the web page or send email to uk-motss-request@diversity.org.uk with only "info uk-motss" in the body of the message.

England

Bisexual groups which may be　　▼♀♥
forming in England
England
Bristol: David c/o BM RiBBiT, London WC1N 3XX (please enclose a stamp for forwarding). Dundee: Cathy c/o Dundee L/G switchboard. Mondays 7-10pm. PO Box 53, Dundee, DD1 3YG. Essex: Jean on 01245 420403. Ilkley: Angela 01943 863 796. Manchester: Straight partners of lesbians, gays, bisexuals. MBG, PO Box 153, Manchester M60 1LP. Newcastle: Bi Women's Group 0191 261 8360.

Local

Bi Community News　　　　　　　　▼🖳
BM RiBBit
London England WC1N 3XX
e-mail: bcn@bi.org
URL: www.bi.org/~ben/
Back issues available on the webpage. National newsletter for UK bisexuals; upcoming events, bi-related publications & films, interviews & articles, cartoons, letters. UK's only regular listing of bi news, groups & events around the country. **Publication(s)***: 12 issues (1 year)*
£8.50
unwages £6.00

Birmingham: Bi Brum　　　　　　　　▼
c/o Abundance, PO Box 5190
Birmingham England B13 90J
tel: Alice: 0121 773 1914
Meets monthly on 3rd Wednesdays 8pm at the Fox Pub (back room), Lower Essex St, Digbeth.

Bristol Bisexual Group　　　　　　　▼
Bristol, Avon England
tel: Sarah 0117-902-1671
Meets socially 1st Tuesdays at 8pm in The Pineapple, St Georges Road, Bristol.

Cambridge Bi Group　　　　　　　▼A🖳
c/o John Dawson
Wolfson College
Barton Road
Cambridge England CB3 9BB
tel: (01223) 335029 (work)
(01763) 226002 (home)
e-mail: cambi@bi.org
URL: bi.org/~combi/
Socials from 8pm at Town & Gown, Northampton St.

Leeds Bisexual Group　　　　　　　　▼
5 Broughton Av.
Harehills
Leeds, Yorkshire England LS9 6BD
Meets Mondays at the Old Red Lion Pub.

Leicester Bi Group　　　　　　　　　▼
Leicester, Leicestershire England
tel: (0116) 2550667 M-F 7:30-10pm
Meets alternate Wednesdays 7:30pm., 45 Kings St.

Liverpool Bi Group　　　　　　　　　▼
LFSG
c/o Friend Merseyside
36 Bolton St.
Liverpool England L3 WBG
tel: (0151) 709 5137
Meets 2nd Mondays. Mixed group, started by bisexuals.

London Bisexual Group　　　　　　▼🖳
PO Box 3325
London England N1 9DN
tel: 081-569-7500
e-mail: LondonBi@bi.org
URL: www.bi.org/~LondonBi
Meets Fridays, 8pm, at London Friend, 86 Caledonian Road N1 (nearest tube, Kings Cross - St. Pancras) Large group, runs other social events.

London Bisexual Women's Group　　▼♀
BM-LBWG
London England WC1N 3XX
Meets Thursdays, 7-10pm, the Wesley House, Wild Court, Holborn. Newcomers 6:45 pm.

Biphoria　　　　　　　　　　　　　　▼
L&G Centre
PO Box 153
Manchester England M60 1LP
tel: (0161) 274-3999
Meets 1st Thursdays 8pm at the L&G Centre on Sydney St., off Oxford Rd. Mixed social/ discussion group. Club night- 1st Saturday after meeting. Cinema Night- 2nd Wednesday each month. Bi Ramble- Escape to countryside one Sunday a month.

🐾 = school　　　　　🎓 = college/university　　　P = professional　　　　　E = educational
A = activist/political　　H = health (incl. HIV)　　📰 = media/press　　　🖳 = Internet resource
The Bisexual Resource Guide 2000　　　　　　　　　　　　　　　　　　　　　*161*

Nottingham Bi Group　▼
Box B, Hiziki
15 Goosegate, Hockley
Nottingham, Nottinghamshire England NG1 1FE
tel: 0115-916-1532
Send SASE for info. Meets 2nd Thursday, 8pm.
in Room 3, International Community Center,
61b Mansfield Road.

Nottingham Women's Bi Group　▼ ♀
Nottingham Women's Centre
30 Chaucer St.
Nottingham, Nottinghamshire England NG1 5LP
Meets 8pm 3rd Tues at above address. Press
buzzer marked "library."

Bisexual Group　▼
Sheffield England
tel: (0114) 275 4387

Staffordshire Bisexual Group　▼
PO Box 362, 2B Hope Street
Hanley S-O-T
Stafford, Staffordshire England ST17 9GH
tel: Lesbian/Gay Switchboard: 0782 266998 for
details
Meets 1st Tues. 8pm at members' houses. Write
or call for details.

Bi Parents' Network　▼
BPN c/o Lisa Geary
Lisa Lovely
c/o BM Rabbit
London England WC1N 3XX
When writing for info, include SASE.

Black Bisexuals' Social Group　C▼
c/o LBG, PO Box 3325
London England N1 9EQ
e-mail: LondonBi@bi.org
Meets 1st Friday in separate room at LGB.

SM/Bi　▼
c/o Central Station
37 Wharfdale Road
London England N1 9SE
e-mail: smbi@andelain.demon.co.uk
Network of bisexuals into S&M, newsletter,
contacts, campaigning, etc. Meets 2nd Sunday
7:30pm. **Publication(s)***: Ungagged Free with*
SAE

MAYBE (Manchester Bi Youth Group)　Y▼
P.O. Box 153
Manchester England M60 1LP
For under 26's.

ComBiNe　▼♥
(Community of Bisexuals in the North East)
PO Box 1JR
Newcastle-Upon-Tyne England NE1
Monthly social/support group for bisexual
women, men, partners of bis & allies. Meets 3rd
Mondays. also women's group.

Newcastle Bisexual Women's Group　▼ ♀
PO Box 1JR
Newcastle-Upon-TyneNE99 1JR England

Bath University:　👫🖥
LGB Society - Square Pegs
Bath England
tel: Tuesdays 6-7pm on Bath (01225) 465793
e-mail: lgb@bath.ac.uk.
URL: www.bath.ac.uk/~su4lgbs/
Regular informal meetings in 4E 3.22on Tues. 6-
7pm.

Birmingham University Lesbian, Gay,　👫♀🖥
Bisexual Society
Birmingham England
tel: (0121) 472 1841x254.
e-mail: LGB@bham.ac.uk
URL: www.bham.ac.uk/lgba/
Meets 8pm Thursdays during termtime at Guild
of Students, LGB Room. Open daily 1-2pm.
There is a separate lesbian & bi women's group
as well.

Maypole Birmingham Lesbian, Bisexual &　Y
Gay Youth Group
Birmingham, West Midlands England
tel: 0800 317780, M-F 5-7pm.
URL: phymat.bham.ac.uk/LGB/westmidlands/
maypole-bhamyth.html
For lgbs under 21. Meets Wed. 7-9:30pm.

Bolton NUS Lesbian Gay & Bisexual Society　👫
Students Union
Bolton Institute of Higher Education
Deane Rd.
Bolton, Greater Manchester England

Bournemouth University LGB Society　👫
Bournemouth, Dorset England
tel: Contact Julia (Wordcode) (Student Welfare
Officer) on (01202) 523755

University of Sussex:　👫▼
Brighton Bi Coffee & Cake Mornings
LGBT Room, Falmer House
BrightonSussex England BN1 9QF
e-mail: sau30@contral.sussex.ac.uk
Meets even weeks on Wednesday during terms at
the LGBT room (232) from 11 am. Non-students
welcome.

Key to symbols:　▼ = bi　　♀ = women　　♂ = men　　☾ = religious/spiritual
♠ = for allies　**M** = for married bis　♥ = for partners of bis　**Y** = youth　　**C** = people of color

University of Brighton: LGB Society   🎓▼
Students Union, Falmer House 232
Brighton, Sussex England BN1 9PH
Meeets Tuesdays 6pm during termtime.

University of Sussex: Bi Group   🎓▼
Falmer House
Brighton, Sussex England
tel: 01273248181
e-mail: sau30@central.sussex.ac.uk
Even weeks, Weds during term, 11am onwards LGBT room (232), Falmer House, U. of Sussex. Non-students welcome.

Bristol Young Lesbian & Bisexual Group   Y ♀
c/o Acro Russez Town Avenue
Redfield
Bristol, Avon England
For girls & women up to 25 who are lesbian, bisexual or questioning their sexuality.

Bromley LGB Social Group   Y
Bromley England
tel: James: (0181) 289-0711 after 6pm.
For under 30s. Meets 2nd & 4th Thursday.

Cambridge University LBG Society   🎓
Students Union
10-12 Trumpington Street
Cambridge England
tel: Termtime: (01223) 333313 Tuesdays 8-11pm;
fax: 01223/323-244
Mondays 9pm at University Centre Bar, Granta Place. Phone first.

Sister Act   ♀ 🖥
PO Box 294
Cambridge, East Anglia England CB4 2XR
tel: 01223 512784
URL: dialspace.dial.pipex.com/town/estate/acb2b/sister
Social club for lesbian & bi women. Weekly events, monthly newsletter.

University LGB Society   🎓
Rutherford SCR
Canterbury, Kent England
tel: Gayline: (01227) 454868, Wed. 8pm-8am.
ÒNot just for students.Ó
Tuesdays 7:30pm during termtime.

Colchester LGB Youth Group   Y
Colchester, Essex England
tel: Switchboard: 01206 869191 (Mon.-Fri. 7-10)
e-mail: alainhea@hotmail.com
For under 25s.

Essex University LGB Society   🎓
c/o Student Union
Colchester, Essex England
Meets Wednesdays at 8pm. Disabled access.

CHB   ▼
Coventry, West Midlands England
Informal group meets in cafe monthly. Write for info c/o Bi Community News, include SASE.

Coventry LGB Youth Group   Y
Coventry, West Midlands England
tel: (0120) 3224090
For those under 21. Meets Saturday 1-4pm.

Derby University: LGB Society   🎓
Derby England
tel: 01332-349333 (Wednesdays 7-10pm)
Meets Thursdays 8pm termtime at the University, Green Lane.

Exeter University: LGB Group   🎓
LGB Officers, Guild of Students
Top Corridor, Devonshire House, Stocker Road
Devon, Devonshire England
tel: (01392) 263541
Meets Fridays 8pm during termtime in Devonshire House.

Happy Families
c/o Community House
7 Netherhall Road
Doncaster England DN6 9QE
tel: Glyn & Richard
(01302) 702601
Support group for lgb parents. Local groups in formation.

Exeter University: LGB Group   🎓🖥
LGB Officers, Guild of Students
Top Corridor, Devonshire House, Stocker Rd
Exeter England
e-mail: lgb@exeter.ac.uk
URL: gosh.ex.ac.uk/services/welfare/lgb.html
Meets alternate Tuesdays (even weeks of term) at Barts Tavern, 53 Bartholomew St West.

Greenwich Gay & Bi Youth   Y♂
Greenwich England
tel: Nigel or James: (0181) 316 4397
For men under 26. Meets Mon. & Fri. 7-9:30pm.

Lancaster University: LGB Society   🎓
Lancaster England
Meets Tursdays 8pm in Chaplaincy Centre.

DeMontfort & Leicester University: LGB Group   🎓
Leicester, Leicestershire England
tel: DeMontfort contact: Ray, LGB Officer: (0116) 2555576. Leicester contact: Jazz: (0116) 2556282x143) or ansaphone (0116) 2555394.
e-mail: lgb@leister.ac.uk
Meets Wednesday 8-10pm during termtime.

🏫 = school   🎓 = college/university   **P** = professional   **E** = educational
A = activist/political   **H** = health (incl. HIV)   📧 = media/press   🖥 = Internet resource
The Bisexual Resource Guide 2000   **163**

Leicester Black Lesbian,   **C**
Gay & Bisexual Group
c/ Leicester LGB Communities Resource Centre
45 King St.
Leicester Leicestershire England
tel: Dylan (Thursdays): 0116 2541747; 0116
2547412
*Monthly meeting at Leicester LGB Communities
Resource Centre, 45 King St.*

Leicester LGB Communities Resource Centre
45 King St.
Leicester Leicestershire England
tel: (0116) 2550667 M-F 7:30-10pm

GYRO Gay Youth 'r' Out   **Y🖳**
36 Boltan St.
Liverpool England L3 5LX
tel: 015-17-089-552 7-10PM (General); 015-17-
094-745 (Fri 8-10PM TV/TS); 015-17-080-224 T/
Th 7-10PM W)
e-mail: gyro@gayyouth.u-net.com
URL: www.personal.u-net.com/~gayyouth/html/
friend_merseyside.htm
*Voluntary organisation offering confidential
help, info & support to lesbians, glbts, & those
unsure, & family & friends.*

Liverpool University/John Moore University: 🌈
Lesbian, Gay & Bisexual Society
Brownler Road
Liverpool England
tel: 0151-7089552 7-10pm
URL: www.personal.u-net.com/~gayyouth/
home.htm
Meets Tues. 8pm during termtime.

Barnet Lesbian, Gay & Bisexual Group
London England
tel: Graham/Andy: (0181) 361 4182; Robert (0181)
349 9579; Roger: (0956) 505 683
*Meets 1st & 3rd Thurs. Old Bull Arts Center,
High St.*

Bexley LGB Group
London England
tel: (0181) 316 5954 M-Th 5-8pm

Divas   **Y ♀**
London England
tel: (0181) 533-2174
*For lesbian & bi women under 21. Meets Fridays
6-8 in Hackney.*

Gemma   **♀**
BM Box 5700
London England WC1N 3XX
*Friendship network of lesbian & bi women with /
without disabilities.*

Hineinu   **🌐**
5 Frome Street
Islington
London England N1 8PB
e-mail: hineinu@weglijo.org
GLB Jewish group.

LG&Bi With Learning Difficulties   **A**
c/o Tim Hart
57a Chester Rd.
London England N19

London Gay & Bisexual Men's Group   **♂**
c/o New Cross Circle Project
308 New Cross Rd.
London England SE14
tel: Sakthi: (0181) 316-5954 M-F 5-8pm
Alternate Wednesdays 7-9pm.

London Gay & Bisexual Women's Group   **♀**
c/o New Cross Circle Project
308 New Cross Rd.
London England SE14
tel: Sakthi: (0181) 316-5954 M-F, 5-8pm.
Alternate Wednesdays 7-9pm.

London Lesbian & Bi Support Group   **♀**
c/o Greenwich MIND
54 Ormiston Rd.
London England SE10
tel: Sakthi: (0181) 316-5954 M-F 5-8pm

Newdykes   **♀ Y**
London England
tel: Jane: 0181-534 6397 or Deb: 0181-514 0452
*For young l/b women or those exploring their
sexuality.*

Newham Out   **Y♂**
London England
tel: Richard: 0181-470 2350 during meeting times.
*Gay & bi men under 25 year olds meets
Wednesdays 7-10, 5 minutes from Upton Park
Tube.*

Outlinks: LGB Youth Project   **Y**
London England
tel: (0171) 378- 8732
*1 on 1 meeting with youth worker. Mixed social
group 7-9pm Tuesdays.*

Shakti
P.O. Box 93
28A Seymour Place
London England W1H 5WH
tel: helpline (171)837-7341
For South Asian lgbt people.

Key to symbols: ▼ = bi   ♀ = women   ♂ = men   🌐 = religious/spiritual
🌈 = for allies   **M** = for married bis   ♥ = for partners of bis   **Y** = youth   **C** = people of color
164   **The Bisexual Resource Guide 2000**

Spectrum   Y
London England
tel: Jennifer/Martin: (0181) 981-5017 Tuesdays
6:30-9:30pm.
Tower Hamlets LGB youth project.

Staying Out   Y
London England
tel: 0181-533-2174
*For LGB people under 21. Meetings Tuesdays 7-
10pm in Hackney.*

Venus Project   C
London England
tel: Avie: (0171) 272 8467; Adrienne (0171) 281-
2121
Black LGB group.

Youth Out   Y
London England
tel: 0181-532-8008
*Waltham Forest LGB people under 25. Meetings
7-10pm Mondays.*

Keele University LGB Society   &*
Lyme, Staffordshire England
tel: (01782) 711411x113
Wed 1-2pm: Nightclub in Students Union.

Manchester University: Stepping Stones &* ⌨
Lesbian, Gay & Bisexual Society
Manchester University Students Union
Oxford Rd
Manchester England M13 9PR
e-mail: lgbsoc@umu.man.ac.uk
URL: www.umu.man.ac.uk/lgbsoc/
Meets weekly.

WILD (Women's Bi & Lesbian   ▼ ♀
Discussion Group)
L&G Centre
PO Box 153
Manchester England M60 1LP
tel: (0161) 274 3814
*Meets 3rd Thursdays 8pm at the L&G Centre on
Sydney St., off Oxford Rd. Social/discussion
group. Also hosts regular social events.*

University of Teeside LGB Group   &*
LGB Officer
Students Union, Borough Rd.
Middlesbrough, Cleveland England TS1 3BA
tel: (01642) 342234

Lesbian, Gay & Bisexual Society   &*
King's Walk, Union Society
Newcastle-Upon-Tyne England
tel: Andrew Smith (LGB Officer): 01 91 232 8402
*Meets 7:30 pm, women's room, 1st floor of union
building, termtimes.*

Northumberland University Gay,   &*
Lesbian or Bisexual Experience (GLOBE)
Newcastle-Upon-Tyne England
*Meets Thursdays at 8pm during termtime in the
Purple Lounge, 1st Floor, Union Building.*

Chameleon Youth   YA ⌨
Norwich England
e-mail: nymhp@dircon.co.uk
scott@pheonix.co.uk
URL: www.dircon.couk/ngmhp/cy/
*LGB Youth up to age 21. Monthly support group
in Norwich UK.*

Nottingham Trent University: &* E
Lesbian, Gay & Bisexual Society
Nottingham, Nottinghamshire England
tel: Stuart: (0115) 9790959
*Meets termtime on Mondays at 7:30pm in
Dryden Street Library (lecture theatre ground
floor) during termtime. Non-students welcome.*

Oxford LGB Youth Group   Y
Oxford England
tel: 01865/243-389
For LGB's under 25.

Oxford University: &*
Lesbian, Gay & Bisexual Society
Student Union
28 Little Clarendon Street
Oxford England

Plymouth Bi Group   ▼
Plymouth EX8 3HS England
e-mail: bisexion@bi.org
Meets Mon. 7-9:30pm, Bretonside.

University of Portsmouth LGB   &* ⌨
Portsmouth, Hampshire England
tel: (01705) 819141
01705 755 866 (nightline, 8pm-8am)
e-mail: mckinnas@ee.port.ac.uk
URL: www.port.ac.uk/~lgb/
*Meets Thursdays 7:30pm, Main Meeting Room,
Allen House, 1st Floor.*

University of Central Lancashire: &*
LG&B Society
Preston, Lancashire England
tel: LGB Officer: (01772) 258382 x225

Southampton: Breakout   Y
Southampton England
tel: (01703) 223344
*Youth project for under 26s. LGBQ. Meets
Thursdays 7:30-9:30pm.*

🖎 = school   &* = college/university   **P** = professional   **E** = educational
A = activist/political   **H** = health (incl. HIV)   🗚 = media/press   ⌨ = Internet resource

Stockport Lesbian, Gay & Bisexual Group YH♂
c/o SMASH
188 Buxton Rd.
Stockport, Greater ManchesterSK2 7AE England
tel: (0161) 487 2020; (0161) 477-4096
Youth group for under 26s, & health project for gay & bi men.

University of Sunderland LGB Society 🔗
LGB, Union Corridor
Wearmouth Hall, Chester Rd.
Sunderland England
tel: (0191) 5145512
(0191) 5157000
Meets Mondays 7:30-9:30pm in "quiet room."

Quaker Lesbian & Gay Fellowship ☯
3 Hallsfield, Ruth, Cricklade
Swindon England SN6 6LR
Bi-positive Quaker group.

Brunel University: LGB Society 🔗💻
c/o Union of Brunel Students
UxbridgeUB8 3PH England UB8 3PH
tel: 01895 462200
Student Union; fax: 01895 810477
e-mail: Brunel.LGB.Society@Brunel.ac.uk
URL: www.brunel.ac.uk/~xxsugsoc/

Cheshire LGB Group
c/o YMCA
3 Winnmarleigh St.
Warrington, Cheshire England WA1 1NB
tel: Sue or Madelane (01925) 32771 8-10pm
Also in Warrington: LGB Helpline: 01925 241994 (live Mondays 7-9pm, other times answerphone).

Henrietta's Out ♀
West Midlands England
tel: Contact (0121) 442 4767
Popular social group for l/b women that has in the past organised non-scene events such as sports, tea dances & canal trips.

Winchester LGB Group
Winchester England
tel: Ken: (01962) 852691; Paul: (01730) 262917
Meets Thursdays 7:30-10:30pm.

Woking LGB Group Y
Woking, Surrey England
tel: Lesley: (01483) 767005
For under 25s. Meets 1st & 3rd Thursdays at Crescent Project, Heathside Crescent.

University of Wolverhampton: 🔗
Lesbian, Gay & Bisexual Students' Group
Student's Union, Wulfruna Street
Woverhampton England WV1 1LY
tel: 01902 322021 (Student Union)

One in Ten Project Y
York England
tel: 01904-612629
For LGB youth under 26. Mondays 7-9pm.

Yorkpride Y
York England
tel: John Knight or Sandra Mitchell: 01904-433723/4.
Youth LGB group. Thursdays 7:30pm.

Dales Information & Support Line
Yorkshire England
tel: David: (01677) 424665. Wednesdays 7-9:30pm.
For gay & bisexual men.

Scotland

National Union of Students - 🔗
East of Scotland
Gay, Lesbian & Bisexual Officer
East of Scotland Area NUS
11 Broughton Market
Edinburgh Scotland EH3 6NU
tel: 0131-558-1541

National Union of Students - 🔗
North of Scotland
Gay, Lesbian & Bisexual Officer
North of Scotland Area NUS
University of Abertay, 158 Marketgait
Dundee Scotland DD1 1NJ

National Union of Students - 🔗
West of Scotland
Gay, Lesbian & Bisexual Officer
Cathcart House, Langside College
50 Prospecthill Rd.
GlasgowG42 9LB Scotland
tel: Gary McNeil: 0141-636 6477

Scotland - National Union of Students 🔗
Scotland
Many Universities & Colleges have LGB Societies. Contact these via your Student Union or Student Association. Many are open to non-students living in the area. There are also groups covering wider areas run in conjunction with the National Union of Students. See other listings in this section.

Key to symbols: ▼ = bi   ♀ = women   ♂ = men   ☯ = religious/spiritual
☙ = for allies   M = for married bis   ♥ = for partners of bis   Y = youth   C = people of color
166   The Bisexual Resource Guide 2000

Local

Edinburgh Bisexual Group ▼
c/o Scottish Centre for Lesbians, Gays &
Bisexuals
58a Broughton Street
Edinburgh Scotland EH1 3SA
tel: 0(1)31-557-3620
*Meets Thurs 8pm, LGB Centre, 58a Broughton
St.* **Publication(s)**: *Ubiquitous*

Glasgow Bisexual Network H▼ 🖳
PO Box 15236
Glasgow Scotland G4 9YF
e-mail: gbn@bi.org
URL: bi.org/~gbn/
*Social support & health information to Bisexuals
& their supporters living in Glasgow. Regular
social meetings held at above address.
Volunteers encouraged. For more info, write
Domenic Aveyard, GBN Group Coordinator, 127
Glenhead Street, Parkhouse, Glasgow G22 6DQ,
Scotland, UK.*

Dundee LGB Switchboard
PO Box 53
Dundee Scotland DD1 3YJ
tel: (01382) 202620
Mondays 7-10pm.

Dundee LGB Youth Group Y
Dundee Scotland
tel: 01382/202-620

Edinburgh University: Biversity ᵍᵍ ▼
c/o BLOGS
60 The Pleasance
Edinburgh Scotland EH8 9TJ
tel: 0131 557 3620 Thurs 7:30-9:30pm
*Meets Thursday evenings 7:30-9:30pm. Meets
weekly during termtime at University of
Edinburgh. Non-students welcome. Large group.*

**Scottish Center for Lesbians, Gays &
Bisexuals**
58A Broughton Street
Edinburgh Scotland EH1 3SA
*Runs GLIB, a lesbigay info bureau (MWF 2-
8pm), & cafe: Nexus, daily 11am-11pm.*

St. Andrew's University LGB Society ᵍᵍ
Fife Scotland
*Meets Mondays 7:30, Management Institute, St.
Mary's Place. Non-students welcome.*

Paisley Forum
Paisley Scotland
tel: Allan Johnstone 0141-842 7200 (9-5 only) or
Strathclyde Switchboard 0141-221-8372.
*Social group for LGB & our allies. Meets at the
Paisley Arts Center, New St., 2nd & 4th Sundays
8:30-10:30.*

Wales/Cymru

Local

Cardiff University: ᵍᵍ ♀
Women's Lesbian & Bisexual Group
c/o Lesbian & Bisexual Center
Cardiff Students' University Union
Park Place
Cardiff Wales CF1 3QN
tel: 01222 396 421 ext498 LGB Officer
*Meets every Wed. 7:30 pm in Meeting Room 3,
4th floor of Students' Union building, Park
Place, Cardiff.*

Lampeter University LG&B Group ᵍᵍ
LGB Officer c/o Student Union
Lampeter, Ceredigion Wales/Cymru SA48 7ED
tel: (01570) 422619 (ask for welfare or LGB
officer; fax: (01570)422480
*Meets Wednesday evenings S.U. building.
Separate caucuses can be organized.*

Swansea University: ᵍᵍ
Lesbian, Bisexual, Gay Society
c/o LGB Offices
Mandela House UCS
Swansea Wales/Cymru SA3 8PP
*Includes Indigo, a weekly lesbian & bi women's
group.*

UCMC/NUS Wales LGB Campaign
c/o 107 Walter Road/ Heol Walter
Swansea Wales/Cymru /Abertawe SA1 5QQ
tel: (01792) 643323

"I was not confused about what I was feeling, which seemed very
clear to me, but rather about what to do about what I was feeling.
What I wanted to do was lie down with her in a field of daisies and
hold her and let her hold me, and then probably kiss. That was
as far as my fantasies went. My confusion came mainly from
what everybody else would think."

—*Joan Baez in* And a Voice to Sing With

🐟 = school   ᵍᵍ = college/university   **P** = professional   **E** = educational
A = activist/political   **H** = health (incl. HIV)   ✑ = media/press   🖳 = Internet resource
The Bisexual Resource Guide 2000   **167**

BiNet USA
The National Bisexual Network

The goals of BiNet USA are to:

▼ Educate on the myths and realities of bisexuality

▼ Facilitate the development of bisexual community

▼ Work for the equal rights and liberation of all oppressed people

▼ Reflect in our organization the ideals that we strive for in the community at large

▼ Build a financially viable and stable organization capable of supporting the needs of the bi community

4201 Wilson Boulevard #110-311

Arlington, Virginia 22203

(202) 986-7186

www.BiNetUSA.org

BiNetUSA@BinetUSA.org

Key to symbols: ▼ = bi   ♀ = women   ♂ = men   ☯ = religious/spiritual
☀ = for allies   **M** = for married bis   ♥ = for partners of bis   **Y** = youth   **C** = people of color
168   **The Bisexual Resource Guide 2000**

USA

national

BiNet USA ▼EA🖳
PO Box 7327
Langley Park MD 20787-7327
tel: 202-986-7186
e-mail: ron@binetaz.org
BiNetUSA@aol.com
URL: www.binetusa.org
*National bisexual network. Collects &
distributes info. on bisexuality; facilitates the
development of bisexual community & visibility;
works for the equal rights & liberation of
bisexuals & all oppressed peoples; multicultural
& political agenda, does media & educational
work, coalition building with gay & lesbian
communities. Open to all. National coordinators:
BiNet News Editor - Gerard Palmieri (biNet
phone); Media Spokesperson - Michael
Szymanski mikeszy@aol.com; Treasurer -
Deborah Kolodny; Secretary - Kris Roehling.
Also has regional delegates who serve as liaisons
to their local regions. For contact info. on your
Regional Delegate, call BiNet's main phone
number. See display ad.* **Publication(s):** *BiNet
News Quarterly newsletter with regular
columns: tips for organizers, news & events of
national & regional interest, resources, activism.*

Bisexual Resource Center
Cambridge MA
See listing under "International."

Midwestern Bisexual Alliance, Inc (MBA) ▼A
P.O. Box 07541
Milwaukee WI 53207
tel: 414-483-5046
515-233-4952
e-mail: bimyke@hotmail.com
*Regional autonomous bisexual corporation
encompassing the entire Midwest. Loose
affiliation with BiNET USA. Empowering
bisexuals in the heartland of America.*

Anything That Moves ▼✐EA🖳
2261 Market Street #496
San Francisco CA 94114-1600
tel: 415-626-5069
e-mail: qswitch@igc.apc.org
URL: www.anythingthatmoves.com
*Non-profit organization publishing a 64-page
magazine for bisexuals: Anything That Moves.
Also a community resource & activist organization.* **Publication(s):** *Anything that Moves 3-4
issues/year.*

Mark Silver (of *Anything That Moves*) with Robyn Ochs
at Creating Change, 1997

Bi Women's Cultural Alliance ▼Y♀AM🖳
PO Box 2254
Washington DC 20013-2254
tel: 202-828-3065
URL: members.tripod.com/~BiWCA
*"Monogamous, duogomous, traditional, feminist.
Not for transgender, s/m, polyamorous, etc."
Groups include:
Jewish Women's Spirituality Group; Bi Women's
Dinner,* **Publication(s):** *"Bi Women's CUltural
Alliance Newsletter" US sub. $10/year.*

Affirmation: United Methodists for Lesbian🌓A🖳
Gay/Bisexual Concerns
PO Box 1021
Evanston IL 60204
e-mail: umaffirmation@yahoo.com
URL: www.umaffirm.org/
*An independent, not-for-profit organization with
no official ties to The United Methodist Church.
Affirmation is 100% supported by contributions
from interested individuals. Tax-deductible
contributions to Affirmation are welcome & can
be sent to PO Box 1021, Evanston, IL 60204.*
Publication(s): *Affirmation Newsletter All
contributors of $25 or more will be considered
members of Affirmation (unless they request
otherwise) & will receive the quarterly
newsletter.*

AIDS Action Committee: Youth Only Hotline YH
tel: 800-788-1234 (M-F 3-10pm)

> "I tried to persuade myself that I
> was three-quarters normal and
> that only a quarter of me was
> queer—whereas really it was the
> other way around."
>
> —*Somerset Maugham, English novelist/
> playwright, 1874-1965*

✎ = school   ✐ = college/university   **P** = professional   **E** = educational
A = activist/political   **H** = health (incl. HIV)   ✐ = media/press   🖳 = Internet resource

American College Personnel   👓🖳**PE**🖳
Assoc. Standing Committee for Lesbian, Gay, Bisexual & Transgender Awareness
One Dupont Circle, NW, Suite 300
Washington DC 20036-1110
tel: 202-835-ACPA; fax: 202-296-3286
e-mail: info@acpa.nche.edu
URL: www.acpa.nche.edu/comms/scomma/sclgbta.htm
The standing committee's list-serv is open to members of the association at listproc@ucdavis.edu, with message "subscribe ACPA-SCLGBA". Publication(s): newsletter: Out on Campus; book: Beyond Tolerance: Lesbians, Gays, & Bisexuals on Campus Newsletter with ACPA membership; book may be purchased from University Press of America, (800-462-6420)—$29.00

American Federation of Veterans, Inc.   **P**
(AmFed Vets)
346 Broadway, Suite 811
New York NY 10013
tel: 212-349-3455; fax: 212-233-6058
National grassroots coalition of GLB veterans' organizations, headquartered in NY. Addresses national issues affecting veterans & the G/L community.

American Library Association: **PE**🖳
Gay, Lesbian & Bisexual Task Force
Robert M. Bird Health Sciences Library
PO Box 26901
Purchasing Department
Oklahoma City OK 73190
tel: 405-271-2036 (nat'l); 718-230-2715 (Michael Miller, NY); fax: 405-271-3297 (nat'l); 718-622-4091 (Michael Miller, NY)
e-mail: sclifton@rex.uokhsc.edu - nat'l
M.Miller@BrooklynPublicLibrary.org - Michael Miller, NY
URL: isd.usc.edu/~trimmer/ala_hp.html
Nation's first GLB professional organization. Awards the annual GLB Book Award (bisexual added to name in 1994). Maintains clearing-house of GLB related bibliographies, directories, reading lists.

American Political Science Association: **P**
Gay, Lesbian & Bisexual Caucus
c/o Shane Phelan
University of New Mexico/Dept. Political Science
Albuquerque NM 87131
tel: 505-277-5104; APSA main #: 202-483-2512
e-mail: sphelan@unm.edu
Holds annual meeting.

American Psychological Association Division 44:

▼ **Committee on Bisexual Issues in**   **P▼**🖳
Psychology
Ron Fox, PhD, Co-Chair
P.O. Box 210491
San Francisco CA 94121-0491
tel: 415-751-6714
e-mail: rcf@wenet.net; m742ehp@aol.com
URL: www.apa.org/divisions/div44/about_us.html#Committee on Bisexual Issues in Psychology
Emily Page, Psy.D., Co-Chair
350 Massachusetts Avenue, #183
Arlington, MA 02474
781-641-3980

▼ **Society for the Psychological Study of**   **P**🖳
Lesbian, Gay, & Bisexual Issues (SPSLGBI)
750 First Street, NE
Washington DC 20002-4242
tel: 202-336-5500
URL: www.apa.org/divisions/div44/
Steven James, PhD, President (1998 - 1999); Esther Rothblum, PhD, President (1999 - 2000).

AT&T Lesbian, Gay & Bisexual United   **EP**
Employees (League)
11900 Pecos St.
Denver CO 80234-2703
tel: 303-538-5324; 1-800-346-LEAG; 202-776-5685
John Klenert, Natl Chair
e-mail: johnklenert@yahoo.com
Addresses workplaces issues affecting LGBT employees or employees with LGBT family members.

BECAUSE Conference (Bisexual   **▼E**🖳
Empowerment Conference A Uniting Supportive Experience) Planning Committee
c/o OutFront Minnesota
310 E. 38th St., Suite 204
Minneapolis MN 55409
tel: 612-822-0128x503 (or talk to receptionist)
e-mail: because@mtn.org
URL: www.mtn.org/~because/index.html
Annual Midwest bisexual 3-day empowerment conference held in Minneapolis,MN last weekend of April. Cooperative planning committee always looking for new blood, fresh ideas & people to speak &/or present at the event. Work often in alliance with Midwest Trans Institute. Contributions welcome. (Note: Robyn Ochs & Fritz Klein keynoting 1999 conference.)

Key to symbols: ▼ = bi   ♀ = women   ♂ = men   ☯ = religious/spiritual
🔖 = for allies   **M** = for married bis   ♥ = for partners of bis   **Y** = youth   **C** = people of color
170   **The Bisexual Resource Guide 2000**

Bisexual, Gay & Lesbian People in Medicine P
American Medical Students Association
1890 Preston White Dr.
Reston CA 22091
tel: 703-620-6600x5,x2

Black Books E▼🖳
Box 31155
San Francisco CA 94131
tel: 415-431-0171; fax: 415-431-0172
e-mail: BlackB@queernet.org
URL: www.queernet.orge/BlackBooks/
*Catalog of products, which give information
"from the erotic world" & which promote
bisexual visibility. Call to order or to make
inquiries. Catalog costs $1. Statement of age
required.* **Publication(s):** *The Black Book is a
bi-annual directory to alternative sexuality
resources in North America. Black Sheets
Magazine is a humorous magazine on
alternative sexuality & popular culture.*

Black Leather...In Color C
874 Broadway #801
New York NY 10003
tel: 212-222-9794; fax: 212-481-944-0
e-mail: nysm-grrl@hotmail.com
*Leather magazine for pansexual POC & friends.
Promoting safe & consensual sex.*
Publication(s): *Black Leather...In Color $20/
yr, sample issue $5.*

Black & White Men Together C♂
1747 Connecticut Avenue NW
Washington DC 20009
tel: 202-452-9173

BLK C🖳🖾
PO Box 83912
Los Angeles CA 90083-0912
URL: www.blk.com/
*National LGB newsmagazines for people of color
in the life: BLK, Blackfire, Black Lace, Kuumba
& Black Dates.*

Blowfish Catalog 🖾🖳
2261 Market St. #284
San Francisco CA 94114
tel: 415-252-4340; fax: 415-252-4349
e-mail: blowfish@blowfish.com
URL: www.blowfish.com
*Catalog of sex toys, videos, etc., which also has
interesting reviews, commentaries, poetry,
artwork. Very bi-positive.* **Publication(s):** *Free
($7.50 each outside the US).*

BMMAMERICA: ♂M🖳▼
Bisexual Married Men of America
e-mail: bmmamerica@umich.edu
URL: www-personal.umich.edu/~dastony/
bmma.html
*Email list for bisexual/gay married/divorced
men/fathers. For more information on the
discussion list, view the homepage, which has
links to members' pages, other bi & gay married
men's groups, general gay/bi/poly links & a
literary lounge w/members' writings.*

COLAGE - Children of YE◊🖳
Lesbians & Gays Everywhere
3543 18th St. #17
San Francisco CA 94110
tel: 415-861-KIDS; fax: 415-255-8345
e-mail: colage@colage.org
URL: www.colage.org
*National support group run by & for the children
of glbt parents. Newsletter, national
conferernces, email lists, & support groups for
children & for adult children of all ages. See also
Family Pride Coalition.* **Publication(s):** *Just
For Us $25 for membership & quarterly
newsletter.*

Delta Lambda Phi (Alpha Chapter) 🕮♂
PO Box 18862
Washington DC 20036
tel: 202-452-7633
*National social fraternity for g/bi & progressive
men. "When it comes to diversity, what others
hide in shame, we boldly embrace in pride."*

✎ = school   🕮 = college/university   P = professional   E = educational
A = activist/political   H = health (incl. HIV)   🖾 = media/press   🖳 = Internet resource

Delta Lambda Phi, Alpha Mu Chapter ⚤ ♂ 💻
PO Box 980280
Ypsilanti MI 48198
tel: 734-781-8098
URL: dlp.org/ or www.emunix.emich.edu/~centaur
*For the University of Michigan, Eastern
Michigan University, & Washtenaw. National
social fraternity for g/bi & progressive men.
"When it comes to diversity, what others hide in
shame, we boldly embrace in pride."*

Democratic Socialists of America: A 💻
Lesbian/Gay/Bisexual Commission
c/o DSA, 180 Varick St., 12th Floor
New York NY 10014
tel: 212-727-8616
e-mail: dsa@dsausa.org
URL: www.dsausa.org
Quarterly newsletter: members of ILGA.
Publication(s): *Socialism & Sexuality*

Digital Queers P 💻
560 Castro St., Suite 150
San Francisco CA 94114
tel: 415-252-6282; fax: 415-252-6290
e-mail: digiqueers@aol.com
info@dq.org
URL: www.dq.org
*National nonprofit group of computer profession-
als & technology aficionados supporting
nonprofit organizations through consultation,
training, & hardware/software upgrades related
to technology. Also a forum for social &
professional networking.* **Publication(s):**
Newsletter in both print & email format.

Dignity USA ☯ 💻
1500 Massachusetts Avenue NW #11
Washington DC 20005
tel: 202-861-0017; fax: 202-429-9808
e-mail: dignity@aol.com
URL: www.dignityusa.org
For glbt Catholics & their family & friends.
Publication(s): *Dignity Journal (with
membership)—quarterly call or email;
membership is $45/year*

Federal GLOBE P 💻
PO Box 45237
Washington DC 20026-5237
e-mail: dian@fedglobe.org
URL: www.fedglobe.org
*GLBT Employees of the Federal Government.
Aims to eliminate prejudice & discrimination
based on sexual orientation in the federal
government through education on GLBT issues.
Particular attention to inclusion of bisexuals.*
Publication(s): *newsletter (bimonthly):
globalview UP to GS6-$12; GS7 to GS11-$24;
GS12 & above-$36*

Ferry Beach Park Assoc. Unitarian ☸ E A
Universalist Camp & Conference Ctr.
5 Morris Ave.
Saco ME 04072
tel: 207-284-8612; fax: 207-283-4465
*Conferences spring, summer, & fall. Includes
conferences for B/L/T women; G/B/T men.
Conferences/staff open & inclusive of queer
adults, youth, children. Camping & dorm space
also available to vacationers not attending
programs. Annual guide to conferences &
programs published in Feb. For more info. see
Unitarian Universalist Association Web Page.*

Gay, Lesbian, Bisexual P 💻
Veterans of America, National
7716 West 26th Street
North Riverside IL 60546
URL: www.glbva.org/
*Many local chapters; support & social activities,
veterans; advocacy, fight anti-gay discrimina-
tion, speaker's bureau.*

Gaylactic Network 💻
PO Box 127
Brookline MA 02146
URL: www.gaylaxians.org/GNetwork/index.html
*Club for LGB science fiction & fantasy fans.
Meets locally in several areas, including Boston
& DC.*

Gill Foundation A
8 South Nevada Avenue #303
Colorado Springs CO 80903
tel: 719-473-4485; 1-800-964-5643
*GLBT funder. Also administers the Gay &
Lesbian Victory Fund for Colordao, which
supports non-glbt progressive organizations.*

GLAAD ✍ A 💻
1360 Mission St., Ste. 200
San Francisco CA 94103
tel: 800-GAY-MEDIA
415-861-2244; fax: 415-861-4893
e-mail: glaad@glaad.org
URL: www.glaad.org
www.glaad.org/glaad/bi-visibility/index.html
*Works for fair & diverse coverage of les/gay/bis,
& fights stereotypical portrayals in the print &
electronic media. To report a defamation, call
hotline at above telephone number.*
Publication(s): *Images
GLAAD Alert (online pub.) Images-quarterly
news magazine for members
GLAAD Alert-weekly activation tool for
grassroots activism*

Key to symbols: ▼ = bi   ♀ = women   ♂ = men   ☸ = religious/spiritual
🕯 = for allies   **M** = for married bis   ♥ = for partners of bis   **Y** = youth   **C** = people of color
172   **The Bisexual Resource Guide 2000**

GLAAD Bi Visibility ▼ A ▨ ▣
Project Team (BVPT)
150 W. 26th St. Suite 503
New York NY 10001
tel: Bill Horn
212-807-1700
e-mail: bi-vis@glaad.org
URL: www.glaad.org/glaad/bi_visibility/
Helping expand GLAAD media monitoring to be
sensitive to bi issues. Call for meeting dates

GLSEN National: Gay, Lesbian & Straight ▣
Teachers Network
121 West 27th St.
New York NY 10001
tel: 212-727-0135; fax: 212-727-0254
e-mail: glsen@glsen.org
URL: www.glsen.org
80 or so chapters.

Harvard University: Gay, Lesbian ↝ P
& Bisexual Alumni/ae Committee of the
Harvard Law School Association
1331-A Pennsylvania Avenue, NW
Suite 8000
Washington DC 20004
tel: 202-371-7334 (Chad Johnson); 206-781-9823
(Kirsten Dodge)
e-mail: Chad Johnson: ChadSJ@aol.com; Kirsten
Dodge: dodgi@perkinscoie.com
Sponsors an annual fellowship to support an
Harvard Law School student who chooses to
spend a summer woking in the field of lesbian/
gay civil rights. Publishes a directory.

Human Rights Campaign A ▣
1101 14th Street, NW
Suite 200
Washington DC 20005
tel: 202-628-4160; fax: 202-347-5323
e-mail: hrc@org
URL: www.hrc.org
National organization lobbies Congress,
participates in elections, mobilizes grassroots
political support for equal rights for lgb
Americans. See ad.

✎ = school   ↝ = college/university   P = professional   E = educational
A = activist/political   H = health (incl. HIV)   ▨ = media/press   ▣ = Internet resource

In The Family: A Magazine for Lesbians, Gays, Bisexuals & Their Relations 🖳
PO Box 5387
Takoma Park MD 20913
tel: 301-270-4771
e-mail: Lmarkowitz@aol.com
URL: www.inthefamily.com
Quarterly magazine addressing g/l/b families. Also sponsors an annual family therapy conference. (Editors note: a really bi-positive magazine to which I happily subscribe!)

Inner Light Unity Fellowship 🕭
400 I St SW
Bethesda MD
tel: 202-544-6588
African-American house of worship for GLBT people. **Publication(s)**: *Coming Out Pagan Quarterly Journal with international readership celebrating glb spirituality/nature religions.*

Island Voice C🖎
PO Box 144
Fordham Station
Bronx NY 10458-0144
tel: 212-862-9474
Publication(s): *Newsmagazine for Carribean-identified lgbt people & friends, speaking to issues affecting all people of the Carribean descent, no matter their colonial history. News stories, interviews, photo essays, literary works, historical events, entertainment & recipes.*

Indiana University, Bloomington: 🔊E🖳
Lambda 10 Project
Office of Student Ethics/Anti-Harassment Programs
705 E. Seventh St.
Bloomington IN 47405
tel: 812-855-4463; fax: 812-855-4465
e-mail: lambda10@indiana.edu
URL: www.indiana.edu/~lambda10
A clearinghouse for educational resources & information pertaining to GLB members of college fraternities & sororities.

Lambda Youth Network YE
369 Third Street Suite B 369
San Rafael CA 94901-3581
tel: 310-821-1139 or 310-216-1312
e-mail: LambdaYN@aol.com
Referrals to national & local resources for lgb youth ages 23 & under. Send $1 & large SASE for a 6-page national referral list. Executive Director: Chris Kryzan.

HUMAN RIGHTS CAMPAIGN

www.hrc.org

Equality through Visibility.

Lavender Caucus: PHAEY
The Lesbian/Gay/Bi Caucus of the SEIU (Service Employees Int'l Union) Western Conference
560 20th Street
PO Box 10593
Oakland CA 94160
tel: 415-821-1142
Focuses on social, on-the-job support, employment, & political issues. Distributes newsletter. All union members welcome at meetings. Biennial conference seeks to educate LGBTs about labor issues & vice versa. Other contacts: Northwest: Marcy Johnsen 206-706-1588 (tel), 206-783-7245(fax), MARCYJ1199@aol.com Southern CA: Bill Strachan nursebear@loop.com 818/985-9115(fax). **Publication(s)**: *Newsletter (occasional) lists upcoming conferences, executive committee meetings, news.*

Lavender Families Resource Network E
PO Box 21567
Seattle WA 98111
tel: 206-325-2643 (V/TTY)
Info, referrals, & emotional support for lgb parents in custody & visitation issues, child rearing, donor insemination & adoption. **Publication(s)**: *Mom's Apple Pie $15 yr. for newsletter.*

Key to symbols: ▼ = bi   ♀ = women   ♂ = men   🕭 = religious/spiritual
🖎 = for allies   **M** = for married bis   ♥ = for partners of bis   **Y** = youth   **C** = people of color
174   **The Bisexual Resource Guide 2000**

Lesbian, Bisexual & Gay United   **PE🖳**
Employees of AT&T (LEAGUE)
290 Davidson Ave.
W1H033
Somerset NJ 08875
tel: National Hotline: 703-713-7820
Peer Support Helpline: 312-230-5324
TDD: 800-855-2880
e-mail: league@leagues-att.org
URL: www.league-att.org
*LEAGUE is an educational & support group at
AT&T that addresses workplace issues affecting
employees who are LGBT or have family,
friends, or colleagues that are.*

Lezbrian: E-mail list   **♀P🖳**
URL: www.library.arizona.edu/users/jueldof/
lesbrian.html
*Electronic forum for discussing professional
issues of interest to lesbian & bi women library
workers. To subscribe, send to
listserv@listserv.acsu.buffalo.edu: "subscribe
LEZBRIAN yourfirstname yourlastname" List
owners: Ellen Greenblatt:
egreenbl@carbon.cudenver.edu; Jerilyn Veldof:
jveldof@bird.library.arizona.edu.*

LGBT Initiatives: Advocates for Youth   **Y**
1025 Vermont Suite 200
Washington DC 20005
tel: 202-347-5700; fax: 202-347-2263
URL: www.youthresource.com
*They have a publication called "I think I'm Bi ...
Now what do I do?" available on the web & as
hard copies. (web address:
www.youthresource.com / library / bisexual.htm)
& "BiYouth Webring." Check out website.*

LiLac: Lesbian, Gay & Bisexual   **P**
Employees of Lotus
55 Cambridge Parkway
Cambridge MA 02142
tel: 617-693-8040 Kay Wilkins/Ron Krouk
e-mail: kwilkins@lotus.com

Lyon-Martin Women's Health Center   **♀EH**
1748 Market Street, Suite #201
San Francisco CA 94102
tel: 415-565-7667
*Primary care services for women, special
sensitivity to lesbian & bisexual women,
including routine physical examinations,
internal medicine, gynecology, family planning,
& prevention & screening. HIV services include
counseling, anonymous testing, prevention
education, support groups, case management,
nutrition counseling, & comprehensive medical
care. Also a parenting program for lesbian &
bisexual parents that provides legal, medical, &
social services information through forums,
workshops, & support groups.*

Momazons   **♀🖳**
PO Box 82069
Columbus OH 43202
tel: 614-267-0193
e-mail: momazons@aol.com
URL: www.glbnet.com/~momazons
*National organization for lesbian mothers &
lesbians who want children in their lives. One of
the organizers says that Momazons is inclusive
of bi women, regardless of the gender of any
current relationship. Membership: $15-$20
sliding scale.*

National AIDS Hotline   **H**
tel: 800-342-AIDS (staffed 24/7); 800-344-SIDA -
Espanol (8am-2am); 800-243-7889 - TTY 10am-
10pm)
*Answers questions on transmission, protection,
testing, treatment. Also referrals & free
publications. Also provide "classroom calls" for
education in schools.*

National Association of Student Personnel   **P🖳**
Administrators: Gay, Lesbian, Bisexual, &
Transgendered Issues Network
Bill Geller
VP for Student & Community Services
University of Maine at Farmington
Farmington ME 04938
e-mail: geller@maine.maine.edu
URL: htt://ecuvax.cis.ecu.edu/~rllucier/
naspaglb.html
*Mission: to increase the acceptance & under-
standing of gay, lesbian, bisexual, &
transgendered faculty, staff, & students & their
allies within the student affairs profession.
Publishes a quarterly newsletter. Holds &
annual conference.*

National Black Lesbian & Gay   **CA🖳**
Leadership Forum
14366 U St., NW #200
Washington DC 20009
tel: 202-483-6786; fax: 202-483-4790
URL: www.nglblf.org@nblglf

National Gay & Lesbian Task Force   **EA📰🖳**
Policy Institute
NGLTF
2320 17th St., NW
Washington DC 20009-2702
tel: 202-332-6483; fax: 202-332-0207
e-mail: ngltf@ngltf.org
URL: www.ngltf.org
*Lobbies, organizes, educates, & demonstrates for
full GLBT civil rights & equality. Holds annual
Creating Change Conference, a skills-building
event for activists.*

✎ = school   ✑ = college/university   **P** = professional   **E** = educational
A = activist/political   **H** = health (incl. HIV)   📰 = media/press   🖳 = Internet resource

National Hotline for Gay, Lesbian,   **Y**
Bisexual & Transgender Youth
tel: 800-347-TEEN
Sponsored by the Indianapolis Youth Group.
Staffed & trained peer youth counselors. Lines
open Sun.-Thurs. 7-10pm, Fri. & Sat. 7pm to
midnight. Confidential & anonymous.

National Inst. for Gay, Lesbian, Bisexual **EYPA**
& Transgender Concerns in Education
P. O. Box 249
Malden MA 02148
tel: 781-321-3569; fax: 617-321-9901
e-mail: kharbeck@aol.com
Nonprofit corporation which provides educators
to go into schools & raise awareness for GLBT
youth & protecting employees who try to help
GLBT youth.

National Lesbian Bisexual Transgender   **C**
Organization of Color
1817 14th Avenue S
Minneapolis MN 55404
tel: 612-871-1273
e-mail: nlbtoc@juno.com

National LLEGO: **CYE**
The National Latina/o Lesbian, Gay,
Bisexual & Transgender Organization
1612 K Street NW, Suite 500
Washington DC 20006
tel: 202-466-8240, Martin Ornelas-Quintero; fax:
202-466-8530
e-mail: aquiLGBT@llego.org
URL: www.llego.org
Dedicated to prodiving assistence & organiza-
tional support to the Latina/o LBGT community
in the US & Puerto Rico. Associations with 100+
organizations: groups serving HIV/AIDS
patients, social/cultural groups, spiritual
groups, university & educational groups, youth
groups.

National Organizers Alliance,   **P**
Les/Bi/Gay/Trans Caucus
715 G St. SE
Washington DC 20003-2853
tel: 202-543-6603; fax: 202-543-2462
e-mail: noa@igc.org
For professional, community, labor, progressive
social change organizers. Annual gathering,
newsletter, pension plan, resource center, job
bank. **Publication(s):** *The Ark (quarterly)*
Subscriptions to newsletter & job bank are $50/
year.

Nat'l Queer Student Coalition, USSA   **A**
1413 K St., NW, 9th fl.
Washington DC 20005
tel: 202-347-USSA or 347-8772; fax: 202-393-5886
e-mail: ussa@essential.org
URL: www.essential.org\ussa\
Caucus of national student lobbying organiza-
tion.

National Union of Jewish Lesbian, Gay,   **E**
Bisexual & Transgender Students
Bernard Cherkasov, Executive Director
1500 Mass. Av., NW
Washington DC 20005
tel: 202-463-7291
e-mail: bcherkasov@hillewl.org
An educational & supportive resource group for
Jewish lgbt students, with affiliate groups on
most major campus & students from all over the
United States & Canada.

National Youth Advocacy Coalition   **Y**
1711 Connecticut Ave., NW
Suite 206
Washington DC 20009
tel: 202-319-7596; fax: 202-319-7365
e-mail: nyac@nyacyouth.org
URL: www.nyacyouth.org
Advocacy, education, & information on GLBT
youth issues; offers resources, technical
assistance, & national referrals.
Publication(s): *Crossroads Twice yearly. No*
charge, but contributions welcome. Call or write
to get on mailing list.

New England Association of Lesbian,   **PA**
Gay & Bisexual Psychologists
P.O. Box 381714
Cambridge MA 02238-1714
tel: Camille: 617-926-5583; Wilfred 617-350-6900
x122
Lesbigay psychologists, counselors, & graduate
students. Provides support, networking,and
mentoring/training for each other & for other
professionals. Also occasionally a forum for
political action on behalf of LGB issues.

OUT! magazine
PO Box 27237
Albuquerque NM 87125
tel: 505-243-2540; fax: 505-842-5114
e-mail: mail@outmagazine.com
URL: www.outmagazine.com
Monthly GLB news magazine. Both the
magazine & web site list GLB resources for New
Mexico. **Publication(s):** *OUT! magazine*

Key to symbols: ▼ = bi   ♀ = women   ♂ = men   ◐ = religious/spiritual
👍 = for allies   **M** = for married bis   ♥ = for partners of bis   **Y** = youth   **C** = people of color
176   **The Bisexual Resource Guide 2000**

Out Youth: Gay, Lesbian, Bisexual &   Y▯
Transgendered Teens
1117 Red River
Austin TX 78701
tel: 512-708-1234; 1-800-96YOUTH; fax: 512-708-1235
e-mail: out@outyouth.org
URL: www.outyouth.org
Helpline 5:30-9:30pm CST; Drop-in Center
Wed.-Sun. 5:30-9:30pm. For email counseling:
support@outyouth.org.

!OutProud!   Y▯
369-B Third Street, Suite 362
San Rafael CA 94901-3581
tel: 415-460-5452; fax: 415-460-5451
e-mail: info@outproud,org.
URL: www.outproud.org
!OutProud! the National Coalition for Gay,
Lesbian, Bisexual & Transgender Youth, has
now merged with the Lambda Youth Network.

Paramour   ✍
P.O. Box 949
Cambridge MA 02140-0008
tel: 617-499-0069
e-mail: paramour@paramour.com
A bi-friendly erotic journal seeking submissions
from artists, writers & photographers.
Circulation 12,000; national distribution. Send
SASE for contributors' guidelines. Subscriptions
$18/4 issues; sample issue $4.95.
Publication(s): *Paramour Quarterly*

PFLAG-USA (Parents, Families & Friends of▯AE⬦
Lesbians & Gays)
See listing under "International."

Pride At Work, AFL-CIO   P
c/o AFSCME International
1625 L St., NW
Washington DC 20036
tel: Van Alan Sheets: 202-667-8237
National coalition of lgbt workers & their
supporters. Includes annual AFL-CIO
concention & labor conference.

"To be individual, my friends, to
be different from others, is the
only way to become distinguished
from the common herd. Let us be
glad, therefore, that we differ
from one another in form and
disposition. Variety is the spice of
life and we are various enough to
enjoy one another's society, so
let us be content."

—*The Cowardly Lion, in L. Frank Baum's* The
Lost Princess of Oz.

Pride Institute   H
14400 Martin Drive
Eden Prairie MN 55344
tel: 1-800-54-PRIDE; fax: 212-243-5565
e-mail: info@pride-institute.com
Inpatient alcohol & drug treatment, intensive
day treatment program for the GLBT commu-
nity.

Rainbow Writers Group   Y✍A
402 Sedgewick Court
Virginia Beach VA 23454
tel: 757-431-0664
e-mail: rainbow@bat.tech.infi.net
A newspaper syndicate dedicated to the
marketing of work by lgbt young people (26 &
younger). Looking for LGBT -themed newspaper
features, opinion pieces, reporting, poetry, very
short fiction, columns & comics.

Reconciling Congregation Program   ☮EY▯
3801 N. Keeler Avenue
Chicago IL 60641
tel: 773-736-5526; fax: 773-736-5475
e-mail: www.rcp@rcp.org
URL: www.rcp.org
Publication(s): *Open Hands*

Seventh Day Adventist Kinship   ☮▯
P.O. Box 7320
Laguna Niguel CA 92607
tel: 714-248-1299
e-mail: sdakinship@aol.com
URL: www.sdakinship.org/
An organization which ministers to the spiritual,
emotional, social, & physical well being of
individuals with diverse sexual orientations who
have ties with the Seventh-day Adventist
denomination along with their families &
friends. Regional groups throughout the US, &
in Canada & Germany.

The Gay, Lesbian, Bisexual,   ⚲
Transgender Education Fund
tel: 612-220-4888
Offers financial assistance to LBGT students.

The GaYellow Pages   ▯
PO Box 533
Village Station
New York NY 10014-0533
tel: 212-674-0120; fax: 212-420-1126 (pls. avoid 11am-6pm M-F)
e-mail: gayellow@banet.net
URL: www.gayellowpages.com
Free listings for LesBiGay groups & services of
all kinds.

✎. = school   ⚲ = college/university   **P** = professional   **E** = educational
A = activist/political   **H** = health (incl. HIV)   ✍ = media/press   ▯ = Internet resource
The Bisexual Resource Guide 2000   **177**

The LEAGUE Foundation   YE▭
John Klenert, Director
2020 K St. NW, Suite 600
Washington DC 20006
tel: 202-776-5685
URL: www.league-att.org/foundate.html
*Formed by LEAGUE of AT&T — scholarship
fund to support youth in the GLBT community
as the attend college or grad school.*

The Society for Lesbian, Gay &   ↩PE
Bisexual Studies
University of Iowa
308 English Philosophy Building
Iowa City IA 52242-1492
tel: 319-335-0454
e-mail: Also: Michael Montgomery:
michael@pucc.princeton.edu (Bi member of the
Board)
*"The encouragement & advancement of lesbian,
gay & bisexual studies in their broadest   ·
sense...through interdisciplinary meetings,
publications, research, schooling, & any other
means it may deem appropriate."*

Trikone   C▱▭
PO Box 21354
San Jose CA 95151
tel: 408-270-8776; fax: 408-274-2733
e-mail: trikone@rahul.net
URL: uts.cc.utexas.edu/~ramakris/
bilinefeb26.html
*A socio-political organization for gay/les/bi
South Asians. Organizes & participates in
several Bay Area events & publishes national
newsmagazine. Send E-mail for events mailing
list.* **Publication(s)**: *published quarterly.*

True Colors, Inc.: Sexual Minority Youth &   YE
**Family Services (Children from the Shadows
Conference)**
PO Box 1855
Manchester CT 06045
tel: 860-649-7386, 888-565-5551
e-mail: cfshadow@juno.com
*Non-profit seeking to improve & enrich the lives
of sexual minority youth & families. Hosts
fabulous annual conference addressing LGBT
youth issues for youth & service providers, plus
semi-annual youth leadershop training
including conflict resolution & leadership skills.
Great source of referrals to youth groups.*

UC Davis: Gay, Lesbian & Bisexual Alumni   ↩
Association
c/o Troy Williams
301 Swift Av. #14
Durham NC 27705-4842

XY Magazine   Y▱
Peter Ian Cummings, Editor/Publisher
4104 24 St. #900
San Francisco CA 94114
tel: 415-552-6668; fax: 415-552-6664
e-mail: xypost@aol.com. Subscription info:
subxy@aol.com
*Bi-monthly breakthrough periodical for young
queers. Includes a wide range of features & news
bites covering music, politics, activism, fashion,
technology & more.*

Youth Resource Online   Y▭EA
e-mail: BCEagleguy@aol.com
URL: www.youthresource.com/support.htm
*National online listings of Queer Youth
Resources. A project of the National Youth
Advocacy Coalition (NYAC).*

The Trevor Project/Helpline   Y▭
tel: 800-850-8078
URL: www.trevorproject.com
*Free, confidential 24-hour hotline for teens to
talk to trained counselors, find local resources &
take important steps on their way to becoming
healthy adults.*

Alabama

Local

Pink Steel, the e-zine for Birmingham   ▭A
& North Alabama
AL
tel: 205-591-1077; fax: 205-591-1077
e-mail: pinksteel@pinksteel.com
URL: www.pinksteel.com
*An online resource guide for glbt North Alabama
including event & service listings, personals,
message board, chat area, & human interest
articles.*

Covenant Metropolitan   ❂▭
Community Church
5117 1st Avenue North
Birmingham AL 35210
tel: 205-599-3363
e-mail: covmcc@aol.com
URL: www.geocities.com/West Hollywood/79031

Gay & Lesbian Information Line:
Lambda Resource Center
Suite 201
205 32nd St. South
Birmingham AL 35233-3007
tel: 205-326-8600
*Information phone/TDD line, Monday-
Saturday, 7pm-10pm.*

Key to symbols: ▼ = bi   ♀ = women   ♂ = men   ❂ = religious/spiritual
◊ = for allies   **M** = for married bis   ♥ = for partners of bis   **Y** = youth   **C** = people of color
178   **The Bisexual Resource Guide 2000**

Steel City Centurions ♂ 🖳
P. O. Box 130938
Birmingham AL 35213
tel: 205-320-1127
e-mail: SCC$Me@aol.com or SCCBear@aol.com
URL: www.gaybham.com/bars/toolbox/scc/
scc.html
*Pan-sexual/non-racial group. General meeting:
1st Sat. each month at Swann Building/BAO
(call for confirmation)
Host bar is the Toolbox (5120 5th Ave. South),
meetings there1st, 3rd, & 5th Sat., 8:30 Levi/
leather/Bear Social Club.* **Publication(s):**
Centurion

HAY (Homosexual Aware Youth) YA 🖳
Huntsville AL
tel: MCCH office: 205-851-6914
e-mail: HAYHuntsville@hotmail.com
URL: members.tripod.com/~HAY_Huntsville/
*Organization for young adults who, together &
with community assistance, meet to provide
support, connection, & action opportunities for
LGBT young adults. Social events, rap groups,
social activism, etc. 1st & 3rd Thursday 6:30 pm.
at the Metropolitan Community Church (near
coner of Sparkman Dr. & Pulaski Pike).*

Rocket City Rainbow Squares 🖳
c/o Rainbows Ltd.
522 Jordon Lane
Huntsville AL 35805
tel: 205-881-6531
e-mail: cwelch@compuserve.com
URL: fly.hiwaay.net/~droberts/rainbow/
*We welcome anyone interested in Western
Square Dancing with or without a partner
regardless of race, religion, sex, national origin,
creed, or sexual orientation.*

Cornerstone Metropolitan Community 🌐 🖳
Church
P.O. Box 6311
Mobile AL 36660
tel: 334-476-4621
e-mail: RevHHL@aol.com
URL: www.geocities.com/West Hollywood/6703
*Meeting place: 2201 Government St. Worship:
Sundays at 11:30am & 7:00pm. Discipleship
program on Wendesdays at 7:00pm. Various
community & support groups meet at the church.
Call for info.* **Publication(s):** *Something in
Common Monthly. Published on the web.
Available in print by mail & in local bars.*

PFLAG Mobile E ♦
957 Church Street
Mobile AL 36604
tel: 334-438-9381 or
334-344-0407
*Meets 2nd Sat. of the month 10:30am at
Cornerstone MCC.*

University of South Alabama: ⚲ 🖳
Gay, Lesbian & Bisexual Alliance
Student Center Room 280
University of South Alabama
Mobile AL 36688
e-mail: GLBAUSA@aol.com
URL: members.aol.com/GLBAUSA/index.html
*Represents student & faculty members concerned
with a variety of issues facing LGB people. USA
students, faculty, & friends of all sexual
orientations, respecting each member's right to
remain private re: his/her orientation. 4 goals:
education, support, service, & social.*

PFLAG Montgomery ♦
P.O. Box 230355
Montgomery AL 36123
tel: 334-265-8533
e-mail: lynnshaw@juno.com

Living Waters 🌐 🖳
Metropolitan Community Church
P.O. Box 3084
2506 Lurleen Wallace Blvd.
Tuscaloosa AL 35401
tel: 205-345-2044
e-mail: ptbears@juno.com
URL: www.geocities.com/West Hollywood/village/
46801
*Open to all believers. Sunday services, 6:30pm.
Wednesday night Bible Study, 6:30pm.*

University of Alabama: Gay, Lesbian, & ⚲
Bisexual Alliance
Ferguson Student Center, 1st Flr
Tuscaloosa AL 35486
tel: 205-348-7210; fax: 205-348-7610
e-mail: Ddonalds@eng.ua.edu
Meets Mondays.

Alaska

The Triangle Network
c/o Alta's Bed & Breakfast
PO Box 82290
Fairbanks AK 99708
tel: 907-389-2582; or 474-3420 (LInda Ross)
e-mail: picaro@mosquitonet.com
*Referrals & references to LBG owned or friendly
travel services in Alaska.*

Local

Fairbanks LesBiGay Hotline
Fairbanks AK
tel: 907-458-5288
*Community information, club event & meeting
schedules, referrals, personals, or just to chat.*

✎ = school   ⚲ = college/university   P = professional   E = educational
A = activist/political   H = health (incl. HIV)   ◁ = media/press   🖳 = Internet resource

Interior AIDS Association　　　　　**HE**
PO Box 71248
Fairbanks AK 99707
tel: 907-452-4222
*Offers medical/dental assistance, "buddies",
meal delivery, library & support. Free &
anonymous HIV testing. Located at 710 3rd Ave.*
Publication(s)*: The Interior Inqueryer Monthly
newsletter includes lesbigay community info. Ed:
Pat Cahill.*

Klondykes, Queens & Company
PO Box 72477
Fairbanks AK 99707-2477
e-mail: kdqco@hotmail.com
*Cabaret & burlesque style performances
featuring local drag artists, musicians, dancers,
actors & writers. Sponsors GLBTQ programming on public TV, local AIDS organizations,
the Imperial Court of Fairbanks, PRIDE & other
community events. "We love to involve everyone
or anyone. We don't care if you've never stepped
foot in a theater before; we can use just about
anyone who can do anything."*

P-FLAG　　　　　**A ⚭**
c/o Into the Woods Bookshop & Coffeehouse
3560 College Rd.
Fairbanks AK 99709
tel: 907-457-3524
*Parents, Families & Friends of Lesbians &
Gays. Meets 3rd Sun. each month, 4-5:30pm at
Into the Woods Bookshop & Coffeehouse.*

University of Alaska - Fairbanks:　　　⚭ 📷
Homophonic Radio
c/o KSUA
University of Alaska Fairbanks
PO Box 750113
Fairbanks AK 99775
tel: 907-474-7054
*Queer music, interviews, news & information;
Sundays 4-7 on KSUA-FM.*

Arizona

BiNet Arizona　　　　　**▼EA🖳**
24 W. Camelback Road, #B-105
Phoenix AZ 85013
tel: 602-280-9074; fax: 602-675-8551
e-mail: binetaz@binetaz.org
URL: binetaz.org
*Provides support groups for women, men, co-
gender, trans, youth & spouses of bis.*
Publication(s)*: BiNet AZ newsletter Monthly
publication.*

Local

The Community Center　　　　**YEH🖳**
24 W. Camelback Road #B-105
Phoenix AZ 85013
tel: 602-234-2572; 265-7283
e-mail: info@phxcenter.org
URL: www.phxcenter.org
*Board voted in May 1998 to drop "Gay &
Lesbian" in order to be more inclusive & changed
their bylaws. Voted for 1st ever out bi as co-chair
of Board of Directors.*

Arizona State University:　　　⚭♂▼🖳
LAMBDA League Coalition
Memorial Union Union, Room 354
Tempe AZ 85287
tel: 602-965-8690
URL: www.osu.edu/studentprgrms/orgs/
lamda_league
*Groups include: Gay & Bi Men's Discussion
Group; Lesbian & Bi Women's Discussion
Group; Act Out (political); Progression (LGBT
graduate Students); BiNecessity (bi discussion
group); UBIQUITY (faculty glbt group)*

GLB Support Group
St. Francis in the Foothills Methodist
4625 E River, Rm 43
Tucson AZ 85718
tel: Dave (facilitator) 520-745-9059; fax: 520-299-
9099
*Open to everyone, not just for religious folks.
Meets Thursdays 7:30.*

Married Gay & Bi Men's Support Group　　**M**
send mail to: MMGBSG
c/o Daniel Overbeck, Ph.D.
5650 E. 22nd St.
Tucson AZ 85711
tel: 520-745-6977; fax: 520-748-2609
*Free, weekly support group facilitated by
professional psychologist.*

Men's Social Network　　　　　♂🖳
4207 N. Limberlost Circle
Tucson AZ 85705-1669
tel: 520-690-9565
e-mail: geraldcurl@aol.com
URL: www.geocities.com/westhollywood/6362
*3-5 social activities per week. Potlucks & pizza
nights. Support group.*

Pima Community College: COLORES　　⚭
2202 W. Anklam Rd.
Tucson AZ 85709
tel: 520-770-9855, or 520-578-8141
*For students. Student advisor: Bob Brodie 520-
206-6781.*

Key to symbols:　　▼ = bi　　♀ = women　　♂ = men　　☽ = religious/spiritual
⚭ = for allies　　**M** = for married bis　　♥ = for partners of bis　　**Y** = youth　　**C** = people of color
180　　　　　　　　　　　　　　　**The Bisexual Resource Guide 2000**

University of Arizona: 🔍E🖥
Bisexual, Gay & Lesbian Association
GALA Building 191
Tucson AZ 85721
tel: 520-621-7585
URL: www.arizona.edu/~bgala/

Wingspan   H🖥
300 E. 6th St.
Tucson AZ 85705
tel: 520-624-1779 (Info line; live 11-7 Mon.-Sat.);
fax: 520-624-0364
e-mail: kbc@azstarnet.com
URL: www.azstarnet.com/public/nonprofit/
wingspan
*7-9pm 1st & 3rd Wednesdays. Bill Maginnis:
520-696-5708.* **Publication(s):** *Center
Newslettter Monthly.*

Arkansas

Local

University of Arkansas: Gay, Lesbian &   🔍
Bisexual Student Association
ARKU 504
Fayetteville AR 72701
tel: 510-575-4633
e-mail: lbsa@comstore.uark.edu or
dmacomp.uark.edu
*Meets Wednsdays at 7pm in ARKU room 311-
South.*

Gay/Lesbian/Bisexual/Transsexual   H
Therapy Group
Psychotherapy Center
210 S. Pulaski
Little Rock AR 72201
tel: 501-374-3605
*Group therapy for queers, led by Dr. Ralph
Hyman; open to everyone listed above. Fee for
service.*

Pals   Y
Psychotherapy Center
210 S. Pulaski
Little Rock AR 72201
tel: 501-374-3605
*Support group for queer teens, led by Dr. Ralph
Hyman.*

Gay & Lesbian Ozarkian Rural Persons
Ken Clodfelter
P.O. Box 384
Salem AR 72576
*Meets in Missouri, Arkansas area for potlucks,
socializing. "Bis are very welcome."*

Rachel Lanzerotti

1995

California

Camp Lavender Hill   Y
PO Box 11335
Santa Rosa CA 95406
tel: 707-544-8150
*Summer camp in Nevada City, CA, for children
(7-17) of GLB families. Counselors are ages 18-
23 & have either grown up in GLB families or
are themselves GL or B. This organization is a
non-profit staffed entirely by volunteers. An
annual golf tournament fundraiser is held on
women's weekend in Guernerville.*

LLEGO California   ACE
P.O. Box 40816
San Francisco CA 94140
tel: 415-554-8436
*A socio-political organization serving glbt
Latinos/as throughout CA. Activities include
Youth Lobby Day in Sacramento (January),
Latino/a AIDS Theater Festival (March), AIDS
Lobby day in Sacramento (April), & Performring
Arts Show (June). Write for more info.*

🐾 = school   🔍 = college/university   P = professional   E = educational
A = activist/political   H = health (incl. HIV)   📰 = media/press   🖥 = Internet resource
The Bisexual Resource Guide 2000   **181**

University of California: & **EM ♥ 🖳**
Lesbian, Gay, Bisexual & Transgendered
Campus Resource Center
Dr. Ronni L. Sanlo, Director
220 Kinsey Hall, Box 951579
Los Angeles CA 90095-1579
tel: 310-206-3628; fax: 310-206-8191
e-mail: snlo@ucla.edu
URL: www.saonet.ucla.edu/lgbt/lgbt.html
The UC system-wide LGBT constituent
organization & umbrella groups. Sponsors
annual conference & seeks to coordinate the
efforts of the various campuses, to provide
communication & leadership of major system-
wide issues.

Central California

SLO Bi Women's Group   ▼ ♀
4650 San Anselmo
Atascadero CA 93422
tel: 805-461-1178

California State University, Fresno: &
Lesbian, Gay, Bisexual & Straight Alliance
5280 N. Jackson
Fresno CA 93740

California State University, Fullerton: &
Lesbian/Gay/Bisexual Association
University Center 256, Box 67
Fullerton CA 92701

California Polytechnic State University: &
Gays, Lesbians, Bisexuals United
Box 234 Student Services
San Luis Obispo CA 93410
Social & support organization, all welcome.

Lesbigay Alliance of Kings & Tulare Counties
PO Box 3881
Visalia CA 93278
tel: 209-733-5242 or 209-583-5242

Northern California

BIPOL   ▼ A
c/o Ka'ahumanu
20 Cumberland St.
San Francisco CA 94110
tel: 415-821-3534

San Francisco Bay Area   ▼ EA ✉
Bisexual Network
2261 Market Street #496
San Francisco CA 94114-1600
tel: 415-703-7977. VMB #1
e-mail: bisrule@igc.apc.org
Umbrella organization providing info &
education about bi resources in the SF Bay Area.
Includes speakers bureau.

Bi-Friendly Network San Francisco/East Bay   ▼
c/o E. Clary
PO Box 1088
Alameda CA 94501
tel: 415-289-2222; 510-523-6532
e-mail: bifriendly@frap.org
7:30pm every Tuesday at Au Coquelet, 2000
University Ave., Berkeley. **Publication(s)***:*
Monthly calendar of events for the Bay area, $12
Sub.

Bi People of Color   ▼ C
Berkeley CA
tel: Pacific Center: 510-548-8283
Meets at the Pacific Center on the 2nd & 4th
Fridays of each month.

Sacramento Area Bisexual Network   ▼ A 🖳
Lambda Community Center
920 20th St., suite 107
Sacramento CA 95814
tel: 916-442-0185 (Lambda Community Center)
e-mail: sacsabn@aol.com
URL: www.geocities.com/westhollywood/Height/
6853/
Political, educational, social, support group for
bi men & women, with meetings, discussion
group. Meets 2nd & 4th Tues. each month, 7-
8.30pm at The Open Book bookstore (916-498-
1004).

Bay Area Bi Women's Group   ▼ ♀ 🖳
PO Box 190493
San Francisco CA 94119
tel: Sue: 510-444-8764
e-mail: asgaya@earthlink.net (calendar info);
sdell99@aol.com (meetings & event planning)
URL: home.earthlink.net/~asgaya/babw.html
Monthly potluck. Come & meet other bi women,
talk & share experiences in an informal setting.
Publication(s)*: Bay Area Bi Women's Calendar*

Bi Phone List
San Francisco CA
tel: 415-597-1992 or 510-433-4701
Joine this phone list to keep abreast of bi events
in the San Francisco Bay Area.

Key to symbols: ▼ = bi   ♀ = women   ♂ = men   ❂ = religious/spiritual
👍 = for allies   **M** = for married bis   ♥ = for partners of bis   **Y** = youth   **C** = people of color
182   **The Bisexual Resource Guide 2000**

Bi-Friendly East Bay ▼🖳
San Francisco CA
e-mail: bifriendly@frap.org
URL: www.frap.org/bifriendly/
Monthly calendar of events in the San Francisco Bay area of interest to bi people. See also Bi-Friendly South Bay. Info: Hew_Wolff@artlogic.com.

Bi Men of Color ▼♂C
San Francisco Bay area CA
tel: Bill: 510-540-0869
Meets twice a month on the 1st & 3rd Fridays.

Jewish Bisexual Caucus ▼☻
c/o James A. Frazin
PO Box 78261
San Francisco CA 94107
tel: Jim: 415-337-4566
e-mail: jf@shibboleth.com
A support & advocacy group welcoming all Jewish (people who identify as Jews, culturally or religiously) bisexuals (or people considering identifying as bisexual) at its monthly gatherings. Mixed heritage people or people who are unsure or exploring bisexual & Jewish identity are warmly welcome also. Meetings announced in BiFriendly Newsletter.

Bi-Friendly South Bay ▼🖳
San Jose CA
tel: 408-793-5131
e-mail: bifriendly@frap.org
URL: www.frap.org/bifriendly/
Meets Tuesdays 9pm at Cafe Babylon, 434 South First St., San Jose (info@southbaybi; www.southbaybi.org). Also parties & events. A project of the South Bay Bisexual Organizers & Activists (SoBOA). See also Bi-Friendly East Bay .

South Bay Bisexual Organizers & Activists E▼🖳 (SoBOA)
San Jose CA
tel: 408-793-5131
e-mail: info@southbaybi.org
URL: www.southbaybi.org
Works to eliminate prejudice & discrimination against bisexual people.

Bi-Friendly Santa Cruz ▼🖳
Santa Cruz CA
tel: 408-477-4150
e-mail: scruz-bi-info@bayview.com
URL: www.bayview.com/scruz-bi/
Social events for bi folk.

Women's Bi-Net of Santa Cruz ▼♀
& The Greater Monterey Bay Area
PO Box 3536
Santa Cruz CA 95063-3536
tel: 408-427-4556

Palo Alto Bi Women's Discussion Group ▼♀
Palo Alto CA
tel: Rebecca 650-961-9590

Bisexual Support & Discussion Group ▼
c/o Spectrum
1000 Sir Francis Drake Blvd. #12
San Anselmo CA 94960-1743
tel: 415-457-1115 X 201; fax: 415-457-2838
e-mail: spectrumVL@aol.com
A new (1998) group that sponsors occasional community forums & hold support/discussion group meetings on the 4th Tuesday of each month, from 7-9pm. Facilitator: Mano Marks. This program is part of a larger collaboration with Bi Life Marin, a program of the Marin AIDS progect. **Publication(s)**: *The Dispatch free quarterly newsletter*

Bisexual Men's ▼♂
Support/Personal Growth Group
Ron Fox, Ph.D., MFCC
PO Box 210491
San Francisco CA 94121-0491
tel: 415-751-6714
e-mail: rcf@wenet.net
Men's therapy group, with focus on communication & relationship issues. Fee.

South Bay/Santa Clara ▼🖳
Mixed Bi Support Group
c/o Billy DeFrank Lesbian & Gay Community Center
175 Stockton Avenue
San Jose CA 95126
tel: Community Center: 408-293-2429; fax: tdd: 408-298-8996
URL: www.southbaybi.org or www.defrank.org
7:30-9pm every Tuesday in Room B. This guided rap & discussion group provides support & referral info to bi men & women.

Bi-Life Marin ▼
c/o Marin AIDS Project
1660 Second Street
San Rafael CA 94901
tel: 416-457-2487 x420; fax: 415-457-5687
e-mail: BiLifeNBay@aol.com
An outreach of the Marin AIDS Project. Provides social events to strengthen the bi community, & provide an environment for bisexual & bi-curious men & women to meet like-minded individuals. Bi-Life also presents educational forums where people meet to discuss important issues of self-discovery.

Cabrillo College: Queer Club 🎓
Student Center, 6500 Soquel Drive
Aptos CA 95003
tel: 408-479-6231

🎒 = school   🎓 = college/university   P = professional   E = educational
A = activist/political   H = health (incl. HIV)   🖾 = media/press   🖳 = Internet resource
The Bisexual Resource Guide 2000   183

Asian & Pacific Islander   C♂🖳
Gay/Bi Men's Support Group
c/o Pacific Center
2712 Telegraph Avenue
Berkeley CA 94705
tel: 510-548-8232; fax: 510-548-2938
e-mail: pacificcenter@gay.net
URL: www.pacificcenter.org
Center sponsors various bi support groups along with speaker's bureau, mental health svcs for couples & individuals, & volunteer opportunities for peer group facilitation. Accredited training site for MFCC internships. Call for info about currently meeting goups. **Publication(s):** *Pacific Currents Quarterly newsletter that includes a free announcement section for other BGLTQ organizations*

Pacific Center
2712 Telegraph Avenue
Berkeley CA 94705
tel: 510-841-6224; fax: 510-548-2938
Center sponsors various bi support groups. Call for info about currently meeting groups. Bi People of Color Group, etc.

University of California, Berkeley:

▼ **Multicultural Bisexual Lesbian Gay**   ⚢
Alliance (MBLGA)
University of California, Berkeley
304 Eshleman Hall
Berkeley CA 94720
tel: 510-642-6942; fax: 510-643-6396
e-mail: mblga@uclink.berkeley.edu
Umbrella group of all UC Berkeley GLBT groups.

▼ **Queer Resource Center**   ⚢
e-mail: events@queer.berkeley.edu
See MBLGA above.

▼ **GLOBE (Gays, Lesbians, Or Bisexuals**   ⚢
Everywhere)
Support & social group for queer & questioning students in the Residence Halls. Meet Tuesdays 8pm in Unit 2's Classroom C (downstairs, near the central unit office).

▼ **Fluid**   ⚢▼
tel: Betsy: 510-643-8429
e-mail: qrc@queer.berkeley.edu
"A bi social & discussion group open to everyone outside extremes." See MBLGA above.

▼ **Cal Asian Lesbian Bisexual & Gay**   ⚢
Alliances Younited (CAL-B-GAY)
Organization for queer-identified Asians/ Pacific Islanders. See MBLGA above.

▼ **Gay, Lesbian, Bisexual**   ☯⚢E🖳
Catholics Support Group
Newman Hall-Holy Spirit Parish
2700 Dwight Way
Berkeley CA 94704
tel: 510-848-7812 or 510-848-7813; fax: 510-848-0179
URL: www.support.net/HolySpirit
Meets 7:30pm 1st & 3rd Thurs of month at Newman Hall at above address.

California State University at Chico: Pride   ⚢E
Bell Memorial Union, Room 210
Chico CA 95929
Student organization providing education, support & social activities for GLB students.

De Anza College: Bisexual, Lesbian,   ⚢
Transgendered, & Gay Association
21250 Stevens Creek Boulevard
Cupertino CA 95014
tel: Advisor: Jean Miller: 408-864-8488

University of California at Davis: ⚢🖳
Lesbian Gay Bisexual Resource Center
University House 105
Davis CA 95616
tel: 530-752-2GLB
URL: lgbcenter.ucdavis.edu/

Black Men's Exchange &   C
Black Women's Exchange
Oakland CA 94609
tel: 510-763-6377

Gaylesta: Gay, Lesbian, Bisexual &   PH
Transgender Psychotherapist's Association
of the Bay Area
5337 College Avenue
Suite #713
Oakland CA 94618
tel: 888-869-4993 (referral service; toll-free); 510-433-9939 (membership & info)
Professional networking, community education, social events & psychotherapist referral service. **Publication(s):** *Gaylesta News A newsletter to inform members of events, ads, classifieds & organization news.*

> Many human beings enjoy sexual relations with their own sex, many don't; many respond to both. The plurality is the fact of our nature and not worth fretting about."
>
> —*Gore Vidal, 1991 (from "The Birds and The Bees" in* The Nation *10/28/91.)*

Key to symbols: ▼ = bi   ♀ = women   ♂ = men   ☯ = religious/spiritual
🖑 = for allies   **M** = for married bis   ♥ = for partners of bis   **Y** = youth   **C** = people of color
184   **The Bisexual Resource Guide 2000**

Mills College: 🔭 ♀ 🖥
Queer Alliance
c/o Associated Students at
Mills College
5000 MacArthur Blvd.
Oakland CA 94613
URL: www.mills.edu/LIFE/ASMC/
MQA/mqa.homepage.html
Committees include: Lesbian Avengers (dedicated to direct action to fight queerphobia & promote LesBiTrans women's issues & visibility on campus & in the larger Oakland community) & BLAST Bisexuals, Lesbians, & Straights Talking (an organization that hopes to educate the straight community about what it means to be gay through movie nights, discussions, & lectures).

San Francisco Pride, 1990.

Robyn Ochs

The P.E.R.S.O.N. Project EA🖥
586 62nd Street
Oakland CA 94609-1245
tel: 510-601-8883; fax: 510-601-8883
e-mail: person@youth.org
URL: www.youth.org/luco/personproject/
Works to ensure that fair, accurate, & diverse information regarding LGBT people is presented to America's youth as a part of public school education. Organizes for reform of curricular policies to make them inclusive of LGBT info & images. News archives: www.glinn.com/news/project.htm.

Lesbian, Gay & Bisexual Awareness EY
Program
PO Box 61011
Palo Alto CA 94306
tel: 408-723-4196 Donna Matthewson
Speaker's bureau, mostly to high school, junior college & college groups, a project of the Billy DeFrank Lesbian & Gay Community Center in San Jose.

Rainbow Community Center of Contra E
Costa County
2637 Pleasant Hill Rd.
Pleasant Hill CA 94523
tel: 925-210-0563
Peer group support, referral services, social opportunities, & educational programs. Contact Cathleen or Diana Barnard at the center for bi-related info. **Publication(s)***: Prism Free monthly newsletter with calendar, articles, ads, center schedule.*

GLSEN/SFBA (formerly BANGLE) PYEA🔭🖥
Box 70554
Point Richmond CA 94807-0554
tel: 510-234-3429
e-mail: boblatham@aol.com
URL: (for GLSEN) www.glsen.org
Advocates equality in education & change in education environments to make them safe & supportive for LGBTQ youth. Works to teach respect for all. People of all occupations & orientations welcome to join. Funded by United Way. Scholarship program. Annual essay Contest. Annual conference. Offers workshops primarily for faculty & administrators. Local chapter of GLSEN, a national org. w/70 chapters. $35/year to join. $15/students or low-income. **Publication(s)***: Star Bangle Spanner Monthly. Lists meetings & school workshops. Articles about GLBT education news. Samples mailed on request.*

Sonoma State University: Bisexual Gay & 🔭
Lesbian Alliance
Rohnert Park CA 94928
tel: Advisor: Matthew Long 707-664-3127
e-mail: matthew_long@sonoma.edu

Spectrum

1000 Sir Francis Drake Blvd. #12 E
San Anselmo CA 94960-1743
tel: 415-457-1115; fax: 415-457-2838
e-mail: SpectrumVL@aol.com
Community center with programs for youth, adults, seniors, men, women, mixed gender groups. Volunteer opportunites. Book discussions. Most programs open to bisexuals. **Publication(s)***: The dispatch free quarterly newsletter*

✎ = school   🔭 = college/university   **P** = professional   **E** = educational
A = activist/political   **H** = health (incl. HIV)   📰 = media/press   🖥 = Internet resource
The Bisexual Resource Guide 2000   **185**

▼ **Lesbian, Gay & Bisexual Parents' Group**
tel: 415-457-1115 x203
See Spectrum above. Occasional events,
including once a year family camp.

▼ **New Horizons**   **Y**
tel: 415-457-1115 X 201
See Spectrum above. Group for TBLG &
questioning people 20-29 years old. Meets 1st &
3rd Mondays 7-9pm.

▼ **Rainbow's End**   **Y**
tel: 415-457-1115 x201
See Spectrum above. For lgbtq youth, 14-23,
Thurs. 7-9pm.

35+ Group   ♂ **C**
c/o GAPA Gay Asian Pacific Alliance
P.O. Box 421884
San Francisco CA 94142-1884
tel: 415-282-GAPA
e-mail: gapa@slip.net
Social/support group for gay/bi API men &
friends. Meets on 2nd Sunday of each month,
150 Eureka St.

Asian Pacific Gay, Lesbian &   **YC**
Bisexual Young People's Support Group
LYFE Program
584 Castro Street #294
San Francisco CA 94114
tel: 415-642-7240; fax: 415-642-7260
For those 21 & under.

BA-CYBERDYKES   ♀ 💻
San Francisco CA
e-mail: ba-cyberdykes-owner@queernet.org
BA-CYBERDYKES is a San Francisco Bay Area
Lesbian/bi discussion list for self-identified
dykes. For more information, send an e-mail
message to majordomo@queernet.org with only
"info ba-cyberdykes" in the body of the message.

BLUR   **Y**
c/o LYRIC
127 Collingwood St.
San Francisco CA 94114
tel: 415-703-6150 or 1-800-24PRIDE
A support & social group for young people (23 &
under) who don't fit into either/or categories of
sexuality. Meets bi-weekly at a local coffeehouse.
Some phone support also available. Contact
LYRIC for more information.

"Ever since I had that interview in
which I said I was bisexual it
seems twice as many people
wave at me in the streets."

—*Elton John, 1980s.*

Cuir Underground   💻
San Francisco CA
e-mail: cuiru@black-rose.com
URL: www.black-rose.com/cuiru.html
A monthly newsletter for the San Francisco Bay
Area pansexual kink communities. 'Pansexual'
refers to all genders & sexual orientations; 'kink'
refers to s/m, leather, fetish, genderfuck & other
forms of radical sexuality.

Gay Asian/Pacific Alliance   **C** ♂ **H** 💻
P.O. Box 421884
San Francisco CA 94142-1884
tel: Infoand events tape 415-282-4272
e-mail: gapa@slip.net
URL: www.slip.net/~gapa
Dedicated to furthering the interest of gay & bi
Asian & Pacific Islander men through
awareness, positive identity development, &
establishing a supportive communtiy. Social,
cultural (chorus, theater, dance), political
awareness, HIV/AIDS advocacy, 35+ group,
publications, scholarship. **Publication(s)***:*
Lavender Godzilla Newsletter

Harvey Milk Institute   👓 **E** 💻
584 Castro St., Suite 451
San Francisco CA 94114
tel: 415-863-7200; fax: 415-863-4740
e-mail: harvmilk@aol.com
URL: members.aol.com/harvmilk
Community-based lgbt institute. In 1998 Melissa
White offered one of the only courses in the world
on bisexuality, entitled "Switch Hit Lit."

Lyric (Lavender Youth Recreation   **Y ▼ H E** 💻
& Information Center)
127 Collingwood St.
San Francisco CA 94114-2411
tel: ofc: 415-703-615; youth talkline: 800-246-
PRIDE or TDD: 341-8812; fax: 415-703-6153
e-mail: office: lyric@lyric.org youth talkline:
lyricinfo@tlg.net
URL: www.lyric.ord
Groups include: 18 & Under: M-F 3-6pm. Young
Women 23 & Under: Mon 7-9; Young Men 23 &
Under: Fri 7-9. All meetings held at above
address. Bisexual rap group, Thurs. 7-9pm (call
for location); 23 & under drop-in Weds. 6-9pm &
Sat. 1-4pm. Lots of youth volunteer opportuni-
ties!

New Leaf/ HIV Mental Health Services   **H**
1853 Market St.
San Francisco CA 94103
tel: 415-626-7000 ext.205
New Leaf provides psychotherapy for HIV-
positive men & women in the LGBT community.
Both long & short-term therapy offered. Bisexual
therapists available on request.

Key to symbols: ▼ = bi   ♀ = women   ♂ = men   ❀ = religious/spiritual
🐾 = for allies   **M** = for married bis   ♥ = for partners of bis   **Y** = youth   **C** = people of color
186   **The Bisexual Resource Guide 2000**

Proyecto Contrasida Por Vida   **CH**
2793 16th St.
San Francisco CA 94103-3633
tel: 415-864-7278; fax: 415-575-1645
Latino/a LGB HIV service agency.

Q Action   ♂**EA▼YH**
2128 15th St.
San Francisco CA 94114
tel: 415-575-1050x777
e-mail: qaction@stopaids.org
*A peer-based group of young gay & bi men (25 &
under) committed to stopping the spread of HIV
in our community.*

San Francisco Bay Times   ✍
525 Bryant Street
San Francisco CA 94107
tel: 415-227-0800; fax: 415-227-0890
e-mail: sfbaytimes@aol.com
*GLBT bi-weekly newspaper for the Bay Area.
This paper has the best (only) regularly
published list of bi (& many other) resources in
the Bay Area.* **Publication(s)***: San Francisco
Bay Times Bi-weekly*

San Francisco Bi Film Festival   ▼✍A🖥
1803 Ninth Ave
San Francisco CA 94122
tel: 415-665-5645
Jeff Ross
e-mail: jtpasty@serius.com
URL: www.serius.com/~jtpasty/bipride
*Annual Bi event. Informational website. Write or
call Jeff Ross, festival director, for more
information.*

San Francisco Network for   ♀**H**
Battered Lesbians & Bisexual Women
3543 18th Street, Box 28
San Francisco CA 94110
tel: voice mail: 415-281-0276
*Brief phone counseling & referrals for women
emotionally, phsyically, or sexually battered by
women lovers. Community education & training
re: woman to woman battering.*

San Francisco State University: ᨆ🖥
Les/Gay/Bi Alliance (LGBA)
Student Union Building M-100A
1600 Holloway
San Francisco CA 94132
tel: 415-338-1952
e-mail: sfsulgba@sfsu.edu
URL: www.sfsu.edu/~sfsulgba
Support, newsletter, events.

Vietnamese Lesbians Gays & Bisexuals   **C**
send mail to: Vietnamese GLB Group
730 Polk Street #4
San Francisco CA 94109
tel: 415-292-3420 ext319
Tony Nguyen ; fax: 415-292-3404

Billy DeFrank   **YCEAH**🖥
Lesbian & Gay Community Center
175 Stockton Avenue
San Jose CA 95126
tel: 408-293-4525; fax: 408-298-8986
URL: www.defrank.org
*A community center with many programs &
courses, from Pink Triangle Traffic School to
Leather schmoozing socials, Baylands Family
Circle, & South Bay Queer & Asian Groups.*

San Jose State University: ᨆ**E**🖥
**Gay/Lesbian/Bisexual/ Transgendered &
Questioning Student Organization**
Box 55 SAS
San Jose CA 95192-0038
tel: 408-924-7820
e-mail: gala@bhs.net
URL: www.sjsu.edu/orgs/GALA/index.html
Social & educational.

South Bay Queer & Asian   **C**🖥
c/oBilly DeFrank Center
175 Stockton Ave.
San Jose CA 95126
tel: 408-293-4525; fax: 408-298-8986
URL: www.defrank.org
*SBQ&A is a support & social group which
provides South Bay Gay Asian & Pacific
Islanders a safe place to come out & be
comfortable with their sexual identity & race. Bi-
monthly meetings in Room C.* **Publication(s)***:
DeFrank News free, monthly*

Inti-Net Resource Center
PO Box 4322
San Rafael CA 94913-4322
tel: 415-507-1739
*Supports loving, committed, ethical, multi-
partner relationships. Workshops, ongoing
groups, speakers bureau, quarterly newsletter.
All sexual preferences welcome.* **Publication(s)***:
Polyamory Quarterly. $20*

University of California, Santa Cruz:

▾ **Gay, Lesbian, Bisexual & Transgender**   ᨆ🖥
Resource Center
Santa Cruz CA 95064
tel: 831-459-2468; fax: 831-459-4387
e-mail: glbtcenter@cats.ucsc.edu
URL: www2.ucsc.edu/glbtcenter/

✎ = school   ᨆ = college/university   P = professional   E = educational
A = activist/political   H = health (incl. HIV)   ✍ = media/press   🖥 = Internet resource
The Bisexual Resource Guide 2000   **187**

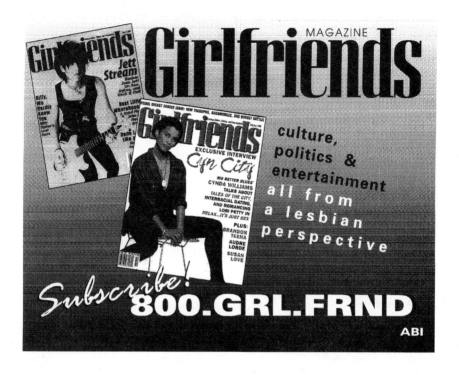

▼**Sappho**　　　　　　　　　　　♀ ⚢
Women's Center
Santa Cruz CA 95060
Group for women who are lesbian, bisexual or questioning.

Stanford University:　　　　　　⚢ 🖥
Lesbian, Gay & Bisexual Community Center
PO Box 8265
Stanford CA 94309
tel: Director: 650-725-4222
e-mail: lgbcc@forsythe.stanford.edu
URL: www.leland.stanford.edu/group/QR/
An information/referral resource, meeting center, & "safe space" for members of Stanford's LGBQTcommunity. Stanford glbt groups include: Bisexual, Lesbian, & Gay Alliance at Stanford (BGLAS): 650-725-4222; OUTLAW - Bisexual, Gay, & Lesbian Law Students Association: 650-723-0362; SUSEQ: Lesbian, Gay, & Bisexual Students, Faculty, & Staff at the School of Education: 650-723-2109

Southern California

Los Angeles Bisexual Support Groups ▼ ♂ ♀ **EA**
Gay & Lesbian Community Services Center
1625 N. Schrader Blvd.
Hollywood CA 90028
tel: 213-993-7400
Co-gender Bi Discussion Group 1st Monday 8-10pm; Bisexual Men's Discussion Group 3rd Thursday 8-10pm; Bisexual Women's Discussion Group 2nd Monday 8-10pm. $2 donation, but nobody turned away for lack of funds.

Bis at the Center/ BiNet　　　　▼E🖥
Long Beach-Orange County
PO Box 20917
Long Beach CA 90801
tel: 800-585-9368 (more #s below); fax: 562-495-7502
e-mail: bisexuals@aol.com
URL: members.aol.com/bisexuals
Meetings held at The Center, 2017 E. 4th St., Long Beach. Support, rap & social group Fridays 8:00 p.m. Also hosts parties & confererences. 562-437-0511 or 562-434-4455.

Key to symbols:　　　▼ = bi　　　　♀ = women　　　♂ = men　　　❂ = religious/spiritual
⚬ = for allies　**M** = for married bis　　♥ = for partners of bis　　**Y** = youth　　**C** = people of color
188　　　　　　　　　　　　　　　　　　　　　**The Bisexual Resource Guide 2000**

BiNet Los Angeles ▼🖳
PO Box 94161
Pasadena CA 91109-4161
tel: 213-882-4402
e-mail: info@BiNetLA.org
URL: \www.BiNetLA.org
Social organization for bis & friends. Meets 3rd Sat. $5 donation requested. Bi Night at Ripples Bar, 1st Fri. of the month in Long Beach. Send SASE for more info.

BiPol San Diego ▼EA
c/o LGMCS
PO Box 3357
San Diego CA 92163
e-mail: kbaker@rohan.sdsu.edu
Meets 1st Tuesday, 8pm, at Lesbian & Gay Men's Community Center (3916 Normal St.), in the Annex. Bisexuals & friends organizing together to educate, promote visibility, & fight homophobia & biphobia.

Bisexual Forum ▼
4545 Park Blvd, Suite 207
San Diego CA 92116
tel: 619-452-2474 or 619-692-2077
e-mail: fritzsd@aol.com
Mixed gender discussion, support & social group; discussions 2nd Tuesdays, 7:30pm. Meets in the auditorium of the Lesbian & Gay Men's Community Services Center, 3916 Normal St., San Diego CA 92103. Meetings open to all.

Bi RAP OC ▼EAM♥
The Center, Orange County
12832 Garden Grove Blvd. Suite A
Garden Grove CA 92843
tel: 714-534-0862 (Center); 562-986-1227 (S. Reese)
Meets: 2nd & 4th Mon each month, 7:30-9pm at the Orange County Center. Facilitated by Steven Reese, focusing on both personal & political issues of importance to all bi, bi-curious & bi-friendly persons & their loved ones. Suggested donation $1-3 donated to the O.C. Center

Married Bisexual Men's Group ▼♂EM
P.O. Box 90814
Pasadena CA 91109
tel: 626-568-7991; fax: 562-495-7502
Married bisexual men's group for men who are or have been in long-term relationships; 8-10-week closed group where bi married men can share their frustrations & strengths with each other. Therapeutic groups & individual counseling also available for youth, adults, families, & couples.

Bi Women's Social Group ♀▼
San Diego CA
tel: 619-259-8019

Bisexual Community Line (San Diego) E▼
San Diego CA
tel: 619-452-2474
Info line for the Bisexual Forum, political action group BiPol, Woman to Woman, Bi West Conference & more. Currently English-language; plans to go bilingual, English-Spanish.

BiNet Santa Barbara - Bi Now ▼
Santa Barbara CA
tel: 805-687-2538
e-mail: BiNetSBBiNow@aol.com
Meets at Chameleon Restaurant at 421 Cota St., Santa Barbara, 2nd & 4th Wednesdays at 6pm. "All openminded & bi-friendly individuals over 21 are welcome. Mostly a social group w/open discussions.

Bisexual Men & Women's Group ▼
c/o Pacific Pride
126 E. Hailey St. #A17
Santa Barbara CA 93101
tel: Lauren: 805-963-3636x127

Bisexual Rap Group ▼
Gay & Lesbian Resource Center
126 E. Hailey St. #17
Santa Barbara CA 93101
tel: 805-963-3636
Meets 1st & 3rd Wednesdays at above address.

Claremont Colleges: 🎓EA🖳
Queer Resource Center
700 N. College Way
Claremont CA 91711
tel: 909-607-1817
URL: classes2.pomona.edu/departments/qrc
Publication(s): *Outspoken - A Literary Magazine*

Orange Coast College: Pride 🎓E
2701 Fairview Road
Costa Mesa CA 92626
tel: 714-432-5738 (student svcs.); 714-432-5613 (advisor)
Weekly meetings during termtime Thurs. 5-6pm.

University of California, Irvine: 🎓EAM♥🖳
Lesbian, Gay, Bisexual Transgender Resource Center
106 Gateway Commons
University of California
Irvine CA 92697-5125
tel: 949-824-3169 (Pat Walsh, Director)
LGBRC office 714-824-3277; fax: 949-824-3412
e-mail: plwalsh@uci.edu
URL: www.uci.edu/~lgbtrc
GLBSU meets Wednesdays, 6-8pm at the LGB Resource Center. Check website for listing of all groups at UCI.

✎ = school 🎓 = college/university P = professional E = educational
A = activist/political H = health (incl. HIV) ✐ = media/press 🖳 = Internet resource
The Bisexual Resource Guide 2000 **189**

University of California, San Diego:

▼ **Lesbian, Gay & Bisexual Peer Counseling** &⟋
Program
La Jolla CA
tel: David Blasband:619-534-3987 Nickie Golden
619-534-3456
e-mail: ngolden@UCSD.edu

▼ **Lesbian, Gay, Bisexual,** &⟋**EA**▣
Transgendered Association
2nd floor, Old Student Center
9500 Gilman Dr.
La Jolla CA 92093
tel: 619-534-4297
e-mail: ucsdlgba@sdcc.13.ucsd.edu
URL: sdcc.13.ucsd.edu/~ucsdlgba/home.html

▼ **Women's Support Group** &⟋ ♀ ♂ **EA**▣
& Gay/Bi Men's Support Group
c/o Psycological & Counseling Services
9500 Gilman Dr.
La Jolla CA 92093
tel: 619-534-3755
e-mail: UCSDlgba@sdcc.13.ucsd.edu
URL: sdcc13.ucsd.edu/~ucsdlgba/support/
support.htm/
UCSD's Psychological & Counseling Services.
Groups available for registered students: a
women's support group Tues. 6-7:30 & Gay/bi
men's support group-(undergrad) Tues. 7-8:30.
Drop-ins welcome.

Asian Pacific Crossroads Orange County ♂ **C**
1919 Beverly Way #304
Long Beach CA 90802
tel: 714-534-0862
For gay & bi API men, meets 3rd Fridays.

Bi Consultation Service ▼**CPEAM**♥**Y**▣
PO Box 20917
Long Beach CA 90801
tel: Gary North: 562-437-0511, or
1-800-585-9368 (1-800-JULY-DOT)
e-mail: bisexuals@aol.com
URL: members.aol.com/bisexuals
One to one counsulatation & small support
groups for people just starting out. Also
information about bi-supportive therapists.
BiMarried men's group. Other specialty groups
created on an as-needed basis.

California State Univ., Long Beach: &⟋**EA**
Lesbian/Gay/Bisexual Resource Center
F04 Room 165, 1250 Bellflower Blvd.
Long Beach CA 90840
tel: 562-985-4585: main line; 985-4588: event line
Mon.-Thurs. 8-5; Fri. 8-noon.

Affirmation: Gay & Lesbian Mormons - ☯**E**▣
Los Angeles Chapter
PO Box 46022
Los Angeles CA 90046
tel: 213-255-7251
e-mail: kelp fish @ aol.com or
AA Saints@aol.com
URL: members.aol.com/LASaints/
Affirmation.html
Sunday evening meetings, monthly social event,
Call ahead. **Publication(s)**: *Affirmation*
Monthly news magazine.

Chingusa - Los Angeles **C**▣
P.O. Box 741666
Los Angeles CA 94004-1666
tel: 213-553-1873
e-mail: chingusai@writeme.com
URL: home.LACN.org/LACN/chingusai/
default2.htm
Korean-American glbt co-gender, multi-
generational & bilingual coalition of 3 sub-
groups: 1st & 2nd generation women, 1st
generation Korean-speaking men; & one-point-
five/second generation English-speaking men.
Twice a year, Chingusai meets as a coalition.

Different Spokes of Southern California ▣
PO Box 291875
Los Angeles CA 90029
tel: 213-896-8235
e-mail: DSpokessc@aol.com
URL: members.aol.com/Dspokessc/index.html
LGB bicycling club. Beginning riders to
advanced. Weekly organized rides & social
events. Please call ahead.
Membership $20 yr. or $35 yr. for a couple.
Publication(s): *Different Spokes Southern*
Calif. Newsletter visit website & click on for
comp. copy

LAAPIS (Los Angeles Asian **C**♀
& Pacific Islander Sisters)
PO Box 86484
Los Angeles CA 90086-0484
tel: 213-969-4084 (voice mail)
e-mail: lapis@aol.com
For lesbian & bi Asian & Pacific Islander
women. Monthly potluck & general meeting, &
support group.

Occidental College: &⟋
Bisexual, Gay & Lesbian Association
1600 Campus Road, Box 5
Los Angeles CA 90041
tel: 213-259-2560

Key to symbols: ▼ = bi ♀ = women ♂ = men ☯ = religious/spiritual
✤ = for allies **M** = for married bis ♥ = for partners of bis **Y** = youth **C** = people of color
190 The Bisexual Resource Guide 2000

University of Southern California: ⚭✐**E**🖥
Gay, Lesbian, Bi Assembly
USC Student Union,
Room 409, University Park Campus
830 Childs Way
Los Angeles CA 90089
tel: 213-740-7619
e-mail: glbausc@usc.edu
cagulada@usc.edu
URL: htttp://www.usc.edu/dept/glba/index.html
Tuesdays 7:30pm @ Peace center of the United
University Church, USC Campus. Includes Bi
Chat .

LA-MOTSS   ✐📁**A**🖥
Los Angeles, Southern California CA
e-mail: owner-la-motss@langevin.usc.edu
URL: langevin.usc.edu/~la-motss
LA-MOTSS is the online social & political forum
for gay/lesbian/bisexual issues in the Los
Angeles/Southern California area. For more
information, view the LA-MOTSS homepage or
send e-mail to majordomo@langevin.usc.edu
with only "info la-motss " in the body of the
message.

California State University, Northridge: ⚭✐**E**🖥
Lesbian Gay Bisexual & Transgendered
Community Resource Center & Lesbian Gay
Bisexual Alliance (LGBA)
18111 Nordhoff St.
Northridge CA 91330
tel: 818-677-5737
e-mail: lgbcrc@csun.edu
URL: www.csun.edu/lgbtcrc

Cerritos College: ⚭✐
Gay, Lesbian, Bisexual Community Services
Cerritos College
11110 Alondra
Norwalk CA 90650
tel: 562-860-2451

Mira Costa College: LesBiGay Alliance ⚭✐**E**🖥
1 Barnard Drive
Oceanside CA 92056-3899
tel: 760-757-2121 x8918 of 1-888-201-8480
e-mail: myeager@mcc.miracosta.cc.ca.us,
fsteffy@mcc.miracosta.cc.ca.us
URL: www.miracosta.cc.ca.us/info/student/
lesbigay/default.htm
Monthly drop-in support group co-facilitated by
peer counselors & students.

Caltech: Lesbigay Union   ⚭✐**E**🖥
Mail Stop 104-58
Pasadena CA 91125
tel: 626-395-8331
e-mail: CLU-request@cco.caltech.edu
URL: www.cco.caltech.edu/~clu/
Open to Caltech students, faculty, & staff.

Cal Poly: Pride Center   ⚭✐**E**🖥
3801 W. Temple Avenue
Pomona CA 91768
tel: 909-869-3064
e-mail: jjowens@csupomona.edu
URL: www.csupomona.edu/~pride_center/

University of Redlands: ⚭✐
Gay, Lesbian, Bisexual Student Union
c/o Student Life
Redlands CA 92373
tel: Advisor: Emily Culpepper, Dir.of Women's
Studies: 909-793-2121, ext. 5103

University of California, Riverside: ⚭✐
Lesbian, Gay, Bisexual & Transgender
Resource Center
250 Costo Hall
Riverside CA 92521
tel: 909-787-2267
e-mail: lgbtrc@ucrac1
Queer Alliance meetings Mondays at 7p.m. Also
various discussion groups. Call for location.

San Diego State University: Lesbian, Gay, ⚭✐
Bisexual & Transgender Student Union
PO Box 45, Aztec Center
San Diego CA 92182
tel: 619-594-2737
Meets Tues. at 6pm at Aztec Center.

Woman 2 Woman   ♀▼
Lesbian & Gay Men's Community Center
3916 Normal St.
San Diego CA 92103-3413
tel: 619-452-2474
Support/discussion group for bi women. Meets
4th Thursdays 8pm at above address.

Pacific Pride Foundation   **Y**
Youth Discussion Group
126 E. Hailey Street #A17
Santa Barbara CA 93101
tel: 805-963-3636
Meets Mon. 3:15-4:15pm.

University of California, Santa Barbara:

▼ **Multicultural Queer Grad Network**   ⚭✐
CAC Box 162
Santa Barbara CA 93106
e-mail: 6500mad@ucsbuxa.ucsb.edu

▼ **Queer Student Union**   ⚭✐ ♀
CAC Box 78
Santa Barbara CA 93106
tel: Women's Center: 805-893-3778

✎ = school   ⚭✐ = college/university   **P** = professional   **E** = educational
A = activist/political   **H** = health (incl. HIV)   📰 = media/press   🖥 = Internet resource
The Bisexual Resource Guide 2000   **191**

Pansocial Center
7136 Matilija Av.
Van Nuys CA 91405
tel: 818-989-3700
Hotline, free counseling & referrals. No meetings being held at present time.

Affirmations/Los Angeles: 🌙E🖳
United Methodists for Gay, Lesbian, Bisexual & Transgendered Concerns
PO Box 691283
West Hollywood CA 90069-9283
tel: 213-969-4664
e-mail: affirm LA @ aol.com
URL: www.umaffirm.org
Meets 2nd Sun. 7pm at Holman United Methodist Church, 3320 W. Adams Blvd., Los Angeles.

Colorado

BiNet Colorado ▼
Denver CO
tel: 303-499-5777
e-mail: binetcolo@aol.com
One of their members is a regional contact for BiNet USA. Call for info & meeting times. Monthly activities.

GLSEN/Colorado E👌
PO Box 280346
Lakewood CO 80228-0346
tel: 303-936-6562; fax: Same # (call first)
e-mail: glsenco@aol.com
A 501(c)(3) group that strives to assure that each member of every school community is valued & respected, regardless of sexual orientation.
Publication(s): *GLSEN/Colorado Newsletter brief quarterly update on activities & news*

Local

Aspen AIDS Project H
Aspen CO
tel: 970-925-2752

Aspen Gay/Lesbian Community Fund
PO Box 3143
Aspen CO 81612
tel: 970-925-2752

Bisexual Women's Voice Boulder ⚭▼♀
Boulder CO
tel: 303-499-5777
e-mail: binetcolo@aol.com

Boulder Gay/Les/Bi Concerned Catholics 🌙
Boulder CO
tel: 303-443-8383

OASOS Program: Y🖳
Coming Out Boulder/ Longmont
3450 Broadway
Boulder CO 80304
tel: 303-413-7504
URL: www.oasos.com
Support, activity group for LGBT/questioning youth 20 & under: Wednesdays 6-9pm in Boulder, Mondays 3:30-5:30pm in Longmont.

University of Colorado, Boulder:

▼ **Gay, Lesbian, Bisexual, Transgender** ⚭🖳
Resource Center
Campus Box 103, Willard #334
Boulder CO 80309-0103
tel: 303-492-1377
e-mail: glbrc@stripe.colorado.edu
URL: stripe.co.orado.edu/~glbrc/Home.html

▼ **Lesbian, Bisexual, Gay &** ⚭
Transgender Alliance
Boulder CO 80309
tel: 303-492-8567
Weekly meetings. Other groups include: Chancellor's LGB Committee; LGB Alumni Association; LGB Advisory Board.

ALSO (All Lifestyles & Outlooks)
Colorado Springs CO
tel: 719-685-4773
Potluck 3rd Sat. 5:30pm church annex. Suppot group at All Souls Unitarian Church.

Colorado College: ⚭E🖳
Gay, Lesbian, Bisexual Alliance
902 N. Cascade
Colorado Springs CO 80946
URL: www.cc.colorado.edu/students/BGALA/
Mixed-gender social & support student group (but not a therapy group), sometimes involved in political action, depending on the interest of its members. Mostly, it creates a community for those who have in common the experience of being different from the dominate heterosexual society. All meetings are confidential & we welcome new people to come to the meetings at anytime!

Colorado College & the University of ⚭
Colorado: Bisexual, Gay & Lesbian Alliance
Colorado Springs CO
tel: 719-471-4GAY
Meets at Pikes Peak Gay & Lesbian Community Center

Key to symbols: ▼ = bi ♀ = women ♂ = men 🌙 = religious/spiritual
👌 = for allies **M** = for married bis ♥ = for partners of bis **Y** = youth **C** = people of color
192 **The Bisexual Resource Guide 2000**

Community Council for Adolescent   **Y**
Development
Pride Center
PO Box 10511
Colorado Springs CO 80932
tel: 719-328-1056
Runs: Inside/Out (a youth support group).

Dignity   ☻
PO Box 1172
Colorado Springs CO 80901
tel: 719-685-5343
e-mail: bud2L@aol.com
For glbt Catholics. 2nd Sun. 11:30 brunch at Colorado Gill. Mass 1st Sat. 7pm at Sacred Heart.

Marriage Transitions   **M**
Colorado Springs CO
Meets 1st/3rd Thurs. 7pm. For glbt people who are, or have been, in a heterosexual marriage.

PFLAG, Colorado Springs   ♨
PO Box 10076
Colorado Springs CO 80932
tel: 719-575-8658
Meetings 2nd Wed. 6:30pm All Souls, 1865 North Academy #D.

Pikes Peak Gay & Lesbian Community   💻
Center: Pride Center
PO Box 607
Colorado Springs CO 80901
tel: 719-471-4429
e-mail: ppglcc2@aol.com
URL: members.aol.com/ppglcc2/cener.htm

Pikes Peak Metropolitican   ☻
Community Church
PO Box 10530
Colorado Springs CO 80932-0530
e-mail: revrost@aol.com
Services at All Souls Unitarian Church. Office at the Pride Center. Rev. Nori Rost.

Prime Timers   ♂
PO Box 38471
Colorado Springs CO 80934
tel: 719-477-1573
For older gay & bi men.

SCIRTS (Southern Colorado Intra-Regional   💻
Transgender Society), Colorado Springs
Colorado Springs CO
tel: 719-491-5860
e-mail: scirts@geocities.com
URL: www.geocities.com/WestHollywood/Heights/4484
Bi-inclusive transgender support organization.

Southern Colorado AIDS Project (S-CAP)   **H**💻
1301 S. 8th St., Suite 200
Colorado Springs CO 80901
e-mail: scap@mdione.net
URL: scap.ppages.com/

Stonewall Democrats   **A**
Democratic Party HQ
103 S. Wahsatch, Suite 102
Colorado Springs CO 80901

Summit Masters
PO Box 6925
Colorado Springs CO 80960-0845
Leather/Levi/Uniform interest.

University of Colorado,   🎓💻
Colorado Springs: BGALA
Colorado Springs CO
tel: 719-262-4105
e-mail: gbala@mail.uccs.edu
URL: www.uccs.edu/~bgala/

Women's Social Group   ♀
Colorado Springs CO
tel: 719-471-4429

Crossroads   ▼
c/o John Barry
3955 E Exposition Ste 408
Denver CO 80209
tel: 303-698-2385
Support group for married bisexual men. Referrals for bi women & spouses.

Denver University: 🎓
Lesbian, Gay & Bisexual Alliance
Box 12, 2055 E. Evans
Denver CO 80208
tel: 303-871-2321

Dignity - Denver   ☻
PO Box 3072
Denver CO 80201
tel: 303-322-8485
Organization for LGBT Catholics. Liturgies Sundays 5pm.

Equality Colorado   **A**💻
PO Box 300476
Denver CO 80203
tel: 303-839-5540;
303-852-5094; crisis line 888-557-4441 toll free in CO only; fax: 313-839-1361
e-mail: equalityco@aol.com
URL: www.tde.com/~equality
Educational & outreach statewide to increase awareness of GLB experience, civil rights & the effect of Amendment 2. Political advocacy, legislative work & PAC. Anti-violence project & training programs. 24 hr crisis line.

💊 = school   🎓 = college/university   **P** = professional   **E** = educational
A = activist/political   **H** = health (incl. HIV)   ▱ = media/press   💻 = Internet resource
The Bisexual Resource Guide 2000   **193**

**Gay, Lesbian & Bisexual E
Community Services Center
of Colorado, Inc.**
PO Drawer 18E
Denver CO 80218-0140
tel: 303-831-6268 (voice/tdd)
*Support groups, counseling,
library, speakers bureau,
youth groups (18-25),
helpline, referrals.Office
located at: 1245 E. Colfax Av.
#125, Denver.*

**Metropolitan Community ☯
Church of the Rockies**
980 Clarkson
Denver CO 80218
tel: 303-860-1819
*LGB religious organization
offers bingo, foodbank &
pastoral counseling. Sunday
& Wednesday services.*

**Metropolitan State ⚢ E 🖳
College of Denver: Gay
Lesbian Bisexual Transgender
Student Services**
CB 39, PO Box 173362
Denver CO 80217-3362
tel: 303-556-6333; fax: 303-556-3896
e-mail: BensenK@mscd.edu
URL: www.mscd.edu/%7eglbss/Welcome.html
Karen Bensen, LCSW, Coordinator.

P-FLAG
Denver CO
tel: 303-333-0286
*Meetings include a rap group for bisexuals &
their families. Meetings are the first Thursday of
each month. Call for location.*

Pagan Rainbow Network ☯
Herbs & Arts Bookstore
2015 E. Colfax Ave.
Denver CO 80218
tel: 303-388-2544
Spirituality circle for LGBT community.

Rainbow Alley Y
919 E. 14th St.
Denver CO
tel: Rebecca Morgan
303-831-0442
Drop in center for GLBT youh 25 & under.

Rocky Mtn. GLB Veterans of America P
PO Box 721
Denver CO 80201-0721
tel: 303-394-2339

BiNet Colorado

**Social Meeting for People with H 🖳
HIV Infection**
Denver CO
tel: 303-860-1819
e-mail: mccrdenver@aol.com
URL: www.mcrockies.org
*Tuesdays 7pm at Metropolitan Community
Church, 980 Clarkson, Denver. For heterosexual,
homosexual & bisexual individuals who just
want to socialize & not dwell on the illness
issues.*

**Fort Lewis College: Gay, Lesbian & Bisexual ⚢
Alliance**
1000 Rim Drive
Durango CO 81301
tel: Prevention Office: 970-247-7097
e-mail: ellison_d@fortlewis.edu

**Gay/Lesbian Association of Durango
(GLAD)**
Durango CO
tel: 970-247-7778

P-FLAG Durango
Durango CO
tel: 970-247-7778

P-FLAG Estes Park
Estes Park CO
tel: 970-586-0941

P-FLAG Evergreen
Evergreen CO
tel: 303-674-4843

Key to symbols: ▼ = bi ♀ = women ♂ = men ☯ = religious/spiritual
♦ = for allies M = for married bis ♥ = for partners of bis Y = youth C = people of color
194 **The Bisexual Resource Guide 2000**

Back Country Betty's ♀
Fort Collins CO
tel: 970-416-1916
Women's outdoor group

Colorado State University: Fort Collins ᴇⁿ
Student Organization for Gays, Lesbians &
Bisexuals
CSU, Box 208, Activities Center
Fort Collins CO 80523
tel: 970-491-7232

Lambda Community Center of Fort Collins ▼ 🖳
147 W. Oak St #2
Fort Collins CO 80524
tel: 970-221-3247
e-mail: lambda@lambdacenter.org
URL: www.lambdacenter.org/
For GLBs in northern Colorado & southern
Wyoming. Support group for gay/bi men meets
Thurs. 7-9pm. Rocky Mountain Youth Group, a
supportive & safe environment for GLB &
questioning youth meets Sun. 1pm. Also mixed
gender Bisexual Support Group.
Publication(s): *Lambda Line Bi-monthly.*

Quiet Corner Bookstore
803 E. Mulberry
Fort Collins CO 80524
tel: 970-416-1916
e-mail: quietcorner@juno.com
Northern Colorado's lgbt & feminist bookstore.

Rocky Mountain Youth Group Y 🖳
c/o Lambda Community Center
1437 E. Mulberry
Fort Collins CO 80524
tel: Andrew
970-221-3247
e-mail: lambda@lambdacenter.org
URL: www.lambdacenter.org
Support group for glbtq youth.

Gayla/Summit County
PO Box 2777
Frisco CO 80443

Colorado State University GLBT Student ᴇⁿ **E**
Services Office
18 Lory Student Center
Ft. Collins CO 80523
tel: 970-491-4342
Resources, referrals, support, education, &
outreach.

Fort Collins Citizens for Human Rights 🖳
(FCCHR)
305 West Magnolia #123
Ft. Collins CO 80521
tel: 970-495-4646
e-mail: fcchr@choice-city.com
URL: www.choice-city.com

Gathering of Womyn
Ft. Collins CO
tel: 970-491-7232

Human Rights Campaign
Ft. Collins CO
tel: 970-223-6431

MCC Family in Christ ❂
Ft. Collins CO
tel: Rev. Mark Lee
970-221-0811
e-mail: MarkLee1@compuserve.com
Sunday services 6pm

Northern Colorado AIDS Project (NCAP) 🖳
Ft. Collins CO
tel: 970-484-4469

Northern Colorado Gay & Lesbian **P**
Employees Network (NCGLEN—Hewlett
Packard)
Ft. Collins CO
tel: 970-679-3010

Rainbow Chorus
Ft. Collins CO
tel: 970-495-3434

Rocky Mountain Youth in Motion
Ft. Collins CO
tel: 970-221-3247

Straight But Not Narrow
Ft. Collins CO
tel: 970-491-7232

Weird Sisters ♀
PO Box F
Ft. Collins CO
tel: 970-482-4393
e-mail: weirdsisters@worldnet.att.net
newspaper for lesbian, bisexual, & alternative
women **Publication(s)**: *Weird Sisters*

Mesa State Gay, Lesbian & Bisexual ᴇⁿ
Alliance
PO Box 2647
Grand Junction CO 81502
tel: 970-241-0894; 970-248-1762; 970-245-4529
e-mail: jzeigel@mesa5.mesa.colorado.edu; or
philhellas@aol.com

P-FLAG Grand Junction
Grand Junction CO
tel: 970-242-8965

Warren McKerrow AIDS Foundation
Grand Junction CO
tel: 970-244-8639

✎ = school	ᴇⁿ = college/university	**P** = professional	**E** = educational
A = activist/political	**H** = health (incl. HIV)	✍ = media/press	🖳 = Internet resource

Western Colorado AIDS Project
Grand Junction CO
tel: 970-243-AIDS

Western Equality
Grand Junction CO
tel: 970-242-8949
Affiliated with Equality Colorado in Denver.

University of Northern Colorado:

▼ **Greeley Gay, Lesbian, Bisexual,**   &⁀**AE**
**Transgender Alliance / GLBT Resource
Center**
UNC University Center
Rm. 2005
Greeley CO 80639
tel: 970-351-1484
*Support & social group for UNC & Greeley
residents. The GLBT Resource Center provides
education & information for the UNC &
Greeley communities. Provides referrals to
local social groups, counseling & medical
services, & supportive religious/spiritual
organizations.*

▼ **Greeley GLBA**
Greeley CO
tel: 970-351-1484

Outfront Youth Group   **Y**
Pueblo Health Department
151 Central Main
Pueblo CO 81003
tel: 719-583-4311

PFLAG Pueblo   ♦
PO Box 4484
Pueblo CO 81003
tel: 719-542-6359

Pueblo After 2   **A**
PO Box 1602
Pueblo CO 81002
tel: 719-542-6359
e-mail: puebloafter2@juno.com
Pueblo's main glbt social/political organization.

Pueblo Metropolitan Community Church   ☯
1003 Liberty Lane (corner Bonforte)
PO Box 1918
Pueblo CO 81002-1918
tel: 719-543-6460

SCIRTS (Southern Colorado Intra-Regional   ▭
Transgender Society), Pueblo
c/o Pueblo MCC
Pueblo CO 81002
tel: 719-546-0480
e-mail: scirts@geocities.com
URL: www.geocities.com/WestHollywood/Heights/
4484
Bi-inclusive transgender support organization.

Southern Colorado AIDS Project (S-CAP)   **H**▭
PO Box 3277
Pueblo CO 81005
tel: 719-561-2616
URL: scap.ppages.com/

University of Southern Colorado: &⁀▭
One in Ten
c/o Associated Student Government
2200 Bonforte Boulevard
Pueblo CO 81005
e-mail: fe1788ke@uscolo.edu
URL: www.uscolo.edu/1in10/

Central Colorado Gay/Lesbian Alliance
PO Box 912
Salida CO 81201

**Gay & Lesbian Alliance of Steamboat
Springs**
Steamboat Springs CO
tel: 303-897-6688

Connecticut

Conn-Bi-Nation: Bi.W.A.   ▼**EA**
(Bisexuals With Attitude)
c/o Project 100 Community Center
1841 Broad St.
Hartford CT 06114
tel: Frances Donovan, 860-246-7093, or
Thom Connolly, 860-726-9306, or
the Community Center 203-724-5542
e-mail: ConnBiNat@aol.com
Statewide bi group. Meets 2nd Sundays at 7pm.

Connecticut Bisexual Women's Network   ▼ ♀
send mail to: GFontaine - CBN
77 Myrtle St.
Shelton CT 06484
tel: 203-922-1058
e-mail: msfontaine@juno.com
*Support group, social gatherings, bi-monthly
publication. Purpose: To bring bisexual women
together so that we do not feel as isolated or
alone. Many of us are married or have male
partners.* **Publication(s)**: *BiWays c/o
GFontaine
msfontaine@juno.com*

Key to symbols: ▼ = bi   ♀ = women   ♂ = men   ☯ = religious/spiritual
♦ = for allies   **M** = for married bis   ♥ = for partners of bis   **Y** = youth   **C** = people of color
196   **The Bisexual Resource Guide 2000**

Connecticut Pride Committee (LGB)　　**A**
c/o GLB Community Center
1841 Broad St.
Hartford CT 06114
tel: Mucha:203-953-1290 203-524-8114
Meets at the Community Center in Hartford.

Connecticut Private High Schools:　　**Y❧E**
Gay/Straight Alliances
CT
tel: 860-649-7386
There are groups at the following schools:
Loomis Chaffee, Windsor; Watkinson School,
Hartford; Choate Rosemary Hall, Wallingfoord.
Call Children From The Shadows at the above #
for contact info. for each school.

Connecticut Public High Schools:　　**Y❧E**
Gay/Straight Alliances
CT
tel: 860-649-7386
There are groups at the following schools:
Brookfield HS; Bunnell HS, Stratford; Conard
HS, W. Hartford; Coventry HS; Danbury HS;
Daniel Hand HS, Madison; EO Smith HS,
Storrs; Guilford HS; Greenwich HS; Hall HS,
W. Hartford; Newtown HS, Newtown; Ridgfield
HS; Southington HS; S. Windsor HS; Staples
HS. Call Children From The Shadows at the #
above for contact info. for each school.

Local

Bisexual Rap Group　　▼
GLB Community Center
1841 Broad St.
Hartford CT 06114
tel: 860-229-6918, Alice
Meets 4th Sundays at 7pm with rotating
facilitators & discussion topics at the GLB
Community Center.

Bi Rap Group　　▼
Triangle Community Center
25 Van Vant St., Box 4062
Norwalk CT 06855
tel: Robin Whiting: 203-855-8646
Meets 2nd & 4th Wednesday 7:30pm.

Danbury Outright　　**Y**
Box 2056
Danbury CT 06810
tel: Joe: 203-837-8215
Facilitated group meets every Mon at 8pm, on
West Conn campus.

Western Connecticut State College:

▼ **Faculty/Staff Alliance for Gay,**　　**↝PE**
Lesbian & Bisexual Concerns
181 White Street
Danbury CT 06810
tel: 203-837-8256 (Jeanne Posner)
e-mail: posner@wcsub.ctstateu.edu
Creates a safer, more supportive climate for
GLB students through education. Conducts
workshops & awareness training for faculty &
staff.

▼ **Lesbian/Gay/Bisexual Student Alliance**　　**↝E**
CTA Dept.
181 White Street
Danbury CT 06810
tel: 203-837-8256 (Jeanne Posner, Faculty
Advisor); fax: 203-837-8525
e-mail: posner@wcsub.ctstateu.edu
Provides support for GLB students on campus
& education to the university as a whole about
these issues.

Gay, Lesbian & Bisexual　　**P◎EA**
Community Center
1841 Broad St.
Hartford CT 06114-1780
tel: Regina Dyton: 203-724-5542; fax: 203-724-
3443
Hours: Monday-Friday 10am-10pm. Provides
safe & supportive meeting space for various
support groups in the LGB community.
Publication(s): *The Center Line Monthly*
newsletter.

Hartford Commission on Gay, Lesbian &　　**A**
Bisexual Issues
c/o City Hall
550 Main Street
Hartford CT 06106
tel: 860-296-7791, Stu Flavel
Meets 2nd Tuesdays 7pm, Rm. 401 City Hall. An
advisory committee to the City Council. Makes
recommendations to Council members regarding
legislation.

Married Men's Support Group　　♂**M**
Hartford CT
tel: 203-264-5605, Norman
For gay & bisexual men. Facilitated by a
therapist. Meets 1st & 3rd Mondays.

Metroline　　✍
Metro Publications
495 Farmington Av.
Hartford CT 06105
tel: 860-233-8334 or toll free 888-233-8334; fax:
860-233-8338
e-mail: mol@hartnet.org
Monthly newspaper.

❧ = school　　↝ = college/university　　**P** = professional　　**E** = educational
A = activist/political　　**H** = health (incl. HIV)　　✍ = media/press　　▢ = Internet resource

Trinity College: EROS   &ᐟ A
(Encouraging Respect of Sexualities)
Student Activities
300 Summit Street
Hartford CT 06106
Gay/Straight Alliance.

University of Connecticut: &ᐟ A
Lambda Law Student Association
School of Law
55 Elizabeth Street
Hartford CT 06105
tel: 860-570-5131, Sandy Goldberg
For GLBT law students, alumni & allies. Meets monthly to support activism around lgbt issues & provide support.

Your Turf Youth Group, Hartford   Y
c/o Gay & Lesbian Health Collective
P.O. Box 2094
Hartford CT 06145
tel: 860-278-4163, Rich
Facilitated group providing support & social connection for LGBT youth. Meets Fridays 7:30-9:30pm at LGB Community Center, 1841 Broad St.

Central Connecticut Youth Group   Y
Middletown CT
tel: 860-347-9514 (Paul)
Provides peer support to LGBT & questioning youth in the greater Middlesex area. Free, Meets Thurs 7-8:30pm in First Church of Christ, Middletown.

. **Wesleyan University:**

▼ **Queer Alliance**   &ᐟ E ♀ ♂ 🖳
c/o WSA
Wesleyan Station
190 High St.
Middletown CT 06459
tel: 860-685-2425; fax: 860-685-2411
e-mail: queer@auk.con.wesleyan.edu
URL: www.con.wesleyan.edu/~queer/queer2.html
Umbrella organization for groups including: LBQ (a women's social group); GBQ (a men's social group), Step One (confidential support group for people questioning their sexuality). Gets speakers on campus,etc. **Publication(s):** *Diva Literary magazine.*

▼ **Bisexual, Lesbian & Gay Awareness**   &ᐟ E
(BILEGA)
e-mail: queer@wesleyan.edu
See Wesleyan Queer Alliance above. Organization that coordinates & gives workshops on lesbigay awareness.

▼ **GBLOCQ**   &ᐟ C
e-mail: queer@auk.con.wesleyan.edu
See Wesleyan Queer Alliance above. Social group for people of color.

▼ **The Queer R.A./Frosh Group**   &ᐟ
See Wesleyan Queer Alliance above. Social & support group between queer-identified Resident Advisors & queer-identified & questioning Frosh.

BGLAD4YOUTH   Y E
c/o AIDS Project New Haven
850 Grand Ave.
New Haven CT 06511
tel: John Ginnetti: 203-624-0947 x232
Provides a safe space for LGBTQ youth in the greater New Haven area to discuss issues of orientation & identity.

New Haven Gay & Lesbian   🖳
Community Center
PO Box 8914
55 Fitch St.
New Haven CT 06532
tel: 203-387-2252
e-mail: NHGLCCweb@aol.com
URL: www.i-out.com/nhglcc
Serving the needs of the GLBT community.
Publication(s): *NGHLCC News Published 6x/year*

Southern Connecticut State University: &ᐟ
LGB Prism
Student Center
501 Crescent St.
New Haven CT 06515

Yale University:

▼ **LGBT Center**   &ᐟ
305 Crown Street
(mailing address: Yale Station, Box 2031)
New Haven CT 06520
tel: 203-432-1585
e-mail: LGB@yale.edu
Located near the corner of Crown & York. Holds Yale LGB Coop archives, & Pathways Peer Counselling staffed exclusively by local gay & lesbian counsellors Tuesdays 9-12pm (203-432-1585).

▼ **Lesbian, Gay, Bisexual,**   &ᐟ E A
Transgendered Cooperative
See LGBT Center above. Umbrella organization at Yale. Sponsors BGLAD & other events & activities. Meets Mondays 9-10pm at Dwight Hall Conference Room on Old Campus.

Key to symbols: ▼ = bi   ♀ = women   ♂ = men   🕮 = religious/spiritual
🜂 = for allies   **M** = for married bis   ♥ = for partners of bis   **Y** = youth   **C** = people of color
198   **The Bisexual Resource Guide 2000**

▼ BiWays ▼ 𝒸 ▱
URL: www.yale.edu/lgb/discussion/biways.html
See LGBT Center above. Discussion / social group for bisexual men & women & allies. Meets in Yale Women's Center, 198 Elm St., Tuesdays 9pm.

▼ Gayalies 𝒸 ♂ ▱
URL: www.yale.edu/lgb/discussion/gayalies.html
See LGBT Center above. Social, support & discussion group for men wishing to discuss gay/bi issues. Topic discussions, social events & activities. Serves as a resource to the communities. Meetings confidential.

▼ Pathways (LGB Peer Counseling) 𝒸 ▱
tel: Maryanne
e-mail: pathways-list@yale.edu
URL: www.yale.edu/pathways/
See LGBT Center above. A counseling hotline for LGB people around their various life issues. Information, referrals & a chance to talk.

▼ Prism: Queers of Color 𝒸 **C** ▱
URL: www.yale.edu/LGB/discussion/prism.html
See LGBT Center above. Discussion (& more!) group for queers of color. Thursdays 9pm at the Women's Center.

Yale Divinity School: 𝒸
Gay Lesbian Straight Bisexual Coalition
409 Prospect Street
New Haven CT 06511
tel: Ralph Thomas Taylor: 203-436-3778
e-mail: ralph.taylor@yale.edu

Yale Lesbian Gay Bisexual 𝒸 ▱
Law School Association (LGBLSA)
Yale Law School
Box 208215
New Haven CT 06520-8215
tel: Associate Dean's Office 203-432-7646
URL: www.yale.edu/lgblsa/contact.htm

Connecticut College: SOUL (Sexual 𝒸 **A**
Orientation United for Liberation)
Box 1295
New London CT 06320
e-mail: soultrain@conncoll.edu
URL: camelZ.conncoll.edu/ccinfo/soul/soul.html
For LGB & questioning people.

Outspoken - Norwalk Youth Group **YAE**
Triangle Community Center
25 Van Zant Street
PO Box 4062
Norwalk CT 06855
tel: 203-227-1755; fax: 203-227-3035
e-mail: dwoog@optonline.net
Weekly support group with 3 co-facilitators, provides safe space for or LGB & questioning, ages 16-22. Support, info, speakers, & an opportunity to involve themselves in the political arena. Meets every Sun 4-6pm at Triangle Center.

Triangle Community Center
25 Van Zant St.
Norwalk CT 06855-1713
tel: 203-853-0600

ANGLE (A Nation for Gay, Lesbian Equality) **Y**
Norwich CT
tel: Ruth: 860-822-8726
Sponsored by PFLAG, Norwich, the group meets weekly.

Quinnebaug Valley Youth **Y**
Quinnebaug CT
tel: Bob Brex: 860-564-6100
Meets Sun. 4-6pm at Quinnebaug Youth & Family Services.

"Just as the existence of biracial and multiracial individuals blurs and utimately eliminates the possibility of generating meaningful hierarchies of distinction between individuals of different racial backgrounds, bisexual people blur distinctions between apparently differing sexual orienations, rendering the hierarchies of value attached to such orienations increasingly meaningless."

—*Beth Firestein*

✎ = school   𝒸 = college/university   **P** = professional   **E** = educational
A = activist/political   **H** = health (incl. HIV)   ✏ = media/press   ▱ = Internet resource
The Bisexual Resource Guide 2000   *199*

University of Connecticut, Storrs:

▼ **BiGALA**   &↗**AE**
Box U-8G, 2110 Hillside Rd.
Storrs CT 06268-3008AA
tel: 860-486-3679
*Student-run group for the college community
with focus on educating the community. Social &
political components.*

▼ **Rainbow Center**   &↗**E**
Martha Nelson, Director
U-8 2110 Hillside Road
University of CT.
Storrs CT 06269
tel: 860-486-5821; fax: 860-486-4484
e-mail: rnbwdir@uconnvm..uconn.edu
*University center for resource for faculty, staff,
students, & alumni. Provides a variety of
information for the LBGTA community.
SafeSpace program. Educational guest speakers.
Resource referral, listserv.*

LGBT/Questioning Youth Therapy Group   **Y**
1022 Farmington Ave
W. Hartford CT 06107
tel: 860-233-6778
e-mail: estrick001@aol.com
*Biweekly group for LGBT/Q youth. Facilitated
by Elliot Strick, MA, LMFT, family therapist.
Explores issues around coming out, family,
sexuality, dating, substance abuse, families,
school & peer relationships.*

University of Connecticut: &↗**P**
Lesbian/Gay/Bisexual Alliance
School of Social Work
1800 Asylum Av.
W. Hartford CT 06117
tel: 860-570-9152 for updated info; fax: 860-241-
9786
*An academic & social support group for LGB
social work students.*

One In Ten Youth Group   **Y**
16 Harbor View Ave
Waterford CT 06385
tel: Marquita: 860-439-2363
*Peer & social support to LGT & questioning
youth in greater New London area. Meets
Sundays 4-6pm in New London.*

Eastern Connecticut State University: &↗**E**
**ABIGAYLE & Friends (Association of
Bisexuals, Gays & Lesbian & Their Friends)**
c/o Unity Center
182 High St.
Willimantic CT 06226
tel: Unity Center: 203-465-5749
*Activities & resources include: a library, peer
counseling, dances, observance of National
Coming Out Day & homophobia seminars in
freshman residence halls.*

Delaware

Black Lesbians in Delaware   **C ♀**
DE
tel: 800-422-0429 or 302-652-6776
*Support Group. Peer support through group
discussion on topics relevant to Lesbian & Bi-
Sexual womyn of African descent. Meets every
2nd & 4th Saturdays from 3-5pm.*

Local

DuPont Bisexual, Lesbian & Gay Network   **P**🖳
DE
tel: Confidential calls: 302-451-4966.
URL: dupontbglad.com
For DuPont employees.

University of Delaware: Lesbian, Gay &   &↗🖳
Bisexual Student Union
Room 304, Perkins Student Center
Academy St
Newark DE 19716
tel: 302-831-8066
e-mail: lgbsu-ud@udel.edu
URL: copland.udel.edu/stu-org/lgbsu/
*Student organization for lgb people & the local
community.*

District of Columbia

BiNetwork DC   ▼**CEY**
Washington DC
See Maryland listings.

Bi Black Females   ▼ ♀ **C**
PO Box 90378
Washington DC 20005
tel: 202-715-6148

"It's preposterous to ask sexual beings to stuff ourselves into the rapidly
imploding social categories of straight or gay or bi, as if we could plot our
sexual behavior on a contentious, predictable curve."

—*Susie Bright (in "Blindsexual," in* Sexual Reality: A Virtual Sex World Reader *(SF: Cleis, 1992), p. 152)*

Key to symbols: ▼ = bi   ♀ = women   ♂ = men   ☯ = religious/spiritual
♦ = for allies   **M** = for married bis   ♥ = for partners of bis   **Y** = youth   **C** = people of color
200   The Bisexual Resource Guide 2000

BiNetwork DC - e-mail list ▼💻
Washington DC
e-mail: majordomo@innovisionmm.com
URL: www.clark.net/pub/stw/bndc.html
Bisexual activists' discussion list to facilitate communication & community building within Washington DC area bi & bi-friendly communities. To subscribe send e-mail to majordomo@innovisionmm.com that reads only: subscribe bndc <your e-mail address>.

The Washington Blade 📰💻
1408 U St. NW
2nd floor
Washington DC 20009-3916
tel: 202-797-7000
URL: www.washblade.com
GLBT weekly newspaper. Covers local, national, & int'l news. **Publication(s):** *weekly*

Whitman-Walker Clinic H💻
1407 S St., NW
Washingon DC 20009
tel: 202-797-3500
e-mail: wwcinfo@wwc.org
URL: www.wwc.org
Non-profit volunteer GL community health organization serving the Washinton, DC metro area. Open to anyone in need of HIV-related services.

American University: 🎓**EA**💻
Gay, Lesbian, Bi, Transgender
& Ally Resource Center
226 Mary Graydon Center
4400 Massachusetts Ave, NW
Washington DC 20016-8164
tel: 202-885-3346; fax: 202-885-3354
e-mail: glbta@american.edu
URL: www.american.edu/other.depts/glbta
Student Grove ("At least 10%) Meet Wed. 8pm in the Gianni Room on campus.

Asian/Pacific Islander C♀
Queer Sisters (APIQS)
c/o Whitman-Walker Clinic
1407 S St. NW
Washington DC
tel: 202-939-7875
Social/support group; focus on issues of being Asian & Gay. Meets 7-9 pm on 2nd & 4th Fridays of each month.

Commerce GLOBE P💻
Washington DC
tel: 202-482-8040
e-mail: ron@fedglobe.org
URL: www.fedglobe.org
Provides info & networking. See Federal GLOBE for description.

DOT GLOBE P💻
PO Box 23239
Washington DC 20029
tel: 202-366-2548
e-mail: ericwdc@aol.com
URL: www.fedglobe.com
GLBT employees at US Dept. of Transportation. See Federal Globe for description.

George Washington University: 🎓
Lesbian, Gay, Bisexual Alliance
c/o Student Activities
800 21st. St. NW, Box 16
Washington DC 20057
tel: 202-994-6555. Call for current contact.
e-mail: lgba@gwu.edu
Open to the public, support, social, awareness.

Georgetown University: Outlaw 🎓
600 New Jersey Avenue, NW
Washington DC 20001
tel: 202-662-9437
e-mail: outlaw@bulldog.georgetown.edu
Fosters greater awareness of legal issues concerning gays, lesbians & bisexuals.

GLB at Labor (Labor Dept.) P💻
2 Massachustts Avenue, NE, #4675
Washington DC 20212
tel: 202-606-6378
e-mail: diane@fedglobe.org
URL: www.fedglobe.org
GLBT employees of the US Dep't of Labor. See Federal Globe for desc.

Interweave: All Souls for LGB Concerns ☯
(Unitarian-Universalist)
c/o All Souls Unitarian Church
16th & Harvard Street, NW
Washington DC 20009
tel: 202-332-5266

IRS GLOBE P💻
PO Box 7644
Washington DC 20044
tel: 202-874-6472
URL: www.fedglobe.org
GLBT employees at the IRS. See Federal GLOBE for description.

Khush - DC C💻
PO Box 53149
Temple Heights Station
Washington DC 20009
tel: 202-728-3870
e-mail: khushdc@geocities.com
URL: www.geocities.com/WestHollywood/4786/
For South Asian LGB people in the DC Metro area. Meets 1st Saturdays at 6pm for GLBT South Asians only, 7pm Social is open to all. Meets at Luna Books 1633p St. NW, in DC, near Metro Circle stop.

✎ = school   🎓 = college/university   P = professional   E = educational
A = activist/political   H = health (incl. HIV)   📰 = media/press   💻 = Internet resource
The Bisexual Resource Guide 2000   **201**

Lambda Sci-Fi: DC Area Gaylaxians
PO Box 656
Washington DC 20044
tel: 202-232-3141
Fans of Science fiction & horror; about half these folks are bi.

Lesbian Services Program of   H ♀ 💻
Whitman-Walker Clinic
1407 S St., NW
Washington DC 20009
tel: 202-797-3500
e-mail: lsp@wwc.org
URL: www.wwc.org
Offers supportive, culturally- sensitive & caring services that address the mental & physical health needs of l&b women. **Publication(s):** *Care Connection Call or write to be put on the mailing list.*

LGB People in Medicine of DC   P
Washington DC
tel: 202-686-4692
Standing committee of American Medical Student Association.

PRIDE - Georgetown University's Lesbian,   👥
Gay & Bisexual Students' Organization
Washington DC 20057
tel: Office of Student Programs: 202-687-3704

Sexual Minority Youth   Y ♀ ♂ EAH 💻
Assistance League (SMYAL)
410 7th St. SE
Washington DC 20003
tel: 202-546-5940 (office)
202-546-5911 (talk line); fax: 202-544-1306
e-mail: smyal@aol.com
URL: www.smyal.org
Youth 14-21; both mixed & single-gender mtgs. 11:30-3 Saturdays. sign language interpretation w/ advance request. free. After-school drop-in M, T, W, F 3-8pm. Talk line weekdays 7-10pm.

> "There is no 'female sexual experience,' no 'male sexual experience,' no unique heterosexual, lesbian or gay experience. There are instead the different experiences of different people, which we lump according to socially significant categlories."
>
> —*Ruth Hubbard (in "There is No Natural Human Sexuality," Sojourner, April 1985)*

US Helping US,   C ♂ HEM 💻
People Into Living, Inc.
811 L St., SE
Washington DC 20003
tel: 202-546-8200; fax: 202-546-4511
URL: www.ushelpingus.org
HIV/AIDS prevention & support services for African-American gay & bi men. Support groups, group therapy, workshops in private homes, & community theatre & forums.

USDA GLOBE   P 💻
1400 Independence Ave, SW
AGBOX 9913
Washington DC 20250-9913
tel: 301-504-1342
e-mail: ron@fedglobe.org
URL: www.fedglobe.org
GLBT employees group at the US Dept. of Agriculture. See Federal Globe for description.

Black Lesbian Support Group   ♀ C 💻
c/o Whitman-Walker Clinic
1407 S St. NW
Washington DC 20009
tel: 202-745-3822
confidential hotline: 202-797-3593
e-mail: blsg@blsg.com
URL: www.blsg.com
Social/ cultural discussion & support group for black lesbian/bi women. Meet every 2nd & 4th Saturday 3-5pm at 1736 14th St. NW. Over 35 group meets 1st Saturdays at 1407 S St. NW. Online chat room in Gay.Com Chat House, Newsletter, Women of Color film festival, Co-sponsors of Sistah Summerfest 98.

Florida

FL-MOTSS   💻
FL
e-mail: FL-motss-request@queernet.org
Discussion of queer issues as they pertain to the state of Florida or its residents. Anyone can join, regardless of state of residence. For info, send an email to the above address.

Local

BiWays ORLANDO: An affiliate of   ▼ 💻
BiNet USA & GLCS of Central Florida
c/o GLCS of Central Florida
714 E. Colonial Drive
Orlando FL 32803
tel: Hotline:407-263-6848 GLCS: 407-425-4527
e-mail: krisr@biways.org
URL: www.biways.org
Support Discussion: Mon 7-9pm at GLCS. BiGathering: Call Hotline for Info. BiVisibility Project: 2nd Mondays, 9:30pm after BiWays.

Key to symbols: ▼ = bi   ♀ = women   ♂ = men   ❂ = religious/spiritual
💧 = for allies   **M** = for married bis   ♥ = for partners of bis   **Y** = youth   **C** = people of color
202   **The Bisexual Resource Guide 2000**

Bayou Bisexual Women ♀ ▼
St. Petersburg FL
tel: Lisa B. Wild: 813-822-2244
Discussion group meets 3rd Friday at 7:30pm at Brigit Books (3434 4th St. N., St. Petersburg). All bi-friendly women welcome. Member group of BiNet, USA.

Fort Lauderdale Bi Friends Meeting ▼ ☺
1164 East Oakland Park Blvd.
Fort Lauderdale FL
tel: Community Center: 954-563-9500
1st & 3rd Thursdays at 7:30 at the Fort Lauderdale G&L Community Center at above address.

Bivouac ▼
c/o 6700 SW 52nd St.
Miami FL 33155
tel: 305-661-2310
Bi-weekly discussion group. Meets 2nd & 4th Saturdays at 7:45pm.

University of Miami at Coral Gables: Gay, ᗌ
Lesbian & Bisexual Community
Smith-Tucker Involvement Center
University Center, Room 209
Coral Gables FL 33124-6923
tel: 305-284-4505; fax: 305-284-5987
e-mail: umglbc@umiami.ir.miami.edu

University of Florida at Gainesville: ᗌ E ⌨
Lesbian, Gay, Bisexual Student Union
Box 30048 JWRU
PO Box 118505
Gainesville FL 32611-8505
tel: 352-392-1665 x310
e-mail: lbgsu@grove.ufl.edu
URL: grove.ufl.edu/~lgbsu
Weekly bisexual discussion groups; library; roommate referral; speakers' bureau; film festivals; speak outs.

GLBT Youth of Miami Y
13732 Biscayne Blvd., Suite 29
Miami FL 33181
tel: 305-892-0057; fax: 305-892-0305
Holds weekly support groups, annual prom for glbt youth, & is one of the groups sponsoring the Sun Confernece, an annual youth conference for all of Florida. Also dances, movie nights. For ages 13-26, & adult volunteers are trained to facilitate support groups & assist at events.

Delta Youth Alliance YE
PO Box 536012
Orlando FL 32853-6012
tel: 407-236-9415
Explicitly includes bisexual people. Rap group Mondays at 6. Ages 13-19.

Gay & Lesbian Community PE ⌨
Services of Central Florida, Inc.
PO Box 533446
Orlando FL 32853-3446
tel: 407-425-4527 - office
407-843-4297 - info; fax: 407-423-9904
e-mail: glcs@glcs.org
URL: www.glcs.org
Located at 714 West Colonial Drive.
Publication(s): *The Triangle newsletter, agency info*

The Family Tree: A Lesbian, Gay, YEA ⌨
Bisexual, Transgender Community Center
PO Box 38477
Talahassee FL 32315
tel: 850-222-8555; fax: 850-222-4211
e-mail: barbara.lynne@juno.com
URL: www.familytreecenter.org
Provides peer & phone counseling, support groups, youth program, social events, community education, resource library, diversity activism, monthly newsletter, website, community outreach. **Publication(s)**: *Branching Out*

Florida State University: ᗌ YCEAM
Lesbian, Gay, Bisexual Student Union
201 Oglesby Union
Tallahassee FL 32306-4027
tel: 850-644-8804
e-mail: lgbsu@admin.fsu.edu
URL: www.fsu.edu/~activity/sga/lgbsu
Discussion Groups, Library, Educational Services, Roommate Referral Service, Open to Everyone. **Publication(s)**: *AWARE Irregular*

Compass YE
1700 North Dixie Hwy
West Palm Beach FL 33407
tel: 561-833-3638; 561-833-8388; fax: 561-833-4941
e-mail: compassinc@aol.com
Lending library, with 4000 books dealing with GLBT & HIV issues, roommate referral service. Call for meeting times. **Publication(s)**: *Compass Points*

"Any woman who feels actual horror or revulsion at the thought of kissing or embracing or having physical relations with another woman should reexamine her feelings and attitudes not only about other women, but also about *herself*."

—*Shere Hite, American sexologist, 1976*

🖎 = school ᗌ = college/university **P** = professional **E** = educational
A = activist/political **H** = health (incl. HIV) ✎ = media/press ⌨ = Internet resource
The Bisexual Resource Guide 2000 **203**

Marcia Deihl

Georgia

Local

BiNet Atlanta   ▼HA🖳
PO Box 5240
Atlanta GA 31107
tel: 404-256-8992 (vm)
e-mail: binet@mindspring.com
URL: www.mindspring.com/~binet/
To bring together LGB & straight communities, work toward eliminating biphobia & prejudice, & provide a suppportive, safe & sane social environment for bi & bifriendly people. Social gatherings at Uban Coffee Bungalow, hiking group, Bi Nature discussion group. Call for schedule. **Publication(s)***: 4-8 page bimonthly newsletter.*

EMORYGLB   🖳A
GA
e-mail: see below
URL: userwww.service.emory.edu/~emoryglb
E-Mail List for Emory University & Atlanta's Internet Community. For more info, view the web page. To subscribe (there is no info file) send email to listserv@listserv.emory.edu with only "subscribe EmoryGLB" in the body of the message.

Emory University: Office of   🖳
Lesbian/Gay/Bisexual Life
Dobbs University Center 246E
Atlanta GA 30322
tel: 404-727-0272
e-mail: schesnu@emory.edu
URL: www.emory.edu/LGBOFFICE/hours.html
Dr. Saralyn Chesnut, Director

Georgia State University BiGALA   P
Jeannie Robertson, Counselor for Faculty & Staff
GSU FASA Services Coordinator, Dept. HR-OED
University Plaza
Atlanta GA 30303
tel: 404-651-4741
e-mail: jrobertson@gsu.edu
Faculty & group.

Georgia Tech: Gay & Lesbian Alliance   🖳
350291 Georgia Tech Station
Atlanta GA 3022-1550
tel: 404-894-5849
e-mail: gala@gatech.edu
URL: cyberbuzz.gatech.edu/gala/
Goal is to provide an environment in which glb people can find support, acceptance & friendship among peers. Also on campus: OUTTECH, a forum for discussing issues of concern to glbt employees of Georgia Tech & for developing strategies to improve the campus climate in relation to those issues.

Spellman Lesbian Bisexual Alliance   ♀
Box 1588
350 Spellman Lane
Atlanta GA 30314
tel: 404-524-8639

West Georgia College: P
Gay, Bisexual & Straight Alliance
Carrollton GA 30118
tel: Mark Faucette, advisor: 770-836-4344

Agnes Scott College: ♀
Lesbian & Bisexual Alliance & Allies
141 East College Avenue
Box 501
Decatur GA 30030
Creates comfortable & safe space for l/b members of the Agnes Scott Community & strives to educate the campus about lbg issues & to raise consciousness & promote acceptance.

Atlanta Asian Pacific Lesbian Bisexual   ♀C🖳
Transgender Network
send mail to: APLBTN
c/o Jennifer Kim
1380 Church St. #C
Decatur GA 30030-1521
e-mail: aplbtn@hotmail.com
URL: userwww.service.emory.edu/~jkim12/
aplbtn/homepage2.html
*A social & support organization for Asian & Pacific Islander
l, b, t, queer & questioning women in Atlanta. Discussion & support group meetings are held 1st Sundays & are for API queer identified women only. We also have social events every 3rd weekend of the month, which are open to anyone in support of APLBTN.*

Key to symbols: ▼ = bi   ♀ = women   ♂ = men   ☻ = religious/spiritual
🜚 = for allies   **M** = for married bis   ♥ = for partners of bis   Y = youth   C = people of color
204   **The Bisexual Resource Guide 2000**

Armstrong Atlantic State University: 🖳
Unity & Diversity League
11935 Abercorn Ext.
Savannah GA 31419
URL: www.armstrong.edu/Activities/Clubs/UDL/
udl.html

Georgia Southern University: Triangle
Statesboro GA 30460

Valdosta State College: Gay & Lesbian
Association
1500 North Patterson
Valdosta GA 31698
tel: Dr. Elza: 333-5771, advisor.
Inclusive of bi folks.

University of Georgia: Lambda Alliance   🖳
Tate Student Center
Athens GA 30602
e-mail: LGBSU@uga.edu.
URL: www.uga.edu/~lgbsu/
75 people at meetings. Social, educational,
speakers bureau. Open to the public.

Hawaii

Local

Bisexual Network   ▼
PO Box 2022
Kapa'a HI 96746
tel: 808-821-1690

Gay & Lesbian Community Center
1566 Wilder Av.
Honolulu HI 96822
tel: 808-951-7000; fax: 808-951-7240
Library, support groups, speakers bureau,
Marriage Project Hawaii.

University of Hawai'i Gay/Lesbian/Bisexual
'Ohana
Honolulu HI
tel: 808-955-6152x3

Gay-Lesbian 'Ohana Maui   🖳
PO Box 5042
Kahului / Maui HI 96733
tel: 808-244-4566
URL: maui-tech.com/glom/
Non-profit organization whose membership is
composed of Maui's glbt community, their
friends, & supporters. If you are
visiting Maui & are looking for fun & exciting
things to do, places to go, people to meet,
(including gay activities, dining, etc.) call hotline
 # (above).

Freedom Network Newsletter   🖳**A**🖂
Lambda Aloha
PO Box 921
Kapaa,Kauai HI 96746
tel: 808-822-7171
e-mail: lambda@aloha.net
URL: www.aloha.net/~lambda
A political Journal for Kauai's Sexual
Minorities. Published on the Web.

Lambda Aloha   🖳
PO Box 921
Kapaa,Kauai HI 96746
tel: 808-821-1690
e-mail: lambda@aloha.net or evolved@aloha.net
URL: www.aloha.net/~lambda

Both Sides Now, Inc.
PO Box 5042
Kahului,Maui HI 96733
tel: 808-244-4566
Dances, picnics, women's gatherings & other
social events. **Publication(s):** *"Out in Maui"*
Monthly.

Bridges: **YE**
LesBiGayTrans Questioning Youth Group
Maui Lesbian/Gay Youth Project
Suite 171, Box 356
Paia HI 96779
tel: Karen: 808-575-2681 (days, evenings,
weekends), or Joe 808-573-1093 (evenings/
weekends)
Weekly support group on Wednesdays in
Wailuku, 7-9pm. Call for location. Provides
education & outreach to adults working with
LGBT youth, classroom presentations, & a
speakers bureau. Offers information, referrals, &
confidential phone contact for youth exploring
their sexual identity.

Idaho

Local

Boise Bisexual Network   ▼♀♥
P.O. Box 15471
Boise ID 83715
tel: 208-331-1101
Meets every Sunday 7pm (8pm during summer).
Support group & social on alternating weeks.
Couples group & a women's group.

Boise State University: Bisexual, Gay &
Lesbian Allies for Diversity (B-GLAD)
Boise ID 83725
tel: 208-385-1223
Meets Fridays during termtime on campus. Open
to the public.

✎ = school   = college/university   **P** = professional   **E** = educational
A = activist/political   **H** = health (incl. HIV)   🖂 = media/press   🖳 = Internet resource
The Bisexual Resource Guide 2000   **205**

Christopher Street Day 1998 in Köln, Germany

The Community Center
919 1/2 N. 27th
Boise ID 83702
tel: 208-336-3870

Triangle Connection:
Bi, Gay & Lesbian Social Group
PO Box 503
Boise ID 83701
tel: Al Dawson, Facilitator: 208-939-2338

Inland Northwest Gay People's Alliance
PO Box 8135
Moscow ID 83843
tel: 208-882-8034
Meets 1st & 3rd Mon. 7pm.

Illinois

Brothers United in Support   H♂C🖵
TPAN
1258 W. Belmont
Chicago IL 60657-3207
tel: 773-404-8726
e-mail: tpanet@aol.com
URL: www.tpan.com
A peer-led social/support for HIV+ gay &
bisexual men of African descent.

Central Illinois LGB Switchboard   E
c/o McKinley Foundation
809 South Fifth Street
Champaign IL 61820
tel: M-F, 7-10pm: 217-384-8040
Staffed by volunteers. Provides support &
resources for the central Illinois area.

Local

Bi-Friendly Chicago   ▼
Box 578404
Chicago IL 60657-8404
tel: 773-509-6401

Bisexual Political Action Coalition   A▼
Chicago IL
tel: 312-458-0983

Chicagoland Bisexual Network   ▼A🖵
PO Box 14385
Chicago IL 60614-0385
tel: 312-458-0983
URL: www.mcs.net/~jcohler/CBN.html
Includes: Bi Womyn's Discussion Group, Bi
Men's Discussion Group, Bi PAAC, Bi Socials,
BiNet USA representation. **Publication(s)**:
Bi...the Way bi monthly newsletter includes local
calendar & local & national news. Submissions
welcome.

Aurora University: GLOBAL (Gays, Lesbians   &⌒
or Bisexuals & our Allies League)
PO Box 5725
Aurora IL 60507
tel: 708-844-3834

Southern Illinois University: &⌒🖵
Gays, Lesbians, Bisexuals & Friends
c/o Office of Student Development
Mailcode 4425
Southern Illinois University
Carbondale IL 62901-4425
tel: 618-453-5151 M-F 5-9pm
e-mail: glbf5151@siu.edu
URL: www.siu.edu/~glbf/

Champaign County
Lesbian, Gay & Bisexual Task Force
Robert Michael Doyle 344-0910
P.O. Box 2511, Station A
Champaign IL 61825-2511

Lavender Prairie News Collective   ♀
P.O. Box 2096, Station A
Champaign IL 61825-2096
One of the longest operating Lesbian/ Feminist
collectives in the U.S. Sponsors a monthly
newsletter for l/b women. They also sponsor
several cultural & social events each year.

OutPost Lesbian, Gay, Bisexual, &
Transgender Community Center
123 W. Church Street
Champaign IL 61820
tel: 217-239-4688
Umbrella Organization for C-U Area. Offers
meeting space, resource center, newsletter, & a
variety of services. Hours; 6-9pm Mon-Fri; 1-
4pm Sat. Hosts Out Zone group for LGBTQ
youth 13-20 years old. Meets Sun, 2 -5pm.

Key to symbols: ▼ = bi   ♀ = women   ♂ = men   ☯ = religious/spiritual
♦ = for allies   M = for married bis   ♥ = for partners of bis   Y = youth   C = people of color
206   **The Bisexual Resource Guide 2000**

OUTRight Support Group
Champaign IL
tel: Carl Graves: 217-367-8691
e-mail: corkscrw@prairienet.org
A support group for those in the glbt community who are in all stages of Coming Out. Meets Thurs. 7pm at the Canterbury House (1011 S. Wright St., Champaign).

Alternative Phone Book 🖥
619 W. Stratford Pl. #406
Chicago IL 60657-2643
tel: 773-472-6319
e-mail: yellow@xsite.net
URL: www.prairienet.org/apb
LGB community listings. Distributed free of charge throughout Chicago.

Amigas Latinas lesbianas/bisexuales ♀ **C**
Chicago IL
tel: 773-267-0976
For Latina lesbians/bisexuals.

Chicago LesBiGay Electronic Resources 🖥
Consortium (CLERC)
Chicago IL
e-mail: webmaster@outchicago.org
URL: www.outchicago.org/index.html

Chicago Metro Area **YEA**
Gay Youth Coalition (C-MAGYC)
3524 N. Southport Ave Suite 172
Chicago IL 60657
tel: 312-409-2655; fax: 312-996-4688
e-mail: cwilso1@uic.edu
An assemblage of college & high school student groups & members of area queer youth service orgs. Goals: To educate & empower LGBT youth on area campuses & to actively work to improve the atmosphere for queer youth on campuses. **Publication(s)**: *MAGYC Newsletter distribution to Chicago are queer student orgs., queer youth social service agencies, & youth hangouts. To order: Brian Hoffmeister 773/506-9389*

DePaul University: Pride DePaul 🎓**EA**
Programs & Organizations Office,
2nd Fl. Stuart Ctr.
2311 N. Clifton Avenue
Chicago IL 60614-3212
tel: 773-687-1878
e-mail: tmeyer1@shrike.depaul.edu

En La Vida 📧**C**🖥
1115 W. Belmont, Suite 2D
Chicago IL 60657
tel: 773-871-7610; fax: 773-871-7609
e-mail: outlines@suba.com
URL: www.suba.com/~outlines/enla-archives/april97/
"The voice of the gay & lesbian community".

Gay, Lesbian & Bisexual Veterans of **PE**🖥
America - Chicago
PO Box 29317
Chicago IL 60629
tel: 773-752-0058
e-mail: jamesdarby@aol.com
URL: www.glbva.org
Publication(s): *The Forward Observer 3 times a year*

Horizons Community Services **YE**🖥
961 W. Montana Avenue
Chicago IL 60614
tel: 773-472-6469; fax: 773-472-6643
e-mail: horizons@interaccess.com
URL: www.horizons-cs.org
Youth services, counseling, support groups, anti-violence project, legal services, speakers service.

Illinois Institute of Technology:

▾ **Gay, Lesbian, Bisexual Student Alliance** 🎓 🖥
3241 S. Federal Street
Chicago IL 60616
tel: 312-808-6400
e-mail: glbsa@charlie.cns.iit.edu
URL: www.iit.edu/~glbsa
Advisor: Doug Geiger, Director of Residence Life. Meets bi-monthly during term time.

▾ **Gay/Lesbian/Bisexual Task Force** 🎓
tel: 312-567-3080

Khuli Zaban ♀ **C**🖥
Chicago IL
tel: 312-409-2753
e-mail: khulizaban@hotmail.com
URL: www.geocities.com/WestHollywood/9993/Khulizaban.html
For South Asian lesbians & bisexual women. Organizes "Color Triangle" - annual meeting on racism in the queer community. **Publication(s)**: *Shamakami To subscribe e-mail juneau2332@aol.com or write to Shamakami, Inc. PO Box 1006, Jamaica Plain, MA 02130. For South Asian esbians & bi women.*

Korean American Lesbian, Gay, Bisexual, **C**
Trans Helpline
Chicago IL
tel: 773-388-2370

Lesbigay Radio/WDNZ AM750 📧
1143 W. Pratt
Penthouse
Chicago IL 60626
tel: 773-973-3999
Mon-Fri 6-9am.

🖉 = school   🎓 = college/university   **P** = professional   **E** = educational
A = activist/political   **H** = health (incl. HIV)   📧 = media/press   🖥 = Internet resource
The Bisexual Resource Guide 2000   **207**

Loyola University:

▼ **Gay, Lesbian & Bisexual Alliance** &⌒**E**⌨
Centenial Forum-Student Union
6525 N. Sheridan Road, Box #25
Chicago IL 60626
tel: 773-973-6910; 312-915-6502
e-mail: bmcclos@luc.edu;mmolone@luc.edu
URL: www.luc.edu/orgs/glaba/
*Offers support & a safe place of LGB & friends
to gather together.*

▼ **Lesbian, Gay, Bisexual Faculty/Staff** &⌒**P**
Association
tel: 773-508-3808

Northeastern Illinois University: LGBA &⌒
5500 N. St. Louis Ave
Chicago IL 60625
e-mail: aaronpk@aol.com
Meets Thursdays.

Pathfinders **Y**
Harriet Tubman Place
5901 W. Fulton
Chicago IL 60644-2111
tel: 312-626-1443
*Lesbigay youth support for those 25 & under,
serving West Side Residents & beyond. Support
groups, housing, coming out, substance abuse
counseling, HIV prevention. Advisor: Kurt Hicke.
2 discussions: 13-18 meets Sat. 3-6pm, 18-25
meets Tues. 6:30-9pm.*

SANGAT Chicago **C**
PO Box 268463
Chicago IL
tel: 773-506-8810; fax: 773-271-4024
e-mail: youngal@aol.com or sangat@juno.com
*LGBT organization & support group for people
from India, Pakistan, Bangladesh, Sri Lanka,
Nepal, Afghanistran, Iran, Burma & other
South Asian countries. Non-profit organization
for international brotherhood/sisterhood for
peace & harmony, regardless of sexual
orientation, religious or boundaries of the
country. Monthly dinner- call for info.*

"Okay, okay. If you're asking am I
one, I'll go that route—good
public relations. If it's good
enough for Gore Vidal and Elton
John, it's good enough for me. I
am bisexual, happy and proud. A
woman in every bed... and a man,
too. Satisfied?"

—*Rock Hudson, American actor 1925-1985*

University of Illinois, Chicago:

▼ **Queers & Associates** &⌒⌨
5706 S University Ave Rm 004
Chicago IL 60637
tel: 773/702.9734 (leave a message with Doris) ;
fax: 773/702.7718
URL: http://student-www.uchicago.edu/orgs/gay-
lesbian/
*For queers & allies at the University. "queer by
nature, nerds by choice" "not just for College
students — we're open to students in the
Divisions & Professional Schools as well as
faculty & staff."*

▼ **Office of Gay, Lesbian, Gay &** &⌒▼
Bisexual Issues
Behavioral Sciences Bldg., Rm. 4078
Chicago IL 60680
tel: 312-413-8619; fax: 312-996-4688
URL: www.uic.edu/depts/quic/oglbc
Open M-F 8:30-4:45.

▼ **Pride (Lesbians, Gays & Bisexuals** &⌒**EA**⌨
Advocating Diversity)
750 S. Halsted
Chicago IL 60608
tel: 312-996-4424
e-mail: pride@uic.edu
URL: www2.uic.edu/stud-orgs/pride/
*Pride is a LGB student organization providing
social, educational & supportive services as
well as events for the UIC community.
Meetings at 312D Northwind, Chicago Circle
Center.*

Wives of Gay Men Support Group ♥ ♀
Chicago IL
tel: PFLAG: 773-472-3079

Northern Illinois University: Lesbian Gay &⌒⌨
Bisexual Coalition
Campus Life Building
190M
DeKalb IL 60115
tel: 815-753-0584
URL: www.niu.edu/student_orgs/lgbc/www-
lgbc.html

Kinheart Women's Center ♀
2214 Ridge Ave
Evanston IL 60201
tel: 708-780-0746
*Friday night programs, coming out groups,
lending library.*

Key to symbols: ▼ = bi   ♀ = women   ♂ = men   ☯ = religious/spiritual
☙ = for allies   **M** = for married bis   ♥ = for partners of bis   **Y** = youth   **C** = people of color
208   **The Bisexual Resource Guide 2000**

Northwestern University:

▼ Gay & Lesbian Univ. Union (GLUU)   🌐**EA** 🖥
c/o Campus Activities Office
Norris University Center
1999 South Campus Drive
Evanston IL 60208-2500
tel: 847-491-8390
V. McCoy
e-mail: bgala@nwu.edu
URL: www.nwu.edu/gluu/index.html
*Providing education on BLG issues, social
opportunities, coming out support & activism
for GLB grad students, faculty & staff.*

▼ BGALA   🌐🖥
1999 Sheridan Road
Evanston IL 60208
tel: 847-491-2375
e-mail: bgala@nwu.edu
URL: www.studorg.nwv.edu/bgala
*Multifaceted organization providing social
opportunities, coming out support, education &
activism for GLB issues.*

▼ QWYR (Queer Women You Rock)   🌐**A** ♀
c/o M. Phillips
614 Clark Street Apt 3e
Evanston IL 60201
tel: 847-869-8465
e-mail: chelle@nwu.edu
*Social group for queer women - in the closet or
out of it. Providing social opportunities,
coming out support & activism for GLB female
grad students, faculty & staff.*

Knox College: Gay, Lesbian   🌐🖥
& Bisexual Community Alliance
Box K-1722
Galesburg IL 61401
URL: knox.knox.edu:5718/~glbcawww/
*Student organization offering support & raising
awareness.*

The Stonewall Group   🖥
Naperville IL 60540-6400
tel: 630-585-3827
e-mail: stnwallgrp@aol.com
URL: members.aol.com/stnwallgrp/stonewall-
main.html
*Meets Tues. 6:30-8pm at DuPage Unitarian
Church, 4S.535 Old Naperville Rd. For those 18+
& out of high school.*

Illinois State University: 🌐🖥
Gay/Lesbian/Bi Pride Resource Phoneline
c/o Student Services
Normal IL 61790-2200
tel: 309-438-2429
URL: www.ilstu.edu/depts/studentlife/RSO/gen/
PRIDE/welcome.html
Meets Wednesday evenings.

QUAD Citians Affirming Diversity   E
P.O. Box 6371
Rock Island IL 62104
tel: 309-797-7986
   Publication(s): *QCAD News Monthly
newsletter about upcoming programs*

University of Illinois, Champaign-Urbana:

▼ Office for Lesbian, Gay & Bisexual &   🌐🖥
Transgender Concerns
322a Illini Union
1401 West Green Street
Urbana IL 61801
tel: 217-244-8863
URL: www.odos.uiuc.edu/gblt/
*Safe, affirming, inclusive place for all
students, faculty, & staff, particularly LGBT
students, faculty, & staff.*

▼ Queers on Campus   🌐**P**
e-mail: qoc@uiuc.edu
*See Office of LGBT Concerns above. Social
organization for UIUC graduate & professional students, faculty, & staff, who are lgbt.
Meetings are very casual—they are opportunities for LGBT people from around campus to
get together & chat. Friends & partners
welcome to all of our activities.*

▼ Illini Union Board Gay, Lesbian, Bisexual   🌐
Transgender Programming Committee
Room 284 Illini Union
tel: 217-333-3663
*See Office of LGBT Concerns above. Sponsors
glb entertainers & educational programs.*

▼ Safe Zone
tel: 217-333-1187
e-mail: Dan: dpohl@uiuc.edu ; Susan:
sbollman@uiuc.edu
*See Office of LGBT Concerns above. Group
formed to educate the campus community
about issues of concern to LGBT people. Meets
Tues. 5:30pm in Conference Room A, Room
280 I.*

▼ Sister Insider   🌐♀🖥
280 Illini Union, Mailbox 41
tel: 217-333-1187
URL: domino.odos.uiuc.edu/counseling_center/
comout.htm
*Weekly social / support group for bisexual
women & lesbians. Run by Spectrum- the
Association of Students for BGLT Concerns.*

🌑 = school   🌐 = college/university   **P** = professional   **E** = educational
A = activist/political   **H** = health (incl. HIV)   📰 = media/press   🖥 = Internet resource

▼ **Ally Network** 👌💻
Sexual Orientation Diversity Association
(SODA) Counseling Center
Urbana IL 61801
tel: 217-333-3704
URL: www.uiuc.edu/ro/safezone/
Queer-friendly & queer faculty & staff at the U
of I. Noticable by the pink triangle labled
"Ally" displayed in
their offices.

▼ **Queer Action Forum** 👌
URU 292 Allen
MC-050 Campus
Urbana IL 61801
tel: 217-332-3336
e-mail: klambert@uiuc.edu

Review: Bi/Gay Married Men's ♂ ♥ **M**
Support & Conversation Groups
send mail to: Jerry Walters - Review
Box 7406
Villa Park IL 60181
tel: 708-524-1323 or 630-627-1990
e-mail: Reviewgrp@aol.com
Informal meetings, about 20 people per meeting.
$2/meeting. Meets in Oak Park. For spouses of
bi & gay partners.

Prairie Flame
P.O. Box 2483
Springfield IL 62705
e-mail: pflame@eosinc.co
LGBT newspaper covering Central Illinois.

Columbia College: GLOBAL 👌**EA**
(Gay, Lesbian, Bisexual Alliance)
623 S. Wabash St. Suite 301
Chicago IL 60004
tel: 312-344-7286; fax: 312-986-8640
e-mail: mjackson@popmail.colum.edu
Dedicated to serving & supporting the needs &
interests of Columbia's LBGT student commu-
nity.

> "What I am—and have been for
> as long as I can remember — is
> someone whose sexuality and
> gender have never seemed to
> mesh with the available cultural
> categories."
>
> —Sandra Lipsits Bem, in Lenses of Gender

Key to symbols: ▼ = bi   ♀ = women   ♂ = men   ☻ = religious/spiritual
👌 = for allies   **M** = for married bis   ♥ = for partners of bis   **Y** = youth   **C** = people of color

Indiana

Local

Bi-Versity ▼
Attn: Holly & Jeff
PO Box 97
Selma IN 47383
tel: 765-287-0395
*Meets 3rd Saturday of each month at Diversity
Center, 1112 Southeastern Avenue, Indianapolis.*

Northwest Indiana Lesbian, Gay, **Y**
Bisexual Youth Group
IN
tel: 219-980-8692

Gay, Lesbian & Bisexual Coalition
PO Box 5731
Bloomington IN 47401
e-mail: the_glbt_coalition@yahoo.com

Gay, Lesbian, & Bisexual Latinos **C**
PO Box 5731
Bloomington IN 47401
e-mail: the_glbt_coalition@yahoo.com

Indiana University:

▼ **OUT (Gay, Lesbian & Bisexual Student** 🎓
Union)
Indiana Memorial Union 48L-M
Bloomington IN 47405
tel: 812-855-5OUT
*Umbrella organization working closely with
various support groups, including "Bi-Ways"*

▼ **Quest (Queers United For Equal Social** **A**🎓
Treatment)
Maggie Schuets
413 E 4th St. Apt 2
Bloomington IN 47409
tel: 812-857-FIRE (3473)
*"Political action group for the university, local,
& state levels. Not a group of white gay &
lesbian middle class students. Bis represented
in group's leadership."*

✎ = school   🎓 = college/university   **P** = professional   **E** = educational
A = activist/political   **H** = health (incl. HIV)   📧 = media/press   💻 = Internet resource

▾ **Office of Gay, Lesbian & Bisexual Student Support Services**
705 E. Seventh St.
Bloomington IN 47405
tel: 812-855-4252; fax: 812-855-4465
e-mail: glbtserv@indiana.edu
URL: www.indiana.edu/~glbtserv/
Office is part of the Office of Student Ethics & Anti-Harassment Programs & the Campus Life Divisions. Includes library & peer support project.

IYG   Y
Box 20716
Indianapolis IN 46220
tel: 317-541-8726; fax: 317-545-8594
Drop-in center offering medical & mental health care & life skills. Trains youth for community outreach. Nat'l pen-pal program for GLB youth.

LGBT Fairness   A
Indianapolis IN
tel: Marla Stevens: 317-582-2910

Lafayette OpenDoors   ⌨
PO Box 1012
Lafayette IN 47905
tel: 765-296-6007
e-mail: opendoors@greaterlafayette.com
URL: www.nlci.com/opendoors
Group for lgb residents of the greater Lafayette area.

Purdue University:

▾ **Ally Association**   ♦ ⚧ ⌨
c/o LesBiGay Network
1001 Stewart Center, Box 642
Lafayette IN 47907-1001
e-mail: ally@expert.cc.purdue.edu
URL: expert.cc.purdue.edu/~ally
Group for queer allies.

▾ **LesBiGay Network**   ⚧ ⌨
1001 Stewart Center, Box 642
Lafayette IN 47907-1001
e-mail: triangle@expert.cc.purdue.edu
URL: expert.cc.purdue.edu/~triangle

Ball State University: ⚧ ⌨
Lesbian, Bisexual & Gay Student Association
Student Center Suite L-2
Muncie IN 47306
e-mail: lbgsa@bsu.edu
URL: www.bsu.edu/students/pride/lbgsa
Publication(s): *Outspoken*

Earlham College: Rainbow Tribe   ⚧
Richmond IN 47374
tel: 765-983-1436; fax: 765-983-1641, Attn: Rainbow Tribe
e-mail: owner-rtribe-l@earlham.edu

Indiana State University: Alliance of   ⚧
Bisexual, Lesbian & Gay Students & Allies
Terre Haute IN 47809
tel: 812-237-6916x1
e-mail: mblgcc@indstate.edu

Citizens for Civil Rights   A⌨
PO Box 2461
West Lafayette IN 47996
tel: 765-523-5767
e-mail: ccr@nlci.com
URL: www.nlci.com/ccr
A group that seeks to enforce civil rights of all citizens in the greater Lafayette area. Works closely in the queer community.

Iowa

Local

Iowa City Bisexual Group   ▼A
c/o Women's Resource & Action Center
University of Iowa
130 N. Madison Street
Iowa City IA 52242
tel: 319-335-1486
For men & women. 2 alternating groups meeting bi-weekly: Bi Discussion Group (safe space for bisexuals to meet & discuss issues), & Bi Action Group (works to increase awareness & acceptance of bisexuality through community action).

QUAD Citians Affirming Diversity   YE♦
IA
See full QCAD listed under Illinois, USA.
Publication(s): *QCAD News Monthly newsletter about upcoming programs*

Gays, Lesbians & Bisexuals of Ames   E
PO Box 1761
Ames IA 50010-1761
tel: 515-232-0000 for meeting times or more info.
Monthly meetings with different topic or speaker.

Iowa State University:

▾ **Lesbian, Gay, Bisexual &**   E⚧⌨
Transgendered Student Services
210 Dean of Students Office
Ames IA 50011
tel: 515-294-1020
e-mail: lgbtss@iastate.edu
URL: www.public.iastate.edu:80/~deanstdt_info/lgbss_home.html

Key to symbols: ▼ = bi   ♀ = women   ♂ = men   ☯ = religious/spiritual
♦ = for allies   **M** = for married bis   ♥ = for partners of bis   Y = youth   C = people of color
212   The Bisexual Resource Guide 2000

▼ **Lesbian/Gay/Bisexual/**   𝐸A 🖳
Transgendered/Allies Alliance
39 Memorial Union
Ames IA 50011
tel: 515-294-2104
URL: www.public.iastate.edu/~LGBA
Weekly meetings, social & educational events.
Open to the public. Check Web site for mission
statement, current plans & upcoming events.

University of Northern Iowa Lesbian, Gay,
Bisexual & Transgendered Alliance
SSC 213
Cedar Falls IA 50614
tel: 319-222-0003
e-mail: mosera9068@uni.edu

GLRC   E
1056 Fifth Ave. SE or
PO Box 1643
Cedar Rapids IA 52406
tel: 319-366-2055

Metropolitan Community Church
Quad Cities
3025 N. Harrison
Davenport IA 52803
tel: 379-324-8281
Sunday service 11AM. Wed 7PM.

Luther College: AWARE
FPO 45
Decorah IA 52101
tel: 319-387-1277

Drake University: Bisexual, Gay,
& Lesbian Alliance
Des Moines IA 50311

Grinnell College: 🖳
Stonewall Resource Center
PO Box U-5
Grinnell IA 50112-0810
tel: 515-269-3327; fax: 515-269-3710
e-mail: srcenter@ac.grin.edu
URL: www.grin.edu/~srcenter/
Open community space for lgbt folks at Grinnell.
Includes a library & meeting rooms. Several
groups including bi-inclusive groups. Paul
Valencic, Director

University of Iowa:

▼ **Gay, Lesbian, Bisexual,**   𝐸A
& Transgender Union & Iowa's Pride
161 Iowa Memorial Union
Iowa City IA 52242
tel: 319-335-3251
Meets alternate weeks during termtime. Free
confidential listening, information & referral
services operated by experienced volunteers
Tuesday & Thursday nights.

▼ **Lesbian, Gay & Bisexual Staff**   PE
& Faculty Association
130 North Madison Street
Iowa CIty IA 52242
tel: 319-335-1125
To support the interests of the LGB community
at the Univ. of Iowa. Open to university
employees. Monthly meetings & ongoing work
in the area of AIDS/HIV+ policy, curricula
development, domestic partnership, &
advocacy/referral.

Morningside College: LGB Student Advisor
Timothy Orwig
1501 Morningside Ave
Sioux City IA 51106
tel: 712-274-5333; fax: 712-274-5101
e-mail: tto001@alpha.morningside.edu

ACCESS line: A Resource for Midwestern   📰
Gays, Lesbians, Bisexuals & Friends
P.O. Box 1682
Waterloo IA 50704
tel: 319-232-6805
A monthly newspaper for, by, about LGB people
in Iowa & surrounding states.

Kansas

The Liberty Press   📰🖳
P.O. Box 16315
Wichita KS 67216-0315
tel: 316-652-7737; fax: 316-685-1999
e-mail: LibrtyPrs@aol.com
URL: ww.libertypress.net
News magazine. Good source for up-to-date info
about groups & happenings in Kansas.

"When the wall of homophobia is just too damn high and the mountain of
intolerance too wide, it's easier to just drop some of the weight, which
usually means elderly gays, queer youth, drag queens, leather folks, sexual
outlaws, bisexuals. I've always believed, to be honest with you, that there is
no dress code for civil rights in this country."

—*Robert Bray, Field Organizer for the National Gay & Lesbian Task Force*

✎ = school   𝐸 = college/university   **P** = professional   **E** = educational
A = activist/political   **H** = health (incl. HIV)   📰 = media/press   🖳 = Internet resource
The Bisexual Resource Guide 2000   **213**

Local

The Freedom Coalition　　　　　　**EA🖳**
PO Box 1991
Lawrence KS 66044
tel: 785-843-1889
e-mail: cubsfan@turnleft.com
URL: www.turnleft.com/freedom/
Meets monthly. Call for schedule. Organizes events, works with schools & community & works for local voters year-round.

University of Kansas, Lawrence:　　🖉🖳
Queers & Allies
423 Kansas Union, Box 13
Lawrence KS 66045
tel: 785-864-3091
e-mail: QandA@raven.cc.ukans.edu
URL: www.ukans.edu/~quanda/
GLB discussion & suppport group.

Flint Hills Alliance　　　　　　　**AE🖳**
PO Box 2018
Manhattan KS 66505-2018
tel: 913-776-6743
e-mail: dtaylor@ksu.edu
URL: www.debtaylor.com/fha
Meets 1st & 3rd Thursdays. **Publication(s):** *The Flint Hills Observer Available online: www.debtaylor.com/observer*

Icebreakers
Manhattan KS
tel: 785-776-3612
e-mail: JENSFOG@FLINTHILLS.COM
Support & discussion group for GLB people.

Kansas State University:　　　　🖉**AE🖳**
Bisexual, Lesbian & Gay Society
PO Box 4783
Topeka KS 66604-0783
e-mail: blgs@ksu.edu
URL: www.ksu.edu/blgs
Open to students, faculty & area residents.

Lifeguard　　　　　　　　　　　　♂
708 SW 6th Ave
Topeka KS 66603
tel: 785-232-3100
e-mail: m4m@aol.com
Open to any men interested in meeting men, regardless of orientation.

Support to Express Yourself　　　　**Y**
708 SW 6th Ave.
Topeka KS 66603
tel: 785-232-3100
For teens, age 13 to ~20s.

Unity & Pride Alliance　　　　　　**A**
1924 SW 13th St.
Topeka KS 66604
tel: 785-272-3792

Kentucky

Local

Centre College: BGLAD　　　　　🖉E
Box 1212
Randy Hayes, Advisor
Danville KY 40422
tel: 606-238-5471
e-mail: hays@centre.edu

Northern Kentucky University: Out-Front　🖉E
10 Campbell Dr.
Oak 1211
Highland Heights KY 41076
tel: 606-572-7874
e-mail: outfront@nku.edu

Transylvania University: TUnity　　　🖉
300 North Broadway
Lexington KY 40508
tel: 606-233-6490
e-mail: tunity@mail.transy.edu
URL: www.transy.edu

University of Kentucky: LAMBDA　　🖉
Patterson Office Tower
Lexington KY 40506
tel: 606-257-3151
Explicitly includes bisexuals.

Louisville Youth Group　　　　　　**Y**
PO Box 4664
Louisville KY 40204
tel: 502-894-9787
Meets bimonthly as a peer support group for self-identified GLB youth age 14-21. Invites speakers to present at the group & holds proms.

University of Louisville: Common Ground　🖉🖳
SAC W301
Louisville KY 40292
tel: 502-635-1905
e-mail: commong@ulkyvm.louisville.edu
URL: www.louisville.edu/rso/commonground

Western Kentucky University:　　　**A**🖉
Lesbian/ Bisexual/ Straight/ Gay Alliance
c/o Dr. Karen Schneider
Cherry Hall Room 20B
1 Big Red Way
Bowling Green KY 42101
tel: 502-745-0111

Key to symbols:　　▼ = bi　　　　♀ = women　　　♂ = men　　　　☯ = religious/spiritual
🖏 = for allies　**M** = for married bis　　♥ = for partners of bis　　**Y** = youth　　**C** = people of color
214　　　　　　　　　　　　　　　　　　　　　　**The Bisexual Resource Guide 2000**

Louisiana

Local

Bi Support Group ▼
c/o Lesbian & Gay Community Ctr
816 North Rampart
New Orleans LA 70116-3010
tel: 504-486-3351(Matthew)
e-mail: kitty@metatron.com

LAMBDA Group, Inc. E🖳
P.O. Box 1911
Baton Rouge LA 70821
tel: 504-383-0777
e-mail: lambdabr@webtv.net
URL: members.aol.com/lambdabr/index.html
Not for profit corporation covering Baton Rouge & the surrounding area, providing programs on LGBT issues & to fight discrimination in the gay & heterosexual community, & to open a community center to facilitate those programs. Baton Rouge Community Center: 504/346-0670 1733 Florida St. **Publication(s)**: *The Lambda Letter Bi Monthly newsletter.*

Louisiana State University: 🎓E
Gay, Bi & Lesbian Supporters United
P.O. Box 16031
Baton Rouge LA 70893
tel: 504-388-5160
e-mail: glsapre@unix1.sncc.lsu.edu
Meets every other Wed. evening in Coates Hall room 212.

University of Southwestern Louisiana: 🎓E
GAYLA, Gay & Lesbian Alliance
P.O. Box 43127
Lafayette LA 70504
tel: 318-482-6401
e-mail: gayla@usl.edu
Affiliated with University of Southwestern Louisiana. Meets 1st & 3rd Wed. each month, 6pm.

Lesbian & Gay Community Center ▼
816 North Rampart
New Orleans LA 70116-3010
tel: 504-522-1103
Community center that has hosted a bi support group. Call for current info. **Publication(s)**: *The Center Line newsletter about the center.*

Tulane University's Bisexual, Gay, & Lesbian 🎓🖳
Alliance
6823 St. Charles Avenue
New Orleans LA 70118
e-mail: bigala@mailhost.tcs.tulane.edu
URL: www.tulane.edu/~bigala

University of New Orleans: GLBSA 🎓
Campus Activities Office - UC 246
New Orleans LA 70148

Maine

Maine Bisexual People's Network ▼AE
PO Box 10818
Portland ME 04104-6818
e-mail: 71612.340@compuserve.com
Resources, referrals, support given. Organization in flux, no current group meetings.

Dial Kids Y
tel: 207-774-TALK
For lgb & questioning youth under 19 years.

Maine GayNet Homepage 🖳
ME
URL: www.qrd.com/maine

Maine Lesbian & Gay Political Alliance AE
PO Box 232
Hallowell ME 04347-0232
tel: 800-556-5472
761-3732 (Portland, ME)
e-mail: mlgpa@javanet.com
Statewide queer political association. Major organizing, strategizing, & campaigns. Leadership varies in bi-acceptance/friendliness. Check for current activities. Monthly newsletter.

Maine Speakout Project for Equal Rights EA
123 Congress St. #1
Portland ME 04101
tel: 207-879-0480
Trains & deploys volunteers state-wide to speak with citizen groups in their towns & regions about their lives & the lives of others who experience discrimination in Maine.

ME Gaynet 🖳EA🗂
ME
e-mail: me-gaynet@abacus.oxy.edu
subscribe me-gaynet
URL: www.qrd.com/maine
Unmoderated. Posts are not reviewed or filtered.

"Like many men, I too have had homosexual experiences and I am not ashamed."

—*Marlon Brando, 1980s.*

🖎 = school   🎓 = college/university   **P** = professional   **E** = educational
A = activist/political   **H** = health (incl. HIV)   📰 = media/press   🖳 = Internet resource
The Bisexual Resource Guide 2000   **215**

National Association of Social Workers,   **PEA**
Sexual Minorites Issues Committee, Maine
Chapter
PO Box 5065
Augusta ME 04330
tel: 207-622-7592; fax: 207-623-4860
e-mail: nasw99me@aol.com
*Assists social workers & other allies advocating
for GLBT people in Maine. Includes engaging in
political activism, lobbying, & providing
education & social service resources to sexual
minority groups & individuals. Strives to
provide Maine social workers with a safe &
supportive environment in which to discuss
sexual minority issues.*

Outright Portland   **YEA**
P.O. Box 5077
Portland ME 04101
tel: 207-828-6560
888-567-7600
*For LGBT & Q young people. Support group
meets Fridays 7:30-9:30pm at 1 Pleasant Street,
4th Floor, in Portland. Other activities
throughout the week-call for more information.
State central office which helps all of the
chapters & covers the toll free phone & from
which staff operate the local chapter activities.*

Rainbow Business & Professional Association   **P**
P.O. Box 6627
Scarborough ME 04070-6627
tel: 207-775-0015
e-mail: wildboys@mainelink.net
*A state-wide, non-profit organization established
to create a gay, lesbian, bi & transgendered
"chamber of commerce" for Maine. Meetings/
dinners held in Greater Portland area, second
Monday of the month.*

Local

Gay/Bi men's potluck (Lewiston/Auburn)   ♂ 🖥
c/o Unitarian Universalist Church
169 Pleasant St.
Attn. Glen Esman
Auburn ME 04210
tel: 207-783-0461; fax: 207-782-3747
e-mail: uuauburn@exploremaine.com
URL: www.maineadv.com
*Gay & Bi men's social group meets for potluck
dinners at 6:30. 1st Mon. & 3rd Tues. of each
month.*

Lesbian Potluck (Lewiston/Auburn)   ♀ 🖥
c/o Unitarian Universalist Church
169 Pleasant St
Auburn ME 04210
tel: 207-783-0461; fax: 207-782-3747
e-mail: uuauburn@exploremaine.com
URL: www.maineadv.com
*L/B women's monthly potluck. Meets in
member's homes. Contact church office for
details.*

Man 2 Man   ♂ **EH**
PO Box 2038
Bangor ME 04402
tel: 207-990-2095
*HIV prevention program for men who have sex
with men. Offers education, HIV testing, support
groups, HIV/AIDS hotline, workshops.*

Outright Bangor   **Y**
Bangor ME 04401
tel: 207-990-2095Shawn Box; 800-429-1481
*Supportive, informative & social meetings for
GLB & Q youth age 22 & under. Safe space for
questions, growth, & fun. Call FMI.*

University of Southern   ⚲ ♀ **EAM** ♥
Maine (USM) Women's Center
131 Campus Center
Bedford ME 04103
tel: 207-780-4996; fax: 207-780-4463
e-mail: ATMCCALL@USM.Maine.edu
*Open Monday thru Friday, 8:30-4. Weekly
"sexual identity" discussion group for issues
related to women. Center has info. about all
queer activities & activism on both campuses.
Center now has a coordinator of lesbian & bi
affairs & plans to expand programs for queer
women.*

Outright Waldo-Knox
Waldo-Knox AIDS Coalition
P.O. Box 956
Belfast ME 04915
tel: 207-338-1427, Lisa
*Meets every other Sunday in Camden for GLB &
Q youth 22 & under. Confidential, supportive,
saf space for growth, discussion & fun. Call or
write FMI. Collect calls ok.*

"...either 'bisexuality' is a very common condition, or another artificial
category concealing the overlaps. What heterosexuals really fear, is not that
'they' — an alien subgroup with perverse tastes in bedfellows — are getting
an undue share of power and attention, but that 'they' might well be us."

—Barbara Ehrenreich, 1989 (in Garber p. 253)

Key to symbols: ▼ = bi   ♀ = women   ♂ = men   ❧ = religious/spiritual
◊ = for allies   **M** = for married bis   ♥ = for partners of bis   **Y** = youth   **C** = people of color
216   **The Bisexual Resource Guide 2000**

University of New England: _E_🖳
Gay/Lesbian/Bi-sexual & Friends
University of New England Biddeford Campus
Biddeford ME 04005
tel: 207-283-2865
Linda Morrison, faculty advisor
e-mail: Lmorrison@mailbox.une.edu
URL: www.une.edu/sl/uclubs.html
_Weekly group open to GLBT students, their
friends & allies. Student handbook lists speakers
bureau, lending library of g/l literature, support
& discussion groups, referral services, special
events, & public relations. Reciprocal referrals
with UNE counseling office. Confidential
hotline. Contact Faculty Advisor Linda Morrison
for meeting times & places._

Bowdoin College: Bisexual, Gay   _&_
& Lesbian Alliance for Diversity (BGLAD)
Moulton Union Info. Desk
Brunswick ME 04011
tel: 207-725-3000 (ask for BGLAD); fax: 207-725-
3477 (attn: BGLAD)
Call for meeting times & places.

Midcoast Outright, Brunswick   **Y**
Brunswick ME
tel: 207-798-4586 Jim
_Provides supportive & affirming spaces for glbt
& questioning youth._

Northern Lambda Nord   **EA**◉🖳
PO Box 990
Caribou ME 04736-0990
tel: 207-498-2088 or 1-800-468-2088 (within
Maine). (answered M, W, F, 7-9), voice/tty.
URL: www.ctel.net/~lambda
_Serving people in northern Maine & northern &
western New Brunswick in Canada. Social
activities, discussion group, speaker's bureau,
newsletter & activities calendar, lending library,
phoneline. Meetings 2nd Thursdays at 6:30pm
(ME), 7:30pm (NB) Gay-Lesbian Community
Services Center, 568 Main St., Caribou.
Religious/spiritual gathering Sundays at the
Community Center._ **Publication(s):**
_Communiqué 6x/year to members & by
subscription. Activities & calendar published
monthly._

Gay OK!   **YCE**
c/o Brian Kaufman
5 South St.
Farmington ME 04938
tel: 207-778-7379; fax: 207-778-7378
e-mail: BJKPMA@aol.com
_Meets weekly for discussion & support. Serving
all of Franklin County._

Q-Squad
Farmington ME
tel: Leave msg at 207-778-7380
_Support group for LGBT community. Serves
Franklin County; based at UM Farmington._

**Rainbow Educational Alliance for Diverse
Individuals (READI)**
c/o Brian Kaufman
5 South St.
Farmington ME 04938
tel: 207-778-7379; fax: 207-778-7378
e-mail: BJKPMA@aol.com
_Student group programs, BGLT events, meetings
& activities._

Bates College: Gay/Lesbian/Bisexual/   _&_
Straight Alliance
Box 77
Lewiston ME 04240
URL: www.bates.edu/

**Lewiston/Auburn Gay, Lesbian, Bisexual
Support Group**
Lewiston/Auburn ME
_Support group for the Lewiston/Auburn area
meets Mon. 7pm at the Unitarian-Universalist
Church on Spring St., Auburn._

Lewiston/Auburn Outright   **Y**
Lewiston/Auburn ME
tel: 207-786-2717
Call about meeting times & places.

University of Maine, Orono:

▼ **Lesbian/Bisexual Support Group**   ♀
Orono ME
tel: 207-581-1425
_Meets Tues., 7-9pm, at Women's Resource
Center, 101 Fernald Hall at UM Orono._

▼ **Wilde-Stein Alliance for**   _&_**EA**🖳
Sexual Diversity
C. Max Hilton Room, Memorial Union
University of Maine at Orono
Orono ME 04469-0000
tel: 207-581-1596
e-mail: wilde.stein@umit.maine.edu
URL: www.ume.maine.edu/~wstein
Call for meeting times & places.

Dignity/Maine   ◉
PO Box 8113
Portland ME 04104
tel: Rosemary or Janet: 207-646-2820;
Laurie: 207-878-0546
_Dignity/Maine offers supportive Masses for
LGBT Catholics & their friends/families. Meets
every Sun. 6pm in St. Luke's Cathedral, side
chapel, 143 State St., Portland. Coffee & dessert
after the liturgy. All replies kept confidential._

✎ = school	_&_ = college/university	**P** = professional	**E** = educational
A = activist/political	**H** = health (incl. HIV)	✍ = media/press	🖳 = Internet resource

The Bisexual Resource Guide 2000

Gay/Lesbian/Bisexual Parents Group
PO Box 10818
Portland ME 04104

Metropolitan Community Church   ❂&
PO Box 1671
Portland ME 04104-1671
tel: 1-888-264-6223
e-mail: cohmcc@hotmail.com
A Christian church founded in & reaching beyond the lgbt community. Inclusive in language as well as orientation. Currently meeting Sundays in rented space at Immanuel Baptist Church, 156 High St., Portland.

The Matlovich Society   E
Portland ME
tel: 207-773-8308
Educational & cultural organization. LGB/ friends committed to sharing our history & providing affirming presentations & discussions. Meets 2nd & 4th Thursdays 7:30pm at the Holiday Inn by the Bay, 88 Spring St.

University of Southern Maine: ⟲EA🖳
Alliance for Sexual Diversity
96 Falmouth Street, Powers House
Portland ME 04103
tel: 207-874-6596
e-mail: usmpride2@usm.maine.edu (listserve)
URL: usmcug.usm.maine.edu/~asd
Programs for bglt & questioning students. Works with other campus groups including a new radical group, "Queer on Campus Coalition," pushing for a Center for Diversity, queer safety on campus, & other supports for queer life.

Gay, Lesbian, Bisexual Discussion Group
Rockland ME
tel: Larry Godfrey: 207-594-2957
Meets 1st & 3rd Fridays, 7-9pm at First Universalist Church, 345 Broadway, Rockland, ME.

"Zeus, to steal boy Ganymede
An eagle's form put on;
And when he wanted the lady Leda
He turned into a swan.

Now some like girls,
and some like boys;
But the moral's plain to see:
If both are good enough for Zeus,
They're good enough for me."

—*Anonymous, Greek poet*

Sister Space   ♀🖳
Saco ME
tel: 207-467-9166
e-mail: msw@ime.net
URL: w3.ime.net/"msu
Support group meets Mon. evenings at Unitarian Church. B/L/questioning women welcome.

Out on Mount Desert Island   🖳
PO Box 367
Southwest Harbor ME 04679
tel: 207-664-0328
e-mail: oomdi@geocities.com
URL: www.geocities.com/westhollywood/heights/5011/index.html
Supporting the Lesbian. Gay, Bisexual, Transgender & allied community of downeast Maine. Very active social/support group. Meets Tuesdays 7pm. Newcomers always welcome.

Colby College: ⟲A🖳
The Bridge- Colby's GLBTA Community
5920 Mayflower Hill Drive
Waterville ME 04901
tel: 207-872-3635
e-mail: bridge@colby.edu
URL: www.colby.edu/bridge/
Call ahead or visit web page for events & meeting times.

SOLO (Senior Older Lesbians Organization)   ♀
PO Box 211
Yarmouth ME 04096
e-mail: footloose@gwi.net
Group meets for potluck dinner, social time, dancing & games. Organizes boat, hiking, & other activities. Open to women in their 40's & beyond, inncluding bi's. Meets 1st Saturday evening of the month, usually at the Durham Quaker Meeting house, Durham, ME. Contact by email for current meeting times & places.

Maryland

Local

BiNetwork DC [DC Metropolitan Area] ▼YEC🖳
PO Box 7657
Langley Park MD 20787
tel: Activities recording: 202-828-3080 or 202-986-7186
e-mail: stw@clark.net
URL: www.clark.net/pub/stw/bndc.html
Active groups include young adults, women's group, bi-friendly dinners, polyamory discussion, People of Color. **Publication(s)**: *"Side Bi Side", a quarterly. $15/year, mail form (on web site) + $15 (personal check/money order) to BiNetwork DC, P.O.B. 7657, Langley Park, MD 20787.*

Key to symbols: ▼ = bi   ♀ = women   ♂ = men   ❂ = religious/spiritual
& = for allies   **M** = for married bis   ♥ = for partners of bis   Y = youth   C = people of color
218   **The Bisexual Resource Guide 2000**

Bi Group   **Y▼A**
Gay & Lesbian Community Center
241 W. Chase St.
Baltimore MD 21201
tel: 410-837-5445; fax: 410-837-8512
Community center sponsors many groups,
including bi group.

Johns Hopkins University: 🔗💻
Diverse Sexuality & Gender Alliance
Merryman Hall
3400 N. Charles Street
Baltimore MD 21218
tel: 410-516-4088; fax: 410-516-4986
e-mail: dsaga@jhu.edu
URL: www.jhu.edu/~dsaga
Events & entertainment, political & social
activities, discussions. **Publication(s)**: *Closet*
Space

Maryland Institute College of Art: ANGLE 🔗
c/o Student Activities
1300 Mt Royal Avenue
Baltimore MD 21217
tel: Student Activities: 410-225-2284
"Awareness Now for Gays, Lesbians &
Everyone."

University of Maryland, College Park: 🔗💻
Lesbian, Gay, Bisexual Alliance
Stamp Student Union
College Park MD 20742
tel: 301-314-8347
URL: www.inform.umd.edu/StudentOrg/lgba/
Weekly "Out Front" meetings for discussion &
planning, mentor program, events.

Hood College: 🔗♀💻
Tolerance, Education & Acceptance
Box 1200
Hood College
Frederick MD 21701
URL: www.hood.edu/student/tea

Towson State University:

▼ Diverse Sexual Orientation Collective 🔗💻
c/o Student Government Association
Towson MD 21204-7097
tel: 410-830-2340
URL: tiger.towson.edu/~bpetr1/DSOC/
index.html

▼ Gay, Lesbian & Bisexual   🔗💻
Issues Committee
c/o David Bergman Chair
English Department
Towson MD 21204-7097
e-mail: Bergman@midget.towson.edu
URL: saber.towson.edu/~tinkler/lgb/
homepage.htm
Addresses issues related to sexual orientation
for students, faculty & staff. Open to all
members of the TSU community.

Massachusetts

Bisexual Resource Center   ▼
Cambridge MA
See listing under "International."

Blue Pride of Massachusetts   **PE**
c/o Kim Rosen, MS 12-21
Blue Cross Blue Shield MA
25 Newport Avenue Ext.
Quincy MA 02171
tel: Kim Rosen, 800-524-4010 ext. 6755
e-mail: rosen_kimberly@bcbsma.com or
kwi2@aol.com
An organization for LGB employees of Blue
Cross & Blue Shield to promote LGB concerns &
create a safe & open environment for LGB
employees.

Building Bridges   **Y**
186 Main Street
Fall River MA 02172
tel: 508-679-0962; fax: 508-676-5592

Color Me Healthy   **HEC♂**
Fenway Community Health Center
7 Haviland St.
Boston MA 02115
tel: David or Craig: 617-927-6300
e-mail: dyoung@hchc.org
Social/support group for gay/bi men of color.
Meets 4th Tues. of every month 6:30 - 8:30pm at
the Fenway Community Health Center.

Coming Out Group
Fenway Community Health Center
7 Haviland Street
Boston MA 02115
tel: 617-927-6200
A co-ed, short term group for men & women in
the process of coming out as gay or bisexual. Call
for meeting times & to arrange an initial
evaluation. Fee-based on sliding scale.

🔖 = school   🔗 = college/university   **P** = professional   **E** = educational
A = activist/political   **H** = health (incl. HIV)   📰 = media/press   💻 = Internet resource

Common Voices ♂ EH
c/o Fenway Community Health Center
7 Haviland St.
Boston MA 02115
tel: 617-927-6400; fax: 617-536-8602
e-mail: livingwell@fchc.org
Free & confidential support & social group for gay & bisexual men. Meets 3rd Thurs. 7-9pm, plus special events. Call for current info.

Delta Project ♂ CAE
Fenway Community Health Center
7 Haviland St.
Boston MA 02115
tel: 617-927-6300
e-mail: dyoung@fchc.org
A group discussing topics each month for gay/bi men. Topics include cultural, social, economic, political & health issues. Meets 3rd Tues. each month 6:30-8:30pm at the FCHC. Contact David Young at 617/927-6300 for more info.

Essence of a Woman ♀ E
c/o Fenway Community Health Center
7 Haviland St.
Boston MA 02115
tel: 617-927-6300
Shantanette Patrice
e-mail: spatrice@echo.org
A sex rap series for women who have sex with women.

Gay & Bisexual Married Men's Support ♂ M 🖳
Group
c/o Bisexual Resource Center
29 Stanhope St.
Boston MA 02116
tel: 617-576-9747; recorded message
e-mail: boston_bmmg@hotmail.com
URL: home.talkcity.com/ConnectionPt/bmmg/
Meets 1st & 3rd Mondays at 29 Stanhope St. from 7:30 - 10:00 pm. Friendly, supportive talk about shared issues.

Gay, Lesbian, Bisexual, YH 🖳
Transgender Youth Initiative
The Medical Foundation
95 Berkeley St.
Boston MA 02116
tel: 617-451-0049; fax: 617-451-0062
e-mail: pss@ma.ultranet.com
URL: www.ultranet.com/'tmf/
Provides resources & technical assistance to groups around Massachusetts that work with GLBT youth or want to address homophobia.

Girlfriends C ♀ E
c/o Cambridge Family & Child Services
929 Mass. Ave
Cambridge MA 02136
tel: Dotè Ridley 617-876-4216
e-mail: grfnos@aol.com
Free, weekly peer support group for lesbians & bi women of color. Meets Saturdays, 10:30am-12:30pm.

HIV-Negative Gay/Bi Men's ♂ HE
Support Group
Fenway Community Health Center
7 Haviland Street
Boston MA 02115
tel: 617-927-6300
e-mail: vlongo@fchc.org
3-session series each month that takes participants through risk assessment & risk reduction strategies. Meets first 3 Tuesdays of each month from 6-8pm at FCHC. Call Vin Longo to register or for more info. at 617-927-6231. FREE.

in newsweekly: New England's ▼ 🖳
Gay, Lesbian & Bisexual Newspaper
544 Tremont St
Boston MA 02116
tel: 617-426-8246; fax: 617-426-8264
URL: www.innewsweekly.com
Serving New England. Covers news & nightlife.
Publication(s): *in newsweekly published weekly. Subscription rate: $140/yr., mailed first class. Also available free at certain community locations. Call to subscribe*

Keshet: Jewish Gay, Lesbian, ✆ AE
Bisexual, & Transgender Advocacy &
Education Group of Boston
10 Arnold Circle, Suite 3
Cambridge MA 02139
tel: 617-576-2309
e-mail: keshet_boston@hotmail.com
To advocate equality & integration of GLBT folks in the Jewsih community to strengthen the Jewish identities of GLBT Jews.

Lesbian & Bisexual Rights Task Force AE 🖳
of the National Organization for Women
214 Harvard Ave
Allston MA 02134
tel: NOW's phone #: 617-782-1056 or 232-1017 (M-F 10-5); fax: 617-232-4162
e-mail: massnow@gis.net
URL: www.NOW.org
Helping to fight racism & homophobia in our communities, while working to expand the diversity of chapter issues, outreach & membership.

Key to symbols: ▼ = bi ♀ = women ♂ = men ✆ = religious/spiritual
🖐 = for allies M = for married bis ♥ = for partners of bis Y = youth C = people of color
220 The Bisexual Resource Guide 2000

MAN TALK ♂ **E**
First Parish Church
Church Green, Church St
Taunton MA 02780
tel: 508-884-8264; fax: 508-884-8273
e-mail: MANTALK@hotmail.com
*Weekly discussion group for men to meet &
interact outside typical gay meeting spots.
Weekly discussion on different subjects suggested
by the group. Open to any gay, bi, or curious
man. Confidential. Taunton: Meets Thurs. 7-
8:30pm at First Parish Church, Church Street,
Brockton: Meets Wed. 7-8:30pm at Unitarian
Universalist Church, 325 West Elm St.. Fall
River: Fri. 7-8:30 Unitarian Soicety, 309 N.
Main St.*

Massachusetts Area South Asian Lambda **C E**
Association (MASALA)
PO Box 1182
Cambridge MA 02142
tel: 617-499-9669
*Discussion / support / social group for South
Asian LGBT folks.* **Publication(s)**: *MASALA
monthly newsletter call for free trial subscription*

Massachusetts Department of Education: **Y E**
Safe Schools Program
350 Main Street
Malden MA 02148-5023
tel: 781-388-3300 x409
e-mail: dbrathwaite@doe.mass.edu
*Massachusetts Dept. of Education project
working in conjunction with the Governor's
Commission on Gay & Lesbian Youth.*
Publication(s): *Gay / Straight Alliances: A
Student Guide 27 minute video - "Safe Schools
Program for Gay & Lesbian Students" - free for
in-state residents. Others send blank 30min
videotape.*

MassQ-Net 🖰🖵
MA
URL: rlserver.wsc.mass.edu/qnet/
*Web page sponsored by the Massachusetts
Governor's Commission on Gay & Lesbian Youth
of GLB contacts at Massachusetts State &
Community Colleges to serve glb members of our
campus communities in a more comprehensive
way.*

Metro Southeast Youth Alliance **Y**
792 North Main St.
Brockton MA 02401
tel: Heather or Richard: 1-888-240-7727
e-mail: jltk80a@prodigy.com
*Questioning & supportive straight youth under
22 yrs. also welcome. Meets every Thursday from
7:00 to 9:00PM at 792 North Main Street.*

Morning Star Metropolitan Community ◐ **AE**
Church
213 Main St.
Cherry Valley MA 01611
tel: 508-892-4320
*Part of the universal fellowship of Metropolitan
Community Churches, Provides support, love, &
gudance in a caring, nonjudgemental, Christian
environment. All welcome.*

National Association of Social Workers, **P E**
**Mass Chapter, Committee on Gay/Lesbian/
Bisexual Issues**
14 Beacon St., Suite 409
Boston MA 02114
tel: Call NASW/Mass at 617-227-9635 for name &
# of current chair.
*Includes a Massachusetts GLB Training
Committee, which does training on how to work
with GLB clients.*

Pride Time 🖎**EA**🖵
66 Charles St. Suite 283
Boston MA 02115
tel: 617-423-1515
e-mail: pridetime@aol.com
URL: www.pinkweb.com
*Cable TV program for the Boston, Cambridge, &
Somerville lesbigay community. Boston: Sat.
7:30pm TV-A3. Cambridge: Thurs. 9pm, TV A-
19. Also publishes the Pink Pages, listing groups,
non-profits, & businesses that welcome the
LGBT community.*

Pridenet 🖵🖰
MA
URL: www.pridenet.com/mass.html
Statewide GLBT Information.

Southcoast Diversity Alliance **YE**🖵
1061 Pleasant St.
New Bedford MA 02740
tel: 508-996-8572; fax: 508-991-8618
URL: www.ultranet.com/~scda/scda.html
*The SCDA is a social support group providing a
safe & nurturing environment for youth, ages 20
& under, questioning & / or LBGT identified.
Program of New Bedford Family Service, Inc.*

SpeakOut: The Gay, Lesbian & Bisexual **YE**🖵
Speakers' Bureau
PO Box 1358
Boston MA 02117
tel: 617-450-9776; fax: 617-236-0334
e-mail: info@glbsb.org
URL: www.glbsb.org
*Very welcoming to bisexuals. Provides speakers
to schools & community groups. Excellent
annual speakers training open to all.*
Publication(s): *The Speaker monthly
newsletter*

🖎 = school   🖰 = college/university   **P** = professional   **E** = educational
A = activist/political   **H** = health (incl. HIV)   🖎 = media/press   🖵 = Internet resource
The Bisexual Resource Guide 2000   **221**

Robyn Ochs

Violence Recovery Program - VRP   **HAE**
Fenway Community Health Center
7 Haviland St.
Boston MA 02115
tel: 617-927-6300 or
800-934-3242
e-mail: rjohnson@fchc.org
*Support & advocacy services for LGBT people.
Services offered to victims of domestic violence,
hate crimes, sexual assault, & police misconduct.
Support groups available include: domestic
violence group, & male survivors of sexual
assault (in conjunction with Boston Area Rape
Crisis Center). All sevices available in Spanish.
Contact office for more info.*

CENTRAL & WESTERN MASSACHUSETTS

Bisexual Women's Discussion   ♀ ▼
Group & Brunches
MA
tel: 413-253-2104 (Dasha)

**University of
Massachusetts, Amherst:**

▼ **Stonewall Center:**   ☌⌒E🖳
**Gay, Lesbian, Bisexual &
Transgender Education
Resource Center**
406G Student Union, Box 41
Amherst MA 01003
tel: 413-545-4824; fax: 413-545-6667
e-mail: stonewall@stuaf.umass.edu
URL: www.umass.edu/stonewall/
*Location: Crampton House/ SW.
Info/referral, education & cultural
programming, speakers bureau for
5-college community. Free library
(including videos). Crisis/
discrimination response, training &
consulting. Activities for graduate
& older
undergraduate students. Also, QueerE, an e-
mail network of GLBT events in the Pioneer
Valley.* **Publication(s)**: *The Blatent Monthly
newsletter of area GLBT events.*

▼ **Bisexual Focus Group**   ▼☌⌒E
e-mail: levchuck@student.umass.edu
*See Stonewall Center above. Affilliated with
the Pride alliance. Meets Sun. 7:30, Campus
center or student union. Directed by L. Feder*

▼ **Alumni Pride Alliance at Amherst**   ☌⌒🖳
URL: www.umass.edu/stonewall/alumni/html
*See Stonewall Center above. To allow alumni
to stay in contact, network, & keep in touch
with the GLB campus community. If you or
someone you know is a GLB alumnus of
UMASS-Amherst, please send name, address,
telephone number, FAX number, e-mail
address, major, degree, & year of graduation
(or as much as you know) to the above address
or email address.*

"If bisexuality is in fact, as I suspect it to be,
not just another sexual orientation but rather a sexuality that undoes
sexual orientation as a category, ... then the search for the meaning of
the word 'bisexual' offers a different kind of lesson. Rather than
naming an invisible, undernoticed minority now finding its place in the
sun, 'bisexual' turns out to be, like bisexuals themselves, everywhere
and nowhere. There is, in short, no 'really' about it. The question of
whether someone was 'really' straight or 'really' gay misrecognizes the
nature of sexuality, which is fluid, not fixed, a narrative that changes
over time rather than a fixed identity, however complex. The erotic
discovery of bisexuality is the fact that it reveals sexuality to be a
process of growth, transformation, and surprise, not a stable and
knowable state of being."

—*Marjorie Garber, in* Vice Versa: Bisexuality and the Eroticism of Everyday Life (NY: Simon & Schuster, 1995)

Key to symbols: ▼ = bi   ♀ = women   ♂ = men   ☣ = religious/spiritual
🍃 = for allies   **M** = for married bis   ♥ = for partners of bis   **Y** = youth   **C** = people of color
222   **The Bisexual Resource Guide 2000**

▼ **Gay, Lesbian, Bisexual**   𝒢⁄**E**
Speakers Bureau
See Stonewall Center above. We talk about our lives as lgbt people & heterosexual allies. We are committed to change through communication.

▼ **Graduate Student Gay,**   𝒢⁄
Lesbian & Bisexual Group
See Stonewall Center above. Group of GLBT graduate students across the campus interested in gathering together to socialize & create connection across departments.

Robyn Ochs

▼ **Lesbian, Bisexual, Gay**   𝒢⁄
Counseling Collective
406G Student Union, Box 41
Amherst MA 01003
tel: 413-545-2645
"Free, confidential peer counseling for local community, supervised by mental health professsionals. Weekly rap group, drop in or phone counseling."

▼ **Lesbian, Bisexual & Gay Political Caucus**𝒢⁄**A**
c/o LGBA, 413 Student Union, Box 41
Amherst MA 01003

▼ **Pride Alliance**   𝒢⁄
RSO Box 66
Amherst MA 01003
tel: 413-545-0154
e-mail: lgba@stuaf.umass.edu
Sponsors info-socials Tuesdays 7-9pm in the Campus Center to provide glbt students with a safe space to socialize & discuss relevant issues. Open to all & a great place to meet people & find community resources if you are just coming out. Also sponsors bisexual (mixed gender) discussion group. Call for more info.

Amherst College:

▼ **Lesbian, Gay & Bisexual Alliance**   𝒢⁄**A**🖳
Heath Center, 204, Box 1817
Amherst MA 01002-5000
tel: 413-542-8106
e-mail: lgbta@unix.amherst.edu
URL: www.amherst.edu/~lbga/
Political, social, support, weekly meetings.

▼ **Queer/Straight Alliance**   𝒢⁄🖳
Amherst MA 01002
tel: 413-582-5714
e-mail: qsa@unix.amherst.edu
URL: www.amherst.edu/~qsa/
A political organization, dedicated to LGBT awareness & fighting homophobia. Meets Tuesdays 8:30pm during termtime in Campus Center 207. All students invited.

Amherst/Pelham Regional High School: **Y**✎
Making Schools Safe for Gay, Lesbian, & Bisexual Students Committee/GSA
21 Mattoon St.
Amherst MA 01002
tel: Michael Bardsley: 413-549-3710

Gay, Lesbian & Bisexual Group of the   ☺
Jewish Community of Amherst
742 Main Street
Amherst MA 01002
tel: 413-256-0160 (Ask for GLB group)
Open to participation by glb Jews & their families. Offers Sabbath & holiday services as well as social, educational & community action programs.

Hampshire College: Queer Campus   𝒢⁄♂
Alliance
Amherst MA 01002
tel: 413-582-5714

Lifecourse Counseling Center   🖳
664 Main Street
Amherst MA 01002
tel: 413-253-2822
e-mail: integsol@valinet.com
URL: www.valinet.com/~lifecour
Individual therapy, education, ongoing groups, transgender support group. Call for current group listing or more info.

Bradford College: Pride   𝒢⁄
Box 547
320 S. Main Street
Bradford MA 01835
tel: 978-496-1662 (Louis)
978-374-7997 (main number for school)
e-mail: lRodrigsley@bnet.bradford.edu
Provides support for students to discuss GLBT issues. Promotes & sponsors educational programs throughout the year. Leave message for Louis at the campus activities office.

✎ = school   𝒢⁄ = college/university   **P** = professional   **E** = educational
A = activist/political   **H** = health (incl. HIV)   ✍ = media/press   🖳 = Internet resource

Fitchburg Public Schools: Gay/Lesbian/   **Y E**
Bisexual Support Group
98 Academy Street
Fitchburg MA 01420
tel: 978-345-3265
Monthly Meetings. Main advisor: Barbara
Christopher.

Venture Out   🖳
PO Box 60271
Florence MA 01062
tel: 413-584-8764
e-mail: ventureout@geocities.com
URL: www.geocities.com/WestHollywood/2956
Activities group based in Western MA.
Publication(s): *A monthly newsletter listing*
events for the month is mailed to each menber.

Unitarian Universalist Lesbian/Gay/Bi   🕊
Support Group
Unitarian Universalist Society of Middleboro
25 S. Main Street
Middleboro MA 02346
tel: 508-947-1935
Regular meetings 1st & 3rd Wed. of month, 7pm.
Very confidential. Good resource for question-
ing/just coming out.

Gay Youth Action   **Y**
PO Box 481
Monterey MA 01245
For GLB & questioning teens, 16-20.

Lesbian, Gay & Bisexual Political Alliance of   **A**
Western Massachusetts
PO Box 1492
Northampton MA 01061
tel: Stacy: 413-549-5829
Political action committee. Advocacy. Monthly
meetings.

Listen Up! This Way Out!   📻
Northampton MA
tel: Chris: 413-256-6794
The international GLB radio newsmagazine
WTTT, 1430am (Northampton) followed by An
Open View at 11:30.

Men With Men   ♂
Room 311, 16 Center Street
Northampton MA 01060
tel: 413-585-1012
Social/discussion group for gay & bi men. Meets
1st & 3rd Fridays 7:30-9pm.

Northampton Area Lesbian & Gay Business
Guild
PO Box 593
Northampton MA 01061-0593
e-mail: nalgbg@westmass.com
A LGB & Allied business association.

Out Now!: Lesbian, Gay & Bisexual Youth   **Y**
Group of Greater Springfield
PO Box 833
Northampton MA 01061
tel: 1-888-429-9990
e-mail: hmrichar@javanet.com
Free, voluntary support group for people under
22. Meets weekly at Trinity Church in Spring-
field. Wheelchair accessible. When you leave your
message, leave any special instructions
regarding calls back. 413-586-2627 M-F 10am-
1pm gets live person. Lifecourse also offers
counseling for bi folks (fee for service).

Smith College School of Social Work: ⚥
Lesbian, Gay, Bisexual Transgendered
Alliance
Lilly Hall
Northampton MA 01063

Smith College: The Lesbian Bisexual   ⚥ ♀ **A** 🖳
Transgender Alliance
Student Government Office
Clark Hall
Northampton MA 01063
tel: 413-585-4907
e-mail: lba@sophia.smith.edu
URL: www.smith.edu/lba
Political & social organization that exists to
serve the Smith LBT & allied community.

Straight Spouse Support Network SSSN   ♥
Northampton MA
tel: Jane Harris 413-625-6033
Support for spouses whose partners are GL or B
in a non-homophobic, confidential environment.
Meets 3rd Tues 7-9pm. New group starting in
Keene, NH meets 4th Sun 2-3:30 pm. Sponsored
by P-FLAG. For locations & info call Jane
Harris 413-625-6033.

Homo-Bi-Hetero Society   **Y**🐾
Northfield Mt. Herman School
Northfield MA 01360-1089
tel: Vicky Greenbaum: 413-498-4440

Smith College: Prism   ⚥ ♀ **C** 🖳
Clark Hall SGA Office
Northhampton MA 01063
e-mail: tstcloud@mail.smith.edu
URL: www.smith.edu/lba/prism
Provides resources to the LBT/Ally/Questioning
women of color community through social events,
films, discussions, & speakers. Meets weekly.

Mount Holyoke College:

▼ Lesbian Bisexual Alliance   ♀ ⚥
   Box 105, Mary Wooley, So.
   South Hadley MA 01075
   tel: 413-538-3822

Key to symbols: ▼ = bi   ♀ = women   ♂ = men   🕊 = religious/spiritual
👐 = for allies   **M** = for married bis   ♥ = for partners of bis   **Y** = youth   **C** = people of color
224   **The Bisexual Resource Guide 2000**

▼ **SYSTA**   ♀ 🎓 C
Box 1943
South Hadley MA 01075
*Lesbian, Bisexual & Questioning Women of
Color.*

Southern Worcester County Bisexual   ▼
Alliance (SWCBA)
PO Box 145
Southbridge MA 01550
*"Open to bis & bi-friendly people of either
gender. In the process of forming a bi support
group, a group for married bisexuals, & a bi/
gay/les walking group. We could use the help of
anyone in the area."*

Gay/Lesbian Info Service
Springfield MA
tel: 413-731-5403

Springfield Technical Community College: 🎓
Gay, Lesbian, Bisexual Alliance
c/o Student Activities
1 Amory Square
Springfield MA 01105
tel: 413-748-3750
*Meets Tuesdays 12:30-1:30 during termtime.
Open to all college-aged people in the greater
Springfield area.*

Westfield State College: Gay/Straight   🎓
Alliance
577 Western Avenue
Westfield MA 01086-1630
tel: Advisors: Brian Cahillane 413- 572-5401,
Kath Bradford 413- 572-5404
URL: rlserver.wsc.mass.edu/qnet/westfield.htm

Williams College: Queer/Straight Alliance 🎓 💻
Student Union
Williamstown MA 01267
URL: wso.williams.edu/orgs/qsa
Meets Mondays 10-11pm during termtime.

Assumption College: Gay & Lesbian   🎓
Discussion Group
500 Salisbury St
PO Box 15005
Worcester MA 01615-0005

Clark University: Lesbian, Bisexual &   🎓
Questioning
c/o Women's Center Collective
Box B-5
Worcester MA 01610-1477
tel: 508-793-7287

Holy Cross College: Allies   🎓 E
1 College St.
Worcester MA 01610
tel: 508-793-3487 (student activities)
*Mixed group (LGBT & straight) with a mission
to educate the Holy Cross community on gay
issues by holding weekly meetings in the Hogan
Center & by organizing events throughout the
year.*

MSM Services Program   H ♂ E
AOW, Inc.
85 Green St.
Worcester MA
tel: 508-770-1308 x32 or 508-775-3773 x32
*Provides specialized assistance & support to G &
B men & other men who have sex with men.
Services offered by professional clinicians who
provide counseling, groups, educational
programs, & social activities. Free & confidential. Funded by the Mass DPH.*

Worcester Polytechnic Institute: BiLAGA   🎓
c/o Student Activities Office
100 Institute Rd.
Worcester MA 01609
e-mail: bilaga@wpi.edu

Worcester State College: Delta   🎓
c/o Student Center
486 Chandler Street
Worcester MA 01602
tel: Student Center: 508-929-8073

EASTERN MASSACHUSETTS

Biversity - Boston   ▼ 💻 EH
29 Stanhope Street
Boston MA 02116
tel: 617-424-9595
e-mail: biversity@blank.org
URL: www.biresource.org/biversity
*Mixed gender network in Boston for bis & allies.
Social events include 2 brunches/month,
discussion groups, movie outings, games nights,
bicycling & lots more. To subscribe to b-monthly
calendar of events by postal mail, write or call
w/your name/address. To subscribe to
Biversity's email list for events only, send email
to biversity-request@blank.org, To discussion
list: biversity-chat-request@blank.org or
biversity-chat-digest-request@blank.org (for a
day's worth of posts in one email. For any
subscription write only the word 'subscribe' (no
quotes) in the body of the message.*

🔎 = school   🎓 = college/university   P = professional   E = educational
A = activist/political   H = health (incl. HIV)   ☰ = media/press   💻 = Internet resource
The Bisexual Resource Guide 2000   **225**

Boston Bisexual Women's Network ▼A ♀
PO Box 400639
Cambridge MA 02140
tel: 617-424-9595
Publishes newsletter. Monthly potluck brunches & other social events. Sells "Bisexual Pride" & visiBIlity buttons. (See our display ad). Periodic bi women's coming out groups. **Publication(s):** *Bi Women sliding scale $20-30 +/-. Bi-monthly, 12-16 pages. Submissions from women welcome.*

Bi People of Color Gatherings C▼
c/o Bisexual Resource Center
29 Stanhope Street
Boston MA 02116
tel: 617-424-9595 (leave message)
617-277-2017
Maria Christina Blanco
e-mail: brctina@shore.net
Maria Christina Blanco
Dinner & Discussion. "A chance to connect & celebrate who we are." 4th Sun. 7-9pm at the Boston Living Center (address above). All genders, diverse ethnicities welcome.

Coming Out as Bisexual ▼🖥
c/o BRC
29 Stanhope Street
Boston MA 02116
tel: BRC Office 617-424-9595
e-mail: info@biresource.org
URL: www.biresource.org
Sponsored by the Bisexual Resource Center. Informal support group for people who think they may be bisexual &/or who are attracted to more than one gender. 1st Wednesday &3rd Tuesday of every month, 7-9pm.

Married Bisexual Women's Support Group ▼ ♀ M
c/o Bisexual Resource Center
29 Stanhope St.
Boston area MA 02116
tel: Debbie Block-Schwenk 617-424-9595
e-mail: starfurry@worldnet.att.net
Open to all bisexual women in long term committed relationships. Meets 2nd Thursday of each month, 7-9:00PM at the Bisexual Resource Center.

Bisexual Women's Rap ♀ E▼
c/o The Women's Center
46 Pleasant Street
Cambridge MA 02139
tel: Women's Center: 617-354-8807
AlternateTuesdays 7:30-9pm, open to all women. Free, open discussion on previously chosen topics.

You Are Not Alone: Straight Spouse Support ♥ E
MA
tel: 781-326-1461
For those who have been or are married to or are living with a homosexual or bisexual partner.. Meets 4th Mondays at Newton-Wellesley Hospital, except on holidays (then meets 3rd Monday). Check phone message for changes.

BAGLY: Boston Alliance of Gay, Lesbian, Y E🖥
Bisexual, Transgendered, & Questioning Youth
PO Box 814
Boston MA 02103
tel: 1-800-42-BAGLY or 617-227-4313; or TTY: 617-983-9845
e-mail: bagly@bagly.org
URL: www.bagly.org/bagly
Youth-run adult-supported social support group for people 22 & under. Weekly meetings Wednesdays 6-9pm at 35 Bowdoin St. in Beacon Hill, Boston & on Sunday afternoons 2-5. Also offers peer-counseling program, speaker's burear, referrals to resources & organizations, & sponsors events & activities for youth. BAGLY is also the primary contact for the GLBT Youth Group Network of Mass.

Boston Area Naturist Group ♂ 🖥
PO Box 180036
Boston MA 02118-0001
tel: 1-800-257-0358
e-mail: bangma@aol.com
URL: members.aol.com/bangma/bangma.htm
Social club for gay & bi men. Non-sexual. Includes all of New England. Call for info & events schedule.

Boston GLASS- Y♂E
Gay & Lesbian Social Services
93 Massachusetts Ave, 3rd fl
Boston MA 02115
tel: 617-226-3349; fax: 617-247-9860
e-mail: GLASS@jri.org
Community Center for LGBT youth, 13 - 25. Formalized programs, discussions, support & social groups. Safe place to meet, talk & hang out. No hassles, no pressures, just a great group of people who understand. Call Patrick Truman at # above for more info.

Boston Prime Timers, Inc. ♂ 🖥
P.O. Box 180010
Boston MA 02118-0001
tel: 617-338-5305
URL: home.earthlink.net/~chuck200/bostonpt.html
For mature gay & bisexual men & their admirers.

Key to symbols: ▼ = bi ♀ = women ♂ = men ☯ = religious/spiritual
🌢 = for allies **M** = for married bis ♥ = for partners of bis Y = youth C = people of color

Alison Bechdel

Boston University Medical Center: 🔍💻
Lesbian, Gay Bisexual People in Medicine
587 Beacon St. #4
Boston MA 02155
e-mail: sycamore@bu.edu
URL: med-www.bu.edu/people/sycamore/lgb/
lgbpm.htm
*Queer group run by medical, public health &
grad students at BU. All are welcome to our
sporadic events.*

Boston University: Spectrum 🔍**E**
Office #6, Student Center,
George Sherman Union
775 Commonwealth Avenue
Boston MA 02215
tel: 617-353-9808
e-mail: lgba@bu.edu
*Phone answered Tues-Thurs & Sun 7-9pm
during termtime. Meetings Mon. 7:30pm in GSU
Alley (basement of 775 Comm. Av.). Films, guest
speakers, etc.*

Dignity/Boston 🌀💻
P.O. Box 408
Boston MA 02117
tel: 617-421-1915
URL: www.dignityboston.org
*For LGBT Catholics. Mass every Sunday at
5:30pm at Church of St. John the Evangelist,
Beacon Hill. Call for info.*

Gaylaxian Science Fiction Society 💻
PO Box 1059
Boston MA 02103
tel: Lynne: 617-253-0133
e-mail: llevine@mit.edu
URL: www.gaylaxians.org
*Bi-friendly club. Meets monthly in members'
homes for potlucks & various activities including
video watching, discussions of books & sharing
creativity.*

Harvard Medical School: Kinsey 2-to-6ers 🔍
25 Shattuck Street
Boston MA 02115
LGB for Harvard Medical School affiliates.

Harvard School of Public Health: Lesbian, 🔍
Gay & Bisexual Alliance
677 Huntington Ave.
Boston MA 02215

Lambda Association of Boston College 🔍
Graduates
Boston MA
tel: 978-777-1710

Lesbian, Gay & Bisexual 💻
Freedom Trail Band of Boston
PO Box 576
Boston MA 02110
tel: Diane 617-926-9730 Roger 508-370-3130
e-mail: frdmtrlbd@aol.com
URL: www.rdrop.com/~lgba/boston/
*Provides music for special events within Lesbian
& Gay community. Entertainment or back-
ground music for potlucks, meetings, celebra-
tions or parties! Perform all year, all over New
England & need twirlers, banner carriers, band-
aides & instruments in all sections. No auditions
required. Call for booking & information.*

🔍 = school   🔍 = college/university   **P** = professional   **E** = educational
A = activist/political   **H** = health (incl. HIV)   📰 = media/press   💻 = Internet resource
The Bisexual Resource Guide 2000   **227**

PO Box 400639
Cambridge, MA 02140

617-424-9595
email: biwomen@biresource.org
http://www.biresource.org/bbwn

Boston

Bisexual

Women's

Network

THE BOSTON BISEXUAL WOMEN'S NETWORK IS A FEMINIST, NOT-FOR-PROFIT COLLECTIVE WHOSE PURPOSE IS TO BRING WOMEN TOGETHER FOR SUPPORT AND VALIDATION. SINCE 1983, BBWN HAS SOUGHT TO PROVIDE A SAFE ENVIRONMENT IN WHICH WOMEN OF ALL SEXUAL SELF-IDENTITIES, CLASS BACKGROUNDS, RACIAL, ETHNIC, AND RELIGIOUS GROUPS, AGES, ABILITIES AND DISABILITIES ARE WELCOME. THE NETWORK IS OPEN TO ALL SELF-IDENTIFIED WOMEN.

BiWomen

"BiWomen", THE NEWSLETTER OF THE BOSTON BISEXUAL WOMEN'S NETWORK, HELPS TO CONNECT BI-FOLK FROM AROUND THE U.S. AND INTERNATIONALLY BY PUBLISHING NEWS, VIEWS, POETRY, ART, FILM AND BOOK REVIEWS, AND LOTS MORE OF INTEREST TO BIS AND OUR FRIENDS. ALL WOMEN ARE INVITED TO SUBMIT ARTICLES FOR PUBLICATION. PEOPLE OF ALL GENDERS WILL ENJOY READING "BiWomen" AND ARE WELCOME TO SEND $25 (MORE IF YOU CAN, LESS IF YOU CAN'T) FOR A ONE YEAR SUBSCRIPTION. CHECKS OR MONEY ORDERS PAYABLE TO BBWN MAY BE SENT TO THE ABOVE ADDRESS.

BBWN ALSO ORGANIZES MONTHLY BRUNCHES AND OTHER SOCIAL EVENTS TO BRING BISEXUAL AND BI-FRIENDLY WOMEN TOGETHER IN THE BOSTON AREA. FOR A FULL LISTING OF EVENTS, CALL, WRITE, SEND US EMAIL, OR CHECK OUT OUR WEBSITE.

BI BUTTONS
FROM BBWN

ONLY $1.50 EACH

TO ORDER, SEND A CHECK OR MONEY ORDER PAYABLE TO BBWN WITH A LIST OF YOUR CHOICES TO THE ADDRESS ABOVE. OR, VISIT THE WEBSITE LISTED BELOW FOR A FULL COLOR LOOK AT ALL THE BUTTONS AND TO ORDER ON-LINE.

www.biresource.org/biproducts

OTHER AVAILABLE BUTTONS:
▼ TWO ROADS DIVERGED IN A YELLOW WOOD . . . AND I TOOK BOTH
▼ IF GOD HAD MEANT PEOPLE TO BE BISEXUAL, THERE WOULD BE TWO SEXES
▼ PLEASE DON'T TELL ANYONE I'M BISEXUAL — I'M TRYING TO BE DISCREET

LUNA: Grupo de Latinas Lesbianas y ♀ **CE**
Bisexuales
c/o Fenway Community Health Center
7 Haviland St.
Boston MA 02115
tel: 617-927-6300
Support group for lesbian & bisexual Latinas.

Massachusetts General Hospital GLBA **PE**
32 Fruit Street - GRBB 030A
Boston MA 02114-2698
tel: 617-726-5687
*Place for glb employees to socialize with each
other; to address work-related issues such as
discrimination, homo- & biphobia, & ignorance;
to educate the hospital community at large to
better serve us; to insure equality in benefits.*

Network for Battered Lesbians ♀ **EA** 🖳
& Bisexual Women
PO Box 6011
Boston MA 02114
tel: 617-695-0877 Hotline:423-SAFE; fax: 617-695-
0877
e-mail: nblbw@erols.com
URL: www.erools.com/nblbw
*Bilingual TTY accessible hotline, free wheelchair
accessible support group, legal & other referrals,
newsletter, community education. Added
Bisexual to their name in 1996.*

Northeastern University: Bisexual, 🖉
Lesbian & Gay Association (NUBiLAGA)
360 Huntington Av., Room 240
Curry Student Center
Boston MA 02115
tel: 617-373-2738
*Meets at 348 Curry Student Center, Northeast-
ern Campus, Boston, Thurs. 6-8 pm during
termtime. Call FMI.*

Northeastern University School of Law: **P** 🖉
Lesbian, Gay & Bisexual Association
Northeastern University
59 Cargill Hall
360 Huntington Ave.
Boston MA 02115
tel: 617-373-2738 (NuBiLAGA)

"It's better to be hated for
what one is than to be loved for
what one isn't."

—*André Gide, French Novelist, 1869-1951.*

Queer Asian Pacific Alliance **C** 🖳
PO Box 543
Prudential Station
Boston MA 02119
tel: 617-499-9531
e-mail: qapa@geocities.com
qapa@ccae.org
URL: www.geocities.com/WestHollywood/heights/
5010
*An organization for lgbt & questioning women &
men of both Asian & Pacific Islander heritages.
Social gatherings first Sundays. To subscribe to
the QAPA email list, send the following message
to majordomo@ccae.org: subscribe qapa-news
<your email address> subscribe qapa<your
email address>To get in touch leave a mssg on
QAPA's voice mail.*

Queercorps **Y** ♂ **AH**
c/Derek Cash
AIDS Action Committee
131 Clarendon St.
Boston MA 02116
tel: 617-450-1MSM
e-mail: queercorps@aac.org
*Queercorps is a community mobilization project
by & for young queer men 25 & under. It
provides a space for young men to talk about the
issues facing them, such as dating, relationships,
& sex; & offers a place to explore HIV prevention
concerns in the context of their lives.*

SASSIE (Sisters Acquiring Safer Sex ♀ **CE**
Information & Education)
c/o Fenway Community Health Center
7 Haviland St.
Boston MA 02115
tel: 617-927-6300
Shananette Patrice
e-mail: spatrice@echo.org
A program for HIV & STD prevention education.

Simmons College: 🖉 **EA** ♀
Lesbian, Bisexual & Allies Association
300 The Fenway
Boston MA 02115
tel: 617-521-2446
e-mail: LBA2@artemis.simmons.edu

SpeakOut: GLBT Speakers Bureau **E** 🖳
P.O. Box 1358
Boston MA 02177
e-mail: glbsbout@aol.com
URL: www.glbsb.org
*Members speak to groups about LGB issues &
personal experiences.* **Publication(s):** *The
Speaker (monthly newsletter) editor: Gilly
Rosenthol, tel: 617/666-2681
send 200-500 word submissions to
gilly@apocalypse.org or Gilly Rosenthol, 36
Francesca Ave., Sommerville MA 02144*

🖎 = school 🖉 = college/university **P** = professional **E** = educational
A = activist/political **H** = health (incl. HIV) 🖎 = media/press 🖳 = Internet resource
The Bisexual Resource Guide 2000 **229**

The Art Institute of Boston: The Alliance   🔗
700 Beacon St.
Boston MA 02215
tel: 617-262-1223
LGB group for students, faculty & staff.

Cape Lesbian, Gay, Bisexual Coalition   **A E**
PO Box 148
Brewster MA 02631
tel: 508-430-9939 (hotline)
    Publication(s): *Directory of gay & gay-friendly businesses & services on Cape Cod call for free copy*

Bridgewater State College: Bisexual,   🔗
Lesbian & Gay Alliance
BSC Campus Center
131 Summer St.
Bridgewater MA 02325
tel: 508-697-1200 x2032

Am Tikva   ☻ E
PO Box 11
Cambridge MA 02238
tel: 617-926-2536
e-mail: amtikva@world.std.com
Boston's congregation of LGBT Jews, offering Sabbath & Holiday services, educational/ discussion groups & social events. Sabbath services on 1st & 3rd Friday of each month at 8pm at the Hebrew School auditorium of Temple Sanai, 50 Sewall Av., Brookline.

ASIA: Asian Sisters in Action   ♀ **CA**
PO Box 380331
Cambridge MA 02238
tel: Priscilla: 617-776-9212
e-mail: jeannie@concord.org
Lesbians, bisexuals & heterosexuals welcome.

Cambridge Lavender Alliance   **A**
PO Box 380884
Cambridge MA 02238
tel: 617-492-6393 Sue Hyde
e-mail: shyde@hgltf.org
A social & political activist organization that focuses on impoving the quality of life for LGBT people in Cambridge.

Harvard University: Association of Lesbian,   🔗
Bisexual & Gay Graduate Students (LBGGS)
Dudley House, Harvard Yard,
Cambridge MA 02138
e-mail: latil@fas.harvard.edu
Social Mixers 8-10pm 1st Thurs. in Graduate Student Lounge of Dudley House, open to anyone. To subscribe send message with name & e-mail address to lbg-request@katla.harvard.edu.

Harvard University: Cornerstone   ☻🔗 **E**
Harvard/Radcliffe Catholic Student Center
20 Arrow Street
Cambridge MA 02138
e-mail: jlandry@pobox.harvard.edu
Bi-monthly gathering to discuss sexual identity & spirituality in a comfortable, non-judgmental atmosphere for Catholic lgb Harvard/Radcliffe students only.

Lesley College: Association of Gays,   🔗 **A**
Lesbians & Bisexuals
29 Everett St.
Cambridge MA 02138-2790
tel: 617-349-8530 (Student Affairs)
For undergraduates.

Lutherans Concerned Metro Boston   ☻ **A** 🖳
c/o University Lutheran Church
66 Winthrop Street
Cambridge MA 02138
tel: 617-876-3256
e-mail: LCMetroBos@aol.com
URL: www.world.std.com/~unilu
Area chapter of Lutherans Concerned North America, a national organization advocating for l/g/b/t inclusion & ordination within the Evangelical Lutheran Church in America. This is a sanctuary organization, meaning identity, attendance, & mailing list information is kept confidential. Group meets once a month at University Lutheran Church. Webmaster is Kathryn Schnaible (schnaibl@fas.harvard.edu or Kls1214@aol.com.)

MIT: Gays, Lesbians, Bisexuals ,   🔗
Transgenders at MIT (GAMIT)
Room 50-306
142 Memorial Drive
Cambridge MA 02139
tel: 617-253-5440
e-mail: gamit@mit.edu
Primarily serving the MIT community, but open to everyone. Coming out group, organization meetings, & social events. Study break: room 50-306, 142 Memorial Drive, Thurs at 9 pm.

Project 10 East, Inc of Cambridge   **YEA** 🖳
Rindge & Latin High School
P.O. Box 382401
Cambridge MA 02238
tel: 617-864-4528; fax: 617-349-6897
e-mail: project10e@aol.com
URL: quniverse.com/p10E
Cambridge Rindge & Latin HS. Gay/straight alliance of students & staff providing education about LGBT community. Conducts peer information workshops & provides counseling & some additional support services for members afternoons & evenings at the Old Cambridge Baptist Church, 1145 Mass Ave.

Key to symbols: ▼ = bi   ♀ = women   ♂ = men   ☻ = religious/spiritual
🔔 = for allies   **M** = for married bis   ♥ = for partners of bis   **Y** = youth   **C** = people of color
230   **The Bisexual Resource Guide 2000**

CAMEN - Cape Ann Gay & Bi Men's ♂
Discussion Group
Cape Ann MA
tel: David Goudreau 978-281-0311

Boston College: Lesbian, Gay & Bisexual ⚭
Community
Box L-112
Chestnut Hill MA 02467
tel: 617-552-2979; fax: 617-555-0050
e-mail: murayda@bc.edu

Concord-Carlisle High School: Spectrum Y✎
500 Walden Steet
Concord MA 01742
tel: Peter Atlas: 978-371-4660
LBG & straight alliance. Call for schedule of programs & events.

New England Gay, Lesbian & Bisexual E🖳
Veterans, Inc.
263 Park Street
Dorchester MA 02124-1334
tel: Cliff: 617-387-2658; Rick: 978-249-5921
e-mail: cliff4vets@aol.com
URL: www.glbva.org
Offers resource referral, advocacy & networking for GLBT military veterans.

University of Massachusetts, Boston: ⚭
Lesbian, Gay & Bisexual Center
c/o Student Life, Harbor Campus
100 Morrissey Blvd.
Dorchester MA 02128-3393
tel: 617-287-7983

Lexington High School: Y✎A
Gay/Straight Alliance
Science Building
251 Waltham Street
Lexington MA 02173
tel: Michael Lerner:
781-861-2362
e-mail: mlerner@sch.ci.lexington.ma.us
Support & social action group for students.

DECPLUS PA🖳
c/o U.S. Manager of Diversity
111 Powdermill Road
Maynard MA 01754
e-mail: DECplus@aol.com
URL: www.ziplink.net/~glen/decplus
DECplus (Digital Equipment Corporation, People Like Us) is an organization for LBGT employess (present & past) of Digital Equipment Corporation, now COMPAQ Computer Corporation. DECplus is in a state of transition due to merger with Compaq & once complete, organization will have a new name to encompass Compaq.

Tufts University: Bisexual, Gay, ⚭
Transgendered, & Lesbian Graduate
Students
Medford MA 02155
tel: 617-727-3770
Provides social network for L/G/B/T Tufts grad students through planned social events.

Tufts University: Lesbian, Gay ⚭E
& Bisexual Resource Center
Carmichael Hall
Medford MA 02155
tel: 781-627-3770; Director: 617-627-5770; fax:
617-627-3574
e-mail: Director's email:
jbrown@emerald.tufts.edu
Provides various services & programming for LGB & straight communities on campus.

Tufts University: Tufts Transgendered, ⚭
Lesbian, Gay & Bisexual Collective
c/o Student Activities
Campus Center
Medford MA 02155
tel: 781-627-3770
Meetings Monday evenings 9-10:30pm. Call for meeting location.

Cape Islands Gay & Straight Y🖳
Youth Alliance (CIGYA)
P.O. Box 805Y
Monument Beach MA 02553-0805
tel: 508-564-4535 Ext. 2
e-mail: pride@capecod.net
URL: www.capecod.net/~fitzmau/gaypride.html
Meetings Wed. 7-8:30pm at 396 Main St. Hyannis, in town of Barnstable, above Puritan clothing. Also workshops, social activities & trips. Youth up to age 22.

University of Massachusetts, Dartmouth: ⚭A
Bisexual, Gay & Lesbian Alliance
PO Box 144, Campus Center
Old Westport Road
N. Dartmouth MA 02747
tel: 508-999-8163
Support for students on campus.

Alliance of Gays, Lesbians & Supporters YE
PO Box H-3031
3 South 6th St.
New Bedford MA 02741
tel: 508-991-8000
Sponsors 3 informal, drop-in chat groups, all meet at the community center on 3 South 6th St. For lgbt & questioning youth 17 & under: alternate Tuesdays 7-9pm. LGBT adults: Mondays from 7-9pm. Women's group: 2nd Tuesday of each month 9-10:30pm.

✎ = school   ⚭ = college/university   P = professional   E = educational
A = activist/political   H = health (incl. HIV)   ✐ = media/press   🖳 = Internet resource
The Bisexual Resource Guide 2000   **231**

Newton South High School Anti-Homophobia/Safe Schools Program ✎ Y
Newton Center MA
tel: 617-552-7547; 617-965-6982

Wheaton College: Lesbian Gay Bisexual Alliance ⚥
Norton MA 02766
tel: Call Student Govt. Assoc. for contact person:
508-286-3815

Salem State College: Gay, Lesbian & Bisexual Peer Action Group of the Salem Community ⚥
Salem MA 01970
tel: 508-741-6436

Cape Cod Community College : LGB Alliance at 4 C's ⚥ EA
#2240 Lyanough Rd.
W. Barnstable MA 02668
tel: John French: 508-362-2131 x4320; fax: 508-375-4018
Meetings on Tuesdays at 1 pm.

Brandeis University: Triskelion ⚥ 💻
c/o Student Center
PO Box 9110
Waltham MA 02254-9110
tel: 781-736-4761
e-mail: trisk@brandeis.edu
URL: www.undergrad.brandeis.edu/~trisk
Organization that holds coming out meetings, support meetings, & organizes social & political events within the Brandeis community.

Wellesley College: ⚥ ♀
Wellesley Alliance of Queers & Straights
Schneider Center, Student Organizations
Wellesley MA 02181
tel: 781-283-2672 (Student Activities)

Wellsley College Lesbians, Bisexuals, Transgendered & Friends ♀ ⚥
106 Central St.
Wellsley MA 02181
tel: Mekusa Rodis 781-283-4753

Michigan

Between the Lines ✎💻
20793 Farmington Rd., Suit 25
Farmington MI 48336
tel: 888-615-7003; fax: 248-615-7018
e-mail: pridepblis@aol.com
URL: www.betweenthelinesnew.com
Statewide LGBT newspaper.

Local

Unscouts: Bisexual Women Support & Social Group ▼ ♀
Ann Arbor MI
tel: Stephanie: w-734-432-4342 or h-734-913-8895.
e-mail: Susan: suhopdu@umich.edu
Informal support/social group for Bisexual & bi-friendly women 21 & over. Meets 1st Sundays 7pm, at Zingerman's Next Door (upstairs) & 3rd Mondays 7pm at Eastern Accents. New members always welcome.

Gay/Lesbian/Bisexual Veterans - Southeast Michigan P
MI
tel: 734-665-6363

Adrian College: Alliance of Bis, Gays, Lesbians & Supporters ⚥
110 S. Mannerle Madison St.
Adrian MI 49221
tel: 517-265-5161x4393

Albion College: Break the Silence ⚥
c/o CPO
Albion MI 49307
tel: 517-629-1469

Grand Valley State University: Out n' About ⚥
Kyle Buchanan
1 Campus Drive
Allendale MI 49401
tel: 616-895-2345
e-mail: out_n_about48@hotmail.com

Alma College: Pride LGB Students ⚥
Kalindi Trietley, Faculty Advisor
614 W. Superior
Alma MI 48801
tel: 248-463-7147 or 517-463-7225

Ann Arbor Gays, Lesbians & Bisexuals
c/o St. Andrews Episcopal church
306 Division
Ann Arbor MI 48104-1497
tel: 734-763-6733
Meets at above address.

Key to symbols: ▼ = bi ♀ = women ♂ = men ☽ = religious/spiritual
🌢 = for allies **M** = for married bis ♥ = for partners of bis **Y** = youth **C** = people of color
232 **The Bisexual Resource Guide 2000**

G/L/B Youth Support Group Y
in Ann Arbor
1705 Washtwnaw
Ann Arbor MI 48104
tel: 734-662-2265
Discuss, watch videos & participate
in recreational & educational
activities within a supportive
environment. For teens through 20.

Poly-Positive 🖳
Ann Arbor MI
tel: Stephanie: 734-913-8895
e-mail: Doug: bolero@ibm.net
URL: www.blackrose.org/~bolero/Poly-
pos.html
Social / support group for
polyamorous people of all orientations. Meets
last Sundays 3pm at Zingerman's Next Door in
Ann Arbor.

University of Michigan 🎓
Lesbian Gay & Bisexual Programs Office
3118 Michigan Union
Ann Arbor MI 48109-1349
tel: 313-763-4186
e-mail: lgbta@umich.edu

Bisexual Married Men's Group ▼🎓♂
Lesbian, Gay, Bisexual & Transgender Affairs
3200 Michigan Union
Ann Arbor MI 48109-1349
tel: 734-763-4186
Meets at university but open to all.

Lavender Information & 🎓**PA**🖳
Library Association
School of Information
304 West Hall
550 East University
Ann Arbor MI 48109
tel: 734-763-4186
e-mail: LILA@board.umich.edu
URL: www.si.umich.edu/LILA/
Active, professional organization for School of
Information students, University of Michigan
libraries & archives staff, & related profession-
als. LILA promotes awarenessof glbt issues
through educational, networking, social &
political activities.

Queer Unity Project 🎓🖳
3116 Michigan Union
530 S. State St.
Ann Arbor MI 48109
tel: 313-763-4186
e-mail: qup@umich.edu
URL: www.umich.edu/~inqueery/qup or www-
personal.umich.edu~mdushand/qup.html
"Fighting homophobia by increasing the
visibility & establishing the rights of LGB
people. "

University of Michigan, Dearborn 🎓🖳
216 ROC
4901 Evergreen Road
Dearborn MI 48128
tel: 313-436-9192
e-mail: umd.lambda@umich.edu
URL: oge.umd.umich.edu/la

Wayne State University: 🎓**E**🖳
Lesbian Gay Bisexual Services
5221 Gullen Mall
573 SCB
Detroit MI 48202
tel: 8313-577-3398; fax: 313-577-3257
URL: www.studentcouncil.wayne.edu/GLBU/
main.html
Student organization. Office in Student Center
Bldg. 756.2. Counseling programs, support
groups, educational presentations, info &
referrals.

Michigan State University: Alliance of 🎓🖳
Lesbian, Bi Gay & Transgendered Students
441 Student Union
East Lansing MI 48824-1020
tel: 517-353-9795; fax: 517-353-4717
e-mail: alliance@pilot.msu.edu
URL: pilot.msu.edu/user/alliance/
Call for weekly support group schedule. Open to
community members & MSU students, faculty &
staff.

> "I don't think there is such a
> thing as a precise sexual
> orientation. I think we're all
> ambiguous sexually."
>
> —*Tennessee Williams, American playwright,*
> *1912-1983*

✎ = school   🎓 = college/university   **P** = professional   **E** = educational
A = activist/political   **H** = health (incl. HIV)   📰 = media/press   🖳 = Internet resource

Michigan State University: Alliance of ✍
Lesbian, Bisexual & Gay Concerns
Brent Bilodeau, Assistant for LGB Concerns
101 Student Services
East Lansing MI 48823
tel: 517-355-8286
e-mail: bilodeau@pilot.msu.edu
Publication(s): Q News MSU's newsletter for
Lesbian, lgbt students.

Affirmations L&G Community Center ▼
Ferndale MI
tel: 800-398-GAYS
e-mail: affirmationsglbt@juno.com
Has "bi & bi-friendly group" that meets 2nd
Wednesdays 7-8:30pm

University of Michigan at Flint: Lesbian, ✍
Gay, Bisexual & Transgender Center
365 UCEN
Flint MI 48502-2186
tel: 810-766-6606
e-mail: lgb@ctr@ucen.flint.umich.edu

Michigan Technological University: ✍🖥
Copper Country Gay, Lesbian, Bisexual &
Transgender Alliance
PO Box 501
Houghton MI 49224
tel: 906-487-3441
e-mail: ccglba@mtu.edu
URL: www.sos.mtu.edu/ccglba

Western Michigan University: ✍🖥
Office for Lesbian, Bisexual, & Gay Issues
A327 Ellsworth Hall
Kalamazoo MI 49008-5074
tel: 616-387-2123
e-mail: OSL_LBG@wmich.edu;
stlf_lbgoffc@wmich.edu
URL: studentworld.wmich.edu/osl/lbg.html

Northern Michigan University: Gay/Lesbian/ ✍
Bisexual Student Union
Box 4, University Center
Marquette MI 49855
tel: 906-277-2409
e-mail: glbsu@nmu.edu

Central Michigan University: ✍ E
Office of Gay & Lesbian Programs
215-B Warriner Hall
Mt. Pleasant MI 48859
tel: 517-774-3637; fax: 517-772-2022
e-mail: michael.l.stemmeler@cmich.edu

Central Michigan University: Prism ✍ E
129 Sloan Hall
Mt. Pleasant MI 48859
tel: 517-774-7470
e-mail: prism@cmich.edu
Social & support organization for GLBs &
friends.

Palland University: Pride Forum ✍🖥
49 Oakland Center
Rochester MI 48309
tel: 248-370-4122; fax: 248-370-4293
URL: www.oakland.edu/prideforum

A. Lorde Collective C
PO Box 1693
Royal Oak MI 48068
tel: 313-863-3396

Dignity Detroit ☯
PO Box 558
Royal Oak MI 48068
"An affirming, loving community of glbt
individuals, their friends & families who gather
to worship in the Catholic tradition."

Northwestern Michigan College: ✍
Triangles & Rainbows
Traverse City MI
tel: 616-922-1512
e-mail: tandrgroup@hotmail.com

Eastern Michigan University: Lesbian, Gay, ✍ P
Bisexual Faculty & Staff Advocacy Coalition
c/o Prof. Michael McGuire
PO Box 980438
Ypsilanti MI 48198-0438
tel: 313-487-0292

Eastern Michigan University: ✍🖥
Lesbian, Gay, Bisexual & Transgender
Support Services Office
c/o Campus Life
201-C Goodison
Ypsilanti MI 48197
tel: 734-487-4149
e-mail: heather.macallister@emich.edu
URL: www.emich.edu/public/vso/lgbt.html

Minnesota

Anti Violence Program & Domestic E
Violence Program
c/o OutFront Minnesota
310 E. 38th St., Suite 204
Minnneapolis MN 55409
tel: 612-822-0127x102
e-mail: outfront@outfront.org (attn: Tommie)
Info, training, advocacy & systems change,
including statewide organizing.

Key to symbols: ▼ = bi   ♀ = women   ♂ = men   ☯ = religious/spiritual
⚗ = for allies   **M** = for married bis   ♥ = for partners of bis   **Y** = youth   **C** = people of color
234   The Bisexual Resource Guide 2000

Lavendar Bar Association P
c/o OutFront Minnestoa
320 E. 38th St., Suite 204
Minneapolis MN 55409
tel: 612-82-1027x103
e-mail: outfront@outfront.org
Legal program of OutFront Minnesota. Legal referrals, info advocacy, etc. Association of legal attorneys & professonals who serve LGBT communities.

Naked Minnesota ♂ 🖳
PO Box 8614
Minneapolis Mn 55408-0614
e-mail: nakedmn@aol.com
URL: members.aol.com/nakedmn
Gay & bisexual nudists. **Publication(s)**: *Naked Minnesota News Monthly newsletter for members only.*

Local

The Bisexual Connection ▼
3534 Girard Avenue, N.
Minneapolis MN 55412-2418
tel: Martin Quam: 612-588-1711
Support & resources for bi, bi-supportive & bi-curious people. Support/discussion potluck 1st Sundays, & social events 3rd Friday. Dates vary if they coincide w/ national holidays. **Publication(s)**: *Bi-Focal (newsletter) Semi-monthly.*

Northland Gay Men's Center ♂
8 North Second Avenue E. #309
Duluth MN 55802
tel: 218-722-8585
Non-profit organization providing services to gay/bi men of the upper Midwest. Open 5-8pm M-F, 9-6 Sat.

Alliance For Justice 🖳
PO Box 124
Mankato MN 56002-0124
tel: 24 Hr. Crisis line: 1-888-989-5223
URL: members.tripod.com/~dawn_1/afj
Serving GLBT victims of crime. **Publication(s)**: *Alliance for Justice Newlsetter A quarterly.*

Mankato State University: Lesbian, Gay, 🎓E
Bisexual Center
MSU 107
PO Box 8400
Mankato MN 56002
tel: 507-389-5131; fax: 507-389-5799
e-mail: lgbu@mankato.msus.edu

Augsburg College: Bisexual, Gay 🎓🖳
& Lesbian Services (BAGELS)
2211 Riverside Avenue
Minneapolis MN 55454
tel: Doug Green, Faculty Adviser: 612-330-1187
e-mail: green@augsburg.edu
URL: www.augsburg.edu/bagels
Student group dedicated to making Augsburg a safe place for GLBT students. Also has a women's group called AWARE.

Brethren/Mennonite Council for ◐🖳
Lesbian & Gay Concerns
PO Box 6300
Minneapolis MN 55406-0300
tel: Jim Sauer: 612-722-6906
e-mail: bmcouncil@aol.com
URL: www.webcom.com/bmc/
Provides support for Brethren & Mennonite glb people & their parents, spouses, relatives & friends. Fosters dialogue between gay/non-gay people in the churches, & provides accurate info about homosexualtiy from the social sciences, biblical studies & theology. The Supportive Congregations Netwropk, a program of BMC, encourages congregations to publicly declare their welcome to lgb people.

Chrysalis: A Center for Women ♀▼🖳
2650 Nicollet Avenue S.
Minneapolis MN 55408
tel: 612-871-0118, TTY 612-871-3652; fax: 612-870-2403
e-mail: info@chrisaliswomen.org
URL: www.chrysaliswomen.org
Women's resource center. Individual & group therapy; legal & mental health resources; various support groups for women & their families, including a coming out support group for lesbian & bi women; an ongoing bisexual support group; & an ongoing lesbian support group.

District 202: A Center for Gay/Lesbian/ YE🖳
Bisexual/Transgender Youth
1601 Nicollet Avenue
Minneapolis MN 55403
tel: 612-871-5559
URL: www.dist202.org
Non-profit youth center. M,W,Th 3-11pm, Fri 3pm-1am, Sat noon-1am; Sun. noon-11pm. Dances, meetings, & weekly movie nights.

🖋 = school   🎓 = college/university   P = professional   E = educational
A = activist/political   H = health (incl. HIV)   📰 = media/press   🖳 = Internet resource
The Bisexual Resource Guide 2000   **235**

H.I.M. Program ♂ H
525 Portland Avenue
Minneapolis MN 55415
tel: 612-348-6641
e-mail: charles.tamble@co.hennepin.mn.us
Safer sex program for men who have sex with men. HIV testing. Sponsors Married Men's Lunch for men age 18 & up, 2nd Friday of the month at a confidential location.

Keshet ☕
3500 Holmes Avenue S.
Minneapolis MN 55408
tel: 612-824-4226
e-mail: ksehetgvah@aol.com
Social & religious organization for Jewish LGBT people.

OutFront Minnesota
310 E. 38th St. #204
Minneapolis MN 55409
tel: 612-822-0127 (24 hr. infoline)
e-mail: outfront@outfront.org
Office open M-F 9-12. "The ultimate resource center. Providing & encouraging programs & services which empower individuals to accept & celebrate their sexual & gender identities & to become proud & active members of the LGBT & the broader community.

Pride Institute Downtown H 🖳
2445 Park Avenue
Minneapolis MN 55404
tel: 1-800-54-PRIDE, 612-874-0833
e-mail: info@pride-institute.com
URL: www.pride-institute.com
Evening outpatient alcohol & drug treatment program.

Project Offstreets Y
212 N. 2nd Street
Minneapolis MN 55401
tel: 612-338-3103; fax: 612-338-7588
Safe space for GLBT street youth. Drop-in time 3-8pm daily; group meeting Tuesday 6 pm.

So What If I Am? Y E
The Bridge
2204 Emerson Avenue S.
Minneapolis MN 55405
tel: 612-377-8800
Support & discussion group for youth ages 10-17 who are questioning their sexual identity. Meets Wednesdays 6:30-8:30pm.

South High School Y ☙
Gay/Lesbian/Bi Support Group
3131 19th Avenue S.
Minneapolis MN 55407
tel: 612-627-2510, ask for school nurse
Only for students of South High.

Speaker's Bureau E
c/o OutFront Minnesota
310 E. 38th St., Suite 204
Minneapolis MN 55409
tel: 612-822-0127x104
e-mail: outfront@outfront.org
Speakers bureau, lobbyists, etc. Run by volunteers. Serves schools, etc. Call for a speaker on any subject.

The Bridge Y
2200 Emerson Avenue S.
Minneapolis MN 55405
tel: 612-377-8800
Resource center for GLBT youth & parents. Support groups, family counseling, social groups.

Twin Cities Men's Center M ▼ 🖳
3249 Hennepin Avenue S., #55
Minneapolis MN 55408
tel: 612-822-5892
e-mail: tcmc@freenet.msp.mn.us
URL: www.tcmc.org
Gay issues support groups; Lots of bi groups, including Friday night supper group for men only; Bisexual Husband & Father's Support Group (meets last Sundays 10am-12:30pm); Bi Night social for men & women (meets 3rd Sat. 7-9pm).

Twin Cities NOW Lesbian Rights Committee ♀ A
1929 South Fifth Street
Minneapolis MN 55454
tel: 612-338-7472
Action-oriented group working on LGBT human rights issues. Many chapters in Minnesota.

University of Minnesota, Twin Cities: ☙ E 🖳
Queer Student Cultural Center
230-A Coffman Union
300 Washington Avenue SE
Minneapolis MN 55455-0396
tel: 612-626-2344; fax: 612-625-9161
e-mail: qscc@tc.umn.edu
URL: www.tc.umn.edu/nlhome/g011/aglbt
An umbrella organization that houses a number of different GLBT groups such as the University Gay Community, University Bisexual & Transgender Community; the Queer Graduate & Professional Association, Straight Friends & Allies of QSCC, Queer Women, & the fraternity Delta Lambda Phi, ALPHA: Allied Lavender Public Health Association. Serving university students at the University of Minnesota Twin Cities.

Moorhead State University: 𝒢↗🖳
Tri-College Ten Percent Society
PO Box 266
Moorhead MN 56563
tel: Larry Peterson: 701-231-8824, Warren Wiese: 218-236-2200
e-mail: lpeterso@plains.nodak.edu or weise@mhd5.moorhead.msus.edu
URL: www.acm.ndsu.nodak.edu/Ten_Percent/
Moorhead State University, Concordia College & North Dakota State University.

University of Minnesota, Morris: Equality   𝒢↗
Group
PO Box 439
Morris MN 56267
tel: Student affairs: 320-589-6080
Advisors: Paul O'Loughlin 320-589-6205, oloughpl@mrs.umn.edu; Peh Ng 302-589-6318, pehng@mrs.umn.edu.

Carleton College: Lesbian, Gay & Bisexual 𝒢↗
Community
1 N. College Street
Northfield MN 55057
tel: 507-646-4000 (Student Affairs)
Weekly meetings. Occasional social events & dances. Contact Carolyn Fure-Slocum, Chaplain: cfureslo@acs.carleton.edu or 507-646-4003.

St. Olaf College: GLOW   𝒢↗🖳
(Gay, Lesbian or Whatever)
1500 St. Olaf Avenue
Northfield MN 55057-1001
tel: 507-646-3923
e-mail: olga@stolaf.edu
URL: www.stolaf.edu/stulife/org/glow
Also alumni group: "AfterGLOW."

St. Cloud State University: Pink Triangle 𝒢↗
Resource Center
Colbert House North
720 Fourth Avenue S.
St. Cloud MN 56301
tel: 320-654-5166

Central High School Gay/Lesbian/Bi/   YA✎
Transgender Support Group
c/o Anne Melaas, Counselor, M.S.
275 N. Lexington Avenue
St. Paul MN 55104
tel: 612-293-8706; fax: 612-293-5433
e-mail: amelaas@mail.central.stpaul.k12.mn.us
Meets weekly during school year. School also has a gay/straight alliance (Megan Vinz, adviser).

Hamline University: Queers & Peers   𝒢↗🖳
Box #1615
1536 E. Hewitt Ave.
St. Paul MN 55104-1284
tel: 612-641-2395
e-mail: gaylesb@piper.hamline.edu
URL: www.hamline.edu/~gaylesb/index.html
Meets Thurs. Manor Hall Basement, Rm 6, "the door with the rainbow colors!" Everyone welcome, regardless of orientation.

Macalester College: Queer Union   𝒢↗
1600 Grand Avenue
St. Paul MN 55105
tel: 612-696-7613; fax: 612-696-6689
Meetings: Sun at 9pm.

Quatrefoil Library   E
1619 Dayton Street
St. Paul MN 55104
tel: 612-641-0969
Library for LGBT people in the Twin Cities. Books, videos, tapes, games, periodicals & archives. M-Th 7-9:30pm; Sat. & Sun. call ahead.

St. Paul Schools Out For Equity Program   Y E
1930 Como Avenue
St. Paul MN 55108
tel: 612-603-4942
e-mail: mtinucci@mail.stpaul.k12.mn.us
Creating supportive school environments for GLBT students, staff & families within St. Paul Public Schools.

Wingspan Ministry   ☯E🖳
St. Paul-Reformation Lutheran Church
100 N. Oxford Street
St. Paul MN 55104
tel: 612-224-3371; fax: 612-224-6228
e-mail: wingspan@aol.com
URL: www.cycerworld.com/spr/wingspan/.htm
LGBT ministry. Worship: Sunday 10:30am. Adult education: Sunday, 9:15am (9:30 in summertime). **Publication(s):** *Soaring With Wingspan A quarterly.*

Woman's Support Group   ♀▼
550 Rice Street
St. Paul MN 55105
tel: 612-871-0118; fax: 612-871-3652
Various support groups for women & their families, including a coming out support group for lesbian & bi women & an ongoing bi support group.

✎ = school   𝒢↗ = college/university   P = professional   E = educational
A = activist/political   H = health (incl. HIV)   ✍ = media/press   🖳 = Internet resource
The Bisexual Resource Guide 2000   237

Mississippi

Camp Sister Spirit   ♀
444 Eastside Drive
Ovette MS 39464
tel: 601-344-1411; fax: 601-344-1411
e-mail: sisterspir@aol.com
Holds some women-only festivals throughout the year. Facilities include: bunkhouses, camp site, cabins, fully equipped shower-house & kitchen, donated library of over 1,500 titles.

Local

University of Southern Mississippi: Gay/   ⚲E💻
Lesbian/Bisexual Student Organization
Box 8741
Hattiesburg MS 39406-9100
e-mail: glbso@usm.edu
URL: www-org.usm.edu/~glbso/
Promotes gay visibility on campus & in community; to educate & end prejudice, discrimination, & homophobia. Meetings: 2nd & 4th Thursdays 7:30pm in Union. Check newsgroup usm.gay.discussion for changes in meeting location.

Safe Harbor Family Church   👁
2147 Henry Hill Drive
Suite 203
Jackson MS 39204-2000
tel: 601-961-9500
Sunday School at 5pm Sun; church service at 6pm Sun. Non-denominational.

Mississippi State University: GLBF, Gays, ⚲E💻
Lesbians, Bisexuals & Friends of MSU
P.O. Box 6220
Mississippi State MS 39762-6220
e-mail: glbf@ra.msstate.edu
URL: www.msstate.edu/org/glbf/
Confidential organization of members from the University & surrounding community. Participates in the Speakers Bureau to educate the general public.

University of Mississippi: ⚲E💻
GLBA, Gay Lesbian & Bisexual Association
University MS 38677
e-mail: glba@olemiss.edu
URL: www.olemiss.edu/orgs/glba/
Primary goal is peer education, to reach as many people as possible with the ideas of tolerance & acceptance.

Missouri

Bisexuals of   ▼CEAM♥
Greater Kansas City (BiG KC)
2 E. 39th St.
Kansas City MO 64111
tel: 816-753-5144 ext. 270; fax: 816-753-0804
BiG KC is a group for information, emotional support & various social functions. Primarily supports bisexuals, but all sexual orientations are welcome. Meetings held 1st & 3rd Tues. 7 pm.

University of Missouri: Triangle Coalition E⚲💻
A022 Brody Commons
Columbia MO 65211
tel: 573-882-4427
e-mail: triangle@showme.missouri.edu.
URL: www.missouri.edu/~triangle

Kaleidoscope
PO Box 411174
Kansas City MO 64141

Men of All Colors Together/Kansas City   ♂💻
Box 412432
Kansas City MO 64141
tel: 816-531-5579
e-mail: kc4mact@aol.com
URL: members.aol.com/KC4MACT

Southwest Missouri State University: Bisexual,⚲
Gay & Lesbian Alliance
901 S. National Avenue
Springfield MO 65804
tel: Advisor: Holly Baggett: 417-837-5206
e-mail: hab845F@upgate.smsu.edu

Pride St. Louis: Annual Celebration of   A
Lesbian, Gay, Bisexual & Transgendered
Pride
PO Box 282C
St. Louis MO 63118
tel: 314-772-8888

Privacy Rights Education Project   A💻
PO Box 24106
St. Louis MO 63130
tel: 314-862-4900; fax: 314-862-8155
e-mail: prepstl@prepstl.org
URL: www.prepstl.org

Montana

Lambda Alliance
MT
tel: 406-243-5922
Call M-F 10-4.

Key to symbols: ▼ = bi   ♀ = women   ♂ = men   👁 = religious/spiritual
👆 = for allies   **M** = for married bis   ♥ = for partners of bis   **Y** = youth   **C** = people of color
238   The Bisexual Resource Guide 2000

PRIDE!
PO Box 775
Helena MT 59624
tel: 406-442-9322
Community center. Information & referrals.

Local

Pridenet   🖳
MT
URL: www.pridenet.com/mt.html
Mailing list, listings for bars, restaurants,
bookstores, accomodations & local groups &
resources.

Montana State University: QMSU   🖉🖳
PO Box 51
Strand Union Building
Bozeman MT 59717
tel: 406-994-4551
e-mail: wwwlambd@gemini.oscs.montana.edu
URL: www.montana.edu/~wwwlambd
Meets Tues 7pm RM145 of Strand Union
Building. Occasional films & guest speakers.

Outspoken   🖳
PO Box 7105
Missoula MT 59807-7105
tel: 406-549-8746
e-mail: outspkn123@aol.com
URL: members.aol.com/outspkn123/index.htm
GLBT newspaper, whose purpose is "to give a
voice to the gay community of Missoula &
surrounding communities." Published 1st
working day each month.

Nebraska

Local

BiNet Omaha   ▼
9505 R Plaza, #106
Omaha NE 68127
tel: 402-592-4250
e-mail: quest15@juno.com

University of Nebraska, Lincoln: 🖉
GayLesBiTrans Resource Center
Rm. 234 Nebraska Union
14th & R Streets
Lincoln NE 68588-0455
tel: 402-472-5144

Nevada

BiNet Nevada   ▼A
c/o Gay & Lesbian Community Center
912 E. Sahara
Las Vegas NV 89104
tel: 702-733-9075

Local

Bi-sexuality Support Group   ▼
1006 E. Sahara
Las Vegas NV 89104
tel: 702-593-4345

Prime Timers Las Vegas   ♂🖳
Las Vegas NV
tel: 702-223-7429
e-mail: primetimer@hotmail.com
URL: www.teleport.com/~pti
Promoting social growth & friendship for
mature gay & bisexual men & their admirers.

University of Nevada, Reno: 🖉AE
Gay, Lesbian, Bisexual Student Union
Mail Stop/056
Reno NV 89557
tel: 702-327-5342 ext. 502 (voice mail)
e-mail: kendall@unr.edu
GLBSU supportas & promotes the understand-
ing of LGBT people, issues & culture through
social interaction, outreach, education,
community service. Membership open to anyone
including, but not limited to, University of
Nevada, Reno students, alumni, & members of
the community of any age.

New Hampshire

Portsmouth NH Bi Women's Resource & ▼♀
Support Group
c/o Portsmouth Women's Health Consortium
379 State St.
Portsmouth NH 03801
tel: 630-431-1669
e-mail: Sue Corcoran: schmoo@nh.ultranet.com
Meets 1st & 3rd Thursdays 7pm.

Concord Outright   Y
PO Box 3466
Concord NH 03302-3466
tel: 603-648-6628
Support group for GLBT youth & their friends
under 22. Meets every Thurs night, 7-9pm at
Unitarian Church, 274 Pleasant St., Concord,
NH.

🖉 = school   🖉 = college/university   P = professional   E = educational
A = activist/political   H = health (incl. HIV)   🖉 = media/press   🖳 = Internet resource
The Bisexual Resource Guide 2000   **239**

Gay & Bisexual Men's Health Project ♂ **EH**
87 Elm St
Manchester NH 03101
tel: 603-623-0710 or
800-639-1122; fax: 603-622-3288
e-mail: breannhaf@aol.com
*The Manchester, NH Gay & Bisexual Men's
Project is a program of the NH AIDS Foundation, offering a weekly support group, a biweekly
social group, quarterly Lifeguards Sexuality
workshops, a yearly retreat, peer HIV prevention
counseling, HIV testing, & outreach to bars &
public sex areas in the region.*

Monadnock Outright **Y**
Penny Culliton
2 Putnam Street
Wilton NH 03086
tel: 603-654-5474 (Chuck Bent)
603-547-2545 (Gordon Sherman)
e-mail: culliton@jlc.net
Gay/straight alliance for social support.

Mountain Valley Men ♂
PO Box 36
Center Conway NH 03814
tel: 207-925-1034-Dave or Paul
e-mail: dfispalp@aol.com
*GB men's social/support group, meets 1st Thurs
6:30pm for potluck dinner & program at the
Center of Hope in Redstone, NH. Monthly
Newsletter.*

Nashua Outright **Y**
443 Amherst Street
Suite 220
Nashua NH 03060
tel: 603-889-8210
e-mail: outrightNH@aol.com (e-mail will change
by 1999)
*For girls & boys 21 & under, all orientations &
genders.*

**NH Gay Info Line: Citizens Alliance for Gay &
Lesbian Rights, Breathing Space**
NH
tel: 603-224-1686
Information on local clubs & meetings.

"I don't care what people do, as
long as they don't do it in the
street and frighten the horses!"

*—Mrs. Patrick Campbell, English actress,
1865-1940.*

PFLAG NH **E**👤
PO Box 386
Manchester NH 03105
tel: 603-536-5522
800-750-2524 (in-state)
e-mail: necad@aol.com
*Concord- 3rd Sun of month 3-5pm at First
Congregational Church, Washington St. door
603-472-4944; No. Country- 3rd Mon at
Lancaster Congregational UUC 7-9 pm 586-
4346; Plymouth- 1st Sun at Plymouth
Congregationalist Church 7-9pm 786-4812;
Seacoast-1st Tues 7-9:30pm at Stratham
Community Church 778-3072, 772-5196, or 772-
3893.*

University of New Hampshire: ♂♂
Campus Gay/Lesbian/Bisexual Alliance
Room 7, Memorial Union Building
Durham NH 03824
tel: 603-862-4522
*Meets weekly in MVB, days & times vary by
semester. Call for info & list of upcoming events.*

Local

Technical Institute of Concord: ♂♂**A**
Campus Pride
c/Ann Marie Durant
PO Box 106
Concord NH 03302
tel: 603-226-1840
Call for meeting times & location.

Dover Gay/Lesbian/Bi/Transgender & 💻
Questioning Support Group
93A Washington St., Apt. 2
Attn: Jasper
Dover NH 03820
tel: Jasper: 603-742-4470; Helpline: 603-743-
GAY2
e-mail: peace@worldpath.net;
aboundwsounds@webtv.net
URL: www.geocities.com/WestHollywood/Village/
1425
*For glbt & questioning people. GLBT helpline for
information, referral, or need to talk. Mon. - Fri.
6-10pm, Sat. & Sun. 9am-2pm. Support group
with monthly activities. Weekly meetings
Sundays at 7pm, Quaker Meeting House,
Central Avenue.*

Dartmouth College: ♂♂
Coalition for Lesbian, Gay & Bisexual
Concerns
Hinman Box 5057
Hanover NH 03755
tel: 603-646-3636

Key to symbols: ▼ = bi ♀ = women ♂ = men 👤 = religious/spiritual
👤 = for allies **M** = for married bis ♥ = for partners of bis **Y** = youth **C** = people of color
240 **The Bisexual Resource Guide 2000**

Dartmouth Rainbow Alliance 　　🖳
e-mail: DRA@Dartmouth.edu
URL: www.dartmouth.edu/~dra
See Coalition for LGB Concerns above. Co-ed
planning meetings, & separate men's & women's
discussion groups.

Gay , Lesbian & Bisexual Programming 　🔗 E 🖳
6181 Collis Center, Room 211
Hanover NH 03755
tel: 603-646-3635; fax: 603-646-1386
e-mail: Margaret.A.Smith@Dartmouth.EDU
URL: www.dartmouth.edu/~peered
www.dartmouth.edu/~glbprog

Bisexual, Gay & Lesbian Alumni 　　　🔗
See Coalition for LGB Concerns above.

Keene State College: 　　🔗 EA 🖳
Keene State Pride
L.P. Young Student Center
Keene NH 03431
tel: 603-358-2639
e-mail: KSCpride@angelfire.com
URL: www.angelfire.com/nh/KscPride/index.html
Meets Thurs. 7pm in Huntress Basement Lounge
(accessible).

Manchester Outright 　　　　　　　Y
816 Elm St., PO Box 344
Mancheseter NH 03101
tel: 603-645-5274
e-mail: manchesteroutrte@hotmail.com
For 21 years old & under. Meets Tuesdays 7-9pm
at Unitarian Universalist Church, 699 Union
St., Manchester.

Manchester Gay & Bisexual Resources 　♂ E
Group
New Hampshire AIDS Foundation
PO Box 59
Manchester NH 03105
tel: Brian: 603-623-0710, or 1-800-639-1122; fax:
603-622-3288
e-mail: briannhaf@aol.com
Meets regularly. Open to, but not limited to,
HIV+ men.

Nashua Pride 　　　　　　　　　　M
427-3 Amherst Street
Suite 113
Nashua NH 03063
tel: Gill: 603-881-9522; fax: 603-881-9522
Meets 1st & 3rd Fridays at the Unitarian
Church in Nashua. 8pm-10pm.

Seacoast Outright: Unitarian Universalists for 👁 Y
L/G/B Concerns
P.O. Box 842
Portsmouth NH 03801-4007
tel: 603-431-1013
800-639-6095 teen crisis line
GLBT & Q youth ages 21 & under. Serves
Southern Maine & New Hampshire youth.
Support group Fri 7-9pm; drop-in center Tues 6-
8pm & Sun 5-7pm. UU Church, Annex, 206
Court St.

New Jersey

Bisexual Network of 　　　▼ ♀ ♂ M ♥ 🖳
New Jersey (BNNJ)
The Pride Center of NJ
211 Livingston Avenue
New Brunswick NJ 08903
tel: Pride Ctr 732-846-2232
e-mail: bnnj-info@plts.org
URL: www.qrd.org/QRD/www/usa/nj/BNNJ
A support & social group open to all bi, bi-
curious, & bi-friendly people & their partners.
Support group every Tuesday 7:30-9:30pm.
Couples support group first Sunday of the month
7:30-9pm. There is also an email list, mostly
announcements. To subscribe, send email to
bnnj-request.plts.org.

GALY-NJ (Gay & Lesbian Youth-NJ) 　　Y 🖳
PO Box 137
Convent Station NJ 07961-0137
tel: 973-285-1595 (helpline); 973-285-5590
(business); 973-285-0889 (TDD); fax: 973-539-8882
e-mail: gaamc@eics.njit.edu
URL: www.qrd.org/QRD/www/usa/nj/GAAMC
Youth group. Meets in South Orange & other
locations.

"The use of the phrase 'sexual orientation' to describe
only a person's having sex with members of their own gender or the other
sex obscures the fact that many of us have other strong and consistent
sexual orientations – toward certain hair colors, body shapes, racial types. It
would be as logical to look for genes associated with these orientations as
for 'homosexual genes.'"

—Ruth Hubbard *("False Genetic Markers," in* The New York Times," *8/2/93.)*

🐦 = school	🔗 = college/university	P = professional	E = educational
A = activist/political	H = health (incl. HIV)	📰 = media/press	🖳 = Internet resource

The Bisexual Resource Guide 2000 　　　　　　　　　　　**241**

Institute for Personal Growth (IPG)   **H**
Dr. Margaret Nichols, Director
8 S. 3rd Avenue
Highland Park NJ 08904
tel: 732-246-8439
New Jersey's largest counseling center serving the Gay, Lesbian,Bisexual & Transgendered community. Insurance accepted, 5 locations in NJ.

Jersey Pride, Inc.   **A🖳**
PO Box 10796
New Brunswick NJ 08906
tel: 732-21-GAY-NJ; 732-214-2965
e-mail: jrsypride@aol.com
URL: members.aol.com/jrsypride
Organizers for New Jersey's LGBT Pride Parade (in Ashbury Park) as well as hosts of the National Coming Out Day Cultural Heritage Festival & a quarterly magazine.

New Jersey Lesbian & Gay Coalition   **A**
PO Box 11335
New Brunswick NJ 08906-1335
tel: 732-828-6772
e-mail: njlgc@aol.com
New Jersey's POLITICAL coalition of LGBT, AIDS & supportive straight organizations.

NJ Alliance of the Deaf
Box 596
Rockaway NJ 07866
tel: 973-857-2555
TTD only or NJ Relay 800/852-7897.

NJ Education Association -   **P**
Lesbian, Gay, Bisexual Caucus
PO Box 314
Roosevelt NJ 08555
tel: 609-448-5215; fax: 609-448-9550
e-mail: carolwchlr@aol.com
Protects the rights & interests of glb association members & their supporters. A network of support & information on lgb issues in education.

Local

Rutgers University, Camden: **⚥**
Lambda Alliance
CMS #68, Rutgers
328 Penn Street
Camden NJ 08102
A support group for glb students at Rutgers.

Gays, Bisexuals & Lesbians (GABLES) of Cape May County
PO Box 641
Cape May NJ 08210-0641
tel: 609-861-1848

Gay Activist Alliance in Morris County   **EA🖳**
PO Box 137
Convent Station NJ 07961-0137
tel: 973-285-1595 (helpline)
973-285-5590 (business line)
973-285-0889 (TDD); fax: 201-539-8882
e-mail: gaamc@eies.njit.edu
URL: www.qrd.org.QRD/www/usa/nj/GAAMC
Meetings at The Morristown Unitarian Fellowship, 21 Normandy Heights Road, Morristown, NJ (near the Morris Museum). The largest gay & lesbian organization in the state. Meets every Monday at 8:45pm with support groups, speakers, dances, socials. Acceptance of bisexuals is improving. "Worth the trip."

Jersey City State College: Gay, Lesbian,   **⚥**
Bisexual & Friends Association
Student Union Bldg.
2039 Kennedy Blvd.
Jersey City NJ 07305

Drew University: Gay, Lesbian, Bisexual &   **⚥**
Straight Person's Alliance
c/o Student Center
Madison NJ 07940

Key to symbols: ▼ = bi   ♀ = women   ♂ = men   ☯ = religious/spiritual
♨ = for allies   **M** = for married bis   ♥ = for partners of bis   **Y** = youth   **C** = people of color
242   The Bisexual Resource Guide 2000

Ramapo College: Gay, Lesbian, Bisexual 🏫
Coalition
c/o Student Activities
505 Rampo Valley Road
Mahwah NJ 07430
tel: 201-825-2800 x547
e-mail: Advisor: mgolsch@ramapo.edu
*Provides support to GLB people. Meetings open
to off-campus community.*

Cumberland County Gay, Lesbian &
Bisexual Alliance (GLOBAL)
PO Box 541
Millville NJ 08332-0541
tel: 609-453-7522
*Positive, safe social & supportive environment
for everyone.*

Rutgers University BiGLARU: 🏫 🖳
Bi/Gay/Lesbian Alliance of Rutgers
University
Rutgers Student Center
SAC Box 91
New Brunswick NJ 08903
tel: 732-932-1306
e-mail: biglaru@mariner.rutgers.edu
URL: mariner.rutgers.edu/biglaru
Open to all.

Rutgers University: 🏫
Bisexual, Gay & Lesbian Outreach Hotline
SAC Box 146
613 George Street
New Brunswick NJ 08903
tel: 732-932-7886

Rutgers University: Gay, Lesbian & Bisexual 🏫
Alumni/ae
PO Box 160
New Brunswick NJ 08903
tel: 732-932-7886

The Pride Center of New Jersey 🖳
PO Box 11335
New Brunswick NJ 08906-1335
tel: 732-846-2232
e-mail: info@pridecenter.org
URL: www.pridecenter.org
*Center located at 211 Livingston Ave., New
Brunswick. A LGBT community center.
Sponsors various discussion/support meetings
for youth, older men, bisexuals, co-dependents,
lesbian mothers, gay men & women in straight
marriages, republicans, educators, families of
G/L/B people, & many other groups.*

Princeton University: 🏫 ▼ 🖳
Lesbian, Gay & Bisexual Alliance
306 Aaron Burr Hall
Princeton NJ 08544
tel: 609-258-4522
e-mail: lgba@princeton.edu
URL: www.princeton.edu/~lgba/
*Includes: Lesbian/Bisexual Task Force, weekly
meetings of Gay/Bi Men & Gay/Bi Women, &
BIG (the Bisexual Interest Group).*

Princeton University: 🏫
Lesbian Gay Bisexual Coordinator
313 West College
Princteon University
Princeton NJ 08544
tel: 609-258-1353; fax: 609-258-3831
e-mail: mseldin@princeton.edu

Raritan Valley Community College: 🏫
Lesbian, Gay, Bi Student Group (GET OUT!)
c/o RVCC Student Activities
P.O. Box 3300
Somerville NJ 08876
tel: 908-526-1200

Rainbow Place of South Jersey 🖳
1103 North Broad St.
Woodbury NJ 08096
tel: 609-848-2455
URL: www.rainbowplace.org
*To advance understanding & acceptance of glbt
people in all areas of society. To establish a sense
of community by providing meeting space,
information services & a support network of
caring individuals. Call for hours of operation &
events. Lesbian, Gay, Bisexual Community
Center, 1103 North Broad Street, Woodbury, NJ
08096.*

Generation Q Y🖳
c/o Rainbow Place
1103 North Broad Street
Woodbury NJ 08096
tel: 609-848-2455
URL: www.rainbowplace.org
*LGBT youth group. Meets at Rainbow Place.
Events, support, etc.*

New Mexico

Bis R Us ▼ ♀
10623 Castillo St., SW
Albuquerque NM 87121
tel: Rachel 505-836-5239
Meets second Sundays for fun & fellowship.

🔑 = school   🏫 = college/university   P = professional   E = educational
A = activist/political   H = health (incl. HIV)   ◢ = media/press   🖳 = Internet resource
The Bisexual Resource Guide 2000   **243**

Common Bond, Inc.   **YE🖳**
POB 26836
Albuquerque NM 87125
tel: 505-891-3647; fax: 505-891-3647
e-mail: commonbond@aol.com
URL: members.aol.com/commonbond/index.html
*LesBiGay Information for Albuquerque & the
NM area. Under 21 group, the only LesBiGay
support group for under 21 teens. Call for more
info.*

Holy Family Anglican Church   **◐🖳**
1701 E. Missouri Avenue
Las Cruces NM 88001
tel: 505-522-7119
505-521-1490
e-mail: lehhar@zianet.com
URL: www.zianet.com/lehhar/index.html
*Inclusive & affirming denomination in
Anglican / Catholic tradition. Welcoming to all
poeple in their journey of faith; social justice
work; discovering God in our culture, language,
sexuality, relationships & occupations.*

Lesbian & Gay Political Alliance   **EA**
P.O. Box 25191
Albuquerque NM 87125
tel: 505-790-2370
*NM's oldest LBG organization. Community
empowerment, visibility, public awareness.
Activities include gay voting guides, educational
videos, special events, & sponsoring legislation.*

New Mexico AIDS Services   **H**
4200 Silver Ave., SE, #D
Albuquerque NM 87108
tel: 505-266-0911
*Referrals to nearest HIV+/AIDS support -service
group. GLBT people can be referred to groups
that include & welcome them.*

Parents & Friends of Lesbians   **♥**
& Gays, New Mexico
various NM
*Various chapters throughout the state, as
follows: PFLAG Alamogordo 505-437-6193;
PFLAG Albuquerque 505-343-7468
(LaneSandy@aol.com); PFLAG Las Cruces /
Dona Ana County 505-522-4056; PFLAG Los
Alamos 505-672-1785; PFLAG Santa Fe: 505-
471-4961; PFLAG Taos: 505-758-8133.*

Local

Emmanuel Metropolitan   **◐◔🖳**
Community Church
P.O. Box 80192
Albuquerque NM 87198
tel: 505-268-0599
e-mail: EMCCAbq@aol.com
URL: www.nmia.com/~sundance
*EMCC has special outreach to the LBGT
community. "We believe in being the hands &
feet of Christ in this world." Social action /
justice. Motto: "Come as you are; believing as you
do." All are welcome. Meets at: 341 Dallas NE,
Albuquerque.* **Publication(s):** *The Advent
Quarterly*

Gay, Lesbian, & Straight   **E**
Education Network of Albuquerque, NM
P.O. Bos 7875
Albuquerque NM 87194
tel: 505-268-1771
505-286-3235
e-mail: doyle@apsicc.aps.edu
*Educational org. for all members of the
community, including LBGTs & others.*

MPower   **♂**
120 Morningside, NE
Albuquerque NM 87108
tel: 505-232-2990; fax: 505-232-2998
e-mail: MPowerABQ@aol.com
*Community Center & community building
program for gay & bi men, 18-29.*

New Mexico Gay Men's Chorus   **🖳**
Turquoise Trail Performing Arts, Inc.
P.O. Box 82206
Albuquerque NM 87198-2206
tel: 505-243-1454
e-mail: crnewslt@trail.com
URL: www.nmgmc.com
*Performing arts group, about 45 members, both
men & women singing men's choral music. 2
concert series / year: June & December. Audience:
about 1000 / series. Members in Albuquerque &
Santa Fe, rehearsals alternate between cities.
Sundays, 3-6 p.m.*

"In another life, dear sister, I too would bear six fat children.
In another life, dear sister, I too would love another woman and raise one
child together as if that it pushed from both our wombs. In another life,
sister, I too would dwell solitary and splendid as a lighthouse on the rocks or
be born to mate for life like the faithful goose. Praise all our choices. Praise
any woman who chooses, and make safe her choice."

—*Marge Piercy*

Key to symbols: ▼ = bi   ♀ = women   ♂ = men   ◐ = religious/spiritual
◔ = for allies   M = for married bis   ♥ = for partners of bis   Y = youth   C = people of color
244   **The Bisexual Resource Guide 2000**

University of New Mexico: Del Otro Lado 🖉
Student Activities Center, Box 100
Albuquerque NM 87106
tel: 505-277-6739
e-mail: smiths@unm.edu
Includes Men's Rap Group, Women's Rap Group,
& Bisexual Rap Group. General discussion
groups & social/political activities.

Lesbians, Bisexuals, Gays 🖉 **EA**
& Friends of New Mexico State University
PO Box 30001
Dept. 3WSP, NMSU
Las Cruces NM 88003
tel: 505-646-4312; fax: 505-646-3725
e-mail: cstephenn@nmsu.edu
Meets Thursdays 7:30pm during termtime in
Rm. 229, English Bldg, NMSU campus. This
group is mostly students, but people of all ages
from the university & community are welcome.

New Mexico State University: 🖉 **PA**
Lesbian & Gay Staff & Faculty at NMSU
Stu Peale, Co-Chair
New Mexico State University Library
Box 30006, Dept. 3475
Las Cruces NM 88003-0006
tel: 505-646-1746; fax: 505-646-7477
e-mail: shpeale@lib.nmsu.edu
Campus org. Membership open to current &
retired faculty, staff, graduate assistants, &
administrators at NMSU. Works for equitable
treatment of LBGT faculty, staff, & students.
Education to the university community, forums
for discussion. Meetings as needed.

Lesbian, Gay, & Bisexual Diversity **P** 🖳
Working Group
MS M704 Los Alamos National Laboratory
Los Alamos NM 87544
tel: 505-665-3364 (voice); fax: 505-665-3891
URL: www.lanl.gov/people/franks/lgblanl.htm
Working group under the Diversity Office at Los
Alamos National Laboratory. Membership
limited to LANL employees & subcontractors.

Los Alamos Bisexual, Gay & Lesbian
Association (LABGALA)
PO Box 338
Los Alamos NM 87544
tel: 505-661-5144
Meets Thursdays at noon.

Southwest Gay Men's Association
PO Box 168
Mesilla NM 88046
tel: 505-522-1390
e-mail: shelmrei@crl.nmsu.edu
Although the group has kept its original name, it
includes gay, bi & lesbian members.

City Different/Ciudad Diferente **P**
Business & Professional Association
P.O. Bos 9951
Santa Fe NM 87504
tel: 505-989-2515; fax: 505-466-6013
URL: www.raodrunner.com/~kurtisa/cdbpa/
Business & professional group inviting LBGT &
friends to join. Business networking, social
contacts, & promorion of GLBT businesses in the
Santa Fe area. Meeting: 3rd Weds.
at the Hilton Hotel; buffet & speaker. Publishes
annual directory & sponsors Business Fair
during Pride week. **Publication(s):** *City*
Different Business Directory annual

Human Rights Alliance **EA**
Santa Fe NM
tel: 505-982-7017
505-982-3301 hotline
Hotline provides names & telephone numbers for
GLB groups in the Santa Fe area.

Rainbow Consciousness 🌀
Santa Fe NM
tel: 505-984-9193
Bisexual men & women are welcome.

Santa Fe Lesbian, Gay & Bi Pride Committee 📧
369 Montezuma #399
Santa Fe NM 87501
tel: 505-989-6672
Community resource & networking group.
Events include Santa Fe LGB Pride, Santa Fe
Gay Film Festival, & National Coming Out Day,
October 11.

New Mexico Institute of Mining & 🖉 🖳
Technology: Gays & Friends
P.O, Box 3681 C18
Socorro NM 87801-3681
tel: 505-835-6297
e-mail: gaf@nmt.edu
URL: www.nmt.edu/~gaf
Easy-going, non-political, social club for GLB
students & friends at New Mexico Institute of
Mining & Technology. Open to anyone else in
Socorro area. Semi-regular monthly meetings.

New York

Student Association of SUNY: 🖉 **PA**
Lesbian/Gay/Bisexual Student Caucus
Student Association of SUNY
300 Lark Street
Albany NY 12210
tel: 518-465-2406; fax: 518-465-2413
Statewide network of l/g/b groups on SUNY
campuses; publish directory; activism regarding
legislative issues affecting lgb SUNY students.

🔧 = school 🖉 = college/university **P** = professional **E** = educational
A = activist/political **H** = health (incl. HIV) 📧 = media/press 🖳 = Internet resource
The Bisexual Resource Guide 2000 **245**

New York City Area

Note: Many of the groups listed below meet at The Lesbian & Gay Community Center, referred to in these listings as:

The Center
The Center's temporary address is:
1 Little West 12th St., New York NY 10011.
It's eventual permanent address will be:
208 West 13th St. [near 7th Ave.]
New York NY 10014.
It is partially wheelchair accessible.

New York Area Bisexual Network (NYABN)

NYABN
c/o The Center
PO Box 497
Times Square Station
New York NY 10108
tel: 212-459-4784 or 212-714-7714 (Bi Request Info Line)
Communications network for bisexual groups; helps new groups form; publishes events calendar. Hosts a wide variety of groups & meetings. Location: Call for info.

The following groups can be reached through NYABN (above), unless otherwise noted:

▼ **Bisexual Youth Initiative, NY**   Y▼AE
Promotes awareness of bisexual issues & events among young people.

▼ **Bi Perspective**   ▼
tel: Bryan: 718-338-1866
e-mail: BFDusini@aol.com
A supportive bisexual discussion & social group. Meets every Sunday, 3-4:30 pm at The Center (see above). Socializing at nearby restaurant afterwards.

▼ **Bi S/M Dungeon Parties**   ▼
For bi & bi-friendly folks. Free w/ Bi S/M Discussion Group membership card. 4th Fri 7-10pm at Hellfire Club, 28 9th Ave (btw 13th & 14th Sts).

▼ **Bi-Ways**   ▼
Variety of social & cultural events. Info on NYABN line. Leave message if you want to plan an event.

▼ **Bisexual Options**   ▼A
tel: 212-969-0702
Activism to increase bi visibility & acceptance in straight & queer communities. Meets 2nd Sunday, 6pm at The Center (see above) & 4th Sunday, 6 pm at Village Star Restaurant (33 7th Ave. at 13th Street).

▼ **Bisexual Public Action Committee**   ▼AE
Educational/activist group fighting for LGB rights.

▼ **Bisexual S/M Discussion Group (BiPAC)**   ▼
Discussion of S/M interests & experiences. Meets 1st Sunday every month, 6-9pm at at The Center (see above). Affiliated with NYABN.

▼ **Bisexual Women's Support Group**   ♀▼
Meets at The Center (see above). Discussion & consciousness-raising group. Wednesdays, 6:30 to 8:00pm. 1st Wed: Personal issues; 2nd & 4th Wed: General; 3rd Wed: Philosophical; 5th Wed (if there is one): Social / Entertainment.

▼ **Gay/Lesbian Identified Bisexuals**   ▼🖳
tel: Bryan: 718-338-1866
e-mail: BFDusini@aol.com
URL: www.glib.com/glib.html
Meets 3rd Sat. 3-4:30 pm at The Center (see above) followed by socializing at a nearby restaurant. Safe space for people exploring their sexuality. Transgendered bisexual people welcome

▼ **The Bi-Social**   ▼
Temporarily suspended until there is a new coordinator. Call NYABN for more info.

▼ **Bi A.A. - Any Which Way We Can**   ▼
Open meeting. Anyone in any kind of recovery is welcome to attend. Meets Saturdays, 6:30 pm at 242 East 14th St., 3rd floor.

▼ **Bisexual 12-Step Program**   ▼
tel: 212-459-4784 (NYABN message line) to confirm meetings & location.
Anyone in any kind of recovery is welcome. Open meetings. Call above # for meeting location.

Bisexual, Gay , Lesbian &   EYA🖳
Transgender Youth of NY (BiGLTYNY)
tel: 212-620-7310 (The Center (see above); ask for Youth Enrichment Services); fax: 212-924-2657 "Y.E.S."
URL: www.gaycenter.ordf/bigltyny.html
Youth-run social & support group for G/L/B/T people under 22. Planning groups & discussion groups meet Saturdays.

Key to symbols: ▼ = bi   ♀ = women   ♂ = men   ☯ = religious/spiritual
🜄 = for allies   **M** = for married bis   ♥ = for partners of bis   **Y** = youth   **C** = people of color

BiRequest ▼🖳
PO Box 396
Ansonia Station
New York NY 10023-0396
tel: 212-714-7714 (recorded
info.)
e-mail: birequest@bi.org
URL: www.bi.org/~bireqst/
*Discussion group for bisexual
& bi-friendly people. Thurs.
6-8pm at NY Spaces, 131
West 72nd Street (between
Broadway & Columbus) in
Studio 1. Wheelchair
accessible. Followed by
socializing at local restaurant. Group outings, dances,
special events, e-mail list.*

Robyn Ochs

NY Bisexual Support Group ▼A
PO Box 2550
Manhattanville Station
New York NY 10027
tel: Martha: 212-865-1854
*Telephone resource for meetings & happenings
in the NY area.*

A Different Drummer Guide ▼🖳
New York NY
e-mail: drum@bway.net
URL: http://www.bway.net/~drum/
*On line listing of bi groups & events in New York
City & surrounding areas.*

Bi Any Other Name Y▼
437 W. 16th St. 2nd Floor
New York NY 10011
tel: 212-414-4740 (Nina Aledort- site director)
*Only bi youth group in NY. Youth Drop-In
Center for ages 15-22 & group meetings Fri. 5-6,
New Neutral Zone.*

Bisexual Information & ▼HP🖳
Counseling Services, Inc. (BICS)
599 West End Avenue, Suite 1A
New York NY 10024
tel: 212-595-8002; fax: 212-877-6314
URL: www.bisexualcounseling.org
*Educational programs/materials, individual/
group/couples therapy. Technical assistance on
bi issues to other non-profits & agencies.
Outreach programs to communities of color,
incarcerated & formerly incarcerated, students,
health professionals. Discussion groups &
graduate internships. Volunteers welcome.
Se habla espanol. Non-profit, tax exempt.*
Publication(s): *Quarterly newsletter: BiLines*

Pride for Youth Y
Long Island Crisis Center
2740 Martin Ave.
Bellmore NY 11710
tel: 516-679-9000 (24 hr. crisis hotline) or 516-826-
0244 (office); fax: 516-781-8306
*24 hr. crisis hotline, counseling, support groups,
peer education, community education, & Fri
night coffeehouse for g/l/b/t youth up to 24. A
free & confidential project of Long Island Crisis
Center.*

SUNY Brockport: Gay Lesbian Bisexual 🎓🖳
Students & Friends Association
350 New Campus Drive
Brockport NY 14420
tel: 716-395-5269
e-mail: glbsfa@earthling.net listserv:
glbsfa@coolist.com
URL: www.acs.brockport.edu/'glbsfa/
*Meetings Mon. at Seymour Cofferhouse, 5:15 -
6:15 pm. Office in Seymour Student Union (B-
21). Open to anyone, student or non-student, in
Brockport area, nothing assumed.*

Albert Einstein College of Medicine: 🎓
Einstein Association of Gays,
Lesbians & Bisexuals
1300 Morris Park Avenue
703 Ullman Building
Bronx NY 10461
tel: 718-722-7130 (Sean Cavanaugh)
*Student & faculty group for lgb folks at Albert
Einstein College of Medicine. Mutual support,
educational outreach to community.*

✎ = school   🎓 = college/university   P = professional   E = educational
A = activist/political   H = health (incl. HIV)   📰 = media/press   🖳 = Internet resource
The Bisexual Resource Guide 2000   **247**

Robyn Ochs

Bronx Lavender   🌀**EA**
Community Center (BLCC)
Poe Building
2432 Grand Concourse, Suite 504
Bronx NY 10458
tel: 718-379-1093; fax: 718-671-0089
e-mail: agoldcrow@aol.com
*Home base of a variety of educational, cultural,
social, political, spiritual, human service, &
health providers, service organizations, agencies
& peer groups. Provides safe space where LGBT
& two-spirited people can meet old & new
friends. New volunteers welcome. Monthly
calendar of events available. Wheelchair
accessible.*

Entre Hombres - The Bronx   ♂**HC**
886 Westchester Ave.
Bronx NY 10459
tel: 718-328-4188; fax: 718-328-2888
*A program of HIV/AIDS (SIDA) education for
Latino gay & bisexual men, operating in Queens
& in The Bronx under the aegis of the Hispanic
AIDS Forum.*

Pride in da Bronx   **Y**
2488 Grand Concourse Suite #326
Bronx NY 10458
tel: 718-364-9529; fax: 718-364-0667
*Drop-in center GLBT & questioning youth in the
Bronx. Includes bi support group.*

Sarah Lawrence College: LGBT Students   👬
Student Activities
Student Affairs Office
1 Mead Way
Bronxville NY 10708

Brooklyn Bisexual   ▼♀**YH**
& Lesbian Youth Sisters
c/o Shades of Lavender, BATF
470 Bergen St.
Brooklyn NY 11217
tel: 718-622-2910; fax: 718-622-2695
*For lesbian/bi youth. Support,
activities, AIDS education, trips,
movies, more. Meets Thursdays, 3-6pm.*

Brooklyn College Lesbian,   **AE**
Gay Bisexual & Transgendered
Alliance (LGBTA)
c/o Student Activities
James Hall
Brooklyn NY 11210-2889
tel: 718-951-4234
*Shelter to g/l/b students. All students,
regardless of race, religion or sexual
orientation, welcome. Office located at 1404
Plaza Bldg.*

Brooklyn PFLAG   **EA**👬
360 Atlantic Avenue #179
Brooklyn NY 11217
tel: 718-646-3390
*Promotes the well-being of GLBT persons, their
families & friends through support, education &
advocacy. Meets 1st Sun. 2-4pm at Union
Temple, 17 Eastern Parkway, Brooklyn.*

Kingsborough Community College: 👬**E**
Gay, Lesbian & Bisexual Alliance
2001 Oriental Blvd.
Brooklyn NY 11235
*Student/academic group focused on GLB issues.
Annual Gay Awareness Day, weekly rap
sessions, end-of-term social events.*

People of Color in Crisis, Inc.   **C**♂**EH**
462 Bergen St.
Brooklyn NY 11217
tel: 718-230-0770; fax: 718-230-7582
*Brooklyn-based HIV/AIDS information &
referral service organization serving African-
American & Caribbean gay & bisexual men.
Providing HIV & Caregivers' support groups,
buddy program, workshops, community forums
& volunteer placement.*

People of Color Queers of   **CA**
Multi-Racial & Ethnic Descent
c/o Audre Lorde Project
85 S. Oxford St.
Brooklyn NY 11217
tel: 718-596-0342
e-mail: alpinfo@alp.org
*Open to anyone who defines themself as a multi-
racial or ethnic Person of Color & queer. Also
involved with OUT FM radio.*

Key to symbols: ▼ = bi   ♀ = women   ♂ = men   🌀 = religious/spiritual
👬 = for allies   **M** = for married bis   ♥ = for partners of bis   **Y** = youth   **C** = people of color
248   The Bisexual Resource Guide 2000

Pratt Institute: Gays, Lesbians & Bisexuals at Pratt 🎓
Office of Student Activities,
Chapel Hall
200 Willoughby Ave.
Brooklyn NY 11205
tel: 718-636-3422

Shades of Lavender ♀ YC
c/o Bklyn AIDS Task Force
502 Bergen St.
Brooklyn NY 11217
tel: 718-622-2910
*Multicultural center in Park
Slope, Brooklyn, for lesbians
& bi women offering self-
help, discussion, workshops,
retreats, etc. Writers
Collective, Bi/Lesbian Youth
under 22 group, Women 20s/
30s group, Narcotics
Anonymous Group, movie nights, 1 on 1. Relapse
prevention councling.* **Publication(s)**: *Shades
Monthly. Events listings.*

Sistahs in Search of Truth, ▼ ♀ CHEA
Alliance & Harmony (SiSTAH)
Cadman Plaza
PO Box 020136
Brooklyn NY 11202-0136
tel: 212-479-7886 or 212-620-7310
e-mail: sistah97@aol.com
*Support organization to address needs of les/bi
womyn of color. Nuturing space affirms, rejoices
& sanction womyn of color in all our diversities.
1st/2nd/3rd Fri 6:30 - 8 pm at The Center (see
above), 208 W. 13th St. Different topics, &
socializing.*

The Audre Lorde Project: CEH
**Center for Lesbian, Gay, Bisexual, Two-Spirit
& Transgender People of Color Communities**
85 S. Oxford Street
Brooklyn NY 11217-1607
tel: 718-596-0342; fax: 718-596-1328
e-mail: alpinfo@alp.org
*Center for lgb, two-spirit & transgender people of
color communities. Classes, groups, events,
political action. Sponsors of 1998 LBTST
Women of Color Organizing Institute - contact
for info on future institutes.* **Publication(s)**:
*Color Life! 4 issues a year: $15 for individuals,
$25 for institutions.*

Unity Fellowship Church ☏C
230 Classon Av.
Brooklyn NY 11205
tel: 718-636-5646
*LGBT church in the Black Pentecostal tradition,
services on Sunday 3:30pm.*

Robyn Ochs

**Zappalorti Society- Gay, Lesbian
& Bisexual Psychiatric Survivors**
tel: 718-442-1838; Bert
*LGBT "Psychiatric Survivors" organized for peer
self-help & mental health advocacy. Meets
Saturdays 2-4pm at the Lesiban & Gay
Community Services Center.*

Dignity- Nassau ☏
P.O. Box 48
East Meadow NY 11554
tel: 516-781-6225
*Support group for LGBT Catholics & friends.
Meets 2nd & 4th Sat. for liturgies & socials.*

Orange County Teen line & 24 Hour Helpline Y
c/o Mental Health Association
20 Wallker St.
Goshen NY 10924
tel: 914-294-7348
e-mail: maj@mhaorangeny.com
*Support group for GLB teens in Orange County
providing local resources & information.*

Hofstra University: Hofstra Lambda Society 🎓
c/o Dean of Students Office
219 Student Center
Hempstead NY 11551
tel: 516-463-3965
Support/rap group for GLB people.

Entre Hombres - Queens C♂H
74-09 37th Avenue, Suite 305
Jackson Heights NY 11372
tel: 718-803-2766
*A program for HIV/AIDS (SIDA) education for
Latino gay & bi men, operating in Queens & the
Bronx, under the aegis of the Hispanic AIDS
Forum.*

🖊 = school   🎓 = college/university   P = professional   E = educational
A = activist/political   H = health (incl. HIV)   ✐ = media/press   ▯ = Internet resource
The Bisexual Resource Guide 2000   **249**

Robyn Ochs

Columbia University: &&ʳ**EA**
Queer Co-op (formerly
Barnard/Columbia
Lesbian, Bisexual, Gay
Coalition)
Columbia University
303 Earl Hall
New York NY 10027
tel: 212-854-1488
e-mail: LGBC@columbia.edu

Columbia University   &&ʳ
Teachers College:
Lesbian, Bisexual, Gay &
Transgender Community
Office of Student Activities
Box 42, 525 W. 120th St.
New York NY 10027

Bi/Hetero Support Groups   **H▼E**
for People Living with AIDS
50 W. 17th St., 8th Floor
New York NY 10011
tel: 212-647-1415
212-647-1420 Hotline; fax: 212-647-1419
Sponsored by the PWA Coalition.

Bisexual Lesbian & Gay Haitians (BLAGH)   **C**
PO Box 1302
New York NY 10159-1302
tel: 718-965-3354
Non pale ni angle ni creolle. Confidentiality
maintained. Support environment for LGB
Haitians living in the U.S.

Center Youth Enrichment Services (YES)   **YEA**
at The Center (see above)
tel: 212-620-7310
URL: www.gaycenter.org
Activities-based empowerment/prevention
program for lgbt youth, 13-22. Theater, art,
writing, TV, journalism, leadership training,
job-seeking, advocacy, referrals.

City College: &&ʳ
Bisexual, Lesbian & Gay Alliance
Convent Avenue & 138th Street
New York NY 10031
Meets in R4/121.

Columbia Center for Lesbian, Gay &   &&ʳ**H**
Bisexual Mental Health
Columbia-Presbyterian Eastside
16 East 60th Street
New York NY 10022
tel: Justin Richardson, Dir., M.D. 212-326-8441;
fax: 212-326-8590
A non-profit program of Columbia University's
Department of Psychiatry. Sponsors research,
educates mental health professionals, & provides
clinical care to promote the well-being of LGB
persons.

Dignity - Big Apple   ☯
P.O. Box 1028
Old Chelsea Station
New York NY 10011
tel: 212-818-1309
National organization of LGBT Roman
Catholics meets Sat. 8 pm. at The Center @ 8pm
for liturgy. Other social, spiritual activities.

Dignity - New York, Inc. Lesbian & Gay   ☯
Catholics
P.O. Box 1554
New York NY 10150
tel: 212-627-6488; Linkline support 212-620-0369;
Liturgy Sunday, 7:30pm at St. Johns-in-the-
Village, 218 W. 11th St. (at Waverly). Social
following service. AIDS ministry available.

Firefighters Lesbian & Gay, Inc.   **P**
at The Center (see above)
tel: 914-762-6261 Gene Walsh
e-mail: fireflag@aol.com
Meets even months 2nd Tues 8pm. Call for
further info.

Gay Asian & Pacific Islander   **C♂EA▢**
Men of NY
PO Box 1608
Old Chelsea Station
New York NY 10113-1608
tel: 212-802-RICE (7423)
e-mail: gapimny@leftnet.net
URL: www.leftnet.net/ˀgapimny/
GAPIMNY provides a safe & supportive social,
political, & educational forum for GBT &
questioning Asian & Pacific Islander men in the
NYC area. Meetings open only to Asian & Pacific
Islander men. Socials are for all men. Meets 3rd
Fri. 8 - 10 pm at the Center (see above).

Key to symbols: ▼ = bi   ♀ = women   ♂ = men   ☯ = religious/spiritual
◐ = for allies   **M** = for married bis   ♥ = for partners of bis   **Y** = youth   **C** = people of color

Gay & Bi Fathers' Forum ♂

at The Center (see above)
tel: 212-721-4216 or
212-768-1358
Group for gay & bi fathers, their partners, & any gay men in a child-nurting environment. Meets 1st Friday of every month for dinner & socializing.

Gay, Lesbian & Affirming ◐▣ Disciples Alliance

1453A Lexington Ave.
New York NY 10128-2506
tel: Ref. Allen V. Harris: 212-289-3016; fax: 212-288-7602
e-mail: aaministry@aol.com
URL: pilot.msu.edu/user/laceyj
Metro NY chapter for lgb, affirming persons related to Christian Church (Disciples of Christ).

Gay Lesbian Bisexual Veterans PA of Greater NY

346 Broadway, Suite 803
New York NY 10013
tel: 212-349-3455; fax: 212-233-6058
Serves needs of glb veterans & service members. Advocates for right to serve openly in the armed forces. Meets 4th Thursdays at 8pm at The Center (see above).

Gay Officers Action League PA▣

P.O. Box 2038
Canal St. Station
New York NY 10013
tel: 212-NY1-GOAL (691-4625)
e-mail: ny1goal@aol.com
URL: www.goalny.org
Fraternal organization open to professionals currently or formerly employed in law enforcement & criminal justice. Other supporters are members of Friends of Goal (FOG). Supports, advocates for membership, empowerment of blg community, social justice. Membership meeting 2nd Tues 7 pm @ The Center (see above)

Gentle Men ♂

at The Center (see above)
tel: 212-501-2034
Group for meeting Bi-Gay men for friendships & relationships through intamacy exercises & speaking from the heart. Meets at The Center 2nd & 4th Fridays @ 8pm.

Hetrick-Martin Institute YEH

2 Astor Place
New York NY 10003-6998
tel: 212-674-2400; TTY 212-674-8695; literature request line x232; fax: 212-674-8650
e-mail: hmi@hmi.org
Non-profit social service agency serving GLBT youth 12-21. Free confidential counseling; after school activities program. Operates Harvey Milk High School. Conducts HIV education for youth at various locations including schools & community groups. Runs Project First Step for homeless street youth. Publishes "You Are Not Alone: National LGB Youth Organization Directory", a directory of 200+ nationwide organizations serving LGB youth.

Iban/Queer Koreans of New York C (Iban/QKNY)

P.O. Box 237, Cathedral Station
New York NY 10025
tel: 718-596-0342x33
e-mail: mudang@ix.netcom.com

Identity House HA

PO Box 572
Old Chelsea Station
New York NY 10011
tel: 212-243-8181
Location: 39 W. 14th St.. Walk-in peer counseling & therapy referral center for the LGB community. Also provides short-term groups, workshops & special events. Call for schedules. Gives therapist referrals. Drop- in COMB-OUT groups for men & women over 40. Small donations for meetings & counselling. Call for further info.

Kilawin Kolektibo C♀

New York NY
tel: 718-706-7220
e-mail: kilawin@aol.com
Pinay lesbian & bisexual identified gathering of sisters.

Korean LGBT Group of New York C

New York NY
tel: English: 718-424-4003 (Pauline Park)
Korean: 212-265-3782 (Hyun Jung Lee)
A social/discussion/support group for LGBT Koreans, Korean Americans & Korean adoptees.

John Jay College: Lambda Association ↝EA

Office of Student Activities
445 West 59th St.
New York NY 10019
tel: 212-237-8738/2 (Student Activities Office)
LBGT student union group. Seeks to educate the student community on LBGT issues.

✎ = school   ↝ = college/university   **P** = professional   **E** = educational
A = activist/political   **H** = health (incl. HIV)   ✍ = media/press   ▣ = Internet resource
The Bisexual Resource Guide 2000   **251**

Lavender Heights
New York NY
tel: 212-465-3100
Washington Heights group welcoming bisexuals.

Lavender Paesans
c/o The Center
tel: 212-267-1434
Italian descent L/G/B group explore their heritage & new world culture. Call for events schedule.

Lesbian/Gay/Bi Info Line
Westchester NY
tel: 914-626-3203
Listing of events 7am-11pm.

LeGaL: Lesbian & Gay Law Association   **P🖥**
of Greater New York Legal Clinic
799 Broadway #340
New York NY 10003
tel: 212-353-9118; fax: 212-353-2970
e-mail: le-gal@interport.net
URL: www.interport.net:/~le-gal
Association of the lesbian & gay legal community in the New York metropolitan area. Free walk-in legal clinic Tuesdays 6-6:30pm at The Center (see above).

Men of All Colors Together/New York   **C♂**
PO Box 907
Ansonia Station
New York NY 10023-0907
tel: 212-330-7678
Group for men of all colors striving to create a multicultural community. Bi-friendly. Meets at The Center (see above). Call 212-620-7310 for new address. General meeting 1st/3rd/4th Fri 8-11pm, Board meeting 2nd Friday.
Publication(s): *MACT Information Bulletin Monthly newsletter of weekly programs, multicultural activities, social & political activities.*

Metropolitan Community Church   **☯**
of New York
446 W. 36th St.
New York NY 10018
tel: Rev. Pat Bumgardner 212-629-7440
A church of LGBT people open to all. Services at 10am & 7pm on Sunday, 7-7:30 on Wednesday.

Network for Realization of the Goddess   **♀☯**
(NRG)
at The Center
tel: 212-348-5738
Meets at The Center on Mondays @ 8pm. Women's Dianic Wicca Spirituality Circle. Open to all women. Practice of Goddess- & Mother Nature-based rituals.

New York University:

▼ **Office of Lesbian, Gay, Bisexual &**   **⚧✓E🖥**
Transgender Student Services
21 Washington Place, 3rd Floor
New York NY 10003-6612
tel: 212-998-4424; fax: 212-995-4116
URL: www.nyu.edu/pages/osa/lgbt

▼ **Queer Union at NYU**   **⚧✓EAH🖥**
21 Washington Place, Box 200
New York NY 10003
tel: 212-998-4938
e-mail: queer-union@nyu.edu
URL: pages.nyu.edu/clubs/QU
A campus organization that deals with the realities of being queer at NYU. Social, political, educational & resourceful. All welcome.

▼ **Bisexual, Gay & Lesbian Law Students**   **⚧✓**
240 Mercer St.
New York NY 10012
tel: 212-996-6574

LGBTIPS: Lesbians, Gay, Bisexuals,   **⚧✓🖥**
Transgenders in Public Service
Wagner Graduate School of Public Services
New York University
New York NY
e-mail: lgbtips.club@nyu.edu
URL: pages.nyu.edu/clubs/lgbtips
Resources & listings of NYU-wide LGBT events.

NOW-NYC Bisexual & Lesbian Rights   **♀A🖥**
Committee
105 E. 22nd St.
New York NY 10010
tel: 212-260-4422 (Jeanne Vacaro, coordinator)
e-mail: nownyc@nyct.net
URL: nyct.net\~nownyc
1st Thursdays. Political action, speakers, workshops. Organizes lesbian/gay pride & activist events.

NY Prime Timers   **♂**
PO Box 291, Midtown Station
New York NY 10018
tel: 212-929-1035
Addresses the needs of mature gay & bi men & their friends. Sponsors social, cultural, intellectual & erotic events. NY chapter of international group.

Orthodykes   **▼♀☯**
at The Center (see above)
tel: 212-627-2629
Group for discussion, socializing & support. For lbt women who identify with Orthodox Judaism. Meets 2nd Wednesdays at 8 pm.

Key to symbols: ▼ = bi   ♀ = women   ♂ = men   ☯ = religious/spiritual
☙ = for allies   **M** = for married bis   ♥ = for partners of bis   **Y** = youth   **C** = people of color
252   **The Bisexual Resource Guide 2000**

Project Reach -- Drop-In Center   **Y**
1 Orchard Street, 2nd fl.
New York NY 10002
tel: 212-966-4227; fax: 212-966-4963
e-mail: prorads@aol.com
> *Multi-racial youth-run drop-in center for GLBT,*
> *heterosexual & questioning youth; counseling &*
> *advocacy programs; discussion groups; referrals.*

Queens Lesbian Gay Bisexual Transgender
Community Center
c/o NYABN (see above)
tel: 718-670-7387

Radical Faeries   ✒ ♂
PO Box 1251
New York NY 10013
tel: 718-625-4505
meeting space:
212-620-7310 or 718-788-0847
> *Meets at the The Center (see above) 4th Fridays*
> *at 8pm. Also ongoing social events & reading*
> *groups.*

Stonewall Veterans' Association   **P**
70-A Greenwich Ave. Suite 120
New York NY 10011
tel: 212-727-1969 or
718-931-4329
> *Meets bi-monthly (even months) on last Friday*
> *at 6 pm at The Center (see above). Veterans of*
> *The Stonewall Rebellion of 1969 who "started it*
> *all."*

TalkSafe Wellness Program   ♂ **H**
412 Sixth Ave. at 9th St.
Suite 401
New York NY 10011
tel: 212-420-9400
> *Free individual, couple & group counseling*
> *program dedicated to helping gay & bisexual*
> *men stay HIV-negative.*

The Door   **H**
555 Broome St.
New York NY 10013
tel: 212-941-9090; fax: 212-941-0714
> *Crisis intervention, long-term counseling, drop-*
> *in center, medical care, alternative high school*
> *for youth, housing referral services, legal,*
> *education/vocational programs for youth 12-20.*
> *Also, support group for g/l/b youth. Program*
> *Hours: Mon 2-8:30, Tues. 3-8:30, Wed. 2-8:30,*
> *Thurs. 2-8:30, Fri. 2-7:30.*

The Neutral Zone: Lesbigay Youth Center   **Y**
c/o Greenwich Village Youth Council
37 Carmine St. #208
New York NY 10014
tel: 212-924-3294
> *Multi-service in-house counseling & referral*
> *service for LGB youth 12-21.*

Triangle Tribe   **Y**
Green Chimney's Children's Services
327 East 22nd St.
New York NY 10010
tel: 212-677-7288; fax: 212-673-1476
e-mail: gpm7@columbia.edu
> *Support group for GLBTQ youth from all*
> *programs within the foster care system. Co-*
> *facilitated by youth & adults. Meets every other*
> *Mon, 7pm at above address. Offers advocacy for*
> *youth in finding queer friendly foster care*
> *placements & GLBTQ training for foster care*
> *professionals.*

Ujima Community   **CH**
c./o The Center (see above)
tel: 212-620-7310 (Dana Rose - Dir. of
Centerbridge)
> *For LGBT people of African descent, using*
> *africological approaches to grief & loss*
> *resolution.*

Uptown Pride   ♂ **YE**
c/o Alianza Dominicana, Inc.
715 W. 179th St.
New York NY 10033
tel: Francisco J. Lazala: 212-795-4226; fax: 212-
795-4285
> *Youth-run group for GBT & Q male youth 13-24*
> *in the Washington Heights area providing*
> *counseling, peer support, & peer mediation -*
> *weekly discussions, social events.*

Veg-Out   **A E**
c/o The Center (see above)
tel: 212-802-8655
> *Pot-luck vegetarian brunch (no meat/eggs/*
> *dairy) for LGB & queer-friendly vegetarians &*
> *wannabees. 4th Sunday 1 - 3:30 pm at The*
> *Center. Additional outside activities. Check 212-*
> *620-7310 for further info.*

Wannabe Dads   ♂ **A**
c/o Center Kids
at The Center (see above)
tel: Will 212-864-6743
James 718-768-2013
> *For men exploring the possibilities of becoming*
> *parents or wanting to be father figures to*
> *children.*

Wazobia   **C A**
P.O. Box 255
New York NY 10116
tel: Nguru
212-690-3705
> *Network of continental African LGBT people in*
> *NY metro area. Meetings at L&G Center. For*
> *support, advocacy, action & community*
> *building. Call for further information.*

✒ = school   ⌇ = college/university   **P** = professional   **E** = educational
A = activist/political   **H** = health (incl. HIV)   ✍ = media/press   ▯ = Internet resource

The Triangle Tribe — Empowering G.L.B.T.Q. Youth In Foster Care

Robyn Ochs

SUNY Purchase: G/L/B/T Union E
c/o Student Activities, Box 1882
Purchase NY 10577
tel: 914-251-6976

Gay/Bi/Lesbian Youth Group YH
ACQC
97-45 Queens Boulevard, Suite 1220
Rego Park NY 11374
tel: 718-896-2500; fax: 718-275-2094
*Free & confidential support groups for
adolescents aged 13-21; deals with coming out.
HIV/AIDS, family issues, safer sex, referrals. A
service of AIDS Center of Queens County. Drop
in group 1st + 3rd Monday, 6-8 pm. Sign-up for
ongoing groups, for 10-14 weeks.*

Gay & Lesbian Switchboard of Long Island
P.O. Box 1312
Ronkonkoma NY 11779
tel: 516-737-1615
516-751-7500 Crisis Line
e-mail: glsbi@aol.com
*All-volunteer info., peer counseling & referral
service. Serves entire LI community with info. &
referrals on g/l/b issues. Switchboard open
7pm-11pm for phone counselling.*

College of Staten Island: Lesbian, Gay, ⚢⌢E
Bisexual & Transgender Alliance
2800 Victory Blvd. Rm. 220
Staten Island NY 10314
tel: 718-982-3107; fax: 718-982-3087
*Campus-wide organization of students, faculty &
staff; focus on providing an affirming environment & educational programming on LGBT
issues.*

SUNY Stony Brook: ⚢⌢**EA**
Lesbian Gay Bisexual &
Transgendered Alliance
Student Union 045A
Stony Brook NY 11790
tel: 516-632-6469; fax: 516-
585-7620
e-mail: pride@ic.sunysb.edu
*Educational, political & social
organization. General meetings
Thurs., support group Wed. All
are welcome.*

Center Lane (Westchester **YE**
Community Services)
200 Hamilton Ave.
White Plains NY 10601
tel: 914-948-1042; fax: 914-
948-2987
*Workshops, theatre, coffee-
houses, trips, & more for g/l/b
youth 21 & under.*

The Loft & Helpline Services **Y🖥**
POB 1513
White Plains NY 10601
tel: 914-948-4922 Helpline
914-948-2932 (reg); fax: 914-948-2987
e-mail: loftcenter@aol.com
URL: www.members.aol.com/loftcenter
*Location: Lesbian & Gay Community Center
180 E. Post Rd., White Plains. 20 groups
providing services to members of the Greater
Westchester Area. Center Lane at the LOFT is a
bi-weekly meeting of GLB youth, 15-21. AA
groups meet on Thursday PM. Al-Anon groups
meet on Sunday PM.*

Meditation for Gays, Lesbians & Bisexuals 🜨
c/o The Center (see above)
tel: 212-799-1245
*Meets 1st & 3rd Wednesdays at The Center.
Guided meditations using the teachings of
Christ, Buddah & Krishna as the guidepost.*

Upstate New York

Capital District Bisexual Network ▼
c/o ABN
342 Madison Ave. #B
Albany NY 12210
tel: 518-462-6138, Box 48
e-mail: stevek@wizvax.net
*Capitol District advocates & activists for
bisexuals in the tri-cities area. Sponsors the bi-
brunch & social space, every 1st & 3rd Sunday
at 11am & Bisexual People's Support Group
Wednesdays 7:30.*

Key to symbols: ▼ = bi   ♀ = women   ♂ = men   🜨 = religious/spiritual
🗲 = for allies   **M** = for married bis   ♥ = for partners of bis   **Y** = youth   **C** = people of color

Bisexual Women's Group   ▼ ♀
PO Box 775
Buffalo NY 14205
tel: 716-882-6519
Women only support group to talk about our lives & our relationships.

Bi Support Group: ▼
Northern Dutchess County, NY
PO Box 531
Rhinebeck NY 12572-0531
Meets monthly or bi-weekly. A respectful & safe environment for bi's to share concerns about our lives, loves, friends, & communities; & our bisexuality. Definitely not for cruising.

Bisexual Discussion Group   ▼
GAGV Community Center
179 Atlantic Ave.
Rochester NY 14609
tel: 716-232-2548
Men & women welcome. Meets last Wednesday of the month 7-9pm at the GAGV Community Center.

Wells College: LBA   ᾔ
NY
e-mail: LBA@henry.wells.edu

Adirondack GABLE
Adirondack Mountains NY
tel: 518-359-7358

Lesbian/Gay/Bisexual   YE
Young People's Meeting
Albany Community Center
Albany NY
tel: 518-462-6138
Albany Community Center also has meetings for GLB adults.

SUNY Albany: ᾔ
Gay, Lesbian, Bisexual Alliance
Campus Center 116
1400 Washington Avenue
Albany NY 12222
tel: 518-442-5672
Meets Tuesdays in room CC375.

Alfred University: Spectrum   ᾔ
c/o Student Activities
Alfred NY

Bard College: BAGLE   ᾔ
(Bisexuals, Activists, Gays, Lesbians, et al)
PO Box 5000
Annandale-on-Hudson NY 12504-5000
tel: 914-758-6822

Binghamton University: ᾔ A 🖳
Queer Students' Union
PO Box 2000
Binghamton NY 13902-6000
tel: 607-777-2202
e-mail: bu-lgbu@io.com (listserv);
bc70322@binghamton.edu
URL: www.sa.binghamton.edu/~qsu
Social & political group for students.

Gay/Lesbian/Bi Resource Line
Binghamton NY
tel: 607-729-1921

Buffalo State College: ᾔ
Lesbian, Gay & Bisexual Alliance
1300 Elmwood Ave
209 Cassety Hall
Buffalo NY
tel: 716-878-6839

Gay, Lesbian, Bisexual Youth Services   Y 🖳
190 Franklin St
Buffalo NY 14202
tel: 716-855-0221
URL: glyns.wny.juno.com

SUNY Buffalo: ᾔ
Graduate Gay & Lesbian Alliance
SUNY Buffalo
Student Union Box 92
Buffalo NY
Open to all LBGT students & their friends. Focus of the group depends on interests of members. Activities in past years include speakers, graduate student conference, workshops on teaching queer subjects & coming out in the classroom, roundtable discussions, socials.

SUNY Buffalo: ᾔ
Lesbian, Gay, Bisexual Alliance
362 Student Union
Buffalo NY 14260
tel: 716-645-3063; fax: 716-645-2112
Support, social, educational, & lesbigay events. Annual film festival. For graduate & undergraduate students.

Hamilton College: ᾔ
Gay, Lesbian & Bisexual Student Alliance
198 College Road
Clinton NY 13323
tel: 315-859-4830

Chautaqua County
Gay, Lesbian & Bi Info Line
PO Box 254
Fredonia NY 14063
tel: 716-679-3560

🖎 = school   ᾔ = college/university   P = professional   E = educational
A = activist/political   H = health (incl. HIV)   ⊠ = media/press   🖳 = Internet resource
The Bisexual Resource Guide 2000   **255**

Chautaqua County Gay, Lesbian & Bi Youth Services   Y
Fredonia NY
tel: Judy Breny: 716-664-2240 or
716-484-8434

SUNY Fredonia:
Gay, Lesbian, Bisexual Student Union
Campus Center
Fredonia NY 14063
tel: 716-673-3149
716-673-3139; fax: 716-673-3390
e-mail: glbsu0000@fredonia.edu
Phone is for student union; leave message with secretary. Provides a relaxed, safe & supportive atmosphere for LGB & their friends as well as educating the campus & community.

SUNY Geneseo:
Gays, Lesbians, Bisexuals, Friends
CU Box 128
Geneseo NY 14454
tel: 716-245-5889
e-mail: glbf@uno.cc.geneseo.edu

Hobart & William Smith College
Pride Alliance
Hobart & William Smith Colleges
Geneva NY 14456
tel: 315-781-GLBF
URL: www.hws.edu/act/pride/
GLBTQ & friends network. Activist organization, seeking to achieve equality for people of all sexual orientations on campus & in the world. Also a social organization, creating a community of glbtq & friends. Also a support network, providing info, resources & a listening ear.

Cornell University:

▼ **Lesbian, Gay, Bisexual**   E
Resource Office
G-16 Anabel Taylor Hall
Ithaca NY 14853-1601
tel: 607-254-4987; 255-8123
e-mail: lgbtro@cornell.edu
URL: htto://LGBROcornell.edu/
G16 Anabel Taylor Hall 10am-4pm.

▼ **Lesbian, Gay, Bisexual**
& Transgendered Coalition (LGBTC)
207 Willard "Straight " Hall
Ithaca NY 14853
tel: 607-255-6482, M-F 10-4PM
e-mail: hor1@cornell.edu
jap19@cornell.edu
URL: glbro.cornell.edu/student/coalition/
lgbtc.edu
Umbrella organization for other GLBT offices. Creates safe atmosphere for LGBT community at Cornell. Educates Cornell & Ithaca community about GLB issues.

▼ **Bridges (Bisexuals ReInventing the** ▼
Definition of Gender & Sexuality)
e-mail: dkw2@cornell.edu
bcu1@cornell.edu
URL: LGBO.cornell.edu/student/coalition/
bridges.html
Provides an atmosphere where bisexual & questioning men & women can comfortably discuss issues. All are welcome! See LGBTC above.

▼ **Dialogue**
e-mail: jhwl3@cornell.edu
URL: lgbro.cornell.edu/student/coalition/
dialogue.html
A multi-faith gathering of LBGT students & friends to grow in faith & spirituality. See LGBTC above.

▼ **Lesbian, Bi & Questioning Women**   ♀
URL: lgbro.cornell.edu/student/coalition/
lbqw.html
LBQ provides a comfortable atmosphere for lesbian, bisexual & questioning women. See LGBTC above.

▼ **Out in the World**
Box 45
Big Red Barn Campus
Ithaca NY 14853
e-mail: OLWmail@cornell.edu
Meets 2nd Thurs @ 8 pm during academic year. Social group.

▼ **ZAP**   EA
tel: 607-257-0570
e-mail: clro2@cornell.edu
URL: Lgbro.cornell.edu/student/zap.html
Panel addressing LBGT community diverse cultures, ethnics & orientation. Q/A session. See LGBTC above.

Ithaca College: BiGAYLA
c/o Student Center
Ithaca NY 14850
e-mail: bigayla@ic3.ithaca.edu
URL: www.ithaca.edu/bigayla
Student organization for glb & heterosexual allies. Meets Tuesdays 8pm in 309 Friends Hall.

Ithaca Lesbian, Gay & Bisexual Task Force
PO Box 283
Ithaca NY 14851
tel: Jeff Popow: 607-347-4605
e-mail: Jeff Popow: jspl@cornelll.edu
Sponsors coffeehouses, a quarterly newsletter, monthly calendar & activities. Coffeehouses held at the parlor of the Unitarian church at East Buffalo & Aurora Sts. on Fridays or Saturdays 8-11pm.

Key to symbols: ▼ = bi   ♀ = women   ♂ = men   ☯ = religious/spiritual
👍 = for allies   **M** = for married bis   ♥ = for partners of bis   **Y** = youth   **C** = people of color
256   **The Bisexual Resource Guide 2000**

LesBiGay Info Line
Ithaca NY
tel: 607-255-6482

J.C.C GLB Support Group   &
POB 20
Janestown NY 14702
tel: 716-665-5220 ext. 204

Coalition for Lesbigay Youth   Y
Kingston NY
tel: 914-255-7123

Unity Through Diversity   Y
27 North St.
Middletown NY 10940
tel: Nancy Simpson 914-343-8838
Support group for g/l/b youth meets every Wed. 6:30-7:30pm at Community Center.

Sojourner's Wimmin's Gathering Space   ♀
PO Box 398
New Paltz NY 12561

SUNY New Paltz: BiGAYLA   &
Student Union Building, 338
New Paltz NY 12561
tel: 914-257-3097

Hartwick College: Bi-Gala+   & 💻
Oneonta NY 13820
e-mail: bigala@hartwick.edu
URL: hartwick.edu/~bigala
Bisexual, Gay & Lesbian Alliance.

State University of New York, Oswego: & EA
BiGALA
Oswego NY 13126
tel: 315-341-2500
e-mail: bigala@oswego.oswego.edu

SUNY Plattsburgh: &
Lesbian, Gay, Bisexual Alliance
Angell College Center
Plattsburgh NY 12901
tel: 518-564-3200; fax: 518-564-3205
e-mail: caji1372@splauna.cc.plattsburgh.edu

Vassar College: Queer Coalition   & A
124 Raymond Av.
Box 3038
Poughkeepsie NY 12601
Social awareness & political umbrella organization for those whose sexual preference is not exclusively hetero or whose gender designation is not limited to their sex. Includes: Gay/Straight Alliance, "HIM" (He's Into Men), Continuum, People of Color Collective, Sisters (the women's Group), First Step (discreet discussion group for those coming out), & ACT 29 (safe place for those whose religion does not approve of their sexuality).

COAP: Come Out & Play   💻
179 Atlantic Avenue
Rochester NY 14609
tel: 716-244-8640
e-mail: coap@welcome.com
URL: www.geocities.com/WestHollywood/2995
Large social group for people in 20s & 30s. No membership dues. Plans parties, weekend trips, & day activities. Meets monthly.

GAGV Lesbian Gay Bi Youth Group   Y
GAGV Community Center
179 Atlantic Ave.
Rochester NY 14609
tel: 716-244-8640
Ages 14-21, group meets every Sunday, 2-4pm at the GAGV Community Center. In 1997-98 they worked on a visible glb mural that remains on display in the local arts district.

Gay Alliance Genesee Valley: EA
Bisexual Support Group
179 Atlantic Ave
Rochester NY 14609
tel: 716-244-8640
5 week support group "Coming to Terms With Bisexuality". Membership in GAGV includes publication. **Publication(s):** *Empty Closet Oldest LGB paper in Upstate NY. Published Monthly. 716/244-9030.*

Lilac Rainbow Alliance for the Deaf
PO Box 20093
Rochester NY 14618
Meets second Saturday of the month at 7pm at 179 Atlantic Ave. Meets at the Gay Alliance.

"Theories of lesbian and gay development have typically regarded establishing a lesbian or gay identity as the end point of the coming out process. Bisexuality was thought to be a transitional experience and identification, whereas, in reality, it can be an endpoint, phase, or place of recurrent visitation."

—Dr. Ron C. Fox *(in BiNet USA presspacket)*

🔥 = school   & = college/university   P = professional   E = educational
A = activist/political   H = health (incl. HIV)   ✍ = media/press   💻 = Internet resource
The Bisexual Resource Guide 2000   **257**

Nayim5　　　　　　　　　　　　　**Y**
Rochester NY
tel: 716-473-6459
Lesbigay Jewish group. youth + adult.

Nazareth College: Lambda Association　　♂
4245 East Avenue
Rochester NY 14618
tel: 716-586-2525
*Monthly meetings in Student Union. Contact
Student Union for more info.*

Rochester Gay Married Men's　　　　**M♂**
Support Group
Box 10041
Rochester NY 14610-0041
tel: Don Hall: 461-3799
*To help men balance being married & being
erotically attracted to men.*

Rochester Institute of Technology:　　♂
Bisexual, Gay & Lesbian Alliance of RIT
PO Box 9887
1 Lomb Memorial Drive
c/o Student Directorate/RITreat
Rochester NY 14623

St. John Fisher College: Bi-GALA+　　♂P
c/o Student Government Association
3690 East Avenue
Rochester NY 14618
*LGB & supportive students & professors whose
main purpose is to bring about a safe environment for those students who are questioing their
sexuality or wish to educate themselves about
LGB concerns.*

University of Rochester: GLBFA　　♂EA⌨
Wilson Commons #101J
Rochester NY 14627
tel: 716-275-9379; fax: 716-473-2404
e-mail: rb012B@uhura.cc.rochester.edu
URL: www.cif-rochester.edu/sa-org/glbfa/
*Serves all members of the University community
in Rochester. Highlights include pride week &
Lambda Alumni Association.*

Upstate New York Gay & Lesbian　　♂E⌨
Intercollegiate Network
c/o Rachael Brister & Lisa Peters
Wilson Commons 101J
Rochester NY 14627
tel: 716-275-9379 & 716-473-2404
e-mail: rb007c@uhura.cc.rochester.edu;
lp002c@uhura.cc.rochester.edu
URL: www.cif.rochester.edu/sa-org/glbfa/
unygalin.html
*UNYGALIN is an organization that allows for
the sharing of ideas on matters that are relevant
to GLB student associations on college campuses.
Focus on creative programming, membership,
retention, budgeting, support services, & campus
visibility.*

Pride Community Center
Syracuse NY
tel: 315-446-4436

Syracuse University: Pride Union　　♂⌨
750 Ostron Avenue
Syracuse NY 13210
tel: 315-443-3599 (helpline)
URL: students.syr.edu/student_orgs/Spec_Int/
GLBSA
*Library, social activities, disussion groups,
referrals, etc.*

Rensselaer Polytechnic Institute:　　♂E⌨
Gay, Lesbian & Bisexual Alliance
Box 146
Troy NY 12181-0146
tel: 518-276-2655 (events line); fax: 518-276-6920
Mark Fax to GLBA Box 68
e-mail: glba@rpi.edu
URL: www.rpi.edu/dept/union/glba/public_html/
index.html
*Group of women & men who meet regularly to
socialize, hear speakers & plan events & other
activities.*

Safety Zone　　　　　　　　　　　　**Y**
Damarise Mann
308 8th Street
Troy NY 12180
fax: 518-272-6561
e-mail: damanse@globalzero.net
GLBT youth drop-in center.

North Carolina

Gay & Lesbian Attorneys of North Carolina　**P**
(GALA)
Chapel Hill NC
tel: 919-956-5600
*"We certainly intend to include bisexual &
transgendered people. But it's not in the name
anymore."*

NC Lambda Youth Network　　　　　**Y**
c/o Duke University
202 Flowers Building, Duke Campus
Durham NC 27708
tel: 919-683-3037
Statewide LGBT youth leadership network.

North Carolina Lesbian, Gay,　　　　**A**
Bisexual & Transgender Pride, Inc.
NC
tel: 919-990-1005
e-mail: ncprideinc@aol.com
*Moves around the state, in a different city each
year.*

Key to symbols:　　▼ = bi　　♀ = women　　♂ = men　　☯ = religious/spiritual
☺ = for allies　　**M** = for married bis　　♥ = for partners of bis　　**Y** = youth　　**C** = people of color
258　　　　　　　　　　　　　　　　　　　　　　　**The Bisexual Resource Guide 2000**

The Front Page　　　　　　　　🖼📖
PO Box 27928
Raleigh NC 27611
tel: 919-829-0181
e-mail: frntpage@aol.com
URL: www.frontpagenews.com
Statewide newspaper which prints statewide directory.

Local

Triangle Area Bisexual Women's Support　▼ ♀
Group
106 Laurel Hill Road
Chapel Hill NC 27514
tel: Sian McLeary 919-933-0485
Support & social activities. Meetings on 3rd Sundays in Durham.

Charlotte Bisexual Support Group　　　　▼
Charlotte NC
tel: Elizabeth: 704-532-9197
"A monthly meeting for confidential support & discussion about issues important to bisexuals is held in the Charlotte area. Open to Bisexuals & Bi-friendly folk." Call in the evening.

Triangle Bisexual Network,　　　　　　▼ ♥
Raleigh Chapter
4205 Pleasant Valley Road, Suite 232
Raleigh NC 17612-2632
tel: 919-856-8370; (919) 406-7555
Serves Wake, Franklin & Johnston counties. Resources, social events. Also a Non-Bi Partners of Bisexuals group.

Community Connections
NC
tel: 828-251-2449

C.L.O.S.E.R. PFLAG/GLBT Ministry　　　🐞
Asheville NC
tel: 336-277-7815
Community Liason Organization for Support, Education & Reform.

Warren Wilson College: GLB Coalition　　🎓
PO Box 9000
Asheville NC 28815

Crape Myrtle Festival
Chapel Hill NC
tel: 919-967-3606
A non-profit fundraiser for the community.

Orange Lesbian/Gay Alliance　　　　　　A
Chapel Hill NC
tel: 919-929-4053
Local political action group.

P-FLAG　　　　　　　　　　　　　　🐞
Chapel Hill NC
tel: 919-929-0192
Parents & friends of lesbians & gays.

University of North Carolina, Chapel Hill:　🎓
Campus Bisexuals, Gays, Lesbians & Allies
for Diversity
CB# 5210
Union Box 39
Chapel Hill NC 27514
tel: 919-962-4401
e-mail: B-GLAD-L@gibbs.oit.unc.edu
Plans activities, including "Coming Out Stories" on National Coming Out Day.

Gay & Lesbian Switchboard
Charlotte NC
tel: 704-565-5075

Mecklenburg GLPAC
Charlotte NC
tel: 704-553-7906
Promoting GLBT equality in Mecklenburg County.

Out Charlotte　　　　　　　　　　　📖
PO Box 32062
Charlotte NC 28232-2062
tel: 704-563-2699
e-mail: OutChar@aol.com
URL: www.outcharlotte.org
Annual cultural festival celebrating the LGBT community as well as film series & cultural events.

PFLAG Charlotte　　　　　　　　　　🐞
Charlotte NC
tel: 704-364-1474

TIME OUT　　　　　　　　　　　　　Y
4037 East Independence Blvd.
Suite G33
Charlotte NC 28205
tel: 704-537-5050
Support group for LGBT youth, ages 13-23, meets Mondays at 7:30pm. Office hours 10-6 Mon-Fri.

B-ME/Black Gay, Lesbian, Bisexual　　　C
Positive Image Exchange
PO Box 48065
Cumberland NC 28331-8065
tel: 910-868-6883; 1-888-886-7423
Organization designed to promote healthy, positive self-image for members of the Black lgbt communities. Especially sensitive to bi/trans issues.

🖼 = school　　　🎓 = college/university　　　P = professional　　　E = educational
A = activist/political　　H = health (incl. HIV)　　🖼 = media/press　　📖 = Internet resource

All About Eve ♀
711 Rigsbee Av.
Durham NC 27701-2138
tel: 919-688-3002
Women's private club.

Duke University:

▼ **Center for Lesbian, Gay, Bisexual & Transgendered Life** &⌐🖥
202 Flowers; Box 90958
Durham NC 27708
tel: 919-684-6607 ; fax: 919-681-7873
e-mail:
lgbcenter@acpub.duke.edu
URL: www.duke.edu/web/queer/
Besides friendly talk & a safe space, the Center has information, magazines, AIDS information, safer sex guides, books, & resource guides. Bag lunch series. Open & staffed M-F 9am-5pm. John Howard, Director.

photo courtesy of the woman in the photo

▼ **Gay, Lesbian & Bisexual Association** &⌐
Bryan Center 101-3
Durham NC 27710
tel: Contact: Seth Persity, President: 919-684-6607
e-mail: koessm@acpub.duke.edu
Undergraduate group.

▼ **Task Force on Lesbian, Gay & Bisexual Matters** &⌐
Robin Buhrke
c/o Vice Pres. for Student Affairs
PO Box 90937
Durham NC 27708
tel: Robin Buhrke 919-660-1000
e-mail: rbuhrke@acpub.duke.edu
Investigate & promotes better conditions for LGB students on campus.

▼ **Duke LGB Discussion Group (E-mail list)** &⌐🖥
e-mail: dukelgb@acpub.duke.edu
For those interested in LGB issues at Duke. Provides gay, lesbian & bi students, faculty & employees at Duke University, friends & supporters, with info about events & courses on campus, & about happenings & events of interest in the world outside. Independent & University sanctioned. To subscribe send email to majordomo@acpub.duke.edu with text "subscribe duke lgb".

▼ **BiGALA Duke** &⌐
Box 61026
Durham NC 27715-1012
e-mail:
BiGALADuke@aol.com
Duke's lgb alumni group. Sponsors events at Homecoming & has a periodic newsletter. Write or e-mail for a registration form. Contact: Lee Golusinski.

▼ **CHUTZPAH: Queer Jews & Friends** &⌐
Ctr. for LGB Life
e-mail: chutzpah@duke.edu
A social group for queer Jews & friends at Duke.

▼ **Gothic Queers** &⌐
Bryan Center 101-3
Durham NC 27710
tel: Seth Persity, President
919-684-6607
e-mail: gothicqueers@duke.edu

▼ **Queer Grads** &⌐AP
Center for LGB Life
Flowers Building
Durham NC 27708
e-mail: queergrads@duke.edu
Active social campus group, open to students (esp. grad & professional students), staff & all others in the Duke LGB community. We are both a social & political organization, offering a variety of activities throughout the year.

▼ **Sacred Worth** ☯&⌐
Attn: Dean Blackburn
Durham NC 27701
e-mail: hdb@acpub.duke.edu
For LGB Christians, any denomination.

Durham Friends Meeting ☯
404 Alexander Rd.
Durham NC 404 Alexander Rd.
Quakers.

Eno River Unitarian Universalist Fellowship ☯
4907 Garrett Rd.
Durham NC

Kerr/Lee Community Center/ Information Line
PO Box 61031
Durham NC 27715
tel: 919-286-1157
For the lgbt & allies community. This organization provides space for glbt organizations to hold meetings, etc. & have an info line.

Key to symbols: ▼ = bi   ♀ = women   ♂ = men   ☯ = religious/spiritual
☄ = for allies   **M** = for married bis   ♥ = for partners of bis   **Y** = youth   **C** = people of color
260   The Bisexual Resource Guide 2000

Queer Jews & Friends ✆
818 Onslow St.
Durham NC
tel: 919-286-7801
Jewish religious & social gatherings.

Emmaus Metropolitan Community Church ✆
PO Box 346
Fayetteville NC 28302-0346
tel: 910-678-8813
e-mail: emmausmcc@aol.com
*New MCC Church in the city that boasts Ft.
Bragg.*

Fayetteville Area Gay Pride A
Fayetteville NC
tel: 910-822-4802; 910-424-7454

Lambda Association of Fayetteville
Fayetteville NC
tel: 910-487-8743
Social group for lgbt folks.

St. Paul's In-The-Pines Episcopal Church ✆
1705 St. Augustine Avenue
Fayetteville NC 28304-5236
tel: 910-485-7098
*"Female pastor VERY friendly to the LGBT
community."*

Alternative Resources of the Triad
Greensboro NC
tel: 336-855-8558
*Operates a hotline, referral center & sponsors
support groups. Hotline operates nightly 7-10pm.*

Gay & Lesbian Adolescent Y
Support System (GLASS)
Greensboro NC
tel: 336-272-6053
Youth support group for ages 15-21.

**Gay, Lesbian & Bisexual Veterans of
America**
130-C N. Walnut Cr.
Greensboro NC 27409

Gay , Lesbian & Straight Education Network
Greensboro NC
tel: 336-271-8428
*Advocates for LGBT staff & students in school
communities.*

Guilford College: ᵍ᷉
Gays, Lesbians, Bisexuals & Allies
PO Box 17725
Greensboro NC 27410

PFLAG ✎E
Greensboro NC
tel: 336-852-8489
Meets 3rd Tues. of every month.

University of North Carolina, Greensboro: ᵍ᷉
Gay, Lesbian & Bisexual Student Alliance
Box 27 Eliot University Center
Greensboro NC 27412
tel: 336-334-4282
e-mail: glbsa@uncg.edu

Down East Gay, Lesbian, Bisexual & 🖳
Transgendered Information Line
Po Box 1691
Greenville NC 27835-1691
tel: 252-551-0316
e-mail: downeastpride@bigfoot.com
URL: www.ecu/edu/org/bglad/dep/
Also put on the Down East Pride Festival.

East Carolina University: ᵍ᷉E🖳
**Bisexuals, Gays, Lesbians, & Allies for
Diversity (B-GLAD)**
c/o Office of Student Leadership Development
109 Mendenhall Student Center, ECU
Greenville NC 27858
tel: 252-328-6149
e-mail: vcbglad@ecuvm.cis.ecu.edu
bglad@mail.ecu.edu
URL: www.ecu.edu/org/bglad/nccp/campuses.html
*For glb & ally students of ECU to meet to further
these issues on campus & in the surrounding
community. Website with very large Index of
GLBT student groups in NC.*

Outer Banks Gay & Lesbian Club
PO Box 1444
Manteo NC 27954
e-mail: outerbanks_glc@geocities.com
*Primarily social glbt oganization. "Recently
more inclusive of bi/trans folks."*

ASPYN - A Safer Place Youth Network Y🖳
PO Box 28913
Raleigh NC 27611-8913
tel: 919-839-2912
*Non-threatening, social outlet for GLB &
questioning youth in Raleigh & surrounding
areas. Meetings facilitated by adults, but run by
the youth.*

National Gay & Lesbian Journalists P
Association - Central Carolina Chapter
Raleigh NC
tel: 919-859-4889

North Carolina Pride PAC A
PO Box 2876B
Raleigh NC 27611-8788
tel: 919-829-0343
LGB political action committee.

Raleigh Hopeline
Raleigh NC
tel: 919-231-4525
Support & crisis hotline.

✎ = school   ᵍ᷉ = college/university   **P** = professional   **E** = educational
A = activist/political   **H** = health (incl. HIV)   ✍ = media/press   🖳 = Internet resource
The Bisexual Resource Guide 2000   **261**

Triangle Community Works ☯
PO Box 5961
Raleigh NC 27650-5961
tel: 919-781-7574
Coaliton w/ member groups dedicated to LGB issues in Raleigh & the triangle area. Gay & lesbian help line any weekday night 7-10pm 919-821-0055.

Winthrop College: ♂⌢
Gay, Lesbian, Bisexual & Ally League (GLOBAL)
c/o Student Activities
Rock Hill NC 29733
tel: Student Activities: 803-323-2247

GROW Resource Line
Wilmington NC
tel: 910-350-8866
Crisis Line: 910-392-7408
G/L/allies resource line.

Alternative Resources of the Triad
Winston Salem NC
tel: 336-748-0031
Operates hotline 7-10pm nightly.

PFLAG ♠
Winston Salem NC
tel: 336-760-8865
Meets 4th Tues. of every month.

Youth Flag Y
Winston Salem NC
tel: 336-765-6694
Support group for youth organized by PFLAG Winston Salem.

North Dakota

North Dakota State University: ♂⌢⌨
Ten Percent Society
see listing under Minnesota (Moorhead State University: Tri-College Ten Percent Society)
Fargo ND
tel: Larry Peterson: 701-231-8824
URL: www.acm.ndsu.nodak.edu/Ten_Percent/

"I think you're confused and you're experimenting. You're experimenting because you'll have to pick one or the other. You have to be one or the other. Either gay or straight. You can't enjoy both. That's impossible."

—Geraldo (in Freaks Talk Back, p. 158.)

Ohio

Kaleidoscope Youth Coalition/Rainbow Y⌨
Pride Hotline & Drop-In Center
PO Box 8104
Columbus OH 43201
tel: 614-294-7886; 614-447-7199 coalition; 1-800-291-9190 hotline
e-mail: support@kaleidoscope.org
URL: www.kaleidoscope.org
Rainbow Pride Hotline 24 hour toll free support & info. line for GLBT youth in Ohio. Drop-in hours: Wed. 8-10pm, Fri 7-10pm at Northminster Presbyterian Church, 203 King Ave. **Publication(s):** *GLBT Youth Resource Guide Resources for youth, educators, counselors, child service agencies.*

Men of Color Outreach Project ♂CE⌨
3458 Reading Road
Cincinnati OH 45229
tel: 513-487-6520; fax: 513-281-0455
e-mail: tpayne@gcul.org
URL: www.gcul.org
Meetings 2nd, 4th Thurs. 6:30-8pm. SIMBA (Safe in My Brother's Arms): meeting/training for men interested in being buddies or peer-to-peer trainers meets 1st, last Fri. 6-8PM. Literary Club meets 1st Mon. **Publication(s):** *Parity 2000 newsletter, Brother II Brother newsletter*

People of All Colors Together (PACT)
OH
tel: 513-395-PACT
e-mail: PACTCINOH@aol.com
Co-chairs- Roger Burgess 591-2833, Jim Wagner 961-4475

Central Ohio

Bi Women for Women ▼♀
PO Box 10814
Columbus OH 43201
tel: 614-299-7764 (Stonewall Union); 614-267-0383 (Nicole)
e-mail: qg@ix.netcom.com
Informal discussion group for bi women, meets 1st Wed. 7:30pm at Stonewall Union.

Buckeye Region Anti-Violence A
Organization (BRAVO)
Columbus OH
tel: 614-268-9622
Compiles hate-crime statistics, aids victims of violence, & battles violence against GLBT people.

Key to symbols: ▼ = bi   ♀ = women   ♂ = men   ☯ = religious/spiritual
♠ = for allies   **M** = for married bis   ♥ = for partners of bis   Y = youth   C = people of color
262   **The Bisexual Resource Guide 2000**

Columbus State GABLE Cougars ‪⁉
Nester 116
550 E. Spring
Columbus OH
tel: 614-227-2637

Diversity of Ohio   **C**
263 Crestview Road
Columbus OH 43202
tel: 614-486-5664
Contact: Sharifa Williams. Statewide coalition of LGBT people of color.

Insight   **P**
PO Box 360821
Columbus OH 43236
GLB professionals.

Ohio Human Rights Bar Association   **P**
PO Box 10655
Columbus OH 43201
GLB lawyers.

PFLAG   **YE**♦⌂
P.O Box 340101
Columbus OH 43234
tel: 614-227-9355
URL: www.geocities.com/WestHollywood/8840
Publishes Resource Guide for GLBT youth, parents, & schools in Columbus & Franklin County area. Includes social service agencies, religious organizations, health & legal resources, support/advice groups, & a bibliography of books, articles, videos, etc. Meets last Sundays, 2pm Unitarian Universalist Church on Weisheimer Rd.

Phoenix Pride Youth Group   **Y**
c/o Southeast Recovery Mental Health Services
1455 S. 4th St.
Columbus OH 43207
tel: 614-444-0800; 614-444-1036
Meets Sat. 11am-1pm & Wed. 6-8pm at Northminster Church, 203 King Ave.

Stonewall Anti-Violence Project   **A**
1160 N. High St.
Columbus OH 43201
tel: 614-299-7764
Compiles hate-crime statistics for the GLB community, aids victims of hate-crimes, & offers self-defense training.

Stonewall Union Center
1160 N. High Street
PO Box 10814
Columbus OH 43201-7814
tel: GLB Hotline 614-299-7764; fax: 614-299-4408
URL: www.stonewall-columbus.org/
GLB community center. Jeff Redfield, Director. Hotline is staffed M-Th 10-7; F 10-5.
Publication(s)*: Stonewall Journal (monthly free publications) & Lavender Listings (yearly free business & resource guide for Columbus area)*

☜ = school   ‪⁉ = college/university   **P** = professional   **E** = educational
A = activist/political   **H** = health (incl. HIV)   ☍ = media/press   ⌂ = Internet resource

The Ohio State University: B-GALA &
1739 North High Street
Columbus OH 43210
tel: 614-292-6200
e-mail: bgala@osu.edu or smith.3023@osu.edu
Student group, meets Wed. 8pm in Ohio Union #G. Queer Lunch Wed. 11am-1pm at Stuff Your Face Pizza, Ohio Union.

The Ohio State University: &
Gay, Lesbian & Bisexual Student Services
464 Ohio Union
1739 North High Street , #340
Columbus OH 43210
tel: 614-292-6206; fax: 614292-4462
e-mail: glbss@osu.edu or
singleton.21@magnus.acs.ohio-state.edu
University office with paid staff & programming budget. Umbrella for several campus GLBT groups.

Ohio Wesleyan University: & E
Gay/Lesbian/Bisexual Resource Center
Hamilton-Williams Campus Center Rm. 225
Delaware OH 43015
tel: 740-368-3196

Ohio Wesleyan University: Pride &
Hamilton-Williams Campus Center
Student Activities Office
Delaware OH 43015
tel: 740-368-3196
e-mail: prideweb@cc.owu.edu
URL: cc.owu.edu/~prideweb

Kenyon College: Allied Sexual &
Orientations & Queer Action (ALSO)
Gambier OH 43022
tel: 740-427-5661

Denison University OUTLOOK A &
Slater Box 2406
Granville OH 43023
tel: 740-587-6696 (Womens Resource Center) 740-587-6366 Leticia Johnson student activities.
Meets in Women's Resource Center first floor Fellows Hall Rm 105. GLBT advocacy group.

Wittenberg University: Spectrum &
PO Box 6100
Springfield OH 45501

Otterbein College: BiGALA &
Westerville OH 43081-2006
tel: 614-823-1258

Muskingum College: &
Alternative Lifestyle Awareness
New Concord OH
tel: 614-826-8091

Northeast Ohio

Akron Area Pride Collective A
Akron OH
tel: 330-657-2977
e-mail: orange@ranbow-akron.com
Meets 2nd & 4th Tues. 7pm. Brian E. Simmons, co-chair. Produces Akron's Annual GLB Pride Weekend.

Akron Les-Bi-Gay Youth Support Y
c/o YWCA
220 S. Bolt St.
Akron OH
tel: 330-258-3652
Sat. 11:30am-1:30pm at Bolt St. Fitness & Recreation.

PRYSM (Akron) Y
East Akron YMCA
100 Goodyear Blvd.
Akron OH 44305-4034
tel: Voice mail: 330-258-3652 or 216-375-2437 (NE Task Force on AIDS)
Discussion/social/support for GLBT teens & adults to age 22. Meets Saturdays 11:30-1:30 at above address.

rainbow-akron.com ⌨
Akron OH
Akron internet service provider that provides www service for Akron, Cleveland, Kent & Medina, OH.

University of Akron: & E ⌨
Lesbian, Gay, Bisexual Union
Gardner Center #14
Akron OH 44325-4601
tel: 330-972-6851
e-mail: lgbu@uakron.edu
include "LGBU" in the subject of email
URL: www.uakron.edu/lgbu/
Open to students & non-students. Meets weekly during termtime. Elm room, Gardner Student Center. **Publication(s):** *LGBU Notebad*

PFLAG Alliance ◊
2541 Pleasant Place
Alliance OH 44601
tel: 440-821-0177, helpline: 800-956-6630

PFLAG Elyria/Lorain County ◊
730 Park Ave.
Amherst OH 44001
tel: 440-988-8215

PFLAG Ashtabula ◊
1710 Walnut Blvd.
Ashtabula OH 44004
tel: 440-964-3350
Meets last Fri. 7pm, Donohoe Center conference room, U.S. 20 East, Ashtabula.

Key to symbols: ▼ = bi   ♀ = women   ♂ = men   ☯ = religious/spiritual
◊ = for allies   **M** = for married bis   ♥ = for partners of bis   **Y** = youth   **C** = people of color

Baldwin Wallace College: Lambda/Allies 🐾🌢
275 Eastland
Berea OH 44017
tel: 440-826-2356
*Contact Director of Student Activities for
meeting times, etc. Lambda is a GLB group.
Allies is a program group of GLB & straight
people. Lambda meets Wednesdays.*

Bowling Green State University: Vision 🐾🖳
University Hall Box 22
Bowling Green OH 43403
tel: 419-372-0555
URL: www.bgsu.edu/studentlife/organizations/
vision
*Regular meetings Wed. 9pm 2nd floor lounge of
Saddlemire Student Services. Also a support
group, VisionLite.*

Bowling Green University: 🐾 ♀
Womyn 4 Womyn
463 Saddlemire Student Services
Bowling Green University
Bowling Green OH 43403
tel: 419-372-2281
e-mail: jhollid@bgnet.bgsu.edu
*Call for meeting times & activities. Contact
Jennifer Holliday at the office, or by e-mail, for
more info.*

ACT UP HA
c/o L-G Center
PO Box 6177
Cleveland OH 44101
tel: 216-861-4946, 888-334-4849

African-American Lesbian/Gay/Bisexual CA
Caucus
PO Box 6177
Cleveland OH 44101
tel: 216-522-1999

Black Pride Planning Committee C
Cleveland OH
tel: 216-522-1999
1st & 3rd Sun., 3-4pm.

Case Western Reserve University: 🐾🖳
Gay, Lesbian, Bisexual Alliance
c/o Thwing Student Office
10900 Euclid Av.
Cleveland OH 44106
tel: 216-754-2215; 216-791-3103; 216-622-2988
(Paul Ellwood)
e-mail: pxe@po.cwru.edu
URL: www.cwru.edu/orgs/glba/GLBA.html
*Group open to non-students also, educational/
social focus. Weekly meetings during termtime.*

Case Western Reserve University: 🐾
Lesbian-Gay-Bisexual People in Medicine
10900 Euclid Avenue
Cleveland OH 44106
tel: 216-368-5871

Cleveland Irish LesBiGay Organization
Cleveland OH
tel: Diane, 216-281-8384, 216-255-2615

Cleveland State University: E🐾🖳
**Lesbian, Gay, Bisexual & Transgender
Alliance**
Cleveland OH
tel: 216-687-4510; 216-615-6570
e-mail: r.gallagher@popmail.csuohio.edu
URL: www.csuohio.edu/gala/index2.html

Equality Ohio A
Cleveland OH
tel: 216-522-1999
*EO is a glbt Political Action Committee. EO
holds meetings at The Center (in Cleveland).*

Lambda Amateur Radio Club P
PO Box 91757
Cleveland OH 44101
tel: 216-381-4774
e-mail: DougBraun@aol.com
*LGBT ham radio operators. Affiliate of amateur
relay league.*

Lesbian & Bi Coming Out Group ♀🖳
c/The Lesbian/Gay Community Services Center
PO Box 6177
Cleveland OH 44101-1177
tel: 216-522-1999 (The Center)
URL: The Center: www.lgcsc.org

PRYSM (Cleveland) Y
PO Box 6144
Cleveland OH 44101
tel: 216-522-1999 or 216-861-5454
*Discussion/social/support for GLBT teens &
adults to age 22. Meets Saturdays 12-2 at
Cleveland Lesbian/Gay Service Center 1418 W.
29th St at Detroit. (#26 bus) Support group for
parents of GLBT youth meets on first Sat of
every month. Drop in nights Wed. 6:30-9pm.*

Sign of the Rainbow
P.O. Box 6253
Cleveland OH 44101
Deaf & hearing impaired organization.

Stonewall, Cleveland
PO Box 5936
Cleveland OH 44101
tel: 216-556-0466
*Meets 1st Mon. 7pm, Cleveland Lesbian-Gay
Center, 1418 W. 29th St. (at Detroit).*

🐾 = school   🐾 = college/university   **P** = professional   **E** = educational
A = activist/political   **H** = health (incl. HIV)   📰 = media/press   🖳 = Internet resource
The Bisexual Resource Guide 2000   **265**

Christopher Street Day 1998 in Köln, Germany.

Twenty Something
PO Box 6177
Cleveland OH 44101-1177
tel: 216-522-1999
Social, discussion, education group for GLB people, ages 18-33. Meets 1st & 3rd Fridays at 8-10 pm, 1418 W.29th St. at Detroit.

Western Reserve Historical Society: Gay & E
Lesbian Archives
Cleveland OH
tel: 216-721-5722
Gay & Lesbian Archives document GLB history in NE Ohio.

Gray Pride E
2373 Euclid Heights Blvd.
Cleveland Heights OH 44106
tel: 216-621-7201x213, 216-381-4774(after 7:30pm), 216-791-8039x328; fax: 216-791-8030
e-mail: DougBraun@aol.com or graypride@juno.com
Meets 2nd Tues., locations TBA. 60+year-olds. Interpreting for the deaf provided upon request.

Lorain Community College: ⚥
Gay, Lesbian, Bisexual Student Association
College Center, 1004 N. Abbe Rd.
Elyria OH 44052
tel: 216-233-7244 x7103

Hiram College: ⚥
Lesbian Gay & Bisexual Union
c/o Student Activities
Box 8
Hiram OH 44234
tel: 330-569-5935
Meets Mon. 7pm during termtime.

Kent State University: ⚥
Lesbian, Gay, Bisexual Union
Kent Student Center, PO Box 17, Rm. 235
Kent OH 44242
tel: 330-672-2068
Meets Thurs. 8pm during termtime on 3rd floor of Student Center, room 318.

Mother Wit ♀
PO Box 265
Kent OH 44240
tel: 330-678-4686
Lesbian & bisexual mothers. This group is for any l/b woman who has ever mothered at anypoint (could be a neice, nephew, or siblings). Women in opposite-sex relationships are welcome.

Bisexual & Married Gay Men ♂ M
send mail to: BMGM
PO Box 770932
Lakewood OH 44107-0041
tel: Doug:216-961-7731
Monthly Support & Social Group. Meets 4th Tues. 7:30 PM

Mentor Center (HUGS East) Rap Group
PO Box 253
Mentor OH 44061-0253
tel: 440-974-8909 (answered live Wed. 7-9pm)
Social & discussion group. Meets Wednesdays 7pm at East Shore Church: 8181 S. Center St. (Ohio 615). The Center serves Lake, Geauga & Ashtabula counties.

Key to symbols: ▼ = bi ♀ = women ♂ = men ☯ = religious/spiritual
🔥 = for allies M = for married bis ♥ = for partners of bis Y = youth C = people of color
266 **The Bisexual Resource Guide 2000**

Asians & Friends, Cleveland　　　　　**C**
c/o Jeff Yu
16465 Heather Lane, Suite 204
Middleburg Heights OH 44130
tel: 216-226-6080 x3
e-mail: silverark@aol.com
URL: www.longyangclub.com/cleveland/
IFW98.html
Social meetings 2nd Sun, business meetings last Sun, potlucks open to general members. Sponsors annual International Friendship Weekend. (Labor Day 1998). **Publication(s):** *Asians & Friends Published spring, summer, fall, winter.*

Oberlin College: Lesbian/Gay/Bisexual/　*&ʔ*
Transgendered Union
Wilder Hall, Rm. 202, Box 88
Oberlin OH 44074-0088
tel: 440-775-8179
Publication(s): *SNAP: It's a Queer Thing*

Oberlin College:　　　　　　*&ʔ* 🖳
Oberlin Lambda Alumni
c/o Oberlin Alumni Association
Bosworth Hall
55 West Lorain Street
Oberlin OH 44074-1044
tel: 440-775-8692; fax: 440-775-6748
e-mail: zola@oberlin.edu
URL: www.oberlin.edu/~alumassc/OLA/
Publication(s): *OLA News www.oberlin.edu/ ~alumassc/OLA/newsletterOLA.html*

PFLAG Akron　　　　　　　　　🔥
723 Tinkers Lane
Sagamore Hills OH 44067
tel: 330-342-5825

PFLAG Cleveland　　　　　　🔥 🖳
14260 Larchmere Blvd.
Shaker Heights OH 44120
tel: 216-556-4317
URL: members.aol.com/pflagcleve/
Meets 2nd Tues, 7:30pm, Trinity Cathedral, E. 22 & Euclid, Cleveland, rear entrance.

John Carroll Allies　　　　　　*&ʔ*
20700 N. Park
Box 9999
University Heights OH 44118
tel: 216-397-2489

College of Wooster:　　　　　*&ʔ*A🖳
Gay Lesbian Bisexual Alliance
College of Wooster
Box C-3166
Wooster OH 44691
tel: 216-287-3868 (Jessica) or 4203 (Alicia)
e-mail: efitzgerald@acs.wooster.edu
URL: www.wooster.edu/glba
Meets Mon. 8pm, Lowry Center Room 119. Advisor is Eileen Fitzgerald. Another group, GABLES, meets Mon. after dinner in Women's Resource Center in Lowry for more personal discussion of G/L/B issues in their lives.

Wayne County Gay, Lesbian, Bisexual Community
Wooster OH
tel: 330-262-4142
Meets 3rd Tues. at Westminster Presbyterian Church House, 353 Pine St, Wooster.

PFLAG Youngstown　　　　　　　🔥
2201 Goleta Avenue
Youngstown OH 44004
tel: 330-747-2696
e-mail: smschild@cc.ysu.edu
Meets 3rd Sun, 3pm, Christ church Presbyterian annex, Hopkins at Canfield (US 62).

Youngstown State University: GALA　　*&ʔ*
Student Government Office
Kilcawley Center
Youngstown OH 44555
tel: 330-742-3591

Northwest Ohio

Ohio Northern University: Open Doors　*&ʔ* 🖳
Ada OH 45810
URL: www2.onu.edu/~stu0037/opend.html
Faculty advisor: Prof. Phil Compton.

Ohio State University:　　　　　*&ʔ*
Bi-Global (Lima Campus)
4240 Campus Drive
66 Galvin
Lima OH 45804
tel: 419-221-1641 x415

PFLAG Toledo　　　　　　　　🔥
PO Box 4619
Toledo OH 43620
tel: 419-244-4421
e-mail: pflag-toledo@geocities.com

"I'm simply trying to live a both/and life in an either/or world."

—*Tom Robinson*

🔥 = school　　　*&ʔ* = college/university　　　**P** = professional　　　**E** = educational
A = activist/political　　**H** = health (incl. HIV)　　🖾 = media/press　　🖳 = Internet resource
The Bisexual Resource Guide 2000　　　　　　　　　　　　　　　　**267**

University of Toledo: Rocket Rainbow &⁄ 🖳
Alliance/ Gay & Lesbian Student Union
3503 Student Union
Toledo OH 43606
tel: 419-530-7975
e-mail: glsu@pop3.utoledo.edu
URL: www.utoledo.edu/~rra_glsu/home.htm
*Meets Thurs. 8pm in Student Union Rm. 3018.
Membership open to both students & non-
students regardless of gender or sexual
orientation.*

Southeast Ohio

Ohio University: GLOBE Gay, &⁄ P🖳
Lesbian, or Bisexual Employees
Athens OH
tel: 740-593-1935
e-mail: cinoman@ouvaxa.cats.ohiou.edu
URL: cscwww.cats.ohiou.edu/~globe
Membership dues are $10/yr.

Ohio University: Lesbian-Gay-Bi-Trans A&⁄ 🖳
Commission of Student Senate
Ohio University
308 Baker, at 20 E. Union Street
Athens OH 45701
tel: 740-593-4049
e-mail: de315496@oak.cats.ohiou.edu
URL: www.ent.ohiou.edu/~senate/LGBC/
*Part of the Student Senate. Serves all students.
Political focus.*

Ohio University: A&⁄
Open Doors: GLBT Student Union
18 N. College St.
Athens OH 45701
tel: 740-594-2385
*Serves all, including straights. A social, support
& (some) political activism group. Meets
Wednesdays 8-10pm in living room of United
Campus Ministry.*

PFLAG Athens 🔥
40011 Carpenter Hill RD
Pomeroy OH 45769
tel: 740-698-2120

Southwest Ohio

BENT ♂ 🖳
PO Box 6370
Cincinnati OH 45206
tel: 812-689-5330
e-mail: Bentoki@aol.com or Bentboy@webtv.net
URL: www.gaynaturists.org/gni.html
*Group of gay/bi male naturists based in
Cincinnati. Members come from ~ 100 miles,
meet at member homes, once a month. Contact:
Gene*

Brother II Brother, Cincinnati, Inc. ♂ **CH**
5531 Hamilton Ave
Cincinnati OH 45224
tel: 513-542-5186 Terry Payne; 513-684-1348
Voice Mail
*Meets monthly. Family of diverse African
American communities dedicated to empowerment, education & improvement of the quality of
life. Seek to create nurturing environment by
organizing & providing social, spiritual, civic &
health care networks. Embraces & affirms all
GLB of African descent.* **Publication(s):**
Brother II Brother newsletter

Cincinnati Youth Group Y🖳
PO BOX 141061
Cincinnati OH 45250-1061
tel: 513-684-8405
e-mail: bearluvr@one.net
URL: www.gaycincinnati.com
*21 & under, trained adult facilitators. Contact:
Missy Sachs.*

Crazy Ladies Center ♀
4039 Hamilton Ave.
Cincinnati OH 45223
tel: 513-541-4198
*A center for the lesbian community & all
feminists. Offers a safe space where diverse
groups of women come together for discussion,
work & education.*

GLSEN/Cincinnati E
PO Box 19856
Cincinnati OH 45219
tel: 513-624-6963; fax: 513-345-5543
e-mail: GLSENcincy@aol.com
*Making schools safe for all students. $35
membership fee (includes both local & national
membership). Meets at the Gay & Lesbian
Community Center of Greater Cincinnati, last
Tues. every other month 7pm.* **Publication(s):**
national newsletter

Greater Cincinnati Gay & Lesbian 🖳
Community Center
Cincinnati OH
tel: 513-241-9400
URL: www.gaycincinnati.com (Rainbow
Cincinnati)

PFLAG Cincinnati 🔥
PO Box 19634
Cincinnati OH 45219-0634
tel: 513-721-7900

Key to symbols: ▼ = bi ♀ = women ♂ = men ☪ = religious/spiritual
🔥 = for allies **M** = for married bis ♥ = for partners of bis **Y** = youth **C** = people of color
268 **The Bisexual Resource Guide 2000**

Tri State Prime Timers   ♂ E 💻
PO Box 20171
Cincinnati OH 45220
tel: 513-956-1939
e-mail: primetimoh@aol.com
URL: www.primetimers.org/
*Mature gay/bisexual men & younger men who
admire mature men. Meets last week of every
month.*

University of Cincinnati: Gay, Lesbian,   👥 💻
Bisexual & Transgender Alliance
PO Box 0136
Cincinnati OH 45221-0136
tel: 513-556-1449
e-mail: ucalliance@hotmail.com
URL: www.soa.uc.edu/org/algbp/
Office in 209 TUC, open 11-3pm.

Dayton Lesbian & Gay Center
Dayton OH
tel: 937-274-1776 (hotline)
*A community based center for lgb people. Hotline
is staffed by volunteers 7-11pm.*

Dignity/Dayton
PO Box 55
Dayton OH 45401
tel: 937-277-7706
*A supportive community of GLBT & allies
within the Catholic community.*

GLSEN/Dayton
572 Towncrest Drive
Dayton OH 45434
tel: 937-427-1578
e-mail: glsenday@aol.com

PFLAG Dayton   👶 💻
PO Box 3721
Dayton OH 45401
tel: 937-640-3333
e-mail: pflagdayton@geocities.com
URL: www.geocities.com/WestHollywood/heights/
5274
*Meets 2nd Tues. 7:30pm, St. John's UCC, 515 E.
3rd St., Dayton.*

Team Dayton
Dayton OH
tel: 937-277-5125
*Sports & cultural opportunities for lgb persons.
Contact Tom Kohn.*

University of Dayton: B-GLAD   👥 E 💻
Dayton OH
tel: 937-229-3141
e-mail: rossman@trinity.udayton.edu
URL: www.udayton.edu/~campus/
bglad_group.htm
*Identity issued support group for lgb people at
Dayton. Weekly meetings. Group advisor is
Kathleen Rossman, OSF.*

Wright State University: Lambda Union   👥
Dayton OH 45435
tel: 937-775-5565; crisis hotline: 937-297-4777
*Meets Thursdays 7:30pm, W047 Student Union.
Office open weekdays 10-5.*

Youth Quest   Y
St Marks Episcopal Church
456 Woodman Drive
Dayton OH 45431
tel: 937-275-TEEN
*An organization for Lesbigay youth under 22
years of age.*

Miami University: 👥
Gay/Lesbian/Bisexual Alliance
PO Box 382
Oxford OH 45056
tel: Roy Boyen Ward: 513-529-4303
*Meets 8pm Thurs. in rm 297 Oppem Hall. Office
is in 381 Shriver Center.*

PFLAG Portsmouth   👶
11 Offnere St
Portsmouth OH 45662
tel: helpline: 740-353-1856

Oklahoma

University of Oklahoma: 👥 AE 💻
Gay, Lesbian & Bisexual Association
Ellison Hall 306
Norman OK 73019
tel: 405-325-4GLB
e-mail: tsj@ou.edu
URL: www.uo.edu/student/glba/
Weekly meetings.

Central Oklahoma Prime Timers   ♂ 💻
5030 North May Ave. #134
Oklahoma City OK 73112
tel: Gene: 405-424-3642
e-mail: gene3642@aol.com
URL: www.primetimers.org/copt/
*A social organization for mature gay & bi men
where mature means men over 30. Younger
partners (21-29 yrs. old) may become associate
members. Monthly meetings & regular organized
group activities. An affiliate of Prime Timers
Worldwide. Monthly newsletter with activity
calendar.*

"I got a girl in every port
and a couple of guys
in every port, too."

—*Sal Mineo, American actor, 1939-1976*

🐾 = school   👥 = college/university   **P** = professional   **E** = educational
A = activist/political   **H** = health (incl. HIV)   ✉ = media/press   💻 = Internet resource
The Bisexual Resource Guide 2000   **269**

Gay Oklahoma Men's Nudist Group ♂ ▣
(GOMN)
4922 Northwest 23rd, Suite 146
Oklahoma City OK 73127
tel: 405-498-6224
405-947-8827
e-mail: GOMN@jam.to
URL: members.theglobe.com/gomn/.html
Mostly gay; bi's encouraged. Strictly a nude male bonding group, not a sex group. **Publication(s)**:
GOMN Digest monthly

Herland Sister Resources, Inc. ♀
2312 N.W. 39th
Oklahoma City OK 73112
tel: 405-521-9696
Mostly for lesbians, but bisexual women are welcome. Small pride store & lending library, & social/support organization.
Open: Saturday & Sunday 1-5pm.
Publication(s): Herland Voice Newsletter

Oklahoma City Gay, Lesbian, Bisexual Community Services Center
2135 NW 39th St.
Oklahoma City OK 73112
tel: 405-524-6000
Provides a meeting space, information, & referrals. Health education & anonymous HIV testing by appointment. M 7-10pm, Tu-Fr 1-10-m, Sat 7pm-midnight.

Red Rock Behavioral Health YEH
Service's Young Gay & Lesbian Alliance
4400 N. Lincoln Boulevard
Oklahoma City OK 73105
tel: 405-425-0399
Has a bifriendly youth group (for those under 25) & offers twice-weekly meetings.

Simply Equal of Oklahoma City EA
PO Box 61305
Oklahoma City OK 73146
tel: 405-521-9696
Political group supportive of glbt issues.

Oklahoma State University: Gay, ✇ EA
Lesbian & Bisexual Community Association
040 Student Union, Box 601
Stillwater OK 74078
tel: 405-744-5252
"Educational, social & political link for people in Stillwater & surrounding areas. Weekly meetings, events, & educational material on GLB & AIDS/HIV issues."

HIV Outreach Prevention & Education
(HOPE)
3503 East Admiral
Tulsa OK 74115
tel: 918-834-TEST
Free, anonymous HIV testing clinic. Medical/educational focus, but runs discussion groups & a Men Having Sex With Men group. LGBT with a (not exclusive) focus on men.

Tulsa Area Prime Timers ♂
PO Box 52118
Tulsa OK 74152-0118
tel: 918-627-2359
e-mail: wesomer@gorilla.net
An affiliate of Prime Timers Worldwide. Social & recreational organization for gay or bi men over 21 in Tulsa & surrounding areas. Monthly meetings at the Pride Center + other activities.
Publication(s): Prime News

Tulsa Oklahomans for Human Rights EA
PO Box 2687
Tulsa OK 74101
tel: 918-743-4297 (Pride Center)
Runs the Pride Center, 1307 East 38th, Tulsa, OK 74135. Sun-Fri 6-10pm, Sat 12-10pm. 10 different organiztions, all bi-friendly. Popular referral center (bars, churches, realtors, doctors, etc.)

Oregon

BiNet, Oregon A▼
PO Box 2593
Portland OR 97208
tel: 541-265-5861
e-mail: geistnologging@hotmail.com
"Bi community building gathering." Focus on coalition building within the bi, gay & straight community. Hosts annual summer campout for Northwest bisexuals.

Local

Bisexual Community Forum ▼A
PO Box 11141
Portland OR 97211
tel: Laury: 503-285-4848
Socials held on 2nd & 4th Wed. 7:30pm at Utopia Cafe, 3320 SE Belmont, Portland.

Key to symbols: ▼ = bi ♀ = women ♂ = men ☯ = religious/spiritual
🖐 = for allies **M** = for married bis ♥ = for partners of bis **Y** = youth **C** = people of color
270 The Bisexual Resource Guide 2000

Portland Bisexual Alliance ▼🖳
PO Box 412
Portland OR 97207-0412
tel: 503-775-9717
e-mail: PBArainbow@aol.com
URL: members.aol.com/pbarainbow
Co-ed meeting 1st & 3rd Fridays 7pm, all ages. Social meetings, political actions, & annual Bi Day rally in June. Meetings at Habit Coffee House 3862 SE Hawthorne, Portland. 503-235-5321. Publication(s): Bisexual Portland Calender, lists all known Portland bi events. Members' newsletter available free by e-mail.

Portland Bisexual Women ▼ ♀
c/o Deborah Samuels
2504 N. Watts
Portland OR 97217
tel: Deborah: 503-283-6433 or Holly: 503-236-0505
e-mail: DebAbz@aol.com
Discussion group for bisexual women or any women wondering about their sexuality. Meets 2nd & 4th Fri. 7-9 at private home.

Bi Women's Caucus of Bradley ▼ ♀
Bradley OR
tel: Amy Gitana: 503-282-9940

Oregon State University, Corvallis: &⌒🖳
Lesbian, Gay, Bi, Transgender Alliance
Corvallis OR 97331-4501
tel: Susan Shaw, Faculty Advisor: 541-737-3082
URL: osu.orst.edu/groups/lgba/
Social group for students, faculty & the public.

Battered Lesbian Support Group ♀ H
Womenspace
Eugene OR
tel: 541-686-6660; 1-800-281-2800
Confidential group for lesbians & bi women who have been physically, sexually or emotionally batttered in their relationships. Not limited to same-sex relationships.

University of Oregon: Lesbian, &⌒YE🖳
Gay, Bisexual & Transgender Alliance
Erb Memorial Union, Ste 34
Eugene OR 97403
tel: 541-346-3360
e-mail: lgba@gladstone.uoregon.edu
URL: gladstone.uoregon.edu/~lgba
On-line newsletter available.

"[Caeser is] every man's wife and every woman's husband."

—*Curio the Elder, Roman writer, 53 B.C.*

University of Oregon: Lesbian, Gay, &⌒Y🖳
Bisexual, & Transgendered Youth Group
Kononia Center
1414 Kincaid St
Eugene OR 97403
e-mail: lgba@gladstone.uoregon.edu
URL: gladstone.uoregon.edu//.lgba/
Sexual orientation drop in groups weekly. Women's, men's & youth groups. Social hours Thurs., monthly potluck. Office hrs. M-F 8-5. Meets Mon. 5-6:30.

Together Works
First Baptist Church
125 SE Cowls
McMinnville OR
tel: Church 503-472-7941
Don Hutchinson 503-434-6266
Support group for LGBs & friends. Activities include discussion on timely topics & social activities. Neutral, safe environment. Oct-Apr at 7pm, May-Sept at 7:30pm, 2nd & 4th Mondays, First Baptist Church.

Oregon Public Employee's Union/Service P
Employee's International Union, Lavender Caucus
c/o Ann Montegue
PO Box 2171
Newport OR 97365
tel: 503-581-1505

African American Gay & Bisexual C♂H
Men's Support Groups
PO Box 3182
Portland OR 97208
tel: 503-417-7991
Discussions about HIV/AIDS, isolation, relationships & ways to build community.

Cascade AIDS Project (CAP) ♂H
Suite 300
620 SW 5th Avenue
Portland OR 92704-1418
tel: 503-223-5907; Gay Hotline 223-2437.
Non-medical services to people whose lives are affected by AIDS in Oregon. Gay & bi men's groups. HIV testing. "Speak to Your Brothers - HIV prevention for gay & bisexual men."

Lesbian Community Project ♀ A
PO Box 5931
Portland OR 97228
tel: 503-282-8090
"Bi inclusive, including bi folk in leadership. " Progressive organization to effect social change. Have socials, dances, annual softball tournament, youth group called "Formerly known as lesbian", bimonthly newlsetter, political action committee.

🎒 = school &⌒ = college/university P = professional E = educational
A = activist/political H = health (incl. HIV) 📰 = media/press 🖳 = Internet resource
The Bisexual Resource Guide 2000 271

Lewis & Clark College: &ᴄ **A E**
United Sexualities
Box 158
0615 Palatine Hill Rd.
Portland OR 97219
e-mail: homophil@lclark.edu
LGB support group for the college community.

Northwestern School of Law & &ᴄ **A**
Lewis & Clark College: Gays, Lesbians or
Bisexuals at Law (GLOBAL)
10015 SW Terwilliger Blvd.
Portland OR 97219
tel: 503-768-6600 (main # for school)
Support & advocacy group (straight friends welcome) for students at Northwestern School of Law & Lewis & Clark College. Frequent meetings & social events, on & off campus.

Oregon Health Services University: &ᴄ
All-Hill Gay, Lesbian, Bisexual Alliance
Portland OR
tel: Scott 503-494-5227 or 503-632-8569
Social gathering once per month. Social interaction for students, faculty, & staff with any connection to OHSU. **Publication(s)***: Just Out Newspaper Published 2x/month. 503-236-1252.*

Portland State University: &ᴄ
Lesbian, Gay & Bisexual Alliance
PO Box 751
Portland OR 97207-0751
tel: 503-725-5681
e-mail: lgba@sg.ess.pdx.edu
Mainly social group. Organizes around queer prom, queer folk festival, etc. Meets every other Friday for lunch, Smith Memorial Center basement. Trying to start a queer studies program.

Reed College: Queer Alliance &ᴄ
Signator QA
3203 SE Woodstock Blvd.
Portland OR 97202-8199
tel: Student Activities: 503-771-1112, ask for the name/# of the current LGBU signator
A social, educational & support group for students, faculty, & staff interested in LGBT issues.

Rosetown Ramblers
Portland OR
tel: 503-234-9944
Square dance club; also rollerskating, country western dancing.

Windfire **Y**
Phoenix Rising
620 SW 5th Avenue, Suite 710
Portland OR
tel: Phoenix Rising: 503-223-8299; SMYRC: 503-872-9664
Social & support group for people under 21 who are GLB or unsure. Meetings are small & informal. Call for times.
Youth meeting SMYRC (Sexual Minorities Youth Recreation Center), 424 E Burnside, Portland, Th 5:30-7:30pm.

Coalition to End Bigotry **A**
PO Box 13144
Salem OR 97309
tel: 603-373-4173, 6-8pm.
Broad-based coalition working to celebrate diversity by actively supporting & securing civil equality for gay men, lesbians & bisexuals. General meetings 3rd Sun.

Willamette University: &ᴄ **E A**
Lesbian, Gay, Bisexual Alliance
c/o Michael Marks
6932, Politics Department
Salem OR 97301
tel: Michael Marks: 503-370-6932; Richard Shintaku: 503-370-6265
Provides & encourage the support, education, & visibility
of glb concerns & issues in the Willamette/TIUA community. Aims to create an awareness & celebration of differing perspectives & lifestyles. Meets Tuesdays, 7pm, Womyn's Center-3rd Floor, University Center 503-370-6692.

Pennsylvania

Local

BiUnity Philadelphia ▼**A**🖳
P.O. Box 41905
Philadelphia PA 19101
e-mail: biunity@netaxs.com
URL: www.bisexual.org/biunity
Organizes: ocial gatherings; Bi Support Groups-men's support group & two women's support/discussion groups; participates in Pride Parades, Festivals, OutFest.

Key to symbols: ▼ = bi ♀ = women ♂ = men ☸ = religious/spiritual
🝱 = for allies M = for married bis ♥ = for partners of bis Y = youth C = people of color
272 The Bisexual Resource Guide 2000

Gay & Lesbian Community Center 🖳
PO Box 5441
Pittsburgh PA 15206
tel: 412-422-0114 (M-F 6:30-9:30pm; Sat. 3-6pm);
fax: 412-422-7913
e-mail: glccpgh@aol.com
URL: trfn.dpgh.org/glcc
*Located at 5808 Forward Avenue, Squirrel Hill.
Meeting spaces, library, youth group (for lgbt,
confused & open-minded youth under 22 meets
Friday nights 7:30, youth line: 422-1663),*
Publication(s): *The Pink Pages + newsletter.
Pink Pages = listings of GLBT oganizations,
business & professional services in the tri-state
area. Newsletter lists events.*

Valley Free Press: 📰
Gay & Lesbian Community News
PA
tel: 610-432-5449
*Local publication for the Lehigh Valley helping
to keep the GL aware of news & import events.*
Publication(s): *monthly, distributed free to
local organizations or call for subscription.*

Muhlenberg University: Rainbow Space ⚭
Allentown PA 18104
tel: 610-432-7571
e-mail: mittlem@muhlenberg.edu
Patti Mittleman, advisor.

Gay, Lesbian, Bisexual Helpline of Altoona E
c/o Family Services
2022 Broad Avenue
Altoona PA 16601
tel: 814-942-8101
*Provides information, referrals, phone
counseling, & one-on-one-counseling. Open M-F
8:30am-4:30pm.*

Gay, Lesbian & Bisexual Task Force
c/o Family Services
2022 Broad Avenue
Altoona PA 16601
tel: 814-944-3583

State College: Coalition of Lesbian, ⚭EA
Gay & Bisexual Graduate Students
c/o Gay & Lesbian Switchboard
PO Box 805
Altoona PA 16804
tel: 814-237-1950 (6-9pm daily)
*An organization of Penn State grad students.
Sponsors educational, social & political
activities.*

Lehigh University: Safe Space ⚭E🖳
c/o Chaplain's Office
110 Johnson Hall, 36 University Drive
Bethlehem PA 18015-3042
tel: 610-758-3877
e-mail: safespace@lehigh.edu
URL: www.lehigh.edu/~safespace
*GLBT & ally program. Speakers bureau,
speaker training, peer counseling.*

Bloomsburg University: Free Spirit ⚭E
Box 95, Kehr Union
Bloomsburg PA 17815
tel: 717-389-4332
717-389-2747, info line; fax: 717-389-2094
*For members of the GLBT community & our
allies - publishes in-house resource guide.*

University of Pitt - Bradford: ⚭E
Bisexual, Gay & Lesbian Alliance (BiGALA)
c/o Director of Student Activities
300 Campus Drive
Bradford PA 16701
tel: Student Activities Office: 814-362-7654
*A student group that sponsors social activities,
speakers, & other programs on campus.*

Bryn Mawr College: ⚭ ♀ AE
Rainbow Alliance
c/o Student Life Office, Bx 1725,C-765
101 North Merion Avenue
Bryn Mawr PA 19010
tel: 610-526-7331
*A social, educational, & political group of LB
students of Bryn Mawr College. Bryn Mawr also
has a confidential Lesbian-Bisexual Support
Group (LBSG) for women, & a speakers' bureau
which will send out speakers upon request.*

East Stroudsburg University: ⚭
Sexual Orientation & University Life (SOUL)
Office of Residence Life
University Center
East Stroudsburg PA 18301
tel: 717-422-3614; or John Judicki: 717-422-3123
e-mail: jjudicki@po-box.esu.edu
*Campus-wide umbrella organization for faculty,
staff & students. Student organization for GLBT
& allies meets bi-weekly. There is also an ally
organzation with approximately 75 faculty, staff
& students.*

Edinboro University of Pennsylvania: ⚭
Identity
c/o Student Government Association
Edinboro PA 16444
*For lesbigay people & allies, dedicated to
breaking down the baricades of sexual
stereotypes & promoting acceptance.*

🖎 = school   ⚭ = college/university   P = professional   E = educational
A = activist/political   H = health (incl. HIV)   📰 = media/press   🖳 = Internet resource
The Bisexual Resource Guide 2000   **273**

Penn State Behrend: ⚢
Trigon: Lesbian, Gay & Bisexual Coalition
Box# 1054
Erie PA 16563
tel: 814-898-6030
e-mail: trigon@psu.edu
URL: www.clubs.psu.edu/trigon/
*Serves glb students, staff, & faculty, & their
allies. Strives to make homosexuality &
bisexuality more acceptable, & is both a support
& social group.*

Gettysburg College: Allies   ⚢E
PO Box 2282
Gettysburg PA 17325
tel: 717-337-6666
e-mail: allies@gettysburg.edu
URL: www.gettysburg.edu/homepage/life/
gusource.html
*A student group supportive of lgb concerns on
campus.*

Bi-GLYAH (Bisexual, Gay, Lesbian Youth   Y
Association of Harrisburg)
PO Box 872
Harrisburg PA 17108
tel: 717-234-0328
e-mail: biglyah@aol.com
URL: www.geocities.com/westhollywood/heights/
28561
*Support group for sexual minority youth in
Harrisburg & surrounding areas. Ages 13-24
welcome. Meets 7pm at c/o St. Michael's
Church, 118 State Street.*

Gay & Lesbian Switchboard of Harrisburg   E
PO Box 872
Harrisburg PA 17108-0872
tel: 717-234-0328
*Information resource center for LGB people.
They publish a gay & lesbian guide to central
Pennsylvania. Volunteers available M-F 6-8pm.*

Harrisburg Youth Group   Y
c/o Gay & Lesbian Switchboard of Harrisburg
PO Box 872
Harrisburg PA 17108-0872
tel: GL Switchboard: 717-234-0328
*Support group for LGB youth, ages 14-25,
Fridays at 7pm at Planned Parenthood
Building, 1514 N. Second Street (lower level) in
Harrisburg.*

Pennsylvania Gay & Lesbian Activists,   A
Harrisburg Chapter
PO Box 349
Harrisburg PA 17108
*Working to end all discrimination based on
sexual orientation.* **Publication(s):** *Gay &
Lesbian Vote Free candidate guide booklet
published year.*

Pennsylvania Gay & Lesbian Activists,   A
Hattboro Chapter
PO Box 764
Hattboro PA 19140
tel: 215-957-1407
*Working to end all discrimination based on
sexual orientation.* **Publication(s):** *Gay &
Lesbian Vote Free candidate guide booklet
published year.*

Haverford College: Bisexual,   ⚢
Gay & Lesbian Alliance (BGALA)
370 Lancaster Av.
Haverford PA 19041
tel: 610-896-1000 (switchboard)
Support group & hotline for students.

Indiana University of Pennsyvania: ⚢
BiGALA
Box 1568-IUP
Indiana PA 15701
tel: 724-463-8541
*Social & political group designed to foster a safe
& supporteive academic & social environment
for the glbt & alllie community of UIP.*

Franklin & Marshall College: ⚢ ▪
Lesbian, Gay, Bisexual, & Allies
PO Box 3320
Lancaster PA 17604-3220
tel: 717-399-6192
e-mail: lgba@acad.fandm.edu
URL: www.fandm.edu/compuslife/organizations/
allies_home.html
*Student-run GLB & ally group which has weekly
meetings/discussions & which sponsors LGB
related activities.*

Pennsylvania Gay & Lesbian   A
Activists, Leigh County Chapter
P.O. Box 20825
Leigh Valley PA 1802
tel: 610-432-5449
*Largest political group in eastern PA - working
to end all discrimination based on sexual
orientation.* **Publication(s):** *Gay & Lesbian
Vote Free candidate guide booklet published
yearly*

Bucknell University: Friends of Lesbians,   ⚢
Gays & Bisexuals (FLAG&B)
Lewisburg PA 17837
tel: 717-524-1609
*A student-run organization which increases
awareness about lesbian, gay & bisexual issues
on campus.*

Bucknell University: ⚢E
Lesbian Gay Bisexual Concerns Office
100 Roberts Hall
Lewisburg PA 17837
tel: 717-524-1609
e-mail: lgb@bucknell.edu

Key to symbols: ▼ = bi   ♀ = women   ♂ = men   ☯ = religious/spiritual
⚢ = for allies   **M** = for married bis   ♥ = for partners of bis   Y = youth   C = people of color
274   **The Bisexual Resource Guide 2000**

Lock Haven University: 🖉
Lesbian, Gay & Bisexual Student League
Office of Human & Cultural Diversity
Box 213, Woolridge Hall
Lock Haven PA 17745
tel: 717-893-2154
e-mail: afreeman@eagle.lhup.edu

Allegheny College: Committee in 🖉 E
Support of Gay, Lesbian & Bisexual People
Box 186
Meadville PA 16335
tel: 814-332-3338; fax: 814-337-0988
Committee of students, faculty, & administrators who work together to educate, bring speakers, offer films, & address concerns that relate to GLB issues specific to the Allegheny Community.

Allegheny College: 🖉
Gay, Lesbian & Bisexual Alumni Caucus
Meadville PA 16335
e-mail: brucel@stratos.net;
jscottvdm@worldnet.att.net

40 Acres of Change YC
c/o Colours
1201 Chestnut St., 5th Floor
Philadelphia PA 19107
tel: Michael Roberson:
215-496-0330
Youth group for & about sexual minority youth of color. Weekly meetings, workshops, parties, trips, & a monthly newsletter. Meets Thursdays, 5:30-7:30 PM

Au Courant ✏🖳
P.O. Box 42741
Philadelphia PA 19101-2741
tel: 215-790-1179; fax: 215-790-9721
e-mail: pridewk@pond.com
URL: www.au-courant.com
Proudly serving the LGBT community for fifteen years.

Colours C
1201 Chestnut St. 5th Floor
attn: Kwami Banks
Philadelphia PA 19107-6732
tel: 215-496-0330; fax: 215-496-0354
e-mail: colours@critpath.org
Primarily dedicated to meeting the needs of LGB people of color. Affiliated group: Positive Brothers group-men of color living with HIV. Same contact information. Meets Mondays, 6:30-8:30 PM. Call Hassan Gibbs at 215/496-0330.
Publication(s): *Colours Bi-monthly. Distributed nationally. Contact office of Mr. Banks for info.*

Diversity of Pride A
315 Spruce St., Suite 227
Philadelphia PA 19107
tel: 215-875-9288 or
215-351-5315
Organizers of the Philadelphia Pride Parade & Festival & OutFest (National Coming Out Day celebration).

Drexel University: 🖉 E
Gays, Lesbians & Bisexuals at Drexel
Creese Student Center, Rm. 3015
MacAlister Hall, 32nd & Chestnut Sts.
Philadelphia PA 19104
tel: 215-895-2063
A GLB social & educational, support group at Drexel.

Encuentros & Encuentros Positivos ♂C🖳
1233 Locust St., 3rd Floor
Philadelphia PA 19107
tel: 215-985-3382; fax: 215-985-3388
URL: www.critpath.org/galaei#services
Encuentros—Support group for HIV-negative Latino GB men meets 6-8pm, 1st & 4th Tues. at GALAEI, 1233 Locust St., third floor.
Encuentros Positivos—Support group for HIV-positive GB latino men meets 6-8pm, 1st & 4th Wednesdays, 1233 Locust.

Gay Married Men's Association (GAMMA) ♂ M
P.O. Box 8501
Philadelphia PA 19101
tel: 215-477-1262
Peer support group for gay & bisexual men who are or were married or who are in relationships with women meets 7:30-9:30 pm 2nd & 4th Wed., $3 requested.

Jewish Bisexuals, Gays & Lesbians (J-BGL)🖉 ✡
Philadelphia PA
tel: 215-238-8864
e-mail: amber215@aol.com or jree@brynmawr.edu
A safe space& social support group for Jewish LBG undergrads, grad students, & their allies. Based at UPenn, supported by Hillel Foundation with members from all over Phila. area.

Lesbian, Gay & Bisexual People in Medicine🖉
LGBPM c/o Lynn Seng
Stemmler Hall, Suite 100
Philadelphia PA 19104-6087
tel: 215-898-3520
e-mail: sengl@mail.med.upenn.edu
Philadelphia chapter of the American Medical Student Association. Social events.

🖉 = school   🖉 = college/university   P = professional   E = educational
A = activist/political   H = health (incl. HIV)   ✏ = media/press   🖳 = Internet resource
The Bisexual Resource Guide 2000   **275**

Lutherans Concerned/ **A**
Philadelphia & Delaware
Valley
3637 Chesnut St.
Philadelphia PA 19147
tel: 215-625-0521: Jim ; fax:
215-625-0521
Potluck Supper Fourth
Sundays, 7pm at Church.
This is a chapter of
Lutherans Concerned North
America (LC/NA), a
nationwide organization
advocating for g/l/b/t
inclusion & ordination
within the Evangelical
Lutheran Church in
America. This is a sanctuary
organization, meaning
attendance & mailing list
information are kept
confidential.

Men of Colour United   ♂**C**
The Colours Organization, Inc.
1201 Chestnut St., 5th Floor
Philadelphia PA 19107
tel: Michael Wickliffe, facilitator
215-496-0330
Wednesdays 6:30-8:30.

Philadelphia Gay News   ✍🖥
505 S. 4th St.
Philadelphia PA 19147
tel: 215-625-8501; fax: 215-925-6437
e-mail: masco@aol.com
URL: www.epgn.com

SALGA- Philadelphia   **EAC**
c/o ASIAC
1201 Chestut, Suite 501
Philadelphia PA 19107
tel: 215-563-2424
e-mail: salga@critpath.org
For GLBT South Asians.

Sexual Minority Youth Center   **Y E**
WIlliam Way LGBT Community Ctr.
Philadelphia PA 19107
tel: 215-545-4005
e-mail: denkulp@aol.com
Education, job training programs, support
groups for sexual minority youth.

Temple University: Lambda Alliance   ↻**E**
Box 116, SAC, 13th & Montgomery (Room 307)
Philadelphia PA 19122
tel: 215-204-5434
Serving bisexual, lesbian & gay students & the
community.

The Attic Youth Group   **Y**
419 South 15th Street
Philadelphia PA 19146
tel: 215-545-4331
Hotline:215-545-2910
e-mail: phaedrus00@aol.com
Provides variety of groups & services for GLBT
& questioning youth age 12-21 including HIV
related resources, coming out group, drop-in
time, counseling, seminars, youth speakers'
bureau, library, newsletter, social groups, etc.

Unity, Inc.   **C**
1207 Chestnut St., Suite 209
Philadelphia PA 19107
tel: Antwine Davis: 215-851-1912; fax: 215-851-
1939
Established to serve as a positive voice of self-
empowerment for the African-American GLBT
communities of the Philadelphia area.

University of Pennsylvania

▼ **Lesbian, Gay & Bisexual Center**   ↻**E**🖥
3537 Locust Walk, 3rd Fl.
Philadelphia PA 19104-6225
tel: 215-898-5044; events line: 215-898-8888
e-mail: center@dolhpin.upenn.edu
URL: dolphin.upenn.edu/~center
University office for the LGB community.
Lending library, programs for staff, faculty &
alumni, campus programming, & speakers
bureau, mentoring program, publishes Out/
Lines newsletter. Director: Dr. Robert
Schoenberg.

Key to symbols: ▼ = bi   ♀ = women   ♂ = men   ☜ = religious/spiritual
🜂 = for allies   **M** = for married bis   ♥ = for partners of bis   **Y** = youth   **C** = people of color
276   **The Bisexual Resource Guide 2000**

▼ **Lesbian, Gay Bisexual Alliance**   👓🖥
243 Houston Hall
3417 Spruce Street
Philadelphia PA 19104-6306
tel: 215-898-5270
e-mail: lgba@dolphin.upenn.edu or
safeplace@dolphin.upenn.edu
URL: dolphin.upenn.edu/~lgba
*Primarily undergraduates. Weekly meetings,
educational & social events during term time.
Bisexual/Gay/Lesbian Awareness Days
(BGLAD) in the spring. Safeplade (small,
confidential) support groups. Listserve &
newsgroup.*

▼ **University of Pennsylvania:**   👓
Lesbian, Gay, Bisexual Social Workers
c/o LGB Center (see above)
*A group for sexual minority students, faculty &
staff of the U. Penn School of Social Work.
Aims to educate, increase visibility & provide
emotional & social suppport for members.*

▼ **Lesbian, Gay & Bisexual**   👓**PE**
Speakers Bureau
c/o LGB Center (see above)
*Open to LGB undergraduate & graduate/
professional students, as well as University
staff & faculty, who would be comfortable
speaking about their lives to groups of people.
Speakers go into classrooms, offices,
fraternities/sororities, as well as area high
schools.*

▼ **Lesbian, Gay & Bisexual Staff/Faculty**   👓**P**
Association
c/o LGB Center (see above)
*Meets 3rd Thursdays to socialize & discuss
issues of mutual issues.*

▼ **PEARL (Penn's Eagerly Awaited**   ♀👓
Radical Ladies)
c/o Penn Women's Center
3643 Locust Walk
Philadelphia PA 19104-6230
tel: 215-898-8611
e-mail: newsgroup: upenn.lambda-grads+pearl
*Social organization for lesbian, bi & other
aware women. Sponsors dances & potluck
dinners. Open to all women at Penn.*

▼ **Queer Law**   👓🖥
Philadelphia PA
URL: www.law.upenn.edu/lgblsa
*Open to students, faculty & staff of the Law
School. Meets regularly both on & off campus.
Confidentiality is respected. Occasionally
sponsors educational &/or political activities.*

William Way Lesbian, Gay, Bisexual &   **A**🖥
Transgender Community Center
1315 Spruce St.
Philadelphia PA 19107
tel: 215-732-2220; fax: 215-732-0770
e-mail: waygay@iamproud.com
URL: www.iamproud.com\waygaycenter
*The William Way Community Center hosts
many political, social & cultural community
organizations. Hours are Mon.-Fri. 12noon -
10pm, Sat. & Sundays 10:30-8:30 pm.*
Publication(s): *Way Gay News Monthly
newsletter.*

Womyn 4 Womyn   ♀**CHE**
The Colours Organization, Inc.
1201 Chestnut St, 5th Floor
Philadelphia PA 19107
tel: Janelle Bond
215-496-0330
*Monthly open discussion forum sponsored by
Womyn 4 Womyn. Call for info.*

After Midnight   **C**
Pittsburgh PA
tel: GLCC: 412-422-0114
*Social club for those in the glbt Black commu-
nity: balls, & other social events.*

Asians & Friends International - Pittsburgh   🖥
PO Box 99191
Pittsburgh PA 15233-4191
tel: 412-521-1368; fax: 412-521-1368
e-mail: afpgh@hotmail.com
URL: www.qrd.org/qrd/www/orgs/afpgh/
index.html
*Annual convention Labor Day weekend, potlucks
2nd Saturdays, movies 4th Fridays. 3 or more
meetings monthly.* **Publication(s):** *Ring of Fire
Monthly magazine.*

Bet Tikvah   ☯
PO Box 10140
Pittsburgh PA 15232-0140
tel: 412-682-2604; 412-681-6818 (recording)
*Synagogue & community for lgb Jews & their
friends. Monthly newsletter.*

Carnegie Mellon University: Allies   👓📖🖥
CMU Student Activities
5000 Forbes Avenue, Box 37
Pittsburgh PA 15238
e-mail: allies@andrew.cmu.edu
URL: www.contrib.andrew.cmu.edu/~allies
*Organization at CMU for people who support glb
peole. Safe space for discussion of sexuality
issues. Includes glb members.*

🖌 = school   👓 = college/university   **P** = professional   **E** = educational
A = activist/political   **H** = health (incl. HIV)   📰 = media/press   🖥 = Internet resource
The Bisexual Resource Guide 2000   277

Carnegie Mellon University: CMU-OUT 👓 🖥
CMU Student Activities, Box 99
5000 Forbes Avenue
Pittsburgh PA 15238
tel: 412-268-8794
e-mail: OUT+@andrew.cmu.edu
URL: www.andrew.cmu.edu:80/user/out/
*Student organization for LGBT people at CMU
that holds dances & monthly discussions.*

Chatham College: ♀ 👓 🖥
Lesbian & Bisexual Alliance
Box 345
Woodland Road
Pittsburgh PA 15232
URL: www.chatham.edu
*Political commitment to promoting visibility of
queer/trans women on campus & bringing this
into the classroom.*

Community College of Allegheny College: 👓
Visions AC
CAC Office of Student Life
808 Ridge Avenue
Pittsburgh PA 15212
tel: 412-237-2675
*A group of students committed to building a
bridge of understanding about glbt concerns on
campus.*

Fifty Plus
c/o Persad
5150 Penn Ave.
Pittsburgh PA 15224
tel: 412-441-9786x231; fax: 412-363-2375
*Lesbigay social group for all of those over &
under 50, working together building an inter-
generational community.*

Gertrude Stein Political Club A
PO Box 70921
Pittsburgh PA 15216
tel: 412-343-2523
*Multipartisan political endorsing organization.
Screening of candidates with respect to women's
rights (esp. reproductive rights) & glbt issues.*

Interweave ☯ 🖥
c/o First Unitarian Church
Ellsworth & Morewood Av.
Pittsburgh PA 15213
tel: 412-343-2523; fax: 412-243-1781
e-mail: kdrust@aol.com
URL: www.pitt.edu/~mcs2/uu/welcome/html
*Activist & social group within the Unitarian
Universalist church. Addresses the concerns of
glbt communities.*

Lesbian & Bisexual Women's ♀
Discussion Group
c/o GLCC
PO Box 5441
Pittsburgh PA 15224
tel: GLCC: 412-422-0114
*Discussion group & social gathering for all
lesbian & bi women. Meets 1st Fridays. $1/
person for use of room.*

Persad Center, Inc. EH
5150 Penn Avenue
Pittsburgh PA 15224-1627
tel: 412-441-9786; fax: 412-363-2375
*Nonprofit outpatient mental health center for
sexual minorities. Clinical counseling &
psychotherapy on issues including AIDS, couples
issues, gender identity, etc. Consultation,
education & speakers available. Sliding scale,
Medicaid & ins. accepted.*

Pittsburgh Affirmation: United Methodists ☯
for Lesbian, Gay & Bisexual Concerns
PO Box 10104
Pittsburgh PA 15232-0104
tel: 412-683-5526
*Network & resourcing group for GLB United
Methodists. A chapter of the national organiza-
tion.*

Planet Q ✍
PO Box 81246
Pittsburgh PA 15217
tel: 412-784-1500; fax: 412-784-1575
e-mail: PlanetQ@aol.com
*Monthly newspaper serving the tri-state lgbt
community.*

Sixth Light Presbyterian Church ☯ 🖥
1638 Murray Av.
Pittsburgh PA 15217
tel: 412-421-2752; fax: 412-421-2784
e-mail: sixthchurch@juno.com
URL: www.hows.net/15217SPC
*A church with active glbt members committed to
working for justice for glbt people.*

Three Rivers Pride Committee A
PO Box 5441
Pittsburgh PA 15217
tel: 412-422-0114, box 3
e-mail: trp@trfn.clpgh.org
URL: trfn.clpgh.org/trp/
*Organizes the annual LGBT PrideFest in June
in Pittsburgh.*

University of Pittsburgh: Rainbow Alliance 👓 🖥
William Pitt Union, Room 500
Pittsburgh PA 15200
tel: 412-648-2105
e-mail: rainbo+@pitt.edu
URL: www.pitt.edu/~rainbo

Key to symbols: ▼ = bi ♀ = women ♂ = men ☯ = religious/spiritual
👍 = for allies M = for married bis ♥ = for partners of bis Y = youth C = people of color
278 **The Bisexual Resource Guide 2000**

Susquehanna University: &✴A🖳
Bisexual, Gay, & Lesbian Alliance of
Susquehanna Students (BGLASS)
c/o Student Life Office
Selinsgrove PA 17870
tel: 717-372-4114
e-mail: hoffman@susqu.edu
URL: www.susqu.edu/orgs/bglass/
Confidential support group for lgb students. The
university also has a Sexual Diversity Awareness
Coalition for allies & friends which raises
awareness of LGB issues on campus.

Above Ground Magazine ✎
524 E. Lancaster Avenue, Suite 642
Shillington PA 19607
tel: 610-378-5554
e-mail: abovgrnd@aol.com
Publication(s): *Published monthly.*

Slippery Rock University: Lesbians, Gays & &✴
Bisexual Alliance
Office of Minority Student Affairs
B101 University Union
Slippery Rock PA 16057
tel: 724-738-2939

Lesbian, Gay, Bisexual, Transgendered
Switchboard of State College
PO Box 805
State College PA 16804
tel: 814-237-1950
Supportive counseling. All-volunteer hotline,
referrals 6-9pm nightly. Open daily 6-9pm.

Swarthmore College: &✴A▼
Swarthmore Queer Union (SQU)
500 College Avenue
Swarthmore PA 19081-1397
tel: 215-328-8000 (switchboard)
e-mail: jsuh2@condor.swarthmore.edu;
dadler1@swarthmore.edu;
scross1@swarthmore.edu
Sponsors parties, social events, political action,
campus awareness. Open to LGBT & question-
ing students. Meetings Wed. at 10 PM in the IC
big room, confidential. Also: Swarthmore
Discussion Group: facilitated group for
discussion/questioning sexuality. Thurs. 10pm
sm IC room. Swarthmore Ourglass (formerly
Fluid Women): Discussion group for bi women.
Swarthmore Peer Conseling: talk with a
supportive student about sexuality issues.
Queer/Straight Alliance.

Pennsylvania State University: &✴🖳
Commission on Lesbian, Gay & Bisexual
Equity
c/o Sue Rankin
313 Grange Building
University Park PA 16802
tel: 814-863-8415
814-863-7696
e-mail: lambda@psu.edu
URL: www.lions.psu.edu/lgb/
A University-wide committee addressing a
variety of issues of concern to lgb people on
campus. "Between Women" & "Between Men"
group meetings for L/Bi women & G/Bi men.

Pennsylvania State University: &✴EA🖳
Lambda Student Alliance
310 Hetzel Union Building
University Park PA 16802
tel: 814-865-3327
e-mail: lambda@psu.edu
URL: www.clubs.psu.edu/lambda
Social, political & educational group. Meets
weekly, plus ongoing support groups & social
events. Speakers bureau: "Straight Talks."
Includes bi support groups.

Pennsylvania State University: Vision &✴🌑
c/o Rev. Carl Symon
Eisenhower Chapel
University Park PA 16802
tel: 814-865-7627
e-mail: cas14@psu.edu
LGBT pastoral group.

Integrity Pittsburgh 🌑
PO Box 3
Verona PA 15147
tel: 412-683-8034; fax: 412-561-6307
e-mail: rosaliew@aol.com
Ministry for the encouragement & nurture of
Episcopalian glbt people & friends for religious
& social groups. 2nd Wednesdays at Calvary
Church (except in summer)

Pennsylvania Gay & Lesbian Activists, A
West Chester Chapter
PO Box 3212
West Chester PA 19381
Working to end all discrimination based on
sexual orientation. **Publication(s):** *Gay &*
Lesbian Vote Free candidate guide booklet
published year.

West Chester University: &✴EA
Safe Space Alliance
Box 233
Sykes Student Union
West Chester PA 19383
tel: 610-436-6949
Meets Thurs. 6pm.

🌑 = school &✴ = college/university P = professional E = educational
A = activist/political H = health (incl. HIV) ✎ = media/press 🖳 = Internet resource
The Bisexual Resource Guide 2000 279

Wilkes University: Ally Intercollegiate   ☙
Organization
c/o Jim Harrington
Wilkes Barre PA 18766
tel: Jim Harrington: 1-800-WilkesU, x4420
e-mail: ally@wilkes1.wilkes.edu
Open to gay students & friends of gay students on college campuses throughout Northeastern Pennsylvania. Currently has over 30 members from 6 local universities & also interacts with & supports a group for high school-aged gay youth. Conducts many social events & educational programs. Meets every other Thurs. 8pm in the Annette Evans Alumni House on the campus of Wilkes University.

Susquehanna Lambda
PO Box 2510
Williamsport PA 17703
tel: 717-327-1411
Social & educational organization. Operates the G/L Switchboard of North-Central PA.

YAL (York Area Lambda)   **EA**
PO Box 2425
York PA 17405
tel: 717-846-6618; 717-846-2560
Educational, political & social group of LGB people in the York area. Dues include newsletter. Focus of group shifts based on membership needs.

Puerto Rico

Madres Lesbianas y Bisexuales   ♀
P.O. Box 190422
San Juan PR 009194-0422
tel: 787-764-9639 (mensajes); fax: same
e-mail: madres.pr@mailexcite.com
Para proveerse un espacio de discusión sobre sus necesidades. También trabajan con las parejas, así como tías, abuelas or mujeres que mantienen alguna relación significativa con niños. Entre otras actividades, realizan talleres y días familiares. [Provides a space for discussion. Also works with relatives, such as aunts, grandmothers, or women who maintain a significant relationship with children. Among other activities are workshops & family days.]

Local

Universidad de Puerto Rico, CODE UPR   ☙
Rio Piedras PR 00931
tel: 787-764-0000x5683
Apoyo a estudiantes lgbt en la Universidad. [Supports LGBT students at the University.]

Fundación Derechos Humanos   **A**
1357 Ashford Av., Box 402
San Juan PR 00907
tel: 787-722-5027
Organización que trabaja en la defensa de los derechos de la comunidad LGBT. [Organization working in defense of the rights of LGBT people.]

Proyecto de Derechos Humanos de LGBT   **A**
[GLBT Human Rights Project]
Box 22029
Estación UPR
San Juan PR 00931
Organización que trabaja en la defensa de los derechos de la comunidad LGBT. [Organization working to protect the rights of the LGBT community.]

Coalición Orgullo Arcoiris [Rainbow Pride   **A**
Coalition]
PO Box 8836
Fernandez Juncos
Santurce PR 00910-8836
Coalición integrada por organizaciones y personas de la comunidad LGBT. Organiza anualmente la Parada de Orgullo en junio y el Día de Concieciación en octubre. [Coalition of organizations & individuals from the LGBT community. Organizes annual Pride Parade & Coming Out Day in Oct.]

Coalición Contra el Artículo 103 y Pro   **A**🖳
Derecho a la Intimidad
Viejo San Juan PR 00903-1003
URL: netdial.caribe.net/~art103/
Tiene como uno de sus objetivos la lucha en contra de la ley que criminiliza las relaciones sexuales consentidas entre personas del mismo sexo, por entender que es un delito sin víctimas y no hace otra cosa que crear un ambiente hostil y legitimar la violencia contra la comunidad lgbt. [Has as one of its objectives the struggle against laws criminalizing consensual sexual activity beteen persons of the samesex, understanding that it is a victimless crime & does nothing more than create a hostile atmosphere & legitimate violence against the lgbt community.]

Rhode Island

Adoption Rhode Island
500 Prospect St.
Pawtucket RI 02860-6260
tel: 401-724-1910; fax: 401-724-9443
e-mail: dsolot@netspace.org
Individual consultation for LGBT issues with respect to adoption.

Key to symbols: ▼ = bi   ♀ = women   ♂ = men   ☮ = religious/spiritual
☙ = for allies   **M** = for married bis   ♥ = for partners of bis   **Y** = youth   **C** = people of color
280   **The Bisexual Resource Guide 2000**

American Baptists Concerned/RI Chapter ☻
RI
tel: Bob: 401-828-9081
Support, advocacy, networking group of LBG &
friends. Meets 3rd Friday, potluck.

Gay & Lesbian Victim Assistance H
311 Dorie Ave.
Cranston RI 02910-2903
tel: 401-781-3990; fax: 401-467-9030
e-mail: w50lbsdfat@aol.com
Non-profit mental health service.

The Speaker's Bureau E
PO Box 5758
Weybosset Hill Station
Providence RI 02902
tel: 401-621-6442
Members meet requests to speak to groups about
LGB issues, personal experiences.

Local

Biprov (formerly Biversity Providence) ▼🖳
P.O. Box 603097
Providence RI
tel: 401-432-2262 (voicemail)
e-mail: majordomo@aq.org subscribe biprov
URL: www.aq.org/~js/biprov/
Mixed gender social group for bis & bi-
questioning people of all ages & genders. One
social event a month in Providence, Rhode
Island (hikes, movies, brunches, etc.) & online
discussion/announcement list. Bi support group
meets 3rd Wed 6:30-8pm at Rochambeau
Library, 708 Hope St—call to verify time, or look
at the schedule on the website.

Bayard, Bessie, Baldwin, Bentley Brunch C
RI
tel: Kathy Townsend-Hurk 401-467-6325
Social group for LGB African-Americans & their
significant others of any race. Monthly potlucks.

Jacks'n'Snacks
RI
tel: Bill Hendrickson 401-944-3896
Support group for lesbigays & friends. Meets
Mon. 7pm in members' homes. Coffee & snacks.

Married Lesbian & Bisexual Women's ♀ M
Support Group
send mail to: MLBWSG - Group III
PO Box 213
Charlestown RI 02813-0213
Informal, discreet group meeting weekly.

Unitarian/Universalist Welcoming ☻A◊
Congregation Committee
Westminster Unitarian Church
119 Kenyon Av., E.
East Greenwich RI 02818
tel: 401-884-5933, or Steve or Dan: 423-0380
Committee within UU church does political work
on LGBT issues within & outside UU commu-
nity. Church is LGBT inclusive.

University of Rhode Island: ⚲
Gay, Lesbian & Bisexual Student Association
c/o Student Senate
346 Memorial Union
Kingston RI 02881
tel: Leave message: 401-874-2097 (women's
center)

Newport Congregational Church (UCC) ☻
Spring & Pelham St.
Newport RI
tel: 401-849-2238
e-mail: nccucc@aol.com
Self-described as open & affirming of LGB
people. 10:30am Sunday services. Performs
commitment services/ceremonies.

Brown University: ⚲E
Lesbian, Gay, Bisexual Resource Center
Box P
Providence RI 02912
tel: 401-863-3145; fax: 401-863-1999
e-mail: kristen_renn@brown.edu

Lesbian, Gay, Bisexual, Transgendered ⚲🖳
Alliance (LGBTA)
Brown University
Box 1930
Providence RI 02912
tel: 401-863-3062
URL: www.brown.edu/lgbta/
Umbrella organization for various LGBT groups
at Brown, sponsors social events.

Lesbian & Bisexual & Questioning ⚲♀
c/o LGBTA (above)
tel: 401-863-2189
Women's Discussion Group.

Lesbian/Gay/Bisexual Staff & Faculty Group ⚲
tel: Jim: 401-861-7978
Social gatherings 3rd Fri. Business meeting 1st
Wed.

Queer Grad Body ⚲
Sarah Doyle Women's Center
185 Meeting Street
Box 1829
Providence RI 02912
tel: 401-863-2189
e-mail: lgb_grad@brown.edu
Meets monthly. Local grad students welcome.

🖎 = school   ⚲ = college/university   **P** = professional   **E** = educational
A = activist/political   **H** = health (incl. HIV)   ☎ = media/press   🖳 = Internet resource

Quest   ⚥
c/o LGBTA (above)
tel: 401-863-3062
Confidential group for people coming out &/or questioning their sexuality.

The Next Thing (TNT)   ⚥ C
c/o LGBTA (above)
tel: 401-863-3062
Lesbigay People of Color Group.

Dignity/Providence   ☮
PO Box 40832
Providence RI 02940-0832
tel: 401-270-4297
Religious & social activities for LGBTs & friends. All welcome.

Gaymers
Providence RI
tel: Al Esposito: 401-521-0283
e-mail: pauliehoff@aol.com
Cards & board games for LGBs. Thursdays 7pm at members' homes.

Integrity   ☮
St. James Church
474 Fruit Hill Av.
North Providence RI
tel: Al Barnaby: 401-353-2079
GLBT Episcopalians. Meets 2nd Sundays 4:30pm.

Johnson & Wales College: GLBA   ⚥
8 Abbott Park Place
Providence RI 02903
tel: 401-598-1129 Karen Fontes
e-mail: glbajwu@aol.com
GLB support group for JWC students.

Rhode Island College: Rainbow Alliance   ⚥
Student Union Info Desk
600 Mt. Pleasant Ave.
Providence RI 02908
tel: Brian: 401-353-2971
Patricia: 401-461-5275
Student-led discussion group.

Rhode Island School of Design: Lesbian,   ⚥
Gay, Bisexual, Transgender Alliance
2 College Street, Box E-6
Providence RI 02903

The Triangle Center   EA
PO Box 6446
Providence RI 02940
tel: 401-861-4590
LGB & Questioning resource center. Works to foster diverse community, offer alternative social activities, education, queer film festival.

YPI   YEH
134 George M. Cohen Blvd
Providence RI 02903-4410
tel: 401-421-5626; fax: 401-274-1990
Offers individual & family counseling; support groups in Providence, Middletown & Wakefield; peer educators on homphobia, HIV, safer sex; HIV-positive youth support group; group for children of GLB parents; GED help.

Bryant College: ⚥ 💻
Gay/Lesbian/Bisexual Students
1150 Douglass Pike
Smithfield RI 02917-1284
tel: 401-232-6389
e-mail: pride@acad.bryant.edu
Weekly meetings, student -led.

South Carolina

Local

Lowcountry Gay & Lesbian Alliance
PO Box 98
Charleston SC 29402

We Are Family   E
PO Box 30734
Charleston SC 29417
tel: 803-937-0020; fax: 803-937-0020
e-mail: Director, Thomas Myers: tmyers@waf.org;
Youth Services, Warren Gress: wgress@waf.org
URL: www.waf.org/
Mission is to encourage straight/gay/lesbian members of our community to value one another through education. Promotes & distributes educational resources, work for the acceptance of gays & lesbians as full members of society, focus primarily on the plight of gay & lesbian children.

University of South Carolina: ⚥ 💻
Bisexual, Gay & Lesbian Association (BGLA)
Box 80098
Columbia SC 29225
tel: 803-777-7716
e-mail: uscbgla@vm.sc.edu
URL: www.sa.sc.edu/bgla/
Student organization at the Univeristy of South Carolina.

Trident Knights Leather/Levi Club, Inc.   ♂
P. O. Box 62302
North Charleston SC 29419
e-mail: HMRQBFH@aol.com
Leather/Levi social & charitable organization

Key to symbols: ▼ = bi   ♀ = women   ♂ = men   ☮ = religious/spiritual
♦ = for allies   **M** = for married bis   ♥ = for partners of bis   **Y** = youth   **C** = people of color
282   **The Bisexual Resource Guide 2000**

South Dakota

Local

South Dakota State 🎓💻
University: Sons & Daughters
PO Box 2815
Brookings SD
URL: www.sdstate.edu/wsds
LGB campus group.

FACES (Free Americans   **A**
Creating Equal Status of
South Dakota)
13121 South Creekview Road
Rapid City SD 57702
tel: 605-343-5577; 800-354-
3417 (toll free in South
Dakota); fax: 605-343-5577
e-mail: facessd@aol.com
Bi-inclusive LGB group.

Augustana College: Out! 🎓💻
Box 1886
Sioux Falls SD 57007
e-mail: out@inst.augie.edu
URL: inst.augie.edu/~out/
Campus LGB group for students, faculty &
allies.

University of South Dakota: Gay, Lesbian & 🎓💻
Bisexual Alliance
U. S. D., Coyote Student Center
414 E. Clark Street
Vermillion SD 57069
tel: Student Activities Office: 605-677-5334
e-mail: glba@sundance.usd.edu
URL: www.usd.edu/student-life/orgs/glba

Tennesee

Local

Bi-Net Nashville ▼
P.O. Box 863
Sewanee TN 37375
Bi-Net Nashville is a volunteer organization for
bisexuals & their friends.

University of Tennessee, Chattanooga: 🎓💻
Spectrum
Chattanooga TN
e-mail: spectrum@cecasun.utc.edu
URL: www.utc.edu/~spectrum/

Robyn Ochs

University of Tennessee, Knoxville: 🎓💻
Lambda Student Union
Box 8529
Knoxville TN 37996
tel: 423-974-4273
e-mail: jrader@utk.edu, lambda@utk.edu
URL: web.utk.edu/~lambda

University of Tennessee, Martin: ALLIES 🎓♦💻
S.T.A.N.D.O.U.T. (Students & Teachers
Against Nontraditional Discrimination &
Observing Universal Truths)
Martin TN
e-mail: allies@mars.utm.edu
URL: mars.utm.edu/~allies

Memphis Area Gay Youth (MAGY)   **Y**💻
PO Box 241852
Memphis TN 38124
tel: 901-335-6249
e-mail: magy@geocities.com
URL: www.geocities.com/WestHollywood/1772
Youth group for ages 13-21.

Rhodes College: Gay-Straight Alliance 🎓💻
2000 North Parkway
Memphis TN 38112
e-mail: bisdj@rhodes.edu
URL: www.students.rhodes.edu/students/clubs/
other/gsa/gsa.html
Very inclusive of bis, according to one bi
member.

University of Memphis: BGALA 🎓💻
Office of Student Orgs., Box 100
Memphis TN 38152
tel: 901-278-5825
e-mail: bgala@cc.memphis.edu
URL: www.people.memphis.edu/~bgala
Organization is alive & well. Feel free to contact
if in vicinity. "University very accepting."

✎ = school   🎓 = college/university   **P** = professional   **E** = educational
A = activist/political   **H** = health (incl. HIV)   📰 = media/press   💻 = Internet resource
The Bisexual Resource Guide 2000   **283**

Middle Tennessee State University: 🔲
Lambda Association
MTSU Box 624
Murfreesboro TN 37132
e-mail: mtlambda@frank.mtsu.edu
URL: www.mtsu.edu/~mtlambda/

Lesbian & Gay Coalition for Justice   A🔲
P.O. Box 22901
Nashville TN 37202-2901
tel: 615-298-5425
e-mail: lgcj@lgcj.org
URL: www.telalink.not/~lgcj/

The Center for Gay-Lesbian-Bi-   YEA🔲
Transgender Life in Nashville
703 Berry Road
Nashville TN 37204
tel: 615-297-0008
e-mail: nashcenter@yahoo.com
URL: nashcenter.org
Nashville area LGBT community center. Hosts a variety of groups - youth, single gender, transgender, mixed gender, etc.

Vanderbilt University: ♊
Grad/Prof/Les/Bi/gay Association
Nashville TN 37240-1111
tel: 615-279-5496
e-mail: vandy_glmsa@hotmail.com
Umbrella organization for the Vanderbilt Gay/ Lesbian Medical Student Association & the Graduate School Lambda.

Vanderbilt University: ♊🔲
Vanderbilt Lambda Association
PO Box 7076 Station B
Nashville TN 37235
e-mail: lambda@ctrvax.vanderbilt.edu
URL: www.vanderbilt.edu/lambda

Texas

Local

Dual Attraction: ▼
The Bisexual Network of Dallas
Dallas TX
tel: 214-522-8306
Meetings 1st & 3rd Tuesdays at the 1st Unitarian Church (Preston at St. Andrews, just north of Mockingbird) in the Religious Education Bldg, Rm. 201.

The Bisexual Network of San Antonio   ▼🔲
PO Box 29171
San Antonio TX 78229-0171
e-mail: bnsa@txdirect.net
BiNetSA@aol.com
URL: www.txdirect.net/users/bnsa/binetsa.html
Purpose of organization is to provide anyone doing research on bisexuality direct access to modern, up-to-date information on everything about bisexuality from personal to political issues. Provide direct access to those who identify as bi, are questioning their sexuality, or would like to educate themselves & their loved ones about bisexuality. Founder- Steven Wolff.

Bisexual Network of Austin   ▼🔲
PO Box 8439
Austin TX 78713
tel: 512-370-9573
e-mail: dave@lim.com
URL: www.bga.com/~bzy/binetaustin.html
Weekly socials & other special events. Bi women's support group; bi men's group, discussion group. **Publication(s)**: *Bi-News bi-monthly. $10/yr.*

Bi-Net Houston   ▼🔲
c/o MCCR Church
1919 Decatur St.
Houston TX 77007
tel: 713-467-4380 or Michelle: 663-7439; voice line 713-461-4380
e-mail: Michelle at mel@owlnet.rice.edu.
URL: www.jps.net/michelle/houbinet.htm
For all men & women exploring their sexuality or already bi-identified. Meets Wed. evenings 7-9pm. Call or e-mail for directions.

Prime Timers: Austin   ♂🔲
PO Box 14892
Austin TX 78716-4692
e-mail: jrdavistx@aol.com
URL: members.aol.com/jrdavistx/primetimers.html
For older gay & bi men.

University of Texas: ♊E🔲
Lesbian, Bisexual, Gay Student Association (LBGSA)
SOC #275
1006 W. Dean Keeton St.
Austin TX 787132
e-mail: lbgsa@www.utexas.edu
URL: www.utexas.edu/students/lbgsa
Provide a social outlet, support & resources for GLBT students, family & friends on campus.

Key to symbols: ▼ = bi   ♀ = women   ♂ = men   ☯ = religious/spiritual
👍 = for allies   **M** = for married bis   ♥ = for partners of bis   Y = youth   C = people of color
284   **The Bisexual Resource Guide 2000**

Trikone-Tejas **C⊠🖳**
PO Box 4589
Austin TX 78765-4589
tel: 512-322-0638
L. Ramakrisnan
e-mail: tricoetejas@geocities.com
URL: www.geocities.com/WestHollywood/3259
*A socio-political organization for gay/les/bi
South Asians. Organizes & participates in
several UTAustin events & shares news via
website. Send E-mail for events/mailing list.*

She Says **🔍 ♀🖳**
c/o LGBSA (above)
e-mail: shesays@www.utexas.edu
URL: www.utexas.edu/students/shesays/
*Social group for bi,lesbian & questioning
women. Meets in the African American Culture
rm in the Texas Union Tues. 7pm.*

University Alliance **🔍EA🖳**
SOC #121
100C West Dean Keaton St.
Austin TX 78712
e-mail: alliance@www.utexas.edu
URL: www.utexas.edu/students/alliance/
*Student group, meets Thurs. 8pm in rm. 296 of
the George I. Sanchez Building.*

Texas A&M University: **🔍🖳**
Gay, Lesbian & Bisexual Aggies
Student Activities
125 John J Koldur Bldg
ATTN: GLBA
College Station TX 77843-1236
tel: 409-847-0321
e-mail: glbaggies@stuact.tamu.edu
URL: stuact.tamu.edu/stuorgs/glba
*Meets Thurs. 7pm - alternates between general
meeting & rap group.* **Publication(s):** *GLBA
Resource Guide resource guide - annual for
A&M students*

Dallas Gay & Lesbian Alliance **EA🖳**
P.O. Box 190712
Dallas TX 75219
tel: 214-528-4233; fax: 214-521-6424
e-mail: dglamail@aol.com
URL: www.divenet.com/dgla
Office hrs M-Th 10-3.

Out Youth Dallas **Y🖳**
P.O. Box 190712
Dallas TX 75219
tel: 214-521-5342 ext. 260
URL: www.divanet.com/dgla/outyouth
*Meet at the activity center of the G & L
Community Center every Thursday at 7:30pm.*

Southern Methodist University: **🔍E🖳**
**Gay, Lesbian & Bisexual Student
Organization**
PO Box 750172
Dallas TX 75275
tel: 214-768-4792
e-mail: Tess Golden tgolden@post.smu.edu
URL: www.smu.edu/~glbso
*Support group for lesbigays at SMU. Meets
Thurs. 5:30pm at the Human Resource/Women's
Center. Speakers on various topics every other
meeting. Active at city & state level in lesbigay
issues.* **Publication(s):** *Gayly Campus Monthly
nesletter*

Walt Whitman Community School **EY**
Dallas TX
tel: 214-855-1535
*GLBTQ High School directed by Becky
Thompson. The opening of the school received
much media coverage.*

North Texas State University: **🔍E🖳**
Courage - Gay, Lesbian & Bisexual Students
c/o Student Center
Denton TX 76203
tel: Hot line:565-6110
Call student center for more info.
e-mail: courage@unt.edu
URL: www.unt.edu
*Meetings for 98-99 Weds at 8pm in the Art
Building, rm 226.
On-line discussion forum, Delta Lambda Phi
activities, lists of local resources on the Courage
website.*

LAMBDA GLBT Community Services **E🖳**
PO Box 31321
910 N mesa
El Paso TX 79931-0321
tel: 915-562-GAYS
e-mail: admin@lambda.org
URL: www.lambda.org/

LAMBDA Services AVP: Gay & Lesbian **E**
Victims' Assistance Hotline
LAMBDA Services (AVP)
PO Box 31321
El Paso TX 79931-0321
tel: 800-259-1536 or
915-562-GAYS; fax: 915-534-7778
e-mail: AVP@lambda.org
*Confidential hotline answered by trained
volunteers to provide info. & referrals to persons
who have experiences violence, discrimination,
harassment, or vandalism.
LAMBDA Services' Anti-Violence Project (AVP)
works to prevent & assist victims of anti-gay
hate.*

✎ = school **🔍** = college/university **P** = professional **E** = educational
A = activist/political **H** = health (incl. HIV) **⊠** = media/press **🖳** = Internet resource
The Bisexual Resource Guide 2000 **285**

Couples with a Gay or Bi Partner ♥ M
901 Lake St.
Fort Worth TX 76102
tel: 817-338-4551
Dr. Rita Cotterly works with couples & can refer individuals to other resources in the area.

Texas Christian University: 👓💻
Gay, Lesbian & Bisexual Network
P.O. Box 297200
Fort Worth TX 76129
tel: 817-921-7160 Prisilla Tate
e-mail: V.Carpenter@tcu.edu
URL: student.tcu.edu/~vcarpenter/triangle
Meets Sun. 5pm at Wesley Foundation Bldg.

Drake University: BGLAD-Bi/Gay/Lesbian 👓
Alliance/Alumni of Drake
3525 Sage Rd, 313
Houston TX 77056
e-mail: bglad@acad.drake.edu

University of Houston: 👓
Gay, Lesbian Bisexual Alliance
PO Box 314
Houston TX 77204-3650

Hub Triangle 💻
Lubbock TX
e-mail: dsphd@hotmail.com
URL: www.geocities.com/WestHollywood/Heights/7439/hubtri.html
Online newsletter for the LBG community.

Texas Tech University: 👓
Gay/Lesbian/Bisexual Students
Box 42031-63
Texas Tech
Lubbock TX 79409
To educate Texas Tech & Lubbock communities on GLB issues. Mostly students, but members of the community (& other TTU students) are welcome. 45 members, 25 active members.

Unity Foundation Gay
& Lesbian Community Center
P.O. Box 15857
San Antonio TX 78212
tel: 210-822-3533
Board meetings at 7pm on the 2nd & 4th Thurs of each month at the library - 6017 Soledad Room 613. Open to the public. Started to provide a home for the social, emotional, & physical well being of all people, primarily LGBT persons in San Antonio.

Utah

Affirmation: Gay & Lesbian Mormons ☯
P.O. Box 526175
Salt Lake City UT 84152
tel: 801-534-869
URL: members.aol.com/wasatchweb
Social & support organization for GLBT people with a Mormon/LDS background, whether they currently identify as Mormon or not. Frequent meetings throughout Utah. Also sponsors Gay Mormon Father's Group that meets separately. See related listing in International section.

Utah Gay/Straight High School Y
Students' Alliance
8457 S Snowville Dr.
Sandy UT 84093
tel: 801-943-0170
This is the High School group that was the center of a storm of controversy.

Local

Weber State University: 👓
Delta Lambda Sapphos Union
2102 University Circle
Ogden UT 84408-2102
tel: 801-625-1639
Weber State's GLBT Student Union.

Utah Valley State College: Freedom Rings 👓
Orem UT
tel: Lee Mortenson: 801-222-8785 or call College general info #: 801-222-8000
LGB group.

Family Fellowship 💧
PO Box 9451
Salt Lake City UT 84109
tel: 801-374-1447
For Mormon families, to help overcome the pain, isolation & divisiveness associated with same-sex orientation within our Mormon families. Quarterly meetings.

First Thursday ♀👓
Salt Lake City UT
tel: 801-467-0052
e-mail: pillarrow@aol.com
Social group for women of all sexual persuasions.

Key to symbols: ▼ = bi ♀ = women ♂ = men ☯ = religious/spiritual
💧 = for allies **M** = for married bis ♥ = for partners of bis Y = youth **C** = people of color
286 **The Bisexual Resource Guide 2000**

Gay & Lesbian Community Center of Utah 🖳
PO Box 1979
Salt Lake City UT 84110
tel: 801-539-8800
URL: www.stonewall.org/
Located at 361 N. 300 West. Coffee shop, library,
& numerous group meetings to be determined.
Will be open M-Th 7am-10pm, F & S 7am-11pm
& Sun 9am-5pm. Hours subject to change.

Vermont

Bisexual Network of Vermont ▼
PO Box 8124
Burlington VT 05402-8124
tel: Kim Ward: 802-229-0112
e-mail: biwarriors@aol.com
Network of individuals throughout Vermont who
are bisexual, multisexual, two-spirited or trans
identified. Monthly social gatherings, sensitivity
training, speakers' bureau in the works. Allies
welcome! **Publication(s)**: *BiNet VT Monthly*
Newsletter

Local

Champlain College: 🖉
Gay/Lesbian/Bisexual/Friends Alliance
PO Box 670
Burlington VT 05402
tel: Becky Peterson at 802-658-0800 x6425
For students only.

Interweave - Unitarian Universalists ☺
Association
First UU Society
152 Pearl Street
Burlington VT
tel: John Byer: 802-863-1818
For glbt people. Meets 2nd Sun. Sept. - June,
downstairs at above address.

Out in the Mountains 📧🖳
PO Box 177
Burlington VT 05402
tel: Barbara Dozetos: 802-434-6486
e-mail: OITM@together.net
URL: www.vtpride.org
If you want to know what's going on in
Vermonts' LGBT communities, pick up this free
paper at many of Vermont's restaurants, stores
& universities. Lists activities & resources.
Publication(s): *Out in the Mountains*

Outright Vermont YE🖳
PO Box 5235
Burlington VT 05402-5235
tel: 802-865-9677, or in state tollfree: 800-GLB-
CHAT (452-2428)
URL: www.members.aol.com/outrightvt/
For GLBTQ youth & allies up to age 22. Call for
location & hours of drop-in center.
Publication(s): *Reaching Out Newsletter by &*
for queer youth

University of Vermont: 🖉🖳
Free to Be: GLBTA
B-163 Billings Student Center
Burlington VT 05405
tel: 802-656-0699
e-mail: jriccio@uvm-gen.EMBA.UVM.EDU
URL: www.geocities.com/westhollywood/heights/
3550/glbta.html

University of Vermont: Gay, Lesbian, 🖉🖳
Bisexual, Transgender Alliance
B-163 Billings Student Center
Burlington VT 05405
tel: 802-656-0699
e-mail: free2b@zoo.uvm.edu
URL: ww.uvm.edu/~fre2b/
Campus & community outreach & resource
center. Meets weekly during termtime.

Castleton State College: P🖉E
One in Ten: Gay, Lesbian, Bisexual Alliance
Castleton VT 05735
tel: Will: 802-468-1401

St. Michael's College: Gay, Lesbian, 🖉
Bisexual, Questioning Support Group
Winooski Park
Colchester VT 05439
tel: Linda Hollingdale or Laura Crain 802-654-
0238

Johnson State College: 🖉
Gay/Straight Alliance
337 College Hill
Johnson VT 05656
tel: 802-635-2356 x2322 (student assoc. office)
e-mail: Bearork@badger.jsc.vsc.edu (Kim Bearor-
contact person)
Holds regular meetings & annual events
including annual ally party.

Lyndon State College: The Beacon 🖉
c/o Student Activities Office
Lyndonville VT 05851
tel: Mary Sue Kelly: 802-626-9371 x6440

🔍 = school   🖉 = college/university   P = professional   E = educational
A = activist/political   H = health (incl. HIV)   📧 = media/press   🖳 = Internet resource
The Bisexual Resource Guide 2000   **287**

Marlboro College: P♀⚥
Gay/Lesbian/Bisexual Group
PO Box A
Marlboro VT 05344-0300
tel: Linda Rice: 802-257-4333
Social group for Marlboro College students, staff, & faculty.

Middlebury College: Middlebury Open ⚥🖥
Queer Alliance (MOQA)
Drawer 9
Middlebury VT 05753-6033
tel: 802-443-5000 x4484
e-mail: MOQA@panther.middlebury.edu
URL: www.middlebury.edu/~MOQA
For students, faculty & staff to communicate on LGBT & Queer lives & living. Weekly meetings. Straight allies & questioning members welcome. Confidential.

Goddard College: ⚥
Gay, Lesbian, Bisexual Alliance
Goddard College
Plainfield VT 05667
tel: 802-454-8311x580
Weekly films, conferences, dances.

Landmark College: ⚥
Gays, Lesbians, Bisexual & Friends Alliance
River Road
Putney VT 05346
tel: Abigail Littlefield: 802-387-6752
e-mail: alittlefield@landmarkcollege.org

Dignity - Vermont ☯
c/o 3 Queensbury Rd.
South Burlington VT 05403-5752
tel: 802-863-1377
e-mail: arodier@prodigy.net
Organization for glbt Catholics.

Virginia

Act Up Virginia A
Richmond VA
tel: Charles 804-353-3261
Meets 1st Mon. at Dominion Place, 1025 West Grace Street.

Virginians for Justice H
P.O. Box 342
Richmond VA 23218-0342
tel: 804-643-4816
Working against Crimes Against Nature law.

Key to symbols: ▼ = bi   ♀ = women   ♂ = men   ☯ = religious/spiritual
🌢 = for allies   M = for married bis   ♥ = for partners of bis   Y = youth   C = people of color
288   The Bisexual Resource Guide 2000

Local

Richmond Bisexual Network (ROBIN) ▼▣
c/o Phoenix Rising - Central
19 N. Belmont Ave.
Richmond VA 23221
tel: 804-257-9159
e-mail: robinsnet@geocities.com
URL: www.geocities.com/WestHollywood/
Stonewall/4409
*"Loosely knit social & support organization for
bi & bi-friendly people."* **Publication(s)**: *Bi-
Lines monthly newsletter, $20/yr.*

Bi Men's Support Group - Charlottesville ▼♂
Charlottesville VA
tel: Kelly: 804-293-8316
e-mail: kmc2f@virginia.edu
Info/support on bi men's issues.

Bi-Nature ▼
Norfolk VA
tel: Bill at 757-490-1719, 6-8pm
*Tidewater bi group meets Thurs. 7:30pm at the
Unitarian Church of Norfolk, 739 Yarmouth St.*

Naturists Across the Blue Ridge States ♂
VA
tel: Radford: 540-639-1747
Nude get togethers for gay/bi men.

Northern Virginia Community College: 🏫
Support & Social Group for Gay Men,
Lesbians & Bisexuals
Alexandria VA 22311
*Meets on the Alexandria Campus in Bisdorf
Building, Room 106.*

Bell Atlantic GLOBE - Northern Virginia P
PO Box 17105
Arlington VA 22216
tel: 703-974-2205
Also a GLOBE branch in Richmond.

SMYAL-NOVA Y
Whitman-Walker Bldg
5232 Lee Highway
Arlington VA 22207-1621

Virginia Tech: Lesbian, Gay, Bisexual, 🏫▣
Transgender Alliance
333 Squires Student Center
Blacksburg VA 24061
tel: 540-231-7975
e-mail: lgba@vt.edu
URL: www.vt.edu:10021/org/LGBTA/
*Meetings Thurs. 8pm during termtime. For
LGBT & straight members of the Virgina Tech &
surrounding communities.*

University of Virginia: ♀
Lesbian, Bisexual & Questioning Women
PO Box 525, Newcomb Hall Station
Charlottesville VA 22904
tel: 804-971-4942
*Meets 7pm at Unitarian House, 808 Rugby Rd.
Open to all women.*

University of Virginia: 🏫
Lesbian, Gay & Bisexual Union
PO Box 525, Newcomb Hall Station
Charlottesville VA 22904
tel: 804-982-2773
Helpline M-Th 5-9pm.

University of Virginia: Lesbians, P🏫
Gays & Bisexuals in Health Care
PO Box 525, Newcomb Hall Station
Charlottesville VA 22904
tel: 804-971-4942

George Mason University: Gay, 🏫▣
Lesbian, Bisexual Transgender Services
Minority Student Affairs
4400 University Drive, Mailstop 2F6
Fairfax VA 22030
tel: 703-993-2895; fax: 703-993-4022
e-mail: pride@gmu.edu
URL: www.gmu.edu/org/pride

Longwood College: UNITY 🏫
Fayetteville VA 23909
LGB campus group.

Mary Washington College: 🏫
Gay/Lesbian/Bi Student Association
Fredericksburg VA 22401
*Open to the public. Meets Wed. 6pm in Chandler
Hall, Rm. 301.*

Interweave ☯
Glen Allen VA
tel: 804-883-6028
*Sponsored by the Unitarian Universalist
Community Church.*

Central Virginia Affirmation ☯
P.O. Box 501
Hanover VA 23069-0501
tel: 746-7279
*Affiliated with Affirmation, a national
organization within the Methodist Church.*

James Madison University: Harmony 🏫
P.O. Box 8119 JMU
Harrisonburg VA 22807
Organization for LBG concerns.

Freddie Mac Gay/Lesbian/Bi Employees P
1914 Wilson Lane
McLean VA 22102
tel: 703-556-8765 (Steve Richards)

✎ = school   🏫 = college/university   P = professional   E = educational
A = activist/political   H = health (incl. HIV)   ✉ = media/press   ▣ = Internet resource

Affirmation: Gay & Lesbian Mormons ☸
Richmond VA
tel: 804-358-3492
e-mail: VAGayLDS@aol.com

Alliance of Black Men ♂ **C**
Richmond VA
tel: 804-342-2957; 804-228-1867

Gay Fathers Coalition ♂
Richmond VA
tel: 804-358-3015
e-mail: GFCRichmond@aol.com
Meets 2nd Tues. 7:30 in the Library Room of the Church of the Holy Comforter. Affiliated with Gay & Lesbian Parents Coalition International.

P-FLAG Richmond ♣
P.O. Box 36392
Richmond VA 23235
tel: 804-744-9016
Parents, Families & Friends of Lesbians & Gays meets second Tues. at the Church of the Holy Comforter (Episcopal) at Staples Mill Road & Monument Ave.

University of Richmond: ↝
The Lambda Coalition
c/o Student Activities, PO Box 11
Richmond VA 23173-0011
Weekly GLB social group. All but one meeting a month are open to anyone in the Richmond community.

Virginia Commonwealth University: ↝
Sexual Minority Student Alliance
Box 75, 907 Floyd Av.
Richmond VA 28284
Open to the public. Meets Wed. during termtime in University Student Commons.

Washington

Equality Washington/Hands Off Washington **A**
1122 E. Pike Street
Suite 3532
Seattle WA 98122
tel: 206-323-5191; fax: 206-323-3560
e-mail: howwf@aol.com
"Would you like to do your part in protecting LGBT civil rights? Call to volunteer for a great cause — YOU!"

Youth Info Line **YEA**
WA
tel: 206-547-7900

Local

Seattle Bisexual Men's Union ▼♂
c/o SBWN
PO Box 30645 Greenwood Station
Seattle WA 98103-0645
tel: 206-728-4533

Seattle Bisexual Women's Network ▼♀
PO Box 30645 Greenwood Station
Seattle WA 98103-0645
tel: 206-517-7767
Bimonthly newsletter. Support & discussion groups, newcomer's meetings, social events. **Publication(s)**: *North Bi Northwest Call for info.*

B-GLAD Group **Y**
Youth Eastside Services
16150 NE 8th
Bellevue WA 98008
tel: 425-747-4YES (4937)
Weekly free drop-in group - currently Thursday 6:30-8pm.

Western Washington University: ↝
Lesbian, Gay & Bi-sexual Alliance
Viking Union, rm. 223
Bellingham WA 98225-9091
tel: 360-650-6120
Student organization which supports & affirms the lives of GLB people & allies.

Evergreen StateCollege: ↝
Evergreen Queer Alliance
T.E.S.C. CAB 314
Olympia WA 98505
tel: 360-866-6000 x6544; fax: 360-866-6793
Regular meetings & social events. Non-students welcome.

Washington State University: ↝ **E** 🖳
Associated Students, Gay, Lesbian,
Bisexual, Transgender, & Allies
Compton Union Building, B-19A
Pullman WA 99164-7204
tel: 509-335-4311
contact: Jason Sloan
e-mail: glba@wsunix.wsu.edu
URL: www.wsu.edu/~glba
Awareness committee holds meetings Tuesdays at 5:10 in the Compton Union Building. Speakers, activities.

Key to symbols: ▼ = bi ♀ = women ♂ = men ☸ = religious/spiritual
♣ = for allies **M** = for married bis ♥ = for partners of bis **Y** = youth **C** = people of color
290 The Bisexual Resource Guide 2000

Washington State University: 戩🖥️
Gay, Lesbian, Bisexual & Allies Program
Compton Union Bldg. B-19A
Pullman WA 99164-7204
tel: 509-335-6428
contact: Melinda Huskey
e-mail: glbap@mail.wsu.ed
URL: www.wsu.edu/glbap
*For GLB students, faculty, staff, & their allies.
Speakers' bureau, newsletter. Center open M-F 8-
5. Student group, meets weekly, open to all.*
Publication(s): *Breaking the Silence: the
GLBAP Newsletter*

Brother to Brother ♂ **C**
c/o POCAAN
607 19th E
Seattle WA 98112
tel: 206-322-7061; fax: 206-322-7204
*Support/networking group for GLBT men of
African descent. Meets 1st & 3rd Mondays, 7pm.*

Dignity/Seattle 🌐
PO Box 20325
Seattle WA 98102
tel: 206-325-7314
*A faith community of GLBT Catholics, their
families, friends, partners. Meets Sundays at St.
Joseph's Church (18th & Aloha, Capitol Hill)
7:30pm*

Freedom Day Committee **A**
1202 E. Pike St., #969
Seattle WA 98122
tel: 206-292-1035
*Organizers of the "Seattle LGBT Pride Parade/
March & Freedom Rally." Call to become a
member & get involved.*

Gay City Health Project ♂ **HE**🖥️
123 Boylston E.
Suite A
Seattle WA 98102
tel: 206-860-6969; fax: 206-860-0195
e-mail: info@gaycity.org
URL: www.gaycity.org
*Sponsors public forums, support groups & other
projects that build community & prevent HIV
infection in gay & bi men.*

Gay Father's Association of Seattle ♂
1202 E. Pike, Suite 1270
Seattle WA 98122
tel: 206-324-4359
*Support group meetings, social activities,
newsletters, resources & forums for parenting &
gay or bi fathers going through transitional
periods in their lives.*

Gay, Lesbian, Bi, Transgendered & **YEA**
Questioning Youth
814 NE 40th Street
Seattle WA 98105
tel: 206-632-0500
*Diverse group of young adults of all sexual
orientations, committed to educating our
communities on subjects affecting GLBTQ youth
& allies.*

Gay, Lesbian, Bisexual Youth of Color **CY**
Discussion Group
1818 15th Av.
Seattle WA 98122
tel: 206-322-2515
*Facilitated by professionals of color. Meets Wed.
6:30pm at Lambert House.*

Gay/Lesbian/Bisexual Youth of Color **Y**
Discussion Group
4620 S. Findlay,
Seattle WA 98136
tel: 206-632-0500

Lambert House **YE**
PO Box 23111
Seattle WA 98102
tel: 206-322-2535 - House;
206-322-2515 - Administration
*Located at 1818 15th Av. (at Denny). GLBT
youth advocacy & drop-in center. We provide
outreach, info & safe space with support to all
youth 14-22 years old.*

Mature Friends
PO Box 30575
Seattle WA 98103-0575
tel: 206-781-7724
*Provides supportive social environment for GLB
people 40 & above. Popular monthly potlucks,
weekly bridge, travel opportunities, garden &
theater groups.*

Queer & Asian - Seattle ♂ **EC**
P.O. Box 14153
Seattle WA 98114
tel: 206-689-6103
e-mail: qasian@drizzle.com
*Supportive network for gay & bisexual Asian
men, fostering leadership & peer support.*

SEAMEC: Seattle Municipal Election **AP**
Committee for Gays, Lesbians, Bisexuals &
Transgenders
1122 E. Pike St. #901
Seattle WA 98122
tel: 206-346-2255
*Independent non-partisan political action
committee which interviews, evaluates & rates
all candidates running for office in Seattle, King
County & Washington State.*

🖊️ = school 戩 = college/university   **P** = professional   **E** = educational
A = activist/political   **H** = health (incl. HIV)   📰 = media/press   🖥️ = Internet resource
The Bisexual Resource Guide 2000   **291**

Seattle Counseling Service for Sexual   **YEH**
Minorities
1820 E. Pine St.
Seattle WA 98122
tel: 206-323-0220 Admin.; 323-1768 Services.
Community mental health service for LGBT folks & youth & children from sexual minority families. Comprehensive crisis intervention & counseling service.

Sistah 2 Sistah   ♀ **C**
c/o POCAAN
607 19th E
Seattle WA 98112
tel: 206-322-7061; fax: 206-322-7204
For LBT women of African descent. Meets 2nd & 4th Sundays 4-7pm.

The Asian Lesbian & Bisexual Alliance   **C** ♀ 💻
PO Box 3302
Seattle WA 98114
tel: 206-689-6155
URL: www.javajungle.com/alba.htm
Also puts out a local newsletter & annual calendar.

University of Washington: Gay, Bisexual,   🔗
Lesbian & Transgendered Commission
HUB Box 104 FK-30
Seattle WA 98115
tel: 206-685-4252
e-mail: asuwgblc@u.washington.edu

OASIS   **YE**
Tacoma-Pierce County Health Dept.
3629 S. D St.
Tacoma WA 98408
tel: 253-798-6060
For GLB & questioning youth 13-24. Offers a drop-in center, support groups, referrals & educational activities.

West Virginia

Local

Rainbow Connections   **Y**
New Connections
1598C Washington Street East
Charleston WV 25311
tel: 304-340-3690
e-mail: rainyouth@aol.com
Support group for young LGBT & anyone else interested in the subject, 15-21 years old. Totally confidential. Run by New Connections, which provides comprehensive youth services. Meets Fridays.

Marshall University: 🔗💻
Lesbian, Bisexual & Gay Outreach Office
137 Pritchard Hall
Huntington WV 25755
tel: 304-696-6623
e-mail: LGBO@marshall.edu
URL: www.marshall.edu/LGBO/
Help students locate gay-friendly housing. Professional counselor on staff. Coming out resources & lending library. Various programs & activities in conjunction with Lambda society.

Marshall University: 🔗💻
Marshall Lambda Society
Memorial Student Center
c/o Office of Student Activities
Huntington WV 25755
tel: 304-696-6623
e-mail: muls@marshall.edu
URL: www.marshall.edu/muls/index.html
Support/education/activism around LGBT issues. Operate speakers bureau in conjunction with LGB Outreach Office, Safe Space Project, & Allies List. Identify supportive faculty & staff, maintain listserve.

Upper Shenandoah Sexual Minority Youth   **Y**
Martinsburg WV
tel: 703/665-0885 (Sara)
For all people 14-21 wishing to discuss issues of sexual identity/orientation, coming out, etc. Facilitated by psychotherapist. 6:45pm Tuesdays; free.

The Gay Switchboard
Morgantown WV
tel: hotline: 304-292-GAY2 304-292-4292
Volunteer service providing information & referral about LGB resources.

West Virginia University: 🔗💻
Bisexual, Gay & Lesbian Mountaineers
PO Box 6444
Morgantown WV 26505
tel: 304-293-8200
e-mail: biglm@wvusa.u92.wvu.edu
URL: www.wvu.edu/~biglm/
Dedicated to serving the needs of LGB students, faculty & staff, as well as members of the greater Morgantown community.

Shepherd College: 🔗
Tolerance, Education, & Acceptance (TEA)
ATT: Student Affairs
Shepherdstown WV 25443
tel: Student Affairs: 304-876-5124
Student group supporting bisexual & homosexual rights.

Key to symbols: ▼ = bi   ♀ = women   ♂ = men   🕭 = religious/spiritual
🔵 = for allies   **M** = for married bis   ♥ = for partners of bis   **Y** = youth   **C** = people of color
292   **The Bisexual Resource Guide 2000**

Wisconsin

In Step Magazine:
Wisconsin's Lesbigay Newspaper
1661 N. Water St. #411
Milwaukee WI 54202
e-mail: instepnews@aol.com
Contains section called "The Guide" with listings throughout the state. Good place to get current info. **Publication(s)***: $35/1 yr. (3rd class); $50/ 1 yr. (1st class)*

Teens Like Us-Dane County's YEA🖳
Lesbian, Gay, & Bisexual Teen Group
Briarpatch
512 E. Washington Avenue
Madison WI 53703
tel: crisis line 608-251-1126 or 608-251-6211; fax: 608-257-0394
e-mail: brpatch@itis.com
URL: www.uwdc.org/briarpatch
An educational/support group for high schol-aged teens who identify as LGB or who are questioning their sexual orientation.

Bi Definition ▼A
PO Box 07541
Milwaukee WI 53207
tel: Steve: 414-483-5046;
e-mail: bidef@netwurx.net
Monthly meetings & other events.
Publication(s)*: Bi All Means Quarterly, $15/ yr, 12 pages*

Local

Bi? Shy? Why? ▼EA
P.O. Box 3221
Madison WI 53701
tel: Outline: 608-255-4297
Meets 1st Mondays. **Publication(s)***: Bi-Lines Quarterly newsletter.*

Lawrence University Bisexual, 🐾
Gay, Lesbian Awareness
Box 599
Appleton WI 54912
tel: 414-832-7503
Provides support to students & larger commu-nity. Offers a meeting place, videos, & print materials. Holds annual Pride conference focusing on a relevant theme.

Lawrence University: Pride 🐾A
c/o Information Desk, Box 599
Appleton WI 54912
tel: 920-832-7051 (Resource Room)
Weekly meetings during the academic year. All orientations welcome.

Frontiers - Gay/Bisexual Men's Outreach ♂
c/o The United
14 W. Mifflin Street, Suite 103
Madison WI 53703
tel: David: 608-274-5959
Discussion/social club for gay & bi men. Monthly forum on various topics such as personal relationships, film & arts, health, politics, books, travel, religion. Also sponsors bridge group, video film circle, dining out, men's rap group, outdoor activities. Annual member-ship dues $20. **Publication(s)***: The New Frontiersman Newsletter mailed monthly to members. Provides info. on upcoming club activities.*

Lesbian, Gay, & Bisexual ☯
Catholic Students & Friends
c/o St. Paul's Catholic Church
723 State St.
Madison WI 53715
tel: Vincent: 608-258-3140

The United E
14 W. Mifflin St.
Suite 103
Madison WI 53703
tel: 608-255-8582-business & general info; 608-255-4297-outline; fax: 608-255-0018
LGBT center. Provides referrals, counseling, & general LGBT information. Maintains the Madison G/.L Resource Center Library, the Speakers' Bureau & men's & women's coming out support groups. Good first contact for non-students. (Students see the LGB Campus Center) Open Mon-Fri, 9am-9pm.

University of Wisconsin, Madison:

▼ **Lesbian, Gay & Bisexual Law Student** 🐾P
Association
Box 17, Room 208, Law Building
123 Bascom Hall
Madison WI 53706
Support & networking group for law students at UW. Provides support system for LGB law students & attempts to recognize & deal with racism, sexism, AIDS, homophobic, outing & a myriad of other issues that affect the legal community & society in general.

▼ **Lesbian, Gay & Bisexual Social Work** 🐾AP
Student Union
Madison WI 53706
tel: Bill-608-263-3660
Provides a forum for LGB students & allies to discuss issues while supporting each other & promoting social justice

---

🐾 = school	🐾 = college/university	**P** = professional	**E** = educational
A = activist/political	**H** = health (incl. HIV)	✉ = media/press	🖳 = Internet resource

Milwaukee, WI, 1995

▼ **Gay, Lesbian & Bisexual Alumni Council** 👓 💻
c/o WAA, 650 N. Lake Street
Madison WI 53706
tel: Russell Betts: 608-262-5895
e-mail: rbetts@facstaff.wisc.edu
URL: www.wisc.edu/waa

▼ **The Lesbian, Gay, Bisexual &** 👓 **E** 💻
Transgendered Campus Center
406 W. Gilman St.
Madison WI 53703
tel: 608-265-3344
e-mail: lgbcntr@macc.wisc.edu
URL: www.stdorg.wisc.edu/lgbcc/home.html
*Good first contact for students. Open at least
half a day every weekday. Maintains Buddy/
Mentor Program, Speaker's Bureau, Queer
Campus News, & a small library.*

▼ **Ten Percent Society** 👓 **E** 💻
PO Box 260394
Madison WI 53726
tel: 608-262-7365
e-mail: tps@tps.StdOrg.wisc.edu
URL: tps.stdorg.wisc.edu
LGBT & straight-friendly.

Support Group Programs **M** ♀ ♂
Counseling Center of Milwaukee
2038 N. Bartlett
Milwaukee WI 53202
tel: 414-271-2565
*$10 fee/group session unless otherwise noted.
Free Space: (women only) exploration of sexual
& affectional orientation. More Space: Support
women who are lesbian-identified. Breaking Up
is Hard to Do: support group for lesbians. Silver
Space: Support group for older lesbians $3
donation. Male Partnered Women — exploration
of needs while dealing with questions of sexual &
affectional orientation. Gay Men's General
Issues: support group on identity/orientation,
intimacy, HIV, relationships, self-esteem.*

University of Wisconsin, Whitewater: 👓 **E** 💻
**IMPACT: Gay, Lesbian, Bi Student Union &
Supporters**
c/o Campus Activities
264 University Center
Whitewater WI 53190
tel: 414-472-5738
e-mail: IMPACT@uwwvax.uww.edu
URL: www.uww.edu/stdorgs/IMPACT/index.htm
*Campus organization addressing issues of
sexual orientation & its effect on campus &
broader society; focuses on growth & development of GLBT people, open to individuals of all
sexual orientations; focuses on campus
education, social activities, & providing support
& resources to glbt students & allies. Office
Address: 309 McCutchan Hall.*

Wyoming

Local

Lambda Community Center of Fort Collins 💻
southern WY
tel: 970-221-3247
e-mail: lambda@lambdacenter.org
URL: www.lambdacenter.org/
*See Colorado listings. For GLBs in northern
Colorado & southern Wyoming.*

University of Wyoming: Lesbian, Gay, 👓
Bisexual & Transgendered Association
PO Box 3625, University Station
Campus Activities
Laramie WY 82071
e-mail: basden@uwyo.edu

Key to symbols: ▼ = bi ♀ = women ♂ = men ☯ = religious/spiritual
💧 = for allies **M** = for married bis ♥ = for partners of bis **Y** = youth **C** = people of color
294 The Bisexual Resource Guide 2000

URUGUAY

Local

Encuentro Ecuménico para la ☯**A**
Liberación de las Minorias Sexuales (EELMS)
Casilla de Correo 1294
Correo Central
Montevideo
tel: 598 2/203-5632
e-mail: fefroq@adinet.com.uy
*Ecumenical, Christian-based organization
dedicated to helping those excluded, oppressed,
isolated. Confidential support groups. Encourages dialogue between social/political/
religious/professional groups promoting human
rights, with particular concern for sexual
minorities.*
"God created diversity & saw that it was good."

Grupo Diversidad LGTTB - Comunidad **A**
Lésbica, Gay Travesti, Transexual Bisexual
Uruguaya
send mail to: Grupo Diversidad LGTTB
Casilla de Correo 7415
Correo Central
Montevideo
tel: 598 2/915-3021
e-mail: clima@adinet.com.uy
*LBGT political activist group; space for support/
self-help.*

VENEZUELA

Movimiento Ambiente de Venezuela **A**
Solis a Munoz, Edificio Augusta,
Piso 1, Oficina D
Caracas 1010
tel: 582 482 41 14; fax: 582 482 63 61
e-mail: accsi@internet.ve

ZAMBIA

LEGATRA: Lesbians, Gays, Bi-Sexuals & **A**
Transgender Persona Association
c/Zambia Independent Monitoring Team
2nd Floor, Muyini House, PO Box 30211
Bombay Road
Kumwala Lusaka
tel: 260-1-236856/7; fax: 260-1-236857
e-mail: zimt@zamnet.zm

ZIMBABWE

Local

BUGLES
P.O. Box 6052
Morningside
Bulawayo
*Bulawayo based social/support group for
lesbians & gay men in Matabeleland.*

Gays & Lesbians of Zimbabwe **HAE**🖳
send mail to: GALZ
P. Bag A6131
Avondale
Harare
tel: 263-4-731736
Crisis Line: 111 404 348; fax: 263-4-731736
e-mail: galz@samara.co.zw
URL: www.icon.co.za/~stobbs/galz.htm
*GALZ has a resource center & office at 35
Colenbrander Road, Milton Park, Harare. GALZ
her numerous projects & sub-committees devoted
to specific campaigns & support work. Frequent
well-attended social events.*

Ngongi Chaidzo **CE**🖳
c/o GALZ
PBag A6131
Avondale
Harare
tel: 263-4-741736
Crisis Line: 111-404348
e-mail: c/o galz@samara.co.zw
URL: www.icon.co.za/~stobbs/galz.htm
*Ngongi Chaido means Great Blessing. Can be
contacted c/o GALZ (above). Recently reformed
with focus on black lesbians. Arranges social
events, as well as safer sex workshops & human
rights training.*

✎ = school	✍ = college/university	**P** = professional	**E** = educational
A = activist/political	**H** = health (incl. HIV)	📰 = media/press	🖳 = Internet resource

The Bisexual Resource Guide 2000 **295**

Final Words

HOW TO ORDER MORE COPIES OF THE GUIDE:

Copies of the Guide are $12.95 each, postage paid. To order a copy, send a check or money order (in US dollars or International Postal Money Order) to: BRC, PO Box 400639, Cambridge MA 02140. Discount rates are available for bulk orders, as follows: 5–9 copies may be discounted 20% ($10.66 each), 10–19 copies discounted 30% ($9.07 each), 20 or more copies 40% ($7.77 each). Inquiries from distributors and bookstores are welcome.

The Bisexual Resource Guide will be updated periodically. The next edition will be the 2002 edition.

REMEMBER, THE BISEXUAL RESOURCE CENTER IS A NON-PROFIT ORGANIZATION.

The Bisexual Resource Center (also called the East Coast Bisexual Network) is a 501(C)3 nonprofit organization. We depend upon your generosity to produce this guide and other materials, and to pay the operating expenses for our small office. All donations are tax deductible. Please consider helping us out.

YOUR HELP IS NEEDED

You are invited (encouraged, begged) to send us suggestions for improving the quality of this *Guide*. Are there books which you think should be listed in the Bibliography? Groups which should be listed? Conferences which should be announced? Let us know.

DISCLAIMER

Neither the Bisexual Resource Center nor Robyn Ochs (nor anyone else) makes any promise about the existence or quality of any group listed in this *Guide*.

About the Editors

Robyn Ochs

Robyn Ochs is an activist based in Cambridge, MA. She teaches courses on bisexual identities and on lesbian, gay & bisexual cultures at Tufts University, and has had her essays published in several anthologies. In addition, she is a public speaker and workshop leader. Please feel free to contact her directly at ochs@bi.org.

Linda Dyndiuk

Linda Dyndiuk lives with her significant other in Somerville, MA, where she enjoys contradancing, drawing and vegetarian cooking. This is her first project in bi-activism.

Same Preference — Different Lifestyles

6th International Bisexual Conference, Rotterdam, Summer of 2000

THE 6TH INTERNATIONAL BISEXUAL CONFERENCE WILL BE HELD IN ROTTERDAM, THE NETHERLANDS IN THE SUMMER OF 2000. WITH THE THEME OF "SAME PREFERENCE, DIFFERENT LIFESTYLES", THE CONFERENCE WILL HOST HUNDREDS OF BISEXUALS, FRIENDS AND ALLIES FROM AROUND THE GLOBE.

IBC6 IS BEING ORGANIZED BY AN INDEPENDENT ORGANIZING COMMITTEE IN CO-OPERATION WITH THE DUTCH BI-NETWORK. THIS THREE-DAY CONFERENCE FEATURES WORKSHOPS, PANELS, PRESENTATIONS, PAPERS AND PERFORMANCE TRACKS.

You can contact us for registration forms, calls for papers, conference particulars, and other information at:

IBC6 Organizing
PO Box 75087
1070AB Amsterdam
The Netherlands

our E-mail address is <ibc6@lnbi.demon.nl>
the IBC6 webste is http://www.lnbi.demon.nl/ibc6/

HOW CAN YOU BE A PART OF BUILDING IBC6?
VOLUNTEER FROM HOME OR IN ROTTERDAM;
DESIGN A PRESENTATION;
MAKE A DONATION;
VISIT OUR WEBSITE, AND
SPREAD THE WORD

GENDER

ACTIVISM

INTERNET

SEXUALITY

SPIRITUALITY

ORGANIZING

SAFER SEX/HIV

PERFORMANCE

RELATIONSHIPS

YOUTH/STUDENT

FILM AND VIDEO

WOMEN'S ISSUES

RESEARCH/THEORY

PERSONAL GROWTH

WRITERS/LITERATURE

TRACK X (OTHER SESSIONS)

NON-BI PARTNERS/FAMILIES

BI'S IN MEDIA/CULTURE/HISTORY

OUR BODIES: DIFFERING ABILITY, HEALTH, IMAGE

GLOBAL/REGIONAL/RACIAL/CULTURAL/CLASS DIFFERENCE

BISEXUAL RESOURCE GUIDE 2000
INDIVIDUAL AND GROUP ORDER FORM

❑ Individual ❑ Group *Please Print*

Name_____

Organization_____

Address_____

_____

City_____State/Province_____

Zip+4/PostalCode_____Country_____

Email_____Website_____

It is our policy to make the Guide accessible to all organizations listed within. However, we must also pay production and mailing costs. If you can make an additional donation, please do so. If your group cannot afford to pay $12.95, please pay what you can. Orders of 5 or more copies may be discounted 20%; 10 or more copies 30%; 20 or more copies 40%.

Quantity:_____Guides @ $12.95 each   subtotal $____.____

Discount (if applicable)   [-] $____.____

Additional Donation (tax deductable)   [+] $____.____

Total amount enclosed (U.S. Dollars) [=] $____.____

❑ Check ❑ Money Order (in US$ or International Money Order)

❑ Visa ❑ MasterCard Card Number _____

Exp.Date_____Signature_____

Mail this form with your payment to:
THE BISEXUAL RESOURCE CENTER (BRC)
P.O. Box 400639
Cambridge, MA 02140

Optional survey questions use additional paper if necessary):

Is this the first edition of the Guide you've purchased? ❑ yes ❑ no

Where or how did you learn about the Guide?_____

Do you have any suggestions or additions for the next edition?

_____

Write to us, call us at (617) 424-9595, visit the BRC and the
Guide at http://www.biresource.org
or send us email at brc@biresource.org
Thank you for your support.

BISEXUAL RESOURCE GUIDE 2000

ORDEN DE PEDIDO PARA INDIVIDUOS O PARA ORGANIZACIONES
❑ Ordenes individuales   ❑ Ordenes para organizaciones
(Por favor escriba en imprenta)

Nombre_____

Organización_____

Dirección_____

Ciudad_____Estado/Provincia_____

Apartado Postal_____País_____

Correo Electrónico_____Página en la Red_____

Es nuestra política hacer que esta guía sea accesible a todas las organizaciones que se encuentran er
la lista. Sin embargo, también tenemos que pagar los costos de producción y de correo. Si usted
pudiera hacer una donación adicional, le agradeceríamos mucho. Si su grupo está imposibilitado
para para pagar $12.95, por favor paguen lo que puedan. Ordenes de más de cinco copias tendrán ur
descuento del 20% o, si son más copias, el descuento será del 40%.

Cantidad:_____Guías @ $12.95 cada una   Subtotal $ ____.____

Descuento (en caso de aplicarse)   (-) $ ____.____

Donación Adicional   (+) $ ____.____

Monto Total Enviado (Dólares de los EE.UU)   (=) $ ____.____

❑ Cheque ❑ Orden de Dinero
(solamente en dólares de EE.UU o en órdenes internacionales de dinero)
❑ Visa ❑ Mastercard Numero de la Tarjeta_____

Fecha de Expiración _____ Firma_____

Por favor enviar este formulario con su pago a:
THE BISEXUAL RESOURCE CENTER (BRC)
P.O. Box 400639
Cambridge, MA 02140

Esta es una encuesta opcional y puede utilizar papel adicional para contestarla si lo necesita:

• Es esta la primera edición de la Guía que usted compra?: ❑ sí   ❑ no

• Cómo se enteró usted de la Guía?_____

• Tiene usted sugerencias o adiciones que hacer para la siguiente edición?_____

Escríbanos, llámanos al (617) 424-9595,
y visita al BRC y su Guía en http://www.biresource.org
o envíanos un correo electrónico a brc@biresource.org

Muchas gracias por su apoyo.

After more than a decade of "marriage" to a woman, Jan Clausen fell in love with a man, stunning herself and the lesbian community to which she had been intimately connected...

Jan Clausen

Apples & Oranges

MY JOURNEY THROUGH SEXUAL IDENTITY

"A visionary and courageous memoir that challenges many of our assumptions about sexual identity and desire." — **Jaime Manrique**, author of *Latin Moon in Manhattan*

"Unsentimental, questing, and deeply funny." — **Catherine McKinley**, editor of *Afrekete: An Anthology of Black Lesbian Writing*

"A brilliant — and stirring — book. Jan Clausen has courageously used her own life as a way of illuminating the crucial issue of 'identity' currently embroiling the culture. Seminal... a true trail-blazer." — **Martin Duberman**, author of *Stonewall*

Available March 1, 1999

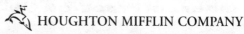

HOUGHTON MIFFLIN COMPANY

ADDENDA TO THE BISEXUAL RESOURCE GUIDE 2000
(yes, already...)

Trying to get a fixed and definitive picture of an ever-changing movement is somewhat like trying to get a large group of young children to sit still for a photo. It just can't be done. The bi and LGBT movements are in a constant state of change. Since we "finished" the Guide, more information has come in. Here it is:

NEW GROUPS:

Sangini
c/o the Naz Foundation India Trust
PO Box 3910
Andrews Gunj
New Delhi 110049
India
011-6859113 or 685-1970/71 Tuesdays 6-8pm
info@naz.unv.ernet.in or
sangini97@hotmail.com
"A lesbian support project providing information, counseling, support & advice. All helpline counselors are lesbians or bisexuals. A support group, open to lesbians and women exploring their sexuality, meets every Saturday 3-6pm.

Jamaica Forum of Lesbians, All-Sexuals, and Gays (J-FLAG)
P. O. Box 1152
Kingston 8,
Jamaica.
Telephone 876 978-1954
Fax 876 978-7876
http://village.fortunecity.com/garland/704/
jflag@hotmail.com
"All-sexual is a term used to indicate that is considers all-sexual behavior to be part of a sexual continuum in which classifications such as "gay," "lesbian" and "bisexual" often cannot be rigidly applied. committed to working towards a Jamaican society in which the human rights and equality of lesbians, all-sexuals and gays are guaranteed. The organisation will engage in initiatives that will foster the acceptance and enrichment of the lives of same-gender-loving persons who have been, and continue to be, an integral part of society. Legal and political advocacy, media watch, counselling, hot-line, referrals, recreation and celebration.

The Rainbow Project
P. O. Box 26122
Windhoek,
Namibia.

Bisexual Network of the Philippines
A new network still in it's formative stage but eager to hear from bisexual and bi-curious men and women from through-out the Republic of the Philippines. All you have to do is register with us to be granted membership. You are welcome to attend any meetings and social events that may be organised or go on our private e-mail list for BiNet Philippines news updates. At present BiNet Philippines is developing social groups in the Manila Metro area and in Cebu City. It is hoped other groups will develop as more people contact BiNet Philippines and get involved. Contact info:
Manila Bi Group: Danny:
sioldan@hotmail.com; Cebu Bi Group:
Brian: argao@rocketmail.com; Web:
www.rainbow.net.au/~ausbinet/binetph.htm.

UPDATES

Kingsborough Community College (NY)
add: Faculty Advisor Don Donin 718-368-5655

Pride in da Bronx (NY)
street address: 2390 Grand Concourse, 2nd floor

Bi Lines, the Newsletter of the Richmond Bisexual Network (ROBIN) will publish its last issue January 1999.

302

Inquires about ROBIN will still be answered via e-mail, s-mail or phone. ROBIN is still active, with a website at www.geocities.com/WestHollywood/Stonewall/4409, e-mail is received at robinsnet@geocities.com, and ROBIN can also be contacted USPS at ROBIN, c/o Phoenix Rising, 19 North Belmont Avenue, Richmond, Virginia.

ADD TO Bi-BLIOGRAPHY:

Helen Eisenbach, Loon Glow. New York: Farrar Straus Giroux, 1998. Straight man falls in love with women who fall in love with women, each other, it turns out. One of these women turns or attention to him for a while. Is she bisexual? Maybe.

E. Lynn Harris, If This World Were Mine. New York: Doubleday, 1997. Several of the male characters in this most recent novel are bisexual, not one of them likeable.

Carole Maso, Ghost Dance. NY: Harper & Row, 1986. About a woman who grows up with a mentally ill mother in a family whose imaginary life is often more powerful than the exterior one. Mother leaves husband and family periodically to spend time with her female love.

Julia Willis, Reel Time. Los Angeles: Alyson Publications, 1998. Dyke drama based in Cambridge, MA, in the early 1990s. Among the characters are a woman who leaves the local lesbian community to go off and marry a man, and a woman who self-identifies as bisexual, has a crush on every woman she meets, but is afraid to act on her feelings. The narrator is not particularly impressed by either woman.

CALLS FOR WRITINGS:

CALL FOR WRITINGS: LESBIAN & BISEXUAL SORORITY WOMEN. The Lambda 10 Project is seeking contributions for their second anthology, specifically focused on being lesbian or bisexual in a college sorority. Lesbian & bisexual women who have been or who are currently members of a college sorority are encouraged to share their personal accounts of sisterhood in relationship to being lesbian or bisexual. We want diverse experiences so we ask women whether "closeted" or "out" in their sorority to share their experience (positive or negative). Straight women also encouraged to submit stories about having a sister "come out" & how that experience impacted the sorority. Lambda 10 Project; Office of Student Ethics/Anti-Harassment Programs; 705 E. 7th Street; Bloomington, IN 47405-3809 or email: lambda10@indiana.edu. See website http://www.indiana.edu/~lambda 10. Deadline: June 10, 1999.

Queer Asian or Pacific American writers: now's your big chance to be published. We're looking for poetry, nonfiction, and fiction submissions for TAKE OUT: Queer Writings from Asian and Pacific America, to be published by the Asian American Writers Workshop in Spring of 2000. The submission is open to all queer people of Asian/Pacific descent in North America; we're especially looking for never-before published poetry, non-fiction, and fiction. Send one hard copy to EACH of the following addresses: QB, 29 Kensington Ave. Apt. 2, Northampton, MA 01060 and HY, Riverhead Books, 375 Hudson Street, NYC 10014 USA. You may send no more than 20 pages of poetry, or 30 pages of short stories/novel excerpts. Include a brief biography and any relevant contact information, including email. Submissions must be received by May 1, 1999 and will not be returned.

And an errata: Change Southern California editor to: "Gary North with Members of BiNet LA and BiNet L.B./O.C.

THAT'S ALL.... FOR TODAY.

303